Criminology

A Canadian Perspective

Rick Linden

University of Manitoba

NELSON

NELSON

Criminology: A Canadian Perspective, Eighth Edition
by Rick Linden

Vice President, Editorial Higher Education:
Anne Williams

Publishers:
Leanna MacLean, Maya Castle

Marketing Manager:
Terry Fedorkiw

Developmental Editor:
Maria Chu

Photo Researcher/Permissions Coordinator:
Jessie Coffey

Senior Production Project Manager:
Imoinda Romain

Production Service:
Cenveo Publisher Services

Copy Editor:
Matthew Kudelka

Proofreader:
Kavitha

Indexer:
BIM Indexing Services

Design Director:
Ken Phipps

Managing Designer:
Franca Amore

Interior Design:
Dave Murphy

Cover Design:
Dave Murphy

Cover Image:
DenisTangneyJr/Getty Images

Compositor:
Cenveo Publisher Services

Library and Archives Canada Cataloguing in Publication

Criminology : a Canadian perspective / [edited by] Rick Linden, University of Manitoba. — Eighth edition.

Includes bibliographical references and index.

ISBN 978-0-17-656206-9 (pbk.)

1. Criminology—Canada—Textbooks. I. Linden, Rick, author, editor

HV6807.C76 2015
364.971   C2014-906362-8

ISBN-13: 978-0-17-656206-9
ISBN-10: 0-17-656206-0

To Christopher, who gave so much and asked so little,
and
to Dan Koenig, a wonderful colleague and friend.

Brief Table of Contents

Contents

CHAPTER 15 Deterrence, Routine Activity, and Rational Choice Theories   407

Rick Linden, University of Manitoba
Daniel J. Koenig, Formerly of University of Victoria

PART 3 PATTERNS OF CRIMINAL BEHAVIOUR   433

CHAPTER 16 Organized Crime   434

Stephen Schneider, Saint Mary's University

CHAPTER 17 Corporate and White-Collar Crime   468

John Hagan, Northwestern University
Rick Linden, University of Manitoba

CHAPTER 18 Cybercrime and Cyberdeviance   500

Michael Arntfield, Western University

Preface

Since it was first published in 1987, *Criminology: A Canadian Perspective* has been used to introduce this field to more than 100,000 students across the country. At that time, most criminology courses in Canada were taught using American texts. It was our intention to provide a text that was written *by* Canadians, *for* Canadians. Over the past three decades, the discipline of criminology has grown from a few widely scattered faculty members to a large community of academics, researchers, practitioners, and students. The eighth edition of *Criminology: A Canadian Perspective* continues to reflect their work. That said, criminology remains a small and underfunded discipline in Canada. As a result, much of the new theoretical and empirical work in the field continues to come from the United States and Europe. This new edition represents our continued effort to provide you with the best Canadian scholarship in combination with the most relevant research from other countries.

Advantages of a Multi-authored Text

The many different theories proposed to explain criminality are continually being revived and revised. Often the popularity of a particular theory owes as much to ideological commitment and academic fashion as it does to its explanatory power. As a result of this unresolved diversity, the pages of many texts are littered with the bodies of straw men, set up only to be sacrificed to the author's favourite approach. The authors of this text are among Canada's leading criminologists. The advantage of a multi-authored text is that the diverse perspectives of criminology can be fairly represented. In this book, each chapter is written by someone who has used the perspective in his or her own research and who understands its strengths and weaknesses.

Organization of the Text

This book is intended as a text for a one-term course in introductory criminology. While the book deals extensively with theories about the causes of crime (which have largely been developed elsewhere), its purpose is to provide students with information about crime in Canada.

The chapters have been organized into three parts. **Part 1: Crime and Society** provides some of the basic information about crime: the sources of criminal law, the legal elements of crime, the sources of information about crime, the social correlates of criminal behaviour, a discussion of women and crime, and a look at victimization and at the role of victims in the justice system. This part provides the student with the background necessary to assess the theories of crime causation presented in **Part 2**. In **Part 2: Explanations of Crime**, all of the major theories are covered, including biological, psychological, and sociological explanations. In **Part 3: Patterns of Criminal Behaviour**, three serious and frequent types of crime—organized crime, white-collar crime, and cybercrime—are discussed. Street crimes such as break and enter, robbery, and assault are discussed throughout the text. This arrangement of chapters is just one way of presenting the material; instructors are encouraged to assign these chapters in whatever order best suits their course needs.

Features of the Text

Each chapter begins with a brief *Introduction* and a list of *Learning Objectives* and concludes with a *Summary* and *Net Work* (Internet activities). *Questions for Critical Thinking* are at the end of each chapter section. This text also features margin notes. In the margins, *Google Terms* refers students to interesting related websites. Also in the margins is a running glossary, which defines the key terms next to the paragraphs in which they first appear. A full *Glossary* and *Bibliography* are at the end of the text.

New to the Eighth Edition

This edition of *Criminology: A Canadian Perspective* provides us with the opportunity to update crime statistics, add new research material, and make some major revisions that have been suggested by reviewers. In this edition, these major revisions include two new chapters:

- Chapter 5, "Correlates of Criminal Behaviour," written by Temitope Oriola, replaces an earlier chapter covering the same topics.
- Chapter 18, "Cybercrime and Cyberdeviance," written by Michael Arntfield, is a new chapter dealing with a relatively new type of crime that has quickly become a major global problem.

We have also made many revisions and updates to the remaining chapters. Chapter 1, "Crime, Criminals, and Criminology," continues to introduce new areas of criminology with the discussion of the new criminological field of surveillance studies. Chapter 3 reflects a number of recent court decisions and has several new Focus boxes. These new boxes discuss assisted suicide; legal issues emanating from the trial of those charged with the murder of Nina Courtepatte in Edmonton; and the controversial issue of the criminalization of the failure to disclose one's HIV-positive status. Besides updating crime statistics, Chapter 4 has added a Focus box on the uses and abuses of police crime figures. In 2014, the federal government introduced legislation creating a Victim's Bill of Rights, and Chapter 7 includes an extensive discussion of this proposal. It also has a new Focus box on Saskatchewan's Adult Restitution and Civil Enforcement Program. Chapter 10 has an expanded discussion of Agnew's work on strain theory and places greater emphasis on the role of strain in white-collar crime. Chapter 11 has a new Focus box dealing with the federal government's controversial Protecting Canadians from Online Crime Act. It has also added an extended discussion of the tragic honour killing of four women from the Shafia family. Chapter 12 now includes a discussion of Wacquant's extension of Bourdieu's work on the bureaucratic field, which includes police, courts, and prisons as part of the right hand of the state; in the same chapter, we have added a discussion of some of the criticisms of critical criminology. A new Focus box in Chapter 13 discusses the moral entrepreneurship of the federal

Liberals' promise to legalize the use of marijuana in Canada. In Chapter 14, we have added a discussion of the consistency between life course theories and social control theory and have updated the research on the role of religion in criminality. A new Focus box in Chapter 15 examines whether moving to a cashless society will mean less opportunity for crime. Chapter 16 has an expanded section applying network theories to organized crime. Chapter 17 has expanded the discussion of workplace health and safety issues and has extensively updated many of the examples of white-collar and corporate crime.

Instructor Resources

About the Nelson Education Teaching Advantage

The **Nelson Education Teaching Advantage (NETA)** program delivers research-based instructor resources that promote student engagement and higher order thinking to enable the success of Canadian students and educators. Be sure to visit Nelson Education's **Inspired Instruction** website at http://www.nelson.com/inspired to find out more about NETA. Don't miss the testimonials of instructors who have used NETA supplements and seen student engagement increase!

Downloadable Instructor Ancillaries

All NETA and other key instructor ancillaries can be accessed through http://www.nelson.com/login and http://login.cengage.com, giving instructors the ultimate tools for customizing lectures and presentations.

NETA Test Bank: This resource was written by Stephen Schneider of Saint Mary's University. It includes over 700 multiple-choice questions written according to NETA guidelines for effective construction and development of higher-order questions. Also included are 320 true/false, and 190 essay questions.

The NETA Test Bank is available in a new, cloud-based platform. **Testing Powered by Cognero®** is a secure online testing system that allows you to author, edit, and manage test bank content from any place you have Internet access. No special installations or downloads are needed, and the desktop-inspired interface, with its drop-down menus and familiar, intuitive tools, allows you to create and manage tests with ease. You can create multiple test versions in an instant and import or export content into other systems. Tests can be delivered from your learning management system, your classroom, or wherever you want. Testing Powered by Cognero for *Criminology: A Canadian Perspective* can be accessed through http://www.nelson.com/instructor. Printable versions of the test bank in Word and PDF versions are available with the instructor resources for the textbook.

NETA PowerPoint: Microsoft® PowerPoint® lecture slides for every chapter have been created by Stephen Schneider of Saint Mary's University. There is an average of 35 slides per chapter, many featuring key figures, tables, and photographs from *Criminology: A Canadian Perspective*. NETA principles of clear design and engaging content have been incorporated throughout, making it simple for instructors to customize the deck for their courses.

Image Library: This resource consists of digital copies of figures, short tables, and photographs used in the book. Instructors may use these jpegs to customize the NETA PowerPoint or create their own PowerPoint presentations.

DayOne: Day One—Prof InClass is a PowerPoint presentation that instructors can customize to orient students to the class and their text at the beginning of the course.

CourseMate

Nelson Education's **Criminology CourseMate** brings course concepts to life with interactive learning and exam preparation tools that integrate with the printed textbook. Students activate their knowledge through quizzes, games, and flashcards, among many other tools.

CourseMate provides immediate feedback that enables students to connect results to the work they have just produced, increasing their learning efficiency. It encourages contact between students and faculty: you can select to monitor your students' level of engagement with CourseMate, correlating their efforts to their outcomes. You can even use CourseMate's quizzes to practise "just in time" teaching by tracking results in the Engagement Tracker and customizing your lesson plans to address their learning needs.

The CourseMate for *Criminology: A Canadian Perspective* was prepared by Alexander Shvarts of Humber College.

Watch student comprehension and engagement soar as your class engages with CourseMate. Ask your Nelson sales representative for a demo today.

Student Ancillaries

CourseMate

The more you study, the better the results. Make the most of your study time by accessing everything you need to succeed in one place. Criminology CourseMate includes:

- An interactive ebook with highlighting, note-taking, and an interactive glossary
- Interactive learning tools, including:
- quizzes
- case studies
- flashcards
- crossword puzzles
- …and more!

Visit http://www.nelson.com/student to start using **CourseMate**. Enter the Online Access Code from the card included with your text. If a code card is not provided, you can purchase instant access at NELSONbrain.com.

Acknowledgements

It has become traditional for authors to thank families for not making demands, and spouses, or close friends, both for moral support and for those unspecified but essential services that writing seems to require. Since my wife and children had already reached their tolerance limit with my work schedule, I decided that I couldn't just disappear into my office and reappear two years later with a book. Thus it is to them that I owe my wise decision to get help from the friends and colleagues who co-authored the text. For the time I did spend writing, I thank for their support Olive, Brad, Chris, Robin, Shawn, Tyler, and Amanda. By the fourth edition, all of my children were old enough that they no longer cared about my working hours. However, their place at my worktable was taken by pets, and I thank Nicholas, Morris, Annie, and Edward for ensuring that each page in this manuscript (back in the days when manuscripts had pages) has been stepped on or slept on by an orange cat. Callie also added some black cat hair to my computer keyboard.

As usual, working with the people at Nelson Education has been a delightful experience. For significant improvements in this eighth edition, I thank Maya Castle and Maria Chu, and Matthew Kudelka for his editorial skills. Jessie Coffey did the photo research and text permissions.

The authors would like to thank the reviewers of the current edition: Joshua Barath, Georgian College; Tara Bruno-Fidler, Western University; Lisette Patenaude, Vancouver Island University; Pamela Nancarrow Snow, Wilfrid Laurier University; Rashmee Singh, University of Waterloo; and James Williams, York University.

The authors continue to benefit from the reviews of previous editions; those reviewers include Bill Avison, Jane Barker, Marilyn Belle-McQuillan, Thomas Bernard, Augustine Brannigan, David Brownfield, Tullio Caputo, Elaine DeCunha-Bath, Sange de Silva, Robert Drislaine, Karlene Faith, Thomas Gabor, Colin Goff, Jim Hackler, Stephanie Hayman, Sheilagh Hodgins, Carl Keane, Gail Kellough, Heather A. Kitchin, John Martin, Robynne Neugebauer, Norman Okihiro, Gary Parkinson, Michael Petrunik, Karen Richter, Vincent F. Sacco, Les Samuelson, Bernard Schissel, Alfredo Schulte-Bockholt, Phillip C. Stenning, Lee Stuesser, Diane Symbaluk, David Ryan, Heather A. Kitchin, and Austin T. Turk.

I would also like to thank each of the authors who contributed to the book. I appreciate your enthusiastic responses to revision suggestions and your efforts to meet deadlines. I continue to enjoy and to learn from your work.

Individual authors wished to make the following acknowledgements: J. Evans (Chapter 4)—"The author wishes to thank the Canadian Centre for Justice Statistics for providing much of the data presented in this chapter."

Rick Linden
University of Manitoba

Crime and Society

Part 1 of this book provides some basic information about crime: the origins of our criminal law, the legal elements of crime, the sources of information about crime, and the social correlates of criminal behaviour.

Chapter 1 introduces you to the discipline of *criminology*, the scientific study of crime and criminals. This chapter examines the role played by rules and shows how these rules are sometimes formalized in laws. The chapter also looks at different ways of defining crime and shows that because crime is socially defined, the definition of crime can change over time. The chapter concludes with discussions of "green" criminology, terrorism studies, and surveillance studies, three of the newest sub-fields of criminology, to show how the discipline continues to evolve.

In Chapter 2, we learn how our legal system has developed as we have evolved from simple hunting and gathering societies to modern industrial ones. With the increased complexity and growth of modern societies comes the need for a formal legal system to maintain order. We also learn why some social harms are defined as illegal while others are not.

The legal elements of a crime are *actus reus* (the physical element) and *mens rea* (the mental element). These are discussed in Chapter 3, along with the defences available to an accused, a history of criminal procedure, and an outline of the social factors affecting the definition of specific types of crime.

We cannot study crime unless we can measure it. Chapter 4 describes how we count crime using official government statistics, victimization surveys, and self-report surveys. None of these methods is completely adequate; you will learn the strengths and weaknesses of each.

Before we can explain a phenomenon such as crime, we must know how it is distributed demographically. In Chapter 5, several correlates of crime are discussed, including age, sex, race, and social class. Chapter 6 considers issues involving women and crime in more depth. The explanations of crime discussed in Part 2 of the book should be judged according to how well they account for these regularities.

Finally, Chapter 7 discusses issues faced by victims of crime. About one in four Canadian adults are victimized by crime each year, and the cost to these victims is estimated at $80 billion a year. Several important international protocols guide the ways in which countries treat victims, but Canadian governments have failed to provide adequate victim services. Instead of investing to support victims and to prevent future victimization, governments have chosen to invest billions of dollars in the traditional institutions of police, courts, and prisons.

1

Crime, Criminals, and Criminology

Rick Linden
UNIVERSITY OF MANITOBA

anadians have an endless fascination with crime. Newspapers and television news broadcasts are saturated with stories about crime and criminals. Movies, television shows, and video games are filled with depictions of violence and other criminal behaviour. While crime is a matter of public concern and a favourite form of entertainment, it is also the subject of serious academic study. This chapter will introduce you to the discipline of criminology, the scientific study of crime and criminals.

Learning Objectives

After reading this chapter, you should be able to

- Define the term *criminology*.
- Understand the different subjects studied by criminologists.
- Explain the role played by rules in our lives and understand how these rules can become formalized in law.
- Understand the different ways of defining crime: a strict legal definition; an expanded legal definition that goes beyond just considering the criminal law; a definition based on the protection of people's human rights; and a definition that places acts of deviance and crime on a continuum ranging from minor acts of deviance to serious offences that almost everyone agrees are wrong.
- Explain how crime is socially defined and how people's ideas about crime change over time.
- Understand the two main theoretical perspectives (conflict and consensus) on how some acts get defined as criminal and others do not.
- Understand the new sub-fields of green criminology, terrorism studies, and surveillance studies.

A Violent Crime: The Sand Brothers

Robert and Danny Sand grew up in an Alberta family with their father, Dennis, and their mother, Elaine. Robert was born in 1978 and Danny was born in 1980. Dennis Sand, who had served time in jail in his youth for a variety of crimes including armed robbery, gave up crime when he was 20 and supported his family through a variety of jobs. He lives in a small Alberta community, where Elaine runs a business and both are respected community members

(Staples, 2002). As youngsters, Robert and Danny were constantly in trouble, along with several of their closest friends, who made up a group composed of the only mixed-race boys in their town. The boys had difficulty in school and were frequently suspended. In junior high they got into more serious trouble, and at age 15 Danny was sent to a youth centre for beating up another student. The boys began to steal cars and use drugs. Journalist David Staples described the situation of the brothers and their friends:

> Their contact with adults was minimal. No teachers, because the teens had all dropped out. No parents, because most didn't live at home. They relied on each other to figure out the world, believing their friends were closer and wiser than any adult. They're all there to protect each other, and they can't see past that, says [one of the mothers]. The teens suffered from the moral blindness of those who have achieved nothing in life and have nothing to lose. But they weren't entirely lacking in vision. They had an inkling of the difference between right and wrong. They certainly understood when someone did wrong to them, or to one of their closest friends. They just didn't see it as a problem to rob or injure someone outside of their group. It was us vs. them, with them being teachers, the RCMP, car owners, property owners, anyone with something they wanted to grab. (Staples, 2002, D2)

In 1998, Robert received a seven-year jail sentence for armed robbery. He became a model inmate, though counsellors said he could never explain why he had committed crimes. Danny also ended up in jail for several crimes, including attacking a police officer. After his release, Danny got involved in another incident that foretold the crime that would result in his death. An Edmonton police officer used his cruiser car to block an alley where Danny was suspiciously parked in a stolen truck. Instead of giving up, Danny sped toward the cruiser and seemed to swerve toward the police officer. After this incident, he joined Robert in Drumheller Penitentiary, where he continued to get into trouble and where he got a tattoo that read "Fearless, Painless, Senseless." After his release, Danny told people that he would never go back to jail.

In October of 2001, Robert was released to a halfway house. He could find only menial work, and he reunited with Laurie Bell, a former girlfriend who was a heavy drug user. He left the halfway house, which violated his parole. On December 18, Robert and Laurie—along with Danny, who was also violating his parole—headed for the Maritimes, where they had vague plans for making a new life. They never made it past Manitoba.

In the midst of a crime spree that included robbing a bank, breaking into homes, and stealing several vehicles, the three made it to the town of Russell, Manitoba. Shortly after midnight on December 21, 2001, Danny drove onto the main highway without first stopping at a stop sign. When RCMP constables Brian Auger and Dennis Strongquill tried to stop the vehicle, Robert fired several shotgun blasts at the police. When the police drove away, Danny chased the police SUV into town. He rammed the SUV after it stopped at the Russell RCMP Detachment. Robert jumped out of the truck and fired at Constable Strongquill, who was trapped in the damaged police vehicle. Four shots hit Constable Strongquill, who died almost immediately.

The RCMP tracked the trio to a motel near Wolseley, Saskatchewan. A police sniper fatally wounded Danny Sand; Robert Sand and Laurie Bell were captured and charged with first-degree murder. While awaiting trial, Robert kept a diary in which he reflected on the shooting:

> I was in one of my moods so I asked to see the pictures again of my case. There are pics of trucks burnt, crashed shot up etc. Homes broken into, property of ours and others and of course pics of the dead cop, shot up cop cars and Dan. Now I've seen them before and without emotion, I've no more tears to shed. But I was looking at this man, on a table. And I started to think, he's just a man, and shouldn't be dead. He had a family and friends, and now he's a body on a table. I realized it's not the man I hated, but the uniform he wore. His flag, colours of war. But seeing him without his uniform I felt bad for the loss of his life. But then I flipped to the pics of Dan, and my thoughts changed. Cause now I felt that the other man is right where he should be. And losses on both sides are to be expected, only Dan took my place. And when I looked upon the cop car I felt pride, and remembered the battle, I remembered how these enemy soldiers fled in fear and [sic] cowardess. I saw how much damage I'd caused to their unit and smiled, from the knowledge that the enemy isn't as strong as they want us to believe. But they should beware that the moment they fly their flag, wear their uniform. That they're at war and people die in war, everyone has their enemies.*

Robert Sand, who physically attacked his own lawyer in court at the end of his trial, is serving a life sentence after being convicted of first-degree murder; Laurie Bell was convicted of manslaughter.

One of the challenges of the discipline of criminology is to make sense of cases such as this one. Why did the Sand brothers live such wild and undisciplined lives? Why did they aggressively pursue Constable Strongquill and his partner? Why did Robert see the world as a war zone? Is there anything we can do to prevent tragedies like this in the future?

Criminologists have considered a wide range of theories to explain crime. Some focus on biology—could Robert and Danny have inherited traits from their parents that made their criminality more likely? Others look at an individual's psychological make-up—were the Sand brothers psychopaths, or could other mental conditions have caused their behaviour? Other theories are sociological—what role did their family and friends play in their violence? Could the schools have done a better job motivating the brothers to study and to become involved in legitimate outlets for their energy? What role did racism and the brothers' poor economic prospects play in their lives?

These questions are very complex, and we may never be able to adequately explain individual cases such as this one. However, even if we could explain the factors that led Robert Sands to kill Constable Strongquill, the same explanation would not apply to another homicide that occurred at about the same time. This case involves Diego Zepeda-Cordera, a Toronto barber, who was a

---

*Excerpt from McIntyre, Mike. (2003). *Nowhere to Run: The Killing of Constable Dennis Strongquill.* p. 195. Winnipeg: Great Plains Publications. Reprinted with permission.

member of the Missionary Church of Christ (Galloway, 2003). His 19-year-old son, Walter, began to behave in a way that troubled Zepeda-Cordera. Walter began going out to bars, smoking, and wouldn't help out around the house. His parents found a satanic magazine in his room. His father became extremely concerned when Walter began to speak in gibberish at a religious meeting. Believing his son was possessed by the devil, Mr. Zepeda-Cordero and a friend tied Walter to two metal chairs in their apartment building. Their minister and many church members came to the home to pray over Walter to exorcise the devil they believed was inside him. Walter remained tied to the chairs, often with duct tape over his mouth, for seven days before he died of dehydration. Although the judge in the case believed that the men genuinely thought Walter was possessed and sought to help him, he sentenced them to four years in jail after they pleaded guilty to manslaughter.

As these two examples suggest, different homicides may have little in common other than the death of a victim. Some involve intoxicated people who stab friends during drinking parties; others involve a settling of accounts among organized criminals; some abusive men kill their wives and children; some corporate executives kill their customers by selling defective products in order to enhance their profits, or kill their employees by providing unsafe working conditions; and some predators kill children after having sex with them. In your criminology course, you will learn about these and many other patterns of criminal behaviour.

A White-Collar Crime: The Downfall of Conrad Black

A very different case illustrates the diversity of the behaviour studied by criminologists. During the spring of 2007, Canadian media covered the trial of Conrad Black and several co-accused, who had been charged in the United States with several offences relating to the fraudulent acquisition of funds that should have gone to shareholders of Hollinger International. The funds instead had been taken by the accused, who were managers (but not owners) of the company.

Black's background was very different from that of the Sand brothers. His father was a wealthy businessman, and Conrad had a very comfortable childhood. As a boy he attended Toronto's Upper Canada College, an elite private school, but was unhappy with its discipline. While at the college, he broke into school offices to steal and alter school records. On one occasion, he and several accomplices stole some final exam papers. Perhaps anticipating his later business career, Black had earlier copied the academic records of all the students, so he knew who would be prepared to pay the most for the exam papers. His motivation was not entirely commercial:

> I was going to reduce the school's whole academic system ... to utter chaos while achieving a spectacular mark for myself having done virtually no work ... By the last week of the school year, I had almost completely undermined the system ... I had more power than our jailers. I penetrated the Masters' Common Room and reassigned the faculty to supervisory tasks by typing up and substituting my own assignment

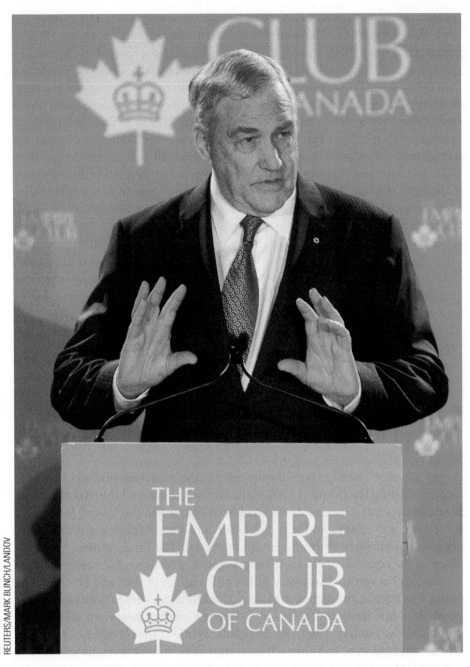

Conrad Black, once the head of Canada's largest newspaper company, spent more than three years in a US jail for fraud and obstruction of justice.

REUTERS/MARK BLINCH/LANDOV

sheet, assuring among other things that our examinations were presided over by the least vigilant people available, the music and printing teachers, as I recall. (Black, 1993, 15)

The scheme unravelled when one of Black's customers confessed to cheating and Black was expelled from the school.

After graduating from law school, Black entered the newspaper business. Along with two partners, he bought a small, money-losing Quebec paper, the *Sherbrooke Record*. Black and his partners quickly discovered a formula that would eventually make them rich. They fired 40 percent of the employees (a step that Black reportedly described as "drowning the kittens" (Plotz, 2001, n.p.), modernized the production process, and began to make a profit. They cut costs relentlessly. When one employee brought Black's partner David Radler a petition signed by newspaper staff complaining about some of the cost-cutting measures, Radler deducted two cents from the man's pay for wasting the piece of paper (Black, 1993). At the same time, Black reports beginning a pattern of behaviour that later led to serious legal problems:

> [At the same time as they were cutting even the most minor expenses at the newspaper] we operated … what amounted to a modest slush fund for our preferred causes and tenuously business-connected expenses. (Black, 1993, 72)

Several times throughout his business career, Black attempted to transfer money from the corporations he ran—but that were owned by public shareholders—to his personal accounts.

Black purchased other small papers and eventually acquired an important British paper, *The Telegraph*, as well as the *Jerusalem Post* and the *Chicago Sun-Times*. He also launched the *National Post* in Canada. Through his corporation, Hollinger International, he ran hundreds of daily papers—including 60 percent of the papers published in Canada—and controlled the world's third-largest newspaper chain (McNish and Stewart, 2004). Black moved to London, England, and in 2001 gave up his Canadian citizenship so that he could accept admission to the British House of Lords and the title Lord Black of Crossharbour. In 2001, shortly after taking his seat in the House of Lords, Black's financial empire began to unravel when he was challenged by investors at Hollinger's annual shareholders' meeting. Some investors wanted to know why their investment in Hollinger was not profitable while Black and other senior executives were getting very wealthy. He was forced to step down from his position as chief executive officer of Hollinger. Meanwhile, an investigation committee established by the board of directors accused Black and other executives of running a "corporate kleptocracy" that had conspired to steal $400 million from Hollinger that should have been paid out to shareholders. The report concluded that "Black and Radler were motivated by a 'ravenous appetite for cash' … and Hollinger International, under their reign, 'lost any sense of corporate purpose, competitive drive or internal ethical concerns' as the two executives looked for ways to 'suck cash' out of the company" (McNish and Stewart, 2004, 288).

While he was under investigation, Black continued to demonstrate the imperious attitude that had characterized his career. In response to criticisms of his extravagance, such as his use of company jets, he responded:

> There has not been an occasion for many months when I got on our plane without wondering whether it was really affordable. But I'm not prepared to reenact the French Revolutionary renunciation of the rights of nobility. We have to find a balance between an unfair taxation on the company and a reasonable treatment of the founder-builder-managers. We are proprietors, after all, beleaguered though we may be. (McNish and Stewart, 2004, 92)

In 2005, criminal fraud charges were filed in the United States against Black and three other executives for conspiring to take funds from Hollinger International for their own personal gain. This was illegal because the corporation was owned by the shareholders, not by the men who ran the company. How did they take the money? Over a period of years, Black had sold off Hollinger's newspapers. When he did so, the buyers paid for agreements that Hollinger would not start competing papers in those markets. However, these noncompete fees were not paid to Hollinger and its shareholders; instead, they went directly to Black and his colleagues, who were alleged to have diverted over $83 million by these transactions. In some cases, the noncompete agreements had not even been requested by the purchasers but had instead been put in the agreement at the request of Black and his colleagues. The money to pay these fees was diverted from the purchase price; thus, the funds that went to Black had essentially been taken from Hollinger's shareholders. In one transaction, Black himself purchased a newspaper from Hollinger; thus, he was actually paid a fee to agree to not compete with himself (McNish and Stewart, 2004). This was done at the expense of Hollinger shareholders, who actually owned the papers being sold.

Black was also charged with misusing corporate money for personal expenses. A key example of this presented by the prosecution at his trial was his use of more than $40,000 of Hollinger money to pay for a lavish birthday party for his wife. Black and his chauffeur were videotaped violating a court order by removing a number of boxes of documents from his Toronto office, so he also faced charges of obstruction of justice. Key to the case against Black was testimony from his partner, David Radler, who had pleaded guilty and received a relatively lenient 29-month sentence in exchange for his testimony against Black.

Black's lawyers claimed that the noncompete payments had been approved by Hollinger's board of directors and were therefore legal. They also claimed that his use of Hollinger funds for parties, trips, and other expenses was legal because the expenses were business-related. For example, his wife's birthday party followed a board meeting and involved contacts with other business people. Also, Black had paid some of the expenses from his own funds to cover the personal component of the event. Finally, they claimed that David Radler was lying in order to get lenient treatment. Indeed, Radler had consistently lied about his involvement prior to his guilty plea, and he had received lenient treatment, so his testimony was vulnerable to those charges by the defence.

In July 2007, Black was convicted on four charges and acquitted on nine others. He was convicted of obstruction of justice because of the documents he had removed from his office. The other convictions related to noncompetition agreements that had not been requested by the buyers of several Hollinger newspapers and to the sale in which Black was paid for agreeing not to compete with himself. He was sentenced to six-and-a-half years in prison and ordered to make restitution of $6.1 million (US). In 2010, after serving two years of his sentence in a Florida prison, the US Supreme Court set aside his fraud convictions and sent the case back to the lower courts for reconsideration, and Black was released from prison on bail. An appeal court upheld both his convictions for fraud and for obstruction of justice. His sentence was reduced to 42 months, and he was ordered back to prison to serve the remainder of his term. He returned to Canada in 2012 and is currently writing a column for the *National Post* (which he had founded) and hosting a television talk show.

Conrad Black and the Sand brothers have little in common except for their criminal convictions. However, these cases show the diverse nature of criminal behaviour and the task faced by theorists who are trying to explain criminality.

What Is Criminology?

The term **criminology** is used in several different ways. Detectives in mystery novels, forensic scientists, and crime analysts on television shows are sometimes referred to as criminologists, as are physicists and chemists who specialize in studying the trajectories of bullets or the ink used in counterfeit money. Most commonly, the term is applied to academics who study crime and the criminal justice system. In this text, we will follow the definition given by two famous American criminologists, Edwin Sutherland and Donald Cressey: "Criminology is the body of knowledge regarding crime as a social phenomenon. It includes within its scope the processes of making laws, of breaking laws, and of reacting to the breaking of laws … The objective of criminology is the development of a body of general and verified principles and of other types of knowledge regarding this process of law, crime, and treatment" (1960, 3). This definition implies that criminologists take a scientific approach to the study of crime.

Why Should We Study Crime?

It is important for us to know more about crime. Social scientists believe it is intrinsically worthwhile to learn more about all aspects of our social lives, including criminal behaviour and society's response to this behaviour. Learning about crime can tell us a lot about our society. For example, the United States has a much higher rate of violent crime—particularly firearms crime—than Canada. The United States also has a much harsher justice system than Canada (see Chapter 15). These differences highlight important value differences between the two countries. Also, just as an understanding of a disease helps medical scientists develop cures, we need to understand crime before we can reduce it. For example, Richard Tremblay tracked the behaviour of children in Montreal as they grew up. He found that boys whose violent behaviour had not declined by age 16 were more likely than other boys to be the sons of young mothers with low levels of education. The Quebec government has used this research to develop support programs for mothers who fit these risk profiles to try to reduce the criminality of their children (Blumstein, 2003). Finally, crime directly or indirectly affects all of us. Many of us have been victims of crime, and all of us pay for the costs of crime and the crime control system.

The Discipline of Criminology

The discipline of criminology includes six major areas: the definition of crime and criminals, the origins and role of law, the social distribution of crime, the causation of crime, patterns of criminal behaviour, and societal reactions to crime.

criminology
The body of knowledge regarding crime as a social phenomenon. It includes the processes of making laws, breaking laws, and reacting to the breaking of laws. Its objective is the development of a body of general and verified principles and of other types of knowledge regarding this process of law, crime, and treatment.

SEARCH FOR:
Criminal Code of Canada

FOCUS

Box 1.1

CRIME AND THE MEDIA

Most Canadians learn about crime through the media rather than from first-hand experience. Media stories shape our views about crime and criminals. Writers of television shows and movies use violence to attract viewers and to sell tickets. Editors and reporters select the crime news we hear and construct the way this news is presented to us in order to attract an audience.

Unfortunately, the picture of crime presented by the media is often inaccurate. For example, most crime is property crime, yet most media stories deal with violent crime. Typical of research in this area was a review of all the crime-related stories reported over two months in an Ottawa newspaper (Gabor, 1994). Over half the stories focused on violent crimes, particularly murders. However, violent crimes made up only 7 percent of reported crimes in Ottawa, and the city averaged just six murders per year. While violent crimes were over-reported, property crimes rarely received much attention, and white-collar and political crimes were almost never discussed.

The portrayal of crime in the fictional media is even more distorted. Consider the partial list of the 221 violent acts depicted in *South Park: Bigger, Longer & Uncut*, the R-rated movie based on the animated series *South Park*:

130 weapons fire (with multiple killings), 18 electric shocks, 10 blows to the body, 8 blood spatterings, 3 burnings, 3 hanging-body scenes, 1 breaking of body in half, 1 assault with chain saw, 1 attempted electrocution, and 1 dog attack. (Media Index, 1999)

The popularity of programs such as the various versions of *CSI* (the original program, set in Las Vegas, has spun off *CSI: Miami, CSI: New York,* and *CSI: Los Angeles*) has affected people's perceptions of the justice system. Some prosecutors have noted the "*CSI* effect", which they believe has caused crime victims and jury members to expect more definitive forensic evidence than is available outside the fictional laboratories of a television show (Dowler, Fleming, and Muzzatti, 2006).

Why do the media misrepresent crime? The primary goal of the media is to make profits by selling advertising. Stories that attract viewers or readers will boost ratings and circulation even if these stories do not represent the reality of crime. The informal news media rule "If it bleeds, it leads" reflects the public's fascination with sensationalized, bloody stories such as mass murders or attacks against helpless senior citizens. Also, some of the media have an ideological agenda favouring "tough on crime" policies, which are more likely to be supported by a public that fears being victimized by violent crime.

The media's misrepresentations of crime have consequences. First, Canadians greatly over-estimate the amount of violent crime and have a fear of crime that is higher than the actual risk of victimization. Second, the media provide a distorted stereotype of offenders. Violent crimes are most often committed by relatives, friends, and acquaintances—not by the anonymous stranger so many of us fear. The media also present distorted views of the racial dimensions of crime. Wortley found that while the crime rate is actually lower among immigrants than those who are Canadian-born, the media perpetuate stereotypes: "One popular columnist, for example, wrote that 'our culture is not used to this type of savagery' and that 'this type of crime is the direct result of choosing too many of the wrong immigrants' ... Another reporter maintained that 'White Canadians are understandably fed up with people they see as outsiders coming into their country and beating and killing them" (2009, 349).

Our fear of crime and our image of the criminal have an impact on government policy. Actual crime trends are irrelevant—if the public feels that crime is out of control, it demands that government do something about it. Crime rates are declining, yet a combination of increasing media coverage of crime and pressure from a variety of interest groups has led the federal government to toughen many laws, including those dealing with immigration, young offenders, and firearms.

The media may also be *contributing* to crime. The linkage between media violence and violent behaviour is complex, and researchers disagree about the degree to which television influences behaviour rather than simply reflecting a pre-existing interest in violence. There is, though, a body of evidence concluding that children who are exposed to extensive television violence are more likely to be violent themselves (Christakis et al., 2013).

There is also anecdotal evidence that the media do play a role in individual cases. For example, Virginia teenager Josh Cooke was a fan of the movie *The Matrix*. He had a large poster from the film in his room and had a trench coat like the one worn by the protagonist, Keanu Reeves's character Neo. He also bought a shotgun similar to one used by Reeves in his movie fight against the "agents." In 2003, Cooke used the shotgun to kill his father and mother and then turned himself in to the police. His defence was that he was attempting to escape the Matrix. Several other killers across the United States have also claimed to have been affected by *The Matrix*. Two of these accused have been found not guilty by reason of insanity (Jackman, 2003).

The news media may also provide patterns for criminal acts such as rampage shootings. In the spring of 2014, North America saw three mass shootings within a two-week period, including the ambush deaths of three RCMP officers in Moncton, New Brunswick. While there were differences between these tragic events, there were also similarities, and some researchers believe that these similarities are a result of media reporting of previous events. The shooters carefully plan their actions based on their knowledge of what others have done. This theory helps explain the similarities between rampage killings and also why these events often occur in clusters. One of the few researchers who has interviewed rampage shooters is Australian forensic psychiatrist Paul Mullen, who sets out characteristics common to many of these killers (Alberici, 2007, n.p.). Typically they are young males who have few friends and few intimate relationships. They are resentful, and they blame others for their unhappiness. Typically, they issue "manifestos," often on social media, outlining their grievances and explaining their killing sprees (Knoll, 2010). Their shootings are a way of getting revenge for the injustices they feel they have suffered. Many plan to commit suicide at the end of the killing spree. They are also gun-obsessed, and firearms play a central role in their lives. Unlike many offenders, they carefully plan out their killings and use what Mullen has termed cultural scripts learned through media reports of previous rampage killings.

While it is obvious that most people who see movies such as *The Matrix* or who read news stories about mass shootings do not commit murders, many researchers believe that media exposure can influence people who are predisposed to commit violence. Researchers who have studied rampage killings have recommended that the media reduce coverage of these events (Knoll, 2010). However, these events draw extensive public interest and high ratings, so there is almost no chance these recommendations will ever be adopted.

What the media ignore about crime may be as important as what they report. Some have criticized the media for failing to cover the story of large numbers of missing women in Canada until Robert Pickton was charged with 26 murders. A missing child from a middle-class home will generate an avalanche of publicity; by contrast, it was not considered important or newsworthy that dozens of lower-class women—many of whom were sex trade workers—had gone missing in Vancouver. Robert Pickton's trial generated international coverage, but the media focused on the gruesome crimes and did not consider broader social issues such as legal policies that were endangering sex trade workers, the structural factor that so many of the victims were Aboriginal, or the state's role in producing socially impoverished neighbourhoods such as Vancouver's Downtown Eastside, where Pickton found most of his victims (Hugill, 2010).

The Definition of Crime and Criminals

Not all social harms are criminal, and not all criminal acts are harmful. Thus we must specify which acts are defined as crimes. There are also questions concerning who should be defined as a criminal for criminological research purposes. Should we include someone who has been charged with a criminal offence but not convicted? What about someone who has committed a crime but not been charged? And how about the person who has been convicted of violating workplace safety laws after an employee was killed on the job, when these laws are not part of the Criminal Code?

The Origins and Role of the Law

It is important to understand the social origins of our laws as well as the role that law plays in society. Why are some acts defined as criminal, while others are dealt with under other types of legislation or are not sanctioned at all?

The Social Distribution of Crime

To understand crime we must know such things as the characteristics of people who commit crimes; trends in the occurrence of crime over time; and differences among cities, provinces, and countries in the rates and types of crime. These and other dimensions of the social distribution of crime help criminologists to understand the causes of crime.

The Causation of Crime

One of the most important questions for criminologists is why some people commit crimes while others live more law-abiding lives. In this text you will learn about a wide variety of explanations of criminal behaviour.

Patterns of Criminal Behaviour

Criminal acts are defined by law in terms of categories such as homicide, theft, and sexual assault. Criminologists have conducted extensive research analyzing the patterns of these offences. Among the questions asked by criminologists are these: Who are the offenders? Who are the victims? Under what social circumstances are offences most likely to occur? What are the consequences for crime victims? How can particular types of crime be prevented?

Societal Reactions to Crime

Historically, societies have responded to crime in many different ways. In Canada, we normally process law violators through a criminal justice system that includes the police, the courts, and the corrections system. Criminologists have studied each of these institutions very extensively.

This text does not cover the criminal justice system, because at most colleges and universities it is covered in a separate course. However, a brief overview of the system will help you understand how people charged with crimes are dealt with. As you will learn in Chapter 3, under the Constitution Act of 1867, the federal Parliament has exclusive jurisdiction over criminal law and procedure. Therefore, the provinces and territories cannot pass or amend the criminal law. However, the provinces are responsible for the administration of justice. Because of this division of powers, the Canadian criminal justice system is quite complex. For example, there are many different levels of responsibility for policing. The federal police force—the RCMP—enforces some federal laws, such as the Controlled Drugs and Substances Act, for which it is responsible in all provinces and territories. It also acts as a provincial police force in all jurisdictions except Ontario, Quebec, and parts of Newfoundland and Labrador, which have their own provincial police forces. The provinces pay the RCMP for these services under provincial policing contracts. The RCMP also acts as a municipal police force in some communities. While most of these are small communities, they also do urban policing under contract in larger communities, most notably in the Lower Mainland of British Columbia. While the City of Vancouver has its own municipal force (like most of Canada's large municipalities), several adjoining cities including Burnaby and Richmond are policed by the RCMP. In 2012, there were almost 70,000 police officers in Canada (Statistics Canada, 2013).

The courts, too, come under both federal and provincial jurisdiction. The provinces are responsible for appointing some judges and for administering the "lower" courts that deal with most criminal cases, including those involving young offenders. Higher-level courts that try serious criminal cases are the responsibility of the federal government, as are the provincial appeal courts. Appeal courts do not try cases, but hear appeals of cases decided by other courts. At the top of the hierarchy of courts is the Supreme Court of Canada, which hears appeals of decisions made by provincial courts of appeal.

Offenders who receive sentences of less than two years are dealt with by the provincial government. This includes offenders who receive community dispositions, such as probation or restitution. Those who are imprisoned go to institutions that are run by the provinces. A sentence of two years or more must be served in a federal institution that is run by the Correctional Service of Canada. This service also supervises offenders who are released into the community prior to the expiration of their sentence. The release decision is made by a separate body, the National Parole Board.

Rules and Laws: The Regulation of Behaviour

All groups have rules. Society cannot function without them—if we are to live and to work with others, rules are necessary. We must also have a reasonable expectation that other people will obey the rules. Think of the chaos that would result if each driver decided which side of the road she would drive on each day, or which stop sign he would decide to obey. Most of the time, most of us conform to the **norms** our group prescribes. Of course, not all members of the group obey all the time. All of you have broken many rules, perhaps some of them important ones. In this text, we shall consider the topic of crime— behaviour that breaks the rules. How do rules get established? Why do people break them? How do groups respond to this violation?

We learn most rules so well that we follow them without thinking about them. Following accepted ways of walking and talking is almost automatic because these norms have been internalized. Often we cannot even specify all the rules that govern a particular behaviour—we just follow them. For example, when you try to learn a foreign language you suddenly become aware of many rules, such as those governing verb tenses, that you aren't consciously aware of when you are using your first language. Other rules are not followed in this routine fashion. Many of us may wish to drive above the speed limit, park illegally, or use marijuana but refrain from doing so because of our fear of penalties, while some people may break these rules whenever they get a chance.

Think of some of the informal rules (or folkways) that govern your conduct. When you were younger, your parents probably tried to persuade you to eliminate some of your favourite habits such as eating with your fingers, dipping food in your milk, and banging your toys on the furniture. These are very basic rules— others can be more complex. For example, how do you address the Queen or the Lieutenant Governor if you meet them? Whose name do you mention first when you introduce your 22-year-old spouse to your 60-year-old employer? What are we to make of these rules, which seem, on their face, to be trivial or silly? Rules help us select from the vast numbers of potential behaviours of which we are capable. Do we bow, kiss, or shake hands as a greeting? Which of two persons holds a door for the other? Who gets served first and last at dinner? How do we handle important milestones such as marriage and death? While the way each society solves these little problems may vary widely, each society has provided solutions.

Not only do these solutions avert potential chaos, but following the rules enhances our sense of belonging. The penalties for not following these rules are

norms
Established rules of behaviour or standards of conduct.

usually informal—the disapproval of family, friends, or colleagues, or perhaps a reprimand from an organization to which the violator belongs. However, we normally don't think of the penalties but continue to obey these rules because we have been taught to obey them and because they are part of belonging to the group.

In our society, not all actions are governed solely by these informal means of social control. Why do some informal rules become more formal regulations or laws? Consider the early days of the automobile. Driving was not regulated, and the only rules of the road were those that applied to horse-drawn carriages. When automobiles were open and speeds slow, drivers gave right of way to other drivers who had higher social status, just as was done when walking down the street. However, as speeds increased and as drivers ranged farther from home, this became impractical and the state had to establish more formal regulations. In such cases, the law exists when order can no longer be maintained through informal rules. The law also deals with behaviour that is too serious to be left to informal mechanisms.

What Is a Crime?

The concept of "crime" has been developed relatively recently (Chapter 2). That does not mean that people didn't do harmful things to one another in earlier times, but this harmful behaviour was handled very differently. Prior to the 18th century, in most societies, offences were handled privately by the wronged individual and his or her family. The early courts in Europe and North America dealt with religious and civil law rather than with criminal law.

The Legal Definition of Crime

The most common definition of crime is a *legalistic* one that defines a crime as an act that violates the criminal law and is punishable with a jail term, a fine, and/or some other sanction. This **legal definition of crime** is satisfactory for most purposes and will fit most of the crimes discussed in this text. However, some criminologists have argued for a sociological definition of crime that encompasses a broader range of harmful behaviour than this strict legal definition provides.

Is White-Collar Crime Really Crime?

Edwin Sutherland was one of the most important figures in the development of criminology. In his famous presidential address to the American Sociological Association in 1939, he argued that focusing only on violations of the criminal law presented a misleading picture of crime. Limiting criminological research to offences such as burglary, assault, and theft—which were dealt with in the criminal courts—led to the conclusion that crime was primarily a lower-class phenomenon. He then pointed out that many **white-collar crimes** were being committed by middle- and upper-class people in the course of their business activities. Criminologists neglected these crimes because they were not dealt with by the criminal courts:

> The crimes of the lower class are handled by policemen, prosecutors, and judges, with penal sanctions in the form of fines, imprisonment,

legal definition of crime
A crime is an act that violates the criminal law and is punishable with a jail term, a fine, and/or some other sanction.

white-collar crime
Crime that is committed by middle- and upper-class people in the course of their legitimate business activities.

and death. The crimes of the upper class either result in no official action at all, or result in suits for damages in civil courts, or are handled by inspectors, and by administrative boards or commissions, with penal sanctions in the form of warnings, orders to cease and desist, occasionally the loss of a license, and only in extreme cases by fines or prison sentences. (1940, 8)

Sutherland argued that even though they are not dealt with in criminal courts, the great harm caused by white-collar criminals made it imperative that criminologists study them. He was suggesting that the legal definition of crime be expanded to encompass the violation of other types of laws.

Human Rights Violations as Crime

Another attempt to expand the definition of crime was made by Herman and Julia Schwendinger (1970), who advocated a definition of crime based on **human rights** rather than on legal statutes. If an action violated the basic rights of humans to obtain the necessities of life and to be treated with respect and dignity, criminologists should consider it a crime. Thus government policies that create poverty and homelessness should be studied as crimes along with other practices that cause social harm, including imperialism, sexism, and racism. Advocates of this approach feel that the criminal law has been established by those in power so that acts committed by powerful people are not criminalized. Therefore, they feel the law is biased against the poor. The Schwendingers' proposal explicitly places criminology on the side of the poor and powerless.

Proponents of green criminology, discussed later in this chapter, take a similar view. Many corporations engage in practices that do enormous harm to the environment and to individuals but that do not violate laws or environmental regulations. For example, multinational companies have built factories in China where environmental regulations are lax (Shuqin, 2010). While legal, many of these factories contribute massive amounts of pollution. Green criminologists argue that practices such as these should be studied, despite their legality, because of the harm they cause (Gibbs et al., 2010).

SEARCH FOR:
Universal Declaration of Human Rights

A Continuum of Crime and Deviance

While few criminologists would limit their work to the strict legal definition of crime, most would not make the definition as broad as the human rights approach suggests. John Hagan (1985) defined crime in a way that reflects how most criminologists view their discipline. Hagan (1985) wrote that a definition of crime must encompass not only violations of the criminal law but also "a range of behaviors that for all practical purposes are treated as crimes (e.g., Sutherland's white-collar crimes), as well as those behaviors that across time and place vary in their location in and outside the boundaries of criminal law. In other words, we need a definition that considers behaviors that are both actually and potentially liable to criminal law" (49). Hagan proposed that deviance and crime be considered on a continuum ranging from the least serious to the most serious acts. Seriousness can be assessed on three dimensions:

- *The degree of consensus that an act is wrong.* Most people feel that mass murder is wrong, but there is much less agreement over using marijuana.

human rights
The minimum conditions required for a person to live a dignified life. Among the rights set out by the Universal Declaration of Human Rights are the right to life, liberty, and security of the person; the right to be free of torture and other forms of cruel and degrading punishment; the right to equality before the law; and the right to the basic necessities of life.

- *The severity of the society's response to the act.* Murder is punishable by death in some societies and by life imprisonment in others. On the other hand, possession of small amounts of marijuana may be ignored by the police, and many US states have legalized or decriminalized marijuana.

- *The assessment of the degree of harm of the act.* Drug use, illegal gambling, and prostitution are often considered to be "victimless" crimes that harm only the offender, while serious crimes of violence are considered to be very harmful.

These three dimensions are usually closely related, but not always. The operators of the Westray Mine, whose unsafe practices resulted in the death of 26 Nova Scotia miners, caused a great deal of harm (Box 17.1). But even though most Canadians would probably agree that this negligence was wrong, none of those responsible for the mine were ever penalized for their actions. This approach recognizes that "the separation of crime from other kinds of deviance is a social and political phenomenon" (Hagan, 1985, 49) and allows criminologists to consider a broad range of behaviours, including some types of deviance that may not be against the law. Hagan's approach is illustrated in Figure 1.1, which shows four major categories of crime and deviance: consensus crimes, conflict crimes, social deviations, and social diversions. Although this book will not specifically consider social deviations and social diversions, the distinction between consensus and conflict crimes is an important one that will be discussed in several chapters.

FIGURE 1.1   **Hagan's Varieties of Deviance**

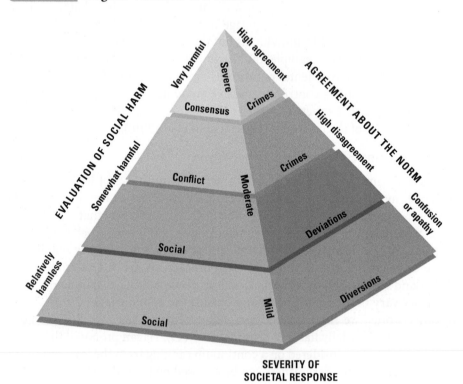

Source: John Hagan. (1991). *The Disreputable Pleasures: Crime and Deviance in Canada*, 3rd ed. Toronto: McGraw-Hill Ryerson, 1991. p. 13. Reprinted with permission.

Crime Is Socially Defined

Can you think of any type of behaviour that *everybody* condemns? Most people might think killing another person is always evil, but this is not the case. Soldiers are considered heroes for killing the enemy during a war. Society allows police officers to kill under some circumstances, and all of us have the right to kill a person who is threatening us with lethal force. Even those who commit what most of us would call murder are not always classified as murderers by the courts. For example, a man may kill his neighbour and be found not guilty by reason of insanity (now called "not criminally responsible on account of mental disorder"). If the same man was sane but intoxicated at the time of the offence, he might be found guilty only of manslaughter. Thus even for an act as serious as killing another person, we must understand the act's social context before we can determine whether it is deviant and how it should be classified.

Other types of crime and deviance are also socially defined. An act is deviant only from the point of view of a set of rules and regulations, and these vary widely from society to society and from group to group. There are some broad similarities in acts that are defined as deviant. For example, most societies, most of the time, disapprove of members killing one another or plotting the violent overthrow of the government. However, there are also great differences between societies and within societies over time. Some societies classify as unlawful acts that are tolerated or even encouraged in Canada, while others permit practices that we condemn. For example, in Saudi Arabia women are not permitted to drive cars or wear short skirts, in Singapore it is unlawful to possess chewing gum (because it is messy), and on some French beaches it is unlawful to wear clothes. All of these practices are quite acceptable here. On the other hand, Canada and most Western countries have laws against helping a terminally ill person commit suicide (though in 2014 Quebec passed a law approving it), while in the Netherlands, doctor-assisted suicide is common.

There is nothing inherent in any act that makes it unlawful. We can define deviance as behaviour that violates the rules, whatever those rules may be. However, this definition leaves us with problems. Whose rules are to be followed? Consider the case of the Muslim father living in Winnipeg who went to court because he wanted his 14-year-old daughter to marry her 27-year-old fiancé. Such a marriage is not permitted by Manitoba law, which sets the minimum age for marriage at 16 (*Winnipeg Free Press*, 1993). Behaviour that was normative from the father's perspective was considered deviant from the province's perspective. What about someone who belongs to an outlaw motorcycle gang? Behaviour that conforms to the standards of that group will often violate the rules of the broader society. The same is true of those who use terrorism to fight what they feel is an unjust political system. If the revolution is successful, they will be heroes. Many political leaders, including Fidel Castro of Cuba and China's Mao Zedong, gained power through violence. However, if the revolution fails, the leaders will be killed or imprisoned. This important question of "Who sets the rules?" will be discussed more fully later in this chapter.

The Relativity of Crime

Since crime is socially defined, the rules can change. A situation in the United States a number of years ago highlighted how changeable the law can be.

Because of pressure from the federal government, many states raised their legal drinking age from 18 to 21. One state did this in stages, with the drinking age rising one year each January 1. In a television interview, a university student whose 18th birthday was in late November described what he was facing for the next three years. Each year, he would be able to legally drink alcohol from his November birthday until midnight on December 31. Since the drinking age changed with the new year, he had to return to soft drinks until the following November when he turned 19. This would go on every year until he was 21, which meant that he could legally drink for less than six months out of the 36 months between his 18th and 21st birthdays.

A more significant example is the fact that several decades ago, the sexual acts of gays and lesbians were prohibited by the Criminal Code and subject to maximum penalties ranging from five to fourteen years (Rodgers, 1962). When former prime minister Pierre Trudeau was the Minister of Justice, he declared that the "state has no place in the bedrooms of the nation" and removed these sections from the Criminal Code. Since that time there have been dramatic changes. Gays and lesbians now have the right to get married, and most of the controversy over gay rights has disappeared.

These examples show that criminal and noncriminal are not two distinct categories. There is an overlap between the two, and the line between them can be ambiguous. We often speak as if the world was divided between criminals and noncriminals. However, we have all broken the law at times—does this mean we are all "criminals"? In fact, phrases like "everybody does it" are used to justify crimes that are committed by "respectable" people (Gabor, 1994), including stealing from employers, not reporting tips and other income on tax forms, and downloading copyrighted material. How do people draw the line between respectable citizens who occasionally do bad things and those they consider "criminals"? What are the implications of thinking of crime as being a matter of degree?

QUESTIONS FOR CRITICAL THINKING

1. Consider Figure 1.1, which shows different types of crime and deviance. Think of behaviours that fit into each of the four categories (consensus crimes, conflict crimes, social deviations, and social diversions). Can you think of examples of behaviours that have moved from one category to another?

2. Look at the way your local newspaper handles crime stories. What picture does the newspaper provide of crime in your community? If you have a tabloid paper (such as the *Toronto Sun*, the *Winnipeg Sun*, or the *Vancouver Province*) in your community, does it handle crime stories in a different manner from other newspapers?

3. Many college and university students have used illegal drugs, and some who work as restaurant servers do not declare all of their income on their tax forms. Should these students be called criminals? Why do you feel they should or should not be called criminals?

Who Makes the Rules? Conflict versus Consensus Theories of Law

Of course the law is not completely subjective or arbitrary. Many criminal laws reflect serious social harms that are illegal in most societies and that most people condemn. However, as you have learned, the exact form of the laws and the specific behaviour prohibited vary greatly in different places and at different times. Why are some acts subject to criminal sanctions while others are not?

One of the most important criminological questions is "Who sets the rules?" Who decided that selling marijuana is illegal while selling cigarettes is respectable? Who determined that an impaired driver who causes the death of a pedestrian can be severely sanctioned, while an employer whose violation of workplace safety rules causes death may receive only a small fine? The issue of how rules come to have a specific content is an important one. There have been two distinct approaches to this question—the consensus and conflict perspectives.

The Consensus Approach

Consensus theorists believe that law represents the consensus of the people. That is, the law reflects the values shared by most members of a society. For example, several Muslim countries have institutionalized sharia law, which is explicitly based on the Koran, so the law reflects those societies' religious values. Similarly, many of the early European settlers in the United States were Puritans who left England for the colony of Massachusetts so that they could freely practise their religious beliefs. Not surprisingly, the legal code of the new colony reflected those beliefs. Much of their legal code of 1648 was taken directly from the Bible, and many crimes were punishable by death. Capital crimes included "idolatry, witchcraft, blasphemy, bestiality, sodomy, adultery, rape, man stealing, treason … cursing or smiting of a parent, stubbornness or rebelliousness on the part of a son against his parents, and homicide committed with malice prepense, by guile or poisoning" (Haskins, 1969, 37). Religious values are not the only ones enshrined in law, but these examples illustrate how values become codified into law.

The consensus view is also supported by the fact that there is a broad agreement regarding many laws, particularly those dealing with street crimes such as robbery, burglary, and murder. Studies that have asked people to rate the seriousness of a broad range of criminal offences have shown considerable agreement among people from Canada and the United States concerning the rankings of these offences (Normandeau, 1966; Akman, Normandeau, and Turner, 1967).

The Conflict Approach

Conflict theorists do not believe that laws reflect a consensus of members of society. Class conflict theorists believe that laws are passed by members of the ruling class to maintain their privileged position by keeping the common people under control. Activities that threaten the powerful are defined as illegal, and the legal mechanism of the state is used to enforce the laws. A historical

consensus theory
Laws represent the agreement of most of the people in society that certain acts should be prohibited by the criminal law.

value
A collective idea about what is right or wrong, good or bad, and desirable or undesirable in a particular culture.

class conflict theory
Laws are passed by members of the ruling class in order to maintain their privileged position by keeping the common people under control.

example shows how the law can be used to further the aims of the politically powerful at the expense of the common people. After the Riel Rebellion in 1885, Hayter Reed, the Assistant Commissioner of Indian Affairs, used the Indian Act to control the Aboriginal population. He deposed many of the chiefs he felt were disloyal and undermined the authority of other Aboriginal leaders by instructing his staff to deal directly with individuals and families rather than with the bands. He also confined Indians to their reserves by ordering the implementation of a pass system that had no justification in law:

> Officials of the [North West Mounted Police] were never comfortable with the absence of any legal foundation for the pass system. The lack of a legal basis in this case undermined the validity of all NWMP operations: they were trying to demonstrate to the Indians that the police enforced a rational system of laws that operated to the benefit of all … In 1893 a circular letter was issued directing all police officers to refrain from ordering Indians without passes back to their reserves.
>
> Hayter Reed would have none of these weak-kneed, legalistic concerns. He urged the police to continue enforcing the pass system on the grounds that the "moral responsibilities of the Indian Department transcended treaty obligations." Reed's views triumphed. By at least 1896 the police had reversed their position. In that year Commissioner Herchmer issued a circular letter instructing police who encountered any Indian without a pass to "use all possible pressure to persuade him to return to his reserve." (Carter, 1990, 153–54)

Reed used the legal system to restrict the movement of Aboriginal people who were believed to represent a threat to the government and to the white settlers who were moving onto the Prairies.

While the pass system has been abolished, the effects of another discriminatory legal intervention targeted at powerless people persist today. Canada has very harsh penalties for the possession and sale of illicit drugs. Though rarely imposed, the maximum penalty for trafficking drugs such as heroin is life imprisonment, and in 2012 the Conservative government passed the Safe Streets and Communities Act, which legislated mandatory prison terms for growing as few as six plants of marijuana if the marijuana was for trafficking purposes.

Why are these drugs punished so severely while other harmful substances such as alcohol and tobacco are legally available? The answer dates back to the early 1900s. Between 1908 and 1929, Parliament passed a series of harsh anti-drug laws, most of which are still on the books. Cook (1969) attributed the severity of these laws to several factors, including racial hostility against Asian immigrants. Not only were the Chinese viewed as inferior, but they had low social status and little power to resist laws that clearly targeted them. While addiction was common among Caucasians, many of whom used opium-based prescription and over-the-counter drugs, the focus of legislators was on those Chinese immigrants who smoked opium rather than on doctors and pharmaceutical companies. Drug laws still disproportionately affect socially disadvantaged Canadians, many of whom are members of racial minority groups. A recent study (Boyd and Carter, 2014) concludes that the police (particularly the RCMP) and the media have misrepresented the dangers of marijuana grow-ops to convince the public that marijuana cultivation poses a

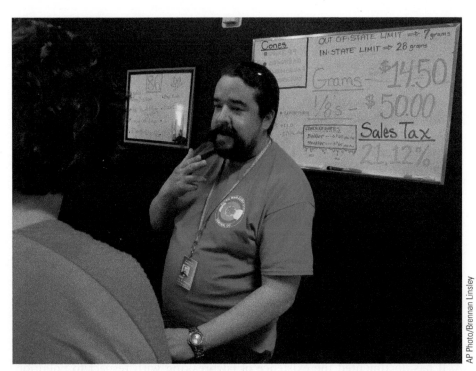

This marijuana store is in Colorado, where voters decided to legalize marijuana sales even while Canada's government was setting harsh mandatory minimum penalties for growing marijuana.

AP Photo/Brennan Linsley

danger to public safety. This campaign has culminated in the very harsh penalties in the Safe Streets and Communities Act at a time when US jurisdictions are legalizing marijuana use.

Both theories of law—consensus and conflict—provide explanations for the development and persistence of some laws. But as Hagan's definition of crime suggests, neither theory provides a *complete* explanation. While many laws benefit the majority of people, other laws benefit the powerful at the expense of the rest of us. Some laws fit into neither category. There is no consensus in Canada about the propriety of marijuana use or gambling, but laws regulating these behaviours do not reflect any particular class interest. Thus, some feel that the most accurate way of describing the process of law formation is group conflict theory. This perspective recognizes that all laws are the result of a political process and that this process typically involves a conflict or a debate among various interest groups. You will learn more about these theories later in this text.

Criminology Is an Evolving Discipline: The Emerging Fields of Green Criminology, Terrorism Studies, and Surveillance Studies

To show how the criminological perspective can help us understand contemporary issues, this chapter concludes with a discussion of three of criminology's newest branches: green criminology, terrorism studies, and surveillance studies. Each of these new areas challenges the discipline by presenting new ways of defining and understanding crime as criminologists engage with significant changes in the world.

Green Criminology

Criminologists are developing a "green criminology" to contribute to the debate about the causes and consequences of environmental destruction and to use their expertise to help address this problem.

Green criminology is rooted in the environmental and animal rights movements, though green criminologists have focused more on environmental issues than on animal rights. These environmental issues include air and water pollution and harm to natural ecosystems such as oceans and forests. Criminologists interested in animal rights study "individual acts of cruelty to animals and the institutional, socially-acceptable human domination of animals in agribusiness, in slaughterhouses and abattoirs, in so-called scientific experimentation and, in less obviously direct ways, in sports, colleges and schools, zoos, aquaria and circuses" (Beirne and South, 2007, xiv; see also Box 1.2). These theorists have introduced the concept of "speciesism," which refers to discrimination against nonhuman animals. Thus green criminology encompasses a broad range of behaviours ranging from acts that are clearly harmful, such as dumping toxic waste in the ocean, to acts that many people consider to be acceptable, such as eating meat or wearing leather shoes.

The range of work done by green criminologists has been outlined this way:

- It has documented the existence of lawbreaking with respect to pollution, disposal of toxic wastes, and misuse of environmental resources.

- It has raised questions relating to the destruction of specific environments and resources in ways that are "legal" but ecologically very harmful to plants, animals, and humans.

- It has challenged corporate definitions of good environmental practice and emphasized the claims of nonhuman nature to ecological justice.

- It has emphasized the dynamic links between distribution of environmental "risk" and distinct communities, particularly how poor and minority populations experience disproportionate exposure to environmental harm.

Jobs such as dismantling ships, which can cause environmental damage and harm to workers, are often contracted to countries where environmental and occupational health and safety laws are very lax and where wages are low. This photo shows workers in Mumbai, India, breaking up ships for recycling as scrap.

AP Photo/Rafiq Maqbool

- It has investigated the specific place of animals in relation to issues of "rights" and human–nonhuman relationships on a shared planet.

- It has criticized the inadequacies of environmental regulation in both philosophical and practical terms.

- It has exposed corporate attempts to stifle environmental critique and dissent through the use of public relations propaganda and strategic lawsuits against public participation.

- It has reconsidered the nature of victimization in relation to environmental changes and events, including social and governmental responses to this victimization.

- It has explored the ways in which law enforcement officials—particularly the police but also environmental protection authorities—have intervened with regard to regulation of fisheries, prosecution of polluters, and conservation of specific environs and species.*

FOCUS

Box 1.2

ANIMAL CRUELTY LAWS IN CANADA

Laws do not just happen: they are the result of a complex social process. The passage of particular laws is influenced by individuals and groups whose interests would be affected by the law. Green criminologists are critical of the fact that the voices of environmentalists are often not heard by politicians, who are also being lobbied by corporate interests that can profit from environmental damage. Current efforts to improve Canada's animal cruelty legislation show how different groups try to ensure that legislation reflects their interests.

Canada has made only minor changes to its animal cruelty legislation since 1892, and there is widespread agreement that stronger laws are needed to prevent animal abuse. Many critics of the current legislation cite an Edmonton case in which two men tied a dog to a tree and beat it to death with a baseball bat. The men were not convicted of animal cruelty because the evidence showed that the dog had died when it was first hit with the bat so it did not suffer cruelty. It is very difficult to get convictions for people who neglect their animals, for the Crown must prove that the neglect is "willful." Thus a farmer whose animals have starved to death will be acquitted unless it can be proved that he or she acted willfully. This is why very few people in Canada have been convicted of animal abuse.

New animal cruelty laws have been before Parliament since 1999. However, the proposed legislation has been opposed by those who fear the laws would affect their livelihoods—hunters, trappers, farmers, and medical researchers who experiment on animals. In 2008, Parliament was faced with two competing bills. The first, S-203, involved minimal changes beyond making the penalties tougher for existing offences. The second, C-229, would have added significant protection for animals. It would have removed the "wilful neglect" provision and would have made it more difficult to kill stray animals. The second bill was supported by many groups, including the Canadian Veterinary Medical Association and virtually all of Canada's humane societies and animal support organizations. On the other side were groups such as the Canadian Sportfishing Industry Association, which claimed that the proposed legislation would jeopardize the $10 billion-a-year sport fishing industry by making it "possible for a Grandfather to face a federal criminal prosecution for taking his grandchildren fishing" (CSIA, 2007). Opponents claimed that the bill would give animals the same legal standing as humans and would encourage animal rights "terrorists" to keep attacking medical researchers (Senate Committee on Legal and Constitutional Affairs, 2006). Proponents of Bill C-229 argued that the bill excluded harming animals for lawful reasons such as hunting and medical experimentation, but this interpretation was challenged by opponents. The Conservative government passed S-203 in 2008, but the bill that would have done much more to protect animals (C-229) has not been passed.

---

*White, Rob. (2007). "Green Criminology and the Pursuit of Social and Ecological Justice." In Piers Beirne and Nigel South (eds.), *Issues in Green Criminology: Confronting Harms Against Environments, Humanity and Other Animals* (pp. 33–34). Portland: Willan Publishing. Reprinted by permission of Taylor & Francis Group.

Green criminologists believe that criminology should study socially harmful actions as well as acts that violate the criminal law. Some environmental harms are illegal. One of Canada's worst environmental disasters was a case of water pollution in Walkerton, Ontario, that caused more than 2,000 people to fall seriously ill and that led to seven deaths. The operators of the water treatment plant who failed to test the water and who falsified test results were successfully prosecuted, but politicians such as former Ontario premier Mike Harris, whose government's policies contributed strongly to the tragedy (O'Connor, 2002) were not prosecuted. However, many actions that are much more serious in the long term, such as the emission of huge quantities of greenhouse gases in the production of oil from Alberta's tar sands (Smandych and Kueneman, 2010), and the clear-cutting of tropical rainforests, are not against the law and may actually be promoted by governments. Green criminologists argue that the damage to the Earth caused by destructive environmental practices can be far more serious than the illegal acts that have traditionally been the focus of criminological study (Lynch and Stretesky, 2007). Global warming could cause mass starvation, migration from countries where drought has caused the collapse of agriculture, and conflict between countries over water resources and food supplies (South, 2010).

Green criminology is grounded in the philosophy of ecological citizenship. This means that notions of morality and rights should be extended to "nonhuman nature" (White, 2007, 35) and that societies should adopt a notion of ecological citizenship that obliges them to recognize that the environment must be protected for future generations. This requires a global perspective because the effects of environmental crimes go far beyond the borders of any single country. This also demonstrates the relativity of crime. Wind and water can easily carry pollution from a country with weak laws and lax enforcement, thereby affecting the health of people in neighbouring countries that may themselves have strong environmental laws and effective enforcement (White, 2011). There are few mechanisms in international law to deal with these transnational issues.

Terrorism Studies

A global perspective is also important in the growing field of **terrorism** studies. Criminologists became more interested in terrorism after the al-Qaeda attacks on the United States on September 11, 2001. Criminologists have looked at several aspects of terrorism, including the recruitment and training of terrorists, the organization of terrorist organizations, links between terrorism and other types of criminality, and the social control of terrorism. Here we will consider two aspects of terrorism studies: the social definition of terrorism and the degree to which Western nations have violated the rule of law in their "war on terror".

terrorism
The illegitimate use of force to achieve a political objective by targeting innocent people.

The Social Definition of Terrorism

There is no universal agreement on the definition of terrorism – the argument is often made that 'one man's terrorist is another man's freedom fighter' (Ganor, 2002). However, a simple definition that captures much of our sense of what terrorism involves is as follows: terrorism is "the deliberate use or the threat to use violence against civilians in order to attain political, ideological and religious goals" (Ganor, 2002, 288).

One reason why an agreed-upon definition is difficult to establish is that "terrorism" is a socially constructed term. Turk has stated the issue:

> Contrary to the impression fostered by official incidence counts and media reports, terrorism is not a given in the real world but is instead an interpretation of events and their presumed causes. And these interpretations are not unbiased attempts to depict truth but rather conscious efforts to manipulate perceptions to promote certain interests at the expense of others. When people and events come to be regularly described in public as terrorists and terrorism, some governmental or other entity is succeeding in a war of words in which the opponent is promoting alternative designations such as "martyr" and "liberation struggle." (2004, 272)

Thus the 9/11 al-Qaeda attack on the United States is generally defined as terrorism by Western countries but is seen by some in other countries as martyrdom for a just cause. The subsequent US invasion of Iraq was not considered terrorism by political authorities in Western countries because the Americans resisted this labelling even though thousands of innocent people were killed during the Iraq War. Actions such as the intensive firebombing of German and Japanese cities by the Allies during the Second World War were not defined as terrorism because those who won the war were able to impose their definitions of these actions.

Another definitional complication is that while we normally consider terrorism to refer to acts committed against a government, the term can also be applied to actions committed by a government against its own people. Joseph Stalin, who ruled the Soviet Union from 1924 to 1953, and Mao Zedong, who controlled China from 1949 to 1976, each killed millions of their own people in order to maintain their political control.

FOCUS

Box 1.3

TERRORISM IN CANADA

Most Canadians are probably unaware that Canada has had problems with terrorism in the past. Kellett (2004) tracked over 400 terrorist incidents in Canada between 1960 and 1992. Most of these incidents involved Canadians attacking domestic targets, and most were committed by two groups: the FLQ and the Sons of Freedom Doukhobors. The FLQ (Front de libération du Québec) were committed to the separation of Quebec from Canada. They financed their political activities through crimes such as credit card fraud and robbery. During the 1960s they were responsible for nearly 100 bombings, including an attack on the Montreal Stock Exchange that injured 27 people. They also kidnapped and murdered Quebec cabinet minister Pierre Laporte in 1970.

The Sons of Freedom Doukhobors were a very different group. They were a pacifist religious group who rejected government involvement in their lives and who refused to pay taxes, to send their children to school, or to register births and deaths. As a result, the British Columbia government removed many of their children from their homes and forced them into residential schools. The group's protests

(continued)

against the government and against other Doukhobors culminated in more than 100 bombings and arson attacks on public facilities such as schools and power lines between 1960 and 1962.

The worst incident of Canadian-based terrorism was the 1985 bombing of Air India Flight 182. A bomb placed in a Boeing 747 in Vancouver exploded over the Atlantic Ocean, killing all 329 people on board. At almost the same time, a bomb placed on another Air India flight from Vancouver exploded at Japan's Narita Airport, killing two baggage handlers. The bombings were blamed on Canadian militant groups supporting a Sikh homeland in India. One man, Inderjit Singh Reyat, pleaded guilty to a charge of manslaughter and building the bombs; he received a 15-year jail sentence. The men accused of placing the bombs, Ajaib Singh Baghri and Ripudaman Singh Malik, were later acquitted. In 2010, Reyat was convicted of perjury in the Baghri and Malik trial and sentenced to an additional nine years in prison.

Terrorist activities have continued over the past decade. In 2006, 18 men were arrested in the Toronto area on charges of planning terrorist attacks in Canada. While not a well-trained or well-organized group, they had plans to detonate several truck bombs and to storm Parliament Hill and behead Prime Minister Stephen Harper. They held training camps north of Toronto (which featured the uniquely Canadian touch of visits to Tim Hortons along with lessons in using firearms and discussions of jihad) and tried to order several tonnes of ammonium nitrate to use in their truck bombs. They were arrested before they got a chance to put any of their plans into action. Eleven of the men were convicted of a variety of charges; their leader received a sentence of life imprisonment.

Most recently, a group of Ottawa men bombed a Royal Bank branch in 2010 to protest globalization, and a Quebec group bombed a Canadian Forces recruiting centre in Trois-Rivières to protest Canada's role in the war in Afghanistan. In 2013, two men were arrested for their involvement in an alleged plot to blow up a VIA Rail passenger train in a case that is before the courts as this chapter is being written.

Terrorism and Rule of Law

Ericson (2007) observed that Western societies have placed a priority on preventing terrorism at all costs: "Normal legal principles, standards, and procedures must be suspended because of a state of emergency, extreme uncertainty, or threat to security with catastrophic potential. The legal order must be suspended to save the social order" (2007, 26). To fight terrorism, the state has assumed greater powers. Enhanced methods of surveillance and control have been put in place, and normal restraints, such as the need for due process and the rights of accused persons, have been ignored in the search for security. For example, the US government has held hundreds of Muslim prisoners in Guantánamo Bay, which is US-controlled territory in Cuba, so that normal American due process rights need not apply. These prisoners are not classified by the Americans as prisoners of war but rather as "unlawful enemy combatants," so the rights provided to prisoners of war by the Geneva Convention also do not apply.

The mandates of Canadian security agencies have broadened since 9/11 (Murphy, 2007). Billions of dollars were added to the budgets of security agencies, including the RCMP, the Canadian Security and Intelligence Service (CSIS), and the Canadian Border Services Agency. New anti-terrorism legislation has expanded the powers of the police and other security agencies. In addition to these new powers, the emphasis on prevention requires that the police use extraordinary tactics, including "the use of paid community informants, extensive community surveillance, broad intelligence-gathering, targeted ethnic and religious profiling, and a preventative security-policing tactic called 'threat disruption'" (Murphy, 2007, 456).

Many governments have violated the rights of some of their citizens in the War on Terror. The most notorious Canadian case involved Maher Arar, a Syrian-born Canadian citizen. Arar was returning from a holiday in Tunisia in 2002 when he was apprehended in New York by US officials. Because of suspected ties to al-Qaeda, he was immediately sent to Syria (a practice known as rendition), where he was tortured in a Syrian prison, likely at the request of US intelligence agencies. He returned to Canada after a year in Syrian custody.

A government inquiry into the Arar case concluded that the RCMP had violated its own policies by providing US authorities with information about Arar that was inaccurate and unfairly negative (Commission of Inquiry into the Actions of Canadian Officials in Relation to Maher Arar, 2006). The RCMP and CSIS did not cooperate with the Department of Foreign Affairs to help secure Arar's return to Canada, and Canadian officials leaked inaccurate classified information about Arar to the media following his return to Canada. The RCMP also concealed information from senior government officials about their handling of the case.

Following the inquiry, the Canadian government formally apologized to Arar and paid him $10.5 million in compensation. US Senator Patrick Leahy's comment on the Arar case offers an eloquent expression of the impact of anti-terrorism programs on the rule of law in many countries: "Maher Arar's case stands as a sad example of how we have been too willing to sacrifice our core principles to overarching government power in the name of security when doing so only undermines the principles we stand for—and makes us less safe" (*Ottawa Citizen*, 2007).

Surveillance Studies

As I am writing the last section of this chapter, parliamentarians in Ottawa are questioning Daniel Therrien, the government's nominee for the position of Canada's Privacy Commissioner. The appointment is controversial because as a government lawyer, Therrien was involved in developing new security legislation, and some of this legislation allowed increased government surveillance of individuals. Some Opposition members and many privacy advocates objected to Therrien's appointment because they did not believe that Mr. Therrien would be a strong privacy advocate.

Why are so many people so concerned about the role of the Privacy Commissioner? Part of the reason is that shortly before his nomination, the government introduced cyberbullying legislation that included requiring telecommunications providers to provide customer information to the police without warrant. Since service providers already respond to 1.2 million requests for customer information each year (Hennessey, 2014), critics are concerned about the privacy implications of giving legal authorities even broader powers.

Governments have always wanted to know more about what citizens are up to, especially in totalitarian countries, where surveillance is often oppressive. However, the technological capacity for surveillance has grown so quickly that massive amounts of personal information are now available. Criminologists, along with scholars from other disciplines, have begun to study the extent and the impact of this surveillance. Four leading Canadian surveillance studies scholars have outlined the problem:

> Today, our lives are transparent to others in unprecedented ways. In Canada, as elsewhere, many kinds of organizations watch what we do, keep tabs on us, check our details, and track our movements. Almost everything we do generates an electronic record: we cannot go online, walk downtown, attend a university class, pay with a credit card, hop on an airplane, or make a phone call without data being captured. Personal information is picked up, processed, stored, retrieved, bought, sold, exchanged. Our lives—or rather, those traces and trails of data, those fragments of reality to which our lives can be reduced—are visible as never before, to other individuals, to public and private organizations, to machines. (Bennett et al., 2014, 3).

What exactly is surveillance? Bennett and colleagues define it as "any systematic focus on personal information in order to influence, manage, entitle, or control those whose information is collected (6).

Governments are relying increasingly on information to govern us, and corporations use our information for their profit. This is not necessarily a bad thing. Government tracking of prescription drug use can help ensure that people are not taking drugs that interact with one another or that addicts are not getting opiate prescriptions written by several different doctors. Police have been able to reduce crime by targeting their efforts on crime hot spots and by monitoring high-risk offenders. Starbucks customers may appreciate having their cellphones receive an electronic discount coupon when they walk near a Starbucks location, and Amazon's suggestions for book purchases based on our buying history can expand our list of favourite authors.

But surveillance can also be harmful. In 2014, Ontario's Privacy Commissioner filed a court action against the Toronto Police Service because they refused to stop releasing information about attempted suicides to other agencies. The action was precipitated by a case involving a woman who missed a Caribbean cruise after she was refused admission to the United States because she had attempted suicide several years earlier. The police had given US officials access to this information. Wealthy people can buy more surveillance than the poor, so offenders may increasingly target neighbourhoods where their actions will not be recorded and monitored. A youthful indiscretion captured in a photo and posted online may cost a person a job when a potential employer views it many years later. Facebook conducted experiments in which they altered the news feeds of hundreds of thousands of subscribers to see if having increased numbers of positive or negative stories altered the tone of users' subsequent posts. Today's unprecedented level of surveillance means that each of us has given up power to the governments and corporations that are collecting and analyzing information about us. Once information has been collected, individuals no longer have control over how it is used.

Bennett and colleagues point out another consequence of the collection of personal information: that information may be used for social sorting, as the data are used to make decisions about our lives. The Ontario woman who had attempted suicide was barred from the United States; the person with a government-issued

Nexus card gets quick passage through airport security screening; the person on welfare or sick leave may be subjected to extra scrutiny to ensure they are not earning extra money. An unintended example of social sorting is provided by Brayne (2014), who found that among people who have been involved with the justice system, the desire to avoid surveillance can limit involvement with institutions such as banks, schools, and hospitals that track and share information. This can impede their reintegration back into society; it can also have impacts on their health, employment, and access to other services.

Surveillance issues are becoming more complex. A major issue is not just the presence of so many surveillance technologies, but the increasing capacity of corporations and governments to link these technologies, as commercial companies aggregate data from multiple sources and as governments establish fusion centres that integrate a variety of different databases to enhance security or to monitor and deliver government services. Drones (small, pilotless aircraft with cameras) are quickly multiplying, and they have unique surveillance capabilities. They are being used globally by military and intelligence agencies; police departments are using them for surveillance and for taking overhead photos of auto accidents and crime scenes; and hydro and pipeline companies are using them to conduct safety inspections on their power lines. When your neighbour can afford a small drone, what privacy rights do you have if he chooses to hover it above your fenced backyard or beside your second-story window transmitting live video of your activities back to his computer screen?

Society has not yet worked out an appropriate balance between privacy rights and the need for more surveillance in order to protect the population or to enable companies to provide better service to customers. This means that surveillance issues will continue to be important and that this new field of criminology will become an important source of theory and data about surveillance and privacy issues.

QUESTIONS FOR CRITICAL THINKING

1. Think of a law that people are currently lobbying to change. What changes are being advocated? Why do some people want to change the law? If anyone is resisting the legal change, why are they offering this resistance? What do you think will be the outcome of this attempt at legal change?
2. Many university students use illegal drugs. Should these students be called "criminals"? Why or why not?
3. What impact would stronger animal cruelty legislation have on meat producers and medical researchers? Do you think that animals should have the same rights as human beings?

● Summary

■ In this text the *term criminology* will refer to the body of knowledge regarding crime as a social phenomenon. It includes within its scope the processes of making laws, breaking laws, and reacting to the breaking of laws. The objective of criminology is to develop a body of general and verified principles and of other types of knowledge regarding this process of law, crime, and treatment.

- The discipline of criminology includes six major areas: the definition of crime and criminals, the origins and role of law, the social distribution of crime, the causation of crime, patterns of criminal behaviour, and societal reactions to crime.

- Our behaviour is strongly influenced by norms, many of which we have internalized. Much of the time we don't even consciously think about the rules that govern our behaviour. Most of the time, rules are enforced through informal means such as the disapproval of our family and friends; however, in some cases the rules are formalized into laws.

- Legally, crime is defined as an act that violates the criminal law and is punishable with jail terms, fines, and other sanctions. Criminologists have expanded on this definition. Discussing white-collar crime, Sutherland said that criminologists should also include violations of other types of laws in addition to criminal law. The Schwendingers proposed that crime be defined as a violation of human rights. Hagan felt that criminologists should consider deviance and crime as a continuum ranging from the minor acts of deviance to serious crimes.

- Crime is socially defined. No behaviour is inherently good or evil, and we must understand the social context of an act before we can determine whether it is deviant and how it should be classified. Also, the form of laws and the specific behaviour that is prohibited vary greatly in different places and at different times.

- Consensus theorists believe that laws represent the will of most of the people in a particular society. By contrast, conflict theorists feel that law reflects power relationships in society, as those with power use the law to help maintain their position. Some laws fit each of these perspectives.

- Like other disciplines, criminology continually moves into new research areas. Three of the newest sub-fields in criminology are green criminology, terrorism studies, and surveillance studies.

NET WORK

A group led by criminologist Delbert Elliott has established a website dedicated to the prevention of violence. The group has assessed over 1200 violence prevention programs and has selected a small number that have a demonstrated ability to reduce violence. Go to the website for Blueprints for Violence Prevention at http://www.blueprintsprograms.com/allPrograms.php. Look at three of the model programs that have been selected by the project. For each of these programs, can you determine what aspect of the child's social environment the program planners are trying to change? What does the success of the three programs you have selected tell you about the causes of crime?

The Social Context of Dispute Settlement and the Rise of Law

Rodney Kueneman and Evan Bowness
UNIVERSITY OF MANITOBA

All human communities have to deal with conflict and develop ways of maintaining social order. In small-scale societies, people lived face-to-face and were known to one another, so when disputes arose, victims or their relatives were responsible for returning harmony to the relationship between conflicting parties. As societies grew in size and complexity, and became increasingly impersonal and unequal, the law emerged as a formal tool for managing discord. In this chapter, we use sociological and historical perspectives to explore the changing social context of dispute settlement. We begin with a discussion of small-scale society, then move to an analysis of the concentration of social power and its relationship to the formation of states and the rise of law. This sets the stage for an analysis of the current weakness in the state's ability to regulate corporate behaviour and its emphasis on street-level crime. We conclude with a consideration of what we see as a return to principles of personal dispute settlement in the form of restorative justice.

Learning Objectives

After reading this chapter, you should be able to

- Understand some of the fundamental differences between small-scale societies and complex industrial societies.

- Trace the changes from community-based dispute resolution processes in small-scale societies to state-controlled processes in more complex societies.

- Explain why knowledge of social context is important in understanding the existence and operation of different dispute settlement systems.

- Understand the emergence and consolidation of social and economic power in human societies and how this concentration has made it difficult to control the actions of those who have power.

- Explain why the rule of law has become a primary force in modern societies and understand the limitations of law as a means of controlling behaviour.

- Discuss how law is shaped by various interests, the limitations of relying on the state to uphold social order, and some of the key threats to contemporary state legitimacy and the rule of law.

- Critically analyze the state's focus on street-level crime.
- Understand the importance of restorative dispute settlement processes in small-scale societies and relate this to their recent reappearance in modern state systems.

This textbook is about crime. It is important to realize that crime does not exist in all societies. In a technical sense, a crime is a violation of a law, and not all societies have had formulated laws. While each society has had to develop a moral order complete with stated expectations for acceptable behaviour, not all societies have developed laws to restrain their members. The formulation of law requires the existence of a central body, such as a **state**, that develops law and enforces compliance with it. This is not only a matter of semantics. For much of human history, social order was maintained by other means.

It is equally important to note that criminal law, as we know it, has not been part of the social fabric for most of human history. In societies without a state, harms between individuals were resolved by various forms of redress. Even in societies with a state apparatus, many disputes are regulated by civil law. Under civil law, the state adjudicates between the parties to the dispute in an effort to repair the damage. Criminal law comes into existence at the point where the state declares itself to be the injured party for certain types of infractions. In its narrowest sense, criminology is concerned with this limited subset of laws and social infractions. But to understand the broad question of social order, it is important to see criminal law in an historical and social context that considers the full spectrum of dispute settlement practices.

The analysis in this chapter follows Lenski (1966), who emphasized the changing **mode of production** in his classification of societies, which had five categories: hunting and gathering, pastoral, horticultural, agricultural, industrial. We will look at the evolution of dispute resolution processes in the context of the major social changes that took place as hunting and gathering societies evolved toward industrial societies. The chapter will show how any discussion of custom, law, and dispute settlement must be placed in its social context if we are to understand how each human society settles the troubles that arise within it. As patterns of societal organization change, new and different forms of dispute settlement emerge.

state
As defined by Max Weber (1864–1920), the state is an institution that claims the exclusive right to the legitimate exercise of force in a given territory through the use of police to enforce laws or the army to maintain civil stability. While there have been stateless societies, most complex societies have state systems of formal government and administrative bureaucracies.

Dispute Resolution in Small-Scale Society

Small-Scale Society and the Origin of Law

For most of human existence, we lived in small hunting and gathering communities. Within these communities, cooperation, mutual aid, and kinship were the essential means of preserving harmony and restoring order. Many of these societies had no centralized structure for decision making, which meant that these communities had to rely on various mechanisms to keep the peace.

The general goal of dispute settlement processes is to restore order. However, the nature of the social order, and the groups that have gained the most advantage as a result of that order, have changed significantly. This chapter will also

mode of production
The dominant form of social and technical organization of economic production in a society. Historically, a variety of modes of production can be distinguished based on both technology and the structure of social relationships.

show how law emerged and evolved to maintain a system of an increasingly unequal distribution of social power. Dispute settlement processes are intimately involved in the structuring of social relationships.

In the next section, the general characteristics of small-scale societies will be described as a prelude to discussing their typical practices for settling disputes. Though such attributes are not present in all small-scale societies, they do appear in virtually all hunting and gathering societies and hence, for the purposes of analysis, are useful as "ideal types."

Without underestimating the often harsh realities of life in small-scale societies, there is no question that such communities were characterized by a strong collective solidarity. Whether they lived in the High Arctic, on the plains, or in the tropical rainforests, hunters and gatherers were well aware that they were part of a natural ecosystem in which there were forces they could not control. They were aware of their individual vulnerability and realized that their collective life was an exercise in mutual survival. The cooperative, mutual-aid character of these societies was not accidental—the near certainty of death for those who lacked the assistance of the group strengthened the group's social cohesion and increased the members' chances for survival.

Another factor that increased solidarity was the relative absence of resource inequality. Living in a subsistence economy where little or no surplus could be generated made it necessary for the group to share the fruits of the day's hunting or foraging. Typically, everyone received an equal and adequate share, regardless of the extent and nature of each one's contribution. In such a distribution system, there may have been collective scarcity if food was not found, but there was never poverty in the sense that some ate while others went hungry. Though a member was not expected to love everyone else, each individual was expected to care for all other members of the community. This ensured that they too would be taken care of in the nonproductive times of their life such as childhood, old age, and sickness. The mutual benefit that characterized social relationships in small-scale societies kept greed and selfishness in check.

The inability to produce or store large amounts of food meant that food gathering was a regular cooperative activity in which all able-bodied members took part. The division and distribution of food to all community members underscored the understanding that everyone had a right to the yield: food was a group possession. The need to move regularly limited the amount of personal belongings a person could accumulate, and since each member had access to the same raw materials, there was little difference in individuals' possessions. There was no individual "self" of the sort so familiar in our society, for the collective interests of the entire group were all-powerful.

The absence of surplus suppressed the emergence of economic stratification and any form of state-like political institution. Small-scale societies had no distinct source of social power or authority independent of the collective will. In such societies, the only form of power available to special individuals was influence, which was based on status derived from hunting skill, sex, wisdom, or generosity, and not on differential access to or accumulation of material resources. Social status was a group property, not a personal attribute. The members of the group could give status and take it away. Hoebel (1973, 82) comments on the position of the Inuit headman: "[He] possesses no fixed

ideal type
A theoretical construct abstracted from experience that brings together observed characteristics of real social relationships. Observed empirical instances are combined to create a social form that has conceptual coherence that is never entirely observed in any actual community but that can be used as a standard against which to compare any real community.

collective solidarity
A state of social bonding or interdependency that rests on similarity of beliefs and values, shared activities, and ties of kinship and cooperation among members of a community.

surplus
The excess of production over the human and material resources used up in the process of production. In simple societies, there was often little if any surplus since the production from hunting and gathering was entirely used up in subsistence. With the development of animal herding and settled agriculture, production exceeded immediate subsistence needs, and social inequality and class division became possible when particular individuals or groups were able to take control of this surplus.

authority; neither does he enter into formal office. He is not elected, nor is he chosen by any formal process. When other men accept his judgment and opinions, he is headman. When they ignore him, he is not." Thus, if an esteemed individual became arrogant or tried to force others to comply in ways that were deemed inappropriate, the group could remove the special status. All aspects of group life worked in a systematic fashion to control and limit the will of the individual in the best interests of the group.

In such close and intimate quarters, members were reluctant to offend one another because of their mutual interdependence. Each member learned to cultivate personal restraint and impulse control in order to prevent the breakdown of a working order. For instance, Colson (1974) shows how these social circumstances fostered the development of forbearance, the avoidance of disputes, the sharing of resources, and the tolerance of human foibles. She relates how the Tonga of Zambia attempted to sidestep controversial issues and how they were reluctant to allow others to drag them into disputes. Their social structure, as well as their fear of attack by sorcerers, worked against outbreaks of violence or other forms of retaliation and contributed to the development of self-restraint.

Colson also notes that the Tonga did not lack "occasion for quarrels and hostility but they learn that they must control their hostility, their greed, and their envy if they are to survive" (61). Such communities could effectively punish any individual who consistently went his or her own way. The self-restraint that members exercised stemmed not only from the close, intimate, and friendly ties that are a product of common life, but also out of the fear of reprisal and the desire to keep hostilities from surfacing and disturbing the business of living.

Dispute Settlement in the Absence of Surplus and Resource Inequality

Of course, disputes still arose in small-scale societies. Newman (1983) provides rich detail concerning the types of disputes that arose among hunter gatherers. For instance, many disputes concerned women. Women were valuable producers, so adultery, failure to honour marriage agreements, and the taking of a woman by an enemy caused serious disruptions. While women were not necessarily considered the property of their fathers or husbands, there was an interest in controlling them as valuable resources in the kin system. Other causes of conflict included improper food distribution, asymmetrical gift exchange, laziness, stinginess, theft, and murder. Theft was an infrequent offence among nomadic foragers because of the relative absence of property. Murders were relatively infrequent and almost always resulted from disputes concerning women.

Regardless of the cause, the major goal of dispute settlement in small-scale societies was to restore harmonious relations between the parties in conflict. It was essential that problems be settled as quickly as possible in mutually agreeable ways so as not to impede group life. The absence of an independent political institution meant that disputants typically had to resolve their differences without an adjudicator (Gulliver, 1979). The community pressured the parties in a dispute to meet and bring an end to the discord. Each party had to exchange information with the other in order to learn the other party's needs and expectations. Through these exchanges, an attempt was made to move toward a mutually agreeable outcome and the restoration of harmony. This approach to discord resulted in a general airing of all the issues that had created friction between the parties. This helped keep the conflict from escalating and brought the dispute to a mutually satisfying conclusion. Potential troublemakers recognized that at some point they would have to confront those whom they had directly harmed. Within this general framework, there was some variation in the types of disputes and the form of the settlement practices.

Self- or Kin-Based Redress

The primary method of redress in small-scale societies was **self- or kin-based redress** (Newman, 1983). The responses available ranged from public criticism, shaming rituals, and temporary ostracism to expulsion from the group, blood feuds, and reprisal killings. Because there was no centralized authority, the injured party had to initiate the dispute process. This does not mean that the victim was free to do whatever he or she wished to an offender. Each society had customary expectations regarding the appropriateness of various reprisals. Too harsh a response could lead to group disapproval and sanctions. When the reprisal was considered more serious than the original offence, the initial offence was expunged and the original offender became the injured party. It is important to emphasize here that self-redress is a regulated social process. The image of small-scale societies as violent and constantly feuding is inaccurate. It is true that disputes did escalate into blood feuds and cycles of revenge killings, but even these proceeded in an orderly fashion. Furthermore, each small-scale society had a body of custom that was coupled with the fear of reprisal; this acted as a brake on escalation by defining the appropriate level of redress for various offences. Clearly defined notions of right and wrong behaviour existed in spite of the absence of third-party authority figures. Formalized civil or criminal law was not necessary for these small, kin-based communities to restore order. An individual who violated a custom suffered the consequences.

self- or kin-based redress
Self-based redress exists where the society allows the harmed party to take matters into his or her own hands in order to seek a settlement. This could be revenge or a successful negotiation of some kind of compensation. Some societies resort to *kin-based* redress, which involves a member of a kin group seeking a settlement on the harmed party's behalf.

During feudal times, disputes were settled by individuals or kinship groups rather than through the involvement of the state.

FOCUS

Box 2.1

TRADITIONAL INUIT AND OJIBWAY DISPUTE SETTLEMENT

The practice in one Inuit village was to call the entire village together and to put the actual event forward as a *hypothetical* event that might happen some time in the future. All people—including the miscreant and his victim—were required to put forward their views as to how things might be handled peacefully and properly were the situation ever to arise. There was no blaming, no pointing of fingers, and no requirement of explanation; nor was there ever any discussion, much less imposition, of either punitive or restitutionary response. At an Ojibway Reserve in my district similar dynamics governed. While the miscreant and his victim were summoned before an Elders Panel, there was never any discussion of what had happened and why, of how each party felt about the other or of what might be done by way of compensation. Nor was there any imposition of punishment. Each party was instead provided with a counselling Elder who worked privately to "cleanse his spirit." When both counselling Elders so signified by touching the peace pipe, it would be lit and passed to all. It was a signal that both had been "restored to themselves and to the community." If they privately arranged recompense of some sort, that was their affair. As far as the community was concerned, the matter was over. While I have not learned what the private counselling did consist of, I have been told that it did not involve retrieval and re-examination of the past in either its factual or emotional facets. It concentrated upon the future, and its spiritual component was central.

As a footnote, such ethics also cast the behaviour of native victims in a very different light. Refusal or reluctance to testify or, when testifying, to give anything but the barest and most emotionless recital of events, may of course have been prompted by fear of the accused, by fear of the court, by love for and forgiveness of the accused or by any other such "sensible" reason (including the possibility, of extreme rarity in my experience, that they are uncomfortable because they are lying). Another reason, culturally foreign to us, could be that giving testimony face to face with the accused is simply considered wrong. It was not part of the traditional processes described above, where in fact every effort seems to have been made to *avoid* such direct confrontation. I recall one Indian woman who repeated her entire story of abuse to me in vivid detail before going into court and then asked me to do whatever I could to have the court send her very dangerous assailant to jail for as long as possible. Ten minutes later she took the witness stand and absolutely refused to say anything of an accusatory nature. When such witnesses regularly ask why they have to repeat their stories in court when they have already told "us" (meaning the police and the Crown), I have come to suspect that it is more than fear or embarrassment at work. I suspect instead that it is perceived as ethically wrong to say hostile, critical, implicitly angry things about someone *in their presence*, precisely what our adversarial trial rules have required … In fact, we have taken this legal challenge into our daily lives, exhorting each person to open up with the other, to be honest and up front, to get things off our chests, etc., all of which are, to traditional native eyes, offensive in the extreme. When they refuse to follow the exhortations of our rules, we judge them as deficient in rule-obedience or, worse still, rule-less. In our ignorance we have failed to admit the possibility that there might be rules other than ours to which they regularly display allegiance, an allegiance all the more striking because it is exercised in defiance of our insistent pressures to the contrary.

Source: Rupert Ross (1989), "Leaving Our White Eyes Behind: The Sentencing of Native Accused." 3 *Canadian Native Law Reporter* 1 at 5–6.

Advisor Systems

A less common method of dispute resolution in small-scale societies was the **advisor system** (Newman, 1983). This was really an extension of the self-redress method of dispute settlement because it was ultimately the victim or kin who enforced any retaliation. Disputants approached advisors, who were typically distinguished warriors, hunters, or speakers. They were mature, although not always the oldest men of the community, and they were regarded as public repositories of wisdom about customs and rituals.

The dispute settlement process was activated when one or both parties sought out one of these high-status figures. They were not required to turn to

advisor system
An extension of the self- or kin-based redress system of dispute settlement. It involves—albeit in a relatively passive way—a third-party decision maker (or makers).

this third party, but it was expected that they would do so. Each party presented its case, and after considering the facts, the advisor recommended what should be done. He interpreted the case with respect to custom, and it was his role to ensure that the social group's conception of appropriate behaviour was protected. He was a moral authority, but he could not enforce compliance. He could, however, attempt to influence the disputants with shaming rituals and compelling arguments. Among some groups, the advisor could take a more active role by indicating which side his own kin group would back in the event of a reprisal. But here, too, the advisor could not direct his kin group; he could only report its position with reference to the dispute. The advisor was, essentially, a communication link between parties, and in that role, he attempted to coordinate a settlement without violence. An advisor gained status by being able to settle disputes before revenge was undertaken. A demonstrated ability to resolve disputes peacefully strengthened his moral authority. If the advisor overstepped his bounds and tried to make his authority too exacting, the community would stop using him as an advisor. In this way, the advisor system was still firmly controlled by the community.

Most hunting and gathering societies relied on self-redress; a smaller proportion developed an advisor system. In general, the dispute settlement processes used by small-scale societies were designed to restore social integration and harmony. These societies tried to contain problems involving members of the community and sought to resolve them through compromise and reconciliation. Any discord created by disputants interfered with the positive relationships among group members, and the group could not afford long-standing rifts of this sort. As Ross (1989) points out, traditional Inuit and Ojibway dispute settlement mechanisms provide a dramatic contrast to the assumptions embedded in the Canadian criminal justice system (see Box 2.1).

On the whole, small-scale societies succeeded very well in avoiding outbreaks of serious trouble. Each member of the community exercised some measure of control over others, so power remained diffuse. The members of the community dealt with discord in such a way that victim and offender could again enter into harmonious interactions after a mutually agreeable settlement of a dispute had been reached.

The Transformation from Small-Scale Society to the State

The Slow Emergence of Social Power and Inequality

In small-scale societies, social **power** was generally shared and was kept under the control of the community as a whole. It was the *group* that moved against the interests of individuals or factions when their actions were viewed as a serious threat to cohesiveness. But new forms of power led to important changes. The emergence of economic surpluses gave rise to "pyramidal" power, whereby a small minority was able to monopolize control of decision making. This was, in effect, the state in its most rudimentary form. The

power
Weber saw power as the ability to realize one's goals despite resistance from others. In small-scale societies, the power to make decisions and affect group life was not institutionalized in social structures, and it was shared by the members of the group. In modern societies, power has become formally encoded in law, and authority (the legitimate use of power) is bestowed by social institutions.

changing role of elders' councils, chiefdoms, and paramount chieftainships (Newman, 1984) points to the slow, progressive development and consolidation of social forms of power that are independent of the community as a whole.

Within the last 6,000 to 8,000 years, as a result of their own development or the invasion of an outside culture, most hunting and gathering societies have been transformed into pastoral, horticultural, agricultural, or industrial societies. At some point during this transformation, the mutuality of face-to-face community-led redress was ruptured. The emergence of the concept of private property slowly and progressively concentrated social power in the hands of a few families and individuals. Privately owned land and livestock meant that the more fortunate members of the community were able to generate a surplus (Newman, 1983). This surplus enabled them to rely less on the community for their survival. In these circumstances, some ancient patriarchs began defining women as property, to secure control of not only their labour but also their reproductive capacity, "in order to ensure that there would be determinate heirs to function as the designatable future owners of individually held accumulations of private property" (Clark and Lewis, 1977, 113).

In small-scale societies, individuals had been expected to discharge their obligations directly to other community members. Slowly, the social elites were able to redirect this exchange to enhance their position in the changing social order. The goods that had been readily available to all members in a simple economy of sharing became distributed in patterns that reflected the stratified nature of pastoral, horticultural, agricultural, and industrial orders. These new modes of production made it increasingly possible for powerful groups and individuals to extract surplus value from those less powerful. The ability of some people to have other people generate personal wealth for them greatly accelerated the formation of structured inequality—that is, patterns of concentrated wealth, resources, and power. Less powerful segments in society found it increasingly difficult to resist those social forces that were compromising their interests.

The state emerged in agricultural society, and it represented the interests of the powerful. The growing size and complexity of social systems gave rise to the need for large bureaucracies and a class of officials whose personal interests became fused with those of the state. Human history was firmly established on a course that would generate hitherto unseen levels of surplus, poverty, and social inequality. The interests of entire groups were devalued and subordinated to the interests of powerful factions and the state. The equality of condition in small-scale societies had been replaced by a class system rife with disparities, and the law became the tool for maintaining that class system.

elder councils
Small groups of respected community members, usually men, who are sought after to determine the best possible outcome of disputes between community members.

chiefdoms
Geopolitical communities ruled by a chief. A chief was the highest political authority in the community and was recognized as having the ultimate power in settling disputes. The chief's decisions were binding, though others may have been required to enforce them. Chieftainships tended to be based on heredity or supernatural knowledge and, chiefs were usually rich men from influential families.

paramount chieftainship
A political system similar to a kingdom that brings together the leaders of a number of partly autonomous villages or communities under the hierarchical rule of a grand chief.

Transformation in the Forms of Dispute Resolution

Changing Forms of Dispute Settlement

As societies changed, so did the types of disputes that arose in them. For example, with the emergence of private property, theft became possible. Also, increased social inequality made theft attractive to the "have-nots." Emerging concepts of rent and contracts led to disputes that required a codified body of civil law. Finally, the emergence of surplus meant that disputes could be settled by the payment of a fine to compensate the party who had been wronged. For example, under Anglo-Saxon law, if a woman was raped, a compensatory fee was paid to either her husband or her father, depending on who exercised the rights of ownership over her at the time of the offence. The fee was not paid directly to the woman herself, because she was not perceived as the person who had been wronged by the act (Clark and Lewis, 1977).

The evolution from social structures such as elders' councils, to chiefdoms, to paramount chiefdoms, and eventually states, set the stage for a legal order of immensely concentrated social power. Increased productive capacity resulted in disputes concerning property, accompanied by increasingly complex legal codifications to deal with them. The creation of chiefdoms and eventually states was accompanied by the emergence of offences such as treason, slander, and libel, and, in general, the possibility for criminal law, defined as offences against the Crown. Any failure to pay taxes or to work on public projects became an offence and a source of litigation.

The transformation of the hunting and gathering social form and the emergence of dispute-settling processes occurred so gradually that the historical actors barely noticed them. However, dramatic social changes were taking place; among them was the beginning of a massive concentration of social power. Once the checks on the accumulation of wealth and power that bound small-scale societies together were undercut, the stage was set for the emergence of a state system.

QUESTIONS FOR CRITICAL THINKING

1. One of the problems with dispute resolution systems based on intervention by the victims or their kinship groups is that they can lead to feuds or vendettas when some parties do not agree with the manner in which a conflict was resolved. How might small-scale societies have avoided prolonging these disputes?
2. Picture three fictitious societies: Society A, which has no surplus or social inequality; Society B, which has a surplus and social inequality; and Society C, which has a surplus but no social inequality. What differences would you expect to see in the types of disputes found in these societies?
3. Pick a social setting, such as at work, on campus, or at home with your family or friends. Does it share any of the key features of small-scale society listed above? For instance, do you feel the presence of mutual-benefit social relations? Is face-to-face interaction the key mode of communication? What gives people "power" in this setting? In what ways does this social setting likely differ from life in an ideal-typical small-scale society?

A Brief History of the Modern State

The emergence of states over the past 3,000 or 4,000 years has created a rich and complex social tapestry. We will outline some of the fundamental changes in the distribution of social power and inequality that occurred during the transition from land-based **feudalism** to the modern capitalist state. These changes set the stage for modern commercial, industrial society. The case of England provides the basis for our discussion of law in Western democratic states because our goal is to understand the social context of legal systems in Canada and the United States. The analysis of law in state systems in other historical circumstances is beyond the scope of this chapter.

A Centralization of Power

Feudalism was a social system based on the tenure of land, which was the dominant form of capital in an agrarian mode of production. The use of land was granted to the vassal or serf in return for military service, compulsory labour, tribute, or, in later years, rent. This relationship, while based on subjection, had a quasi-familial tone, and the lord had a duty to protect and feed his serfs in hard times. The lord controlled the use of the land, and a serf could lose the right to use it only for neglect of the land or failure to meet obligations.

As feudalism developed, the notion of collective responsibility was replaced with that of individual responsibility, and money settlements and fines were used to settle serious disputes. Compliance with these was through local custom, since no centralized source of power had emerged to enforce them. Once Anglo-Saxon lords were able to consolidate some power in England, they began to develop a body of law to deal with disputes. Under this system, trial by ordeal (using such methods as walking on hot coals or reaching into boiling water to pick up a pebble) was the means of establishing guilt or innocence for those who could not find some other way to settle a dispute. The pattern is clear: dispute settlement practices used in small-scale societies were being continuously undermined and replaced by feudal lords and their laws.

Following the Norman Invasion in 1066, William the Conqueror declared himself the "supreme landlord" of all England, so that all individuals who held land held *his* land. Over succeeding centuries, the English kings slowly expanded and consolidated their power over the feudal landscape. The Norman kings saw themselves as the injured party when a crime was committed because the harm was against their peace. Thus, compensation was paid to kings, lords, and bishops rather than to kinship groups. Since some crimes were now against the Crown, the current system of criminal law became a reality. The Crown replaced the victim as the injured party, and compensation to the victim's family was replaced by punitive fines payable to the Crown.

A central authority had emerged in England to replace the authority of feudal lords. The king's system of Royal Courts and Royal Writs created a **common law** that became available to all individuals who sought the jurisdiction of the Crown rather than that of their family or local lord. As Jeffery (1969) has stated, "The family was no longer involved in law and justice. The State was the offended unit, and the State was the proper prosecutor in every case of crime." The law and the courts played a pivotal role in this undertaking to consolidate centralized political and economic power. The growth of trade and the rise of the merchant class also contributed to the decline of the feudal system and to the rise of towns and cities at the expense of the rural manors. Cities began to arise during the reign of King John (1199–1216), and though they were situated on land controlled by feudal lords, they fell under the jurisdiction of the Crown. A new system of social relationships developed based on commerce rather than on feudal obligations.

The Coalition of Merchants and Monarchs: The Rise of the Merchant Class

William the Conqueror created a state apparatus in England when he made all nobles take an oath to establish him as their feudal overlord. With this came the power to create laws to govern the kingdom, Royal officials to protect the king's interests, and Royal Courts to dispense the king's justice. The state apparatus emerged from existing feudal relations. While feudalism was dominant, the king used the state to defend the common interests of feudal lords. However, the breakdown of feudal obligations and the feudal tax system also meant a loss of revenue for the Crown, which needed to find new ways to finance the state and its military. This was accomplished by going outside the feudal system to negotiate loans with merchants, using land as collateral. This was at a time when merchants were gaining considerable power through the expansion of trade.

The kings wanted their power consolidated and needed political support and financial assistance; the merchants wanted a unified and safe trading area (Chambliss, 1969; Hall, 1969a). The state would become the vehicle that the Crown and its merchant allies used to overcome resistance to the new social order. In return for the support of the merchants, Henry VIII conceded that Parliament would have control over tax revenues and the legislative function. Thus the state, which was staffed by the **bourgeois class**, would become the mechanism for change by statute. Laws would be passed by Parliament.

The rising bourgeois class benefited from this new arrangement because they were able to gain greater access to land. When Henry VIII expropriated church lands, more than one-sixth of the land in England was removed from its connection to feudalism. Henry sold this land to friends and allies, for whom he created peerages with seats in the House of Lords. This more than doubled the king's revenues, placed a large block of land outside feudal control, and made it available for purchase. The feudal system continued to decline during the transition to capitalism; many lords were tied into feudal land arrangements of rent, which forced them into financial ruin. Eventually, their lands too were freed of feudal ties and became part of the commodity market, to be bought and sold as private property in the interest of profit. Then in 1540, Henry VIII gave his support to the Statute of Wills, which made most land in England transmittable by will. The role of the Crown had changed from that of shared owner of land under feudalism to that of land regulator via the state, which was becoming a separate and sovereign entity.

The labour of serfs, who had been tied to the land under feudalism, was freed from the land, as were the lords. In addition, much of the land that had been controlled by the church was also made available as commons for serfs to graze their animals. However, the new owners enclosed a great deal of this land for wool production and thoroughly disrupted the lives of the commoners. The right of commoners to hunt, fish, and gather wood on their lord's manor was extinguished under the new property relations. For instance, the Black Act

bourgeois class
The term *bourgeois class*, or *bourgeoisie*, was used by Marx to refer to the capitalist or ruling class in modern societies.

of 1723 increased the number of offences for which the courts could impose the death penalty; these harsh measures were seen as necessary to compel the common people to abandon these feudal practices (Thompson, 1976). The new land regulations displaced the rural workforce, which became the new urban workforce in the factories made possible by technological innovation.

These fundamental changes gave increased importance to commerce and money. The close and personal ties of fealty and its reciprocal duties and obligations were eclipsed by the abstract, anonymous transactions of money in commercial enterprise. The growth of banking institutions, the use of paper currency, and other instruments of credit created new occasions for theft by trusted third parties. The famous Carrier's Case of 1473 made it clear that the law of theft would need to be refined in order to prevent intermediaries from keeping goods put in their possession for transport (Hall, 1952). International trade, spurred by Britain's colonial empire, also necessitated an expansion and refinement of the concept of theft. Hall (1969b) recounts how the law governing embezzlement was enacted to make theft of paper money and commercial bonds a crime. When a business was run by members of a household, behaviour was regulated by custom and family ties. However, as businesses grew, they needed to hire employees from the community who had no other ties to the owners. Transactions between anonymous parties would henceforth be regulated by law because of the absence of customary ties between them.

Law and Transition to Capitalism

During the mid-1500s, the king sought to further consolidate power, and he found that he could make great inroads into the common law by throwing his support behind the merchant class. In return for taxes and loans, the Crown placed the power of the state behind the laws of commerce and enforced these laws. Tigar and Levy (1977) documented this new alliance, in which the merchant class supported the legislative and judicial power of the Crown in exchange for the development of legal mechanisms that would strengthen their class position and increase their fortunes. This guaranteed a primary role for law and lawyers in the new industrial, capitalist mode of production. The king's support of merchant law as the law of the land helped stabilize the necessary social and legal conditions for commerce. The merchant class had supported the Crown's aspirations because its members needed a stable legal system in order to conduct their affairs.

The growth of commerce, spurred by the **Industrial Revolution** and the expansion of trade, required greater uniformity and enforceability of trading arrangements. Towns, cities, and even nation-states realized that a system of laws, and a court system to apply them, would be essential if trade was to stabilize and grow. The volume of trade, its growing impersonality, the practice of joint ventures, and the long distances involved in international trade created the need for a mechanism to secure the interests of traders. Legal contracts, which had existed since Roman times, became the dominant mechanism that would tie social relationships together in the new social order. Tönnies (1887)

Industrial Revolution
A period of social transformation from the mid-1700s until the mid-1800s, marked primarily by new manufacturing technologies and a harnessing of new forms of energy, such as coal and steam.

argued that modern society came to exist as a superior power to enforce the terms set out in the contracts of merchants and capitalists. Lawyers grew in number and importance as new contract forms were developed to meet the increasingly complex trade arrangements of the time. The power of the nation-state was solidified around the interests of commerce, and the role of custom and kinship was eroded. The basis for the new social order was predicated on law, in both commercial and criminal realms.

The power of the bourgeois class in Parliament grew as the landed aristocracy's power waned. Peasants and workers were not represented in this early Parliament, and as a result, the modern state developed under the influence of the bourgeoisie. The rise of the labour movement would come later, but the power of organized labour has never matched that of organized business (Miliband, 1969). While advances have been made in democratizing the state apparatus, it remains a political and legal structure to protect the interests of property.

Contemporary State Power

As feudalism and the power of the monarchy declined, the state became the dominant institution regulating social order and settling disputes. State decisions were backed by the military and police. The state was the superior force behind the contractual arrangements of business and property, and it ensured that the terms of those arrangements were observed.

Law has become the dominant means of regulating human affairs. Legislation and administrative directives are the legal apparatus on which nation-states are now based: property, commerce, real estate, labour, and contractual agreements are all regulated by law. Municipalities and corporations are governed by law, the protection of the environment is regulated by law, and disputes over persons and property are handled through family, civil, and criminal law. In short, the law is the principal means whereby human activity is prohibited, permitted, or required, and the state is intimately enmeshed in the modern social order.

Interest Groups and the Law

As shown in earlier sections, the merchant class has long succeeded in promoting and protecting its interests, and in doing so it has shaped both the state and its laws. But business interest groups are not the only ones that approach the state to promote their interests. A variety of cultural, ethnic, minority, class, economic, and political interest groups also lobby the state. These diverse groups are often at odds with one another, and the state cannot satisfy everyone. Choices need to be made. Given the nature of electoral politics, the state is under some pressure to promote the values and interests of the majority as well as those of powerful minorities in order to maintain legitimacy and popularity.

Drug legislation is one example of how the state responds to various forms of outside pressure. According to Becker (1963), drug legislation in the United States was the result of the efforts of a civil servant, Harry Anslinger, whom Becker "described as a moral entrepreneur" who strongly pushed an anti-drug agenda. And according to Shirley Small (1978), who researched Canadian narcotics legislation, strong anti-Asian racism was a motivating force in campaigns for harsh drug laws. Comack (1985) has shown that these anti-Asian sentiments are best understood as having been grounded in labour disputes, which were addressed in racial rather than class terms.

Graham's (1976) analysis of amphetamine legislation demonstrated the operations of special interests. Despite strong support from the American public and the president, attempts to change the Federal Drug Administration's (FDA) control of amphetamine production failed because of pressure from powerful drug companies that were profiting from drugs sold illegally into the street drug market. A legislative remedy would have done much to promote the common good with regard to this significant problem, but the power of a lobby group that gave huge donations to political campaigns stifled the attempted changes.

Analyses of the history of rape legislation (Brownmiller, 1975; Clark and Lewis, 1977; Kinnon, 1981) show how oppressive and patriarchal laws were enacted to protect the transmission of property in the male line of descent. Fathers used rape laws to avoid transferring property to men of whom they disapproved but who had taken their daughters by bride capture. They also sought compensation for the reduction of bride price they suffered because their daughters were no longer virgins. Husbands wanted to secure control over their wives' reproductive capacity to ensure that they transferred their property to their own sons. As a consequence of all this, women and children became the property of the man of the household, and the act of rape became an offence against the husband. Over time, and as the result of feminist activism, sexual assault has been redefined as a crime against the woman who has been victimized; in some jurisdictions, including Canada, a husband can now be prosecuted for raping his wife. This, of course, means that women have succeeded in having themselves redefined as persons and not merely as the property of their fathers or husbands. But there is still a great deal of dissatisfaction regarding the ability of the law and the justice system to protect women from sexual assault.

A Failure to Regulate

The preceding section showed that law creation is heavily influenced by the pressure that various interest groups bring to bear on the state. **Transnational corporations** are among the most powerful of these groups. Many of these corporations have amassed so much economic power that they are hard to regulate. Some corporations are exceeding the rates of growth of national economies, and this scale gives them considerable power to resist state regulatory efforts. When a government is too restrictive in its regulatory policies, a transnational corporation can relocate operations to another country with laws more to its liking. When environmental regulations are too strict, or when occupational safety rules are too rigid, a corporation can close its production operations in that country and head somewhere else. It is clear that corporations are responsible for environmentally damaging practices that are harmful

transnational corporation
A corporation that has sales and production in many different nations. Because of their multinational reach, these corporations are often thought to be beyond the political control of any individual nation-state.

to individuals, societies, and nature itself and that these harms are not being effectively controlled by the state and the rule of law. The following accounts of victims of avoidable harms help make the point.

Reasons, Ross, and Paterson (1981) analyzed numerous instances in which Canadian workers were needlessly exposed to risks in the workplace that resulted in injury and death. Many of these dangers were known to employers and were avoidable, which led Reasons and colleagues to suggest that these casualties were "victims without crimes." In the same vein, Dowie (1977) reported that the design problems of the Ford Pinto that resulted in passenger injury and death were known by the auto manufacturer, that these problems could have been addressed by cost-effective measures, and that the corporation chose not to make the improvements. Internal Ford memos revealed that the costs of design changes had been compared to the costs of potential litigation for death, dismemberment, and injury and that the company had decided to put Pinto passengers at risk. It is hard to conceive of the death and injury created by the Pinto as accidental when such injury and death were anticipated and could have been avoided. It could be argued that these deaths were homicides and that such harmful behaviour ought to come under the purview of the Criminal Code. Ford was, in fact, charged with homicide for one of the Pinto-related deaths, in Indiana, but it was acquitted by a jury. This kind of reckless corporate behaviour persists (see Chapter 17). Clearly, today's consumer-citizen is not being protected under the rule of law from dangerous corporate misbehaviour.

The courts could move in the direction of holding corporations and their managers accountable for harms such as the one that took place in Cook County, Illinois. In 1985, three former executives of a silver-recycling plant were convicted of murder; each received a sentence of 25 years in prison and a fine of $10,000 for the death of an employee. The company had exposed workers to cyanide gas by intentionally concealing warnings of hazards from immigrant workers. It is believed that these murder convictions were the first in the United States of corporate officials in a job-related death. To date, however, governments have not pursued a vigorous policy of bringing such corporate harms under the appropriate sections of the Criminal Code (see Chapter 17). This case turned out to be a rarity and not a harbinger of greater corporate accountability.

Another clear example of the state's failure to control industrial corporate activity involves the asbestos industry. Asbestos is a heat-resistant mineral that has been used primarily in building insulation. The substance has known carcinogenic and disease-causing properties that, according to WHO estimates, kills 107,000 people annually (WHO, 2010). According to Brodeur (1985), the industry had been aware of the health hazards related to the inhalation of asbestos particles since the 1930s but had withheld this information from workers and did not take steps to improve workplace safety. Juries have found asbestos corporations responsible, and this has unleashed a flood of litigants; the estimated total cost of all claims in the United States is as high as $265 billion (Carroll et al., 2002). At least 73 companies have filed for bankruptcy due to asbestos litigation (Carroll et al., 2005). In an attempt to avoid bankruptcy, many companies have offered to settle asbestos claims out of court in exchange for a maximum ceiling on their liability. In this situation, the state finds itself struggling to balance the rights of individuals to damages on one hand, with the needs of corporations to keep their businesses running and protect their workers from unemployment on the other.

What makes the asbestos example especially troubling is that, while people were clearly harmed with malice and intent, those responsible were not prosecuted by the criminal law. Reasons and colleagues have made a compelling case that many "accidents" in the workplace are not unforeseen and therefore are not accidental. In their view, these harms should be conceptualized as "assaults on workers" and fall under the Criminal Code rather than OHS legislation: "It has been revealed that asbestos companies continued to expose workers to that substance in spite of the fact that they had had evidence concerning its fatal effects for some thirty years. Such conscious, premeditated, and rational behaviour undoubtedly led to thousands of deaths and disabilities. Nonetheless, asbestos companies are only liable to civil lawsuits" (1981, 6). And even though asbestos damages are handled through **tort law**, some states, such as Florida and Texas, have introduced laws that impose barriers on potential plaintiffs who wish to pursue litigation. This is arguably due to the burden these lawsuits place on the courts, in that they have driven up the legal system's operating costs. As other jurisdictions consider similar "tort reform" legislation, and as those who have been harmed by asbestos continue to line up for justice, it remains to be seen whether the state is prepared to hold corporations responsible under the law for their reckless and harmful behaviour.

Transnational corporations exist to make profits for investors, and those profits have often been maximized by reckless and dangerous behaviour. The serious harm to employees, customers, and the environment that has resulted suggests that powerful human actors are currently operating beyond the control of law. Marchak (1991) described some of the serious harms stemming from the creation of **free trade zones** within Third World countries. Countries create free trade zones within their borders to attract corporations. The corporations that establish branch plants within these zones have often been able to negotiate highly favourable terms, including freedom from taxation, exemptions from labour and environmental legislation, and flexible labour regulations that allow them to hire workers very cheaply. One of the more harmful practices described by Marchak is the use of noncitizen, female workers from neighbouring states in microchip production and in the garment industry. For example, "Singapore has imported Malaysian, Thai, Filipina, and Indonesian women as guest workers. These women have no citizen rights and no civil rights, and are deported if their eyesight or productivity fails to please, or if markets slow down" (147). When they are sent back home, they receive no compensation or benefits and typically face severe financial, social, emotional, and health difficulties.

At present, many such harms cannot be brought to the courts for remedy because the state has not defined them as violations of existing law. One might ask whether the modern state has truly established the rule of law when actions like these are not subject to regulation and control. In some important ways, the legal power of states has been superseded by the economic power of corporations. The law cannot impose order in areas of social life where the state does not establish its jurisdiction. The absence of protection from the raw economic power of corporations places citizens in harm's way.

tort law
The branch of law concerning noncontractual wrongs against individuals. Examples include negligence, trespassing, nuisance, and defamation. Tort lawsuits are filed by a plaintiff who seeks compensation for damages purportedly caused by some defendant.

free trade zone
A specially designated geographical area within a nation that is exempt from the regulations and taxation normally imposed on business. These zones are intended to facilitate cross-border production and trade. Zones like these are found along the US–Mexico border, where they are referred to as *maquilladoras*.

Snider (1999, 2000) has described in detail many acts of corporate impropriety in Canada as well as the steps the Canadian government has taken to "make corporate crime disappear." She notes that "the significance of the disappearance of corporate crime speaks volumes about the potential of state law to harness capital. The corporate counter-revolution illustrates how profoundly dependent the promulgation and enforcement of nation-state law is on the balance of powers operating within a society" (1999, 204). She describes how, when unions or social movements are strong, such as in Scandinavia, corporate "downsizing and decriminalization will be resisted longer and more effectively" (204). When they are weak, as in Canada and the United States, corporate wrongdoing is increasingly decriminalized and less and less scrutinized. She adds that progressive social movements have a vital role to play in pressuring states to use law as a mechanism for controlling harmful corporate behaviour. This makes it all the more urgent that we critique the state's failure to protect us from corporate crime (see Chapter 17).

A Coming Crisis in State Legitimacy?

A core function of the law is to foster a willingness to obey the rules. The rule of law depends in large measure on the willingness of the majority of citizens to comply with legal prescriptions and prohibitions. In other words, the citizenry must perceive the state as legitimate. So it is essential that the state system be seen as providing peace, security, good government, and protection from harm. Any state that fails to live up to its end of the social contract will eventually face a **crisis of legitimacy**, which can lead to civil unrest and threaten the state's power. In situations of widespread, sustained disobedience, the social control arms of the state may be unable to cope or even be overwhelmed. In many quarters, dissatisfaction is growing with the nation-state system because of its evident failure to regulate seriously harmful behaviour. Some examples of potential sources of delegitimizing the state include the following:

1. The underregulated business practices of major corporations have introduced massive amounts of toxins into the air, water, soil, and food chain, with severe and profound consequences for human health. The soaring incidence of cancers, birth defects, and other human-caused forms of misery is a clear sign that the state has not been providing basic security from harm. Its limited effectiveness in regulating corporate behaviour is of growing concern. The responsibility to curb the harm caused by irresponsible corporations properly falls within the jurisdiction of the state, given that corporations are created by charters of incorporation approved by the state. Yet the US government has abandoned its right to control corporations—a right that it had been assigned by law when they were first brought into being (Grossman and Adams, 1993). This ineffectiveness may make people critical not only of the corporations but also of the state itself.

2. Systematic and profit-driven assaults on entire ecosystems have resulted in loss of diversity, loss of habitat, species extinctions, and deformities of plant and animal life forms. The cumulative consequences are so serious that they threaten the integrity of the world's ecosystem. This has been referred to as an "ecocide" (Broswimmer, 2002). The fact that such destructive behaviour

crisis of legitimacy
A situation where the state no longer maintains the authority to govern. Sometimes referred to as a legitimation crisis. A number of factors can contribute to such a crisis, for which there are only two possible resolutions: (a) the state regains legitimacy, or (b) a new governing body is instated.

is not criminalized undermines the legitimacy of the nation-state system. Citizens expect the state to protect them and future generations from human-created sources of harm.

3. Economic inequality is approaching extremes. Today, the world's 85 richest individuals own the same amount of wealth as the combined bottom half of the entire global population (Oxfam, 2014) and there have been growing calls for some form of state intervention into the distribution of wealth. The state has the legal means to limit class disparities through taxation policies that would redistribute wealth so as to provide basic security, health, and social justice for a greater number of people. Such progressive legislation had been used in the past, and there are increasing calls for its reintroduction. True, private wealth is private property, but it is important to remember that the notion of private property is a human invention regulated by the nation-state. The failure of nation-states to control egregious disparities of wealth has denied a large part of humanity a decent standard of living. This invites contempt for an unfeeling state apparatus, which in turn brings into question the legitimacy of the status quo and those institutions that make it possible.

These are not hypothetical concerns; we have seen signs of social upheaval, both domestically and abroad. For instance, the "Arab Spring," a wave of revolutionary uprisings in northern Africa and the Middle East, began in late 2010 when a Tunisian street vendor set himself on fire to protest the crippling unemployment plaguing the nation under then-president Zine el Abidine Ben Ali. Over the next three years, hundreds of thousands of protesters took to the streets in many countries across the region; their demands ranged from changes in specific state policies to a complete dismantling of existing governments. These demonstrations have been both nonviolent and violent. Since then, hundreds of thousands of protesters have died in struggles against police and the military. These actions have had a significant impact, spurring regime changes in Tunisia, Egypt, Libya, and Yemen and rebellions in other states, including Syria. There have been victories against oppressive states; however, grassroots efforts to democratize the region have largely faltered, and many of the fundamental issues that inspired the uprisings remain unresolved.

Closer to home, and inspired by the Arab Spring, the Occupy Movement began on September 17, 2011, in Zuccotti Park in Manhattan's financial district. For two months, participants lived in tents as they banded together to voice their concerns about growing income and wealth inequality, the weakening of democracy, and the rise of corporate power. The movement called on citizens to take back the economy and to fight for a more equitable and inclusive society. This demonstration, which went by the name "Occupy Wall Street," took as its slogan "We Are the 99%"—a reference to it members' shared opposition to concentration of wealth in the hands of a tiny ultra-wealthy global elite. The Occupy Movement has inspired international demonstrations, including a Global Day of Action on October 15, 2011, when people in more than 80 countries participated, including in at least 20 Canadian cities. It remains a powerful generator of social action and continues to grow social demonstrations from the grassroots.

These marchers were part of the Idle No More protest in Ottawa. They were marching in support of some young people who had marched 1600 kilometers from the Whapmagoostui First Nation in northern Quebec to Ottawa in support of the movement.

This message is echoed by the Idle No More movement, which Attawapiskat Chief Theresa Spence galvanized during her hunger strike in January 2013. Chief Spence called for a nation-to-nation conversation with Prime Minister Stephen Harper about omnibus legislation the federal government had introduced, which included controversial changes to the Navigable Waters Protection Act. A key issue here was that the changes would reduce protections for rivers, lakes, and coastlines. At the time, controversial projects such as the Enbridge Northern Gateway pipeline were raising concerns within Aboriginal communities. The Idle No More movement was born out of a rejection of complicity in the ongoing history of colonialism and natural resource exploitation. Idle No More has led to protests, flash mobs, and teach-ins across the country, and has heightened awareness of issues facing Indigenous peoples in Canada.

SEARCH FOR:
"The Path of Protest"

Being "Tough" on Street Crime, but Soft on "Suite" Crime

In small-scale societies, every member had direct access to processes of redress; today, not everyone can afford to seek remedy through the courts. Furthermore, some serious harms are not currently subsumed under the law, and without a crime, there are few means available for victims to seek redress. Ever since feudalism gave way to capitalism, the legal process has been controlled and administered by the state, which has come to play the central role in dispute settlement. In small-scale communities, the interests of *all* members formed the basis of customary practice; today, in Western industrial societies, the interests of corporations have been given a special place in law. This has placed ordinary citizens at risk and made it more and more difficult to constrain corporations from systemically harming workers, consumers, and the ecosphere.

The state's failure to regulate harmful behaviours has resulted in growing cynicism about the "rule of law." In this regard, we should turn our gaze to what the law *does* focus on. Clearly, corporations are weakly regulated, but meanwhile, the Canadian federal government is highly vocal about its efforts to curb street-level crime. This loud talk of being "tough on crime," protecting the rights of law-abiding victims of crime, and slamming shut the "revolving prison doors" has meant increased funding for policing and prison expansion, even though crime rates are declining (see Chapter 4). Similarly, the federal agenda has enacted legislative changes such as the Safe Streets and Communities Act, which has imposed mandatory minimum jail sentences for many offences, tighter restrictions on pardons, and eliminated accelerated parole review. The question, as framed by Paula Mallea (2011), has become "will Stephen Harper's billions for his Tough-On-Crime-Agenda make our streets any safer?" The answer to this question is likely no (see Chapter 15).

Yet those who will be processed by the criminal justice system will be those already socially marginalized in an increasingly unequal world. And these policies have proven ineffective in the past and in other countries, such as the United States, where mass incarceration policies are now being scaled back. And the resources the government has earmarked for these changes are needed elsewhere, especially in building stronger communities through social programs and crime-prevention strategies that are "smart," rather than simply "tough" on crime.

Full Circle: Restorative Justice and a Return to Original Forms of Dispute Settlement?

Many critics of the current justice system have advocated returning to a fundamentally different approach that is intended to restore social relationships rather than simply punishing 'criminals.' Advocates of restorative justice seek to return the focus of the justice system to repairing the harm that has been done to the victim and the community. A key element of restorative justice is the involvement of the victim and other members of the community as active participants in the process. The focus of the restorative justice approach is to reconcile offenders with those they have harmed and to help communities *reintegrate* victims and offenders. The source of peace and order lies in a strong, active, and caring community, and proponents of restorative justice feel that a more humane and satisfying justice system can help to rebuild communities that may have been weakened by crime and other social ills.

Canada and New Zealand have led the way in the field of restorative justice. This is due at least in part to the influence of Aboriginal people in these two countries. Rupert Ross (1996) discusses some of the steps undertaken in Aboriginal communities which placed a renewed emphasis on healing as the community response to individual wrongdoing. Many community leaders view the restorative justice approach as a way to restore harmonious relationships and to foster the development of healthy communities.

The restorative approach is not just limited to Aboriginal communities. The Young Offenders Act and its successor, the Youth Criminal Justice Act, mandated youth courts to look for alternative measures to traditional punishment, and options such as restitution, alternative dispute resolution, victim–offender reconciliation, community group conferences, and sentencing panels are being used much more frequently for both juvenile and adult offenders. Braithwaite and Mugford (1994) have discussed some of the ways in which the traditional practices of shame, reintegration, and healing might be introduced into modern urban settings. As outlined earlier, there are important differences in the make-up of small-scale and modern communities. When an offence occurs within the intimacy of small-scale communities it typically involves a victim and an offender who have an established bond. The trouble between them has weakened or shattered the bond, and the dispute settlement process seeks to restore the bond to the satisfaction of both parties and to reintegrate the offender into the community as a member in good standing. In modern communities, no such bond exists between many victims and offenders who are, more often than not, strangers to each other until the offense creates a connection between them. The goal of the restorative approach within this context is not to re-establish a nonexistent earlier bond; rather it is to intervene in such a way that the parties to the conflict can transform the negative ties they have to each other into positive ties. In this sense, conflict can actually create the opportunity for the establishment of positive bonds between former strangers whereas the normal adversarial court practice would solidify their interconnection into a permanent negative tie between them. In other respects, the similarities are worth noting. Not only are the offender and the victim touched by the offence, so too are their immediate circles of family and friends. To the extent that the restorative justice approach can mobilize these "communities of care" (Johnstone, 2002, 51) in support of the healing process and involve them in the development of a solution that they also endorse, a larger community can be created where none existed previously. The restorative approach helps to empower the victims of crime in any community and increases their participation in the dispute resolution process rather than requiring them to surrender their voice to lawyers. While it is too soon to know the degree to which these practices will replace more punitive methods of justice, it is clear that these traditional ideas are being actively reconsidered.

FOCUS

Box 2.2

RESTORATIVE JUSTICE: PRESENT PROSPECTS AND FUTURE DIRECTIONS

There is a difference of opinion as to whether restorative justice can work in communities that do not have strong social ties prior to the commission of an offence. Elmar Weitekamp sees it as follows:

Looking at the newest developments of restorative justice within the context of existing justice systems, one finds that they resemble in fact very old and ancient forms of restorative justice as used in acephelous [without governing chiefs or leaders] societies and other forms of humankind: family group conferences, family conferences, peace circles, community circles, or circle hearings as used by indigenous people such as the Aboriginals, Maori, Inuit, the Native Indians of North America and African peoples. The new concepts and models treat crime as an offence against human

(continued)

relationships, recognize that crime is wrong and when it happens can further alienate the community, the family of the victim and the offender and lead to damage, disrespect, disempowerment and feelings of insecurity. The chance of the restorative justice approach is to recognize the injustice, so that in some form, equity will be restored, thus leading the participants of this process to feel safer, more respected and more empowered. It is somewhat ironic that, at the beginning of the new millennium, we have to go back to methods and forms of conflict resolution which were practised some millennia ago by our ancestors. (325)

In this view, we need to recover the restorative practice and apply it to our efforts to repair the damage done and restore peace between parties to a dispute. There is no call for a change in the overall make-up of social relationships or other social practices of modern society. This view may be overly optimistic regarding the ability of the restorative justice principle by itself to restore peace among offenders, their victims, and their communities of care. Barbara Gray and Pat Lauderdale do not think that restorative principles will be sufficient:

Restorative justice is dependent on the foundational traditional preventative structures and practices that work together to create justice and prevent injustice. Focusing on the restorative aspects of justice without incorporating the preventative mechanisms creates injustice, for it breaks the Circle of Justice and leaves individuals and the community without the necessary cultural foundational structures to heal and prevent crime. (218)

Their point is that restorative principles are but part of a much larger social fabric that has other ways to contribute to the achievement of a Circle of Justice within the community. "The preventative mechanisms are found within the traditional teachings—for example, in ceremonies, songs, dances, stories, kinship relations, and healing and warrior societies" (218).

Teachings within traditional societies promote the development of the "good mind" in each member by implanting "the concepts of love, unity, peace, equity, coexistence, cooperation, power, respect, generosity, and reciprocity" (218). Each member of the community is encouraged to use these concepts, to live in accordance with their teachings, and to retain "balance by respecting and protecting each other and the rest of the natural order" (217).

The foundational narratives of many American Indian nations contain teachings about how humans are to live with each other and the rest of the natural world. They also provide the blueprints for societal structures: the political and spiritual form of governance, kinship relations, and specific duties and responsibilities in maintaining justice within the community. One has a duty to self and to the community to prevent injustice ... The duties and responsibilities of each person in the society are given and reaffirmed every time the people come together for ceremonies and social activities. (219)

The Great Law of Peace [of the Haudenosaunee], then, is a system of checks and balances that depends not only on people not wanting to commit a transgression, but on people understanding and having the will to prevent others from breaching the peace. (220)

From this perspective, attempts to use the restorative aspect without providing the work necessary to build a larger set of preventative peace-keeping practices is unlikely to be adequate to the task.

Sources: Elmar G.M. Weitekamp, "Restorative Justice: Present Prospects and Future Directions," in *Restorative Justice: Theoretical Foundations*, ed. Elmar G.M. Weitekamp and Hans-Jürgen Kerner (Portland: Willan, 2002); "The Great Circle of Justice: North American Indigenous Justice and Contemporary Restoration Programs," *Contemporary Justice Review* 10, no. 2 (June): 215–25, reprinted with permission of the publisher, Taylor & Francis Group, 2007.

It is enticing to imagine that the use of a limited set of restorative justice principles could help repair the damage caused by anonymity, excessive individualism, a heightened form of self-interest, the erosion of cohesive communities, the competitiveness and materialism of modern society, and great inequalities of power and wealth. This is the attraction: we can repair the damage between people who are estranged from one another without repairing the social fabric that made them indifferent strangers in the first place. While this is a small contribution to building community cohesion, it should not be underrated. There is genuine value in creating justice—the foundation for

This photo shows a training session for a restorative justice program that is being implemented to help resolve disputes within a school system.

Photo by Ann Hermes/The Christian Science Monitor via Getty Images

apology and forgiveness—and in creating peace and goodwill in the social circles that were disrupted by the harm done.

QUESTIONS FOR CRITICAL THINKING

1. Proponents of restorative justice advocate that we move away from legalistic, punishment-oriented ways of dealing with social conflict. Do you think this will work in our contemporary society? Can you think of examples of restorative justice programs in your own community?
2. This chapter has discussed the role played by special interest groups in the passage and enforcement of particular laws. What are some of the laws that reflect the interests of some groups at the expense of others? What are some examples of laws that reflect the consensus of most members of society?
3. Assume you live in a small city. A local chemical company has been found to be improperly disposing of hazardous wastes by burying them underground. The wastes have leached into local wells and contaminated the water supply. Some say the company should be prosecuted and its operations shut down; however, the company is the largest employer in the community. Describe several ways in which the community might approach this problem. What sort of outcome is most likely?

Summary

- For most of human history, we lived in small groups. Because individuals lacked the resources to live independently, such societies were coercive in their enforcement of codes of conduct.

- In small-scale societies, disputes were typically settled by the parties to the dispute or by their kinship groups. The individual was expected to show a considerable degree of self-restraint, because the survival of the group depended on the cooperation of all its members.

- While people in small-scale societies were relatively equal to one another, changes in methods of production led to new social formations in which some families and individuals gained greater access to material surplus. This led to the growth of social power, the stratification of society, and the emergence of rulers. This in turn eventually gave rise to the state.

- The rise of the central authority of the state undermined local kinship-based methods of resolving disputes. Harms were now seen as having been done to the ruler, who had displaced the actual victim.

- As the merchant class grew, social life became increasingly regulated by contracts, which were regulated and enforced by a strong central state. The interests of the capitalist class became central to the modern state, and the rule of law became the dominant means of regulating all aspects of human affairs.

- Law is created through a process where various interest pressure the state. Many laws recently have been created, or have not been created, to benefit large corporations.

- The ineffectiveness of the nation-state system to provide peace, security, good government, and protection from harm to large portions of humanity threatens to undermine the legitimacy of the rule of law. Signs of a coming crisis in state legitimacy have appeared recently, such as the Arab Spring and the Occupy Wall Street and Idle No More movements.

- In recent years, we have seen a return to restorative justice practices that are similar to those used in small-scale societies.

NET WORK

You have learned in this chapter that one of the major trends in criminal justice is the return to methods of restorative justice. To earn more about methods of restorative justice, go to the Correctional Service of Canada website at http://www.csc-scc.gc.ca/publications/092/005007-5500-eng.pdf. This will give you access to a report called Satisfying Justice written by the Church Council on Justice and Corrections. Using this report, answer the following questions:

1. What do the authors mean by "satisfying justice"? How can you use this concept to understand the dissatisfaction most Canadians seem to have with our current criminal justice system?

2. Describe four different types of restorative justice programs, and give an example of each.

Criminal Law

Simon N. Verdun-Jones
SIMON FRASER UNIVERSITY

3

C riminology is concerned with crimes and the individuals who commit them. Criminologists must acquire a basic understanding of the criminal law because it is this body of legal rules and principles that designates which types of behaviour should be prohibited and punished and whether those persons who are accused of committing crimes should be convicted and officially labelled as criminals.

Learning Objectives

After reading this chapter, you should be able to

- Define a crime.
- Identify the sources of Canadian criminal law.
- Distinguish between regulatory offences and "true crimes."
- Analyze criminal offences in terms of the *actus reus* (physical) and *mens rea* (mental) elements.
- Understand the differences between subjective and objective *mens rea* requirements.
- Describe the different ways in which a person may become a party to a criminal offence.
- Identify the basic components of the inchoate crimes of counselling, attempt, and conspiracy.
- Describe the major defences that may be raised in response to a criminal charge: not criminally responsible on account of mental disorder, mistake of fact, mistake of law, intoxication, necessity, duress, provocation, and self-defence.

What Is a Crime?

For a lawyer, the definition of a **crime** is remarkably simple: namely, the coupling of a *prohibition* against certain conduct with a *penal sanction* (such as imprisonment or a fine). In Canada, all crimes are the products of a legislative process and are contained in statutes such as the *Criminal Code*. Some crimes may reflect a social consensus that certain conduct is wrong and should be punished (for example, murder and sexual assault). Other crimes may not be based on such a consensus, and a significant proportion of Canadians may not consider them to be inherently wrong and deserving of punishment (for example, assisting a terminally ill patient

crime
Conduct that is prohibited by law and that is subject to a penal sanction (such as imprisonment or a fine).

to commit suicide when he or she is in great pain). While legislators must wrestle with the ongoing task of trying to bring the criminal law into line with emerging community notions of crime and justice, the police and the judiciary are required to enforce the existing criminal law, regardless of their own private views as to whether particular conduct should or should not be defined as a crime (see Box 3.1). While it is important to be aware of the intensely political nature of the process of enacting legislation dealing with crime and punishment, such considerations fall outside the scope of a chapter dealing with the existing criminal law.

FOCUS

Box 3.1

CONFLICT OF VALUES: SHOULD THERE BE A CONSTITUTIONAL RIGHT TO A PHYSICIAN-ASSISTED SUICIDE?

Section 241(b) of the *Criminal Code* makes it an indictable offence to aid and/or abet an individual to commit suicide. While many argue that the great value that Canadians place on the sanctity of human life requires an absolute prohibition on assisted suicide, others assert that it should be a basic human right for an individual to request that a physician assist her or him to end their life if they are suffering from a terminal illness and wish to die with dignity. How should this conflict of values be resolved under the Canadian *Charter* of Rights and Freedoms?

In *Rodriguez v. British Columbia (Attorney-General)* (1993), the Supreme Court of Canada rejected a *Charter* challenge to section 241(b) by a narrow 5–4 majority vote. The case was brought by Sue Rodriguez, a 42-year-old woman who was suffering from amyotrophic lateral sclerosis (or Lou Gehrig's disease). Most people die from this disease within three to five years of the first symptoms appearing. Death is often the result of respiratory failure or pneumonia, and the steady loss of the ability to function independently during the passage to death is frequently a source of extreme physical and emotional distress. Ms. Rodriguez requested a declaration that section 241(b) of the *Criminal Code* was invalid because it violated her rights under the Canadian *Charter* of Rights and Freedoms and was seeking judicial recognition of a constitutional right to a physician-assisted suicide. The Supreme Court of Canada rejected her request.

The majority of the Court took the view that an absolute prohibition on assisted suicide was the only effective means of preventing the abuse of vulnerable individuals who may be pressured into requesting a physician to end their lives. A challenge under section 7 of the *Charter* was rejected because, in the view of the majority, denial of the right to an assisted suicide did not constitute a violation of "principles of fundamental justice": indeed, the majority of the Court asserted that the sanctity of life was a principle of fundamental justice that was

protected by section 241(b). Justice Sopinka stated that section 241(b) underscores the interest of the state in "protecting life" and "reflects a policy of the state that human life should not be depreciated by allowing life to be taken."

It was also argued that section 241(b) infringed the equality provision of the *Charter* (section 15). Rodriguez's counsel had asserted that, since it is no longer a crime to attempt suicide in Canada, able-bodied individuals may decide to take their own lives when faced with a terminal illness that is causing them extreme distress, but such an option is not available to individuals whose physical limitations make it unfeasible for them to commit suicide without the assistance of a physician. According to this view, section 241(b) discriminates on the basis of physical disability and, therefore, violates section 15 of the *Charter*. However, the majority of the Court declined to decide whether section 15 of the *Charter* was infringed by section 241(b) but stated that, even if the equality rights of individuals living with a disability were infringed, the provision would still be justified as a reasonable limitation under section 1 of the *Charter*.

In the years following the *Rodriguez* decision, physician-assisted suicide (under strict legal controls) has been legalized in the Netherlands (2001), Belgium (2002), and Luxembourg (2008) and in four U.S. states (Montana, Oregon, Vermont, and Washington). Should the Supreme Court of Canada reconsider its decision in *Rodriguez*? It will certainly have the opportunity to do so in *Carter v. Canada (Attorney-General)*, a case that the Court recently (January 2014) decided to hear on an appeal from the British Columbia Court of Appeal.

Gloria Taylor was a leading member of a group of plaintiffs in the *Carter* case, which involved an action brought in the Supreme Court of British Columbia to seek a declaration that section 241(b) of the *Code* is invalid under the *Charter*. Like Sue Rodriguez, Gloria Taylor had been diagnosed with ALS. Ms. Taylor was seeking the right to have a physician assist her suicide if she came to the point where her symptoms and reduced quality of life were no longer bearable:

> I do not want to die slowly, piece by piece. I do not want to waste away unconscious in a hospital bed. I do not want to die wracked with pain.

In *Carter v. Canada (Attorney General)* (2012), Justice Lynn Smith of the BC Supreme Court granted the application by Gloria Taylor and others for a declaration that section 241(b) of the *Criminal Code* is invalid. She ruled that section 241(b) infringed sections 15 and 7 of the *Charter* and that it was not "saved" by section 1 because it was not a reasonable limitation on those rights. As it turned out, Gloria Taylor died in hospital of natural causes on October 4, 2012. However, the BC Court of Appeal allowed the Government of Canada's appeal and set aside the decision of Justice Lynn Smith, stating that it was bound by the decision of the Supreme Court of Canada in *Rodriguez* to reaffirm the constitutional validity of section 241(b). The Supreme Court will decide whether its decision in *Rodriguez* should be reaffirmed or overturned when it issues its ruling in the *Carter* case.

Do you think that the Supreme Court should reverse its previous decision in *Rodriguez* and grant Canadians a right to a physician-assisted suicide? Should the Supreme Court have the power to overturn its own decisions, thereby creating uncertainty in the law? Would granting this right undermine the sanctity-of-life principle and set Canadians on a "slippery slope" that would lead to the abuse of weak and vulnerable individuals who might be persuaded to kill themselves to avoid becoming a burden on their families or on society? Alternatively, is it possible to establish a regulatory process that would ensure that only those terminally ill individuals who are competent to make informed end-of-life decisions and who are not being subjected to illicit pressure are granted the right to a physician-assisted suicide? If so, what criteria should be required before a request for a physician-assisted suicide is granted, and what type of procedure should be followed in order to avoid abuse of the weak and vulnerable? Should the procedure be left to physicians to operate or should it be controlled by a judge?

Further Reading: *Carter v. Canada (Attorney-General)* (2012), 287 C.C.C. (3d) 1 (B.C.S.C.). http://canlii.ca/en/bc/bcsc/doc/2012/2012bcsc886/2012bcsc886.html.

Carter v. Canada (Attorney-General), (2013), 302 C.C.C. (3d) 26 (B.C.C.A.). http://www.canlii.org/en/bc/bcca/doc/2013/2013bcca435/2013bcca435.html.

What Is Criminal Law?

The body of jurisprudence known as **criminal law** includes not only the definitions of the various crimes and the specification of the respective penalties but also a set of general principles concerning criminal responsibility and a series of defences to a criminal charge. The focus of this chapter will be on the general principles underlying Canadian criminal law and the major defences that have been developed both by the Parliament of Canada and by judges in the course of deciding specific cases that have come before them.

The Sources of Criminal Law

A basic question about criminal law is "Where does it come from?" There are two primary sources of Canadian criminal law: (1) legislation, and (2) judicial decisions that either interpret such legislation or state the "common law."

Federal Legislation and Criminal Law

Since Canada is a federal state, legislation may be enacted both by the Parliament of Canada and by the legislatures of the various provinces and territories. However, under the terms of the Canadian Constitution, there is a distribution of specific legislative powers between the federal and provincial or territorial levels of government. Under the terms of the *Constitution Act*, 1867, the federal Parliament has the exclusive jurisdiction to enact "criminal law and the procedures relating to criminal matters." One might think that it is

criminal law
A body of jurisprudence that includes the definition of various crimes, the specification of various penalties, a set of general principles concerning criminal responsibility, and a series of defences to a criminal charge.

relatively simple to define the term *criminal law* for the purpose of interpreting the scope of the federal criminal law power under the *Constitution Act, 1867*. However, this task is not quite as straightforward as it may appear at first glance. It was noted above that a crime can normally be defined by two basic elements: (1) a *prohibition* against certain conduct, and (2) a *penalty* for violating that prohibition. However, when the courts are required to decide whether Parliament has enacted legislation that legitimately falls within the scope of its criminal law power, a third element must be added to the definition of a crime. More specifically, the Supreme Court of Canada has ruled that the prohibition and penalty must be directed against a "public evil" or some form of behaviour that is having an injurious effect on the Canadian public. If any of these three elements is missing, the legislation may not be considered to fall within the legitimate scope of the federal criminal law power; indeed, it may be ruled invalid insofar as it intrudes into areas of legislative authority that have been specifically allocated to the provincial and territorial legislatures. Consider the problem of environmental pollution. In the case of *Hydro-Québec* (1997), the Supreme Court of Canada held that the Parliament of Canada could use its criminal law power to enact legislation that imposes penalties on those individuals who engage in serious acts of pollution. The particular legislation in question in this case was the Canadian Environmental Protection Act, R.S.C. 1985, c. 16. In the words of Justice La Forest, "Pollution is an 'evil' that Parliament can legitimately seek to suppress." Therefore, the Canadian Environmental Protection Act was considered to constitute "criminal law" because the Parliament of Canada was unequivocally concerned with the need to safeguard public health from the devastating consequences of toxic pollution. If the Supreme Court had ruled that this statute was not a genuine exercise of the Parliament of Canada's criminal law power, then the Court would have ruled that the Act was invalid. Similarly, in *R. v. Malmo-Levine; R. v. Caine* (2003), the Supreme Court of Canada ruled that Parliament had the authority to prohibit the simple possession of marijuana. Even though simple possession may be viewed as a "victimless crime," the criminal law power may nevertheless be used to protect the users of marijuana from self-inflicted harm. The "evil or injurious or undesirable effect" that Parliament sought to address was "the harm attributed to the non-medical use of marijuana." The Supreme Court, therefore, upheld the constitutional validity of the relevant provisions of the Narcotic Control Act, R.S.C. 1985, c. N-1.*

What important pieces of legislation has the Canadian Parliament enacted in the field of criminal law? Undoubtedly, the most significant federal statute dealing with both the *substantive criminal law* and the *procedural* law relating to criminal matters is the *Criminal Code*, R.S.C. 1985, c. C-46 (first enacted in 1892). "Substantive criminal law" refers to legislation that defines the nature of various criminal offences (such as murder, manslaughter, and theft) and that specifies the various legal elements that must be present before a conviction can be entered against an accused person. The term also refers to the legislation that defines the nature and scope of such defences as provocation, duress, and self-defence.

---

*This Act was repealed in 1996. Possession of marijuana is now prohibited by section 4 of the *Controlled Drugs and Substances Act*, S.C. 1996, c. 19 (which came into force on May 14, 1997).

The term **criminal procedure** refers to legislation that specifies the procedures to be followed in the prosecution of a criminal case and that defines the nature and scope of the powers of criminal justice officials. For example, the procedural provisions of the *Criminal Code* classify offences into three categories: (1) *indictable offences*, (2) offences punishable on *summary conviction*, and (3) *"mixed" or "hybrid" offences*, which may be tried either as indictable or as summary conviction offences. These provisions then specify the manner in which these different categories of offences may be tried within the system of criminal courts. For example, they spell out whether these offences may be tried by a judge sitting alone or by a judge and jury, and indicate whether they may be tried before a judge of the Superior Court or by a judge of the Provincial (or Territorial) Court. Indictable offences carry the most serious penalties upon conviction of the accused. The procedural provisions of the *Criminal Code* are also concerned with defining the nature and scope of the powers of such officials as police officers. For example, these provisions stipulate the nature and scope of the powers of the police in relation to the arrest and detention of suspects. Likewise, the *Criminal Code* articulates the powers of judges in relation to the important task of sentencing convicted offenders.

In addition to the *Criminal Code*, a number of other federal statutes unquestionably create "criminal law." These include the Controlled Drugs and Substances Act, S.C. 1996, c. 19, and the Youth Criminal Justice Act, S.C. 2002, c. 1.

Federal and Provincial or Territorial Regulatory Legislation: Quasi-Criminal Law

Under the *Constitution Act*, 1867, the provincial and territorial legislatures have been granted exclusive jurisdiction to enact legislation in relation to such issues as health, education, highways, liquor control, and hunting and fishing. This legislation may be enforced through the imposition of "a fine, penalty or imprisonment." At first blush, it may seem that the use of punishments of these types would persuade the courts to treat such legislation as criminal law—an area of legislative authority that is reserved exclusively for the Parliament of Canada. However, such regulatory legislation does not constitute "real" criminal law for the purpose of the distribution of powers under the Constitution because such legislation lacks the necessary element of "public evil" that was discussed earlier. Indeed, regulatory legislation is concerned with the orderly regulation of activities that are inherently legitimate (such as driving a vehicle or operating a business). Criminal law is directed towards the control of behaviour that is considered inherently wrong (namely, **"true crimes"** such as theft, assault, sexual assault, and willful damage to property). **Regulatory offences**, therefore, are quite distinct from the "true crimes" that arise under the *Criminal Code* or the Controlled Drugs and Substances Act, and they are, therefore, classified as quasi-criminal law ("quasi" means seeming, not real, or halfway).

Regulatory offences are generally far less serious in nature than "true crimes." Indeed, the maximum penalties that may be imposed for violation of regulatory offences are generally no more than a fine or a maximum term of imprisonment of six months, or both.

Regulatory offences are also included among a broad range of federal statutes that regulate activities that fall within the jurisdiction of the Parliament of

criminal procedure
A body of legislation that specifies the procedures to be followed in the prosecution of a criminal case and that defines the nature and scope of the powers of criminal justice officials.

"true crime"
A "true crime" occurs when an individual engages in conduct that is not only prohibited but also constitutes a serious breach of community values; as such, it is perceived by Canadians as inherently wrong and deserving of punishment. Only the Parliament of Canada, using its criminal law power under the *Constitution Act*, 1867, may enact a "true crime."

regulatory offences
Regulatory offences arise under legislation (either federal, provincial, or territorial) that regulates inherently legitimate activities connected with trade, commerce, and industry or with everyday living (driving, fishing, etc.). These offences are not considered to be serious and usually carry only a relatively minor penalty upon conviction. Indeed, many regulatory offences are sanctioned by means of a ticketing system, and the fines may often be paid online.

Canada: for example, the Competition Act, R.S.C. 1985, C. c-34; the Fisheries Act, R.S.C. 1985, c. F-14; the Food and Drugs Act, R.S.C. 1985, F-27; the Safe Food for Canadians Act, S.C. 2012, c. 24; the Species at Risk Act, S.C. 2002, c. 29; and the Tobacco Act, S.C. 1996, c. 13. Along with the quasi-criminal offences created under provincial and territorial legislation, these federal regulatory offences contribute to a vast pool of quasi-criminal law that is becoming increasingly complex. Most lawyers are only acquainted with a fraction of the hundreds of thousands of regulatory offences that exist under both federal and provincial or territorial legislation. However, ignorance of the law is no excuse for those who commit regulatory offences.

Judge-Made Criminal Law

The second major source of criminal law in Canada is the large body of judicial decisions that either interpret criminal legislation or expound the "common law"—a term that refers to that body of judge-made law that evolved in areas not covered by legislation. Parliament cannot provide for every possibility or provide comprehensive definitions of every term used in the legislation it enacts. Therefore there is always great scope for judicial interpretation of the *Criminal Code*. For example, in section 380 of the Code, Parliament has created the offence of fraud. According to section 380, fraud may be committed by "deceit, falsehood, or other fraudulent means." However, the term "other fraudulent means" was left undefined, and it was left to the Supreme Court of Canada to provide a working definition in the case of *R. v. Olan, Hudson and Hartnett* (1978), namely, "all other means which can properly be stigmatized as dishonest."

common law
The body of judge-made law that has evolved in areas not covered by legislation.

Terri-Jean Bedford is one of the current and former sex trade workers who challenged the constitutionality of Canada's prostitution laws. In 2013 the Supreme Court of Canada upheld their challenge and gave the federal government one year to change this legislation.

THE CANADIAN PRESS/Colin Perkel

In discussing the common law it is important to recognize that, historically, much of the English criminal law, upon which the *Criminal Code* of 1892 was loosely based, was developed by judges who were required to deal with new situations that were not dealt with by the legislation of the day. In Canada, one common law offence still exists—contempt of court. With the exception of contempt of court, the *Criminal Code* (section 9) has, since 1954, stated that judges cannot create any new common law crimes. However, judges have developed a number of common law *defences* that were not dealt with by legislation. For example, Canadian courts have developed a defence of necessity even though it is not mentioned in the *Criminal Code*; hence, necessity is known as a common law defence. Section 8(3) of the *Criminal Code* preserves any common law "justification," "excuse," or "defence" to a criminal charge "except in so far as they are altered by or are inconsistent with this act or any other act of the Parliament of Canada." This provision is significant because it means that common law defences, such as necessity, may still be developed by Canadian judges.

Impact of the Canadian *Charter* of Rights and Freedoms on Criminal Law

The enactment of the Canadian *Charter* of Rights and Freedoms as part of the *Constitution Act*, 1982, heralded a dramatic new era in the relationship between judges and the elected members of the Parliament of Canada and the legislative assemblies of the various provinces and territories. As an entrenched bill of rights, the *Charter* empowers judges to declare any piece of legislation to be invalid—and of no force or effect—if the latter infringes on an individual's *Charter* rights (such as the presumption of innocence [section 11(d)] or the right not to be deprived of the right to life, liberty, and security of the person except in accordance with the principles of fundamental justice [section 7]). Canadian judges have demonstrated a willingness to use this extraordinary power when they believe it is absolutely necessary to do so. For example, in *Canada (Attorney General) v. Bedford* (2013), three current or former sex trade workers (including Terri Jean Bedford) sought a declaration that a number of *Criminal Code* provisions relating to prostitution* were invalid under section 7 of the *Charter* because they put the physical security of sex trade workers at risk by denying them the opportunity to employ protective measures (such as hiring security guards or screening clients) that would ensure their physical safety. The Supreme Court of Canada agreed with the Ontario Superior Court of Justice that the *Criminal Code* provisions at issue should be declared invalid and of no effect. Chief Justice Beverley McLachlin stated, on behalf of the Supreme Court, that "the impugned laws deprive people engaged in a risky, but legal, activity of the means to protect themselves against [the] risks of disease, violence and death" at the hands of "pimps and johns." The Supreme Court

Charter
The Canadian *Charter* of Rights and Freedoms, enacted by the Canada Act 1982 (UK) c. 11. (See glossary for extended definition.)

---

* Sections 210 (keeping or being in a bawdy-house), insofar as this provision related to prostitution; 212(1)(j) (living on the avails of prostitution); and 213(1)(c) (communicating in public for the purpose of prostitution).

suspended the implementation of the ruling for one year in order to permit the Parliament of Canada to enact new legislation which would regulate prostitution in a manner that does not place the physical security of sex trade workers at risk.

However, the courts are bound to take into account the provisions of section 1 of the *Charter*, which permit Parliament or the provincial or territorial legislatures to impose "such reasonable limits [on *Charter* rights] as can be demonstrably justified in a free and democratic society." This provision requires Canadian courts to engage in a balancing act in which they must decide whether the infringement of an individual's *Charter* rights can be justified in the name of some "higher good." For example, in *R. v. Sharpe* (2001), the Supreme Court of Canada ruled that certain aspects of the child pornography provisions of the *Criminal Code* (section 163.1) infringed the accused person's right to "freedom of thought, belief, opinion and expression"—a right that is guaranteed by section 2(b) of the *Charter*. However, the Court also ruled that the child pornography provisions constituted a "reasonable limitation" on the accused's section 2(b) right and were, therefore, justified under section 1 of the *Charter*. On the other hand, in the *Canada (Attorney General) v. Bedford* case (2013), the Supreme Court held that the *Criminal Code*'s violation of the right of sex trade workers to personal security could not be justified under section 1 as a reasonable limitation on that right.

The Basic Elements of a Crime: *Actus Reus* and *Mens Rea*

In the decision of the Supreme Court of Canada in *Mabior* (2012), Chief Justice McLachlin restated one of the most basic principles of Canadian criminal law:

> A criminal conviction and imprisonment, with the attendant stigma that attaches, is the most serious sanction the law can impose on a person, and is generally reserved for conduct that is highly culpable—conduct that is viewed as harmful to society, reprehensible and unacceptable. It requires both a culpable act—*actus reus*—and a guilty mind—*mens rea*—the parameters of which should be clearly delineated by the law.

The study of criminal law invariably begins with the statement that every criminal offence can be analyzed in terms of two major elements: namely, *actus reus* and *mens rea*. These terms are derived from the Latin maxim, *actus non facit reum nisi mens sit rea* (which, translated literally, means that an act does not render a person guilty unless his or her mind is also guilty). This principle means that an accused person may not be convicted of a criminal offence unless the prosecution can prove the following beyond a reasonable doubt:

(a) that a particular event or state of affairs was "caused" by the accused person's conduct (*actus reus*); and

(b) that this conduct was simultaneously accompanied by a certain state of mind (*mens rea*).

In essence, the concept of *mens rea* refers to the mental elements of an offence, while the term *actus reus* refers to all the other elements that must be proved by the Crown. However, an important gloss must be placed on this seemingly simple formulation—namely, the *actus reus* of a criminal offence includes an element of voluntariness. As Justice McLachlin said, in delivering the judgment of the majority of the justices of the Supreme Court of Canada in the case of *Théroux* (1993):

> The term *mens rea*, properly understood, does not encompass all of the mental elements of crime. The *actus reus* has its own mental element; the act must be the voluntary act of the accused for the *actus reus* to exist.

The *Actus Reus* Elements of a Crime

In general, it is possible to divide the *actus reus* into three separate components:

(a) conduct (a voluntary act or omission constituting the central feature of the crime);
(b) the surrounding or "material" circumstances; and
(c) the consequences of the voluntary conduct.

For example, in order to prove that an accused person is guilty of the offence of assault causing bodily harm (section 267 of the *Criminal Code*), the Crown must establish that the accused applied force to the body of the victim (conduct); that the force was applied without the consent of the victim (circumstances); and that the application of force caused bodily harm (consequences). Bodily harm is defined in section 2 of the *Criminal Code* as meaning "any hurt or injury to a person that interferes with the health or comfort of the person and is more than merely transient or trifling in nature." For example, a swollen face and bleeding nose have been considered to constitute "bodily harm," and Canadian courts have also ruled that the term even includes psychological harm.

There are some significant exceptions to the division of the *actus reus* into three elements. For example, perjury (section 131 of the *Criminal Code*) is an offence that does not require proof of any consequences. Provided the accused person knowingly makes a false statement with intent to mislead a court, he or she will be guilty of perjury even though not a single person actually believed the false statement. However, consequences do constitute a crucial element of the *actus reus* of most criminal offences. Consider the offences of dangerous operation of a motor vehicle causing death, or dangerous operation of a motor vehicle causing bodily harm (section 249 of the *Criminal Code*); these carry maximum penalties of 14 and 10 years, respectively. In contrast, the "simple" offence of dangerous operation of a motor vehicle (where the Crown does not have to prove the consequences of death or bodily harm) carries a maximum penalty of only five years. Occasionally, the *actus reus* of an offence does not contain the requirement that the accused engage in conduct of any kind; instead, the Crown must prove that the accused was found in a particular "condition" or "state." For example, it is an offence, under section 253 of the *Criminal Code*, to be in "care or control" of a motor vehicle while one's ability to operate the vehicle is impaired by alcohol and/or another drug or when

actus reus
All the elements contained in the definition of a criminal offence, other than the mental elements (*mens rea*).

one's blood-alcohol level exceeds 80 milligrams or alcohol in 100 millilitres of blood. This offence does not require proof that the accused person was actually driving the motor vehicle: indeed, the vehicle may be stationary. However, the offence will be established if the accused person's intoxicated condition creates a *risk* that the vehicle might be set in motion and thereby pose a danger to people or property. As Justice Fish, of the Supreme Court of Canada, stated in *Boudreault* (2012):

> "care or control", within the meaning of s. 253(1) of the *Criminal Code*, signifies (1) an intentional course of conduct associated with a motor vehicle; (2) by a person whose ability to drive is impaired, or whose blood alcohol level exceeds the legal limit; (3) in circumstances that create a *realistic risk*, as opposed to a *remote possibility*, of danger to persons or property.

Undoubtedly, the objective of Parliament when enacting section 253 was *preventative*. It permits police officers to intervene in a potentially dangerous situation and eliminate the risk to people and property created by the presence of an intoxicated person who is in charge of a motor vehicle.

An important question to address is whether a failure to act (an omission) can qualify as the conduct element of the *actus reus* of an offence. The answer is that a failure to act can constitute a crime only if the accused was under a pre-existing legal duty to act. A good illustration is the duty owed by a parent to a small child to provide the latter with the "necessaries of life"—for example, by feeding the child and providing him or her with necessary medical care (section 215 of the *Criminal Code*). Under Canadian criminal law, there is no duty to rescue a stranger who is in serious danger. However, there is a duty to rescue when the person in danger is a child or spouse of the accused person or is in some other relationship that imposes a duty to act (for example, a prisoner is owed such a duty by the officer in charge of the jail). Some have argued that the criminal law is seriously deficient insofar as it does not require every adult citizen to take active steps to rescue a person who is in danger provided, of course, that the rescue may be undertaken without an unreasonable degree of danger to the rescuer. However, it may be very difficult to enforce such a duty in practice. For example, suppose a radio message is broadcast reporting that volunteers are needed to help rescue children in a collapsed school. Should everyone who hears that message be legally required to forsake what they are doing and rush to the scene of the disaster?

A final point to be made about the *actus reus* component of an offence concerns the requirement that the accused's conduct be voluntary. If a driver is repeatedly stung by a swarm of bees and crashes his or her vehicle, the accident will be considered the consequence of a series of reflex actions that were beyond the driver's control; clearly, they did not flow from the free exercise of his or her will. Similarly, if an accused person's consciousness is impaired to such an extent that he or she is unable to control his or her actions, it may be concluded that there was no *actus reus* of any criminal offence because the accused acted involuntarily. When this situation occurs, the accused may raise the defence of automatism. Automatism is a rare defence and may be successfully raised only in a very limited number of situations. For example, if an individual is hit on the head and immediately thereafter enters a state of impaired consciousness and assaults another person, he or she may claim the benefit of the defence of automatism—provided it is established that the assault constituted an involuntary action. In practice, automatism is a particularly difficult defence to assert successfully because, in the *Stone* case (1999), the Supreme Court of Canada ruled that the burden of proving the defence is placed on the accused person who raises it (normally, the Crown is required to prove every element of the *actus reus* and *mens rea* components of an offence). Stone had been charged with the murder of his wife, following a series of provocative statements she had directed at him. The accused had stabbed his wife 47 times but claimed that, at the time, he was in a state of dissociation following the shock of the "psychological blow" that had been inflicted on him by his spouse's hurtful words. More specifically, he stated that a "whoosh" sensation had swept over him and that he was unaware of what he was doing. Ultimately, the jury concluded that the claim of automatism had not been proved by Stone. However, Stone was convicted of manslaughter rather than murder because the jury concluded that there had been provocation (within the meaning of section 232 of the *Criminal Code*). Stone's conviction of manslaughter was later affirmed by the Supreme Court of Canada, where Justice Bastarache stated that the plausibility of a claim of automatism in such cases is significantly reduced if the victim is alleged to be the "trigger" of the violence directed at him or her. A successful defence of automatism presupposes that accused persons are plunged into such a state of impaired consciousness that they are barely aware of what is happening around them. In Stone's case, the accused responded directly to what he perceived to be insults, and the jury evidently believed that his actions were those of a man who knew where he was and what he was doing.

The *Mens Rea* Elements of a Crime

Basically, *mens rea* refers to all the mental elements (other than voluntariness) that the Crown must prove (beyond a reasonable doubt) in order to obtain a conviction for a criminal offence. *Mens rea* is rather like a chameleon insofar as it changes its nature from one offence to another. Obviously, the *mens rea* for murder is very different from that required for theft. Furthermore, *mens rea* is not one mental state but rather a combination of mental states; indeed, it is necessary to analyze the *mens rea* required in relation to each of the three elements of the *actus reus* of any particular crime—that is, conduct, circumstances, and consequences.

The requirement that the prosecution prove *mens rea* reflects basic values that Canadians hold in relation to civil liberties. In essence, the *mens rea* requirement ensures that only those defendants who are morally blameworthy are convicted of "true crimes" under the *Criminal Code*. As Justice McLachlin said in the Supreme Court of Canada's decision in *Théroux* (1993),

> *Mens rea* [...] refers to the guilty mind, the wrongful intention, of the accused. Its function in the criminal law is to prevent the conviction of the morally innocent—those who do not understand or intend the consequences of their acts.

mens rea
The mental elements (other than voluntariness) contained in the definition of a criminal offence.

Subjective and Objective *Mens Rea*

There are two very distinct types of *mens rea* requirements in Canadian criminal law: (1) subjective and (2) objective.

Subjective *mens rea* is based on the notion that accused persons may not be convicted of a criminal offence unless (a) they *deliberately intended* to bring about the consequences prohibited by the law, (b) *subjectively realized* that their conduct might bring about such prohibited consequences but recklessly continued with that conduct in spite of their knowledge of the risks involved, or (c) were wilfully *blind* in that they deliberately closed their minds to the obvious criminality of their actions. As Justice McLachlin explained in the Supreme Court of Canada's decision in *Creighton* (1993),

> The requisite intention or knowledge may be inferred from the act and its circumstances. Even in the latter case, however, it is concerned with "what was actually going on in the mind of this particular accused at the time in question."

Subjective *mens rea*, therefore, constitutes a requirement that the accused *deliberately chose to do something wrong*.

Objective *mens rea* is predicated on the principle that accused persons should be convicted of certain offences, not because they intended to bring about the prohibited consequences or acted recklessly, but rather because *reasonable* people, in the same situation, would have appreciated that their conduct created a risk of causing harm and would have taken action to avoid doing so. Here the fault of the accused does not lie in deliberately choosing to do something wrong; instead, the culpability lies in the fact that the accused person had the capacity to live up to the standard of care expected of a reasonable person and failed to do so. As the Supreme Court of Canada stated in *Beatty* (2008): "objective *mens rea* is based on the premise that a reasonable person in the accused's position would have been aware of the risks arising from the conduct. The fault lies in the absence of the requisite mental state of care." Who is the "reasonable person"? The answer to this question is simply that it is up to the judge or jury (if there is one) to decide what is reasonable in all the circumstances of the case, and no doubt, they call upon their own life experience to determine what they think is reasonable. This means that it is always difficult to predict whether a judge or jury will determine that a specific defendant in a criminal trial acted reasonably.

In the *Creighton* case (1993), Justice McLachlin emphasized that the "moral fault of the offence must be proportionate to its gravity and penalty." In other words, the most serious crimes, carrying the most severe penalties, should generally be based on a subjective *mens rea* requirement. Significantly, in the case of *Martineau* (1990), the Supreme Court of Canada ruled that the crime of murder is so serious and carries such a high degree of stigma that criminal responsibility for this offence must be based on subjective *mens rea;* indeed, the Court stated that the *Charter* requires that the Crown prove either that the accused deliberately intended to kill or, at the very least, subjectively foresaw that his or her conduct was likely to cause death. However, in *Creighton* (1993), the Supreme Court held that responsibility for manslaughter could be based on

subjective *mens rea*
The *mens rea* elements of a criminal offence are considered to be subjective if they are based on a determination of "what actually went on in the accused person's mind." The forms of subjective *mens rea* are intention and knowledge; recklessness; and wilful blindness.

objective *mens rea*
The *mens rea* elements of a criminal offence are considered to be objective if they are based on a determination of whether a reasonable person, in the same circumstances and with the same knowledge as the accused, would have appreciated the risk involved in the accused's conduct and would have taken steps to avoid the commission of the *actus reus* elements of the crime in question.

an objective *mens rea* requirement because the degree of stigma and the penalties attached to it were considerably less severe than is the case for murder. In Creighton's case, the accused had injected a quantity of cocaine into the arm of the victim. In order to convict Creighton of manslaughter, the Crown first had to prove that he had intentionally committed an unlawful act that had resulted in death. The unlawful act was the offence of trafficking in narcotics (trafficking includes the act of administering a drug), and there was no doubt that the victim died as a direct consequence of the injection. The *mens rea* for so-called unlawful act manslaughter is objective in nature. Therefore, the second task confronting the Crown was to prove that any reasonable person would have foreseen the risk of non-trivial bodily harm as a consequence of committing the unlawful act. The Supreme Court of Canada had no doubt that Creighton was correctly convicted of manslaughter because any reasonable person who administered a dangerous drug intravenously would foresee the risk of some degree of bodily harm.

There are three forms of subjective *mens rea* that the Crown may be required to prove in a criminal prosecution: (1) intention and knowledge, (2) recklessness, and (3) wilful blindness.

Section 155(1) of the *Criminal Code* provides a typical example of the subjective *mens rea* requirement of intention and knowledge; indeed, it provides that an individual commits incest if, knowing that another person is "by blood relationship his or her parent, child, brother, sister, grandparent or grandchild," he or she intentionally has sexual intercourse with that person. Usually, the *Criminal Code* will require the Crown to prove a specific mental element in addition to intention and knowledge. Take, for example, the offence of first-degree murder. Section 31(2) of the Code states that this offence is committed when murder is both "planned and deliberate." In order to convict an accused person of murder, the Crown must establish that this person either intended to kill or intended to inflict bodily harm that he or she knew was likely to cause death and was reckless (did not care) whether death ensued or not (section 229(a)). However, if the offender is to be convicted of first- as opposed to second-degree murder, then normally the Crown must also prove that the killing was planned and deliberate in the sense that the accused did not act impulsively and was following some pre-existing plan to kill someone. Intoxicated defendants who are found to have the necessary *mens rea* for murder will often be acquitted of first-degree murder because they acted on impulse or without thinking about what they were going to do ahead of time; these accused persons will instead be convicted of second-degree murder.

Recklessness is a form of subjective *mens rea* where the accused knows that his or her conduct could cause certain prohibited consequences but deliberately proceeds with that conduct because he or she does not care one way or the other. Take the crime of arson. Section 434 of the *Criminal Code* states that a person who "intentionally or recklessly causes damage by fire or explosion to property that is not wholly owned by that person" is guilty of an indictable offence and may be sentenced to a maximum of 14 years in prison. If Nero throws a lighted cigarette onto a haystack, realizing that there is a good chance the haystack will catch fire, he will be convicted of arson even if he can demonstrate that he did not start the fire deliberately and that, in fact, he hoped very sincerely that there would not be any blaze as a consequence of his actions. Nero is guilty of arson because his recklessness constitutes one of the forms of *mens rea* that is necessary for conviction under the terms of section 434.

Wilful blindness is the final form of subjective *mens rea*. It exists where accused persons have every reason to make some kind of inquiry as to whether there are circumstances that would render their conduct criminal but deliberately choose to shut their eyes to the obvious because they wish to avoid being convicted of an offence. As the Supreme Court of Canada stated in *Briscoe* (2010): "wilful blindness imputes knowledge to an accused whose suspicion is aroused to the point where he or she sees the need for further inquiries, but deliberately chooses not to make those inquiries." Wilful blindness is treated as being the same as actual knowledge of a circumstance that incriminates the accused person.

Objective *mens rea* has been applied to a significant number of offences under the *Criminal Code*. For example, the following offences have all been characterized by the courts as requiring proof only of objective, rather than subjective, *mens rea:* manslaughter, dangerous operation of a motor vehicle, assault causing bodily harm, and criminal negligence causing death or bodily harm. However, it is important to bear in mind that the courts have consistently stated that accused persons may not be convicted of "true crimes" under the *Criminal Code* merely because they were "careless" in the sense that their conduct fell below the standard of care expected of a reasonable person acting prudently in the same circumstances as the accused. As Justice McLachlin said in the *Creighton* case (1993), "The law does not lightly brand a person as criminal." Indeed, in *Roy* (2012), the Supreme Court of Canada emphasized that the *minimum standard* for objective liability is a *marked departure* from the standard of care expected of the reasonable person acting prudently. Furthermore, the Supreme Court of Canada has repeatedly stated that the courts should apply a "modified objective test" in such cases. This means that a judge or jury (if there is one) must ask what the accused person in the case before them actually knew about the circumstances surrounding their actions. The judge or jury must then decide whether the accused's behaviour constituted a marked departure from the standard of care expected of a reasonable person who faces the identical circumstances as the accused and who is armed with exactly the same knowledge of those circumstances. Suppose, for example, an accused person suffers a brain seizure while driving a vehicle and he or she crosses over the centre of the road and causes a fatal collision with a car that is travelling in the opposite direction. On the face of it, straying over the centre line and causing a collision constitutes a marked departure from the standard of care expected of a reasonable person. However, if the accused did not know that he or she was likely to suffer from a seizure, there would be no conviction on a charge of dangerous operation of a motor vehicle causing death [section 249(4) of the *Criminal Code*]. A reasonable driver, with no knowledge of the likelihood that he or she might suffer a seizure, would have behaved in the same way as the accused. However, the situation would be very different if the accused person knew that he or she was liable to experience a seizure or was subject to sudden fainting spells and nevertheless continued to drive a motor vehicle without having first obtained medical clearance to do so. Clearly, a reasonable

FOCUS

Box 3.2

CONVICTION OF FIRST-DEGREE MURDER ON THE BASIS OF WILLFUL BLINDNESS

The case of *Briscoe* (2010) illustrates the principle that wilful blindness will be treated as being equivalent to guilty knowledge even with respect to a charge of first-degree murder, the most serious crime in the *Criminal Code*. Briscoe was charged with first-degree murder on the basis that he had aided and abetted (assisted or encouraged) the commission of murder by another person. Under section 21(2) of the *Criminal Code*, an individual who aids/abets another to commit a crime is liable to conviction for that crime.

Briscoe drove a group of youths led by a 19-year-old man, Laboucan, to a deserted golf course. Riding with Laboucan and his associates were two young women who had been lured into the vehicle by the lie that they would be taken to a party. At the golf course, one of the young women, 13-year-old Nina Courtepatte, was brutally raped and killed by Laboucan and his gang. Briscoe, who did not

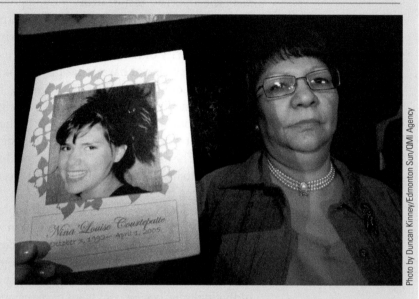

Nina Courtepatte was a young woman who was sexually assaulted and brutally murdered near Edmonton, one of over 1,000 Aboriginal women who have been murdered in Canada since 1980. Michael Briscoe was convicted after a second trial of first-degree murder even though he did not participate in the murder because he provided assistance to those who actually committed the killing and did so with wilful blindness as to their intentions.

Photo by Duncan Kinney/Edmonton Sun/QMI Agency

participate directly in the rape and murder but stood by and watched, was nevertheless charged with kidnapping, aggravated assault, and first-degree murder on the basis that he aided and abetted Laboucan and his associates to commit these crimes.

Apart from driving the victim to the scene of her death, Briscoe provided Laboucan and his associates with items from the trunk of his vehicle that were later used as the murder weapons (a hammer, a pair of pliers, a wrench and a pipe). Also, Briscoe had heard Laboucan tell the youths in his group that he "would like to find someone to kill someone," and he knew that Laboucan was violent. The trial judge acquitted Briscoe on the basis that it had not been proved that he actually knew what Laboucan had in mind when Briscoe drove Nina Courtepatte to the golf course. However, the Supreme Court of Canada agreed with the Alberta Court of Appeal that there should be a new trial because the trial judge had not considered whether Briscoe was willfully blind with respect to Laboucan's murderous plan.

Justice Charron stated that "the evidence cried out for an analysis on wilful blindness" and pointed out that Briscoe's own statements to the police suggest that "he had a strong, well-founded suspicion that someone would be killed at the golf course and that he may have been wilfully blind to the kidnapping and prospect of sexual assault." At his new trial, in April 2012, Briscoe was convicted of first-degree murder, kidnapping, and sexual assault.

Do you think the Crown should have been able to obtain a conviction of first-degree murder even though it could not prove that Briscoe actually knew that Laboucan planned to kill the victim whom he (Briscoe) transported to the scene of the homicide?

Further Reading: *R. v. Briscoe*, [2010] 1 S.C.R. 411. Available at http://www.canlii.org/en/ca/scc/doc/2010/2010scc13/2010scc13.html.

R. v. Briscoe 2012 ABQB 239. Available at http://www.canlii.org/en/ab/abqb/doc/2012/2012abqb239/2012abqb239.html.

person armed with this knowledge would never attempt to take a vehicle on the road; therefore, the accused's conduct would almost certainly be considered a marked departure from the standard of care expected of the reasonable person.

Although it may appear somewhat harsh to convict individuals of serious crimes on the basis of objective *mens rea*, it is clear that the courts have weakened the objective test of liability by requiring that the judge or jury take into account the subjective knowledge accused people have of the relevant circumstances surrounding their actions. Furthermore, if an accused person lacks the normal capacity of the reasonable person to appreciate that his or her conduct might create a risk of harm, that person may not be convicted of a crime, even if it is based on proof of objective *mens rea*. For example, suppose a 20-year-old man has a mental age of 10 and he hits a neighbour with a metal bar. Tragically, the neighbour dies from his injuries. In the case of a person without a severe disability, it would be relatively easy for the Crown to prove a charge of manslaughter. The *mens rea* requirements are objective in nature. The accused must be proved to have intentionally applied force to the victim, and the Crown must then proceed to establish that a reasonable person would have foreseen the risk of non-trivial bodily harm. Any reasonable person would foresee the risk of fairly serious bodily harm if an attack is carried out with a metal bar; therefore, most accused persons would be routinely convicted of manslaughter.

However, if the accused is so developmentally disabled that he or she cannot foresee that their actions may cause non-trivial bodily harm, then that individual may not be convicted of manslaughter. The essence of culpability in objective *mens rea* is the notion that the accused had the capacity to foresee— and avoid—the risk of physical harm but did not do so. If the accused lacks this basic capacity, to convict him or her of manslaughter would amount to punishing someone who lacks any blameworthiness. In *Creighton* (1993), the Supreme Court of Canada ruled that such an outcome would infringe the fundamental principles of justice that are enshrined in the *Charter* (section 7).

Mens Rea and Regulatory Offences

Earlier in this chapter, a distinction was drawn between regulatory offences ("quasi-criminal law") and "true crimes." Where "true crimes" are concerned, the Crown usually has to prove the required *mens rea* of the offence beyond a reasonable doubt. However, most regulatory offences are considered to be offences of strict liability. This means that the Crown only has to prove the *actus reus* elements of the offence; the onus is then on the accused to prove, on the balance of probabilities, that he or she was not negligent (or that he or she "acted with due diligence"). The rationale for strict liability is that it would be extremely difficult to conduct effective prosecutions of regulatory offences if the Crown were required to prove that accused persons were negligent. Usually, the accused person has the best knowledge of the steps that he or she has taken to comply with the regulations that apply to his or her field of manufacturing or business activities, and so on. Therefore, it is fair to require the accused to present this evidence and prove that he or she acted with the due diligence expected of a reasonable person in the same circumstances. Furthermore, the penalties for regulatory offences are comparatively lenient, since they rarely include imprisonment as a realistic sentencing alternative. In any event, strict liability is infinitely preferable to a regime of absolute liability, in which the accused is not permitted to claim a lack of *mens rea* as a defence.

In the *Wholesale Travel Group Inc.* case (1991), the accused had been charged with the regulatory offence of false or misleading advertising, under the federal Competition Act, R.S.C. 1970, c. C–23. The Act clearly imposed strict liability insofar as it permitted the accused to raise a defence of having acted "with due diligence." Essentially, the defence would be available where the accused proved that the "act or omission giving rise to the offence" was the "result of error" and that he or she "took reasonable precautions and exercised due diligence to prevent the occurrence of such error." It was contended before the Supreme Court of Canada that, because strict liability requires accused persons to prove their innocence, it infringed the presumption of innocence enshrined in section 11(d) of the *Charter*, and was, therefore, invalid. However, the Supreme Court of Canada ultimately held that strict liability was not invalid under the provisions of the *Charter*. The *Wholesale Travel Group Inc.* case is, therefore, a decision of great importance since it has affirmed the legitimacy of the basic principles of liability that are at the heart of the vast network of regulatory legislation that governs the everyday lives of all Canadians.

A vast number of regulatory offences have been enacted by the federal and provincial/territorial legislatures in Canada. In addition, countless bylaws have been created by municipalities across Canada, acting on the authority delegated to them by the respective provinces and territories. Many of the provincial/territorial regulatory offences and most of the bylaw infractions are prosecuted by means of a ticketing system (for example, the dispensing of speeding and parking tickets is a practice that is well known to Canadians). Furthermore, approximately 2,000 federal regulatory offences have been designated as "contraventions" under the *Contraventions Act, S.C. 1992, c. 47*, thus enabling prosecution through provincial/territorial ticketing systems.

Becoming a Party to a Criminal Offence

Individuals can be convicted of criminal offences even if they are not the persons who actually commit them. For example, section 21(1) of the *Criminal Code* provides that anyone is a party to a criminal offence who (1) actually commits it, (2) aids another person to commit it, or (3) abets (encourages) any person to commit it. In a homicide case the person who actually commits the offence would be the individual who physically kills the victim. However, a person who intentionally provides assistance and/or encouragement is liable to be convicted of murder on the same basis as the actual killer. Section 21(1), therefore, provides the courts and, in particular, prosecutors with a significant degree of flexibility. Take, for example, the notorious case of *Pickton* (2010). William Pickton was involved in one of the most horrific series of murders in any country in modern times. In this case, though the evidence appeared to indicate that Pickton had committed the murders himself, the defence suggested that others may have been involved in the killings. The Supreme Court of Canada held that section 21(1) places the person who aids and or abets a murder on exactly the same footing as a person who actually commits it. Therefore, it does not matter whether members of the jury believed that Pickton actually committed the murders himself or whether he aided and/or abetted others to do so: in either case, he should be convicted of murder. Section 22 of the *Criminal Code* provides a similar degree of flexibility to the courts insofar as it provides that a person who counsels ("procures," "solicits," or "incites") another to commit a crime becomes a **party to that crime** even if "the offence was committed in a way different from that which was counselled" (section 22 of the *Criminal Code*).

An individual may also become a party to a criminal offence that has been committed by other people when he or she had previously formed a common intention with them to commit a crime. Section 21(2) of the *Criminal Code* deals with the situation in which two or more persons have agreed to commit a crime and to assist one another in carrying out this "common purpose." Each of these individuals is considered a party to any offence committed by the other person(s) who entered the original agreement provided (1) that this other offence was committed in order to carry out the "common purpose" and (2) that these individuals either knew or ought to have known that the commission of this other offence "would be a probable consequence of carrying out the common purpose." Suppose that Chuzzlewit, Dedlock, and Murdstone agree to commit a robbery and to help one another in carrying out this "common intention." Murdstone—without consulting his colleagues in crime—kills one of the robbery victims. In these circumstances, Chuzzlewit and Dedlock would be convicted of manslaughter if they either knew or ought to have known that inflicting non-trivial bodily harm on the intended victim(s) would be a probable consequence of implementing their common intention to commit robbery. Since robbery necessarily involves an element of violence or threatened violence, any reasonable person would foresee the probability that someone may be seriously hurt; therefore, Chuzzlewit and Dedlock would almost certainly be found guilty of manslaughter. The use of the phrase "or ought to have known" indicates that the *mens rea* elements are objective in nature; this means that the scope of potential liability under section 21(2) is remarkably broad. The only exception to this form of objective liability arises where the offence of murder is concerned. Since the Supreme Court of Canada has ruled [in *Martineau* (1990)] that an accused person may be convicted of murder only where there was an actual intention to kill or subjective foresight of the likelihood of death, Chuzzlewit and Dedlock would be convicted of murder only if they subjectively realized that death was a probable consequence of carrying out their common intention to commit robbery.

One question that immediately springs to mind when discussing section 21(2) is whether an individual who agreed with others to commit a crime and to provide the necessary assistance to achieve his goal should be entitled to change his or her mind and withdraw from the common intention. The answer is that an individual may withdraw from the common intention, but may do so effectively only when he or she gives unequivocal notice to the other party or parties of his or her wish to abandon the criminal enterprise. Once effective notice has been given, the individual is no longer liable for any subsequent crimes committed by the other party or parties in pursuit

party to a crime
The *Criminal Code* specifies that one is a party to—and liable to conviction of—a criminal offence if one actually commits it, aids and/or abets it, becomes a party to it by virtue of having formed a common intention with others to commit a crime, or counsels the commission of an offence that is actually committed by another person.

of the common intention. However, in *Gauthier* (2013), the Supreme Court of Canada added a new prerequisite for raising the defence of abandonment of the common intention: the defence will only be successful if the accused person demonstrates that a reasonable effort was made to neutralize the effects of her or his participation or to prevent the principal offender from committing the offence.

The Use of Criminal Law as a Preventative Tool: Inchoate Offences

The criminal law permits the police to intervene and arrest those who, in some way, demonstrate that they are about to embark upon the commission of a serious crime. If members of a gang of professional kidnappers agree to abduct a particular victim and to hold him or her to ransom, the police do not have to wait until the abduction is actually carried out before they intervene. Even though the kidnapping may exist only in the intentions of the members of the gang, it is undoubtedly legitimate for the state to punish them for having participated in a conspiracy to commit kidnapping. Conspiracy is an **inchoate crime** (literally, a crime "in embryo"); once their agreement to commit a crime has been reached, the accused may be convicted of the crime of conspiracy even though the offence they originally planned to commit is never brought to fruition. Other inchoate crimes are criminal attempt and counselling an offence that is not committed.

Inchoate crimes raise questions about the civil liberties of those who are charged with having committed them. It is generally accepted that the criminal law should not punish people simply for entertaining evil thoughts. However, society does have the right to prevent individuals from translating their evil thoughts into criminal acts. The problem lies in defining the point at which the state is justified in laying a charge against someone who has not yet committed the crime that he or she has in mind. Basically, accused persons must take some form of action that manifests their intention to commit a crime; in counselling, the accused must encourage another person to commit a crime; in attempt, the accused must take a substantial step toward completion of a crime; and, in conspiracy, the accused must enter into an agreement to commit a crime.

Counselling an Offence That Is Not Committed

According to section 22 of the *Criminal Code*, it is a crime to **counsel** another person to commit an offence that is not ultimately brought to fruition. Since the main focus of the offence is on the accused person's intentions, it does not matter that no one is actually influenced by the accused person's efforts to procure, solicit, or incite someone to commit a crime. Furthermore, once their counselling action is completed, accused persons cannot escape criminal conviction merely because they change their minds and renounce their criminal intent. Box 3.3 illustrates how technological change can affect the interpretation and application of the criminal law.

inchoate crime
A criminal offence that is committed when the accused person seeks to bring about the commission of a particular crime but is not successful in doing so. The three inchoate offences in the *Criminal Code* are attempt, conspiracy, and counselling.

counselling
Procuring, soliciting, or inciting another person to commit a crime.

FOCUS

Box 3.3

COUNSELLING CRIME OVER THE INTERNET

Courts are constantly faced with the need to adapt the criminal law to deal with the many opportunities that rapidly developing communication technologies create for novel methods of committing crimes. *R. v. Hamilton* (2005) furnishes a noteworthy example of a case in which the Supreme Court of Canada very cautiously adapted the existing principles of criminal law to deal with a situation in which it was alleged that the Internet had been used to communicate information that was likely to incite other individuals to commit criminal offences.

Hamilton had used the Internet to sell computer files and documents to a number of individuals. These files contained detailed instructions for bomb making and burglary, as well as a program that generated credit card numbers that might be used for fraudulent purposes. Hamilton was charged with counselling the commission of four offences that had not in fact been committed—namely, making explosive substances with intent, doing anything with intent to cause an explosion, break and enter with intent, and fraud. At his trial, Hamilton readily admitted that he had read a computer-generated list of the files concerned but denied that he had actually read the contents of those files. Although he had generated some credit card numbers, he had never used them and there had been no complaints from the bank concerning their misuse.

At his trial, the judge acquitted Hamilton of all the charges against him because, in her view, Hamilton never intended that the persons to whom he sent the computer files should actually commit the offences described in them. The Crown took the case to the Supreme Court of Canada, which articulated the *mens rea* that must be proved before an accused person may be convicted of counselling an offence. According to Justice Fish,

> the *mens rea* consists in nothing less than an accompanying *intent* or *conscious disregard of the substantial and unjustified risk inherent in the counselling*: that is, it must be shown that the accused either intended that the offence counselled be committed, or knowingly counselled the commission of the offence while aware of the unjustified risk the offence counselled was in fact likely to be committed as a result of the accused's conduct. [at para. 29] (Emphasis in original)

Prior to the *Hamilton* case, the courts had always applied the principle that, in order to obtain a conviction for counselling, the Crown must prove that the accused person actually intended that the offence be committed. However, the Supreme Court ruled in *Hamilton* that an accused person may also be convicted if he or she was *extremely reckless* as to the likelihood that the offence would be committed. Nevertheless, even with this expanded definition of the necessary *mens rea*, the Supreme Court affirmed Hamilton's acquittal on all the counselling charges except the charge of counselling fraud. The Supreme Court ordered a new trial on the charge of counselling fraud because it took the view that the trial judge should have found that Hamilton had the necessary *mens rea* for this offence. The Supreme Court noted that Hamilton had sent an e-mail "teaser" to various individuals in which he advertised software that could generate "valid working credit card numbers." Justice Fish noted that Hamilton "sought to make 'a quick buck' by encouraging the intended recipients of his Internet solicitation to purchase a device that generated credit card numbers easily put to fraudulent use." Furthermore, the Supreme Court emphasized that Hamilton knew very well that "the use of false credit card numbers is illegal." Therefore, even if Hamilton had not actually wanted the purchasers of the files to commit the offences described in them, he was at the very least extremely reckless as to the risk that the files were likely to incite the purchasers to commit the offence of fraud.

Do you agree with the Supreme Court of Canada's decision to expand the scope of the *mens rea* for counselling an offence to include extreme recklessness? Should this decision have been left to Parliament or was it appropriate for the Supreme Court to modify the existing law to meet the challenge posed by the use of the Internet to communicate information that is likely to incite individuals to commit potentially serious crimes? Do you think Parliament should amend the *Criminal Code* to make it easier to obtain convictions in such cases? For example, should individuals such as Hamilton be made criminally liable for the *negligent* transfer of files that turn out to contain information as to how to commit offences even though they may not have actually read the files in question?

Criminal Attempt

The offence of **criminal attempt** is focused on an accused person's intention to commit a crime that is never realized. Section 24(1) of the *Criminal Code* provides that "everyone who, having an intent to commit a crime, does or omits to do anything for the purpose of carrying out his intention is guilty of an attempt to commit the offence whether or not it was possible under the circumstances to commit the offence." Clearly, the *mens rea* of criminal attempt is nothing short of an actual intent to commit an offence. The *actus reus* of attempt is any step taken by the accused toward the completion of the offence, provided that this step goes beyond "mere preparation" and is not considered to be "too remote" from the completed offence. For example, buying a train ticket with a view to travelling to another city in order to rob a bank would be considered "mere preparation" and "too remote" from the completed robbery to justify convicting the accused of a criminal attempt. However, if the accused person actually reaches the front doors of the bank before being arrested by the police, it is clear that the *actus reus* of the offence of attempted robbery has been established. Unfortunately, it is often very difficult to predict exactly where the court will draw the line between mere preparation and an act that warrants conviction for a criminal attempt. It should also be emphasized that a criminal attempt may be committed even though it is impossible for the accused to commit the complete offence that he or she has in mind. For example, if someone tries to steal a motor vehicle that has been totally disabled by its owner, that person is guilty of attempted theft even though it was impossible for that person to take the vehicle from the spot where it had been parked. Similarly, if an accused person mistakenly shoots a wax dummy, believing it is an enemy, that person is guilty of attempted murder. What is important is that the accused person seriously intended to commit the crime and that there is a real likelihood that, having failed on this particular occasion, the accused will try again and, perhaps, be more successful on that subsequent occasion.

Conspiracy

The crime of **conspiracy** is established when two or more individuals form a common intention to commit a crime. The Crown must also prove that each individual charged with conspiracy actually intended to put the common design into effect. The *actus reus* of conspiracy is the agreement to engage in criminal conduct, while the *mens rea* component consists of the intent not only to enter into this agreement but also to implement it. Suppose two individuals apparently agree to murder a third party. However, it later turns out that one of these individuals was actually an undercover police officer who never had any intention to act on this supposed agreement. In this case, neither of the individuals may be convicted of conspiracy. The police officer lacks the necessary *mens rea* for conspiracy, and the other individual cannot be convicted of this offence because the Crown must prove that there are at least two persons who seriously intended to implement the plan to commit murder. On the other hand, if there are two or more individuals who agree to commit murder and who fully intend to carry out their homicidal plans, they will be convicted of conspiracy even if an undercover officer is also part of this group. As long as a minimum of two

criminal attempt
A criminal attempt occurs when an individual does—or omits to do—anything for the purpose of carrying out a previously formed intention to commit a crime. The conduct in question must constitute a substantial step towards the completion of the crime that is intended.

conspiracy
An agreement by two or more persons to commit a criminal offence.

individuals intend to carry out an agreement to commit a crime, there is a conspiracy. Conspiracy is a crime that provides the Crown with a number of distinct advantages. For example, certain types of evidence may be accepted at the joint trial of a group of alleged co-conspirators that would never be admitted against specific members of that group if they were tried separately. In effect, there is always the danger of "guilt by association" in conspiracy trials.

QUESTIONS FOR CRITICAL THINKING

1. Why does Canadian criminal law place so much importance on the requirement that the Crown prove the relevant *mens rea* elements of a criminal offence? Would it not make more sense for the state to intervene and deal with offenders solely on the basis of the fact that they have committed the *actus reus* of an offence (a harmful or potentially harmful act or omission)?

2. Pluto is driving his car down a steep hill in a large city. He discovers that his brakes are not functioning, and the vehicle starts to gain speed. In the near distance, a group of schoolchildren are crossing the road ahead. To avoid colliding with these children, Pluto steers his speeding car onto the sidewalk. Pluto is aware that there is an elderly man on the sidewalk, but he is confident that he can avoid hitting him. Tragically, at that moment, Pluto suffers a "fainting spell," and while he is unconscious, his car not only strikes and kills the man on the sidewalk but also returns to the road and injures five of the schoolchildren, who are on the clearly marked crossing. There is evidence that Pluto had experienced brief "fainting spells" before but that he did not consider them serious. After the accident, it is discovered that Pluto probably suffers from a mild form of narcolepsy (a neurological condition that may cause an individual to experience uncontrollable episodes of sleep). Is Pluto guilty of dangerous driving causing death and dangerous driving causing bodily harm?

3. Should the criminal law be used as a preventative tool? Should the police be able to intervene and bring individuals to the criminal courts before those individuals have actually committed the crime(s) they are planning to carry out? Do the existing inchoate offences in the *Criminal Code* strike an acceptable balance between the demands of public security and the civil rights of accused persons?

Defences to a Criminal Charge

Conviction for a "true crime" should not occur unless the accused person is considered blameworthy. Just because individuals engage in conduct that, from an objective point of view, is either actually or potentially harmful does not mean they should be punished under the provisions of the criminal law. Indeed, the requirement of *mens rea* ensures that the Crown must first prove a culpable mental state or the prosecution will fail. In addition to the *mens rea* requirement, several distinct defences may be raised by an accused person

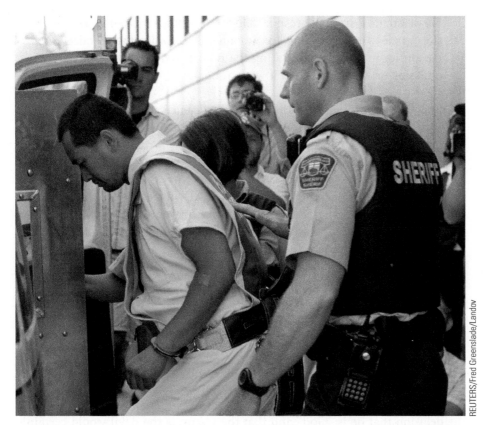

Public outcry about the possibility that Vince Li would eventually be released was one of the factors that led to more restrictive laws dealing with people found NCRMD.

REUTERS/Fred Greenslade/Landov

in a criminal trial. Some of these defences, such as mistake of fact, basically amount to a denial that the Crown has proved the necessary *mens rea*, but other defences, such as duress, may be raised successfully even though the accused possessed the necessary *mens rea* for the offence that has been charged. Essentially, a patchwork of defences has evolved as a means of ensuring that those individuals who have a justification or excuse for their conduct are either acquitted of criminal charges or are treated more leniently (for example, by conviction for a less serious offence).

Mental Disorder as a Defence to a Criminal Charge

In the Supreme Court of Canada's decision in *Winko* (1999), Justice McLachlin said:

> In every society, there are those who commit criminal acts because of mental illness. The criminal law must find a way to deal with these people fairly, while protecting the public against further harms. The task is not an easy one.

In Canada, this difficult task is undertaken through the application by the courts of the special defence of **not criminally responsible on account of mental disorder (NCRMD)**. The current test that must be used in deciding whether an accused should be found NCRMD is articulated in section 16(1) of the *Criminal Code*:

NCRMD
The special verdict of "not criminally responsible on account of mental disorder." In order to be found NCRMD, it must be proved on the balance of probabilities that, because of mental disorder, the accused lacked the capacity to appreciate the nature and quality of the act or omission in question or to know it would be considered morally wrong by the average Canadian.

> No person is criminally responsible for an act committed or an omission made while suffering from a mental disorder that renders the person incapable of appreciating the nature and quality of the act or omission or of knowing that it was wrong.

The first requirement of the NCRMD defence is that the accused was suffering from a "mental disorder" at the time of the alleged offence(s). The Supreme Court of Canada has adopted an extremely broad definition of mental disorder, but in practice, only those accused persons who, at the time of the alleged offence, were experiencing the symptoms associated with a severe mental disorder are likely to be found NCRMD (for example, the hallucinations and or delusions that may be caused by schizophrenia or bipolar affective disorder). Indeed, the criteria specified in section 16(1) of the *Criminal Code* are very restrictive: namely, that the accused was rendered incapable either of appreciating the physical nature and quality of the act or omission in question or of knowing that the act or omission is considered morally wrong by the everyday standards of the ordinary Canadian. Most individuals living with serious mental disorders understand the physical nature of their conduct (for example, most would realize that stabbing someone in the heart will cause death). Similarly, the majority of these individuals are capable of knowing that their conduct would be "morally condemned by reasonable members of society" [as Justice Arbour of the Supreme Court of Canada put it in the *Molodowic* case (2000)]. However, an individual who, as a result of a mental disorder, is under the delusion that he is "God" and that the victim is the devil would certainly not have the capacity to know that killing the victim would be considered morally wrong—as was the case in *Landry* (1991). Significantly, section 16(1) does not extend the benefit of the NCRMD defence to mentally disordered persons who claim that—as a consequence of mental disorder—they succumbed to an irresistible impulse to commit a crime; provided such individuals were capable of understanding what they were doing and that it was wrong, they are not considered to be NCRMD in Canadian criminal law.

The very narrow scope of the NCRMD defence ensures that relatively few accused persons may raise it successfully at their trial. It is significant that section 16 places the burden of proving the NCRMD defence on the shoulders of the accused person if he or she raises it at trial. In this situation, the accused has to prove the defence on the balance of probabilities. Although this provision infringes the presumption of innocence, enshrined in section 11(d) of the *Charter*, the Supreme Court of Canada ruled, in the *Chaulk* case (1990), that this infringement of the accused person's right was justified as a reasonable limitation under section 1. The Court took the view that it would be impractical to require the Crown to prove beyond a reasonable doubt that the accused was not mentally disordered—particularly in light of the fact that an accused person may refuse to cooperate with a psychiatrist nominated by the Crown to report to the court on the accused's mental condition.

Accused persons who are found NCRMD are not acquitted in the technical sense of that word. Indeed, section 672.1 of the *Criminal Code* states that a verdict of NCRMD constitutes a finding that "the accused committed the act or omission that formed the basis of the offence with which the accused is charged but is not criminally responsible on account of mental disorder." NCR accused may be granted (1) an absolute discharge, (2) a conditional discharge, or (3) an order holding them in custody in a psychiatric facility. A recent amendment to the *Criminal Code* (s. 672.64), which came into effect in April 2014,* empowers the court, following a finding of NCRMD, to designate the NCR accused person a "high-risk accused" if he or she committed a serious personal injury offence and:

(a) the court is satisfied that there is a substantial likelihood that the accused will use violence that could endanger the life or safety of another person; or

(b) the court is of the opinion that the acts that constitute the offence were of such a brutal nature as to indicate a risk of grave physical or psychological harm to another person.

The main consequence of this designation is that the NCR accused person must be kept in strict custody in a hospital and not allowed any temporary absences unless (1) he or she is escorted and (2) there is no undue risk to the public. Only the court may lift the "high-risk accused" designation.

One reason for this amendment to the law was the case of Vince Li, who gruesomely murdered a fellow passenger on a Greyhound bus travelling through Manitoba in 2008. Li was diagnosed as living with schizophrenia, and psychiatrists agreed that at the time of the homicide, Li's psychotic state led him to believe that the victim was an alien. Li was found NCRMD and committed to the Selkirk Mental Health Centre. Shortly after arriving at the Centre, he was authorized to take secure walks outside the facility. Many members of the public complained about the walks and about the possibility of Li's eventual release. The new legislation sought to restrict the freedom given to some accused who are found NCRMD and to provide more opportunities for victims to be involved in review board hearings.

Section 672.54(a) of the *Criminal Code* has been interpreted as providing that, unless a court or review board determines that an NCR accused person constitutes a "significant threat to the safety of the public," then it *must* order an absolute discharge. In *Winko* (1999), the Supreme Court of Canada ruled that the threshold for justifying the imposition of restrictions on the liberty of a person who has been found NCRMD is very high:

> A "significant threat to the safety of the public" means a real risk of physical or psychological harm to members of the public that is serious in the sense of going beyond the merely trivial or annoying. The conduct giving rise to the harm must be criminal in nature.[†]

General Defences to a Criminal Charge

Mistake of fact may constitute a defence to a criminal charge if it causes the accused to erroneously believe that the circumstances facing him or her did not render his or her actions criminal. For example, if a woman participates in

mistake of fact
Mistake of fact may be a defence where the accused person acts under the influence of an honest mistake in relation to any of the elements of the *actus reus* of the offence charged.

Not Criminally Responsible Reform Act, S.C. 2014, c. 6

†An amendment in 2014 incorporated this definition into the *Criminal Code* and added some clarifying words: "a significant threat to the safety of the public means a risk of serious physical or psychological harm to members of the public—including any victim of or witness to the offence, or any person under the age of 18 years—resulting from conduct that is criminal in nature but not necessarily violent." (s. 72.5401).

a marriage ceremony with a man, erroneously believing that her first husband is dead, she would not be guilty of the crime of bigamy. The central element of the *actus reus* of bigamy is that one of the parties to a marriage ceremony is already married. If the accused honestly believed that she was a widow, then—in the circumstances as she perceived them to be—she was not committing a prohibited act because she was no longer married to her first spouse. When the accused operates under a mistake of fact, he or she is really stating that the Crown has failed to prove the necessary *mens rea* of the offence.

One of the most controversial uses of the defence of mistake of fact used to occur when an accused person who was charged with sexual assault claimed that he honestly believed he had the complainant's consent, even though he was mistaken. However, section 273.2(b) of the *Criminal Code* (enacted in 1992) states that mistaken belief in consent will not be a valid defence to a charge of sexual assault unless the accused took "reasonable steps, in the circumstances known to the accused at the time, to ascertain that the complainant was consenting." By requiring the accused person to act reasonably, this amendment to the Code has considerably reduced the opportunities for abuse of the defence of honest belief in consent. For example, in *Crangle* (2010), the accused had initiated sexual intercourse with his twin brother's sleeping girlfriend. The victim initially thought that the accused was her boyfriend, but as soon as she realized his true identity, she strongly objected to his actions. The accused claimed that he had an honest—albeit mistaken—belief that the victim had consented. The trial judge rejected this defence because Crangle had done nothing to make his identity perfectly clear to the victim; undoubtedly, he had failed to take reasonable steps to ascertain whether there was consent.

While honest mistake of fact constitutes a valid defence to a criminal charge, a mistake concerning the nature or scope of the criminal law does not absolve an accused person of criminal liability. Section 19 of the *Criminal Code* makes it clear that ignorance of the law is no excuse. This is a harsh rule but an inevitable one, since it would be impossible for the Crown to prove actual knowledge of the relevant legal principles. There are some exceptions to this rule. One of the more important exceptions arises when an official who is charged with the administration of certain types of regulatory legislation gives erroneous legal advice. If the accused person reasonably relies on this advice, he or she may take advantage of the defence of "officially induced error."

FOCUS

Box 3.4

THE CRIMINALIZATION OF THE FAILURE TO DISCLOSE ONE'S HIV POSITIVE STATUS

Section 265(3)(c) of the *Criminal Code* states that consent to the application of force or the threat of force is rendered invalid if it was obtained by fraud. The Supreme Court of Canada ruled in *Cuerrier* (1998) that an individual who has tested positive for HIV (the human immunodeficiency virus that causes AIDS, acquired immune deficiency syndrome) and who engages in unprotected sexual intercourse with another person without disclosing his or her HIV positive status is guilty of fraud. Therefore, any consent given to sexual activity on the part of that other person is invalid if that consent would not have been given had the other person been made aware of the individual's HIV positive status. Since transmission of HIV threatens the life of the other person, the Supreme Court of Canada has ruled that a charge of aggravated sexual assault may be laid under section 273 of the *Criminal Code*.

There is considerable debate as to the wisdom of criminalizing individuals who live with HIV positive status and who engage in sexual intercourse without disclosure of that status. Changes in the treatment of HIV have greatly reduced the likelihood that the virus can be transmitted. ART (antiretroviral therapy, consisting of a "cocktail" of drugs) effectively suppresses HIV and reduces the risk of transmission of the virus to minimal levels. A person who is receiving ART will have a low viral load (a minimal level of HIV in the blood) so that the risk of transmission of HIV is very small. Some maintain that an individual who is HIV positive, but who owing to ART has a low viral load, should not be convicted of aggravated sexual assault if he or she engages in unprotected intercourse without disclosure of his or her HIV positive status. In the case of *Mabior* (2012), the Supreme Court of Canada had the opportunity to reconsider its ruling in *Cuerrier* in light of the evidence relating to the impact of ART and its ability to reduce viral load.

Mabior was charged with nine counts of aggravated sexual assault because he had failed to disclose his HIV-positive status to nine women with whom he had sexual intercourse. Mabior had been receiving ART and his viral loads were low, thereby reducing the risk of transmission of the virus. The Supreme Court of Canada set out the requirements for conviction of an accused person in Mabior's situation. Chief Justice McLachlin summarized the Court's ruling as follows:

> … to obtain a conviction under ss. 265(3)(c) and 273, the Crown must show that the complainant's consent to sexual intercourse was vitiated by the accused's fraud as to his HIV status. Failure to disclose (*the dishonest act*) amounts to fraud where the complainant would not have consented had he or she known the accused was HIV-positive, and where sexual contact poses a significant risk of or causes actual serious bodily harm (*deprivation*). A significant risk of serious bodily harm is established by a realistic possibility of transmission of HIV. On the evidence before us, a realistic possibility of transmission is negated by evidence that the accused's viral load was low at the time of intercourse and that condom protection was used. However, the general proposition that a low viral load combined with condom use negates a realistic possibility of transmission of HIV does not preclude the common law from adapting to future advances in treatment and to circumstances where risk

factors other than those considered in the present case are at play.

Ultimately, Mabior was convicted only of the three charges that concerned acts of sexual intercourse that had taken place *without the use of a condom*. Having low viral loads was not considered sufficient *per se* to eliminate "a realistic possibility of transmission" of the virus: in order to achieve that objective, the accused must also use a condom.

The *Mabior* case raises many questions. Is it an appropriate use of the criminal law to punish individuals who live with HIV for engaging in unprotected sexual relations and failing to disclose their HIV-positive status? Chief Justice McLachlin, on behalf of the Supreme Court, clearly took the view that this conduct is an appropriate target of the criminal law. The Supreme Court concluded that engaging in fraud and subjecting the other party in a sexual encounter to a serious risk to their life is blameworthy.

The Supreme Court also stated that failure to disclose infringes basic values enshrined in the Canadian *Charter* of Rights and Freedoms. It has been asserted by some that criminalization of the failure to disclose HIV positive status will discourage individuals living with this condition from seeking testing and treatment. However, Chief Justice McLachlin stated that the Court had not been presented with evidence that would prove this assertion to be true.

Critics of the *Mabior* decision have focused on the lack of certainty as to the precise meaning of "a realistic possibility of transmission" of HIV. The risk of transmission depends on the nature of the sexual act in question. In *Mabior*, the Supreme Court considered only the risk associated with vaginal intercourse. The very complexity of assessing the risk for different types of sexual acts renders it most likely that expert witnesses will disagree in the courtroom. Critics have also questioned whether the Supreme Court had understood the scientific evidence concerning the risks of transmission when the individual has low viral loads. Why, if there is a low viral load and a very small risk of transmission, did the Court also impose the requirement that an individual living with HIV must use a condom?

Do you agree that the criminal law should be used to punish individuals who do not disclose their HIV positive status? Do you think there are public health measures that might be taken that would be more effective as a means of reducing the transmission of HIV and other diseases?

Further Reading: *R. v. Cuerrier*, [1998] 2 SCR 371. Available at: http://www.canlii.org/en/ca/scc/doc/1998/1998canlii796/1998canlii796.html

R. v. Mabior, [2012] 2 SCR 584. Available at: http://www.canlii.org/en/ca/scc/doc/2012/2012scc47/2012scc47.html

Vandervort, L. 2013. "HIV, Fraud, Non-Disclosure, Consent and a Stark Choice: *Mabior* or Sexual Autonomy." *Criminal Law Quarterly* 60, no. 2: 301–20.

For example, if a factory inspector tells a manufacturer that it is acceptable to modify a certain safety device, it would clearly be unfair to convict that manufacturer of a violation of the relevant occupational safety legislation. If the manufacturer reasonably relied on the advice of the factory inspector and committed what a court later concludes is a regulatory offence, then the defence of officially induced error will come to the rescue of the manufacturer.

Intoxication is a complex and highly problematic defence. A high proportion of violent crimes are committed by individuals who have abused alcohol and/or other drugs, and the great majority of the inmates in Canada's prisons have been diagnosed with a substance abuse disorder. If the scope of a defence of intoxication were drawn too broadly, many violent offenders would escape criminal liability even though they were considered to have ingested alcohol and/or other drugs voluntarily. One of the main effects of alcohol (and some other drugs) is to cause disinhibition—a condition in which the accused may be rendered less able to control his or her conduct. However, the courts have consistently ruled that intoxication may not be raised as a valid defence by accused persons who simply claim that alcohol and/or other drugs impaired their ability to control their conduct. Instead, the intoxication defence focuses on whether the accused's state of intoxication (from alcohol and/or other drugs) prevented him or her from forming the necessary *mens rea* for the crime in question.

The defence of intoxication is primarily a "common law" defence in that it was developed by the courts in the absence of any legislation that defined its nature and scope. Traditionally, the defence has applied only to those offences that required proof of a complex form of *mens rea* known as "specific intent." Therefore, the defence of intoxication may reduce the severity of a charge (for example, from murder to manslaughter or from robbery to assault). On the other hand, it has been a long-standing principle that intoxication is not a valid defence to a charge of such "basic intent" offences as assault, sexual assault, or damage to property (mischief).* The legal rationale for maintaining the distinction between crimes of specific and basic intent is that intoxication does not normally impair people to the extent that they do not even have the minimal degree of *mens rea* required to assault someone or to damage property. Even extremely intoxicated people have some degree of awareness of what they are doing, and the acts of committing an assault or damaging property require only a very minimal degree of intent. On the other hand, assaulting someone with the specific intent to kill (murder) or forcefully taking something from another individual with the specific intent to steal (robbery) are acts that require a considerably more complex pattern of thought, and intoxication may well prevent the accused from forming the necessary specific intent that is required for conviction of these serious crimes.

If the ingestion of alcohol and/or other drugs precipitates a psychosis (a condition in which an individual loses contact with reality), should the accused person be able to assert the defence of NCRMD, under section 16 of the

intoxication defence
Intoxication caused by alcohol and/or other drugs may be a defence if it prevents the accused from forming the intent required for a specific intent offence, such as murder or robbery.

---

*Even if the accused person is so intoxicated that he or she is in a state that is similar to extreme mental disorder or automatism, section 33.1 of the *Criminal Code* denies the accused person any defence to a charge of a basic intent offence (such as sexual assault) that involves violence or a threat of violence

Criminal Code? In the case of *Bouchard-Lebrun* (2011), the Supreme Court of Canada ruled that, if the substance-induced psychosis is only short-lived and the accused person quickly recovers when the substance leaves his or her body, then he or she may not raise the NCRMD defence. However, if the accused person has a pre-existing mental disorder that is exacerbated by the ingestion of alcohol and/or other drugs or if there has been a long-standing pattern of substance abuse that has caused significant changes to the brain, then the substance-induced psychosis may provide the basis for a successful defence of NCRMD.

The defences of **necessity** and **duress** are based on the notion that it would be unfair to convict individuals of a criminal offence if they did not have a genuine choice at the time they committed it. As the Supreme Court of Canada put it in *Ruzic* (2001), "it is a principle of fundamental justice that only voluntary conduct — behaviour that is the product of a free will and controlled body, unhindered by external constraints — should attract the penalty and stigma of criminal liability." In a moral sense, individuals who act under the constraints of duress or necessity do not so voluntarily, and hence, the defences of duress and necessity are said to be based on "moral involuntariness." Both defences are conceptualized by the courts as "excuses" rather than "justifications"; as Justice Dickson said, in the Supreme Court of Canada's decision in *Perka* (1984), "An 'excuse' concedes the wrongfulness of the action but asserts that the circumstances under which it was done are such that it ought not to be attributed to the actor." Self-defence, by way of contrast, is considered to be an action that is justified. In *Ryan* (2013), the Supreme Court of Canada compared the rationale for self-defence with that for duress and necessity:

> Despite its close links to necessity and duress, self-defence, on the other hand, is a justification … It "challenges the wrongfulness of an action which technically constitutes a crime" … In determining whether the defence is available, less emphasis is placed on the particular circumstances and concessions to human frailty and more importance is attached to the action itself and the reason why the accused was justified in meeting force with force.

Necessity is a common-law defence that arises when the accused person can avoid some disaster or calamity only by breaking the law. In *Perka* (1984), Justice Dickson provided an example of such a situation:

> The lost Alpinist who, on the point of freezing to death, breaks open an isolated mountain cabin is not literally behaving in an involuntary fashion. He has control over his actions to the extent of being physically capable of abstaining from the act. Realistically, however, his act is not a "voluntary" one. His "choice" to break the law is not true choice at all; it is remorselessly compelled by normal human instincts.

The "evil" that the accused person seeks to avoid must be greater than the "evil" involved in the breaking of the law, and the accused must have no reasonable legal alternative but to break the law. Take the case of a surgeon who

necessity
Necessity may be a defence to a criminal charge when the accused person commits the lesser evil of a crime in order to avoid the occurrence of a greater evil.

duress
Duress may be a defence to a criminal charge when the accused was forced to commit a crime as a consequence of threats of death or serious bodily harm made by another person.

is contemplating the surgical separation of conjoined twins who share vital organs, such as the heart or the lungs. Without an operation to separate the babies, both of them will ultimately die. However, the operation will save one of the twins, while inevitably killing the other. Is the surgeon justified in killing one twin in order to save the other? In these particular circumstances, one can assume that the defence of necessity would be available to the surgeon should he or she ever be charged with murder.

When claiming the defence of necessity, defendants may point to any circumstances that constitute a threat to life or limb. Where the defence of duress is raised, defendants are asserting that their power of choice is being overborne by another human being. In the *Hibbert* case (1995), the Supreme Court of Canada ruled that duress, like necessity, was a defence that was based on the concept of "normative involuntariness." Section 17 of the *Criminal Code* sets out the requirements for the defence of duress; however, in the case of *Ruzic* (2001), the Supreme Court of Canada ruled that some of these requirements were so restrictive that they could result in the denial of the defence to an individual who was not blameworthy. As a result, the court struck down these requirements as invalid under the *Charter.*‛ The Supreme Court then held that the courts should apply the "common law" defence of duress. The main elements of this defence are that the accused had been subjected to a threat of death or serious bodily harm directed either toward the accused or toward another person (such as a child or spouse). The threat must be so serious that the accused believes it will be carried out, and the court must be satisfied that it would have caused a reasonable person, placed in exactly the same position as the accused, to act as he or she did. Finally, it should be established that the accused had no obvious "safe avenue of escape." After all, if the accused had the option to escape from the person who was making threats, he or she cannot now claim that he or she was acting involuntarily.

In the *Ruzic* case, for example, the accused was charged with importing a narcotic and use of a false passport. Two kilograms of heroin had been found strapped to her body when she arrived at Pearson Airport in Toronto. Ruzic admitted the offences but asserted that she had acted under duress. Her story was that she lived with her mother in Belgrade (in the former Yugoslavia) and that she had been persistently threatened by a "paramilitary" man who physically assaulted and sexually harassed her. The man had a reputation for extreme violence, and he informed Ruzic that she must take a consignment of heroin to Toronto. When the accused protested, the man threatened to harm her mother. At the time of these threats, law and order had largely broken down in Belgrade, and Ruzic said she did not inform the Belgrade police of the threats against her mother because they were "corrupt and would do nothing to assist her." The jury acquitted Ruzic on both charges, and the Supreme Court of Canada ultimately upheld the acquittal. Ruzic had met all the requirements contained in the common law defence of duress. She clearly believed that she had absolutely no alternative to bringing the heroin into Canada. If she had not done so,

---

‛The Supreme Court did not declare invalid the requirement that the accused person not be a member of a gang or conspiracy which brought about the alleged situation of duress nor did it address the list of 22 offences (ranging from murder to robbery and arson) which Parliament has excluded from the benefit of the defence. However, section 17 only applies to those who actually commit the offence (as opposed to those who are parties to offence by way of aiding/abetting, etc.).

her mother might have been seriously harmed or killed, and seeking the assistance of the local police would have been a futile gesture given the particular circumstances in Belgrade at that time.

In *Ryan* (2013), the Supreme Court of Canada ruled that the threat that is at the core of the defence of duress must be one that is specifically made in order to coerce the accused person into committing a crime. Duress cannot be raised as a defence in situations where the real issue is self-defence. In *Ryan*, the accused was the "victim of a violent, abusive and controlling husband" and had counselled an undercover RCMP officer to kill her husband. The Supreme Court ruled that duress was not available to her.*

Other important defences are provocation and self-defence. **Provocation** is only a partial defence. It may be raised only when the accused is charged with murder. If provocation is raised successfully by the accused, he or she is convicted of manslaughter rather than murder. In *Tran* (2010), Justice Charron of the Supreme Court of Canada noted that "the accused's conduct is partially *excused* out of a compassion to human frailty." The defence is available even though the accused undoubtedly possessed the *mens rea* for murder. Under the terms of section 232 of the *Criminal Code*, murder may be reduced to manslaughter if the accused killed "in the heat of passion caused by sudden provocation." Before the defence may be raised successfully, it must be established that the provocation was of a kind that would be "sufficient to deprive an ordinary person of the power of self-control." The ordinary person would be someone with the same objective characteristics as the accused (for example, race, gender, and age), and the alleged provocation must be viewed within the specific context of the interaction between the accused person and the victim (for example, whether there has been any past history between them). In *Thibert* (1996), the Supreme Court of Canada stated that the ordinary person in that particular case would be "an ordinary person who was a married man, faced with the breakup of his marriage," who had been taunted by the man with whom the accused person's spouse had recently decided to live. In the *Tran* case (2010), Justice Charron asserted that the "ordinary person" test had been enacted by Parliament in order to encourage "reasonable and non-violent behaviour" and that it was a means of upholding the standard of self-control and restraint" that is expected of Canadians.

Once the accused person has satisfied the objective "ordinary person" test, he or she has to establish that the alleged provocation was "sudden and unexpected" and that it in fact caused the accused person to act in anger "before there was time for his or her passion to cool."

The *Stone* case (1999), discussed earlier in connection with automatism, constitutes a typical case of provocation insofar as the accused killed the victim immediately following a series of hurtful insults (which included raising doubts about the paternity of his children and denigrating his sexual prowess). Clearly, the jury believed that an ordinary husband would be likely to lose the power of self-control in such circumstances and that Stone must be considered to have responded to sudden provocation before there had been time for his passion to cool.

provocation
Provocation may be a partial defence to a charge of murder (if successful, it reduces the offence from murder to manslaughter). The required elements of provocation are (1) that the accused responded to a wrongful act or insult that was of such a nature that an ordinary person would have been likely to lose the power of self-control, and (2) that the accused acted "on the sudden and before there was time for his (or her) passion to cool."

*However, the Supreme Court entered a stay of proceedings that prevented her retrial on a charge of counselling murder.

Self-defence is frequently raised as a defence to charges of assault or homicide. Recent amendments to the *Criminal Code* have simplified the law that defines the circumstances in which self-defence and defence of property will be accepted as complete defences to criminal charges.

Section 34 of the *Criminal Code* states that a person may use a reasonable amount of force in self-defence if she or he reasonably believes that they or another individual are the target of actual force or that a threat of force is being made against them. The section also sets out the factors that the courts must take into account in considering whether an accused person's use of force in self-defence was reasonable in all of the circumstances of the case. The factors listed in section 34, which are not exclusive, are: the nature of the force or threat; the extent to which the use of force was imminent and whether there were other means available to respond to the potential use of force; the person's role in the incident; whether any party to the incident used or threatened to use a weapon; the size, age, gender, and physical capabilities of the parties to the incident; the nature, duration and history of any relationship between the parties to the incident, including any prior use or threat of force and the nature of that force or threat; any history of interaction or communication between the parties to the incident; the nature and proportionality of the person's response to the use or threat of force; and whether the act committed was in response to a use or threat of force that the person knew was lawful.

Although the self-defence provisions of the *Criminal Code* have been dramatically overhauled, the large body of case law concerning the "old" provisions is still relevant, particularly with respect to the issue of whether the accused person's conduct was reasonable. The Supreme Court of Canada has consistently emphasized that the basic issue is whether the particular accused person acted reasonably in light of the specific circumstances that faced him or her at the time of the assault upon him or her and in light of her or his perception of those circumstances. For example, the Supreme Court of Canada has emphasized the need to ensure that women who are the victims of domestic violence are judged by the standards of "reasonable women" who face the same circumstances of ongoing abuse and not by the standards of "reasonable men" brawling in a bar. In the *Lavallee* case (1990), the accused had shot her abusive male partner (Rust) in the back of the head. Rust was leaving Lavallee's room just after he had physically assaulted her and threatened her with death.

At Lavallee's trial for murder, a psychiatrist gave expert testimony concerning the so-called battered wife syndrome in order to help the members of the jury determine whether the accused woman's beliefs and actions were reasonable in light of her experience of chronic abuse at the hands of her partner. The psychiatrist asserted that Lavallee "had been terrorized by Rust to the point of feeling trapped, vulnerable, worthless and unable to escape the relationship despite the violence." This witness concluded that Lavallee's shooting of Rust should be viewed as "a final desperate act by a woman who sincerely believed that she would be killed that night." The jury acquitted Lavallee. The Supreme Court of Canada later upheld the acquittal and ruled that the trial judge had acted appropriately in permitting an expert witness to testify about the "battered woman syndrome" as a means of assisting the members of the jury to assess the reasonableness of Lavallee's beliefs and actions.

self-defence
Section 34 of the *Criminal Code* states that a person may use a reasonable amount of force in self-defence if she or he reasonably believes that they or another individual are the target of actual force or that a threat of force is being made against them.

In a later case, *Malott* (1998), the Supreme Court of Canada suggested that this type of evidence should be presented to the jury in order to assist them in understanding at least four separate issues: (1) why an abused woman might remain in an abusive relationship, (2) the nature and extent of the violence that may exist in an abusive relationship, (3) the woman's ability to perceive when her partner was dangerous, and (4) whether she believed on reasonable grounds that she could not otherwise preserve herself from death or serious bodily harm. Section 35 also permits an individual to use force in defence of his or her real property (house, apartment, land) and/or personal property, provided the force used is reasonable in the particular circumstances.

QUESTIONS FOR CRITICAL THINKING

1. It has been suggested that the defence of provocation should be abolished because it is frequently raised in the context of family violence (see, for example, the *Stone* case in this chapter). Do you think there is any place for a defence of provocation in a modern *criminal code*?
2. Do you think self-induced intoxication should ever be a defence to a crime of violence? What are the arguments for and against permitting defendants to raise a defence of intoxication? For example, is it fair that an intoxicated person may kill someone and be sentenced to two years' imprisonment while a sober person who deliberately kills another will be convicted of first- or second-degree murder and be sentenced automatically to life imprisonment?
3. Daphne has lived with Apollo for 10 years, during which he has, on various occasions, subjected her to physical assaults, some of which have inflicted serious injuries (such as extensive bruising to the body, a broken nose, and concussion). One night, Daphne returns home late from an evening meeting and Apollo becomes furious with her. He yells that he is "going to fix her once and for all." However, Apollo is so drunk that he passes out on the couch. Daphne goes to the kitchen and picks up a sharp knife. She then returns to the room where Apollo is sleeping and stabs him to death. Would Daphne be able to raise a successful plea of self-defence if she were charged with murder or manslaughter?

Summary

- A crime consists of a prohibition against certain conduct and a penal sanction (such as imprisonment or a fine).
- The sources of criminal law are (1) legislation and (2) judicial decisions.
- Under the terms of the Canadian Constitution, the Parliament of Canada has the exclusive authority to enact "criminal law and the procedures relating to criminal matters."

- There is a significant difference between "true crimes" that arise under the *Criminal Code* and regulatory offences that arise under regulatory legislation enacted both by the various provinces and territories and by the Parliament of Canada.

- The enactment of the Canadian *Charter* of Rights and Freedoms has given judges the power to invalidate criminal law that unjustifiably infringes on an accused person's *Charter* rights.

- Each criminal offence can be analyzed in terms of its *actus reus* and *mens rea* elements.

- The *actus reus* generally consists of three components: conduct, circumstances, and consequences.

- *Mens rea* may be subjective or objective.

- Subjective *mens rea* may consist of intention and knowledge; recklessness; or wilful blindness.

- Objective *mens rea* is based on the requirement that there be a marked departure from the standard expected of the reasonable person acting prudently.

- An individual may become a party to a criminal offence in a number of different ways: by actually committing an offence, by aiding and/or abetting an offence, by becoming a party to an offence by way of common intention, and by counselling an offence that is committed.

- Three inchoate offences permit the police to intervene before a particular crime is committed: counselling an offence that is not committed, criminal attempt, and conspiracy.

- A successful defence of not criminally responsible on account of mental disorder (NCRMD) is not an acquittal. It is a finding that the accused person has committed the act or omission in question but may not be held criminally responsible on account of mental disorder.

- The most important defences to a criminal charge include mistake of fact; intoxication; necessity; duress; provocation; and self-defence.

NET WORK

Basic legal research is increasingly conducted online. The federal government and the governments of the provinces and territories operate websites that offer swift access via the Internet to the full text of legislation and the decisions of the courts. In addition, a number of commercial electronic database services, such as *BestCase*, *CriminalSource*, *Criminal Spectrum*, *QuickLaw*, and *LawSource* provide information concerning legislation, cases, and legal literature (journal articles and textbooks). You should be able to gain access to these databases through your university or college. If you have such access, a useful exercise might be to search for Canadian criminal cases in which the courts have discussed the defence of duress.

You can explore the powerful electronic tools that are available for research into Canadian criminal law by visiting the website of the Canadian

Legal Information Institute. This website provides easy access to federal and provincial/territorial legislation and court decisions. In addition, the website provides access to the decisions of various federal and provincial/territorial boards and tribunals (such as the Canadian Human Rights Tribunal and the Human Rights Tribunal of Ontario). It also contains links to various external websites that may be of particular value to students (for example, the debates of the House of Commons *Hansard* or the *Canada Gazette*, which provides "Canadians with their rightful access to the laws and regulations that govern their daily lives"). The website address for the Canadian Legal Information Institute is http://canlii.org. Using this website, find the report of the following case: *R. v. Tomlin*, 2014 ONCA 357 (CanLII), decided by the Ontario Court of Appeal on May 6, 2014.

The website operated by the Department of Justice Canada is particularly useful. This site provides not only detailed information about the activities of the Department of Justice and federal developments concerning criminal law but also access to all federal legislation and regulations. The website address for the Department of Justice Canada is http://www.canada.justice.gc.ca. To locate legislation and regulations, click onto "The Laws Site" on the home page.

Using the Department of Justice Canada website, see what information is available concerning Bill C-14, the Not Criminally Responsible Reform Act, *which* received Royal Assent on April 10, 2014.

Find the relevant website for the courts in your own province or territory (for example, in Ontario, log on to http://www.ontariocourts.on.ca/en/sitemap.htm, or, in British Columbia, log on to http://www.courts.gov.bc.ca). Both the Ontario and BC websites provide links to all of the other provincial and territorial court websites in Canada. As an exercise, find out if, during the period 2000 to 2013, your own provincial or territorial court of appeal decided any cases concerning the offence of theft (section 322 of the *Criminal Code*).

Counting Crime

John Evans*

This chapter is about statistics on crime and criminal justice. Over the past century, those who have tried to understand crime have relied heavily on statistical descriptions of criminal behaviour, criminals, and the criminal justice response. What we know about crime depends on the quality, coverage, reliability, and validity of our measures of crime.

This chapter describes how social scientists count crime. After discussing the problems of the validity and reliability of our measures of crime, we introduce the long-standing debate over whether crime statistics accurately reflect the amount of crime in Canada or whether they merely reflect the activities of the criminal justice system. To help you to understand the strengths and weaknesses of Canadian crime statistics, we describe how the administrative records of the police, courts, and prisons are turned into measures describing the amount of crime and the characteristics of offenders and victims. This process involves developing clear procedures concerning units of count, levels of data aggregation, definitions, data elements, and counting procedures. Particular attention will be paid to the most commonly used measure of crime: the Uniform Crime Report system (UCR). The UCR is based on crimes reported to the police across the country. Finally, the chapter describes victimization surveys and self-report studies. These provide data that are complementary to those produced by the UCR.

Learning Objectives

After reading this chapter, you should be able to

- Describe how the administrative records collected in the criminal justice system are turned into statistics about crime and the characteristics of offenders and victims.
- Understand the problems of reliability and validity associated with measures of crime and offenders.
- Understand the system that produces Canadian crime and criminal justice statistics.
- Describe the trends in Canadian crime rates over the past five decades.
- Describe the strengths and weaknesses of victimization and self-reported criminality surveys and understand how these two methods enhance our understanding of the problem of crime in Canada.

*The first edition of this chapter was written with Alexander Himelfarb.

Controversies over Counting Crime

The first concern of those who first sought to measure crime was coverage: how can we obtain data about the amount and nature of crime in a society? As the official sources of statistics have increased, and as creative methodologies for data collection have advanced, reliability and validity have become the most pressing concerns. In simple terms, are the methods and techniques involved in gathering statistics strong enough that anyone following the procedures would produce the same counts (reliability)? And do the statistics collected count what they purport to count (validity)?

Imagine a situation in which you wished to test a theory of crime causation. For example, what aspects of communities create pressures to greater criminality? Let us say that your theory predicts higher crime rates in big cities than in small towns. You are then going to need statistical data on the amount of crime in these two types of settings. How do you get these counts? You could consult police statistics. Police gather vast amounts of information on suspects, incidents, arrests, and charges. These data are often used by criminologists to test their ideas. However, there have always been problems with police statistics. When police officers are dispatched to a call, each officer must use his or her own judgment to decide whether a crime has been committed or whether the call is unfounded. If the officer determines that there has been an offence, a report will be filled out by the officer and processed by police department staff. Most police departments then send the data from each incident to the Canadian Centre for Justice Statistics (CCJS), a division of Statistics Canada. Police are supposed to follow a uniform set of rules (the Uniform Crime Reporting Rules) in recording criminal incidents or calls for service. Yet it has been discovered that different police departments often use different rules for recording their information. In fact, individual police officers exercise a good deal of discretion in what they decide to record and how they record it. There may be doubts, then, about the reliability of the statistics derived from police records. However, there is perhaps an even more fundamental problem: Are suspects criminals? Are those arrested and charged criminals? Are all incidents that are recorded actual crimes, and are these incidents a complete count of crimes? Do the data provide a valid count of crime?

A particular difficulty arises in crime counts because as the reliability of a statistical measure increases, its validity as a count of crime often decreases. Thus, while the police certainly never detect or become aware of all crimes, and despite enormous problems of reliability, their counts of crime are likely to be a far more valid reflection of the amount of criminal behaviour than are counts of convictions or counts of prisoners. The criminal justice system operates as a funnel: only some fraction of incidents result in a police record of a criminal incident, only a portion of recorded incidents result in suspects identified, only a portion of suspects are arrested or charged, only a portion of charges result in conviction, and only a portion of convictions result in incarceration (see Figure 4.1). The farther you go into the system, the more confident you can be that the count is accurate and reliable and that it is a decreasingly valid representation of all criminal behaviour. Also, there are built-in biases because some crimes

methodology
Refers to the study or critique of methods.

reliability
Identifies one of the standards (another being validity) against which the tools used to measure concepts are judged. Reliability refers to consistency of results over time.

validity
The extent to which a tool or instrument (questionnaire, experiment) actually measures the concept the researcher claims to be interested in and not something else.

crime rate
Criminologists calculate crime rates (or rates of incarceration, conviction, or recidivism) by dividing the amount of crime by the population size and multiplying by 100,000. This produces the standard rate per 100,000; occasionally it is useful to calculate a rate per million or some other figure when looking at less frequently occurring offences.

FIGURE 4.1   The Crime Funnel: Break-and-Enter Offences Processed
through the Canadian Criminal Justice System, 2009

ALL BREAK AND ENTER: Offences reported and not reported to the police.
There were an estimated 640, 000 break and enters
in 2009.

REPORTED: 54% were reported to the police.

CHARGED: For about every 17 offences that occur, 1 person is charged.

CONVICTED: For about every 56 offences that occur,
1 person is convicted.

SENTENCED: For about every 122 offences that
occur, 1 person is sentenced to
custody.

Note: This diagram illustrates the processing of break-and-enter offences through various stages in the criminal justice system.
For cautions about these data, see Box 4.3 , Summary and Cautions: Using Victimization Survey Data and Data from the UCR and the
Court Surveys.

Sources: Adapted from Statistics Canada, special tabulation, unpublished data, Uniform Crime Reporting (UCR1) Survey, Canadian
Centre for Crime Statistics, 1998 to 2009.

(and some criminals) are more likely than others to be reported and to result
in arrest, charge, conviction, and a sentence to incarceration. For example,
murderers are more likely to be arrested and to go to jail than are corporate
criminals or shoplifters. The farther you go into the system, the more obvious
it becomes that you are counting something about how the system itself operates; you are counting official decisions about crime and criminals. Statistical
descriptions of the prison **population** may provide valid indicators of one way
that a society responds to crime. These descriptions, however, do not provide a
valid measure of the amount and the nature of crime.

How have criminologists handled these problems? For a long time, they
acknowledged the problems and then, when they needed data, they pretended
the problems away. Kaplan's "law of the hammer" holds that when you give
a small child a hammer, he or she discovers that everything needs pounding.
Similarly, social scientists have often been accused of letting their methods
or the most readily available statistics dictate their theories. Social scientists
often find out what they are able to discover most easily and build their theories
around this limited information. Many of the early theories of criminology
discussed elsewhere in this text were built upon a rather uncritical acceptance
of official sources of statistics. Many early criminologists used prisoners to

population
Refers to all members of
a given class or set. For
example, adult Canadians,
teenagers, Canadian
inmates, and criminal
offenders can each be
thought of as a population.

study the differences between criminals and noncriminals. Some used police records of arrest or charge; some used court records. These criminologists rarely asked the following questions: Are all criminals equally likely to get arrested? To be charged? To be put in prison? Even when criminologists recognized the limits of the available information, they used these unreliable and often invalid measures because this was all they had.

In the 1960s and the 1970s, a number of sociologists and criminologists focused their attention on the systematic biases of past theories built on official records. New theories suggested that official records showed us how the criminal justice system operated to create crime and criminals. The statistics revealed information about the police, about the courts, and about whom they selected for their attention and worst punishments. Arrest, charge, and conviction were parts of a formal labelling process, a ceremony of degradation in which a person was formally stigmatized. These labelling or social reaction theories (see Chapter 13) asked why certain people were more often selected for this process and then studied the consequences of this process for these people. The same "crime statistics" that had been used to describe the behaviour of criminals were now being used to describe the official agents of social control. Criminologists are increasingly becoming polarized. Many seem to be returning to the conservative criminology of the past, to the acceptance of official records as a reasonable indicator of crime, and are focusing on explaining crime for the purpose of controlling it. Others, influenced by some variant of "critical" criminology (see Chapters 11 and 12), see crime statistics as simply part of the government's control mechanism, a way of characterizing the crime problem, a means of self-justification, and a reflection of more fundamental structural inequalities.

Are crime statistics whatever one makes of them? Are statistics simply a resource to tell lies or support one's own favoured position? Yes, sometimes. But they need not be. Theories about crime and facts about crime are built simultaneously, are mutually dependent, and shape one another. Theory without facts is indistinguishable from ideology; facts without theory are often implicit ideology; statistical facts without theory are numerology, often bent to ideological ends. Theorists and policy-makers have often been guilty of using statistics to their own ideological ends, using crime counts to show that we are going through a crime wave, or using the same counts to show how we are living through a wave of repression. We live in an age when numerical values have a certain magic and a power to convince us, to make arguments seem true. Statistics can be dangerous if we do not know how to examine them critically.

For example, imagine that you read, in some credible source, that violence in Canadian society has risen by 100 percent over the past decade. Before you set off to explain this "fact," or before you turn your home into a fortress, you should ask just what is being counted as violence. Is it crimes? *Some* crimes? Political dissent? Violence by the state? Domestic violence? What theory or ideological assumptions have guided this choice of "fact"? And how good are the facts? How well and consistently have they been counted? Are they reliable and valid?

What have social scientists and policy-makers done about the lack of good crime information? Nearly 50 years ago, the American sociologist

theory
A set of concepts and their nominal definitions or assertions about the relationships between these concepts, assumptions, and knowledge claims.

ideology
A linked set of ideas and beliefs that act to uphold and justify an existing or desired situation in society.

Ned Polsky (1967) argued that our understanding of crime would never be significantly advanced if we relied on statistical data. He was concerned that sociologists and criminologists relied too heavily on remote sources of information. They remained too distant from the criminals they wished to understand. He advocated field research through which social scientists live among, and learn from, the criminals themselves. Not surprisingly, few have followed Polsky's lead. Rather, most have worked to improve the quality of statistics based on official sources, to specify the valid uses of these statistics, and to develop innovative methodologies to complement official data and to fill gaps. Despite the problems, criminological theory and criminal justice policy remain heavily dependent on statistics about crime and the criminal justice system. This is not to say that there are not many other ways to advance our understanding of crime. This, however, is not a methods chapter. Qualitative techniques and other methods of studying crime should be examined elsewhere.

One can distinguish three broad types of criminal justice statistics: statistics about crime and criminals, statistics about the criminal justice system and its response to crime, and statistics about perceptions of crime and criminal justice. Theory and policy require statistics about the decisions of those who break the law, about the decisions of those who maintain it, and about what people think of all of this.

Statistics on the Criminal Justice System

The criminal justice system produces an enormous amount of raw data in the form of police reports and records, the recorded decisions of prosecutors and judges, the administrative records of prisons and penitentiaries, and the recorded decisions of parole boards and probation and parole services. From these administrative records the Canadian Centre for Justice Statistics (CCJS) has developed a sophisticated system of statistics on the criminal justice system.

From Records to Statistics

Administrative records are not statistics. Records are concerned with individual cases and are intended primarily to help practitioners make decisions about these individual cases. Statistics are aggregated; they are concerned with what is common among individual cases. Statistics are meant to provide information about larger questions: planning and evaluation, policy and program development, and theory building and testing. While good records are the base, the conversion of records into statistics requires a number of conceptual decisions. The potential clients or users of the statistics must decide what it is they want to know and how they plan to use the information. Statistical systems should be built to address enduring theoretical and policy concerns.

Specifically, the following issues must be addressed before records can be converted into statistics: unit of count, levels of aggregation, definitions, data elements, and counting procedures.

administrative record
A collection of information about individual cases.

levels of aggregation
Refers to how data are to be combined. Do we want city-level, provincial, or national data?

data element
Specification about what, exactly is to be collected.

counting procedure
A consensus on how to count units and data elements.

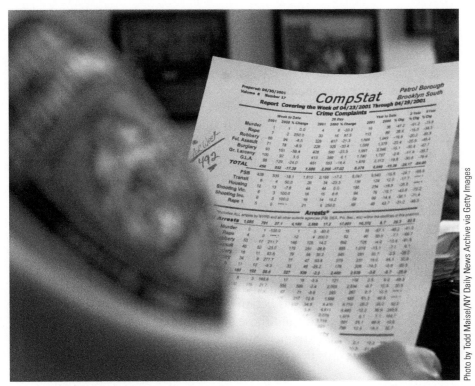

At this CompStat meeting, police officials use crime statistics to plan crime reduction initiatives.

Photo by Todd Maisel/NY Daily News Archive via Getty Images

Unit of Count: Consensus about What It Is That We are Counting

In the course of everyday activities, police may count many different things: suspects, offences, charges, or calls for service. Typically, they work with occurrences. An occurrence may involve several offenders, several victims, and/or several offences. The unit we wish to count in a statistical system will depend on whether we are trying to learn something about police workload or productivity, or crime or victims. Recently, for example, there has been a growing awareness among policy-makers and criminologists that victims have been an ignored unit of count and that we know little about their characteristics. Some units of count are specific to a particular sector. For example, the prison sector can count inmates; the court sector, convictions; and the police, suspects.

Levels of Aggregation: Consensus about How to Combine Data

A crucial decision is the level at which we want our statistics. For example, do we want to combine police records for a city? Do we want to combine statistics for an entire province? Or region? Or the nation? To the extent that we want to generalize our theories or develop or evaluate national policies, we are likely to want national statistics. But several criminologists have warned that the further you move from those who produce the data and the more you try to combine data from different sources, the more questionable is the result. They prefer the richer and more detailed information available from local police to the abstracted, less complete data available about national policing.

Definitions: Consensus about How to Define What is Being Counted

While the Criminal Code provides a common set of definitions for counting crime, there remains a good deal of discretion regarding when an incident of crime is truly an incident, or even what, for example, constitutes "inmate." If one wishes to count inmates, should one count those who are temporarily absent, or those on remand, or those in community correctional facilities, or those who have committed criminal acts and have been assigned to mental institutions? Common definitions are essential. This is not merely a technical issue. Depending on how the terms are defined, you can inflate or deflate the statistics; you can make it appear that crime is higher or lower, or that there are more or fewer prisoners.

Data Elements: Consensus about What Specific Information Should be Collected

While the police will need certain kinds of information to help them in their investigative activities, this information will be far more detailed than, and sometimes quite different from, what is needed as aggregated statistics. Similarly, the police in one jurisdiction may, for their own good reasons, maintain records quite different from those of other police departments. As understandable as this is, it is extremely difficult to build aggregated statistics out of different types of records that may be incompatible.

Counting Procedures: Consensus on How to Count Units and Elements

If an offender goes on a break-and-enter spree and hits six houses in an evening, how many offences should be counted—six (one offence per house) or one (a singular spree)? Or if, during a break and enter, an offender is confronted by the home owner and assaults him or her, is this one or two offences? If one, which offence should be counted? If we agree that the most serious should be counted, how do we determine seriousness?

Canadian Criminal Justice Statistics

The questions or issues of unit of count, levels of aggregation, definitions, data elements, and counting procedures are at the base of much of the technical and critical literature on criminal justice statistics. In Canada, attempts to answer these questions have long been the responsibility of our national statistical agency, Statistics Canada. More recently, the federal and provincial governments have created a national institute—the **Canadian Centre for Justice Statistics (CCJS)**—which is a division of Statistics Canada and is governed by a board of directors of senior officials responsible for justice.

A major challenge for the CCJS is achieving agreement on priorities such as whose needs should be met. Crime statistics are used by different people and for different purposes: criminologists and researchers want to build and test theories, policy-makers and analysts want to identify problems and develop and test solutions, and administrators and program managers want to plan and run their operations and to monitor and evaluate their programs. Most important, statistics serve the public interest by keeping people informed and by providing some measure of public accountability. Good statistics are important, but they are important in different ways for different users.

Canadian Centre for Justice Statistics
A division of Statistics Canada, formed in 1981, with a mandate to collect national data on crime and justice.

Canada has reasonably good national data on criminal justice inputs such as resources and expenditures. The data are now far better when it comes to outputs such as incidents, arrests, charges, convictions, and dispositions. The CCJS has developed and improved the Adult Criminal Court Survey, a census of courts in Canada. Since 2009, the survey has collected data from jurisdictions representing about 95 percent of the national criminal court caseload. Correctional statistics are the most accurate because we can count the number of prisoners in Canada and provide some information on their social characteristics. This can be quite useful for projecting future inmate populations and for planning future facilities and services. When linked to other data, these data can also be useful for developing correctional policy. For example, how much are we using incarceration, and are we doing so in the most useful and appropriate ways?

Data on prisoners, however, do not tell us much about crime and criminal behaviours. They tell us about the criminal justice system. The confusion comes when people equate "criminal" with "prisoner." Some people are more likely to be caught; some people are more likely to be charged; some people are more likely to be convicted; and some people are more likely to be sentenced to prison or to a penitentiary. We know too much about how people get selected for incarceration to assume that prison statistics tell us very much about crime.

But what can such data show? Figure 4.2 shows the growth in the number of adults incarcerated in Canada between 1978–79 and 2012–13. In this period, the adult inmate population increased from 21,834 to 39,679. Unfortunately, there is no national count of youth in custody. Statistics Canada does not have youth custody data from Nova Scotia, Quebec, Saskatchewan, and Nunavut.

SEARCH FOR:
"Justice and Crime"
Statistics Canada

FIGURE 4.2   **Average Daily Count of Adults in Custody**

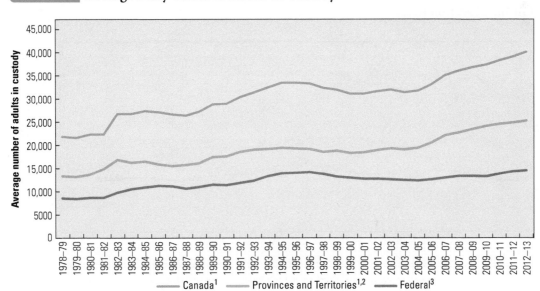

Notes: 1. Province/Territory and Canada totals exclude Prince Edward Island, Northwest Territories, and Nunavut for comparison between years. 2. Provincial and territorial counts may include federal sentenced offenders in a provincial or territorial facility. 3. Federal counts may include provincial/territorial offenders in a federal facility and those temporarily detained in a federal facility.

Source: Statistics Canada, Canadian Centre for Justice Statistics, Correctional Services Surveys, Adult Key Indicators Report.

Obviously, these figures are important for administrative and planning purposes. But do these figures tell us something about growing crime in Canada? No. Do they tell us something about harsher or more punitive sentencing practices? No. In fact, if we look at the rate of incarceration (per 100,000 adult Canadians), we see that much of the growth in the penitentiary population can be accounted for by the growth of the Canadian population (Figure 4.3).

International comparisons are difficult and problematic. That said, they do tell us that Canada incarcerates people at a much higher rate than most Western European nations but at a much lower rate than the United States, where more than 2.3 million people were incarcerated in 2012. This is an incarceration rate of 716 per 100,000 US residents, up from 411 in 1995 (Bureau of Justice Statistics, 2012) and six times the Canadian rate of 118 per 100,000 in 2012–13. Note that this Canadian figure is a much lower rate than that shown in Figure 4.3 below. The difference is that the figure of 118 is based on the total population whereas the data in Figure 4.3 are based on the adult population. For international comparisons, the total population base is typically used.

Some have compared Canadian to Western European incarceration rates to argue that Canada is too punitive, that too many people are being put behind bars and put there for too long. Others have argued that it simply means Canada has more serious crime than many other nations. The debates flourish. Statistics do not provide the answers; they indicate only where problems may exist.

How Much Crime?

It should come as no surprise that criminologists have had difficulty counting crime. Crime is typically a secretive activity. When people commit crimes, they

FIGURE 4.3 **Adult Incarceration Rates**

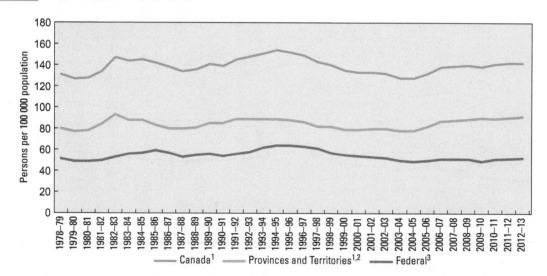

Notes: 1. Incarceration rates for provinces/territories and Canada exclude Prince Edward Island, Northwest Territories, and Nunavut for comparisons between years. 2. Provincial and territorial counts may include federal sentenced offenders in a provincial or territorial facility. 3. Federal counts may include provincial/territorial offenders in a federal facility and those temporarily detained in a federal facility.

Source: Adapted from Statistics Canada, Criminal victimization in Canada, 2004, Juristat, 85-002-XIF2005007, vol. 25 no. 7 (November 2005), http://www.statcan.gc.ca/bsolc/olc-cel/olc-cel?catno=85-002-XIE&lang=eng.

FIGURE 4.4 **International Incarceration Rates, OECD Countries**

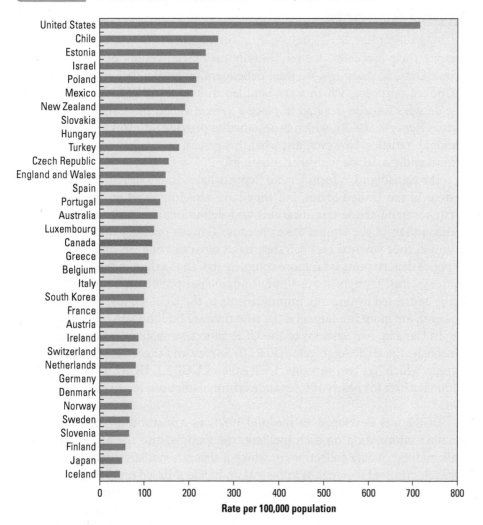

Source: Walmsley, R. World Prison Population List (10th edition), International Centre for Prison Studies. http://www.prisonstudies.org/sites/prisonstudies.org/files/resources/downloads/wppl_10.pdf. Reprinted by permission.

try to avoid becoming part of the count of criminals. (They do not want to become a statistic!) The "best" crime is one that no one knows about, and no criminal justice system will ever be able to ferret out all crimes and all criminals. Some crimes are harder to detect than others, and some criminals are harder to apprehend and convict. Criminologists have long recognized that the major problem of counting crime is the so-called **dark figure of crime**—that is, crime that remains unreported, unrecorded, and largely unknown. In response to this problem, criminologists have developed a variety of ways of counting crime, or at least for describing crime patterns and trends. They have tried to rationalize and improve official statistics, but they have also developed approaches that do not depend on official counts of crime. In the next section, we look at official records, victimization surveys, and self-report studies as sources of data about crime.

dark figure of crime
The amount of crime that is unreported or unknown.

Official Statistics: Canadian Uniform Crime Reports

Despite their problems, we rely heavily on official counts of the amount of crime. Until 50 years ago, we were dependent on local police records collected for police purposes, which were handled differently in each locale. For over five decades Canada has had in place a system called the Canadian Uniform Crime Reports (UCR), which is designed to provide uniform and comparable national statistics. However, just what this system counts has been subjected to almost endless debate within criminology.

The Canadian Uniform Crime Reports have drawn heavily from a similar system in the United States, but they have also improved on the US system. First, common crime classifications and definitions are easier to arrive at in Canada than in the United States because Canada operates under a common criminal code whereas each US state has a separate code. Second, the coverage of police departments is far more complete in Canada than in the United States. Both systems, though, share some fundamental problems. Some of these are being addressed by ongoing improvements to the UCR survey; others, though, however, are more fundamental because they are built into all official statistics.

In Canada, two versions of the UCR collection instrument operate simultaneously: the UCR Aggregate (UCR1.0) Survey and the UCR2 Incident-Based Survey, which has two versions, UCR2.0 and UCR2.1. UCR1.0, which collects summary data for nearly 100 separate criminal offences, has been in place since 1962.*

UCR2 was developed in the mid-1980s as a method of collecting more detailed information on each incident, the victims, and the accused persons. This method of data collection, in which a separate statistical record is created for each criminal incident, is known as an incident-based reporting system.

A revised version of UCR2, known as UCR2.1, was introduced in 1998. This survey introduced certain efficiencies for police services and lowered the response burden by eliminating or simplifying UCR2 variables (Statistics Canada, 2010). In 2004, yet another version, UCR2.2, was introduced to add new violations and other variables.

Let us look more closely at the "seriousness rule." A number of studies (Nettler, 1974; Silverman and Teevan, 1975; Silverman, 1980; de Silva and Silverman, 1985) have documented some of the problems in the recording and scoring rules and how these rules are applied. Specifically, the studies have examined the implications of the "seriousness rule," which holds that only the most serious crime is to be scored in an incident involving several crimes. The concerns this rule creates are threefold: first, it deflates the total crime count, since less serious crimes are not counted separately; second, it inflates serious crimes as a proportion of the total; and third, the way in which seriousness is scored is problematic because not enough qualitative data about the crimes are recorded to use a sophisticated scale of seriousness. See Box 4.1 for a discussion of the main UCR categories and the most serious offence rule.

Uniform Crime Reports (UCR)
Since 1962, Statistics Canada has published the Uniform Crime Reports based on a standardized set of procedures for collecting and reporting crime information.

seriousness rule
If there are several crimes committed in one incident, only the most serious crime is counted. UCR1.0 uses the seriousness rule.

---

*The description of the UCR is based on the CCJS website: http://www.statcan.ca Search for UCR.

FOCUS

Box 4.1

UCR CATEGORIES AND THE MOST SERIOUS OFFENCE RULE

Violent incidents involve offences that deal with the application, or threat of application, of force to a person. These include homicide, attempted murder, various forms of sexual and nonsexual assault, robbery, and abduction. Traffic violations that result in death or bodily harm are included under Criminal Code traffic incidents.

Property incidents involve unlawful acts with the intent of gaining property but do not involve the use or threat of violence against an individual. Theft, breaking and entering, fraud, and possession of stolen goods are examples of property crimes.

Other Criminal Code incidents involve the remaining Criminal Code offences that are not classified as violent or property incidents (excluding traffic). Examples are mischief, bail violations, disturbing the peace, arson, prostitution, and offensive weapons.

Total Criminal Code incidents is the tabulation of all violent, property, and other Criminal Code incidents reported for a given year.

Most Serious Offence

The UCR1.0 Survey classifies incidents according to the most serious offence (MSO) in the incident. In categorizing incidents, violent offences always take precedence over nonviolent offences. Within the violent and nonviolent categories, offences are then sorted according to the maximum sentence under the Criminal Code. The UCR Survey scores violent incidents differently from other types of crime. For violent crimes, a separate incident is recorded for each victim (categorized according to the most serious offence against the victim). If, for example, one person assaults three people, then three incidents are recorded. If three people assault one person, only one incident is recorded. For nonviolent crimes, one incident (categorized according to the most serious offence in the incident) is counted for every distinct or separate occurrence. Robbery is one exception to the above scoring rule. Robbery is categorized as a violent offence. Unlike all other violent offences, one occurrence of robbery is equal to one incident, regardless of the number of victims. The reason for this exception is that robbery can involve many people who could all be considered victims. In a bank robbery with five tellers and 20 customers present, 25 incidents of robbery would be counted if the normal scoring rule for violent incidents were applied. This would seriously overstate the occurrence of robbery. Thus, the total number of incidents recorded by the UCR Survey is not a census of all violations of the law that come to the attention of police. Rather, it is equal to the number of violent crimes (other than robbery) plus the number of separate occurrences of nonviolent crimes (and robberies).

Actual Incidents

When a crime is reported to the police, the incident is recorded as a "reported" incident. Police then conduct a preliminary investigation to determine the validity of the report. Occasionally, crimes reported to the police prove to be unfounded. Unfounded incidents are subtracted from the number of reported incidents to produce the number of "actual incidents." Numbers and rates of crime are calculated on the basis of "actual incidents" categorized according to the most serious offence.

Source: Adapted from Statistics Canada, special tabulation, unpublished data, Uniform Crime Reporting (UCR1) Survey, Canadian Centre for Crime Statistics, 1998 to 2009.

Concerns have also been expressed that the crime categories used are too general, allowing too many different kinds of acts to be recorded in the same way. For example, thefts and attempted thefts are recorded under the same category.

Furthermore, as previously indicated, it is not always entirely clear just what it is we want to count. In Canada, the count of crimes includes violations of the Criminal Code, violations of other federal and provincial statutes, and violations of some municipal bylaws. Many of these criminal and quasi-criminal laws are not what most Canadians think of as crime. When most people think of crime they are thinking about particular offences. They are not thinking about the Criminal Code and the full range of behaviours legally defined as criminal. When we seek to count crime, we are invariably struck with a complex mix of these two sets of definitions. For this reason,

gross counts of crime may be very misleading. For example, in 1969 the Ouimet Report pointed out that total convictions for all criminal offences in Canada increased by an alarming 2500 percent between 1901 and 1965. The report added, however, that 98 percent of the increase was accounted for by summary convictions—less serious crimes—particularly traffic offences. Thus, much of the apparent increase in crime actually reflected the increased use of automobiles in Canada during this period. With the report of the gross crime counts alone, most people would no doubt have had horrific visions of violent predators preying on innocent victims, rather than the more accurate vision of careless motorists abusing one another and pedestrians. For these reasons, UCR programs count offences within particular offence categories so that each offence can be examined separately.

Another often-cited problem is that the Canadian UCR treats property crimes and personal crimes differently. Several property crimes, even if they involve different victims, may be recorded as a single offence if they are considered part of the same incident. This is not the case for personal offences. However, even for personal offences, the UCR1 survey collects very little information about victims and offenders. The CCJS has sought to rectify this by developing the UCR2, which as we saw above collects data on characteristics of the victim and the accused as well as characteristics of the incident itself. As a result of the most serious offence scoring rule, less serious offences are undercounted by the aggregate survey. However, the incident-based survey allows up to four violations per incident, permitting the identification of lesser offences.

By 2009, the response rate from police respondents to the UCR surveys was virtually 100 percent. UCR2 data provide a rich source of information for Canadians. Continuity with the UCR aggregate survey data is maintained by converting the incident-based data to aggregate counts at year end.

The question remains, however, whether the new and improved Canadian UCR will provide us with an accurate count of crime or even a reasonable indicator of crime and crime trends. Can official statistics ever tell us about total crime? Are official statistics useful only for understanding the criminal justice system?

We have discussed the Canadian UCR under the heading of criminal justice statistics because these official data may tell us more about police activities than about crime. "Official violations" statistics are, in part, a product of policy decisions within the criminal justice system—that is, decisions about which criminal infractions deserve the most police attention and resources. Furthermore, crime statistics are the product of individual police decisions made in the exercise of police discretion regarding what crimes are serious enough to attend to, record, and pursue. In fact, the ways in which police and police departments apply crime recording and scoring procedures reflect, to some extent, the policing style and policy of the particular police department. Because combining or comparing statistics from different departments is highly problematic, the CCJS has developed elaborate rules and procedures for collecting and verifying data.

Police statistics are also shaped by public perceptions, concerns, and fears. The police depend on the accounts of victims and witnesses. In other words, victims and witnesses must recognize an act as a criminal justice matter, must

gross counts of crime
A count of the total amount of crime in a given community, making no distinction between crime categories.

believe it to be of sufficient seriousness to warrant a report to the police, and must believe that reporting the act is worthwhile—all this before the police make their decisions about how to respond to and record an act (see, for example, Shearing, 1984).

Official crime statistics, then, are shaped by both commonsense and legal definitions of what constitutes crime. These statistics reflect the decisions of many people, not simply the behaviours of criminals. Official counts of crime will change as legal definitions change, as commonsense definitions change, and as the priorities of agents of law enforcement change. For example, if Parliament made premarital sex illegal, we could well expect a rather sharp increase in crime. Would this be reflected in official crime counts? To the extent there are no direct victims to bring these offences to police attention, the answer is probably no. Much would depend on the priority attached to enforcement of this offence.

Consider two less hypothetical examples. As official statistics reveal to us increasing rates of family violence, theoretical explanations of the crisis in the nuclear family abound. But has the incidence truly increased, or have Canadians become less tolerant of such behaviour and more willing to bring such incidents to police attention? Have police become more sensitive to the seriousness of the problem and more likely to record the incidents as crimes? In other words, has the incidence of family violence increased, or have the definitions and reporting and recording behaviours changed? For those students wanting more statistical and substantive information on this topic, the CCJS website has a wealth of excellent studies on family violence and victimization of women.

Over the past decade, there has been an increase in the rate of police-reported drug offences in Canada. The rate in 2013 was 13 percent higher than it was a decade previously. The rate of possession offences for other drugs increased 80 percent, driven by increases in Quebec, BC, and Ontario. The rates of possession of cannabis (+28%) and cocaine (+8%) also increased, along with offences involving the trafficking, production, or distribution of cocaine (+13%) and other drugs (+10%). Offences involving the trafficking, production, or distribution of cannabis were the only drug offences to see a decrease compared to their rate 10 years previously (−35%), with the largest decreases recorded in BC and Quebec.

Why have there been these changes in drug offences? Has their use really increased that much or have the priorities of law enforcement agencies shifted as well? One factor contributing to the increase in cannabis offences may be the effort to shut down marijuana-growing operations (grow-ops) across the country now that hydroponic gardening has enabled Canadian growers to supply an increasing share of the domestic market and to export to the United States, often in exchange for cocaine for the Canadian market. Because statistics for victimless crimes such as drug use are as much a result of police priorities and budgets as they are of the amount of criminal behaviour, official statistics may not tell us much about the actual prevalence of these behaviours.

What, then, *can* the UCR tell us? The total Criminal Code offence rate nearly doubled, from 2,771 offences per 100,000 Canadians at the inception of the UCR in 1962 to 5,019 in 2013. Figure 4.5 shows the trend line during this

FIGURE 4.5   **Total Criminal Code Offences Reported to Police by Most Serious Offence, Rate per 100,000 Canadians, 1962–2013**

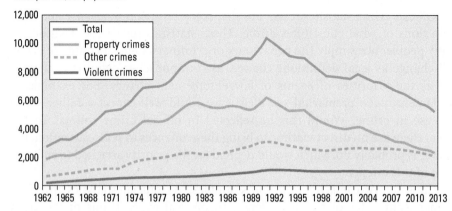

Source: For years 1962–2005: Adapted from Maire Gannon, Crime Statistics in Canada, 2005, Juristat, Vol. 26, no. 4, p. 16 (2006), http://www.statcan.ca/bsolc/english/bsolc?catno=85-002-X&CHROPG=1; For years 2006-2009: Adapted from Mia Dauvergne and John Turner, Police-reported crime statistics in Canada, 2009, Juristat, Vol. 30, no. 2, p. 25, (2010), http://www.statcan.gc.ca/pub/85-002-x/2010002/article/11292-eng.htm.

period. Both violent and property crime rates increased steadily until 1992 and then declined or stabilized through 2013. Violent crimes (1,092 per 100,000 in 2013) were consistently much lower than property crimes (3,146 per 100,000).

Those who work with crime statistics generally refer to *crime rates* when they wish to take into account the size of the population. The crime rate is simply the number of incidents for every 100,000 Canadians. References to rate rather than incidence, ensure that comparisons from jurisdiction to jurisdiction, or over time, do not reflect changes in population size rather than differences in criminal behaviour.

In 2013, Canada had 505 homicides (first- and second-degree murder, manslaughter, and infanticide) and 642 attempted murders. Together, these crimes accounted for less than half of 1 percent of reported violent incidents. The national homicide rate declined to 1.44 per 100,000 in 2013, marking an 8 per cent decrease from the previous year and the lowest homicide rate recorded since 1966 (see Figure 4.6).

Crime has been declining in recent years. The crime rate rose from 1962 to 1991 but has generally declined since then (see Figure 4.7, which shows the levels of all recorded offences for the period 1962 to 2013. The police-reported crime rate in 2013 was the lowest recorded since 1969, and was 33 percent below the police-reported crime rate in 2003.

Crime Severity Index

To address the matter of the crime rate being driven by high volumes of less serious offences, the CCJS developed crime severity indexes (CSI). CSI values are available from 1998. The crime severity index is calculated by assigning each offence a weight derived from actual sentences given by the criminal courts. The more serious the average sentence, the greater the weight. Thus,

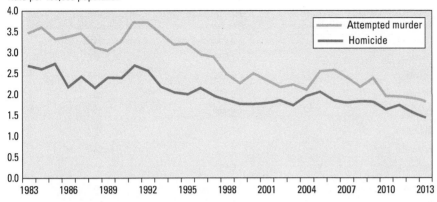

FIGURE 4.6   **Homicide Rate per 100,000 Canadians, 1961–2013**

Source: Adapted from Statistics Canada, Homicides peaked in mid-1970s, Juristat, Vol. 30, no. 3, p. 7 (2009), http://www.statcan.gc.ca/pub/85-002-x/2010003/article/11352-eng.pdf.

more serious offences have a greater impact on the severity index. Figure 4.7 shows the crime severity indexes from 2003 to 2013.

In 2013, the Crime Severity Index (CSI), which measures both the volume and the seriousness of police-reported crime in Canada, declined for the tenth year in a row, dropping to 68.7. This was a 9 percent decrease from 2012 and a 36 percent decrease from 2003 (Boyce et al., 2014). (For a full account of these new indexes, including a youth crime severity index, see Dauvergne and Turner, 2010.) Table 4.1 shows the crime rates and crime severity values for most of Canada's largest cities for 2013. The city rankings on the two measures are very similar.

Remember that all these data are based on reports to the police. But what can we say about crime rates given all the cautions with which we began this chapter? How much crime remains hidden to the police? Which crimes? How

FIGURE 4.7   **Police-Reported Crime Severity Indexes, Canada, 1998–2013**

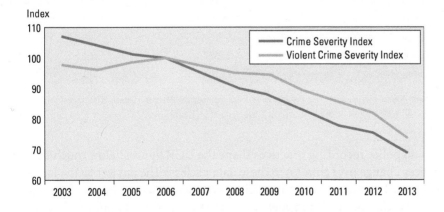

Source: Statistics Canada, special tabulation, unpublished data, Uniform Crime Reporting (UCR1) Survey, Canadian Centre for Crime Statistics, 1998 to 2009.

TABLE 4.1   Crime Rate and Crime Severity Index Values, by Census Metropolitan Area, 2013

Census Metropolitan Area	Crime Rate	Crime Severity Index
Regina	8,069	109.3
Kelowna	7,680	92.6
Saskatoon	7,958	99.1
Thunder Bay	6,392	80.6
Winnipeg	5,368	83.2
St. John's	6,464	78.4
Edmonton	6,743	84.5
Vancouver	6,897	90.3
Saint John	4,986	60.4
Halifax	5,326	68.6
Abbotsford	6,109	80.7
Brantford	6,242	83.7
Victoria	5,408	59.1
London	5,225	67.2
Canada	**5,190**	**68.7**
Moncton	5,913	66.1
Sudbury	4,685	66.9
Barrie	3,712	42.8
Kingston	4,848	54.6
Montreal	4,072	65.9
Calgary	4,268	60.4
Windsor	4,399	61.3
St. Catharines	3992	57.5
Hamilton	3,786	55.1
Kitchener	4,336	56.8
Peterborough	4,489	54.4
Trois-Rivieres	3,875	60.3
Ottawa	3,615	52.1
Guelph	3,557	43.0
Quebec	3,257	46.5
Toronto	2,941	47.1

Source: Adapted from Dauvergne, Mia, and John Turner. Police-reported crime statistics in Canada, 2009, *Juristat*, Vol. 30, no. 2 (2010), Table 4, p. 29, Table 6, p. 32.

much do police recording practices shape the UCR figures? How much do these practices change over time? Are these data useless? The answer to the last question is no. For example, the homicide statistics collected by the CCJS reflect the actual number of homicides fairly accurately. It is also probable that certain other offences that are of high priority within the criminal justice system, and which victims are likely to report, are relatively well captured by the UCR program. Motor vehicle theft is the best example of this type of offence. In sum, we can learn something about the incidence of crime from these data, but we are not sure how much.

FOCUS

Box 4.2

THE USES AND ABUSES OF POLICE CRIME FIGURES

The government [is] extremely fond of amassing great quantities of statistics. These are raised to the nth degree, the cube roots are extracted, and the results are arranged into elaborate and impressive displays. What must be kept ever in mind, however, is that in every case, the figures are first put down by a village watchman, and he puts down anything he damn well pleases. – Attributed to Sir Josiah Stamp, 1840-1841, H.M. collector of Inland Revenue.

Perhaps. But most reports come from citizens and not from the "watchman," and now there are elaborate rules for recording crime figures.

In cooperation with police departments, Statistics Canada has established rules governing the collection of data, complete with coding manuals, and has assigned individuals the task of verifying the reports from which the data are extracted. Local quality control measures are in effect for respondents of crime surveys to minimize the underreporting of crime. In addition, Statistics Canada runs a number of automated checks to ensure data completeness and accuracy.

However, elaborate and sound procedures developed and refined over decades can be subverted by managers determined to show their police forces in a more favourable light. Recently, the United Kingdom's Statistical Authority has withdrawn its "gold standard" status from police figures. Police crime figures can no longer be used as national statistics until the forces can demonstrate that the quality of the data meets national standards. Allegations include claims that the Metropolitan Police have understated sexual offences by as much as 25 percent. Other "fiddling" techniques have included downgrading offences to less serious ones or persuading victims not to make a complaint. In some cases, crimes were only recorded if they were solved. Other offences were kept off the books if the offender could not be traced (UK Statistical Authority, 2014).

Similar dubious practices have recently been documented for Chicago, Illinois, and Los Angeles, California. In Chicago, it is alleged that new police managers, under political pressure from the mayor to show that their policing practices were working, downgraded many homicides to death investigations or caused them to disappear altogether. Other crimes were similarly downgraded, all to show that crime figures were better than in the previous year (*Chicago Magazine*, May 2014).

These inaccurate counts do a disservice to everyone, not least police departments. Crime data are a powerful resource that can be used to target police patrols and develop partnerships with other sectors in the community—partnerships that can and should assist with prevention and enforcement. Even calls for service can be a powerful resource.

A very simple example of using crime data to direct resources involved one community in which two nearly identical apartment complexes generated vastly different numbers of calls for service (10 versus 150). The situation was closely examined, and the only significant difference between the two complexes was the quality of the management. The police chief met with management, and eventually the situation improved: calls for service were reduced so that each complex generated around 10 calls for service per month (Engstad and Evans, 1980).

More recently, many police department websites have made crime data available in map form so that citizens can see which crimes are reported in which neighbourhoods throughout the city. In some cases, citizens can file an incident report online.

And, going much further, some police forces are turning to "predictive policing." A computer program analyses crime data and predicts where certain types of crime are likely to occur. Officers use these data and their own knowledge to deploy to particular places. The program, PrePol, is being aggressively marketed and is being used by a number of forces, including the LAPD and the Seattle police. No comprehensive evaluation of the program is yet available.

As data storage and analysis continue to get easier and cheaper, many other data analysis techniques will be developed to mine the wealth of data that incident reports contain. Some of these techniques are discussed in more detail in Chapter 15 of this text.

Sources: Adapted from Perreault, Samuel, and Shannon Brennan. Criminal Victimization in Canada 2009, *Juristat*, Vol. 30, no. 2, p. 5 (2010), http://www.statcan.gc.ca/pub/85-002-x/2010002/article/11340-eng.htm.

We can be more confident that if police departments across Canada are recording and reporting crimes relatively consistently, then the UCR data give us a picture of what crimes the police are processing. For example, in the 1980s, changes in policy limited police discretion in laying charges when handling domestic violence incidents. This policy has produced more official incidents of such assaults, reflecting changes in police practice if not changes in criminal behaviour (see Chapter 6). Some optimists would argue that the UCR indicates trends in crime. The less optimistic say no, there is too much we do not know about victim reporting behaviour, about the exercise of police discretion in deciding what is criminal and what is not, about police recording and reporting practices, and about the nature and seriousness of the offences captured by the UCR. Out of these concerns have emerged attempts to develop other ways of counting crime. The most important of these is the victimization survey.

QUESTIONS FOR CRITICAL THINKING

1. Crime rates in Canada declined between 1999 and 2013. How would you account for this decline? You might wish to read ahead in Chapter 5 for possible answers to this question.
2. The media do not accurately portray the nature and extent of crime in Canada. Can you find examples in your own community of media distortions of crime? Why do the media behave in this way? What are the consequences of these distortions?

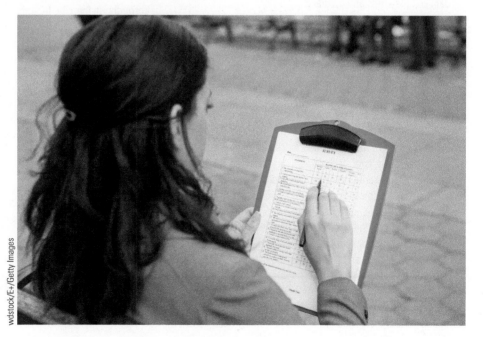

Surveys asking Canadians about their crime victimization provide valuable knowledge about crime in Canada.

wdstock/E+/Getty Images

3. To what extent do official statistics measure the amount of crime in society? What are the major biases in official statistics?

Victimization Surveys

Victimization surveys ask people whether they have been victims of acts that the Criminal Code defines as criminal. They are asked to describe the nature and consequences of their victimization experiences; to describe the criminal justice response; to indicate whether victims or others brought the incidents to official attention, and if not, why not; and to indicate their perceptions of and attitudes toward crime and criminal justice in Canada. The first large-scale victimization survey in Canada was carried out in 1982 by the Ministry of the Solicitor General of Canada and Statistics Canada. Those interested in the methodological developments for the first large-scale victimization surveys can read Catlin and Murray (1979), Evans and Leger (1978), and Skogan (1981).

Since 1988, Statistics Canada has conducted a victimization survey about every five years (1988, 1993, 1999, 2004, and 2009) as part of the General Social Survey. For the 2009 survey, telephone interviews were conducted with a random sample of approximately 19,500 people, aged 15 and older, living in the 10 provinces. The three territories were also covered, using a different sampling design.

Respondents were asked for their opinions concerning the level of crime in their neighbourhood, their fear of crime, and their views concerning the performance of the justice system. They were also asked about their experiences with criminal victimization. Respondents who had been victims of a crime in the previous 12 months were asked for detailed information on each incident, including when and where it occurred, whether the incident was reported to the police, and how they were affected by the experience.

Not all crimes can be captured through this survey method. One need not be a methodologist to recognize that murder cannot be included in such a survey. Nor can consensual crimes for which there are no direct victims—drug use, gambling, and the like. These consensual crimes are not captured very well through official data or through victimization surveys. Similarly, those crimes designed to keep victims unaware that they have been victimized cannot be captured accurately in victimization surveys (or official data sources). Fraud, embezzlement, employee pilferage, price fixing, and the wide range of consumer, corporate, and white-collar crimes were not included in the survey. The eight categories of crime included were sexual assault, robbery, assault, break and enter, motor vehicle theft, theft of household property, theft of personal property, and vandalism. The major findings of the 2009 survey are outlined in Box 4.3. The 2014 survey is being conducted at the time of writing. Results should be available on the CCJS website in mid-2015.

victimization survey
A survey of a random sample of the population in which people are asked to recall and describe their own experience of being a victim of crime.

sample
A group of elements (people, offenders, inmates) selected in a systematic manner from the population of interest.

FOCUS

Box 4.3

CRIMINAL VICTIMIZATION IN CANADA, 2009: HIGHLIGHTS

- The 2009 General Social Survey (GSS) found that just over one-quarter of Canadians aged 15 years and older reported being the victim of a crime in the preceding 12 months. This proportion was similar to that in 2004, when the previous victimization survey was conducted.
- Seven in 10 self-reported victimizations were nonviolent. Of the 8 offences measured by the GSS, theft of personal property was the most common.
- Overall rates of self-reported violent victimization remained stable between 2004 and 2009, as did the rates of sexual assault, physical assault, and robbery.
- Overall rates of self-reported household victimization also remained stable between 2004 and 2009. However, motor vehicle thefts declined 23 percent while break-ins increased 21 percent.
- Self-reported rates of violent and household victimization in 2009 were higher in western Canada, particularly

Manitoba and Saskatchewan, than in the eastern part of the country.
- Younger Canadians reported higher rates of violent victimization than older Canadians. The rate of violence reported by 15-to-24 year olds was almost 15 times higher than the rate for individuals 65 years or older.
- Just under one-third of Canadians (31 percent) who had been victimized reported their victimization to police, down slightly from 2004 (34 percent). Break-ins and motor vehicle thefts were more likely than other types of victimizations to be brought to the attention of authorities.
- In 2009, the vast majority (93 percent) of Canadians felt somewhat or very satisfied with their personal safety from crime, similar to the GSS findings from 2004.

Source: Adapted from Statistics Canada, Criminal victimization in Canada, 2004, Juristat, Vol. 25 no. 7 (2005), http://www.statcan.gc.ca/bsolc/olc-cel/olc-cel?catno=85-002-XIE&lang=eng.

Note that of the incidents identified, just under one-third (31 percent) had been reported to the police or had otherwise come to police attention. Allowing that the victimization survey cannot capture the entire "dark" figure missed by the UCR, the survey data do reveal that many more Canadians are victimized by crime than is revealed by official statistics.

As most would guess, a large proportion of unreported crime is relatively trivial—the kinds of incidents that most of us would not expect the police to devote time or resources to investigating. For example, a few dollars stolen by somebody within the household, a toy stolen from the porch, or an umbrella stolen from a restaurant are the kinds of common incidents that are rarely reported. Nonetheless, as Table 4.2 shows, more serious incidents may often go unreported. For example, in the 2004 Victimization Survey, 92 percent of

TABLE 4.2   **Incidents Reported to Police, 1993, 1999, 2004, and 2009**

Incidents	1993	1999	2004	2009
Theft personal property	42	35	31	28
Robbery	46	46	46	43
Physical assault	33	37	39	34
Break and enter	68	62	54	54
Motor vehicle/parts theft	50	60	49	50
Theft household property	43	32	29	23
Vandalism	46	34	31	33

Source: For 1993–2004 data: Adapted from Gannon, Maire, and Karen Mihorean. Criminal Victimization in Canada, 2004, *Juristat*, Vol. 25, no. 7 (2006), Figure 11, p. 17 (2006), http://www.statcan.gc.ca/bsolc/olc-cel/olc-cel?catno=85-002-X20050078803&lang=eng; For 2009 data: Adapted from Perreault, Samuel, and Shannon Brennan. Criminal Victimization in Canada 2009, *Juristat*, Vol. 30, no. 2, p. 15 (2010), http://www.statcan.gc.ca/pub/85-002-x/2010002/article/11340-eng.htm.

those who had been sexually assaulted did not report the incident to the police. Women assaulted by people they knew indicated that fear of revenge was one of the reasons they failed to report. Figure 4.8 presents the major reasons for failing to report to the police in the 2009 survey.

Where incidents produced great financial loss to the victim, reporting was far more likely, even more likely than for those incidents that resulted in pain or injury but no loss. Reporting property crimes, particularly when the loss was over $1,000, is less an act of justice (or even revenge) than a far more utilitarian act—seeking redress, recompense, or recovery. On the other hand, 83 percent of victims of violent crime felt it was their duty to report to the police. Figure 4.9 displays the data on reasons for reporting from the 1999 survey.

The survey data confirm many of the concerns about official sources of crime data. Some crimes are more likely to come to police attention than others. Some categories of victims are more likely to report their victimizations, and some categories of offenders (for example, family members) are less likely to be reported. In general, it is only through such knowledge that we can begin to understand the UCR data and the dark figure of crime. Because victimization surveys are based on victims' perceptions and experiences, and because they

FIGURE 4.8 **Reasons for Not Reporting Victimization to Police, 2009**

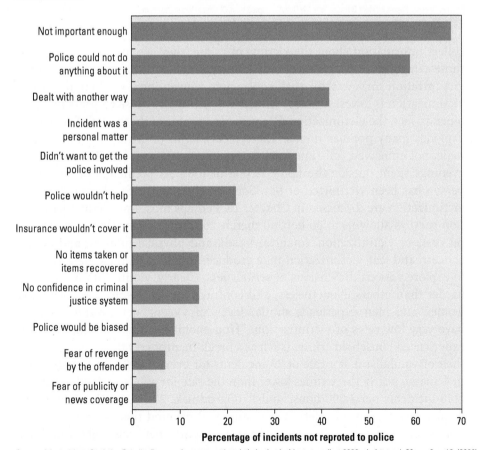

Source: Adapted from Statistics Canada, Reasons for not reporting victimization incidents to police, 2009, *Juristat*, vol. 30, no. 2, p. 16, (2009), http://www.statcan.gc.ca/pub/85-002-x/2010002/article/11340-eng.pdf.

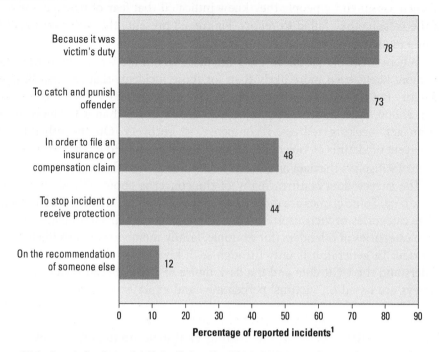

FIGURE 4.9 **Reasons Given for Reporting to Police**

Source: "Victims Report Incident Because 'It Is My Duty,'" adapted from, "Criminal Victimization in Canada, 1999," *Juristat* 20, no. 10 (1999): 12, http://www.statcan.gc.ca/pub/85-002-x/85-002-x2000010-eng.pdf.

collect information about the victims of crime, they are useful in identifying those categories of people most at risk of criminal victimization. For example, victimization surveys show that, contrary to conventional wisdom, the risk of victimization is lowest for older Canadians, especially those 65 years of age or older. In fact, the victimization data provide a profile of the victim of crime that explodes many popular myths. The typical victim of crime is young, single, male, not employed full-time, and living an active social life. The number of evenings spent outside the home is one of the best predictors of whether a person has been victimized or not. Some of the reasons for these patterns of victimization are discussed in Chapter 15. Perhaps most important, victimization surveys allow us to go beyond merely counting crime. They provide data on costs of victimization, financial losses, and physical injuries, and on the concern and fear victimization may produce. In addition, these data allow us to explore various dimensions of seriousness. Clearly, victimization hits some harder than others. Nonetheless, and contrary to most people's expectations, women and men experience similar levels of violent victimization. Seniors have very low rates of victimization: "Households with only senior residents experienced household crimes (such as a break-in, property theft, motor vehicle theft or vandalism) at a rate of 87 incidents for every 1,000 senior households in Canada, nearly three times lower than the rate for all Canadian households (248 incidents per 1,000 households)" (Ogrodnick, 2007, 15). This is reflected in their perceptions of safety, as the survey also found that "seniors' satisfaction with their personal safety improved slightly between 1999 and 2004. The vast majority (92%) of seniors reported feeling satisfied with their overall level of safety from crime in 2004, compared to 89% reported in 1999. This increase closes the gap between seniors and younger Canadians, resulting in fairly consistent levels of satisfaction with their personal safety (92% compared to 94%)" (Ogrodnick, 2007, 17).

Victimization surveys cannot measure all crimes. They are dependent on the vagaries of human memory and are subject to the kinds of criticisms levelled against any survey, including the fact that some people may not tell interviewers the truth. Victimization surveys are dependent on respondents' ability not only to recall incidents and their details, but also to place the incidents correctly in time. We know that respondents are fallible. And, as Skogan (1978) suggests, well-educated, articulate respondents are more likely than others to talk to interviewers and to give rich and full accounts of their victimization experiences, thus perhaps biasing the data. There is reason as well to be cautious about interpreting data on domestic and sexual assaults that have been collected through surveys. Respondents may well be reluctant to discuss such experiences with an interviewer. Also, the methodology is still relatively young. Special methods will be needed to get data about rural victimization and victimization of Aboriginal Canadians. Special methodologies are also required to measure white-collar crime, consensual crime, and what has come to be called enterprise crime—organized crime and the crimes of organizations and the state. More information is also required on the psychological and emotional impact of victimization.

Despite the limitations, these data provide us with the opportunity to go beyond counting incidents and to gain some understanding of what it is we are counting. The data are an essential complement to other sources of crime statistics.

Self-Report Studies

Yet another approach to generating data on the nature and distribution of crime is the self-report study. The people who know the most about crime are those who break the law. Rather than relying on police data, which will inevitably be incomplete, or on the knowledge of victims, why not just ask criminals what they do and how often they do it? Many sociologists have done this, most commonly through questionnaires given to students in junior and senior high schools. A classic study done by Travis Hirschi (1969) in the San Francisco area is typical of self-report studies (you will read about some of the results of this study in Chapter 14). Hirschi took a random sample of all the junior and senior high school students in Richmond, California, and administered questionnaires to 5,545 students. The survey was a very lengthy one, and we will consider here only the questions measuring delinquent behaviour. The students were asked six questions about their illegal conduct; for each, they were asked to check off one of the following responses: "A. No, never"; "B. More than a year ago"; "C. During the last year;" and "D. During the last year and more than a year ago." The delinquency questions were:

- Have you ever taken little things (worth less than $2) that did not belong to you?
- Have you ever taken things of some value (between $2 and $50) that did not belong to you?

self-report study
A method for measuring crime involving the distribution of a detailed questionnaire to a sample of people, asking them whether they have committed a crime in a particular period of time. This has been a good method for criminologists to determine the social characteristics of offenders.

FOCUS

Box 4.4

SUMMARY AND CAUTIONS: USING VICTIMIZATION SURVEY DATA AND DATA FROM THE UCR AND THE COURT SURVEYS

Victimization Surveys

These surveys provide rich data, but remember that they collect information on a limited set of crimes—eight in the Statistics Canada surveys. Uniform Crime Report (UCR) surveys cover more than 100 offence types. When considering these data, use caution. Refer back to Figure 4.1, "The Crime Funnel." The 2009 victimization survey estimated that there were 630,000 break and enters in Canada. Note that these are break and enters of households. Break-and-enter offences against businesses are not included. Thousands of break and enters are therefore excluded from the victimization survey but are included in police and court data. This affects each subsequent item in the funnel. The figure is an illustration only.

Defining Courts-Based Data and Police Incident-Based Data

Police

The procedures used to collect UCR data have been discussed earlier in this chapter.

Courts

The purpose of the Adult Criminal Court Survey (ACCS) and the Youth Court Survey is to provide a national database of statistical information on the processing of cases through the adult and youth criminal court systems. The surveys consist of a census of Criminal Code and other federal statute charges dealt with in adult criminal courts and youth courts. In 2008–9, the ACCS represented approximately 95 percent of the national adult criminal court caseload. The Youth Court Survey has 100 percent coverage.

Counting Procedures

The basic unit of count for the Court Surveys is a case. A case is one or more charges against an accused person or corporation, where the charges receive a final disposition on the same date. Charges are linked to a case on the basis of the accused identifier and the date of the last court appearance.

Most Serious Offence and Decision Rules

When a case has more than one charge, it is necessary to decide which charge will be used to represent the case (since a case is identified by a single charge). In multiple-charge cases, the "most serious decision" rule is applied. Decisions are ranked from the most to the least serious as follows: (1) guilty, (2) guilty of a lesser offence, (3) acquitted, (4) stay of proceeding, (5) withdrawn, dismissed, and discharged, (6) not criminally responsible, (7) other, and (8) transfer of court jurisdiction.

In cases where two or more offences have resulted in the same decision (e.g., guilty), the "most serious offence" rule is applied. All charges are ranked according to an offence seriousness scale, which is based on the average length of prison sentence and rate of incarceration. If two charges are tied according to this criterion, information about the sentence type (e.g., prison, probation, and fine) is considered. If a tie still exists, the magnitude of the sentence is considered.

Comparisons between Courts and Police UCR Survey Data

Counts from the UCR survey for offences cleared by charge are not comparable to the Adult Criminal Court Survey (ACCS) figures for charges disposed of. There are many reasons for this. In part, it is the result of the scoring rules used by the UCR survey. The UCR survey counts violent offences by the number of victims in the incident; nonviolent offences are counted by the number of separate incidents.

For example, two persons break into a house and subsequently commit vandalism and theft. This would be considered as one police incident. Assuming the charges were laid and the matter proceeded to court, there would be a minimum of six charges—three charges for each accused.

In addition, the differences in the "most serious offence" rule between the courts and police surveys can result in court cases and police incidents being represented by different offences even though they may have been part of the same crime.

Furthermore, the published UCR figures include offences involving youths, while the ACCS case counts include only the very few youth offences that have been transferred to adult court (less than 100 per year).

Moreover, information is captured in the UCR with the laying of a charge, while in the ACCS information is captured upon the court rendering a decision. This time lag in data collection between the two surveys further affects comparability.

- Have you ever taken things of large value (worth over $50) that did not belong to you?
- Have you ever taken a car for a ride without the owner's permission?
- Have you ever banged up something that did not belong to you on purpose?
- Not counting fights that you may have had with a brother or sister, have you ever beaten up on anyone or hurt someone on purpose?

Hirschi looked at responses to these delinquency questions and compared them with other measures, including such things as students' reports of their friends' behaviour, and their family and school relationships, in order to shed some light on what caused some students but not others to become delinquent. He was using self-report studies to try to overcome some of the weaknesses of police data. In most cases, the results of self-reporting have supported the view that there are systematic biases.

Because self-report studies supposedly avoid these biases, they have been particularly important in research and theory on the causes of crime and delinquency, especially the relationship between social class and crime. For a long time, these studies were not very carefully scrutinized. A major project to determine the reliability of self-report studies was carried out by Hindelang, Hirschi, and Weis (1981). They concluded that the self-report method does demonstrate that people are willing to report crimes, both those known and those not known to officials, and that respondents' reports are internally consistent. A difficulty arises in that it appears that different populations answer self-report questions in different ways. Lower-class males and black males in the United States study are more likely to underreport their own criminal behaviour than are middle-class white males. Similarly, in Canada, Fréchette and LeBlanc (1979, 1980) confirm that while self-report studies do uncover much hidden delinquency and raise questions about the biases in official statistics that show the preponderance of lower-class crime, previous self-report studies have also masked the fact that lower-class crime is typically more serious and persistent.

In 2006, Canada participated in the International Self-Reported Delinquency Study, which was conducted in over 30 countries. Canada's study was conducted in Toronto schools, sampling youth in Grades 7 to 9. According to the International Youth Survey, over one-third (37 percent) of students in Grades 7 to 9 in Toronto reported having engaged in one or more delinquent behaviours in their lifetime, through either acts of violence, acts against property, or the sale of drugs. The lifetime prevalence was higher among boys (41 percent) than among girls (32 percent) (Savoie, 2007).

There are two related problems with self-report studies. First, it would appear that those who are typically law abiding are more likely to report completely their occasional infractions than are the more committed delinquents to report their more serious and frequent infractions. Second, differences between official statistics of delinquent behaviour and self-report data may reflect not simply biases in official data, but biases in the self-report method as well. The official data are likely to include more serious offences, and self-report data are more likely to include more minor infractions, as you can see from the items used in Hirschi's studies (Note that the dollar amounts in Hirschi's questions reflect the value of the dollar in the 1960s.)

There are a number of other, more technical problems with self-report studies. For example, there are sampling problems—it is difficult to get "hard-core criminals" in a sample for several reasons, including the fact that they are less likely than other youth to be in school, where most of these surveys are administered. A recent study, however, did show moderate agreement between self-reports and official data for a group of serious delinquents. (Piquero, Schubert, and Brame, 2014). There are also disagreements regarding which offences to select, which produce the most reliable and valid data, and which scoring procedures best suit the uses of the data (see Hindelang, Hirschi, and Weis 1981; Thornberry and Krohn, 2000). Although self-report studies are never likely to be an instrument for counting crimes, recent methodological refinements have enhanced their potential to address fundamental questions about crime and the correlates of crime.

Another use of self-report studies is to examine trends. In Ontario, the Centre for Addiction and Mental Health has conducted surveys every two years since 1977. Large samples of students in Grades 9 through 12 fill out anonymous surveys on their use of alcohol and drugs. The data show that both drug and alcohol use have been declining over time (Boak et al., 2013).

Self-report data can be used for other purposes as well. By using formal self-report surveys such as Hirschi's or by interviewing criminals in prison or in other, less restrictive situations, we can learn a great deal about their motivations for committing crimes and the techniques they use to commit crimes. This information can help us understand the causes of crime and how to prevent it. In later chapters of this book you will read about many of the lessons that criminologists have learned from talking to criminals.

The Future of Crime and Criminal Justice Statistics

The importance of good statistics for planning, policy-making, and administration has long been recognized within the criminal justice system. The founding of the CCJS is a recognition—in a country with shared jurisdiction for criminal justice—of the importance of developing national commitment and national strategies for producing and sharing criminal statistics.

New information technology holds great promise for improving the official records that form the basis of most criminal justice statistics on prisons, courts, and police. Only through a nationally coordinated effort can we avoid the danger of developing incompatible systems in each province (or worse, each municipality) of the sort that feed many different criminal justice systems and inhibit the continued development of a coordinated national system of justice.

The methods for counting crimes are still in their formative stages. Some, like the UCR, will be derived from official records (designed in accordance with UCR rules) and will, therefore, suffer the limitations of all such official statistics. Nevertheless, recent advances in police management information systems and crime classification systems hold great promise for providing us with a measure of calls for police service, police caseloads, and police activity. The richer information from the UCR2 will help here. Other methods, like victimization surveys, will draw on people's experiences and will, therefore, suffer the limitations of all such surveys. Significant progress has been achieved in Canada in the development and refinement of victimization surveys and self-report studies.

How much crime is there in Canada, and what are the trends? Is it bad and getting worse? Do we have cause for alarm? Are things good and getting better? Do we have cause for complacency? Depending on your bias and prejudices, the state of the art allows you to find some evidence and numbers to justify either extreme. But with the improvements in our knowledge about crime and the development of new methods, we are coming to recognize the complexity of the questions. When taken together, the UCR and the victimization surveys encourage neither alarm nor complacency. Overall, there is certainly less serious crime than most Canadians assume based on media accounts and the high visibility of sensational incidents. At the same time, we are starting to uncover some particular kinds of serious incidents that have remained hidden for too long. Sexual assault and family violence are two important examples. Much more work is needed. Only through an integrated program of criminal justice statistics that recognizes the limits of any one source of information will we be able to build powerful theories of crime and sound policies and programs for crime prevention and control.

QUESTIONS FOR CRITICAL THINKING

1. Victimization surveys reveal that many crimes, including serious violent crimes, are not reported to the police. Why not? What is the significance of this for society?
2. In 2010, former Conservative Public Safety Minister Stockwell Day tried to explain why his government was increasing spending on prison construction even though crime rates were declining. His response was that the prisons were needed because of increases in unreported crime. Can you figure out why this response was nonsensical?
3. How are self-report studies used in criminology? Can you find examples of the use of self-report data in later chapters of this book?

Summary

- Statistics can help us better understand the nature and extent of crime in Canada. But to interpret these crime statistics properly, we must understand their strengths and weaknesses.
- The quality of official statistics varies depending on their sources. Corrections data are the most reliable and valid because the task of counting prisoners can be done accurately. On the other hand, crimes known to the

police, the most commonly used statistics, will always be biased by inconsistencies in reporting and recording, although the CCJS is very stringent about verifying data.

■ Administrative records can be the basis of statistics if clear procedures are developed about units of count, levels of data aggregation, definitions, data elements, and counting procedures.

■ The Canadian Uniform Crime Report (UCR) system is designed to provide uniform and compatible national statistics. There is much debate about just what is counted. Some hold that the UCR provides a reasonable estimate of crime rates. Others hold that what is being measured is criminal justice processing.

■ The crime rates provided by the UCR, based on crimes reported to the police, have declined since the peak year of 1991. Both violent and property crimes have declined. The police-reported crime rate in 2013 was the lowest recorded since 1969, 33 percent below the police-reported crime rate in 2003.

■ Victimization surveys provide an alternative and complementary method of measuring crime. These surveys ask random samples of the population about their victimization experiences. They also provide data on such important issues as reasons for reporting and not reporting crimes to the police.

■ Self-report studies are not serious rivals of either the UCR or victimization surveys as a method of measuring crime. However, they do have a useful place in answering specific questions related to understanding the causes and correlates of crime.

■ Developing Canada's national statistics will take continued effort and commitment from all the actors in the system. The CCJS has made great progress, and the statistics now available are much better than they were 10 or 20 years ago.

NET WORK

Canadian crime statistics are compiled by the Canadian Centre for Justice Statistics, which reports the annual number of crimes reported to the police. Go to the Statistics Canada website and find the *Juristat* report "Police-Reported Hate Crime in Canada, 2012." What are hate crimes? Have they been increasing? Why do you think the rates of hate crimes vary so much across Canada's major cities (CMAs)?

Correlates of Criminal Behaviour

5

Temitope Oriola
UNIVERSITY OF ALBERTA

This chapter focuses on **correlates** of criminal behaviour. Correlates of crime are variables that are connected with crime. A correlate is "a phenomenon that accompanies another phenomenon and is related in some way to it" (Hartnagel, 2012). Generations of research in criminology have examined socio-demographic variables that are correlated with crime. These include offenders' age, gender, ethno-racial background, and socio-economic status, and the spatial location of offences. This chapter explores how these variables or correlates are associated with crime. The aim is to answer questions such as these: Who is likely to be involved in crime? How is crime gendered? What does age have to do with criminality? Does race have any relationship with crime?

It is important to understand that correlation is not the same as causation. Thus, while the correlates we will be examining are in some ways connected with criminal behaviour, they do not necessarily *cause* crime. No single factor explains any particular crime. Each correlate should be viewed as one of a much more complex assortment of factors that contribute to criminal acts. Thus, a change in a correlate of crime may not necessarily lead to a change in crime. Six major correlates of crime are examined in this chapter: age, gender, race, drug and alcohol use, socio-economic status, and spatial location.

Learning Objectives

After reading this chapter, you should be able to

- Describe the major correlates of criminal behaviour.
- Explain the trends and patterns of age and gender distribution of criminal behaviour.
- Demonstrate an understanding of the relationship between race and crime.
- Explain the reasons for the overrepresentation of Aboriginal peoples in the criminal justice system through the colonial model, trauma transmission model, and critical race theory.
- Critique cultural theories of Aboriginal overrepresentation in crime.
- Analyze the relationship between drug and alcohol use and crime.
- Demonstrate an understanding of the complex interplay of socio-economic status and crime.
- Explain how crime rates vary by spatial location or geographic region in Canada.

> **correlate**
> A phenomenon that accompanies another phenomenon and is related in some way to it.

◯ Age as a Correlate of Criminal Behaviour

Young people are disproportionately represented in crime generally and in violent crime in particular. Figure 5.1 shows the age distribution of persons accused of crime in 2011. It illustrates an established pattern: criminal activity intensifies in adolescence and young adulthood and declines thereafter (Hartnagel, 2012). The exceptions are political crimes, corruption, and other white-collar crimes; all of these require structural opportunities and employment opportunities that are not yet available to young people.

Figure 5.2 shows that while persons aged 35 to 89 were responsible for 41 percent of all cases completed in adult criminal court in 2011–12, persons aged 18 to 34 were involved in 59 percent of all cases (Boyce and Cotter, 2013). Most crimes committed by Canadian youth are nonviolent (Perreault, 2013). Theft under $5,000 is the most common offence committed by youth (18% of all youth Criminal Code offences excluding traffic violations). This crime often involves shoplifting (Perreault, 2013). The most common violent crime among Canadian youth is Level 1 assault (11%). Level 1 assaults are assaultive acts that do not cause any physical harm to victims. Other violent crimes frequently committed by youth in 2012 were uttering threats (4%), assault level 2 (3%), and robbery (approximately 2.5%) (Perreault, 2013). Assault level 2 is the category of assaults that involving carrying, using, or threatening to use an imitation or real weapon (Dauvergne, 2009). The 2012 data also show that Canadian youth were heavily involved in crimes such as cannabis possession (10%), administration-of-justice violations (10%), and mischief (11%). Administration-of-justice violations include failure to report to court, while mischief is the crime of vandalism. It involves unlawful interference with somebody else's property, thereby

FIGURE 5.1   **Persons Accused of Crime, Aged 12 to 65 Years, 2011, Canada**

Source: Brennan, Shannon, "Police-reported crime statistics in Canada, 2011," chart 15 (2012). Ottawa: Statistics Canada. Available online at: http://www.statcan.gc.ca/pub/85-002-x/2012001/article/11692-eng.htm (accessed on May 26, 2014).

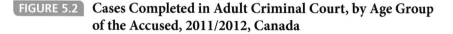

FIGURE 5.2 **Cases Completed in Adult Criminal Court, by Age Group of the Accused, 2011/2012, Canada**

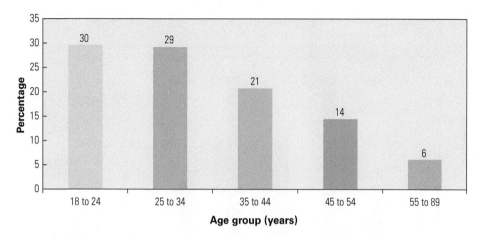

Note: Includes information on accused persons aged 18 to 89 years at the time of the offence. Data exclude cases involving companies and those in which the age and/or the sex of the accused was unknown. A case is one or more charges against an accused person or company that were processed by the courts at the same time and received a final decision. Data exclude information from superior courts in Prince Edward Island, Quebec, Ontario, Manitoba, and Saskatchewan as well as municipal courts in Quebec due to the unavailability of data.

Source: Boyce, Jillian. Adult criminal court statistics in Canada, 2011/2012, chart 3, *Juristat* (2013), http://www.statcan.gc.ca/pub/85-002-x/2013001/article/11804/c-g/desc/desc03-eng.htm.

causing damage. Most serious youth crimes were down in 2012: there were 12 fewer youth-perpetrated homicides in 2012, and robbery (–8%), and assault levels 2 and 3 (–10%) also declined (Perreault, 2013). Only 44 percent of youth accused were formally charged in 2012, a continuation of a trend toward diversion that began in 2003, when the Youth Criminal Justice Act was introduced (Perreault, 2013).

Homicide represents less than 1 percent of violent crimes committed by Canadian youth (Taylor-Butts and Bressan, 2006) but is worth discussing because of its seriousness. Figure 5.3 shows the percentage of persons of various age categories accused of homicide in 1991 and 2012. Persons aged 12 to 24 committed 40 percent of all homicides in Canada in 2012 and 36 percent of homicides in 1991. In contrast, only 13 percent (2012) and 8 percent (1991) were committed by people aged 50 and above. Persons aged 12 to 24 made up only 13 percent of the Canadian population in 2012 and 14 percent in 1991, while persons aged 50 and above constituted 34 percent of the population in 2012 and 30 percent in 1991. Fifty-nine youth per year were charged with homicide between 2000 and 2009 (Mahony, 2011a). This was an increase from 52 youth per year between 1991 and 2001 (Dauvergne, 2002).

Woodworth, Agar, and Coupland (2013) found that youth homicide offenders were more likely than adults to victimize strangers. They also found that youth are more likely than adults to commit homicides as a group rather than as lone individuals. This suggests that peer influence is a critical factor in youth violence. The rate of violent youth crime in Canada is two to three times lower than the rate among American youth (Li, 2008).

Why Do Young People Commit More Crimes Than Adults?

Matza (1964, 22) first drew attention to the notion of **maturational reform**—that there is a reduction in criminal offending as individuals get older.

maturational reform
The fact that people are less likely to commit crime as they grow older.

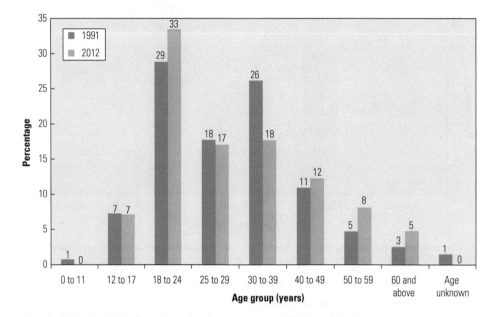

FIGURE 5.3 Percentage of Persons Accused of Homicide by Age Group, 1991 and 2012, Canada

Note: Homicide includes Criminal Code offences of murder, manslaughter, and infanticide; includes all persons who are accused (by police) as having committed a homicide. Data in this figure do not necessarily agree with data from the Uniform Crime Reporting Survey, where youth accused include a small number of persons under the age of 12.

Source: Statistics Canada. Table 253-0003 - Homicide survey, victims and persons accused of homicide, by age group and sex, Canada, annual (number), CANSIM (database).

The basic explanation for maturational reform is that adolescence is a period of transition marked by ambiguity. Young people at this stage are neither children nor adults and may not be fully committed to conventional values. Their infractions, Matza argues, are temporary. The confusion, marginality, and "in-between-ness" of adolescents' social position may be conducive to criminal behaviour, for these provide little incentive for noncriminal lifestyles; adults, by contrast, enjoy greater incentives to conform, such as jobs and marriage (Hartnagel, 2012). For instance, money is required to participate in the consumerist youth culture of Western societies (Greenberg, 1979, cited in Hartnagel, 2012). Young people may shoplift or steal if their parents are unable or unwilling to pay for the latest phones and tablets. Hartnagel also suggests that older people may have become more skilled at avoiding detection, and that as they age, they may be physically unable to engage in certain kinds of criminal behaviour.

The notion of maturational reform encompasses three factors that may cause crime to decline. First, aging brings physiological limitations. Second, the formation of various types of social bonds, such as work, marriage, and children, means that individuals have other people who depend on them to make the "right" choices. Third, maturational reform involves a more socially responsible trajectory of human agency. A relatively simple example of this is that beyond a certain age, "getting wasted" on weekends may no longer sound as attractive a course of individual or group action as it is for younger people.

The notion of maturational reform is intertwined with life course theory. Life course theory is concerned with the "role of age-graded transitions and social controls" (Salvatore and Markowitz, 2014, 629). Life course theorists articulate how social bonds (Chapter 14) such as attachment to a spouse, pursuit of education, and the onset of major life events or turning points such as having children or stable employment help reduce the likelihood of involvement in crime (Salvatore and Markowitz, 2014; Laub and Sampson, 2001). Laub and Sampson (2001) offer a life course theoretical framework for understanding desistance from criminal behavior. They argue that desistance is an underlying causal process whose end product is reducing or ending involvement in criminal activity. Some of the major factors over the life course that contribute to desistance from crime are "aging; a good marriage; securing legal, stable work; and deciding to 'go straight,' including a reorientation of the costs and benefits of crime" (4). For most individuals, many of these watershed moments take place in adulthood, and they are believed to contribute to reduced criminal offending (Salvatore and Markowitz, 2014; Laub and Sampson, 2001).

Life course theorists have begun to study the "romance–crime nexus" (Larson and Sweeten, 2012, 606). Larson and Sweeten examined the effect of breakup of nonmarital romantic relationships on the offending patterns of 10,438 young people aged 17 to 21 in the United States. They found that male offending increases after the breakup of a nonmarital romantic relationship, but that breakup is not associated with female offending. Also, young people who enter into a new relationship after a breakup avoid engaging in criminal activities but increase their alcohol consumption and illicit drug use.

Gender as a Correlate of Crime

Have you ever wondered why most criminals are males? This section focuses on four key questions in the gender distribution of police-reported crime. First, what is the proportion of females accused of crime compared to males? Second, what are the percentages of females and males under the supervision of correctional services at the provincial and federal levels? Third, what is the gender distribution of convicted persons who have been designated "dangerous offenders" in Canada? And fourth, is there evidence supporting the notion of role convergence between males and females as regards crime? The answers to these questions provide a gendered picture of criminality.

SEARCH FOR:
Women and the Criminal
Justice System: Juristat

Females are less likely to be charged with criminal offences. The past three decades have seen an increase in the number of females charged with criminal involvement—21 percent of adults charged with a Criminal Code offence in 2009 versus 15 percent in 1979 (Mahony, 2011b). Despite the increase, males are still greatly overrepresented in crime. The level of involvement of males and females varies by type of crime. In 2011–12, for instance, males made up 81 percent of all persons in cases completed in the adult criminal court (Boyce, 2013). Males made up 98 percent of the accused in sexual assaults and 91 percent of weapons offences; females were most commonly accused of theft (35 percent) fraud (30%), and possession of stolen property (27%). Aside from cases involving property offences, females were most frequently involved in cases for prostitution (34%) and failure to appear in court (23%). Females had higher rates of offending than men for drug possession (52%) and prostitution (51%). Data from 2008–9 indicate that the "most serious" charges against females in adult courts were theft (17%), assault level 1 (11%), impaired driving (10%), failure to comply with a court order (9%), breach of probation (7%) and fraud (7%) (Mahony, 2011b, 27). The charges against females in youth court were similar to those of adult females (27).

Gartner, Webster, and Doob (2009, 182) found that women's imprisonment has not increased in the past few decades in Canada despite significant media attention to female crime and a perceived increase in incarceration rates of women. Figure 5.4 shows that females make up 23 percent of all admissions to youth correctional services. Also, 85 percent of the 413,951 admissions to adult correctional services in 2011–12 were men. Females made up 7 percent of those in federal custody (which indicates sentences of at least two years), 19 percent of those sentenced to probation, and 20 percent of those given conditional sentences in 2011–12 (Perreault, 2014). According to Mahony (2011b), there are gender dynamics at the prosecution and sentencing stages. Women were less likely than men to be found guilty of a crime (59 percent versus 68 percent). Only 28 percent of cases involving men were stayed or withdrawn compared with 37 percent of cases involving women. After a finding of guilty, 26 percent of women were sentenced to jail compared with 37 percent of women. Adult female sentences were generally shorter those given to male counterparts.

FIGURE 5.4   **Youth Custody and Community Services (YCCS), Admissions to Correctional Services by Age Group and Gender in 2011/2012, Canada**

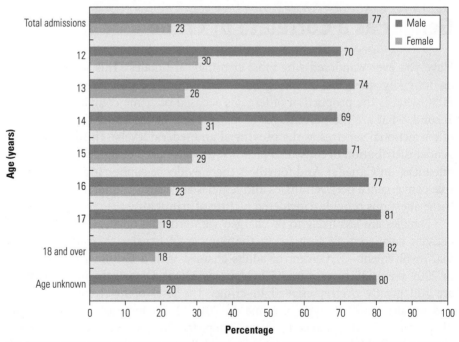

Note: Data represent the total for all reporting jurisdictions, rather than a complete national total, because data for some jurisdictions are incomplete or not available. Admissions are collected each time a person begins any type of custodial or community supervision and describe and measure the case flow in correctional agencies over time. The same person can be included several times in the admission counts where the individual moves from one type of legal status to another (e.g., from open to secure custody) or re-enters the system in the same year. Thus, admissions represent the number of entries within a fiscal year to sentenced custody, to remand, and to community supervision regardless of the individual's preceding or following legal status.

Source: Statistics Canada. Table 253-0003 - Homicide survey, victims and persons accused of homicide, by age group and sex, Canada, annual (number). Available at: http://www5.statcan.gc.ca/cansim/a26?lang=eng&retrLang=eng&id=2530003&paSer=&pattern=&stByVal =1&p1=1&p2=-1&tabMode=dataTable&csid= (accessed: June 10, 2014).

Why do women receive more lenient treatment in the courts? One reason is that males commit more serious crimes, especially more violent offences. A second factor that influences court decisions is female offenders' responsibility for young children (Kruttschnitt, 2013).

Women and Violent Crime

As shown in Figure 5.5, 89 percent of persons accused of homicide in 2012 were male (Boyce and Cotter, 2013). Males tend to murder other males. Most homicide victims are males (71%) (Figure 5.6). The category "dangerous offender" also sheds light on those considered most violent among the population convicted of serious crime. Canada's dangerous offender law (section 753 of the Criminal Code) separates out the most aggressive criminal recidivists among those who have been convicted of a violent and/or sexual criminal offence. A person who has been classified a dangerous offender can be held in prison for an indeterminate period. Dangerous offenders represent 3 percent of the incarcerated population. Of nearly 500 persons held in 2013 under the "dangerous offender" law, only one was a woman.

FIGURE 5.5   **Distribution of Persons Accused of Homicide by Gender, 2012, Canada**

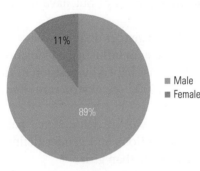

Note: Homicide includes Criminal Code offences of murder, manslaughter, and infanticide; includes all persons who are accused (by police) of having committed a homicide. Data in this figure do not necessarily agree with data from the Uniform Crime Reporting Survey, where youth accused include a small number of persons under the age of 12.

Source: Statistics Canada. Table 253-0003 - Homicide survey, victims and persons accused of homicide, by age group and sex, Canada, annual (number). Available at: http://www5.statcan.gc.ca/cansim/a26?lang=eng&retrLang=eng&id=2530003&paSer=&pattern=&stByVal=1&p1=1&p2=-1&tabMode=dataTable&csid= (accessed: June 10, 2014).

FIGURE 5.6   **Distribution of Victims of Homicide per Gender, 2012, Canada**

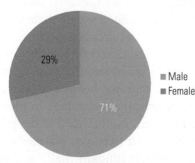

Note: Homicide includes Criminal Code offences of murder, manslaughter, and infanticide.

Source: Statistics Canada. Table 251-0011 - Youth custody and community services (YCCS), admissions to correctional services, by sex and age at time of admission, annual (number). Available at: http://www5.statcan.gc.ca/cansim/a26?lang=eng&retrLang=eng&id=2510011&paSer=&pattern=&stByVal=1&p1=1&p2=-1&tabMode=dataTable&csid= (accessed: June 10, 2014).

Both males and females are more likely to be killed by males. Females are more than twice as likely as males to be killed by their spouse (Mahony, 2011a; Ansara and Hindin, 2010). When a woman commits a violent crime, it is often against someone closely related to her. Victims of female acts of violence in 2009 were the spouse or some other intimate partner (46%), an acquaintance (29%), a stranger (14%), or a family member (12%) (Mahony, 2011a, 21). Males are more likely to direct their violence at acquaintances, especially when the crime is homicide.

Heimer and De Coster (1999) have made an important contribution to our understanding of the gender gap in violent crime by examining structural positions and cultural processes, including social learning. They conclude that:

1. Violent delinquency is a function of the social learning of violent definitions by both males and females.
2. There are gender differences in the process of learning violent definitions. Direct parental controls such as aggressive discipline influence violent definitions for males to a greater degree than for females, while indirect parental controls, such as emotional attachment to family, influence girls' learning of violent definitions but not boys'.
3. Direct parental controls such as supervision of the youth's friendships help reduce violent delinquency in boys but have no importance for violence committed by girls.
4. Girls who accept traditional gender definitions have lower rates of violence; such ideational notions have no influence on violence by boys.
5. Violence by boys and girls is shaped by position in the social structure, but the influence of position in the social structure over criminal behaviour in boys and girls differs.
6. Boys have higher rates of violent delinquency partly because they tend to learn more violent definitions and gender definitions and have greater experience with violent crime than girls.
7. Boys tend to learn more violent definitions than girls because of their experience with violence and lower levels of emotional attachment to their families (Heimer and De Coster, 1999, 302–3).

Studies of structural disadvantage factors, such as poverty, on male violent crime have produced fairly consistent results: the most violent males are those who are the most disadvantaged. Steffensmeier and Haynie (2000, 428) found that structural disadvantage variables (poverty, income inequality, a female-headed home, etc.) were also associated with female violent crimes. More specifically, they found that structural disadvantage had "significant effects" on robbery and homicide and modest effects on the rates of larceny, burglary, and aggravated assault rates committed by women. Even so, structural disadvantage has a greater impact on men's criminal behaviour than on women's. Marriage has been found to attenuate criminal behaviour in men (Laub and Sampson, 2001). For disadvantaged women, motherhood is the primary factor reducing drug use and delinquent behaviour (Kreager, Matsueda, and Erosheva, 2010).

The pathway to criminality is fundamentally gendered (Chapter 6). Daly (1992) describes five pathways for women's involvement in crime:

1. "Harmed and harming women": These women have endured abuse and have had a difficult family life. The abuse was likely perpetrated by an

adult male, and they may have been abandoned or abused by their mother. They suffered the loss of loved ones when they were young, and they are regarded as "out of control" by family members. They resorted to substance abuse, particularly in their early teens. Daly argues that such women commit crimes when intoxicated or because they are unable to control their anger.

2. "Battered women": These women's criminal activities are precipitated by an abusive partner. Relationships with violent men are the defining factor in the criminal activity of such women.

3. "Street women": These women suffered serious levels of abuse in childhood or in present relationships. What distinguishes "street women" from "harmed and harming women" is street involvement. Street women are street-involved and engage in various survival mechanisms, such as prostitution, drug selling, and theft. Such women tend to have longer criminal histories and are more likely to have spent time behind bars.

4. "Drug-connected women": These women have engaged in illicit drug use and sale in part because of their relationships with people, usually family and partners, who were involved in drugs. Such women are not necessarily drug-addicted, nor do they have long criminal histories (see also Kruttschnitt, 2013).

5. "Other women": This category refers to persons with no history of unfavourable family life, who have not suffered abuse, and who are not street-entrenched, but who are engaged in crime for economic gain.

Is There Evidence for the Role Convergence Hypothesis?

The study of gender differences in criminal behaviour has a long history (Walklate, 2012). Lombroso and Ferrero (1895, 27) provided some the earliest explanations for gender differences in crime. These focused on supposed "pathological anomalies" and the sexualization of female offenders. These issues persisted for many decades—for example, in the work of theorists such as Freud (1933) and Pollak (1950) (see Chapter 6).

These biological theories have been challenged. Criminologists have shown that explanations for gender differences in criminal behaviour are embedded in social structure, particularly its patriarchal traditions and the attendant gender roles. Those roles are well-defined, so that males and females are held to widely divergent standards and expectations with regard to what constitutes appropriate behaviour (Hartnagel, 2012; Hagan, Gillis, and Simpson, 1985).

The home in particular is a site of acculturation and gender contestation. It is in the home that boys and girls learn appropriate behaviours. While the power control theory developed by Hagan, Gillis, and Simpson (1985, 1987) is discussed more fully in the next chapter, we can note here that they concluded that girls are subjected to greater control than their male siblings in the same household. Daughters are objects of control, and the main instrument of control is the mother, who is assigned that role by her husband. This cuts across social classes, albeit with varying intensity (1987). Male children from the employer class are more delinquent than their female counterparts in part because they are not as tightly controlled by the mother and are not deterred by the risk of punishment (1985). It follows that gender equality has begun to bridge sex differences in crime, for it is freeing females from excessive control:

"When daughters are freed from patriarchal family relations, they too become delinquent" (1987, 814).

Gender roles are produced by and reflect the structures and ideologies of society (Cotter, Hermsen, and Vaneman, 2011). Societal expectations, and the widely acknowledged double standards for women, have implications for how women and men live their lives, navigate social settings, and behave in general. The influence of societal standards and gender roles can be expected to extend to delinquent or criminal behaviour (Hartnagel, 2012). In theory, then, when there is a convergence of the roles and duties of the sexes, a decline in gender differences in crime should also occur. This **role convergence hypothesis** posits that as women leave the domestic sphere for the world of wage labour, there should be an increase in female crime. Some have suggested that the expansion of employment opportunities for women should lead to an increase in female property crime (Simon, 1975).

The gender gap in crime has declined, but much depends on the time periods and on the offences that are considered (Kruttschnitt, 2013). Crime statistics indicate a growing involvement of women in some types of violent crime; however, this is not supported by self-report studies. Stevens, Morash, and Chesney-Lind (2011) found that young girls in 2000 were twice as likely to be charged as their 1980 counterparts, while the pattern for boys had remained constant. Policing and other bureaucratic practices may play a major role in the increasing numbers of women charged with both property (Steffensmeier and Streifel, 1992) and violent offenses. Some have argued that the gender gap is shrinking because of a *reduction* in *male* criminal behaviour (Rennison, 2009). Lauritsen and colleagues examined data from 1973 to 2005 and concluded that police practices were not solely responsible for the narrowing gender gap. They argued that the gender gap had narrowed in recent times because of a decrease in male offending rates and an increase in violent offending among females, especially in terms of crimes such as aggravated assault, robbery, and simple assault (Lauritsen, Heimer, and Lynch, 2009, 386). According to their study, the greatest increase in female involvement was in minor property offenses such as shoplifting, credit card fraud, and passing bad cheques. This perhaps reflected the feminization of poverty more than any changes in gender roles (see Chapter 6).

Given the increased numbers of women in the labour force, one area in which role convergence might be expected is corporate crime. But despite the increase in the number of women in nontraditional corporate positions, women are not as engaged in corporate crime as men. A study of criminal convictions for corporate crime in seven federal districts in the United States found that 14 percent of men's cases involved indictments against organizations while only 1 percent of women's cases involved the same (Daly, 1989). In terms of occupational crime, however, Daly found that the female share of bank embezzlement was nearly 50 percent. Daly also found that 60 percent of the female bank embezzlers worked as tellers and that 90 percent were involved in some form of clerical duties. This suggests that women occupied positions that presented few opportunities for serious financial crime. This has implications for the scale of the embezzlement committed by women; men were better positioned in their organizations to steal more. Most of the male criminals but almost all of the

role convergence hypothesis
The hypothesis that as the work roles of women become similar to those of men, so will their involvement in crime.

female criminals were "little fish" (789). This is generally consistent with female involvement in theft and related property offences at the street level. Also, Daly found that men were more likely to commit occupational crime in concert with others, whereas women often acted on their own. Acting in a group may increase the magnitude and seriousness of (white-collar) crime. Additionally, women (36%) were twice as likely as men (18%) to cite financial need for their families as the main motivation for their white-collar crime.

More recent research has supported Daly's findings on gender patterns in corporate crime. Women's pathways to corporate criminality were found to be "relational" For instance, a study by Steffensmeier, Schwartz, and Roche (2013) found that one-third of women defendants had a personal relationship—typically spousal—with a male mastermind. The second pathway for women's corporate crime was "utility"—that is, these women were occupying positions that made them the "conduit or instrument of manipulation" of financial data rather than the persons behind the criminal behaviour. In this study, 68 percent of the women had been charged as co-conspirators. Steffensmeier and colleagues found that three-quarters of women participated in the white-collar crime because of pressure or directives from male bosses. In some cases, they were co-signers of fraudulent tax returns filed by a male spouse.

Most female participants in criminal conspiracies received lower rewards from their crimes than their male counterparts. The women who received high compensation for their criminal activities were the spouses of male masterminds. Steffensmeier and colleagues also found that there were no all-female conspiracies; fewer than 10 percent of corporate offenders were women, and women earned far less than men in corporate crime even when they had a high rank in the organization and played a prominent role in the fraudulent scheme. Overall, women were only involved in petty corporate crime; men were involved in both petty and major corporate crime.

QUESTIONS FOR CRITICAL THINKING

1. What is a correlate of crime?
2. Why are youth overrepresented in police-reported crime statistics?
3. Discuss how the notion of maturational reform is used to explain why older people are less involved in crime than are youth.

Race and Crime

Race is not as strongly related to crime as age and sex (Hartnagel, 2012). Research on the interplay of race and crime in Canada (Pederson, Malcoe, and Pulkingham, 2013; Wortley and Owusu-Bempah, 2011; Fitzgerald and Carrington, 2010; Henry and Tator, 2005) is not nearly as extensive as in the United States (Peterson, 2012; Peterson and Krivo, 2010; Shedd and Hagan, 2006). This is partly because police in Canada rarely report information on race (Owusu-Benpah and Millar, 2010, 97). The exception is information about Aboriginal offenders.

An attempt in 1990 by Statistics Canada to collect data on the race of offenders was rejected because of lack of cooperation from most police organizations and because of broad criticism of the policy (Hartnagel, 2012). The idea of collecting race and crime statistics has been controversial in Canada (Wortley and Tanner, 2003; Wortley, 1999; Johnston, 1994; Roberts, 1994). Wortley (1999) has summarized this debate. Opponents of race-based crime statistics believe that the idea should be abandoned because of the poor quality of police-reported crime statistics, the difficulties inherent in measuring race, and the possibility that such statistics would be used to justify racist theories of crime and, consequently, discriminatory treatment of minorities (263). On the other hand, supporters of these statistics argue that race-based data are required to verify the accuracy of claims that certain groups are receiving differential treatment in the criminal justice system; that such statistics may provide tools to challenge biological theories and other ideas about the race–crime relationship; and that banning the collection of race-based, police-reported data will not prevent the spread of racist ideology (265). Support for the collection of race-based crime statistics has continued in more recent times on similar premises (Millar and Owusu-Benpah, 2011; Owusu-Benpah and Millar, 2010).

The evidence that does exist suggests that some minority groups are overrepresented in police-reported crime statistics. This overrepresentation is believed to be present in all Western societies (Tonry, 1997), though the specific groups that are overrepresented vary by jurisdiction. In Canada and Australia, for instance, Aboriginal people are overrepresented. In the United States, New Zealand, Germany, and Turkey, African Americans, Maoris, and Turks and Kurds respectively are overrepresented. In Canada, the minority groups that are over-represented vary by location. In Greater Toronto, for example, Blacks are overrepresented, while Aboriginal people are overrepresented on the prairies.

Evidence from surveys and self-report studies (Wortley and McCalla, 2007) point to differential outcomes for various ethno-racial groups in Canada's criminal justice system. Wortley and Owusu-Bempah (2011) found that Blacks are 6.5 times more likely than whites to state that they know a friend or family member who has been racially profiled by the police (401). They conclude that "black racial background appears to be a master status that attracts police attention and significantly contributes to police decisions to conduct street interrogations" (402). Also, Blacks are more likely to perceive police stops as unfair, and this may have an impact on their demeanour in encounters with the police. A Toronto survey conducted by Wortley and Tanner (2005) found that Black high school students who were not involved in any criminal or deviant activity were four times more likely to report being stopped and six times more likely to be searched by police than their white colleagues who were also not involved in crime. Fitzgerald and Carrington's (2011) analysis of the National Longitudinal Survey of Children and Youth (NLSCY) found that Aboriginal, Black, and West Asian youth were three times more likely to report contact with the police. The same study found that the least delinquent minority youth had the greatest contact with police, so delinquency involvement does not explain why they were stopped and/or searched by police. Fitzgerald and Carrington (473) also found that though youth who were involved in violent delinquency had a higher probability of contact with the police, this variable did not reduce the effect of race on contact with police.

Mascoll and Ranking reported that a majority of Black Toronto police officers who participated in a focus group discussion stated that they had been stopped and searched by their colleagues "for no other reason than the colour of their skin" when they were off duty (cited in Tanovich, 2006, 1–2). The Commission on Systemic Racism in the Ontario Criminal Justice System (1995) found a differential pattern in how citizens are stopped by police. Nineteen percent of Chinese male residents, 25 percent of white male residents, and 43 percent of Black male residents reported having been stopped in the previous two years. The study also reported that "there was widespread perception among Black, Chinese and White Torontonians that judges discriminate on the basis of race" (1995).

Similar data have been put forward by the Office of the Correctional Investigator, the government-appointed oversight agency for Correctional Service Canada. In a 2012–13 report, the agency stated that in 2013, 40 percent of inmates in federal prisons were non-Caucasians. Since 2003, according to Barrett (2013), there has been a 90 percent increase in the Black population of Canadian federal prisons while the Caucasian population has declined by 3 percent. Overall, Canadians of African descent now comprise 10 percent of the federal inmate population although they are less than 3 percent of the general Canadian population. A case study by the Correctional Investigator, Howard Sapers, indicated that Black inmates were concerned about "prejudicial attitudes by some corrections staff" who assumed they were gang members. Barrett notes that this assumption is believed to have contributed to the disproportionate number of Black prisoners in maximum security facilities, segregation placements, use of force by prison staff, more charges while in prison, and a lower likelihood of being paroled despite lower rates of recidivism (Barrett, 2013).

Evidence from the United States shows a similar pattern of differential arrests and sentencing disparities. Blacks are arrested for drug offences at 2 to 11 times higher rates than whites, and Black offenders receive sentences that are 10 to 20 percent longer than those given to white offenders for the same crimes (Peterson, 2012, 307). According to The Sentencing Project (2014), there are 2.2 million persons in US prisons or jails, and more than three-fifths of them are minorities. Current estimates are that one out of 17 white men, one out of 6 Latino men, and one out of 3 Black men will go to prison at some point in their lives. Similar statistics for women show that one in 111 white women, one out of 45 Latino women, and one out of 18 Black women will be incarcerated at some point in their lives.

It is widely contended that in the United States, the death penalty is discriminatory. Cohen and Smith (2010) analyzed the social and geographic distribution of candidates for the death penalty. They found that accused persons of minority background in urban centres surrounded by majority white suburban counties were more likely to receive the death penalty. Missouri has handed down more death sentences than the three larger states of New York, California, and Florida. Yet a death sentence is rarely handed down in three districts dominated by minorities: the District of Columbia, Puerto Rico, and the Southern District of New York. "These three federal districts account for 55 of the 460 death-authorized cases but are not responsible for a single death sentence" (465). This analysis suggests that when offences that are punishable by death are held constant, whether the death penalty is applied depends on the race of the accused and the community where the offence was committed.

There are two competing explanations for the overrepresentation of minorities in the criminal justice system: the **differential offending hypothesis** and the **differential treatment hypothesis**. The differential offending hypothesis states that there are actual differences between racial groups in terms of the incidence, level of seriousness, and persistence of offending patterns (Fitzgerald and Carrington, 2011; Owusu-Benpah and Millar, 2010). The differential treatment hypothesis (Fitzgerald and Carrington, 2011) states that structural inequality in the administration of justice, from police patrols to courtrooms to correctional services, is responsible for the overrepresentation of minority groups in the criminal justice process. Fitzgerald and Carrington (453) divide the differential treatment hypothesis into three parts:

1. The police often give closer attention to people who meet certain social criteria (young lower-class males), and minority group members may disproportionately be included in these groups.
2. Certain social spaces tend to experience greater police surveillance than others—for example, areas with concentrated social disadvantage marked by relatively high levels of unemployment, poverty, and social disorder—and these areas are often inhabited by newer immigrant groups and poor minorities (see also Sampson, Raudenbush, and Earls 1997).
3. The police may be influenced by race or ethnicity in the exercise of their discretion and authority. This includes decisions about whether or not to stop, search, or arrest a suspect. Contact with police is typically the first step in the criminal justice process.

differential offending hypothesis
There are actual differences between racial groups in terms of the incidence, level of seriousness, and persistence of offending patterns.

Aboriginal Peoples and the Canadian Criminal Justice System

Aboriginal people are overrepresented in the criminal justice process. They are 4 percent of the Canadian population and 6 percent of the Canadian youth population, but they make up a much higher proportion of the prison population. Figure 5.7 shows how the share of Aboriginal youth in custody has increased since 1997–98. Aboriginal female youth are more highly overrepresented in youth custody. In 2010–11, 24 percent of the male youth population in custody and community services were Aboriginal males; Aboriginal females represented 34 percent of female youth admitted to custody and community services. Aboriginal adults are also greatly overrepresented in the prison population. In 2010–11, 91 percent of persons in custody in the Northwest Territories were Aboriginal, compared to 47 percent of the general population (Figure 5.8). The situation is similar in other provinces and territories—for example, in Saskatchewan (78% versus 12%), Yukon (74% versus 23%), Manitoba

differential treatment hypothesis
Structural inequality in the administration of justice (from police patrols to courtrooms to correctional services) is responsible for the overrepresentation of minority groups in the criminal justice process.

FIGURE 5.7 Representation of Aboriginals (Male and Female) in Total Admission to Youth Custody and Community Services (YCCS), 1997–98 to 2011–12, Canada

Note: Indicates whether the youth is Aboriginal. Aboriginal identity includes North American Indian, Métis, and Inuit, whether registered or not. Note that this variable is self-reported and that data availability varies among jurisdictions. For Canada, data represent the total for all reporting jurisdictions rather than a complete national total, because data for some jurisdictions are incomplete or not available. Totals for secure and open custody include Youth Criminal Justice Act (YCJA) and Young Offenders Act (YOA) based admissions; admissions are collected each time a person begins any type of custodial or community supervision and describe and measure the case flow in correctional agencies over time. The same person can be included several times in the admission counts where the individual moves from one type of legal status to another (e.g., from open to secure custody) or re-enters the system in the same year. As such, admissions represent the number of entries within a fiscal year to sentenced custody, to remand, and to community supervision regardless of the individual's preceding or following legal status.

Source: Dauvergne, Mia. Adult correctional statistics in Canada, 2010/2011, chart 7, Statistics Canada. Available at: http://www.statcan.gc.ca/pub/85-002-x/2012001/article/11715/c-g/desc/desc07-eng.htm (accessed on December 20, 2013)

FIGURE 5.8 Aboriginal Adult Admissions to Custody, by Province and Territory, 2010–11, Canada

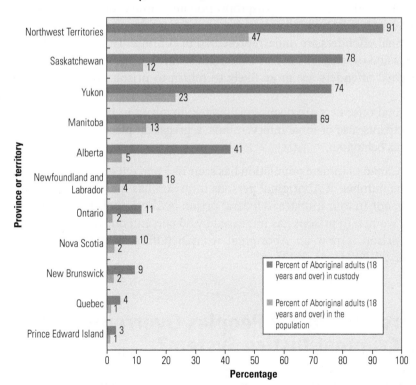

Note: Excludes admissions to custody in which Aboriginal identity was unknown. Excludes British Columbia and Nunavut due to the unavailability of data. Population estimates based on 2006 Census data.

Source: Statistics Canada. Table 251-0012 - Youth custody and community services (YCCS), admissions to correctional services, by sex and aboriginal identity, annual (number). Available at: http://www5.statcan.gc.ca/cansim/a26?lang=eng&retrLang=eng&id=2510012&paSer=&pattern=&stByVal=1&p1=1&p2=-1&tabMode=dataTable&csid= (accessed: June 10, 2014)

(69% versus 13%), and Alberta (41% versus 5%). The Canadian Criminal Justice Association (2000; cited in Greenberg, Grekul, and Nelson, 2012, 237) has provided a summary of the problems confronting Aboriginal peoples in the Canadian criminal justice process:

1. Aboriginal accused are more likely to be denied bail.
2. More time is spent in pre-trial detention by Aboriginal people.
3. Aboriginal accused are more likely to be charged with multiple offences and often for crimes against the system (failing to appear).
4. Aboriginal people are more likely not to have representation at court proceedings.
5. Aboriginal clients, especially in northern communities where the court party flies in on the day of the hearing, spend less time with their lawyers.
6. Aboriginal offenders are more than twice as likely to be incarcerated than non-Aboriginal offenders.
7. Aboriginal Elders, who are the spiritual leaders, are not given the same status as prison priests and chaplains in all institutions.
8. Aboriginal people often plead guilty because they are intimidated by the court and simply want to get the proceedings over with.

A more recent report by the Office of the Correctional Investigator (2012, 6) reported that:

1. Aboriginal offenders serve disproportionately more of their sentence behind bars before first release.
2. Aboriginal offenders are underrepresented in community supervision populations and overrepresented in maximum security institutions.
3. Aboriginal offenders are more likely to return to prison on revocation of parole.
4. Aboriginal offenders are disproportionately involved in institutional security incidents, use of force interventions, segregation placements, and self-injurious behaviour.

While Canada's inmate population has seen 16.5 percent growth in the past 10 years, the number of Aboriginal persons in prison has increased by 46 percent. Today, one in four inmates in federal prison is Aboriginal. The number of Aboriginal women in prisons has increased by 80 percent; one in three women in federal prison is now an Aboriginal woman (Office of the Correctional Investigator, 2012; Barrett, 2012).

Why Are Aboriginal Peoples Overrepresented in the Criminal Justice System?

SEARCH FOR:
The Aboriginal Justice
Inquiry of Manitoba: Volume 1

Several explanations have been offered for the overrepresentation of Aboriginal peoples in the criminal justice system. They include cultural theories, the colonial model, the trauma transmission model, and critical race theory.

Cultural Theories

Cultural theories of crime examine the traits, characteristics, or way of life of an identifiable group to explain the involvement of members of that group in the criminal justice process. Such theories analyze the development of a subculture (or counterculture) that runs contrary to the dominant culture. Research on the prevalence of violence in poorer segments of society has a long history (Wolfgang and Ferracuti, 1967). For instance, Anderson's *Code of the Street* (1999) captures the subculture of the inner city, the quest for respect, and the potential for interpersonal violence (see Chapter 10).

There are two major strands in cultural theories of Aboriginal overrepresentation in the criminal justice process. The first views Aboriginal cultures as inherently violent. Martin (1992, 16, cited in Snowball and Weatherburn, 2008), for instance, argues that though external "intervention" is responsible for some of the issues relating to violence in Aboriginal cultures, violence is

> also deeply rooted in cultural values relating to such matters as the high stress on personal autonomy, on appropriate behaviour for each sex, on notions of morality, on how individuals are seen to be related to wider social groupings, on the appropriate expression of emotions such as anger, and how individuals are expected to act upon the world in order to achieve their ends or redress wrongs done to them. (218)

The second strand comes close to cultural conflict theory (see Chapter 11). This perspective views Aboriginal cultures as different from the dominant Euro-Canadian culture in content and/or manner of expression (Hartnagel, 2012). Aboriginal cultures' emphasis on sharing, and their traditional approaches to dispute resolution—which emphasize mediation and healing—are viewed as unsuited to the adversarial system imported from Europe. The common law system's norms, values, and procedures are alien to Aboriginal peoples and predispose them to conflict with the law (Dumont, 1993).

Cultural explanations for the overrepresentation of Aboriginal people in the criminal justice system are problematic for several reasons. First, they presuppose a monolithic Aboriginal culture when in fact, Aboriginal peoples and their cultures are diverse. Second, a static Aboriginal culture is assumed; Aboriginal culture is presented as a calcified relic of the past and hence as uninfluenced by the dominant culture in which it exists. Third, there seems to be an assumption that there is a particular kind of behaviour that constitutes *Aboriginal behaviour*. Fourth, cultural explanations inadvertently pathologize Aboriginal peoples' cultures. Underlying that is a presumption that there is an objective standard that makes Aboriginal cultures delinquent. Such explanations are simplistic and do not fully engage with a bi-dimensional phenomenon: the process of incorporating Aboriginal cultures without allowing them access to legitimate opportunity structures in Canadian society. Aboriginal people, like all Canadians, are inundated with the prevailing ideas and ideals about socially desirable material goods in our consumerist culture. Aboriginal unemployment numbers are higher than for other Canadians. This suggests several factors are involved: deculturalization from Aboriginal ways of life; acculturation or assimilation into Euro-Canadian ways of life; and structural exclusion. As Young argues in *The Exclusive Society*

These North West Mounted Police members from Fort Macleod are shown visiting Calgary in 1886. The NWMP were established to keep order during the European settlement of western Canada.

Glenbow Archives NA-5656-3

(1999, 81), there can be *"cultural inclusion and structural exclusion"* (italics original) as two sides of a coin in a group's relationship with the wider society. Consequently, scholars increasingly give attention to *structural explanations* of Aboriginal overrepresentation in crime statistics.

Structural Theories

Structural theories situate the locus of criminality in the historical context and prevailing structures of society rather than in individual or group pathology. The key argument is that institutional arrangements—particularly the distribution of socially valuable resources such as education and jobs—and the routine functioning of the criminal justice system are major explanatory factors for ethno-racial representation in crime statistics. The judgment of the Supreme Court of Canada in *R v Gladue* (1999) provides a backdrop to structural explanations of the overrepresentation of Aboriginal peoples in the criminal justice system:

> The background factors which figure prominently in the causation of crime by aboriginal offenders are by now well known. Years of dislocation and economic development have translated, for many aboriginal peoples, into low incomes, high unemployment, lack of opportunities and options, lack or irrelevance of education, substance abuse, loneliness, and community fragmentation. These and other factors contribute to a higher incidence of crime and incarceration.

This statement is sociological rather than legalistic. The Supreme Court notes the "unique systemic or background factors which may have played a part in bringing the particular aboriginal offender before the courts."

Three structural explanations are examined here. They are the colonial model, historic trauma transmission model and critical race theory.

The Colonial Model

The colonial model was made popular by Frantz Fanon (1963; 1967). More recent works by Tatum (1994), Agozino (2003), and Gabbidon (2010) have shed more light on the link between colonialism and crime. The colonial model is a socio-psychological perspective. It focuses on the intersection of "structural oppression, alienation and three adaptive forms of behaviour—assimilation, crime or deviance, and protest" (Tatum, 1994, 34). Tatum's typology includes four stages of colonization. In the first, the territory of one racial group is invaded by another. The goal in this phase is to acquire valuable resources such as gold or furs. In the second stage, a colonial society is formed. At this stage, processes of cultural imposition, cultural disintegration, and cultural re-creation occur. Cultural imposition means that the Native populations are forced to adopt the values and ways of life of the colonial power. This leads to the collapse or decentring of the norms and values of the colonized group. As a consequence, a society develops in which the old norms and values have given way to different values that inferiorize the Native population. In Canada, this stage of Aboriginal colonization was carried out by residential schools, which were established in the 1870s and eventually numbered over 130 (Truth and Reconciliation Commission, 2014). The residential schools made systematic efforts "to assimilate Aboriginal children into mainstream society by removing the 'Indian within them'" (Charles and DeGagné, 2013) through a process of "aggressive civilization" (Rand, 2011, 56). The physical and sexual abuse suffered by Aboriginal children was an arguably unintended consequence of implementing the schools' main objective.

In the third stage, Native peoples find themselves governed by representatives of the colonizer's power, such as the police and military. In Canada, the North-West Mounted Police (later renamed the RCMP) set out to pacify the Aboriginal population so that the West could be settled (Kelly and Kelly, 1973). That forceful effort has strongly shaped the relationship between law enforcement agencies and Native populations. During this third stage, minor infractions by the dominated group are likely to come to the attention of law enforcement, given that the latter's mission is to pacify the group. This reduces the likelihood that colonized populations will cooperate with the police and perceive them as fair, which has implications for whether or not people obey the law (Jackson and Bradford, 2010; Tyler, 1990). Fourth, the colonial society develops a caste system based on race. As a result, access to socially valuable resources such as land, jobs, and education is shaped by racial considerations. This provides opportunities for settler populations and an economy of disadvantage for natives. Concentrated disadvantage increases the likelihood of criminal behaviour (Thompson and Gartner, 2014; Peterson, 2012; Sampson, Raudenbush, and Earls, 1997).

These four processes have psychological and social consequences for the colonized population. One consequence is what Wright (1994, 20) calls mentacide — the "deliberate and systematic destruction of a group's minds with the ultimate objective being the extirpation of the group." Each member of the colonized group bears the burden of proving that he or she is not inferior to the dominant group and is a well-adapted member of the colonial society (Gabbidon, 2010). Another consequence is "cultural limbo," or double alienation. A colonized population is routinely and forcefully expected to shed its Native identity, language, and customs. The Native people are thus neither fully themselves nor part of the colonizer's racial group. They occupy an in-between state that is both confused and confusing.

The resulting alienation and ambiguity may manifest itself in crime, particularly through self-hate (Gabbidon, 2010). Self-hate may be evident in the desire of the colonized not to identify with their traditional customs, which have been discursively rendered primitive. The self-hate may also be projected to the group: "The alienation can result in attacks against the people that the colonized now hate the most: *themselves*" (6; italics original). When people are alienated from their group, the consequence may be horizontal violence in the dominated community. Horizontal violence refers to violent acts by a person within his or her social class. Overtly violent crimes are rarely between classes. Scholars have only recently begun to focus on the physical and sexual abuse *between* students (in addition to abuse by staff against students, which had been the subject of earlier studies) in the residential school system (Charles and DeGagné, 2013).

Most of the violent acts reported to police, including homicides, are intra-class—usually, committed by people of lower socio-economic status on members of their own social category. This is partly a result of internalized anger caused by blocked opportunity and the development of self-destructive coping mechanisms such as alcoholism and drug abuse (Gabbidon, 2010; Tatum, 1994; Brownridge, 2010). High rates of psychiatric disorders, hypertension, and various serious crimes, particularly homicide, are common in oppressed communities (Tatum, 1994). The colonial model of crime focuses on how the conditions fostered by colonialist expansion generate particular institutional arrangements that produce a kind of subject who is susceptible to committing (violent) crimes. While the colonial model seems rather deterministic, it does not necessarily negate human agency. Rather, it demonstrates that colonialism has consequences for human psyche and actions, such as criminal behaviour. It also indicates that historical context matters when we examine criminal statistics.

Historic Trauma Transmission Model

This model is closely related to the colonial model in that it emphasizes the social and psychological consequences of colonialism. Cynthia Wesley-Esquimaux and Magdalena Smolewski (2004) are leading proponents of the historic trauma transmission model as it relates to Aboriginal communities in Canada. The model explicates the "aetiology of social and cultural diffusion that devastated Aboriginal communities for so many years" (65). The focus is on how historic trauma manifests itself socially and psychologically. In particular, this model demonstrates how "acculturation (and a loss of the social self) is often associated with alcoholism, drug addiction, family disintegration and suicide" (66). As is shown in this chapter, many of these variables, such as drug misuse (see below) are correlated with crime.

This model argues that when a group of people experience physical extermination, cultural genocide, and colonial subjugation, members of the group develop "learned helplessness" (66). This is a shared form of fatalism in which members of a group believe that no action on their part can alter the course of their lives. "Such a person or group becomes passive, inactive and hostile, ascribing social failures to personal, internal causes and blaming themselves for their helplessness (internal attribution). This internal attribution of failure results in decreased sense of self and social esteem" (66).

Traumatic memories are passed from one generation to the next down four main avenues (76). First, through biological channels, which include inherited predispositions to post-traumatic stress disorder (PTSD) and fetal alcohol spectrum disorder (FASD). These conditions have been linked to some Aboriginal youths' inability to articulate thoughts as well as to their confusion with adjudication processes (Greenberg, Grekul, and Nelson, 2012). Second, traumatic memories are passed on through storytelling and other culturally sanctioned behaviours. Third, historic trauma is passed on as a direct result of violence, deficient parenting, the acting out of abuse, and other social ills. Fourth, there are psychological avenues involving memory, individual recollections of pain, suffering, and debilitating social conditions (66).

Qualitative studies have consistently linked the residential school system to abuse and suicidal thoughts in Aboriginal communities (Charles and DeGagné, 2013; Rand, 2011). This supports the notion of trauma transmission. A recent quantitative study (Elias et al., 2012) lends support to the historic trauma transmission model. That study used a First Nations sample of 2,953 Manitoba adults. About one-third of the sample had attended residential school; the rest had not. Attendance at residential schools was associated with a history of abuse. Abuse was also more common among respondents who had not attended residential schools but whose parents or grandparents had done so. Overall, the historic trauma transmission model provides a context for understanding the socio-genesis of the conditions in Aboriginal communities that face severe social problems, including crime.

Critical Race Theory

The earliest strands of this theory are found in the works of Derrick Bell (Delgado and Stefancic, 2012). Critical race theory emerged in the 1980s as a counter-hegemonic strategy. It challenges the policies and dynamics and taken-for-granted assumptions of institutional power. It adopts a **social constructionist approach** to race, the law, and justice. A social constructionist approach questions the idea that there is a social reality that is observable or measurable, positing instead that multiple realities pervade the social world. In other words, crime is what a society defines it to be and is not an objective fact.

The notion of "legal indeterminacy" is central to critical race theory. This concept means that "not every legal case has one correct outcome" (5). In other words, court decisions are not always predictable: an accused person may be given a long term in prison for the same criminal behaviour for which another accused person was acquitted. Critical race theory focuses on racial subordination, racism, and discrimination. It also examines the intersection of race, gender, and class in the criminal justice process.

Critical race theory makes several assumptions. These include the idea that the law reflects the dominant group's norms and values and favours that group. It also presupposes that the enforcement and interpretation of the law is subjective. That is, the law is not colour-blind. The theory also holds that racism in the justice process is not an aberration; rather, it is "normal." The theory also assumes that though the average member of society views the law as something tangible, like the weather, the law is in fact not an objective entity. Its enactment, enforcement, and interpretation are subjective processes; as a result,

social constructionist approach to crime
This approach questions the idea that there is an observable or measurable social reality, but rather proposes that a crime is whatever a particular society defines it to be.

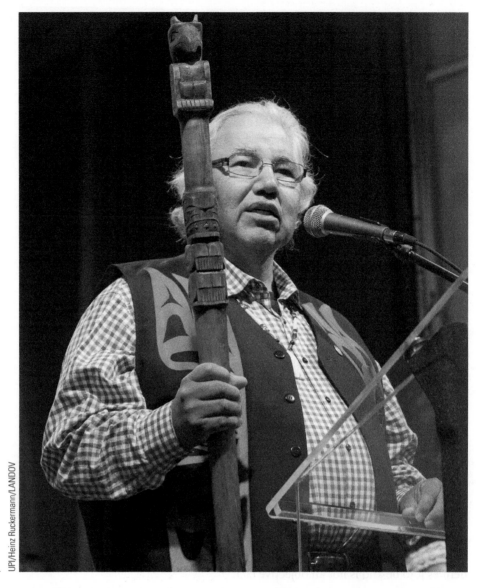

The Honourable Justice Murray Sinclair is the chair of the Truth and Reconciliation Commission, which was established to help deal with the consequences of the residential school system. Justice Sinclair also made an important contribution to Canada by co-chairing Manitoba's Aboriginal Justice Inquiry.

UPI/Heinz Ruckermann/LANDOV

groups that are not well situated to make, enforce, and interpret laws often bear the brunt of the criminal justice system. So from this perspective, Aboriginal people are overrepresented in the criminal justice system because of their systematic exclusion from the conventional opportunity structures of society and because of overpolicing and harsh sentences.

Mirchandani and Chan (2002, 9) have emphasized the need for a shift in analysis from "race" to "racialization." **Racialization** is a process whereby "categories of the population are constructed, differentiated, inferiorized and excluded" (Anthias, 1998, 7). It comprises the processes by which meanings are attributed to particular objects, features, and processes of individuals and/ or groups, in such a way that those features are given special significance and carry a set of additional meanings (Miles, 1989, 70). Essentially, this process leads to the construction of "races as real, different and unequal in ways that

racialization
A process in which categories of the population are constructed, differentiated, inferiorized, and excluded.

matter to economic, political and social life" (Commission on Systemic Racism, 1995). For Tanovich (2006, 14), racialization involves the following:

- Selecting some human characteristics as meaningful signs of racial differences.
- Sorting people into races on the basis of variations in these characteristics.
- Attributing personality traits, behaviours, and social characteristics (e.g., criminality) to people classified as members of particular races.
- Acting as if race indicates socially significant differences among people.

Race or racialization remains a critical variable in the criminal justice system. For instance, "race structures citizen views of the police" (Cao, 2011, 14). This is supported by research conducted by Wortley and Owusu-Bempah (2011), Shedd and Hagan (2006), and Henry and colleagues (2000), among others. Aboriginal people and visible minorities in particular are more likely to hold negative views of the police and other criminal justice agencies, though perceptions and experiences vary among groups (Sprott and Doob, 2014). There are consequences for criminal justice when suspects believe—rightly or wrongly—that their race or racialization played a role in their arrest, sentence, or treatment in custody. First, it may attenuate the legitimacy of the criminal justice process (Wortley and Owusu-Bempah, 2011; Cao, 2011). Second, those who feel discriminated against are less likely to trust the agents and agencies of criminal justice (Cao, 2011). This is a question of public confidence. People who have no confidence in the police are less likely to cooperate with them, to report criminal activity, to serve as witnesses, to engage in jury duty, and so on. Confidence in the police is important because only a small fraction of crime is discovered by police officers; most crimes that come to the attention of the police are reported by the public.

Canada's Truth and Reconciliation Commission was established to help in "rebuilding and renewing Aboriginal relationships and the relationship between Aboriginal and non-Aboriginal Canadians." It aims to understand and document the impact of the residential school system and its intergenerational consequences in Aboriginal communities (TRC, 2014).

SEARCH FOR:
Truth and Reconciliation
Commission of Canada

Drug and Alcohol Misuse as a Correlate of Crime

The use of illicit drugs is strongly correlated with street crimes including murder, robbery, auto theft, and mischief (Buxton et al., 2009). Drugs such as cocaine, crack, and heroin are often involved in debates about the drug–crime nexus (Bennett and Holloway, 2005, cited in Hartnagel, 2012). Seventy percent of offender release suspensions involve alcohol and other substances (Weeks et al., 1994). More recently, Public Safety Canada (2014) has estimated that three out of four inmates enter custody with substance abuse issues and that for around 50 percent of federal inmates, "there is a direct link between their substance use and criminal behaviour."

Three factors link drug and alcohol use and crime. First, efforts to support an addiction can lead to involvement in crimes; second, individuals may commit crimes because they are under the influence of drugs or alcohol (Pernanen et al., 2002; Buxton et al., 2009); third, the mere possession of illegal drugs in and of itself is a crime. Drug possession accounts for 4.8 percent of police-reported crime in British Columbia (Buxton et al., 2009).

This analysis is closely related to Goldstein's (1985) model, which suggests that drugs cause crime in three ways: psychopharmacological, economic compulsive, and systemic. First, the psychopharmacological dimension means that drugs have the capacity to change behaviour and make people break laws. People under the influence of substances such as alcohol, stimulants, or barbiturates become "excitable" and "irrational" (494). Examples of psychopharmacological violence include spouse or child abuse and barroom brawls. Other consequences resulting from a substance user's state of intoxication may lead to contact with the police, although a large volume of such incidents go unreported. Second, the economically compulsive dimension implies that crime may be committed in order to secure drugs to feed a habit. Thus, a chronic drug user may resort to robbery, prostitution, shoplifting, or drug dealing to support her addiction, especially for relatively expensive drugs such as cocaine and heroin, which are also noted for their addictiveness. Third, the systemic dimension indicates that "violence is intrinsic to involvement with any illicit substance" (497). In other words, being involved in the sale and use of banned commodities like cocaine or heroin invariably connects individuals with a complex web of interactions with criminal actors and networks. Goldstein (497) lists some of the ways that engagement in illicit drug distribution or sale may enmesh people in criminal interactions and activities:

1. Disputes over territory between rival drug dealers.
2. Assault and homicides committed within dealing hierarchies as a means of enforcing normative codes.
3. Robberies of drug dealers and the usually violent retaliation by the dealer or his/or bosses.
4. Elimination of informers [as a routine business activity].
5. Punishment for selling adulterated or phony drugs.
6. Punishment for failing to pay one's debt.
7. Disputes over drugs or drug paraphernalia.
8. Robbery violence related to the social ecology of copping areas [neighbourhoods reputed for drug distribution or sale].

More recent evidence lends support to Goldstein's (1985) drug-violence model. For instance, the annual expenditure by British Columbians on cannabis is estimated as between $443 million and $564 million (Werb et al., 2012). Attempts by criminal syndicates to exploit the illegal drug trade often generate violence. For example, the Quebec biker wars between 1994 and 2002 led to violent clashes between Hells Angels and the Rock Machine over who would have access to the lucrative wholesale drug distribution trade in Quebec, particularly in Montreal (Schneider, 2013). By the end of 1997, there had been 313 violent incidents, including 81 bombings and 71 attempted murders (Criminal Intelligence Service, Canada 1998; cited in Schneider, 2013). Clearly, homicides and other violent criminal activities associated with the drug trade are major issues confronting law enforcement agencies in Canada, where increases in organized-crime-related homicides have been recorded (Schneider, 2013) despite the overall decline in Canada's murder rate since 1966 (Perreault, 2013; Mahony, 2011).

While individual illicit drug users may not appreciate the level of violence involved in getting their fix, the multifaceted connection between the demand for illegal drugs and crime is well-established. A self-report study of 667 illegal drug users in Edmonton, Montreal, Quebec City, Toronto, and Vancouver found that participants were involved in drug dealing (27%) and property crimes (16%), particularly theft (Manzoni et al., 2007). The study also found that crack use was associated with property crime in Toronto and that cocaine use and sex work were closely related in Montreal and Quebec City (Manzoni, Fischer, and Rehm, 2007).

The yearly Canadian Alcohol and Drug Use Survey (CADUMS) measures the use of alcohol and illegal drugs by Canadians aged 15 and over (Health Canada, 2014). The most recent report presents findings from the 2012 survey. Its results show that 78% of Canadians reported drinking alcohol the previous year. More men (83%) than women (74%) indicated past-year alcohol use. Drinking patterns also varied by province. Quebec (82.1%) and Nova Scotia (72.3%) were on the high and low ends of past-year alcohol consumption in Canada. Age of initiation to alcohol ranged from 16.2 years among 15 to 24 year olds to 18.6 among Canadians aged 25 and over. However, adults drank at a rate that was 10 percent higher than youth (80% versus 70%).

Alcohol consumption is directly correlated with multiple social harms, including crime (Rehm and Room, 2009). Participants in the 2012 CADUMS survey were asked whether they had experienced any of four harms—being verbally abused, feeling threatened, being emotionally hurt or neglected, and

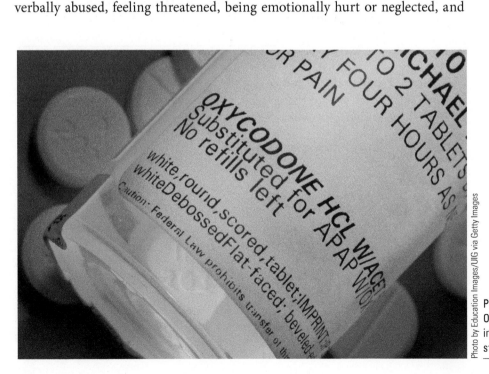

Photo by Education Images/UIG via Getty Images

Prescription drugs such as Oxycontin and Oxycodone are increasingly being sold on the street and used by addicts.

being physically hurt—due to somebody else's drinking habits. Overall, one in seven respondents (14%) reported suffering one harm because of somebody else's drinking. About 2.2 percent of respondents reported that they had been physically hurt; 6.3% felt threatened; 7.1% felt emotionally hurt or neglected; 8.9% suffered verbal abuse.

Cannabis use is becoming increasingly "normalized" in Canadian society (Duff et al., 2009, 536). Even so, it remains a legally contentious issue. Survey participants were asked about their use of cannabis; 41.5 percent indicated that they had used cannabis at some point in their lives. That was a 3 percent reduction in lifetime cannabis use from the 2004 Canadian Addiction Survey (CAS). New Brunswick (9%) and British Columbia (14%) were at the lower and upper ends of cannabis use among Canadian provinces in 2012. The average age of initiation to cannabis use in Canada was 16.1 years in 2012. This was up from 15.6 years in 2004. The increase in age at first consumption or initiation is important, because early substance use is predictive of abuse as well as dependence (Hingson, Heeren, and Winter, 2006). Cannabis is one of the three main substances (including alcohol and tobacco) used by young people (Clark, 2009).

Figure 5.9 shows that other illicit substances are being used in Canada at significantly lower rates. For instance, the 2012 survey found that the past-year use of ecstasy was 1%; hallucinogens (including salvia), 1%; and cocaine or crack, (estimated) 1%. Participants were asked about their use of cocaine or crack, speed, ecstasy, and hallucinogens (including salvia or heroin but excluding cannabis) (Health Canada, 2014). About 2% of participants reported using one of these banned substances in the past year. Males reported using illicit substances at a rate nearly three times that of females. Youth were found to use illicit substances at a rate five times higher than that of adults (6.5% versus 1.2%).

FIGURE 5.9   **Percentage of the Population Using Drugs in the Past Year, 2010 and 2012**

Note: 2012 estimate suppressed due to high sampling variability.

Source: Canadian Alcohol and Drug Use Monitoring Survey (CADUMS), 2012. Available at: http://www.hc-sc.gc.ca/hc-ps/drugs-drogues/stat/_2012/summary-sommaire-eng.php (accessed: June 11, 2014).

Students rarely use substances other than cannabis, alcohol, and tobacco (Clark, 2009). Street youth, however, often report rates of illicit drug use (cocaine, ecstasy, etc.) and associated risks that are higher than the national average for both their peers and the general population. In a study conducted with youth from Vancouver and Victoria, Duff and colleagues (2009, 519) identified three "high risk" categories: the club and "party drug" scenes, street-entrenched users aged 19 and over, and street-involved youth aged 15 to 19. The use of illicit substances has implications for contact with the law. These drugs have a negative impact on lives (68%). That impact is felt on relationships (48%), finances (26%), and school-related activities (20%). Eight percent of club drug users reported having "legal problems" (534).

In their At-Risk Youth Study of 991 street-involved young people in Vancouver, Lianping and colleagues (2013) reported that police confrontations were associated with daily cannabis use, daily heroin use, crack pipe/syringe sharing, public drug use, and drug dealing. These findings suggest that the possession and/or use of illegal substances increases the likelihood of encounters with police. These encounters may result in the young person being processed in the criminal justice system, particularly now that the government has intensified its efforts to reduce the supply and use of illegal drugs. Illicit drug use also has a positive correlation with mortality. According to BC Vital Statistics (2005), for instance, the Downtown Eastside, where drug use is high, has a mortality rate seven times higher than for Vancouver as a whole (cited in Buxton et al., 2009, 450). Life expectancy in this neighbourhood is nine years lower for men and three years lower for women (BC Vital Statistics, 2005).

Another increasing concern is the misuse of prescription medication. The United States and Canada have been ranked first and third vis-à-vis consumption of prescription opioids per capita (Fischer et al., 2009, 57). The same study indicates the level of abuse of medical prescription drugs. The sale of drugs for money and the exchange of prescription drugs for nonprescription drugs is especially prevalent in Toronto and Victoria. Such exchanges include prescription opioids and other drugs such as cannabis and crack. Fischer and colleagues also found found that 77 percent of study participants in Toronto and 80 percent in Victoria were involved in this illicit trading. They concluded (63) that prescription opioids are often used concurrently with illegal substances like crack and cannabis. Also, the delineation of drug dealers from users was a false one: drug users in the Toronto-Victoria study were often dealers, and vice versa (65).

Socio-economic Status and Criminal Behaviour

Historically, the lower classes have been seen as responsible for crime. In eighteenth-century Paris and London, there were concerns about the proliferation of "dangerous" or "criminal classes" in society (Silver, 1967). These concerns were expressed in Canada and the United States in the nineteenth and twentieth centuries (Boritch and Hagan, 1987; Myrdal, 1962). The early dangerous classes were unemployed single people involved in crime (Silver, 1967). The term "underclass" (Myrdal, 1962, 1963) has become more prominent in common and scholarly discourse to explain criminal activity; it refers to the cultural underpinnings of people at the margins of society. The underclass is defined by "poverty, crime, poor education, dependency, and teenage out-of-wedlock childbearing" (Lenmann, 1986, 41, cited in Hagan, 1992, 2). This category often has political and racial connotations (Hagan, 1992).

Police-reported statistics primarily identify lower-class offenders, and social disorganization theories (Chapter 14) identify crime with lower-class communities. This view was challenged when Edwin Sutherland (1940) brought attention to white-collar crime; this was followed two decades later by the pioneering self-report delinquency studies conducted by Nye and Short (1957; Nye, Short, and Olson, 1958). Nye and colleagues concluded that class had no statistically significant relationship with delinquency. This generated a major debate that was influenced by a research review by Tittle, Villemez, and Smith (1978), who concluded that the negative association between socio-economic status (SES) and crime was small and had declined over the previous four decades.

The relationship between SES or class and crime is complex (Wright et al., 1999; Clelland and Carter, 1980; Tittle and Meier, 1990). Official statistics and self-report studies often provide divergent results about SES–crime relationship (Tittle, Villemez, and Smith, 1978).

The term "socio-economic status" is increasingly being used as a substitute for the Marxian term "class" in social science research generally and criminology in particular (see Tittle and Meier, 1990), albeit not without some objections (see Hagan et al., 1985). SES is typically measured as a composite of three key variables—education, income, and occupation (APA, 2014).

Criminologists now recognize that people with low SES are overrepresented in police-reported statistics partly because the criminal behaviour of the "middle and upper crime class systematically escaped official notice" (Gaylord and Galliher, 1988, 68). John Hagan made an important statement about the class–crime debate in his 1991 American Society of Criminology (ASC) presidential address. He argued (1992, 9) that the "relationship between class and crime is class and crime specific." That is, various classes are involved in different kinds of criminal behaviour because they have differential access to opportunity structures for committing crime. Male children of employer-class parents were found to be more likely to commit copyright violations (Hagan and Kay, 1990), while theft was common among young people from poorer families (Sabates, 2008).

Wright and colleagues (1999) made three fundamental findings concerning the link between SES and crime or delinquency. First, the link between SES and crime is an indirect one that operates through mediating variables, which include people's attitudes, behaviours, neighbourhood, peer networks, family conditions, cultures, economic opportunities, and so on. Second, low SES promotes delinquency—that is, it serves as a catalyst for delinquency because it causes alienation, financial strain, and aggression even while reducing individuals' educational and occupational aspirations. Third, and rather counterintuitively, high SES promotes delinquency by reducing adherence to conventional values while increasing social power and risk-taking behaviours. Wright and colleagues concluded (190) that there are causal links between SES and delinquency (i.e., through the mediating factors above) but "little overall correlation." The three analytic distinctions they made are crucial for us to understand the findings of studies discussed below.

Recent work supports the idea that the SES–crime relationship depends on the type of crime being studied. Recall that the three SES measures are education, income, and occupation. For instance, Aaltonen and colleagues (2012) examined police-reported data about violence committed by men in Finland between 2005 and 2007. They found that having no secondary education, earning low income, and being unemployed increased the risk of committing violent acts.

Property crimes in the United States are committed mostly by uneducated males (Lochner, 2004). Increased educational attainment has been found to reduce theft, burglary, drug offences, and vandalism (Sabates, 2007). Partner abuse in New Zealand has been linked to poverty and poor educational achievement in adolescence (Moffitt and Caspi, 1999). Sabates (2008) used data from the United Kingdom to investigate the conviction rate for three cohorts of people born between 1981 and 1983. According to that study (404), an increase in educational attainment led to "3.7, 56.1 and 6.7 fewer convictions per 1000 students for burglary, theft and vandalism and drug-related offences, respectively." The same study found that theft convictions were reduced by 1,233; convictions for vandalism and drug offences by 148; and convictions for burglary by 85. This translated into £3.2 million savings on victim services and health care in each of the three local education authorities that were studied.

In the United States, high school completion reduces the likelihood of incarceration by 3 percent for Blacks and by 1 percent for whites (Lochner and Moretti, 2004). Over the life course, people with higher levels of education are less involved in crime than those with lower levels of education (Hansen, 2003). The association between education and crime is not one-dimensional: older and better educated people generally commit more sophisticated crimes, while younger and uneducated people commit crimes that require few or no skills (Lochner 2004; Levitt and Lochner, 2000).

Aaltonen and colleagues (2012, 1206) contend that education is the "most robust predictor of both male-to-male and male-to-female violence," with the least educated males committing higher levels of violence against females and other males. Sabates (2008), however, cautions that education does not necessarily reduce violent crime, as violent crime is more closely related to poverty (Ludwig et al., 2001). Aaltonen and colleagues (2012, 1207) conclude that the most violent men are overwhelming from low SES.

Employment is another crucial SES variable. Sampson and Laub (2005) argue that finding a stable job is a watershed event that reduces recidivism. Conversely, high unemployment rates lead to intensification of criminal acts (Arvanites and Defina, 2006). Evidence from the United States (Lin, 2008) and Belgium (Hooghe et al., 2011) indicates that areas with high unemployment rates experience higher levels of violent and property crime. There is a gender dynamic in terms of employment and intimate partner violence (IPV). IPV is higher in homes where husbands are unemployed and wives are employed (MacMillan and Gartner, 1999). Women with low household incomes and low levels of education face a higher risk of intimate partner violence (IPV)

(MacMillan and Kruttschnitt, 2005). This implies that IPV generally declines with high SES (Abramsky et al., 2011). However, IPV and general crime often have distinct risk factors. Aaltonen and colleagues (2013) found that unemployment is correlated with property crime but not violent crime and drunk driving. Other studies caution that transitioning to stable employment is a *result* of desisting from crime, rather than a *cause* of desisting from crime (Skardhamar and Savolainen, 2014).

Spatial Location as a Correlate of Crime

Studies of crime and place show that different streets, neighbourhoods, cities, states/provinces, and countries have different patterns of crime.

It can be difficult to compare police-reported statistics from various countries. These difficulties relate to criminal code differences, policing practices and capabilities, the relationship between the police and the public, and the latter's willingness to report criminal behaviour, among other factors (Hartnagel, 2012). Homicide statistics are often used to compare different jurisdictions, because those data are fairly comparable across different jurisdictions. Homicides, after all, are more likely than other crimes to be reported and to be investigated by authorities (UN Office on Drugs and Crime, 2011). Also, there are similarities in how homicide is defined and counted across different countries—at least relative to many other types of offences (Nivett, 2011).

Figure 5.10 presents data on homicide rates in selected countries (Boyce and Cotter, 2013). The United States has the highest rate of homicide among its peer

FIGURE 5.10   **Homicide in Selected Countries, 2011**

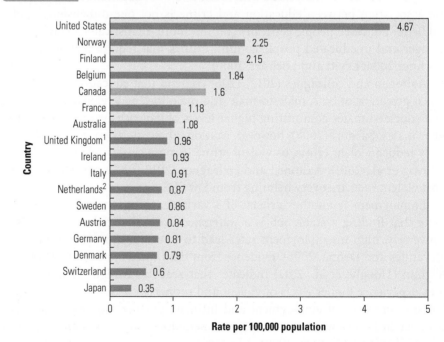

Source: Boyce, Jillian and Cotter, Adam. Homicide in Canada, 2012, chart 4, *Juristat*, (2013), http://www.statcan.gc.ca/pub/85-002-x/2013001/article/11882-eng.htm

countries—4.7 per 100,000. The United States recorded 14,827 murders in 2012. Canada's homicide rate—1.6 per 100,000—is nearly three times lower than that of its neighbour. Police in Canada reported 543 homicides in 2012 (Boyce and Cutter, 2013). Homicide made up less than 1 percent of all violent crimes in Canada in 2012 and is at its lowest level since 1966 (Perreault, 2013; Boyce and Cotter, 2013). Most other peer countries shown in Figure 5.9 have even lower homicide rates than Canada (Boyce and Cotter 2013). Developing countries tend to have higher homicide rates (de Souza and Miller, 2012; Pridemore, 2011). However, most homicide studies focus on developed countries (Morris and Graycar, 2011). Property crimes are generally higher in developed countries; developing countries tend to have higher rates of violent crime (Hooghe et al., 2011).

Different regions in Canada have very different patterns of crime. Figure 5.11 shows how the provinces and territories rank on the 2012 Crime Severity Index (CSI). The territories have the highest rates of crime, followed by Saskatchewan and the other the western provinces. Ontario, Quebec, and the Atlantic provinces reported relatively similar crime rates.

FIGURE 5.11 **Police-Reported Crime Severity Index by Province and Territory, 2013, Canada**

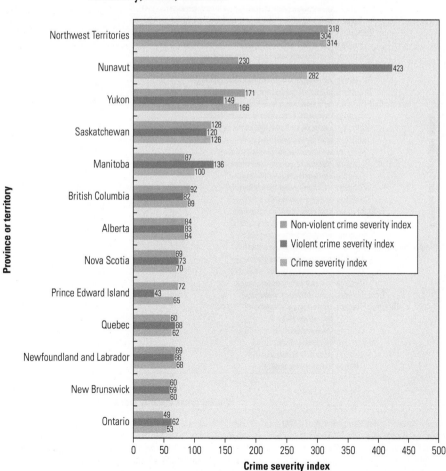

Source: Boyce, Gillian, Adam Cotter, and Samuel Perreault. 2014. Police Reported Crime Statistics in Canada, 2013. Juristat. Ottawa: Canadian Centre for Justice Statistics.

Figure 5.12 shows the violent crime severity index (CSI) in census metropolitan areas. In 2012, Winnipeg (145) had the highest violent CSI; Saskatoon (126) and Thunder Bay (119) were second and third respectively (Perreault, 2013). Thunder Bay had the highest homicide rate in 2012; Winnipeg ranked second. The three largest Canadian cities—Toronto, Vancouver, and Montreal—had lower violent, property, and total crime rates than many smaller or mid-sized cities, including Winnipeg and Saskatoon. There is also an interesting rural–urban differential: rural areas have higher violent crime rates than larger urban centres but lower property and total crime rates (Francisco and Chenier, 2007).

The relationship between neighbourhood characteristics and crime is a hot topic among criminologists today (Peterson, 2012; Sampson, Raudenbush, and Earls, 1997; Weinrath, Young, and Kohn, 2012). Current evidence from the United States indicates that neighbourhood matters. There is evidence, for example, that violent juvenile criminal behaviour declines when families

FIGURE 5.12   **Police-Reported Violent Crime Severity Index, by Census Metropolitan Area, 2013, Canada**

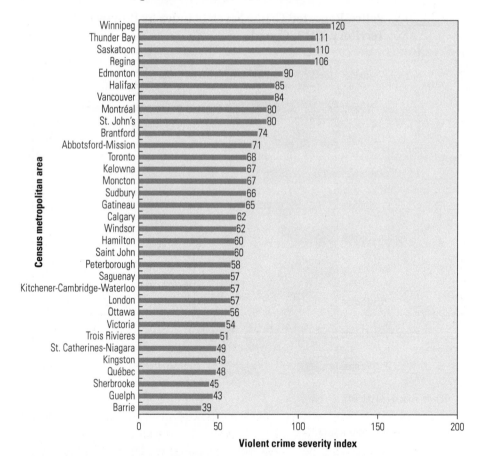

Note: The Oshawa Census Metropolitan Area (CMA) is excluded from this chart due to the incongruity between the police service jurisdictional boundaries and the CMA boundaries. Police-reported statistics may be affected by differences in the way police services deal with minor offences. In some instances, police or municipalities might chose to deal with some minor offences using municipal bylaws or provincial provisions rather than Criminal Code provisions. The base index was set at 100 for 2006 for Canada; Gatineau (1): refers to the Quebec part of the Ottawa–Gatineau CMA; Ottawa (2): refers to the Ontario part of the Ottawa–Gatineau CMA.

Source: Boyce, Gillian, Adam Cotter, and Samuel Perreault. 2014. Police Reported Crime Statistics in Canada, 2013. Juristat. Ottawa: Canadian Centre for Justice Statistics.

move to wealthier neighbourhoods (Ludwig, Duncan, and Hirschfield, 2001). Peterson (2012) argues that residential segregation—the occupation of distinct built spaces by specific ethno-racial groups—which leads to "ecological dissimilarity" in terms of available resources and opportunities in these various ethnic enclaves, is responsible for the racial gap in police-reported crime in the United States. "A large part of the racial difference in neighbourhood crime is because Whites and Blacks often live in ecologically dissimilar areas" (311).

The development of collective efficacy theory by Sampson and colleagues (Sampson, 2012; Sampson, Raudenbush, and Earls, 1997) has shed light on the link between spatial location and crime. Collective efficacy refers to "social cohesion among neighbours combined with their willingness to intervene on behalf of the common good" (Sampson, Raudenbush, and Earls, 1997, 918). The theory is based on research involving 8,782 Chicago residents in 343 neighbourhood clusters. The neighbourhoods studied were ethno-racially diverse. Latinos, Blacks, and whites each made up one-third of residents.

Sampson, Raudenbush, and Earls (1997) sought to understand why violence was concentrated in some neighbourhoods and why the composition of neighbourhoods was important. They found that crime is not randomly distributed; rather, it is a consequence of structural disadvantage and limited collective efficacy. "Three dimensions of neighbourhood stratification—concentrated disadvantage, immigration concentration and residential mobility—explain 70% of variation in collective efficacy across neighbourhoods" (923). They also found that high socio-economic status, homeownership, and age are all associated with increased levels of collective efficacy. Residential stability helps increase collective efficacy; by contrast, gender, ethnicity, and years spent in the neighbourhood are not associated with collective efficacy. Collective efficacy is crucial, for it demonstrates residents' willingness to work together for the common good. Neighbourhoods with high levels of collective efficacy are more likely to prevent violent incidents and break down of order.

An Arizona study of youth aged 8 to 17 highlights the distinction between solo offending and co-offending (group offending) (Schaefer, Rodriguez, and Decker, 2014). Youth are more likely to co-offend when a neighbourhood has racially/ethnically similar peers, is more stable, and is less disadvantaged. This suggests that racial homogeneity, residential stability, and resource availability help reduce crime by lone individuals but paradoxically *increase* crime carried out by groups (Schaefer, Rodriguez, and Decker, 2014). In other words, the mutual trust and solidarity generated by residential stability, availability of resources, and ethno-racial similarity also provide an incentive for criminality by individuals acting in groups.

Neighbourhood context and characteristics have been used to explain criminal behaviour in some Canadian cities. Thompson and Gartner (2014), for example, examined the social ecology of homicide in Toronto. They found that economic disadvantage and the proportion of residents in the age cohort 15 to 24 were positively correlated with homicide in that city. In other words, neighbourhoods with higher numbers of young people, higher levels of unemployment and poverty, and lower educational attainment had higher rates of homicides.

As noted earlier, Aboriginal people are overrepresented at every stage of the criminal justice process. This phenomenon has been linked to the characteristics and social contexts of the urban neighbourhoods in which Aboriginal people live. Fitzgerald and Carrington (2008) found that Aboriginal people are more likely to live in higher crime neighbourhoods, which increases the likelihood that their behaviour—criminal and noncriminal—will attract the attention of the authorities. The consequence is that Aboriginal people are seven times more likely than non-Aboriginal people to be identified as offenders (545). Also, socio-economic disadvantage and residential mobility (structural features) play a significant role in Aboriginal crime rates. The overrepresentation of Aboriginal people in police-reported crime statistics in Winnipeg, Saskatoon, and Regina is a function of their living conditions in those cities (La Prairie, 2002).

Ex-offenders tend to live in resource-poor parts of cities and to return to the same neighbourhoods after their release (Kirk, 2012). A US study found that offenders have higher chances of recidivism when they return to neighbourhoods with low socio-economic status (Kubrin and Stewart, 2006). Generally, changing neighbourhoods and routines after incarceration reduces the chances of reoffending (Kirk, 2012). Kirk (2009) found that the likelihood of reincarceration declined by 1 percent for every 10 miles parolees moved from their previous neighbourhood. Sharkey and Sampson (2010) found that although the likelihood of engaging in violent crime increased among adolescents who changed neighbourhoods within Chicago, those who moved outside the city experienced a reduction in their violent behaviour.

Policing practices in neighbourhoods are fundamental to crime detection and police-reported crime. Sacks (1972) used the concept of "incongruity procedure" to describe the conduct of police work: "the police are occupational specialists on inferring the probability of criminality from the appearances persons present in public spaces" (282–3). This is a matter of socially sorting who is "in place" and who is "out of place" (Sacks, 1972). In other words, police match spaces with faces or appearances. This is particularly relevant in cities that have racially segregated neighbourhoods (Peterson, 2012). Incongruity procedure involves "appearential ordering," or drawing inferences about people's behaviour from the appearances they present in public spaces (Lofland, 1973, 48–49; Sacks, 1972). Decisions about who looks suspicious, who possesses drugs, or who is in the wrong neighbourhood are sometimes made on the basis of appearential ordering. This micro-sociological process entails considering a potential suspect's manner of dress, hair arrangement, facial cues, gait, speech and overall demeanour.

However, appearential ordering may be cumbersome in urban settings because in the "modern city, appearances are chaotic, [while] space is ordered" (Lofland, 1973, 82). Appearential ordering has declined and spatial ordering has become predominant in modern cities as a result of socio-economic, political, demographic, and technological changes (56–66). This has contributed to the designation of some spatial locations as "high-risk" neighbourhoods and thus warranting greater scrutiny, which in turn may contribute to the crimes that are discovered in such areas.

Conclusion

This chapter has examined six correlates of crime: age, gender, race, drug misuse, socio-economic status, and spatial location. None of these correlates in and of itself explains criminal behaviour. Overall, crime rates arise from a complex interplay of macro-sociological, community, family, and individual factors. At the structural level, criminologists recognize the importance of factors such as socio-economic conditions, housing, and access to employment, education, and other valuable resources in the social production of crime and criminals. These structural factors reflect the broader political economy of societies (Sampson et al., 1997) and transcend individual characteristics, neighbourhoods, regions, and other units of analysis.

QUESTIONS FOR CRITICAL THINKING

1. Discuss the four explanations for Aboriginal overrepresentation in the criminal justice process.
2. What is the relationship between drug misuse and crime?
3. Using the collective efficacy theory, analyze the relationship between spatial location and crime.

Summary

- This chapter examines six correlates of crime: age, gender, race, drug and alcohol misuse, socio-economic status, and spatial location.
- In all societies, younger people commit more crime than older people. Most types of crime peak during the teen years and decline steadily thereafter. However, the peak is later for some types of violent offences and for white-collar and corporate crimes.
- Women commit less crime than men, particularly for serious and violent offences. While females have increased their level of involvement in crime since the 1960s, most of this increase has been for minor offences such a shoplifting and low-level fraud, which many researchers believe reflects the feminization of poverty over that period of time.
- In most countries, there are racial and ethnic differences in crime. These differences are due to some combination of differential offending and differential treatment by the justice system. Criminologists have developed a number of theories to explain differential offending by minority groups, including these: cultural theories, the colonial model, trauma transmission model, and critical race theory.
- Drugs and alcohol are major contributors to crime. There are three factors linking drug and alcohol use and crime: efforts to support addictions can lead to involvement in crimes; an individual may commit crimes because

they are under the influence of drugs or alcohol; and the possession of illegal drugs in and of itself is a crime.

■ The linkage between socio-economic status and crime is complex and varies by type of crime. The best evidence suggests that violent crimes and many other types of street crime are disproportionately committed by people from the lower classes, while upper-class people are disproportionately involved in serious forms of white-collar and corporate crimes.

■ Different countries, provinces, cities, and neighbourhoods have very different rates of crime. There are a variety of different explanations for these differences.

NET WORK

Statistics Canada provides a great deal of information about crime and its correlates over the Internet. To learn more about correlates of crime, first go to the Statistics Canada home page at http://www.statcan.ca/start.html. Under "Browse by Subject," click on "Crime and Justice," then "Crimes and Offences," then "Summary Tables." Then click on the table "Crimes by Type of Violation, by Province and Territory." Using the data in this table, answer the following question:

1. How do the provincial and territorial crime incidents and rates vary across the country when you compare all Criminal Code violations, violent Criminal Code violations, and property crime violations? How do drug violations vary across the country?
2. Then click on the table "Homicide Offences, Number and Rate, by Province and Territories." Using the data in this table, answer the following question:
3. How do the provinces rank in terms of the number of homicide offences in 2013? Does their rank vary depending on the year?
4. Then click on the table "Victims and Persons Accused of Homicide, by Age and Sex." Using the data in this table, answer the following question:
5. Look at homicide victims; what is the five-year trend for male and female victimization? Is the trend the same for male and female victims under the age of 12? What about for male and female victims ages 18 to 24? Other age categories?

Feminism and Criminology

Elizabeth Comack
UNIVERSITY OF MANITOBA

6

Like other academic disciplines, criminology has been a male-centred enterprise. Despite the use of generic terms such as "criminals," "defendants," and "delinquents," most of criminology has really been about what men do. As a consequence, women have been rendered invisible in much criminological inquiry. When women are looked at as offenders, their small numbers relative to men have typically been used to justify or rationalize this neglect. In 2011, for instance, only one in five persons accused by Canadian police of a Criminal Code offence was female (Brennan, 2012). When women were looked at as victims, violence against them was traditionally not a major area of concern. Official statistics on crime indicated that offences such as rape were relatively infrequent, and victim surveys reported young males to be the group most at risk from crime. Perhaps even more significant is that even though the subject matter of criminology has been men, criminologists have done very little work on men *as* men. In short, they have neglected to consider the "maleness" of their subjects. Over the past four decades, there has been a growing awareness of the implications these omissions hold for the discipline. This has come about largely through the feminist engagement with criminology: the efforts of feminist criminologists to move women—and an analysis of gender—from the periphery to the centre of criminological inquiry. The purpose of this chapter is to recount this history with a view to clarifying the kinds of issues and questions that are now commanding criminologists' attention.

After reading this chapter, you should be able to

- Explain the various theories that have been developed to understand women's involvement in crime.
- Understand the social, cultural, and legal factors that pertain to the issue of male violence against women.
- Appreciate some of the connections between a woman's law violations and her history of abuse.
- Evaluate the claim that women are "men's equals" in violence and some of the problems raised with using the Conflict Tactics Scale to research violence between intimate partners.
- Appreciate the gains to be made in addressing the connections between masculinity and crime.

The Invisibility of Women

The feminist engagement with criminology began over 40 years ago when pioneers in the discipline, such as Marie-Andrée Bertrand (1967) and Frances Heidensohn (1968), first called attention to criminology's amnesia when it came to women. Heidensohn (1968, 171), for instance, described analyses of women and crime as "lonely uncharted seas" and stated the need for a "crash programme of research which telescopes decades of comparable studies of males." In its initial phases, however, the feminist engagement with criminology consisted of a critique of existing approaches to explaining crime. This critique took two paths. Initially, writers like Dorie Klein (1973) and Carol Smart (1976, 1977) focused attention on the sexism of the small body of theories that had been developed to explain women's crime. Other writers soon broadened the focus to include the invisibility of women in the mainstream theories within the discipline.

Theories of Women's Crime

The Conservative Approach

Historically, a particular pathway can be followed when tracing the initial attempts to explain women's criminality. It begins with the publication of Lombroso and Ferrero's *The Female Offender* in 1895 and is followed by Thomas's *The Unadjusted Girl* in 1923, Glueck and Glueck's *Five Hundred Delinquent Women* in 1934, and Pollak's *The Criminality of Women* in 1950. Each of these works reflected a conservative approach to understanding differences in criminality between men and women. Specifically, "difference" was rooted in biology. Women were viewed as "naturally" inferior to men, and that inferiority was used to explain women's criminality.

For example, in applying the concepts of atavism and social Darwinism (see Chapter 8), Lombroso and Ferrero suggested that women possessed limited intelligence. They were also less sensitive to pain than men, full of revenge and jealousy, and naturally passive and conservative. Women's natural passivity, for instance, was caused by the "immobility of the ovule compared to the zoosperm" (Lombroso and Ferrero, 1895, 109). Atavistically, women were seen as displaying fewer signs of degeneration than men. The reason, according to Lombroso and Ferrero, was that women (and nonwhite males) had not advanced as far along the evolutionary continuum as (white) males and so could not degenerate as far. Given that women were relatively "primitive," the criminals among them would not be highly visible. However, those women who were criminal were cast as excessively vile and cruel in their crimes. They combined the qualities of the criminal male with the worst characteristics of the female: cunning, spite, and deceitfulness. Lacking the "maternal instinct" and "ladylike qualities," criminal women were seen as genetically more male than female.

First published in 1923, Thomas's (1967) work on female delinquency was premised on a similar kind of biological determinism. Thomas suggested that

sexism
Attributing to women socially undesirable characteristics that are assumed to be intrinsic characteristics of that sex.

conservative approach
An approach that understands "difference" between men and women as biologically based sex differences. Women are viewed as "naturally" inferior or unequal to men.

human behaviour was based on four "wishes": for adventure, security, response, and recognition. These wishes corresponded to features in the nervous system, which were expressed as biological instincts of anger, fear, love, and the will to gain status and power, respectively. However, Thomas asserted that men's and women's instincts differed both in quantity and quality. Since women had more varieties of love in their nervous systems, their desire for response was greater than men's. According to Thomas, it was the need to feel loved that accounted for women's criminality, and especially for prostitution.

Glueck and Glueck (1934) continued in this same tradition with *500 Delinquent Women*. The Gluecks described the women in their study as a "sorry lot. Burdened with feeblemindedness, psychopathic personality, and marked emotional instability, a large proportion of them found it difficult to survive by legitimate means" (299). The view of criminal women as "Other" is clearly evident in the Gluecks' work: "This swarm of defective, diseased, antisocial misfits … comprises the human material which a reformatory and a parole system are required by society to transform into wholesome, decent, law-abiding citizens! Is it not a miracle that a proportion of them were actually rehabilitated?" (303).

Pollak's (1961) work attempted to account for what he described as the "masked" nature of women's crime. Skeptical of the official data on sex differences in crime, Pollak suggested that women's crime was vastly undercounted. He put forward the view that female criminality was more likely to be hidden and undetected. Women were more often the instigators than the perpetrators of crime. Like Eve in the Garden of Eden, they manipulated men into committing offences. Women were also inherently deceptive and vengeful: they engaged in prostitution, they blackmailed their lovers, as domestics they stole from their employers, and as homemakers they carried out horrendous acts on their families (like poisoning the sick and abusing children). According to Pollak, woman's devious nature was rooted in her physiology. While a man must achieve erection in order to perform the sex act, and hence will not be able to conceal orgasm, a woman can fake orgasm. This ability to conceal orgasm gave women practice at deception. Pollak also suggested that female crime was caused by the vengefulness, irritability, and depression women encountered as a result of their generative phases. For example, menstruation drove women to acts of revenge by reminding women of their inferior status (and their ultimate failure to become men) (see Box 6.1). The concealed nature of their crimes, the vulnerability of their victims, and their chivalrous treatment by men who could not bear to prosecute or punish them, all combined to "mask" women's offences. When these factors were taken into account, according to Pollak, women's crimes were equal in severity and number to those of men.

As Heidensohn (1985, 122) notes, these early approaches to explaining women's crime lent an aura of intellectual respectability to many of the old folktales about women and their behaviours. They reflected widely held assumptions about "women's nature," including the good girl/bad girl duality and a double standard that viewed sexual promiscuity as a sign of "amorality" in women but "normality" in men. Relying on "commonsense" anecdotal evidence and circular reasoning—that is, "things are as they are because they are natural, and they are natural because that is the way things are" (Smart, 1976, 36)— the early theorists failed to call into question the structural features of their

FOCUS

Box 6.1

THE "WOMAN PROBLEM"

In the following passage, Otto Pollak offers us an illustration of a male-centred view of what has been traditionally referred to as the "woman problem" and its relationship to female criminality.

The student of female criminality cannot afford to overlook the generally known and recognized fact that [women's] generative phases are frequently accompanied by psychological disturbances which may upset the need satisfaction balance of the individual or weaken her internal inhibitions, and thus become causative factors in female crime. Particularly because of the social meaning attached to them in our culture, the generative phases of women are bound to present many stumbling blocks for the law-abiding behaviour of women. Menstruation with its appearance of injury must confirm feelings of guilt which individuals may have about sex activities which they have learned to consider as forbidden. As a symbol of womanhood, it must also, because of its recurrent nature, aggravate any feeling of irritation and protest which women may have regarding their sex in a society in which women

have had, and still have, to submit to social inequality with men. In both instances, it must lead to a disturbance of the emotional balance of the individual and this becomes potentially crime-promoting. Pregnancy in a culture which frowns upon illegitimacy and fosters in large sectors of society limitation in the number of children or even childlessness must become a source of irritation, anxiety, and emotional upheaval in many instances. The menopause in a society which makes romance and emotional gratification the supreme value in a monogamous marriage system must be experienced, at least by married women, frequently as a threat to the basis of their emotional security if not to their general marital existence. In view of these cultural implications of the generative phases and their psychological consequences, it is difficult to understand why the existing literature contains so little discussion of their possible crime-promoting influence.

Source: Otto Pollak, *The Criminality of Women* (New York: A.S. Barnes, 1961), 157–58. Originally published by University of Pennsylvania Press (Philadelphia) in 1950.

society and the gendered nature of the roles of men and women. Instead, sex (a biological difference) and gender (a cultural prescription) were equated as one and the same, with the "ladylike qualities" of the middle- and upper-class white woman used as the measuring rod for what was inherently female. In the process, the theories constructed were not only sexist but classist and racist as well.

While we can look back on these early theories of women's crime with some amusement, it bears noting that the kinds of assumptions and beliefs reflected in them have not disappeared. As Klein (1973, 7) comments, "The road from Lombroso to the present is surprisingly straight." Throughout the 1960s, researchers continued to rely on the assumptions and premises of the earlier approaches (see, for example, Cowie, Cowie, and Slater, 1968; Konopka, 1966). Following in the footsteps of Pollak, a more contemporary version of this conservative approach to understanding the difference between men and women links hormonal changes associated with women's menstrual cycles to their involvement in crime.

Premenstrual syndrome (PMS) has been described as a condition of "irritability, indescribable tension, [and a] desire to find relief by foolish and ill-considered actions" that is thought to occur during the week or two prior to the onset of menstruation (Frank, cited in Osborne, 1989, 168). Some 150 different symptoms (behavioural, psychological, and physiological) have been associated with PMS, and estimates of its incidence vary from 20 to 95 percent of the female population. There are no biomedical tests for determining the existence of PMS; it is the only "disease" not dependent on a specific type of symptom for its diagnosis. Nevertheless, PMS has been argued to be a cause of violent behaviour in women who suffer from it. It gained popularity as a cause of women's criminality in the 1980s, when PMS was introduced in two British court cases as a mitigating factor in homicide, enabling the women to receive more lenient sentences (Luckhaus, 1985). Sandie Smith was convicted on a reduced charge of manslaughter and given three years' probation plus mandatory progesterone treatments. Christine English pleaded guilty to manslaughter with diminished responsibility and received a one-year conditional discharge. She was also banned from driving for a year (she had run her boyfriend over with a car).

While research linking PMS to women's criminality has been criticized for its methodological deficiencies (Morris, 1987), feminist criminologists have questioned the validity of framing explanations for women's criminality that isolate the source of the problem in women's bodies, thereby ignoring the cultural meanings (especially with regard to menstruation) and social contexts that are at play (Kendall, 1991, 1992). So long as women are pathologized as "sick" or "diseased," the broader structural factors that impinge on women's lives—and are thereby implicated in their offending behaviours—will be ignored.

The Liberal Approach

In the 1970s, theories of women's crime began to shift toward a more sociological orientation. Rather than focusing on biology, attention turned to culture. In this liberal approach, differences between men and women are not necessarily innate or inborn, but are learned by individuals through the process of socialization. It is the culture that marks off the differences between men and women by proscribing certain roles and behaviours as "male appropriate" and "female appropriate." In this way, "gender" has been separated from "sex" and made the key focus of inquiry.

This liberal approach to understanding difference took the form of role theory as an explanation for female criminality. Hoffman-Bustamante (1973), for example, suggested that the lower rate of delinquency of girls can be accounted for by differential socialization and childrearing practices. Whereas boys are encouraged to be aggressive, outgoing, and ambitious and are allowed greater freedom, girls are taught to be passive and domesticated and are more closely supervised. Since girls are taught to be nonviolent, they do not acquire the skills, technical ability, or physical strength to engage in violent acts such as gang fighting. When women do engage in violent behaviour, their actions reflect their greater domesticity. For example, women who murder are more likely to use kitchen knives than guns. The finding that women are more likely to be charged with shoplifting offences was similarly explained with reference to their gender roles and socialization. Women are traditionally the consumers in society, and when they steal, girls are more likely to take small items like make-up. Role theory, then, offered an explanation in terms of the differential gender socialization for both the types and nature of offences that females commit.

liberal approach
Distinguishes sex (biological) from gender (cultural) and sees differences between men and women as resulting from gender roles and socialization patterns.

Another version of role theory was put forward by Hagan and his colleagues (Hagan et al., 1979, 1985, 1987) in the form of a power-control theory of sex and delinquency. Power-control theory is intended to explain the sex differences in delinquency by drawing linkages between variations in parental control and the delinquent behaviour of boys and girls. More specifically, Hagan and his colleagues suggest that parental control and adolescents' subsequent attitudes toward risk-taking behaviour are affected by family class relations. They distinguish two ideal types of family: the patriarchal family, in which the husband is employed in an authority position in the workforce and the wife is not employed outside the home, and the egalitarian family, in which both husband and wife are employed in authority positions outside the home. Hagan and his colleagues suggest that in the former, a traditional gender division exists whereby fathers and especially mothers are expected to control their daughters more than their sons. Given the presence of a "cult of domesticity," girls are socialized to focus their futures on domestic labour and consumption activities while boys are prepared for their participation in production activities. In the latter form, parents redistribute their control efforts so that girls are subject to controls more like those imposed on boys. "In other words, in egalitarian families, as mothers gain power relative to husbands, daughters gain freedom relative to sons" (1987, 792). The authors predict that these different family forms will produce differing levels of delinquency in girls: "Patriarchal families will be characterized by large gender differences in common delinquent behaviours, while egalitarian families will be characterized by smaller gender differences in delinquency" (1987, 793).

Smart (1976) has commented that role theory can offer only a partial explanation of women's crime. Because of a failure to situate the discussion of gender roles in broader structural terms, little attention is devoted to why socialization patterns are gender differentiated and how they have come to be that way. In the absence of a structural analysis, it is too easy to fall back on explanations that view such differences as biological, and not social, in their origins: "role is destiny" can therefore act as a ready substitute for "biology is destiny" (Morris, 1987, 64). While Hagan and his colleagues endeavour to place role theory in a broader structural context (by attending to the labour force participation of parents), they make an important assumption: if a woman is working for wages, there will be "equality" within the household. Their formulation does not pay enough attention to the nature of women's paid work and to other variables that might be in operation (such as how power and control may be exercised between males and females within the household).

In addition to engaging in critical evaluations of the specific theories that had been developed to explain women's involvement in crime, feminist criminologists drew attention to the invisibility of women in mainstream approaches within the discipline.

The Mainstream Theories of Crime

Since the 1970s, mainstream approaches to explain crime have come under increasing scrutiny. Writers such as Leonard (1982), Heidensohn (1985), Morris (1987), and Naffine (1987) have highlighted the general failure of mainstream theories in criminology to adequately explain or account for women's involvement in crime; "mainstream" was, in effect, "malestream."

For example, in explaining crime in relation to the strain that results from the disjunction between culture goals (such as monetary success) and institutionalized means (education, jobs), Merton's anomie theory (see Chapter 10, "Strain Theories") reflected a sensitivity to the class inequalities that exist in society. The same could not be said, however, with regard to an awareness of gender inequalities. If lower-class individuals were more likely to engage in crime because of a lack of access to the institutionalized means for achieving monetary success, then it follows that women—who as a group experience a similar lack of access—should also be found to commit crime as a consequence of this strain. This is not the case.

Like strain theory, Sutherland's differential association theory is presented as a general theory of crime (see Chapter 13). In focusing on the processes by which individuals learn definitions of the legal codes as either favourable or unfavourable, Sutherland posited the existence of a "cultural heterogeneity" in society with regard to pro- and anti-criminal associations. While this cultural heterogeneity accounted for men's involvement in crime, women were the anomaly or exception in that they displayed a "cultural homogeneity." In Sutherland's view, women were more altruistic and compliant than men. As Naffine (1987) has noted, Sutherland missed a great opportunity when he neglected to explore this apparent cultural homogeneity in females. Given his critical outlook on the individualism and competition that he felt characterized American society, an examination of women's conformity could have provided Sutherland with clues to better understand crime and its causes.

Hirschi's work on social control theory is also characterized by a neglect of the female (see Chapter 14). While other criminologists focused their attention on explaining deviance, Hirschi set out to explain conformity. In this regard, since women appear to be more conformist than men, it would have made sense to treat women as central to his analysis. Nevertheless, though he collected data on female subjects, Hirschi set these data aside and—like his colleagues—concentrated on males.

With the advent of the labelling and conflict theories during the 1960s and 1970s, the potential for a more inclusive approach to crime increased. Yet, while Becker's labelling perspective raised the question of "Whose side are we on?" and advocated an approach to deviance that gave a voice to those who were subject to the labelling process, it was never fully realized in the case of women. Similarly, Taylor, Walton, and Young's *The New Criminology* (1973), which offered up a devastating critique of the traditional criminological theories, failed to give any mention to women.

In general, when sex differentials in crime are considered by the mainstream theorists, the tendency has been to rely on stereotypical constructions of masculinity and femininity: men are aggressive, independent, daring, and adventurous; women are submissive, dependent, and compliant. In the process, female law violators are classed as a rather "dull lot." Even in their deviance, they are less interesting than men. Moreover, such stereotypical depictions of women have been considered "so obvious" that they require no further discussion (see, for example, Cohen, 1955, 142)—let alone theoretical or empirical concern.

We saw in Chapter 5 that females commit less serious offences, in smaller numbers, and with less frequency than males. Criminologists have typically responded to these findings by formulating their theories to account for only male crime and delinquency. The ramifications of this tendency have been spelled out by Gelsthorpe and Morris:

> Theories are weak if they do not apply to half of the potential criminal population; women, after all, experience the same deprivations, family structures and so on that men do. Theories of crime should be able to take account of both men's and women's behaviour and to highlight those factors which operate differently on men and women. Whether or not a particular theory helps us to understand women's crime is of *fundamental*, not marginal importance for criminology. (Gelsthorpe and Morris, 1988, 103, emphasis added)

The Generalizability Problem

One issue raised by this problem with the mainstream theories of crime is referred to by Daly and Chesney-Lind (1988) as the **generalizability problem**: Can theories generated to explain male offending be modified to apply to women? Several criminologists responded to this problem by attempting to make the mainstream theories of crime "fit" women. For example, Leonard (1982) reformulated Merton's strain theory, suggesting that females may be socialized to aspire to different culture goals than males—in particular, relational ones concerning marriage and having children. If this is the case, then women's low rate of criminality would be explained by the relatively easy manner in which females can realize their goals. Nevertheless, as Morris (1987) notes, such a formulation relies on an idealized and romanticized version of women's lives. Not only does it display an insensitivity to the strains and frustrations associated with women's familial role, but it also fails to acknowledge the economic concerns that women confront. Such efforts to revise mainstream theories of crime to include women have been referred to as the "add women and stir" approach. Part of the difficulty with this endeavour is that women are presented as afterthoughts, not as integral to the arguments being developed (Gelsthorpe and Morris, 1988). A more significant problem with this effort is captured by Naffine (1997, 32): "The point of these exercises has been to adapt to the female case, theories of crime which purported to be gender-neutral but were in fact always highly gender specific. Not surprisingly, the results have been varied and generally inconclusive."

The Gender-Ratio Problem

A second issue raised by the feminist critique of mainstream criminology is one that Daly and Chesney-Lind (1988, 119) refer to as the **gender-ratio problem**. Why are women less likely than men to be involved in crime? What explains the sex difference in rates of arrest and in the variable types of criminal activity between men and women? Attention to the gender-ratio problem sparked a plethora of studies in the 1970s and 1980s on the processing of men and women by the criminal justice system (see, for example, Scutt, 1979; Kruttschnitt, 1980–81, 1982; Steffensmeier and Kramer, 1982; Zingraff and Thomson, 1984; Daly, 1987, 1989). The main question that guided much of this research stemmed from Pollak's assertion that criminal justice officials exercised "chivalry": Are

generalizability problem
Raises the issue of whether mainstream theories of crime—which have largely been developed with men in mind—can be made to "fit" women.

gender-ratio problem
Poses the question of why there are sex differences in rates of arrest and types of criminal activity between men and women.

women treated more leniently than men? As with the generalizability problem, the answers to this question have been mixed. For instance, research that supports the chivalry hypothesis indicates that when it does exist, chivalry benefits some women more than others—in particular, the few white middle- or upper-class women who come into conflict with the law. Also, chivalry appears to apply only to those female suspects who behave in a stereotypical fashion, that is, "crying, pleading for release for the sake of their children, claiming men have led them astray" (Rafter and Natalizia, 1981, 92). In this regard, Rafter and Natalizia have argued that chivalrous behaviour should be seen as a means of preserving women's subordinate position in society, not as a benign effort to treat women with some special kindness. Naffine (1997, 36), however, points to a larger problem with this research. By turning on the question of whether women were treated the same as or differently from men, the chivalry thesis (and its rebuttal) took men to be the norm: "Men were thus granted the status of universal subjects, the population of people with whom the rest of the world (women) were compared."

The Women's Liberation Thesis

While research on the chivalry thesis was drawing the attention of criminologists in the 1970s and 1980s, another thesis began to attract considerable attention. The women's liberation thesis posits that women's involvement in crime will come to more closely resemble men's as differences between men and women are diminished by women's greater participation and equality in society. As reflected in the work of Simon (1975) and Adler (1975), this thesis suggests that changes in women's gender roles will be reflected in their rates of criminal involvement. Simon suggested that the increased employment opportunities that accompanied the women's movement would also bring an increase in opportunities to commit crime (such as embezzlement from employers). Adler linked the apparent statistical increase in women's crime to the influence of the women's movement and suggested that a "new female criminal" was emerging: women were becoming more violent and aggressive, just like their male counterparts.

Naffine (1997, 32) refers to the thesis that "women's liberation" causes crime in women as "perhaps the most time-consuming and fruitless exercise" in criminology. The many empirical difficulties with the thesis were discussed at some length in Chapter 5. For feminist criminologists, the main difficulty with the women's liberation thesis—as with the chivalry thesis—was that it posed a question that took males to be the norm: Were women becoming more "liberated" and thus more like men, even in their offending?

Given the difficulties encountered in efforts to respond to the generalizability and gender-ratio problems, many feminist criminologists saw the need to "bracket" these issues for the time being in order to understand better the social worlds of women and girls (Daly and Chesney-Lind, 1988, 121). Cain (1990) took this suggestion further. She noted that while feminist criminologists needed to understand women's experiences, there were no tools in existing criminological theory with which to do this. Cain therefore advocated a "transgressive" approach, one that started from outside the boundaries of criminological discourse.

Criminalized Women

For many feminist criminologists, starting from outside criminology has meant resisting the temptation to fashion theories of women's involvement in crime that take crime categories (such as crimes against the person or crimes against property) as their starting point. As writers such as Smart (1989), Laberge (1991), and Faith (1993) have pointed out, "crime" is not a homogenous category. There are notable differences between women in the nature and extent of both their criminal involvement and their contacts with the criminal justice system. As well, crime categories are legal constructions, the end result of a lengthy process of detection, apprehension, accusation, judgment, and conviction. They represent one way of ordering or making sense of social life. Crime categories are also premised on a dualism between "the criminal" and "the law-abiding," which reinforces the view of criminal women as "Other" and thereby misses the similarities that exist between women. In this respect, criminal women are in very many ways no different from the rest of us. They are mothers, daughters, sisters, girlfriends, and wives, and they share many of the experiences of women collectively in society. Since crime is the outcome of interactions between individuals and the criminal justice system, writers like Laberge (1991) have proposed that we think in terms of "criminalized women" rather than "criminal women."

In these terms, women may commit a variety of crimes for a variety of reasons; there is no single or special theory for their criminality. As Carlen (1985, 10) has emphasized, "The essential criminal woman does not exist." In contrast to the conservative and liberal approaches that have dominated criminologists' thinking about the "difference" between men and women, a **feminist approach** understands "difference" as rooted in the structure of society. More specifically, the lives of criminalized women are located within a broader social context characterized by inequalities of class, race, and gender.

With regard to class location, criminalized women tend to be young, poor, undereducated, and unskilled. They are most likely to be involved in property crimes. Johnson and Rodgers (1993, 98) suggest that "women's participation in property offences is consistent with their traditional roles as consumers and, increasingly, as low income, semi-skilled, sole support providers for their families. In keeping with the rapid increase in female-headed households and the stresses associated with poverty, greater numbers of women are being charged with shoplifting, cheque forging and welfare fraud."

In contrast to the women's liberation thesis, feminist criminologists have suggested that increases in women's involvement in crime are more directly connected with the "feminization of poverty" than with women's emancipation. Indeed, several writers have called attention to how government cutbacks to social assistance have left increasing numbers of women and children at risk (Chunn and Gavigan, 2014; Mosher, 2014; Crocker and Johnson, 2010). In the Province of Ontario, for example, social assistance payments were cut by 21.6 percent in 1995, "workfare" programs were implemented, and a zero tolerance policy on welfare fraud was put in place. The feminization of poverty has been accompanied by the "criminalization of

feminist approach
Understands "difference" between men and women as structurally produced by inequalities of class, race, and gender that condition and constrain women's lives.

poverty." Next to murderers, individuals convicted of welfare fraud now have the greatest likelihood of receiving a sentence of incarceration. A 1997 study of 50 welfare fraud convictions found that 80 percent of those found guilty were sentenced to time in prison (Martin, 1999). One individual caught up in this process was Kimberly Rogers (see Box 6.2).

SEARCH FOR:
Justice with Dignity—includes articles and information on the inquest on the death of Kimberly Rogers

FOCUS

Box 6.2

INQUEST TO PROBE HOUSE-ARREST DEATH

SUDBURY—If Hazel St. has seen better days, the evidence of that era is long gone. The short street where Kim Rogers lived and died in destitution is a mix of warehouses and run-down old homes just south of the courthouse where an inquest into her death begins today.

The 40-year-old woman lived for three years on the top floor of a red brick house across the road from a parking lot. When she moved in, the west-facing window might have seemed like a bonus, flooding the small bedroom with bright light.

But by August, 2000, she was eight months pregnant. As temperatures soared to 30°C and the sun's unforgiving rays bounced off the unshaded street, she must have longed each day for the respite of nightfall.

Because this apartment—its living room with a view of a wall, its narrow kitchen with a peeling gray linoleum and rusting appliances, its tiny bathroom windowless—was her prison.

In April, she was put under house arrest after pleading guilty to defrauding the welfare system of $13,000, which she drew in 1996–99 while also collecting $49,000 in student loans.

A few years earlier, this would not have been considered an offence.

"The whole concept of being on welfare and getting a student loan—that didn't used to be illegal until this government came in," said Janet Gasparini, executive director of the Sudbury Social Planning Council. "There are many success stories that came out of people who did what she did."

By 1996, it was a crime.

"I'm very sorry it happened," Rogers said as she pleaded guilty in the Ontario Court of Justice on April 25, 2001. Mr. Justice Greg Rodgers sternly pointed out that she had engaged in "almost four years of deception and dishonesty."

"I am satisfied you did not lead an opulent lifestyle, even with these two sources of income, but welfare is there for people who need it, not for people who want it, who want things and who want money."

Rodgers sentenced her to a jail term in her home of six months, followed by 18 months' probation. She would be allowed to leave for medical or religious reasons, to report to a supervisor, and to shop for the necessities of life, to be done only on Wednesdays between 9 a.m. and noon.

Rogers was also ordered her to pay back the full amount to the Ontario Works program, which was already "clawing back" $52 a month from her $520 monthly cheque.

But the criminal conviction triggered an automatic three-month suspension of benefits, a penalty introduced by the Harris government and subsequently stiffened in April 2000, when a "zero-tolerance policy on welfare cheats" raised the penalty to lifetime suspension.

These are among the policies that will go under the microscope at the five-week inquest, presided over by coroner David Eden.

"We cannot live in a society where we say at some point we would stop supporting people," said Gasparini, whose organization has been granted standing but denied legal aid.

The Social Planning Council has been told to piggy-back on the resources of two national coalitions with standing—one headed by the Canadian Association of Elizabeth Fry Societies, the other by the Ontario Social Safety Network. Gasparini said her organization offers the only community perspective and should have been granted separate legal representation.

"Two government ministries, the municipality and the police department will all be represented by lawyers paid with taxpayers' dollars," she said. "It's imperative to have a local voice to tell about the impact of these policies."

Rogers' family has chosen not to participate. Her mother, Meryl Caetano, said she knows she's going to be upset by the public airing of personal details of her daughter's life.

"To me, she's my daughter and I loved her," she said.

Still, she said, she can't argue with the need to examine what led to Rogers' death. "I think it should be taken seriously. These things shouldn't happen to anyone."

Reports on the physical cause of death will be among the first evidence to be led by coroner's counsel Al O'Marra. It points to a suicide, sources told *The Star* soon after the tragedy.

(continued)

Rogers had attempted suicide before, in 1996, before enrolling at Cambrian College, from which she graduated in 2000 with a social services diploma. Her most recent employment was with a call centre, chasing people who had defaulted on their long-distance charges—a job she quit in January 2001, because of the stress of dealing with abusive customers.

By early May, Rogers had no food. The local food bank would allow only one visit a month, and she had been there just before Easter. She was behind on her $450 monthly rent, and her drug card had been suspended so she could not obtain medication prescribed for depression and nausea.

"I am unable to sleep because of my situation," she said in a May 23 affidavit. "I am very upset and I cry all the time."

Some responded. Her landlord agreed to reduce her rent to $300 a month until her circumstances improved. The estranged father of her unborn child came up with a "one-time" payment of $300 for her rent. Friends gave her food.

Workers for the Elizabeth Fry Society and the Social Planning Council scrounged for help, with limited success. Her family doctor intervened to get her drug card reinstated.

Toronto lawyer Sean Dewart launched a constitutional appeal on her behalf and persuaded Madam Justice Gloria Epstein to reinstate her benefits in the interim.

In a May 31 ruling, Epstein found that "for a member of our community carrying an unborn child" to be homeless and deprived of basic sustenance is a situation that would adversely affect the public—"its dignity, its human rights commitments and its health care resources."

Rogers still had five months of house detention. She would last only two. Residents of a downstairs apartment said she had been dead several days when her body was found Aug. 9 in her bed, a little more than a month before her baby was due.

Last week, neighbours said they felt the treatment she received was harsh.

"She would have been better off in jail," said Mary Lou Fabbro, owner of a nearby stained-glass business.

The death reflects poorly on our society, she said. "We need to take care of each other."

Source: Kate Harries, "Inquest to Probe House-Arrest death," *Toronto Star*, October 15, 2002. Reprinted with permission—Torstar Syndication Services.

Locating women's involvement in crime in its broader social context also involves attending to racial inequality. Aboriginal people in Canada are disproportionately represented in crime statistics, but the over-representation of Aboriginal women in Canadian prisons is even greater than that of Aboriginal men (Dauvergne, 2012; Perreault, 2009; Sapers, 2013). Aboriginal women are incarcerated for more violent crimes than non-Aboriginal women. And alcohol has played a role in the offences of twice as many Aboriginal women in prison as Aboriginal men (La Prairie, 1993; Comack, 1996). The historical forces that have shaped Aboriginal communities—colonization, economic and political marginalization, and forced dependency on the state—have culminated in a situation where violence and drugging and drinking have reached epidemic proportions in many Aboriginal communities (Hamilton and Sinclair, 1991; Royal Commission on Aboriginal Peoples, 1996). As Monture Angus (1999, 27) has noted, "Aboriginal people do not belong to communities that are functional and healthy (and colonialism is significantly responsible for this fact)."

Gender inequality and its links to race and class help explain prostitution or sex trade work (Brock, 1998; Bruckert and Parent, 2014; Seshia, 2005). According to Johnson and Rodgers, women's involvement in prostitution is a reflection of their subordinate social and economic position in society: "Prostitution thrives in a society which values women more for their sexuality than for their skilled labour, and which puts women in a class of commodity to be bought and sold. Research has shown one of the major causes of prostitution to be the economic plight of women, particularly young, poorly educated women who have limited *legitimate* employment records" (Johnson and Rodgers, 1993, 101, emphasis in original).

The structured inequalities in society that shape and constrain the lives of criminalized women provide an important backdrop for understanding their involvement in crime. As Carlen (1988, 14) notes, women make their lives in conditions that are not of their own choosing. In their efforts to transgress criminology, feminist criminologists have become increasingly aware that to understand women's lives we must bring into view women's experiences of violence at the hands of men. This violence needs to be understood as a manifestation of **patriarchy**—that is, the systemic and individual power that men exercise over women (Brownmiller, 1975; Kelly, 1988).

Violence Against Women

At the same time that feminist criminologists were criticizing criminology for its neglect of women, feminists in the women's movement were raising the issue of male violence against women. This issue had historically not been a matter of societal, legal, or academic concern.

The Cultural Construction of Rape

With regard to the lack of societal concern about male violence against women, feminists questioned assumptions and beliefs that dominated the public's understanding of sexual violence. The **cultural construction** of rape, for example, was riddled with myths and misconceptions about the nature of the act itself, as well as with stereotypical images of "true" rape victims and offenders. These myths and stereotypes—and their limitations—included the following:

- *Women "ask for it" by their dress or their behaviour.* The absurdity of this claim is revealed when we apply the same logic to victims of robbery (see Box 6.3).

> **patriarchy**
> A system of male domination that includes both a structure and an ideology that privileges men over women.
>
> **cultural construction**
> A perspective on a subject that is shaped by cultural assumptions rather than having a natural or objective basis.

FOCUS   Box 6.3

WAS HE ASKING FOR IT?

In 1975, *Harper's Weekly* carried the following response to an American Bar Association finding that few rapists are punished for their crime. The article asks us to imagine a male complainant in a robbery case undergoing the same sort of cross-examination that a female complainant in a rape case does.

"Mr. Smith, you were held up at gunpoint on the corner of First and Main?"

"Yes."

"Did you struggle with the robber?"

"No."

"Why not?"

"He was armed."

"Then you made a conscious decision to comply with his demands rather than resist?"

"Yes."

"Did you scream? Cry out?"

"No. I was afraid."

"I see. Have you ever been held up before?"

"No."

"Have you ever given money away?"

"Yes, of course."

"And you did so willingly?"

"What are you getting at?"

"Well, let's put it like this, Mr. Smith. You've given money away in the past. In fact, you have quite the reputation for philanthropy. How can we be sure you weren't contriving to have your money taken by force?"

"Listen, if I wanted—"

"Never mind. What time did this holdup take place?"

(continued)

"About 11 p.m."

"You were out in the street at 11 p.m.? Doing what?"

"Just walking."

"Just walking? You know it's dangerous being out on the street that late at night. Weren't you aware that you could have been held up?"

"I hadn't thought about it."

"What were you wearing?"

"Let's see—a suit. Yes, a suit."

"An expensive suit?"

"Well—yes. I'm a successful lawyer, you know."

"In other words, Mr. Smith, you were walking around the streets late at night in a suit that practically advertised the fact that you might be a good target for some easy money, isn't that so? I mean, if we didn't know better, Mr. Smith, we might even think that you were asking for this to happen, mightn't we?"

- *Rape is a sexual act brought on by a man's uncontrollable sexual urges, which cannot be halted once a woman has "turned him on."* Such a view not only depicts male sexuality in a distorted way but also ignores the element of physical coercion and the effects of fear and threats on the woman.

- *When women say no they really mean yes.* This belief suggests that women are expected to be coy and flirtatious and that men are encouraged not to take no for an answer. In these terms, it legitimates the act of rape.

- *If a woman has had sexual relations in the past, she will be less credible when she says she didn't consent to sex.* This myth suggests that "bad girls" or "loose women" deserve to be raped.

- *Women cannot be trusted.* For instance, they will make false accusations against innocent men. Casting all women as inherently untrustworthy acts to silence survivors and exonerate rapists.

- *The act of rape really has little long-term impact on the woman.* So long as the harm of rape is denied, society can continue to ignore the issue and its effects on women's lives.

- *Men who commit "real" rape are an "abnormal" group in society.* Attributing rape to the actions of a small, disturbed minority in society effectively lets men as a group off the hook. Rape is thus cast as an isolated problem for psychologists and psychiatrists to deal with or is narrowly defined as a "women's issue"—not an issue that all of us need to confront.

Smart (1989, 28) has described this cultural construction of rape as "phallocentric," by which she means "the prevailing dominance of the masculine experience of, and meaning of, sexuality. Sexuality is comprehended as the pleasure of the Phallus, and by extension the pleasures of penetration and intercourse—for men." Clearly, the more prevalent such phallocentric myths and stereotypes about sexual violence are in society, the more far-reaching will be their consequences.

For perpetrators of sexual violence, these myths and stereotypes can translate into less chance of detection, higher acquittal rates, and lighter sentences. In 2009, for instance, only 3 percent of sexual assaults were reported to police in Canada, and of those 3 percent, less than 20 percent were brought to trial (Statistics Canada 2010, 2011a, 2011b). Once failure to complain and to charge are taken into account, the likelihood that someone who commits a sexual assault will be convicted of an offence is less than 1 percent (Busby,

2014). Studies also show that many rapists do not even believe they have done anything wrong. Scully and Marolla's (1984) interviews with men convicted of rape found that a large proportion of the men either denied having sexual contact with the victim or admitted to sexual acts but did not define their behaviour as rape. The men tried to demonstrate that their victims were willing and, in some cases, enthusiastic participants. One man convicted of attempting to rape a prison hospital nurse claimed: "She semi-struggled but deep down inside I think she felt it was a fantasy come true" (535). Another man who had hid in his victim's closet and later attacked her while she slept maintained that while the victim was scared at first, "once we got into it she was ok." He believed he had not committed rape because "she enjoyed it and it was like she consented" (536). A third man who beat his victim admitted that "I did something stupid. I pulled a knife on her and I hit her as hard as I would hit a man," yet he still maintained: "But I shouldn't be in prison for what I did. I shouldn't have all this time [sentence] for going to bed with a broad" (537).

For survivors of sexual violence, rape myths can mean a "double victimization." Survivors not only endure the humiliation and degradation inherent in the act itself, but may experience further humiliation if they report the crime to the authorities. Also, since phallocentric cultural beliefs suggest that rape is the woman's fault, survivors may feel responsible for their own victimization. As Smart (1989, 35) has argued, "The whole rape trial is a process of disqualification (of women) and celebration (of phallocentrism)." For women generally, the cultural construction of rape can produce feelings of fear and vulnerability that impose restrictions on their daily activities. One study, for example, reported that 24 percent of women (compared with only 3 percent of men) stay at home at night because they are afraid to go out alone (Johnson, 1996). Another study (Statistics Canada, 2005) found that 27 percent of women worried for their personal safety when they were home alone at night, compared to only 12 percent of men. And twice as many females as males worried when taking public transit alone at night (58% versus 29%).

QUESTIONS FOR CRITICAL THINKING

1. To what extent is the "cultural construction of rape" evident in films, music videos, advertising, and other aspects of Canadian culture? To what extent does it influence your own thinking about sexual violence?
2. In what ways have rape myths and stereotypes been evident in law and legal practice?
3. Identify some of the controversies surrounding violence against women

The Law's Role in Condoning Male Violence Against Women

Recognition of the pervasiveness of these phallocentric myths and stereotypes led to a questioning of the role that the law has played in condoning male violence against women. Feminists noted, for example, that women have historically been viewed as the "property" of men. The law upheld this view by granting husbands certain legal rights, in particular, the "right to consortium" and the "right to chastise" their wives.

Consortium generally refers to the companionship, affection, and assistance that one spouse in a marriage is entitled to receive from the other. According only husbands the right to consortium meant that wives had a legal obligation with respect to the "consummation of marriage, cohabitation, maintenance of conjugal rights, sexual fidelity, and general obedience and respect for his wishes" (Dobash and Dobash, 1979, 60). This right was reflected in Canadian law until 1983. Under the old rape law, a rape was defined as having occurred when "[a] male person has sexual intercourse with a female person *who is not his wife*, (a) without her consent, or (b) with her consent if the consent (i) is extorted by threats or fear of bodily harm, (ii) is obtained by impersonating her husband, or (iii) is obtained by false and fraudulent representations as to the nature and quality of the act" (s. 143, emphasis added). It made no sense, under the law's logic, to prevent men from "consorting" with their own property; wives did not have the legal right to say no.

Besides granting a husband immunity from rape charges, the rape law reinforced the cultural construction of rape. For instance, reflecting the belief that "women cannot be trusted" when they claim they have been raped, the legislation included a corroboration requirement, whereby the accused could not be found guilty in the absence of corroborating evidence (such as cuts and bruises) supporting the testimony of the complainant. As well, under the doctrine of recent complaint, it was assumed that a woman who complained at the first reasonable opportunity was more credible or believable than one who complained some time after the rape had taken place. Because the key element in establishing the guilt of the accused in rape cases was consent, the focus of the trial rested on the woman's credibility. Her moral character came under the scrutiny of the court in the attempt to determine whether she could be believed when she said she did not consent. Defence lawyers were permitted to ask questions about the past sexual history of the complainant, reinforcing the belief that women who have had sexual relations in the past are "less credible" when they say they didn't consent to sex.

With regard to the right to chastise, the law historically has given a husband the authority to use force in order to ensure that his wife fulfilled her obligations. The only restraint the law placed on a husband was that he had to apply that force in a moderate manner. When husbands went too far, and their wives died as a result, the British courts were inclined to leniency. Yet if a wife killed her husband, it was considered a "species of treason" akin to killing the king, for she was going against his authority (Edwards, 1985). The law, in essence, reflected and reinforced patriarchal relations between men and women. This view continued to inform legal practice into the latter part of the 20th century. Because police officers were inclined to view violence in the home between intimate partners as a "private trouble" that was not the law's business, they were reluctant to intervene or to define the situation as a criminal matter.

Criminology's Complicity

Within criminology, male violence against women was similarly not seen as a social problem. Official statistics suggested that crimes like rape were relatively infrequent. Victim surveys—which asked respondents whether they had been victimized by crime—indicated that the group most at risk of crime victimization was young males, not women. When criminologists' attention did turn to crimes like rape, the focus was on the small group of men who had been convicted and incarcerated for the offence, and these men were typically understood as an abnormal and pathological group. Much of traditional criminology, then, tended to mirror the cultural construction of rape. In his "classic" study of forcible rape, for example, Amir (1967, 1971) introduced the notion of "victim precipitation." The concept suggests that some women are "rape prone" (because of their "bad" reputation) and that others invite rape through their "negligent and reckless" behaviour (by going to bars or hitchhiking) or their failure to react strongly enough to sexual overtures. Amir's work essentially blamed the woman for the violence she encountered.

Breaking the Silence

In combination, the absence of societal, legal, and academic concern about the issue of male violence against women had the effect of silencing women. One of the main goals of the women's movement as it gained momentum in the 1970s was to break this silence. As women came together to share their stories, and with increasing efforts devoted to provide support and services to women (such as rape crisis centres, crisis lines, and shelters for abused women), it soon became evident that the incidence of sexual violence far exceeded what was reported in crime statistics. In 1980, for example, the Canadian Advisory Council on the Status of Women (CACSW) estimated that one in every 5 Canadian women would be sexually assaulted at some point in her life and that one in every 17 would be subjected to forced sexual intercourse. Yet only one in 10 sexual assaults was ever reported to the police (Kinnon, 1981). That same year, the CACSW released its report, *Wife Battering in Canada: The Vicious Circle*. MacLeod (1980), the report's author, estimated that every year, one in 10 Canadian women who is married or in a relationship with a live-in partner is battered. Yet when this finding was reported in the House of Commons (on May 12, 1982), it was met with laughter from members of Parliament. Public outrage ensued, and over the next decade, wife abuse was gradually transformed from a "private trouble" into a "public issue."

The growing awareness of male violence against women led to pressures for legislative reform. Two major changes occurred in 1983. First, the old rape law was repealed and three new categories were added to the offence of assault: sexual assault (s. 246.1); sexual assault with a weapon, threats to a third party, and bodily harm (s. 246.2); and aggravated sexual assault (s. 246.3). Under this new legislation, husbands could now be charged with sexually assaulting their wives, limitations were placed on the ability of the defence to ask questions about the past sexual history of the complainant, the corroboration requirement was dropped, the doctrine of recent complaint was formally removed, and there was provision for a publication ban on any disclosure of the identity of the complainant. These changes were designed to redress the apparent gender inequities in the law and to reduce the trauma experienced by the complainant during the trial in an attempt to encourage the reporting of cases. Second, a national directive was issued to encourage police to lay charges in wife assault cases (previously, the decision was left to the wishes of the complainant) and police training was upgraded to emphasize sensitive interventions in cases of wife assault. These reforms led to increases in the number of charges for domestic assault. In Winnipeg, for instance, there were 629 domestic assault charges laid in 1983; by 1989, the number had increased to 1,137 charges laid (Ursel, 1994).

The Montreal Massacre

The reality of violence against women was made most evident on December 6, 1989, when a gunman entered a classroom at the École Polytechnique in Montreal, separated the men from the women students, declared, "You're all a bunch of feminists," and proceeded to gun them down. Fourteen women were killed that day and 13 others wounded. The gunman's suicide letter explicitly identified his action as politically motivated: he blamed "feminists" for the major disappointments in his life. Police also found a "hit list" containing the names of prominent women (see Box 6.4). The Montreal Massacre served to reinforce what women's groups across the country had been arguing for decades: that violence against women is a widespread and pervasive feature of our society. It takes many forms, including sexual harassment in the workplace, date rape, violent sexual assaults, incest, and wife abuse.

While the murder of 14 women in Montreal has understandably received the attention it deserves, it is also noteworthy that the violence women encounter at the hands of men has become "routine." In 1993, Statistics Canada released the findings of the Violence Against Women Survey (VAWS). The first national survey of its kind anywhere in the world, the VAWS included responses from 12,300 women (see Johnson, 1996). Using definitions of physical and sexual assault consistent with the Canadian Criminal Code, the survey found that half (51%) of Canadian women had experienced at least one incident of physical or sexual violence since the age of 16. The survey also confirmed the results of other research in finding that women face the greatest risk of violence from men they know. "Almost one-half (45%) of all women experienced violence by men known to them (dates, boyfriends, marital partners, friends, family, neighbours, etc.), while 23% of women experienced violence by a stranger (17% reported violence by both strangers and known men)" (Statistics Canada, 1993, 2). The VAWS also found that 29 percent (or 3 in 10) of ever-married women had been assaulted by a spouse.

Missing and Murdered Women

The gendered *and* racialized nature of violence has become more of a public issue now that attention has begun to focus on the numbers of missing and murdered women in Canada. In 2004, Amnesty International published a report, *Stolen Sisters*, that called attention to the violence encountered by Aboriginal women and pointed to the role that cultural and systemic discrimination played in perpetuating this violence, thereby impeding their basic human right to be safe and free from violence. The report noted that Aboriginal women are

FOCUS

Box 6.4

A TIME FOR GRIEF AND PAIN

Montreal

Fourteen women are dead for one reason: they are women. Their male classmates are still alive for one reason: they are men. While gender divides us in thousands of ways every day, rarely are the consequences of misogyny so tragic.

I found out about the murders early yesterday morning. I came home from dinner with friends about 1 a.m., and listened as usual to my answering machine. It was the last message that gave me a jolt. It was a good friend telling me that there would be a vigil last night for the 14 women who had been killed at the University of Montreal.

Not believing my ears and desperate for news, I turned on the radio. I ended up listening to an open-line show. The talk was about relationships between young men and women these days.

Most of the callers were men. They blamed the murders on everything from drugs and condom distributors in high schools to women who have made men feel insecure. Many callers said they did not understand what had happened. It's all very well and fine to be misogynous, said one caller, but you can't lose your head.

I realized, as I was listening to this show, that I was trembling. So were the voices of the female callers. I felt something I had not experienced in a long time: fear of being alone in my apartment. There were sounds at the window I would normally ignore. Now I could not. Immobilized, I was afraid to stay alone and afraid to go out.

It does not matter that the man who decided to kill 14 women—and he clearly did decide to do that—killed himself afterward; it is not of him I am afraid. I am afraid of what he represents, of all the unspoken hatred, the pent-up anger that he expressed. Hatred and anger that is shared by every husband who beats his wife, every man who rapes his date, every father who abuses his child, and by many more who would not dare.

It happened at the École Polytechnique in Montreal but it could have been anywhere.

It would be a great mistake, I think, to see this incident as some kind of freak accident, the act of a madman that has nothing to do with the society in which we live. The killer was angry at women, at feminism, at his own loss of power. He yelled: "You're all a bunch of feminists" on his way to killing 14 women.

Now there is little that is comforting to say to women. It is a time for grief for all of us; grief for those who have died, and pain at being reminded of how deep misogyny still runs in our society.

Source: Diana Bronson, "A Time for Grief and Pain," *Globe and Mail*, December 8, 1989, A7. Reprinted with permission of the author.

---

five times more likely to die as a result of violence (23). It also documented many of the cases of missing and murdered women—including the disappearance of women from the streets of Vancouver's Downtown Eastside. In 2005 the Native Women's Association of Canada (NWAC) launched the *Sisters in Spirit* initiative, which was aimed at addressing the root causes, circumstances, and trends of missing and murdered Aboriginal women and girls. By March 2010, NWAC had gathered information about the disappearance or death of more than 580 Aboriginal women and girls across Canada (NWAC, 2010). A more recent database compiled by the RCMP has increased that figure to 1,181 missing or murdered Aboriginal women and girls (RCMP, 2014).

Between 1978 and 1992, some 60 women, many of them Aboriginal and involved in the street sex trade, were reported to have vanished from Vancouver's Downtown Eastside, known as Canada's "poorest postal code." As Hugill (2010) notes, however, Vancouver's crisis of missing and murdered women generated very little interest on the part of the media and the criminal justice system prior to 1998, and it was not until 2001 that police formed a Missing Women Joint Task Force to investigate these cases. In February 2002 this new unit raided the Port Coquitlam pig farm of Robert Pickton, who was eventually charged with the murder of 27 women. In December 2007 he was

SEARCH FOR:
Native Women's Association of Canada

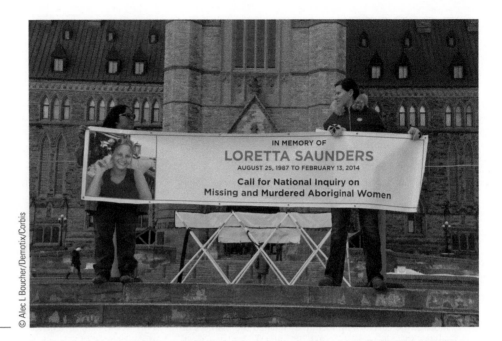

Many protesters across the country have demanded a government inquiry into hundreds of murdered and missing Aboriginal women.

convicted of the second-degree murder of six women and sentenced to life imprisonment.

Events such as these confirm that male violence against women continues to be a serious social problem in Canadian society. They also raise concerns about the effectiveness of the criminal justice system in responding to this pressing problem.

Recent History of Law's Response to Violence Against Women

As the 1990s unfolded, many feminists became uncertain as to whether engaging with the criminal justice system to combat male violence against women was having the desired outcome. With respect to sexual assault, it appeared that the phallocentric myths and stereotypes surrounding rape were continuing to pervade the practice of law. Some judges, for instance, were making statements in court that suggested their decisions were being influenced by these myths. In a British Columbia case heard in 1991, the judge made the following statement in his written decision: "The mating practice, if I may call it that, is less than a precise relationship. At times no may mean maybe, or wait awhile" (*R v Letendre*, cited in Boyle, 1994, 141). In June 1998, an Alberta Court of Appeal judge upheld a lower court's acquittal of a man charged with sexually assaulting a 17-year-old girl. In his decision, the judge commented on the clothing worn by the young woman (a T-shirt and shorts), noting, "It must be pointed out that the complainant did not present herself to [the accused] in a bonnet and crinolines" (*R v Ewanchuk*, 1999). Several decisions by the Supreme Court of Canada also raised concerns over the law's treatment of sexual assault cases.

In a 1991 ruling on the cases of *Seaboyer* and *Gayme (R v Seaboyer*, 1991), the Supreme Court struck down section 276 of the Criminal Code. Known as the "rape shield" provision, section 276 was included in the 1983 sexual assault law with the aim of preventing a woman's sexual conduct from being used to discredit her testimony. The Supreme Court ruled that, while laudable in its intent, the provision went too far and could deny the accused the right to a fair trial. Critics took exception to this decision because it left the question of whether evidence of the complainant's past sexual history would be admissible in court to the discretion of the trial judge. In response, Parliament introduced Bill C-49 in 1992, which was designed to amend the 1983 sexual assault legislation.

Under this new legislation, the rules of evidence now state that evidence that the complainant had previously engaged in sexual activity, whether with the accused or with any other person, is not admissible to support an inference that the complainant was either more likely to have consented to the sexual activity in question or was less worthy of belief. Also, a new test for judges has been provided for determining whether a complainant's sexual history may be admitted at trial. Bill C-49 also provided a definition of "consent" as it applies to sexual assault cases—"the voluntary agreement of the complainant to engage in the sexual activity in question" (s. 243.1 (1))—and specified the conditions under which there is "no consent" (for instance, where the complainant is incapable of consenting to the activity by reason of intoxication or where the complainant expresses, by words or conduct, a lack of agreement to engage in the activity). The bill also placed restrictions on the defences available to those accused of sexual assault: the onus was now on the accused to show that he or she took "reasonable steps" in the circumstances to ascertain that the complainant was consenting [s. 273.2 (b)].

The Supreme Court's ruling in *R v O'Connor* (1995) had even more profound implications for survivors of sexual assault. Bishop O'Connor was a priest and principal at a residential school near Williams Lake, British Columbia, where four Aboriginal women attended and worked. In 1991, the women laid charges of rape and indecent assault against O'Connor for incidents that occurred at the school between 1961 and 1967. The charges were stayed by the trial judge in 1992 when the Crown failed to release to the defence counsel the women's residential school records and all therapy and medical records since the time they had left the school (none of these records were in the Crown's possession). When the case reached the Supreme Court, the Court overturned the stay and ordered a new trial for O'Connor, but gave exceptionally large scope to defence access to complainants' records held by third parties. After the Court's decision, women's shelters and rape crisis centres found themselves being subpoenaed to turn over all files and counselling records relating to cases before the courts, and criminal defence lawyers were being advised by their association that they would be "negligent" if they did not subpoena complainant's files (Busby, 1997).

The Supreme Court's ruling in *O'Connor* meant that confidential records, as well as personal diaries, letters, and the like, could now all be accessed. The ruling had special implications for the work of therapists and rape crisis counsellors, who could now be required to hand over any and all records or notes relating to a complainant in a sexual assault case. Critics noted that such materials are not designed to be a written record of allegations; they are maintained for therapeutic, not evidentiary, purposes. For example, one of the issues regularly dealt with in therapy sessions is the need to explore feelings of guilt or shame that a woman may experience after a rape. In the hands of the court, this could be taken as evidence of "consent" or "complicity" on the part of the woman. To this extent, the *O'Connor* decision supports the old rape myths: that women lie or make false allegations and that they cannot be trusted. One of the main effects of the ruling was the silencing of women. Women who were sexually assaulted now had to decide whether they would seek counselling or initiate criminal prosecution of their assailant (Busby, 1997, 2006).

In May 1997, in response to concerns raised over the *O'Connor* decision, Parliament passed Bill C-46 to limit the access of defendants to confidential records of complainants in sexual assault cases. The bill established more restrictive grounds for access, required the defence to establish that the records were relevant to the case at hand, and restricted the disclosure to those parts that were important to the case. Only a few months after its passage, the legislation was constitutionally challenged as a violation of the fair trial guarantees of the Charter and struck down by two lower courts. In 1999 the Supreme Court rendered its decision on this question in *R v Mills* (1999). While the Court held that the legislation governing the disclosure of records did not violate an accused's constitutional rights, some commentators, such as Gotell (2001, 340), argued that the decision did tame the meaning of the legislation: "To the extent that this decision eases the statutory test for disclosure put in place by Bill C-46, Canada remains a jurisdiction where women's claims of sexual violation can be discounted through records production."

More recently, in February 2011, a Manitoba judge came under heavy criticism for his decision to sentence a man convicted of sexual assault to a conditional sentence of two years less a day. The assault by the 40-year-old man against a 26-year-old Aboriginal woman had taken place along a darkened highway near Thompson, Manitoba, in 2006. The Crown had argued for a three-year prison sentence, but the judge disagreed, saying that the man's actions "had the characteristics of a clumsy Don Juan" and that "this is a case of misunderstood signals and inconsiderate behaviour" (*R v Rhodes* 2011). The judge also described the situation as one in which "sex was in the air," in that the man and his friend had met the woman and her girlfriend that night outside a bar under "inviting circumstances." He also noted that the women were wearing tube tops with no bra, high heels, and make-up. The trial judge's decision was overturned on appeal, and after a retrial, the man received a sentence of three years' imprisonment. Nevertheless, the announcement of the initial decision, which came just one week after a Toronto police officer apologized for telling a crowd of university students at a safety session not to "dress like sluts" if they wanted to avoid being raped (Anderssen, 2011), led critics to suggest that the cultural construction of rape was still very much in operation.

This recent history of the law's treatment of sexual assault highlights a number of tensions. For one, there appears to be tension between the courts, whose decisions become binding as case law, and Parliament, which, in passing statute law, has endeavoured to be sensitive to the concerns raised by women's constituencies across the country. For another, there is a tension within the law with regard to competing rights, in particular, the right of a defendant to a fair trial compared to the right of a complainant to privacy. Clearly, the extent to which the legal system will be able to resolve these tensions and thereby offer women and men equal protection and treatment under the law is a matter of ongoing debate.

Although the national directive to police forces in 1983 resulted in increasing numbers of domestic assault charges entering the criminal justice system, several provinces took further steps to respond to the problem of wife assault. In Winnipeg, for example, a specialized Family Violence Court was established in 1990. The number of spousal assault cases dealt with by this court rose from 1,302 in 1990–91 to 3,543 in 1993–94, a 172 percent increase (Ursel, 1998). A large part of this increase was attributable to the implementation of a zero tolerance policy on domestic violence by the Winnipeg Police Service in 1993. Under this policy, police were instructed to lay a charge when there were reasonable grounds to believe that a domestic assault has occurred, whether or not the victim wished to proceed with the matter and even in circumstances where there were no visible injuries or independent witnesses. The zero tolerance policy resulted in increasing numbers of men—and women—being charged. However, a high proportion of charges resulted in a dismissal or stay of proceedings. One Winnipeg study, for instance, found that 80 percent of charges against women and 51 percent of those against men were subsequently stayed by the Crown (Comack, Chopyk, and Wood, 2000). While the intent of this more rigorous charging protocol was to assist victims of domestic violence (who are predominantly women), zero tolerance opened the way for "double-charging" to occur—that is, both partners ended up being charged with an offence when police were called to the scene. Comack and colleagues found that double-charging occurred in 55 percent of the cases they studied involving women accused and in 10 percent of those cases involving men. Stays of proceedings were even higher in these cases (88 percent and 70 percent, respectively). Wood (2001) found that the zero tolerance charging appeared to have a racialized impact. Prior to 1993, white men had been more likely than Aboriginal men to be charged with domestic violence, but after the implementation of the police protocol in 1993, Aboriginal men were more likely to be charged with domestic violence. In a similar vein, other researchers have showcased the differential impacts of mandatory charging and no-drop prosecutorial policies on immigrant and refugee women, particularly those with precarious legal status (Martin and Mosher, 1995). In sum, while the changes that have occurred within the criminal justice system have a symbolic value—they carry a strong message of society's unwillingness to tolerate wife abuse—feminists have questioned whether system, which is punitive and adversarial by nature, is the most effective means for combating the problem (see, for example, Snider, 1991, 1994).

Blurred Boundaries: Women as Victims and Offenders

Breaking the silence around male violence against women has had an impact on how feminist criminologists understand the lives of criminalized women. Clearly, violence against women both reflects and reinforces women's inequality

SEARCH FOR:
Canadian Association of
Elizabeth Fry Societies

in society in relation to men. As *The War Against Women* (1991, 9) report noted, "The vulnerability of women to violence is integrally linked to the social, economic and political inequalities women experience as part of their daily lives." How, then, does this gender-based violence figure in the lives of criminalized women?

Several studies carried out in the 1990s revealed the extent of abuse experienced by criminalized women. Research conducted for the Task Force on Federally Sentenced Women, for instance, found that 68 percent of women serving a federal term of imprisonment in Canada had been physically abused as children or adults and that 53 percent had been sexually abused at some point in their lives. Among Aboriginal women, the figures were considerably higher: 90 percent said they had been physically abused and 61 percent reported sexual abuse (Shaw et al., 1991, vii and 31). Another study of women in a provincial jail found that 78 percent of the women admitted over a six-year period reported a history of physical and sexual abuse (Comack, 1993).

Qualitative research conducted by feminist criminologists explored women's accounts of their lawbreaking and its connections to abuse (see, for example, Gilfus, 1992; Adelberg and Currie, 1993; Sommers, 1995; Ritchie, 1996). *Women in Trouble* (Comack, 1996) was built around the stories of 24 women who were incarcerated in a provincial jail. The women's stories revealed the connections between a woman's law violations and her history of abuse to be complex. Sometimes the connections are direct, as in the case of women who are criminalized for resisting their abusers. Janice, for instance, was serving a sentence for manslaughter. The offence occurred at a party:

> I was at a party, and this guy, older guy, came, came on to me. He tried telling me, "Why don't you go to bed with me. I'm getting some money, you know." And I said, "No." And then he started hitting me. And then he raped me. And then [pause] I lost it. Like, I just, I went, I got very angry and I snapped. And I started hitting him. I threw a coffee table on top of his head and then I stabbed him. (Janice, cited in Comack, 1996, 96)

Sometimes the connections become discernable only once a woman's law violations are located in the context of her struggle to cope with the abuse and its effects. Merideth, for example, had a long history of abuse that began with her father sexually assaulting her as a young child and that extended to several violent relationships with the men in her life. She was imprisoned for writing cheques on her bank account when she didn't have the money to cover them. The cheques were used to purchase "new things to keep my mind off the abuse":

> I've never had any kind of conflict with the law. [long pause] When I started dealing with all these different things, then I started having problems. And then I took it out in the form of fraud. (Merideth, cited in Comack, 1996, 86)

Sometimes the connections are even more entangled, as in the case of women who end up on the street, where abuse and law violation become enmeshed in their ongoing, everyday struggle to survive. Brenda had this to say about street life:

Street life is a, it's a power game, you know? Street life? You have to show you're tough. You have to beat up this broad or you have to shank this person, or, you know, you're always carrying guns, you always have blow on you, you always have drugs on you, and you're always working the streets with the pimps and the bikers, you know? That, that alone, you know, it has so much fucking abuse, it has more abuse than what you were brought up with! . . . I find living on the street I went through more abuse than I did at home. (Brenda, cited in Comack, 1996, 105–6)

This kind of work subsequently became known as pathways research— a term that has been applied to a variety of different studies, all of them sharing the effort to better understand the lives of women and girls and the particular features that led to their criminal activity (see, for example, Chesney-Lind and Rodriguez, 1983; Miller, 1986; Arnold, 1995; Heimer, 1995; Chesney-Lind and Shelden, 1998). In drawing the connections between women's law violations and their histories of abuse, pathways research led to a blurring of boundaries between "offender" and "victim" and raised questions about the legal logic of individual culpability and law's strict adherence to the victim/offender dualism in the processing of cases (not only for women but also for poor, racialized men; see Comack and Balfour, 2004). It also had a decided influence on advocacy work conducted on behalf of imprisoned women. For instance, *Creating Choices*, the 1990 report of the Canadian Task Force on Federally Sentenced Women, proposed a new prison regime for women that would incorporate feminist principles and attend to women's needs (see Shaw, 1993; Hannah-Moffat and Shaw, 2000; Hannah-Moffat, 2001; Hayman, 2006). The near-complete absence of counselling services and other resources designed to help women overcome victimization experiences (see Kendall, 1993) figured prominently in the Task Force's recommendations.

THE CANADIAN PRESS/The Waterloo Region Record–David Bebee

Grand Valley Institution for Women near Kitchener-Waterloo is one of the new prisons for women built by the federal government in recent years.

As Snider (2003, 364) notes, feminist criminologists succeeded in reconstituting the criminalized woman as the "woman in trouble." Less violent and less dangerous than her male counterpart, she was more deserving of help than punishment. When women did engage in violence, it was understood as a self-defensive reaction typically committed in a domestic context (Browne, 1987; Dobash and Dobash, 1992; Jones, 1994). Nevertheless, while the concept of blurred boundaries and the construct of the woman in trouble were important feminist contributions to criminology, they had particular ramifications for the ability of feminist criminologists to counter competing knowledge claims—ones founded on representations of women not as victims but as violent and dangerous.

The Violent Woman

One decisive event that challenged the blurred boundaries between victim and offender was the Karla Homolka case. In July 1993, Homolka was sentenced to 12 years in prison for her part in the deaths of two teenage girls, Kristen French and Leslie Mahaffy. Homolka's sentence was part of a plea bargain reached with the Crown in exchange for her testimony against her husband, Paul Bernardo. The Crown had entered into this plea bargain prior to the discovery of six homemade videotapes that documented the sexual abuse and torture of the pair's victims—including Homolka's younger sister, Tammy. Bernardo was subsequently convicted of first-degree murder, kidnapping, aggravated sexual assault, forcible confinement, and offering an indignity to a dead body. He was sentenced to life imprisonment in September 1995 (McGillivray, 1998, 257).

During Bernardo's trial, the real challenge came in trying to explain the role of Homolka, the prosecution's key witness. As Boritch (1997, 2) notes, "Among the various professionals who commented on the case, there was a general agreement that, as far as serial murderers go, there was little that was unusual or mysterious about Bernardo. We have grown used to hearing about male serial murderers." Homolka, however, was the central enigma of the drama that unfolded, transforming the trial into an international, high-profile media event.

The legal documents and media accounts of the case offered two primary readings of Homolka. The first reading constructed her as a battered wife, one of Bernardo's many victims (he had also been exposed as "the Scarborough rapist"). A girlish 17-year-old when she met the 23-year-old Bernardo, Homolka had entered into a relationship that progressed to a fairytale wedding (complete with horse-drawn carriage) and ended with a severe battering (complete with darkened and bruised raccoon eyes). According to this first reading, Homolka was under her husband's control and had no agency of her own. Like other women who find themselves in an abusive relationship, she was cast as a victim and diagnosed as suffering from the battered woman syndrome, a psychological condition of "learned helplessness" that ostensibly prevents abused women from leaving the relationship (Walker, 1979, 1987). The representation of Homolka as a battered wife and "compliant victim" of her sexually sadistic husband (Hazelwood, Warren, and Dietz, 1993) was meant to bolster her credibility as a prosecution witness and validate her plea bargain. This first reading was met with strong resistance in the media and public discourse, leading to the second reading. Journalist Patricia Pearson (1995), for one, vigorously countered the picture of "Homolka as victim" and instead demonized her as a "competitive narcissist" willing to offer up innocent victims (including her own sister) to appease the sexual desires of her sociopathic husband. Despite their divergent viewpoints, both of these readings relied on the discourse of the "psy-professions" (psychology, psychotherapy, and psychiatry) to make sense of Homolka.

Feminist criminologists countered both of these readings. For instance, they pointed out that women are seldom charged with murder and that when they do kill, they are most likely to kill their male partner. Also, while Homolka's middle-class background and lifestyle set her apart from the vast majority of women charged with criminal offences, her efforts to conform to the standard feminine script (dyed blonde hair, fairytale wedding) put her in company with a host of other women. But these claims were seldom heard. Instead, the cry that "Women are violent, too!" grew louder, even to the point of arguing that women's violence was quantitatively and qualitatively equal to that of men.

In a widely publicized book, *When She Was Bad: Violent Women and the Myth of Innocence*, Pearson (1997; see also Dutton, 1994; Laframboise, 1996) argued not only that "women are violent, too" but also that their violence can be just as "nasty" as men's. Following on the footsteps of the 1950s criminologist Otto Pollak, Pearson (20–21) suggested that women's violence is more masked and underhanded than men's violence: women kill their babies, arrange for their husbands' murders, beat up on their lovers, and commit serial murders in hospitals and boarding houses. Nevertheless, argued Pearson (61), when their crimes are discovered, women are more likely to receive lenient treatment from a chivalrous criminal justice system. In a fashion that hearkened back to other early criminologists, Pearson (1997, 210) also stated: "Female prisoners are not peace activists or nuns who were kidnapped off the street and stuck in jail. They are miscreants, intemperate, wilful and rough."

Pearson drew support for her position from studies that use the Conflict Tactics Scale (CTS) to measure abuse in intimate relationships. Developed by US researcher Murray Straus and his colleagues (Straus, 1979; Straus, Gelles, and Steinmetz, 1980), the scale is a quantitative instrument that consists of 18 items and measures three different ways of handling interpersonal conflict in intimate relationships: reasoning, verbal aggression, and physical violence. The scale categorizes items on a continuum from least to most severe (for example, "discussed an issue calmly" and "cried" to "threw something," "hit with a fist," and "used a knife or a gun"). Respondents are asked how frequently they perpetrated each act in the course of conflicts or disagreements with their partner within the past year, and how frequently they were on the receiving end. These self-reports of perpetration and victimization are then used to construct estimates of the rate of violence used by male and female partners. Most criminologists who have employed the CTS have found equivalent rates of violence by women and men (Steinmetz, 1981; Straus and Gelles, 1986; Brinkerhoff and

Lupri, 1988; Kennedy and Dutton, 1989). Such findings have led to the conclusion that there is a sexual symmetry in intimate violence; that is, that women are just as violent as men.

Despite the scale's popularity, however, it has been heavily criticized (see, for example, DeKeseredy and Hinch, 1991; Dobash et al., 1992; Schwartz and DeKeseredy, 1993; Johnson, 1996). Criminologists have noted that the CTS is an incomplete measure of intimate violence for the following reasons:

- It measures only incidents of violence and thus ignores the social context of the violence (such as whether a woman is acting in self-defence).

- It situates items only in the context of settling quarrels or disputes and thus misses assaults that "come out of the blue" or are motivated by the desire to control another person.

- It relies on self-reports of violence and may thereby underestimate the incidence of violence by males (who are more likely to under-report).

- It fails to make adequate distinctions between the severity of different forms of violence (for example, "tried to hit with something" is defined as "severe," while "slapped" is defined as "minor").

- It does not capture the outcome of the violence (for example, the degree of injury incurred by the participants).

Pearson, however, argued that these methodological concerns amount to unwarranted attacks by feminists and their supporters, who were invested in a gender dichotomy of men as evil and women as good. In this regard, unlike earlier, conservative-minded criminologists, Pearson asserted that women were no different from men. While feminists were intent on gendering violence by drawing its connections to patriarchy, Pearson (1997, 232) was adamant that violence be *de-gendered*: violence was simply a "human, rather than gendered, phenomena," a conscious choice, a means of solving problems or releasing frustration by "a responsible actor imposing her will upon the world" (23).

The claims made by writers like Pearson, in combination with the difficulties encountered with using the CTS as a measure of violence between intimate partners, led feminist criminologists to seek alternative strategies for determining whether, in fact, women are "men's equals" in violence. To explore qualitative differences in men's and women's violence, for example, Vanessa Chopyk, Linda Wood, and I drew a random sample of 1,002 cases from police incident reports involving men and women charged with violent crime in Winnipeg over a five-year period at the beginning of the 1990s. While studies that use the CTS have concluded that a sexual symmetry exists in intimate violence (men are as likely as women to be victims of abuse, and women are as likely as men to be perpetrators of both minor and serious acts of violence), we found that a different picture emerged in police incident reports (Comack, Chopyk, and Wood, 2000, 2008). First, the violence tactics used by men and women differed in their seriousness. Men were more likely to use physical strength or force against their female partners, while women were more likely to resort to throwing objects (such as TV remote controls) during the course of a violent event. Second, female partners of men accused of violence used violence themselves in only 23 percent of the cases, while male partners of women accused of violence used violence in 65 percent of the cases. This finding suggests that the violence that occurs between intimate partners is not "mutual combat." Third, almost one-half (48%) of the women accused—as opposed to only 7 percent of the men accused—in partner events were injured during the course of the event, adding weight to the argument that violent events between men and women are not symmetrical.

Finally, in incidents involving partners, it was the accused woman who called the police in 35 percent of the cases involving a female accused, compared with only 7 percent in those involving a male accused. If we interpret calls to the police as a form of "help-seeking behaviour" on the part of someone in trouble, this finding suggests that in more than one-third of the cases involving a woman accused, she was the one who perceived the need for help. Nevertheless, the woman ended up being charged with a criminal offence.

These findings are supported by data from the General Social Survey conducted by Statistics Canada, which show that the scope and severity of spousal violence is more severe for women than for men. Female victims of spousal violence were more than twice as likely as male victims to be injured (42% versus 18%). Women were almost seven times more likely to fear for their lives (33% versus 5%) and almost three times as likely to be the targets of more than 10 violent episodes (20% versus 7%) (Mahony, 2011, 10). In countering the arguments made by writers like Pearson, then, feminist criminologists placed the issue of women's violence and aggression in a different context (see also Chan, 2001; Mann, 2003; Morrissey, 2003; Comack and Brickey, 2007).

While women are certainly capable of violence, these findings suggest that they are not "men's equals." Writers like Pearson are to be credited for pointing to the "culture of victimhood" that is produced when feminists rest their understandings on dualistic constructions such as "victim versus offender." Yet in her efforts to call attention to women's capacity for violence, Pearson goes to the other extreme. By casting women as scheming, underhanded manipulators who engage in violence "to defend their aspirations, their identity and their place on the stage" (Pearson, 1997, 20), she effectively replaces the "men as evil" image that she so roundly criticizes feminists for with a "woman as evil" imagery.

TABLE 6.1   **Theories of Women's Crime**

Theory	Theorists	Key Elements
Early theorists	Lombroso/Ferrero, Thomas, Glueck/Glueck, Pollak	Women's "inherent nature" and their natural inferiority to men account for the nature and extent of their criminality.
Sex role socialization	Hoffman-Bustamante	Differential socialization of females is reflected in the types of offences they commit and the nature of their participation in crime.
Power-control theory	Hagan/Simpson/Gillis	Gender differences in delinquency can be explained by variations in parental control. Girls in patriarchal families will be less free to deviate than those in egalitarian families.
Women's liberation thesis	Adler, Simon	Women's changing gender roles are reflected in the nature and extent of their criminal involvement. Women are becoming "more like men"—more aggressive and violent—and have greater opportunities to commit crime.
Intersectionality theories	Carlen, Chesney-Lind, Comack, Daly, Gilfus, Morris, Naffine	Structured inequalities of class, race, and gender (including experiences of male violence) condition and constrain the lives of criminalized women.

◯ **Gendering Crime**

The feminist critique of criminology and the effort to draw attention to the gendered nature of women's lives led to calls to "gender" crime more broadly. Women, it was argued, were not the only ones with a gender; men's lives too needed to be understood in gendered terms. In this regard, critics pointed out that while criminology had long been characterized by its neglect of the female, the discipline's ability to explain male patterns of criminal activity were just as troublesome. Since the 1990s, various criminologists have responded by initiating studies of men, masculinity, and crime.

One criminologist who has taken up this project is Messerschmidt (1993, 1997, 2004, 2012). In his endeavour to contribute to a "feminist theory of gendered crime" (1993, 62), Messerschmidt designed a theory that situates men's involvement in crime in the context of "doing" masculinity. Following on the work of West and Zimmerman (1987), gender is viewed as a "situated accomplishment." While sex is the social identification of individuals as man or woman, gender is the accomplishment of that identification in social interaction: "we coordinate our activities to 'do' gender in situational ways" (1993, 79). In the process, individuals realize that their behaviour is accountable to others and so construct their actions "in relation to how they might be interpreted by others in the particular social context in which they occur" (1993, 79). In a culture that believes there are but two sexes—male and female—this accountability will involve living up to the gender ideals that have been tied to each sex—that is, behaving "as a man" or "as a woman" would in a given social situation. Because we accomplish masculinity and femininity in specific situations (though not necessarily in circumstances of our own choosing), these are never static or finished products.

Messerschmidt borrows the concept of "hegemonic masculinity" from the work of Connell (1987, 1995, 2000). Connell was interested in how a particular gender order—a "historically constructed pattern of power relations between men and women and definitions of femininity and masculinity" (Connell, 1987, 98–99)—comes to be reproduced in society. Connell suggested that male dominance in the gender order is achieved through the ascendancy of a particular idealized form of masculinity that is culturally glorified, honoured, and exalted. Hegemonic masculinity therefore references not just a set of role expectations or identity; it is a "pattern of practice" (Connell and Messerschmidt, 2005, 832). Different from a male sex role, this cultural ideal may not correspond with the actual personalities of the majority of men, and it may well not be "normal" in a statistical sense, for only a minority of men may enact it. In these terms, exemplars such as sports heroes, movie stars, and even fantasy figures (such as Rambo and The Terminator) offer representations of masculinity that come to be normative in the sense that they embody "the currently most honored way of being a man." This requires all other men to position themselves in relation to these representations (Connell and Messerschmidt, 2005, 832).

Messerschmidt argues that it is in the process of "doing" masculinity that men simultaneously construct forms of criminality. He explains: "Because

hegemonic masculinity
A particular idealized form of masculinity that is culturally glorified, honoured, and exalted. For example, associating "the masculine" with physical strength, aggression, independence, ambition, lack of emotion, and heterosexuality.

types of criminality are possible only when particular social conditions present themselves, when other masculine resources are unavailable, particular types of crime can provide an alternative resource for accomplishing gender and, therefore, affirming a particular type of masculinity" (1993, 84). Messerschmidt subsequently put his theory to work to understand varieties of youth crime, street crime, corporate crime, sexual harassment in the workplace, wife beating, and rape (Messerschmidt, 1993). Key to his analysis is the thesis that gendered power is central to understanding why men commit more crimes and more serious crimes than women: crime is one practice in which and through which men's power over women can be established, and the different types of crime men may commit are determined by the power relations among them (1993, 84).

QUESTIONS FOR CRITICAL THINKING

1. How does the way in which the "difference" between men and women is understood influence our understanding of women's involvement in crime?
2. How does making gender a central focus of criminological inquiry affect the ways in which criminologists study men's involvement in crime?
3. Is use of the criminal justice system the most effective strategy for responding to the problem of violence against women?

Summary

- One of the primary aims of the feminist engagement with criminology has been to bring women into view. This has involved a re-evaluation of the accumulated knowledge about criminalized women, the nature of their offending, and the claims made about their "differences" from males. In the process, mainstream criminologists have been forced to consider how their traditional subject matter—men and male criminality—has influenced their theories and research.

- Feminist criminologists have argued that understanding women's involvement in crime requires an awareness of the larger social context, specifically, the structured inequalities of class, race, and gender that condition and constrain the lives of criminalized women.

- Breaking the silence around male violence against women has meant questioning the ways in which societal and legal responses reinforce and reproduce the problem.

- Making women more visible in criminology requires not simply letting women into the mainstream of the discipline but developing alternative ways of conceptualizing and studying the social world so that the interests and concerns of both men and women are included. In the process, the criminological enterprise is itself transformed.

NET WORK

Are you interested in finding more information about the issues of domestic violence and sexual assault? To find a variety of sites that deal with these issues, first visit the Canadian Women's Virtual Information Centre home page at www.womennet.ca. Here you will find various links to domestic violence sites and sites dealing with sexual assault. Using these links or any of the links found throughout this chapter, answer the following questions:

1. Describe some of the programs that are offered in Canada to serve survivors of domestic violence and sexual assault.
2. Identify some of the controversies concerning domestic violence. Can you find sites on the Internet that present different perspectives on this problem? How can you assess the validity of the information presented on different websites?

Victimology, Victim Services, and Victim Rights in Canada

7

Irvin Waller
UNIVERSITY OF OTTAWA

For centuries, the traditional system of law enforcement, criminal justice, and corrections has focused on catching, convicting, and, in some cases, fining or incarcerating offenders. The role of the victim has been limited to calling the police, collaborating with the police investigation when asked, and acting as a witness in the court case. But the conversation is shifting as federal, provincial and municipal governments begin to focus on prevention of harm to victims and providing services and rights for victims of crime.

Many criminologists blame political pressure from victims of crime for the increases in incarceration that politicians have implemented, particularly in the United States, over the past four decades. In Canada, the federal government has justified its actions as giving precedence to the rights of victims of crime over the rights of offenders. The government has focused on increasing penalties, particularly for those serving long sentences; but it has also established the Ombudsman for Crime Victims, and in 2014, it introduced a Bill of Rights for Victims.

Victimologists argue that offering empathy and expanding services and rights for victims of crime would decrease the desire of victims for punishment. They also stress that crime victims' rights would be upheld most strongly if governments invested in effective ways to *prevent* victimization; this would best be achieved by governments investing in proven prevention methods and moving away from ineffective and costly responses to crime such as reactive policing, mass incarceration, and long prison sentences.

Victims of crime are often described as the orphans of criminal justice. They are also the orphans of criminology. Many criminology students still graduate without having learned what we know about victims or about the needs and human rights of victims. This means students may be misled by many myths about victims, including the extent to which victims actually want more severe punishment.

Learning Objectives

After reading this chapter, you should be able to

- Discuss the risk of being a victim of crime and comprehend the key components of the harm suffered by victims of crime.
- Outline the way in which the traditional system of police, courts, and corrections in Canada limits the role of the victim to complainant and witness.

NEL

- Identify the key laws and international standards that provide the vision for the shift from the traditional criminal justice system to a system that embraces the needs and human rights of victims.

- Propose specific and basic ways for police to meet the needs of victims, including victims of gender-related crimes and violence against children.

- Specify the ways in which restitution from the offender, civil remedies, restorative justice, and compensation from the state will repair damage to victims.

- Debate ways for victims of crime to have their basic human rights respected in criminal courts.

- Understand the key components of system-wide strategies for stopping violence and repeat victimization.

- Justify actions likely to shift crime policy from the traditional system to one that embraces reducing victimization and providing services and rights for victims of crime.

This chapter is organized around four key areas of modern victimology: (1) prevalence, impact, and needs of victims; (2) the origins of victimology and international standards; (3) policing, victim services and compensation, courts, and restitution; and (4) how to rebalance the justice system to respect victims' human rights.

Prevalence, Impact, and Needs of Victimization

As you learned in Chapter 4, flaws in police crime statistics have led criminologists to collect information from victimization surveys. These surveys are conducted annually in many other countries, but in Canada they are conducted only every five years, and they do not receive the attention they deserve from criminologists, the media, or politicians.

A summary of some of the data on risk of victimization provided by Statistics Canada victimization surveys is outlined in Box 7.1. The main source of data about the prevalence of victimization in Canada among adults 15 years and older is the General Social Survey (GSS). This survey shows the following

- Over one-quarter of adult Canadians are victimized each year by one of the crimes included in the survey.

- This rate of victimization has not changed significantly over the past 20 years.

- Adult victims of violent crimes are young (the age group of 15–24 has reported being victimized more than 15 times more often than the 65 and older age group); more likely to be male, except for sexual assault; and more likely to be Aboriginal (Perrault and Brennan, 2010).

FOCUS

Box 7.1

A SNAPSHOT OF VICTIMIZATION IN CANADA

On average, each year in a Canadian city of 1,000,000 persons interpersonal crime will cause victims $2.5 billion in costs and pain and suffering, including that suffered by 60,000 adult victims of assault, 16,000 adult victims of sexual assault, and 18,000 adult victims of thefts from or of cars. Additionally, it is important to recognize the following: Fewer than one in three victims will call the police to report the crime, and an even lower proportion will report the offence of sexual assault.

- Fewer than three percent of victims will see "their" offender convicted.
- Local urban police services will cost $240 million out of local taxes while other policing services will cost $160 million and correctional services will cost $180 million out of federal and provincial taxes. Expenditures on victim services and rights in Canada, on the other hand, are a tiny $10 million, often paid out of a tax on fines.

- With some important exceptions, police are unlikely to inform victims of the availability of services such as property repair, volunteer victim support, restitution, or compensation.
- Those working with victims are paid less than half the salary of police officers.
- Most eligible victims will not know of or receive restitution or compensation.
- Victim impact statements do not impact sentences.
- Victims do not have remedies for their rights, though this may change with the inclusion of complaint procedures in the 2014 federal Bill of Rights.

Sources: Statistics Canada General Social Survey 2004, Statistics Canada General Social Survey 2009, and Statistics Canada General Social Survey 1999

Table 7.1 shows the rates of victimization for seven of the offences included in the Statistics Canada GSS for the last five years in which the survey was undertaken—1988, 1993, 1999, 2004, and 2009. These rates confirm small increases in robbery and physical assault. They also show some increases and decreases for property crime in terms of the various types of theft and vandalism; specifically, they show an increase between 1999 and 2004, with a small decrease between 2004 and 2009.

Repeat victimization of the same victim (or victim's household) has often been observed in victimization surveys. According to the 2004 Statistics Canada Survey, of those who stated that they had been victimized by a crime during the preceding 12 months, 40 percent reported that they had been victimized more than once.

As in other countries, these surveys show victimization to be concentrated in certain areas, families, and individuals. For example, males aged 15 to 25 who are not married and who go out from their residence are much more likely to be victims of most crimes. In Canada, Aboriginal people are much more at risk.

Impact of Victimization

Crime causes financial loss, injury, and emotional pain and trauma to victims. These harms to victims can also extend to persons such as the spouse, parents, and friends of the victims. Some of the consequences of victimization include injuries such as cuts and broken bones, diseases (STDs, AIDS, etc.), and pain; emotional trauma, which can manifest itself as anger, fear, shock, depression,

repeat victimization
The phenomenon of a person being a victim of a crime more than once.

harm to victims
The direct impact of crime on victims includes harm, such as loss, injury, pain, and emotional trauma. These can be exacerbated by the victim's experience with the police, courts, corrections, and others.

TABLE 7.1 **Rates of Victimization in Canada (1988, 1994, 1999, 2004, 2009)**

Year of Survey	Sexual Assault	Robbery	Physical Assault	Subtotal	
		Rates of Victimization (Per 1000 Population Age 15 Years and Older)			
1988	n.a. (16?)	13	68	n.a. (97?)	
1993	16	10	67	93	
1999	21	9	81	111	
2004	21	11	75	107	
2009	24	13	80	117	

Year of Survey	Break and Enter	Motor Vehicle Theft/Parts	Theft of Household Property	Vandalism	Subtotal
		Rates of Victimization (Per 1000 Households)			
1988	54	51	48	63	216
1993	51	37	48	56	192
1999	48	41	62	66	217
2004	39	44	88	77	248
2009	47	34	83	74	238

Sources: Statistics Canada General Social Survey 2004, Statistics Canada General Social Survey 2009, and Statistics Canada General Social Survey 1999

or post-traumatic stress disorder and can lead to physical symptoms; and financial loss due to stolen or damaged property, medical care costs, or loss of wages.

In 2011, Justice Canada released a report showing the tangible costs and pain and suffering to victims of crime (Zhang, 2011). This report concluded that the total annual cost of harm to victims in 2008 was $83 billion (Table 7.2). While

TABLE 7.2 **Estimates of Costs of Crime for Victims, 2008**

Victim Costs—Tangible Costs	$ (millions)
Health care	1,443
Productivity losses	6,734
Stolen/damaged property	6,143
Total tangible victim costs	14,320
Selected Services—Tangible Costs	**$ (millions)**
Victim services and compensation Programs	451
Shelters for victims	254
Other expenditures related to crime	238
Total selected services costs	943
Victim Costs—Intangible Costs	**$ (millions)**
Pain and suffering	65,100
Loss of life (homicides)	3,055
Total intangible victim costs	68,155
Grand Total	83,418

Source: Costs of Crime in Canada, 2008, Summary Table 1: Estimated Tangible Costs of Crime in Canada, 2008 http://www.justice.gc.ca/eng/rp-pr/cj-jp/victim/03/princ.html. Department of Justice Canada, 2003. Reproduced with the permission of the Minister of Public Works and Government Services Canada, 2014

TABLE 7.3   Costs of Criminal Justice in Canada, 2008

Criminal Justice System Costs	$ (millions)
Police	12,000
Court	1,000
Prosecution	528
Legal Aid	373
Corrections	5,630
Total	19,531

Source: Costs of Crime in Canada, 2008, Appendix A: Criminal Justice System Costs http://www.justice.gc.ca/eng/rp-pr/cj-jp/victim/03/princ.html. Department of Justice Canada, 2008. Reproduced with the permission of the Minister of Public Works and Government Services Canada, 2014

tangible costs exceeded $14 billion, the intangible costs of pain and suffering exceeded $68 billion. This study estimated annual expenditures on services for victims at a modest $750 million.

These costs can be exacerbated by "secondary victimization," which refers to costs and trauma experienced by victims when they collaborate with the police, courts, and correctional systems as witnesses. Some of this victimization relates to time and expense of meeting with police or going to court. Some is emotional as feelings and fears are stirred by revisiting what happened. Some reflects dissatisfaction with the way victims are treated by the system.

Expenditures on police, courts, and corrections are rising and have now reached nearly $20 billion in Canada (Table 7.3) (Parliamentary Budget Officer, 2013). It is estimated that between 50 and 60 percent of police costs are used to respond to 911 calls made by or on behalf of crime victims (Waller, 2008; Skogan and Frydl, 2004). Additional police costs—probably close to 20 per cent—are incurred by the detectives investigating crimes. Some politicians assign these expenditures on policing, in addition to the costs of criminal courts and corrections, as costs incurred by victims, but in fact these are costs incurred by taxpayers generally, and not always for harms to victims. However, police costs have doubled in the past 10 years. In addition, both police and jail costs are expected to continue rising faster than other government expenditures.

Needs of Crime Victims

International organizations such as the International Association of Chiefs of Police (IACP, 2008), researchers working on victims' needs, and victim organizations largely agree on eight core needs of victims of crime. These are articulated under three broader categories: support, justice, and governance (see Table 7.4).

Right to Recognition

Victims need to be recognized. Crimes are committed against people—they are not just an affront to the state. Human faces are associated with every robbery, rape, and assault. These are the faces of persons suffering loss, injury, and trauma at the hands of an offender who inflicted the harm.

Right to Information

Victims need to be provided with information. They need to know which services are available to them and what rights they have to recover reparation.

rights of crime victims Legislators in different countries and intergovernmental agencies such as UN have recognized various fundamental principles of justice and rights for victims of crime, such as the right to be informed, to receive restitution, and to be present when decisions such as bail or sentencing are being decided in court.

TABLE 7.4   **Core Rights for Victims of Crime and Likely Responses**

Core Needs for Victims of Crime	Right to Legislation and Implementation to Provide
Support	
1 Recognition and emotional support	Trained informal and professional crisis support and counselling
2 Information on criminal justice, their case, services, and personal developments	Timely information on law enforcement, criminal justice and corrections; case; assistance; and expected developments
3 Assistance to access practical, medical, and social services	Advocacy and assistance with repair, practical, social, and other services
Justice	
4 Help to pay bills caused by victimization	Emergency funds and restitution from offender, compensation from state, and paid medical and mental health care
5 Personal safety and protection from accused	Prevention of revictimization and protection from accused
6 Choice to voice in justice	Choice to participate and be represented to defend safety, reparation, truth, and justice
Good Government	
7 Best public safety	Modern strategies that reduce crime and prevent victimization
8 Implementation	Performance measures and surveys of victims as clients

Source: Irvin Waller, Rights for Victims of Crime: Rebalancing Justice (New York: Rowman and Littlefield, 2010), 28–33.

They also need information regarding the police investigation, as well as the prosecution in criminal court if the offender is caught.

Right to Assistance

Victims, wherever they live, need to be informed of services, to be given access to these services, and to have them adequately funded. Specific services are required for victims of specific crimes; for example, rape victims, child abuse victims, and robbery victims require different types of services. Different types of services are also needed as the victims' needs evolve over time.

Right to Reparation

Victims need help to recover financially from their crime victimization. Some of this recovery should be through **restitution from the offender**. Some may be paid in **compensation from the state**. Some may come from civil suits against the offender or a third party.

Right to be Protected from the Accused

Victims need to be protected from the accused, and not just through incarceration of the offender. Child victims and victims of domestic abuse are vulnerable to being revictimized by the offender. The state needs to intervene to ensure this does not happen.

Right to Participation and Representation

Victims need to be able to participate and to be represented in the criminal justice process, whenever their personal interests are affected. Those interests may relate to restitution, information, privacy, justice, and of course their own safety. This goes beyond a victim impact statement, which only allows the victim to discuss the impact of the crime on them.

restitution from the offender
Victims of any type of crime may request that the offender pay the victim money as reparation for financial or other losses caused by the crime.

compensation from the state
Victims of crimes who suffered physical or other injuries may apply to an agency in most provinces to receive lump sum or monthly payments according to provincial legislation.

Right to Effective Policies to Reduce Victimization

Governments need to implement programs that are known to be effective in preventing the first victimization and any repetition. It is not enough to simply punish offenders after the fact.

Right to Implementation

A victim does not have a right unless there is a remedy. Many of the principles of justice and bills of rights in Canada (and in other countries) have not been adequately implemented, and the provisions for remedy are limited or nonexistent. The 2014 federal legislation provides some rights with an untested complaint process.

QUESTIONS FOR CRITICAL THINKING

1. What is a victimization survey? Do these surveys show violent crime to be decreasing or increasing?
2. What are the main impacts of crime on victims? What are the estimates of the financial and other costs to victims?
3. How have expert organizations such as the International Association of Chiefs of Police and victim assistance organizations articulated the main needs of victims of crime?

The Origins of Victimology and International Standards

In the 1960s, pioneers of what would become victimology and victims' rights began seeking changes in the treatment of victims of crime. Their motives centred on a concern for victims. Some of these pioneers, shocked by the treatment of victims of violence against women, founded rape crisis centres and refuges for battered wives. The first organizations formed by crime victims—particularly by the parents of murdered children—began to demand reforms to police practices, court procedures, and parole decision making (Amernic, 1984). Other reformers had different motivations. Some started victim–witness assistance programs to support the traditional system of criminal justice by attempting to increase the proportion of crime victims going to police and cooperating with prosecutors. Some promoted victim–offender mediation and restorative justice programs in an effort to make the traditional system less harsh on offenders. Some undertook the first victimization surveys to develop better data on the extent of crime.

These disparate groups became part of an international movement that brought together advocates for victims' services and rights, many of whom worked in academe or in the trenches with victims. Initially they were fighting for changes within their own countries, but soon they discovered that the problems of victims crossed national borders.

In 1979, a non-governmental organization, the World Society of Victimology (WSV), was formed to allow all the various researchers,

Several international organizations, including the UN, have been strong advocates for adopting evidence-based crime prevention programs.

Mo Peerbacus/Alamy

policy-makers, and service providers to pursue their common interests and to exchange their knowledge and experiences. This group has organized regular symposiums and sponsored courses for graduate students.

Magna Carta for Victims

The WSV quickly began to put social science knowledge, human rights principles, and international collaboration to work by influencing the UN. In 1985 the UN General Assembly adopted a landmark resolution that recognized that crimes are not just against the state but also do harm to victims. It called for a shift away from the traditional criminal justice approach toward one that would emphasize both prevention of victimization and respect for the human rights of victims of crime. Every government in the world is part of the UN General Assembly, so every government has endorsed this resolution, whose "technical" name is the UN General Assembly Resolution 1985 A/30/44 on the Declaration of Basic Principles of Justice for Victims of Crime and Abuse of Power.

The resolution commits governments to (1) implement basic principles of justice for victims of crime and abuse of power and (2) prevent victimization through a series of comprehensive measures, which include attacking social causes and fostering individual responsibility.

The UN Declaration is organized under these rubrics:

- Information on criminal justice, their case, and services
- Assistance to access practical, medical and social services
- Guidelines and training for police, health and other services
- Reparation through restitution and state compensation
- Right and access to justice (voice in justice)

This UN Declaration has become the benchmark for basic services and rights for victims. It is often referred to as the Magna Carta for victims of crime because through it, for the first time, the UN has endorsed their basic human rights. It has also shifted the traditional system from its obsession with the courtroom battles to comprehensive efforts to end victimization and to provide services to crime victims.

However, this shift is happening extremely slowly. The traditional system of police, courts, and corrections is vast as well as resistant to change. In part, criminology has perpetuated this by focusing on the negative aspects of sentencing and prisons without providing alternatives.

Origins of Victims Rights Policies in Canada

The first seeds of policies to help victims in Canada were sown in the 1960s. In 1967, Saskatchewan joined jurisdictions such as New Zealand, the UK, and California in providing compensation to victims of violent crime. In the 1970s the first criminological monographs on crime victims were published on victims of burglary (Waller and Okihiro, 1978) and rape (Clarke and Lewis, 1977). These studies remain models of what criminology can do to focus efforts on the prevention of crime, including violence against women, and to change the response to victims.

In 1981 the US National Organization for Victim Assistance and the Canadian Council for Social Development organized a major international conference in Toronto with significant funding from the federal and Ontario governments to discuss the topic of assistance for victims of crime. That conference led to a federal–provincial task force of public servants. In 1983, that task force made a number of recommendations, including these:

1. Gather survey data on numbers of victims
2. Provide information for victims
3. Provide services for victims
4. Provide restitution, compensation, and property return
5. Protect victims from intimidation
6. Provide victim impact statements to assist with restitution, and hold trials within a reasonable time
7. Pay for services using a fine surtax on offenders
8. Monitor the implementation of recommendations

However, this report had been produced behind closed doors by public servants working for the traditional system, and it did not reflect the growing body of social science knowledge about victims. The committee's lack of attention to participatory justice and to the emotional trauma experienced by victims meant that its report neglected the importance of victim participation in justice processes, prevention of victimization, and mental health services.

In the United States, in stark contrast, the President's Task Force (1982) followed a much more scientific and more transparent procedure and arrived at a much broader and more comprehensive set of recommendations. It recommended ways in which the traditional system could be used to help meet the needs of crime victims. It also included major sections on mental health, as well as a draft constitutional amendment that would provide victims with standing equivalent to that of the offender at critical stages in the criminal justice process such as bail and sentencing.

In an attempt to do better than the provincial task force, Ontario's Justice Ministry organized a transparent consultation to review its recommendations.

This new consultation heard from groups representing victims of crime, including the parents of children killed by drunk drivers as well as victims of sexual assault (Ontario, 1984). The recommendations arising from this exercise addressed two important needs that had been overlooked by the public servants: to prevent crime, and to provide legal standing for victims in the criminal justice system. Unfortunately, the province's Attorney General, Roy McMurtry, on the advice of his officials, chose not to implement these additional recommendations, which would have aligned government policy more with the needs of crime victims than with the needs of the traditional system.

Tensions between the Traditional and Human Rights for Victims

Canada supported the efforts in 1985 to get the UN General Assembly to adopt the declaration discussed earlier by organizing a preparatory meeting. However, two issues have impeded full respect for the basic human rights for victims of crime. One is resistance to change within the traditional system. The other is the gap between social science researchers and the lawyers who manage the traditional system. Unfortunately, the groups responsible for proposing and implementing reforms are part of the legal bureaucracy, which is committed to the traditional system. In Canada, this gap is sustained and exacerbated by a lack of transparency in the development of policies to meet victims' needs. This contrasts with developments in the UK and the United States, particularly at the national level.

Manitoba, in 1986, was the first province to adopt legislation to provide services and some limited rights for victims of crime. This was inspired by pioneering legislation in Massachusetts, which established a compensation program that included a statement of standards for services as well as a central office to implement those standards. These and later federal legislative initiatives led to a system of fine surcharges to fund some victim services. Some assessments of these services suggest they are a patchwork; judges often do not order the victim fine surcharge. Unfortunately, there has not been sufficient research to measure the gap between what was promised and what was delivered.

In 1988 the federal and provincial ministers agreed to a Canadian Statement of Principles of Justice in an effort to "Canadianize" the UN Declaration. Though inspired by the UN resolution, this agreement fell far short of the UN position on issues of restitution, compensation, services, and a role for the victim in criminal justice.

The principles were associated with important but limited moves by most provinces to adopt legislation to provide some services for victims of crime. But these laws were often weak, and strong responsibility centres were not established to implement them. This was particularly true of Ontario. On June 11, 1996, An Act Respecting Victims of Crime—Victims' Bill of Rights was proclaimed law in Ontario. The act was described by the Ontario Ministry of the Attorney General as "a set of principles that guide how justice system officials should treat victims at different stages of the criminal justice process." The same act created an Office for Victims of Crime, but its role was limited to advising the Attorney General on victims' issues. Unfortunately, this ministry was dominated by lawyers from the traditional system, who seemed to have

victim fine surcharge
A monetary penalty similar to a fine, which can be assessed at sentence or added to a fine such as in a traffic violation, but can only be used by the government to fund services for victims.

little interest in meeting the needs of victims and who were not familiar with current social science research and methods. As a result, there were no rights because there were no remedies. The government made promises but did not provide a way for victims to ensure that promises are kept.

Though the intentions were good, these initiatives were very weak. A Canadian parliamentary committee reviewed progress on victims' services and published 17 recommendations to improve the situation (Canada, 1998). The committee held town hall meetings in different constituencies across Canada and listened to both crime victims and experts. Their report, *Victims: A Voice Not a Veto*, made significant recommendations for reform, including the creation of an adequately funded, high-level leadership centre and reforms to the basic principles.

When criticized by the Parliamentary Committee (Canada, Standing Committee, 2000), the federal, provincial, and territorial governments revised their principles in 2003 to those set out in Box 7.2. As with too many of the reforms in Canada, this was not a transparent process with input from experts and practitioners. While they included some obvious good principles, they were not drafted to facilitate effective ways to measure their implementation, as had been requested by the Parliamentary Committee. They also overlooked such basic issues as assistance to access services (other than information); help obtaining reparation, such as restitution and compensation (other than information); providing victims with a voice in justice; effective policies to prevent victimization; and ways to ensure and monitor implementation. Once again the results were disappointing, as the process was not open to victims' groups or experts in measuring outcomes.

Some modifications have been made to the Criminal Code and to the Youth Criminal Justice Act to protect the privacy of victims, encourage restitution orders in criminal courts, and allow victim impact statements. However, the lack of attention to social science research measuring the impact of these changes means that little is known about the extent to which these provisions are, or are ever likely to be, used extensively.

Ontario has only recently started to use the victims' justice fund—the fund into which victim surcharges are paid—to expand victim services. In 2007, Ontario's Provincial Ombudsman undertook an inquiry into compensation for victims of violent crime. His report, tabled just before an election, labelled the system as "Adding Insult to Injury." The Ontario Attorney General responded by appointing the retiring Chief Justice of Ontario, Roy McMurtry, to investigate and make recommendations. His report measured the current services and compensation for victims of crime against the internationally agreed standards of the UN Declaration on Basic Principles of Justice. It made several practical recommendations for improvements, such as getting police to provide victims with information about victim services, using surveys of victims to measure gaps in the delivery of services, and so on. Ironically, McMurtry is the same person who more than 20 years earlier had resisted basic changes to fundamental rights for victims. His more enlightened and informed views in the recent report have still not been implemented by the current Attorney General for Ontario.

Justice Canada launched an awareness campaign in 2010 called Victims Matter. It included a tool for identifying services for victims by postal code. While this is a start, these improvements fall far short of developments in comparable jurisdictions, as we will see in the next section.

SEARCH FOR:
Victims Matter

SEARCH FOR:
Federal Ombudsman for Crime Victims

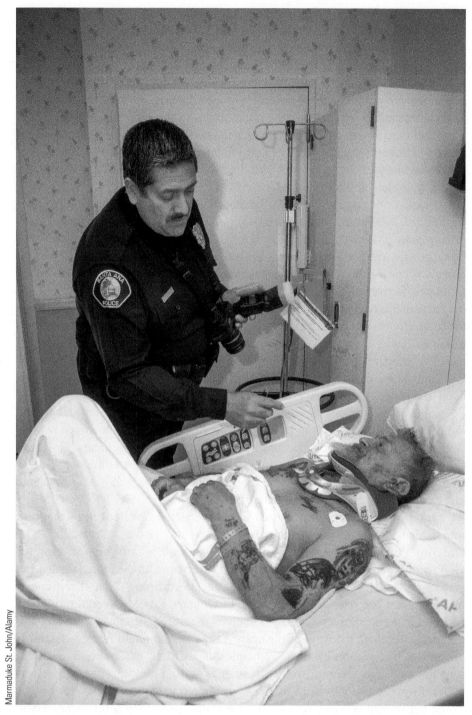

Marmaduke St. John/Alamy

The personal costs of violent crime are very high. The costs to society include hospital costs, justice system costs, and lost productivity. Victims like this one face personal trauma, loss of income, and months of suffering. This is why many groups are advocating increased compensation and services for crime victims.

The Federal Ombudsman for Victims and the Bill of Rights for Victims

In 2007 the federal government established the office of the Federal Ombudsman for Victims of Crime (FOVC) to defend the rights of victims and to bring about systemic change at the federal level. The person appointed as ombudsman serves a three-year term with a staff of fewer than 10 and an equally small budget.

The first appointee had to set up the office from scratch while dealing operationally with complaints (most of them concerning parole and provision of information) and identifying areas where reforms were needed.

The second appointee has served into two mandates. She has worked on two important reports that have helped shift the conversation in Canada toward victims. These reports have focused on restitution, the victim fine surcharge, victim impact statements, and the federal Bill of Rights. In June 2013, she organized a national meeting that brought together victims, victims' advocates, and academics to look at areas for improvement. The report of this meeting has been published on the FOVC website as *Moving the Conversation Forward*. It covers eight areas:

1. Criteria for who is a victim of crime
2. Equitable access to tangible supports for victims
3. Meaningful case information to victims
4. Awareness of and collaboration across the network of victims' services
5. Visibility of victims' voices
6. Prevention and safety
7. Equity of treatment before the law
8. Equity across all regions of the country.

The same report calls for a more influential role for the FOVC and makes specific proposals for a federal Bill of Rights. In 2014, Prime Minister Stephen Harper announced legislation "to give victims of crime a more effective voice in the criminal justice system." Box 7.2 highlights the five key elements in the proposed legislation.

FOCUS

Box 7.2

CANADIAN VICTIMS BILL OF RIGHTS

In April, 2014, the federal government introduced a bill — The Victims Bill of Rights Act — to create statutory rights at the federal level for victims of crime, including complaint mechanisms.

Right to Information About:
The status of the investigation and the criminal proceedings;

The criminal justice system, the programs and services that are available to victims of crime;

Reviews while the offender is subject to the Corrections process, or hearings after the accused is found not criminally responsible on account of mental disorder or unfit to stand trial, and the decisions made at those reviews and hearings;

The complaint procedures that are available to them when their rights have been infringed or denied;

Right to Restitution
To have the courts consider making, in all cases, a restitution order against the offender;

To have a restitution order entered as a civil court judgement that is enforceable against the offender if the amount owing under the restitution order is not paid.

Rights to Protection:
To have their security and privacy considered by the appropriate authorities in the criminal justice system;

To protection from intimidation and retaliation;

To request testimonial aids (e.g. giving evidence in court by closed circuit television);

Right to Participation:
To convey their views about decisions to be made by authorities in the criminal justice system that affect the rights of victim's rights under this Act and to have those views considered;

To present a victim impact statement and to have it considered;

Right to Complain
Requirement for federal departments to create mechanisms for victims to complain if their rights have been infringed

Separate from the bill, the federal government has proposed subsidies to facilitate complaint mechanisms by provinces in a manner that is consistent across Canada.

Most experts and victims' groups are positive about this law and its provisions but are also disappointed with what it does *not* include. For example, the sections in the legislation on the right of victims to information do not state what the police should do to provide information. Also, the legislation does not extend the right to information to helping victims access services such as victim assistance or sexual assault crisis centres. Providing the right to restitution should increase its use by the courts, but the bill does not go far enough in requiring the offender to provide the court with information about his or her ability to pay. The bill also does not require parole boards to consider whether the offender has paid restitution. Furthermore, the onus is on the victim to bring a civil action, and this can be a complex process. In some US states, the state plays an active role in recovering the money. For example, in Vermont the state pays the restitution up to a specified amount and then sues the offender to recover the monies when necessary. The bill's section on the right to protection provides some improvements but does not specify how this protection is to be provided. The right to participation provides for limited input from the victim while continuing to allow victim impact statements. The text on complaint procedures is a start but does not identify which government department is responsible for implementing which section of the law, nor does it set any standards for these complaint procedures. If funding from the federal government is provided to provinces, then there may be some consistency in the way victims can complain across Canada.

The Federal Ombudsman for Victims of Crime has called the proposed legislation a "Cornerstone for Change" and has welcomed the proposed act, but has gone on to call for many improvements because the act addresses only 4 of the 30 areas of need identified by the ombudsman.

Perhaps the act's most significant weakness is that it does not specify a clear way of evaluating whether it has been properly implemented. In the United States in 2004, the federal victims' rights law included a requirement for the General Accounting Office (GAO) to monitor the implementation; as a result, the GAO has been able to recommend—on the basis of evidence—many improvements to police officers, prosecutors, and judges. Because these recommendations have been backed by evidence, the improvements have generally been made.

The rights in the bill do not refer to services, assistance, or compensation, which are the items generally considered to require the most funding. Also, funding from the federal government is very limited at this stage.

The bill's other major weakness is that it includes no reference to preventing violence. Yet current evidence suggests that a shift in funding could achieve a 50 percent reduction in the number of victims and savings of billions of dollars in taxes (see Waller, 2014).

A Comparison of Canada to Other Jurisdictions

In the United States, the federal Victims of Crime Act was adopted in 1984 to increase victim assistance services and criminal injuries compensation across the country. This legislation included the creation of the powerful and independently funded Office for Victims of Crime (OVC), which allocates close to $1 billion every year for victim assistance and compensation.

This law has brought about dramatic improvements by ensuring that every state has a system for providing compensation to victims of violent crime and by multiplying the availability of victim assistance programs. It has also fostered research, training, and advocacy to improve rights and services for victims. In 2013, $9 billion was available in the OVC fund. Such funds come principally from fine surcharges against wealthy corporate offenders, of which the largest so far was the $1.2 billion Pfizer paid when settling allegations of fraud around Bextra and three other drugs. This shows how federal funds can be used to channel services, compensation, training, advocacy, and much more to victims of crime.

In 1994 the Violence Against Women Act was passed in the United States; it has since been reauthorized several times. This act established the Office on Violence Against Women as part of the US Department of Justice. That office is specifically mandated to improve services for female victims; its programs its are tailored to issues of gender and to protecting victims from the accused.

In 2004 the United States adopted the Crime Victim Rights Act, which provided six rights in federal courts, including the right to restitution and the right to be heard. The same act required the GAO to review how the act was operating and to recommend improvements. As a result, police, prosecutors, judges, and others have made significant improvements to services for crime victims federally. This is an important model for how social science research can improve practice.

In 2001, all member governments of the European Union (EU) adopted service standards for victims of crime. These standards cover a number of areas, including information, services, and mediation. To ensure implementation, a performance monitoring mechanism has been established that includes independent monitoring—paid for by the EU—five years after the target dates for implementation. This independent monitoring has found many gaps. One important recommendation has been that "the role of the victim throughout the criminal justice process ... be respected and recognised as equal to that of the accused" (Victims Support Europe, 2010).

On October 4, 2012, the 27 EU nations established minimum standards regarding the rights, support, and protection of victims of crime. This has advanced victims' rights for 500 million people and ensures that all victims of crime in Europe will have access to information and assistance and be able to get these across national borders. Certain basic rights in criminal proceedings are now guaranteed, and protections are now provided, particularly for women, children, and vulnerable victims.

The EU standards are more than political wishful thinking. They have sufficient teeth to get implemented, and they encompass training, sharing of best practices, and data to evaluate whether victims' needs are being met. If it is possible to get agreement so many countries on both standards and ways to get them implemented, then Canada should be able to adapt this model across 10 provinces and 3 territories.

In Table 7.5, the Canadian Bill of Rights is compared to the US federal Victim Rights Bill and the EU directive. The table shows the general areas in which the articles will require governments to meet the minimum standards. This table is organized around the analysis in Chapters 1 and 2 of *Rights for*

TABLE 7.5   **Comparison of the Canadian Victims Bill of Rights to the EU Directive Using the Eight Core Needs**

	Core Needs of Victims	2004 US Federal Victim Rights Act	2012 EU Directive	2014 Canada Victims Bill of Rights
1	Recognition and emotional support	Recognition of victims and families; fairness; right to avoid delay	Recognition of victims and, in case of homicide, family (2)	Recognition of victim and immediate relations
2	Information on criminal justice, case, services, and developments	Right to notice of hearings	Information (3–7)	Information, including correctional
			Referral by competent authority to victim support (8)	
3	Assistance to access practical, medical, and social services		Comprehensive support (9)	
			Special assistance for vulnerable (1, 18–24)	
4	Help to pay bills caused by victimization	Right to full and timely restitution	Restitution (called compensation) from the offender (16)	Restitution, including a form but victim to enforce
			Restorative justice—respecting victim rights (12)	Information only within correctional system
			Information on State Compensation (part of 9)	Information only
5	Personal safety and protection from accused	Right to be reasonably protected from accused.	Protection of victims with special protection needs, including women, children, and vulnerable (18–24)	Some protection, including testimonial aids
6	Choice to voice in justice	Rights to be present and get legal advice	Rights limited mainly to national law (10–17)	Right limited to victim impact statement, access to parole
7	Best public safety		Information to prevent repeat victimization (part of 9)	
8	Implementation	Right to court enforcement of rights: complaints, training, funding; evaluation of implementation by General Accounting Office	Training, data, cooperation and 5 year reports (26–31)	Only complaints

Source: Irvin Waller. *Rights for Victims of Crime: Rebalancing Justice.* (New York: Rowman & Littlefield, 2010), p. 37, Figure 2.1. Reprinted by permission of Rowman & Littlefield Publishing Group.

Victims of Crime of the core needs of victims. Clearly, the US law focuses on both rights and their implementation by the courts. It shows that the EU directive is impressively comprehensive and includes a commitment to evaluate every five years the extent to which its implementation achieves its goals of supporting and protecting victims.

The model law discussed below goes even further to recommend a central office to lead implementation, standards that identify who is responsible for implementation, training for those charged with implementation, and, importantly, evaluation by social scientists to gauge whether victims are getting the services.

QUESTIONS FOR CRITICAL THINKING

1. Why is it so difficult for governments to shift to implement the UN Declaration?

2. What is the role of federal Ombudsman for Victims of Crime?
3. What are key advances in the Canadian Bill of Rights for Victims over the Canadian Basic Principles?

Policing, Victim Services, Reparation, Courts, and Prevention

Victim Services and the Police

More and more victims in Canada no longer go to the police. If they do, most will not get information on services, assistance, and support. Even when the police start an investigation, few victims will obtain reparation, protection, or go on to a criminal court—let alone get what they consider justice.

In Canada, the percentage of victims of crime reporting their victimization to the police has been dropping. In 2009, only 31 percent reported to the police, down from 37 percent in 1999 and more than 40 percent earlier. The details of this decline are shown in Table 7.6. The drop in reporting rates experienced in Canada has not occurred in the United States or in England. It is not clear why this decline has occurred in Canada, but one hypothesis is that fewer victims report because services and compensation are not available or well known. The UK, the United States, and the Province of Quebec, which *have* maintained

TABLE 7.6 Percentage of Crime Victims Reporting to Police by Offence (1988, 1994, 1999, 2004, 2009)

Year	Sexual Assault	Robbery	Physical Assault	Subtotal	
1988	n.a.	32	35	n.a.	
1993	10	46	33	44	
1999	n.a.	46	37	31	
2004	8	46	39	33	
2009	n.a.	43	34	29	
Year	Break and Enter	Motor Vehicle Theft/Parts	Theft of Household Property	Vandalism	Subtotal
1988	72	58	44	46	45
1993	68	50	43	46	48
1999	62	60	32	34	44
2004	54	49	29	31	37
2009	54	50	23	35	36
Year	Theft of Personal Property	Total Victimization			
1988	37	n.a.			
1993	42	42			
1999	35	37			
2004	31	34			
2009	28	31			

Sources: Statistics Canada, Criminal Victimization in Canada, 2009, *Juristat*, 30, no. 2. Ottawa, ON: Canadian Centre for Justice Statistics, 2010; Statistics Canada, Criminal Victimization in Canada, 2004, *Juristat*, 25, No. 7. Ottawa, ON: Canadian Centre for Justice Statistics, 2005; Statistics Canada, Criminal Victimization in Canada, 1999, *Juristat*, 20, No. 10. Ottawa, ON: Canadian Centre for Justice Statistics, 2000.

their reporting rates, all have more consistent services and larger compensation payments than the rest of Canada.

In the 2004 and 2009 victimization surveys, adult Canadians who were victims of crime were asked why they did *not* report the crime to the police. The question assumed that everyone would want to report. The most frequent reasons for not reporting included that the crime did not seem important enough, that the police could not do anything about it, that the crime would be dealt with in another way, that the incident was a personal matter, or that they did not want the police involved.

Surveys in other countries ask why victims *do* call the police; that is, they do *not* assume that everyone wants to report. The annual and extensive National Crime Survey in the United States shows that victims report to police because (1) victims of violence want to ensure their personal safety and ensure that others aren't victimized, and (2) property crime victims want to recover stolen property, get damages repaired, and collect insurance. Punishment of the offender is the least frequent reason why victims contact the police (Waller, 2010, 60–62).

The Canadian surveys confirm a common finding in countries similar to Canada: most women who are victims of sexual assault or rape do not report their victimization to the police. Specialized surveys exist to measure violence against women and violence against children, but these are not undertaken regularly in Canada (Waller, 2010, 59–60). In the United States, these surveys have found that around 800,000 adult women are victims of forcible rape each year and that only 18 percent report to the police. In a disproportionate number of these rapes, the victim is a college or university student. As many as one in five female students will graduate from university after being a victim of rape while on the university campus. Typically, the perpetrator is a male student in the same university (Fisher and Sloan, 2007).

Another common finding from government surveys is that most victims who report to the police will not see their offender identified or arrested (Waller, 2008, 14; 2010, 60). Overall, less than 4 percent of victims in Canada will see "their" offender convicted (Figure 7.1).

Police services in Canada are proud of their orientation toward providing service to their communities, but they have not focused on services to victims in any significant way. A major reason for the loss of confidence in the police in Canada is the lack of protocols detailing how an officer responding to a 911 call should respond. The Ontario Police Services Act sets out six principles that structure 911 call responses, but only one of the principles refers specifically to respect for victims of crime. This has not yet been accompanied by the sort of procedures and assessments that the International Association of Chiefs of Police (IACP) sees as essential to making crime victims a focus of policing. The Ontario Police Services Act (Ontario, RSO, 1990) requires police services to be delivered in accordance with the following principles. It is the fourth principle that is most relevant to our discussion.

1. The need to ensure the safety and security of all persons and property in Ontario.
2. The importance of safeguarding the fundamental rights guaranteed by the Canadian Charter of Rights and Freedoms and the Human Rights Code, 1981.

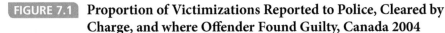

FIGURE 7.1 **Proportion of Victimizations Reported to Police, Cleared by Charge, and where Offender Found Guilty, Canada 2004**

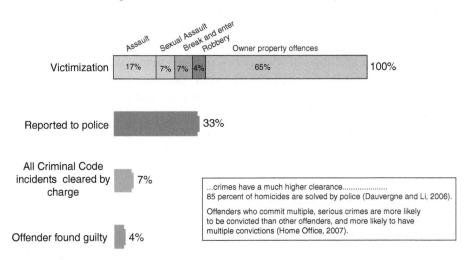

Sources: Adapted from Maire Gannon and Karen Mihorean, "Criminal Victimization in Canada, 2004," *Juristat* 25, no. 7 (2005); Mikhail Thomas, "Adult Criminal Court Statistics, 2003/2004," *Juristat* 24, no. 12 (2004); Julie Sauvé, "Crime Statistics in Canada, 2004," *Juristat* 25, no. 5 (2005).

3. The need for cooperation between the police and the communities they serve.
4. The importance of respect for victims of crime and understanding of their needs.
5. The need for sensitivity to the pluralistic, multiracial, and multicultural character of Ontario society.
6. The need to ensure that police are representative of the communities they serve.*

Most Canadian police services have established crime victim services units. These units vary from municipality to municipality. Some are crisis units with mental health workers, who sometimes work in teams with police officers; others are victims' service units staffed by workers with mental health training. Still others are composed of a professional executive and trained volunteers. No systematic data are available on how many victims of what offences are served by these units or on the results of their efforts.

Another reason for the drop in confidence in the police is the failure of police to improve how they respond to female victims of sexual assault despite many high-profile failures. In Ontario, the Bill of Rights for Victims includes the right for a victim of sexual assault to get an officer of the same gender, but there is no evidence that this is ever implemented. Despite the IACP guidelines and the law in Ontario, victims of sexual assault continue to miss out on basic respect from the police. The Jane Doe case is only one well-known example of a woman not being warned that a serial rapist was operating near her residence and then not being well treated by the investigators with the Toronto Police Service (Waller, 2010, 148–49). Recently, the Toronto Police Service sent an

---

*This is an unofficial version of Government of Ontario legal materials. http://www.e-laws.gov.on.ca/html/statutes/english/elaws_statutes_90p15_e.htm#BK0

officer to talk to students at York University; he told them they were more likely to be raped if they dressed like sluts. This caused so much outrage that people took to the streets of Toronto and Ottawa to protest.

Many senior Canadian police officers are members of IACP, which is the largest professional body for police leadership in North America. It has a sustained interest in spelling out what police services should do to enhance their response to victims of crime. In 1983, IACP developed its own guidelines, which, among other things, drew attention to the need to respond to female victims of sexual assault with female officers.

In an effort to overcome lack of leadership and implementation, IACP worked with the US Office for Victims of Crime to develop and implement a "21st Century" strategy (see Box 7.3) to enhance the police response to victims of crime (IACP, 2008; Waller, 2010, Ch. 3). In 2008, IACP developed a full set of tested procedures that were ready for implementation and that could be used in Canada (Waller, 2010, 55–76). It proposed some simple, obvious, and practical ways to improve services to victims. For example, every officer responding to a 911 call should make the victim aware of which services are available to them with a short and simple informational brochure or wallet card (already a practice in England and Wales). Also, officers should be trained to listen to the victim with sensitivity and to provide emotional support. The guide was field tested both in Charlotte-Mecklenburg, North Carolina (population 800,000) and in other smaller police departments.

The IACP strategy encourages police leaders to enforce implementation by all police officers and to ensure police support for victim assistance agencies outside the police service. The proposals include simple, non-time-consuming services that responding police officers can provide to victims. In Canada, some police services ask the officer to check a form if they provided information to a victim, but it is well known that this is not enough to get victims the

FOCUS

Box 7.3

INTERNATIONAL ASSOCIATION OF CHIEFS OF POLICE GUIDE TO RESPECT VICTIMS OF CRIME

The Strategy Package includes an implementation strategy, toolkit, and training so that police can enhance their response to victims of crime. It emphasizes leadership, partnering, training, and performance monitoring. Here are the seven stages:

1. *Safety*: Protection from perpetrators and assistance in avoiding re-victimization

2. *Support*: Assistance to enable participation in the criminal justice system processes and repair of harm

3. *Information*: Concise and useful information about victims' rights, criminal justice system processes, and available victim services

4. *Access*: Ability to participate in the justice system process and have ready availability to support services

5. *Continuity*: Consistency in approaches and methods across agencies through all stages of the criminal justice process

6. *Voice*: Opportunities to speak out and be heard on specific case processing issues and larger policy questions

7. *Justice*: Receiving the support necessary to heal and seeing that perpetrators are held accountable.

Source: Adapted from International Association of Chiefs of Police, *Enhancing Law Enforcement Response to Victims: A 21st Century Strategy* (Alexandria: International Association of Chiefs of Police, 2008).

information they need. While there are small victim service groups in police agencies in Canada, the mainstreaming of an appropriate response by police to victims falls far short of what is needed and what is possible.

A significant shift is needed in the way Canadian police respond to victims of crime. This better way of meeting the needs of victims and encouraging more reporting of crime need not be costly. Waller (2010, 75–76) proposes the following four steps for Canadian police to reach international standards in their response to victims of crime:

1. Improve the proportion of victims reporting to police and assess progress by holding officers accountable for providing information in a timely manner to victims.
2. Develop and follow protocols to better meet the needs of victims who are women, children, Aboriginal, or disabled.
3. Develop a timetable to implement the IACP strategy package to make victims a primary concern of law enforcement.
4. Ensure independent surveys of victims who report to the police to monitor the extent to which their core needs for information, referral to services, and protection among others are being met.*

Services for Victims of Crime

Canadian provinces provide health services without charge to all residents of Canada. Thus health services for physical injuries, disease, or pregnancy incurred as a result of crime are provided to all victims in Canada. While this is similar to countries such as the UK, it is markedly different from the US model, where victims can incur significant medical and hospital costs that may or may not be reimbursed by state compensation programs.

Crime victims also need emotional and psychological support following their victimization. Victims are likely to turn to their friends and family immediately following the crime to ask for advice: Where should they turn? Who should they call? What should they do?

The most universally recognized mental health issue surrounding victimization is post-traumatic stress disorder (PTSD). Following a crime, it is normal to feel shock, numbness, and disorientation. PTSD is diagnosed when these symptoms persist. Sufferers of PTSD usually have difficulty sleeping, mentally relive the experience, and feel a need to avoid normal situations that trigger memories of the original trauma. We do not know the degree to which services in Canada are adequately equipped to handle victims who suffer PTSD. If victims have private insurance through a large employer such as a corporation or government, they may be able to get a limited number of sessions with a therapist, but most victims with PTSD or other emotional trauma require much more.

Victim assistance services are expanding in Canada, but we do not know the degree to which victims are aware of these services, the adequacy of these services, or what proportion of victims access them.

Statistics Canada attempted to conduct a complete census of victims' service providers in Canada and estimated that there were 884 providers (Allen, 2014). This may sound like a lot, but it reflects the reality that there is a patchwork of

---

*Waller, Irvin. Rights for Victims of Crime: Rebalancing Justice. (New York: Rowman and Littlefield, 2010).

services with many gaps. The study found that 40 percent of the service providers were based in police agencies, 23 percent were based in the community, 8 percent were based in the courts, and 17 percent were sexual assault crisis centres. These agencies had more than 3,000 paid employees, who, along with volunteers, served more than 400,000 victims annually. This represented about 10 percent of adults known to have been victimized, according to the Statistics Canada victimization survey. Remember, though, that we do not know how many others were not informed of these services who could also have benefited from them. Table 7.7 provides an overview of the services in Ontario.

London, Ontario, has long been at the forefront of services for victims of domestic violence, such as child abuse and wife battering. In 1972, the London Police Service began collaborating with the University of Western Ontario to establish police–social worker teams to respond to family violence—the police officer to control the situation and the social worker to help the family resolve its problems. After forming an inter-agency team to look at complementary programs, the city pioneered a battered wife advocacy clinic, world-renowned innovations in its court systems, and, more recently, an effective program called the 4th R to stop violence against women (Institute for Prevention of Crime, 2009; Crooke et al., 2008).

TABLE 7.7 **Services for Victims of Crime in Ontario**

Core Need	2006 Draft Convention (Article)	Services
Support		
1	Recognition of victims, co-victims, good samaritans (1)	
2	Information (7)	Victim Assistance & Referral Services (VCARS), Victim Quick Response Program (VQRP), SupportLink
3	Assistance (8)—referral by police	
	Assistance (8)—short term	Victim Support Line (VSL)
	Assistance (8)—medium term	Sexual Assault/Rape Crisis Centres (SACs)
	Special assistance because of age, gender, disability, race (3)	Sexual Assault/Rape Crisis Centres (SACs), Domestic Violence Court (DVC) Program, Partner Assault Response (PAR) Programs, Internet Child Exploitation (ICE) Counselling
Justice		
4	Restitution from offender (10)	
	Restorative Justice (9)—respecting victim rights	
	Compensation from state (11)	Victim Quick Response Program (VQRP), Criminal Injuries Compensation Board (CICB)
5	Protection of victims, witnesses, and experts	Victim/Witness Assistance Program (VWAP), Child Victim/Witness Program
6	Access to justice and fair treatment	
Good Government		
7	Commitment to reduce victimization	
8	Implementation	

Sources: Ontario Ministry of the Attorney General, OVSS Programs. http://www.attorneygeneral.jus.gov.on.ca/english/ovss/programs.asp#crisisAssistance; I. Waller, *Rights for Victims of Crime: Rebalancing Justice* (Toronto: Rowman & Littlefield, 2011).

From a 2012 survey, we know that on one day there were 12,000 residents in battered wife shelters in Canada. About half were women, the other half dependent children (Mazowita and Burczycka, 2014). About 380 women and 220 children were turned away on just that one day for reasons of lack of space or other problems faced by the women.

For victims of sexual assault, there are a number of sexual assault or rape crisis centres scattered across Canada, mainly in urban areas. Though there is little systematic research on these centres, they likely provide services as good as similar centres in other countries, where research has shown that they are important to victims (Waller, 2010). What *is* known is that they are typically not funded on a permanent basis and that despite the importance and effectiveness of their work, the salaries of staff are significantly lower than those of other justice professionals (police, lawyers, judges, etc.).

One interesting model for responding to victims of sexual assault is Nina's Place in Burlington, Ontario. Nina's Place provides specialized health care, police services, and agency referrals for women and men who have experienced sexual assault within the past 72 hours and recent domestic violence. The support is available whether the survivor has involved the police or not. It is named in memory of Nina de Villiers, the victim of a tragic assault in Burlington in 1991. Nina's Place is open 24 hours a day, 7 days a week, and the services are free (Nina's Place, 2011). The services offered by Nina's Place include a physical examination and treatment of any physical injuries, the collection and recording of evidence of the assault (forensic evidence within 24 hours) that could be used if the victim decides to involve the legal system, testing and counselling for possible pregnancy, risk assessment and safety planning, follow-up medical care and referral to community agencies, and counselling.

Basic responses to assist victims of crime in Canada lag behind those in other countries. Waller (2010, 95–96) proposes the following measures to bring Canada up to international standards:

1. Increase funding significantly and pay professional salaries for the full range of victim support services, including those for victims of sexual assault and domestic violence.
2. Develop and implement professional standards for support services along the lines of those in the UK.
3. Ensure that professional care for mental health trauma is available at no cost to the victim.
4. Schools and universities should teach citizens to provide emotional support to victims of crime.
5. Conduct surveys to measure the gaps between the core needs of victims and the services provided to them.*

Restitution from the Offender, Compensation from the State, and Civil Remedies

Crime often involves direct financial loss, costs of services, and loss of quality of life. Victims have several potential ways to obtain reparation to recover these losses:

---

*Waller, Irvin. Rights for Victims of Crime: Rebalancing Justice. (New York: Rowman and Littlefield, 2010).

1. An order of restitution made in a criminal court
2. A civil suit brought against the perpetrator of the crime
3. A civil suit brought against a third party whose negligence may have contributed to the crime
4. Restorative justice
5. A payment made by a state/provincial compensation board

Restitution from the Offender

Though restitution is available through criminal and juvenile courts, it is not known how often it is considered appropriately, ordered, or paid. We do know that programs such as a model program in Saskatchewan (Box 7.4) and various best practices in the United States result in some restitution being ordered and paid.

Experts have identified key steps to get restitution paid, but these have not yet been applied in Canada. According to the US National Crime Victim Centre (2009; Waller, 2010, 101–4), restitution would be paid if jurisdictions followed seven steps:

1. Victims request restitution in writing.
2. Victims demonstrate losses.
3. The offender's assets, income, and liabilities are identified at the beginning of the justice process.
4. Restitution payments are made automatic.
5. Payments are monitored.
6. Compliance is enforced.
7. Restitution payments are made the priority over other government payments such as fines.*

FOCUS

Box 7.4

ADULT RESTITUTION AND CIVIL ENFORCEMENT PROGRAM, SASKATCHEWAN

A unique provincial program in Saskatchewan has two components—the Adult Restitution Program and the Restitution Civil Enforcement Program. The Ministry of Justice and Attorney General operates these programs to help victims receive restitution (http://www.justice.gov.sk.ca/victimsservices).

The Adult Restitution Program provides information to victims about restitution, monitors payments, works with offenders to help ensure payments are made, and works with probation officers and prosecutors to enforce restitution orders. This program ensures the Crown is aware that the victim has suffered financial loss as a result of the crime and of the extent of the loss. A court will generally only order restitution if the amount of loss is "readily ascertainable."

The Restitution Civil Enforcement Program assists victims with the civil enforcement of restitution orders. The program pursues civil enforcement of the restitution order on the victims' behalf (when a supervised order has expired or in the case of stand-alone restitution orders). This may include, but is not limited to, the garnishment of the offender's wages and bank accounts, and seizure of personal property.

These are pilot projects being funded by the Department of Justice. Nova Scotia is currently establishing a new Restitution Program modelled on Saskatchewan's Adult Restitution Program to assist victims in obtaining restitution payments.

Source: Adapted from Saskatchewan, Restitution Civil Enforcement Program, Justice and Attorney General, 2011

---

*Waller, Irvin. Rights for Victims of Crime: Rebalancing Justice. (New York: Rowman and Littlefield, 2010).

Restorative Justice

There are several models for restorative justice; most involve the victim and offender meeting with a professional coordinator or mediator. The goal is to reconcile the two parties.

Restorative justice was pioneered internationally in the region around Waterloo, Ontario, by Mennonites in the 1970s. In 1981, when the US National Organization for Victim Assistance came to Toronto for their annual conference, Ontario was a leader in restitution and supported victim–offender reconciliation programs across the province. At that time, the Church Council on Justice and Corrections took up the challenge of spreading restorative justice models across Canada. However, these are more often pioneering projects rather than comprehensive policy. By 2010, Nova Scotia had achieved one of the most extensive networks of restorative justice for juvenile offenders.

Though popular among criminologists, restorative justice models have not achieved their potential. As with many other victim innovations, the system has resisted these options. Furthermore, the victims' movement has been quick to stress that victims are not always given the same attention as the offender. Restorative justice has become an international movement in which there is more often talk in university classrooms than action in practice.

Nevertheless, research by Strang and Sherman (2007) using random control trials in Australia and the UK has demonstrated that victims prefer restorative justice to the traditional system and that, on average, offenders who go through this process are less likely to reoffend. Their data have reinforced the work by the National Association for Victim Support Schemes and Restorative Solutions to train practitioners across England and Wales.

Compensation from Government

In 1967, Saskatchewan became the first province to provide compensation to victims of violence. Since then, many provincial governments have established compensation programs to ensure that victims of violence are compensated for their losses. However, it seems that many victims are not aware of these programs. In Ontario, for example, fewer than 4,000 victims apply each year—a relatively small proportion of those estimated to be eligible. When a person is injured or killed as a result of a violent crime, the maximum (lump sum) awarded is $25,000. Also, a victim who is unable to work due to the victimization may only be awarded a maximum of $1,000 per month to cover this loss. That is equivalent to $50 a day. The Ontario program pays an average of $8,000 for pain and suffering and over $7,000 when funeral expenses are required. Quebec pays significant amounts for temporary loss of wages and for rehabilitation, using a scheme that parallels workers' injury compensation. Table 7.8 compares the main types of awards in the two programs. Overall, Quebec pays an average close to $12,000 for about 6,000 cases, whereas Ontario is more modest at about $7,000 for about 3,500 cases. Both provinces pay administrative costs to run these programs, which add several million dollars to the overall costs.

TABLE 7.8   **Criminal Injuries Compensation in Ontario and Quebec: Total Awards by Name of Benefit in Millions of Dollars**

Ontario (2012–13)		Quebec (2012)	
Pain and suffering	$23.9		
		Rehabilitation	$9.8
Loss of wages	$0.4	Loss of work	$25.4
		Social and economic stabilization	$2.0
Funeral expenses	$0.4	Funeral expenses	$0.2
		Permanent disability	$36.5
Total	$24.7		$73.9

Note: These exclude medical expenses and legal expenses.

Source: © Queen's Printer for Ontario, 2014. Reproduced with permission. First column in table is drawn from CICB data. Second column is obtained by permission from the CIBC's Integrated Financial System (IFIS) as of December 6, 2013.

Victims of violence in the UK are informed about compensation and can use a website (www.cica.gov.uk) to make a claim. The website provides instructions on how to make a claim and indicates that the awards range from $1,000 to $800,000. Because the UK code of practice requires the police to inform victims about support services (also, they are required to inform the services that the person has been victimized), proportionately more victims get much larger awards than in most jurisdictions.

To bring restitution and compensation up to international standards, some significant investment and rethinking will be needed in Canada. After looking at what has been achieved in other jurisdictions, Waller (2010, 113–14) says that Canada should do several things to establish a similar standard, including the following: implement key steps to collect restitution from offenders; ensure that compensation paid by the state meets the costs and "pain" of victims from violent crime; provide mediation and restorative justice programs that respect the core needs of victims; and support research informing victims how to get restitution, civil suit orders, compensation, and restorative justice

Human Rights for Victims in Criminal Courts

In Canada's criminal and youth courts, victims are still limited to the role of witness, though some are allowed to submit a victim impact statement. The impact statement is usually a written statement, but in some cases it is a brief oral statement. Having said this, there are no data on the number of victims who are informed of this option or who take advantage of it.

In France, the United States, and some other countries, and in the International Criminal Court (of which Canada is an active partner), there is more scope for victim representation and participation. France has provided victims a role in the court system for over 40 years. Victims have legal standing in the courtroom and are represented as a civil party in the criminal justice system. This combination of criminal and civil proceedings allows victims to defend their interests in the pursuit of truth, reparation, public safety, fair sentencing, and other issues simultaneously. Victims can raise concerns about personal safety and compel a more thorough investigation of the offences against them. Many cases in the French system result in restitution orders, which are paid. When this measure is "bound" to the court, the victim has a more tangible and enforceable agreement—to which the accused and the victim can agree—than is typically the case in restorative justice.

France is no longer alone in employing this civil/criminal system. Belgium, Germany, Japan, and Korea are some of the countries that in the past decade have mobilized this system by providing legal assistance to victims.

In the United States, the federal Justice for All Act, passed in 2004, provides extensive rights to protect victims and facilitate restitution. In 2008, the State of California adopted Marsy's Law, which expanded victim's rights in that state. Both these laws provide models that may be adapted to Canada over the next few years. However, some people oppose these initiatives because of concerns that they might compromise the rights of the accused.

The International Criminal Court, of which Canada is a signatory, provides even more extensive rights for victims in a system that continues to provide offenders with rights under an adversarial system (see Table 7.9).

Table 7.10 provides a schematic of the current Criminal Code and Youth Criminal Justice Act and compares it to the US Justice for All Act (Waller, 2010). The Canadian Corrections and Conditional Release Act provides some additional rights to victims.

It is striking how many initiatives to support victims have been implemented in other countries but not in Canada.

Stopping Violence Against Victims and Preventing Repeat Victimization

By far the best way to reduce the $83 billion harm to victims (Zhang, 2011) is to prevent victimization in the first place by investing in what we know will reduce crime. In a recent book, Waller (2014) draws upon research brought together by the World Health Organization, many leading criminologists, and government agencies to show that we have the knowledge to reduce violence against women, street violence, property crime and child abuse by 50 percent or

TABLE 7.9   Participation and Representation in the International Criminal Court

Support
Victims are protected and supported
Victims are given responses sensitive to gender, age, and other issues
Justice
Victim participation and representation (grouped) is paid by legal aid in adversarial trial and sentencing
Restitution is paid to victims through trust funds funded by offenders and others
Good Government
Trust funds contribute to awareness and prevention
Permanent infrastructure is paid for by governments with performance assessments

Source: Irvin Waller, *Rights for Victims of Crime: Rebalancing Justice* (New York: Rowman and Littlefield, 2010), 126–30, figure 6.4.

TABLE 7.10 **Comparison of Provisions for Victim Rights in the US Federal Justice for All Act with the Criminal Code and the Youth Criminal Justice Act**

Justice for All Act (U.S., 2004)	Criminal Code	Youth Criminal Justice Act
1. The right to be reasonably protected from the accused.		
2. The right to reasonable, accurate, and timely notice of any public court proceeding, or any parole proceeding, involving the crime or of any release or escape of the accused.		
3. The right not to be excluded from any such public court proceeding, unless the court, after receiving clear and convincing evidence, determines that testimony by the victim would be materially altered if the victim heard other testimony at the proceeding.		
4. The right to be reasonably heard at any public proceeding in the district court involving release, plea, sentencing, or any parole proceeding.	Section 672.5 (14) Victim Impact Statements Right to have read at sentencing.	Sections 50–51 Victim Impact Statements Right to have read at sentencing.
5. The reasonable right to confer with the attorney for the government in the case.		
6. The right to full and timely restitution as provided in law.	Section 83.17 (2) Restitution Judge has discretion	Section 42-2-F Restitution Judge has discretion
7. The right to proceedings free from unreasonable delay.		
8. The right to be treated with fairness and with respect for the victim's dignity and privacy.		

Source: Adapted from Irvin Waller, *Rights for Victims of Crime: Rebalancing Justice* (New York: Rowman and Littlefield, 2010), 121–24.

more for a reinvestment of about 10 percent of what we are presently spending on reactive policies (Waller, 2014). As we saw earlier, expenditures on policing, courts, and corrections are at $20 billion and rising. By reinvesting $2 billion smartly, we could probably reduce losses to victims by $40 billion.

School-based programs are among the best ways of reducing delinquency involvement.

Jim West/Alamy

Several experimental projects have allowed sophisticated random control evaluations. They have demonstrated that it is indeed possible for government to tackle the negative life experiences of persons at risk of offending to help them to live their lives without victimizing others (Waller, 2014). For instance, a Canadian initiative, Stop Now and Plan (SNAP), helps children and parents regulate youth aggression. This program has been subjected to rigorous evaluations, many of which have demonstrated positive outcomes among children under the age of 12. Effective crime prevention programs can save a great deal of money. For example, a cost analysis of the well-known Perry Preschool Program found that every dollar spent on effective prevention programs saves at least seven dollars. These savings came from lower costs to victims, reduced justice system costs, lower welfare costs, higher taxes paid by program participants who had higher incomes than non-participants, and reduced special education costs (Schweinhart, 2003; Waller, 2014; Institute for Prevention of Crime, 2009, 2.1).

Equally impressive have been the outcomes of evaluations of programs to prevent child abuse and subsequent adolescent offending. These programs have different names—Perry Pre-school Program, Public Health nurse visitation programs, and Triple P (Positive Parenting Program). These programs can help parents in difficult situations raise their children in a more consistent and caring way.

In 2011, the US Justice Department announced the creation of a new website, crimesolutions.gov, to help taxpayers judge the effectiveness of state and local anti-crime programs. The cost–benefit analyses of these programs have been very impressive, showing a huge return on investment. This is known as the "prevention dividend." The work by the Washington State Institute on Public Policy, conducted for the legislature of the State of Washington, is an important and continuing source of additional and detailed updates. We can also look to England's Youth Inclusion Projects, a series of programs developed to reach the most difficult teenagers and significantly reduce their offending. The UK did not wait to retest the Youth Inclusion Projects. Instead, it multiplied them in 72 low-income housing estates with an evaluation. When they succeeded again, they doubled the projects. Canada's National Crime Prevention Centre still funds only limited replications of these projects. The time is long overdue to invest in a national program that would draw from the successes achieved in other countries.

Youth are involved in many of the sexual assaults that occur in elementary and secondary schools, universities and colleges, and neighbourhoods in Canada. Fortunately, Canadian research confirms that when we change male attitudes toward violence and women, we can expect to reduce most common types of violence against women. One strategy that stands out is the "4th R", which was tested through a large-scale random control trial in Canada. It changes the attitudes of teenagers in high school regarding alcohol and drug abuse, violence, and sexual assault against women. This program was developed by a partnership of the University of Western Ontario and the City of London, Ontario, described earlier in this chapter (Crooke et al., 2008; Institute for Prevention of Crime, 2009, 1.2; Waller, 2014).

Some successful models for reducing crime focus on reducing the risk to victims. The first proven prevention of residential burglary occurred in Seattle in the 1970s; more than 50 percent of residential burglaries were avoided. A similar strategy in Kirkholt, England, achieved similar results: it focused on repeat burglary victims and achieved a reduction of over 80 percent (Waller, 2008, 53–66).

WHO, the UN Commission on Crime Prevention and Criminal Justice, the US National Research Council, and the 2007 Alberta Task Force on Reducing Crime have called for a three-pronged approach to reduce victimization. This approach combines enforcement with prevention as well as community treatment for persons at risk of offending. All of the involved organizations stress the importance of mobilizing key agencies such as schools, social services, housing authorities, and the police to collaboratively develop solutions to the problems, implement those solutions, and follow up with careful evaluation of the results.

One successful approach is to establish a task force that analyzes what we are currently doing, identifies the gaps compared with best practice, and recommends necessary actions. This is exactly what the Province of Alberta did in 2007, and as a result it became the leading jurisdiction in North America in implementing the best approaches to reducing crime. It launched a three-pronged, evidence-based strategy of enforcement, treatment, and prevention while also committing an additional $500 million over three years as part of a comprehensive long-term strategy. The program was implemented by a permanent leadership centre called the Community Safety Secretariat, which was composed of senior officials assigned to the centre on a permanent basis. The program was to be evaluated using indicators of reduction in victimization and harm to victims. Unfortunately, the secretariat's small budget and also its highly cost-effective investments were cut in 2013, thus shifting Alberta back to policies that allow crime and expenditures on police and prisons to grow.

Another spectacular yet little-known and non-replicated Canadian example is the Winnipeg Auto-Theft Suppression strategy (see Chapter 15) which is saving Winnipeg residents about $40 million each year in auto insurance premiums.

A growing number of municipalities, including Edmonton, Montreal, Ottawa, and Waterloo Region, have established permanent leadership centres to diagnose problems and implement solutions. However, these cities have not made the financial investment that research shows is required to provide successful programs.

We now know a great deal about how to stop people from becoming victims of crime. Waller (2014) has identified a number of ways in which we can do better at reducing the number of victims.

1. Shift crime policies to pre-emptive strategies orchestrated by a small secretariat to diagnose problems and to mobilize key sectors such as schools, housing, and policing,
2. Invest adequately in programs that have demonstrated their effectiveness, such as repeat victimization programs, compulsory curricula—such as the 4th R to reduce sexual assault, Triple P to stop child abuse, and the strategies used in Winnipeg to reduce car theft and now street violence.
3. Continue to tackle alcohol and drug abuse among younger adults.

QUESTIONS FOR CRITICAL THINKING

1. What actions would the police need to take to meet the needs of victims of crime?
2. Identify one way other than a victim impact statement that would provide victims with a way to protect their interests in criminal courts.
3. Given current knowledge about violence prevention, how would you shift government resources to reduce the number of victims of violence?

Systemic Ways to Shift, Reinvest, and Rebalance Justice for Crime Victims

In the first section of this chapter, we described the impact of crime on victims. In the second section, we saw the origins of the victimology movement in Canada and the development of international standards. In third section, we saw areas where Canada could advance toward those standards to better meet the needs of crime victims.

Throughout this chapter we have seen that the traditional criminal justice system has long resisted making the changes that research shows are required to reduce victimization and to improve the lives of victims. That system has even resisted the recommendations of the 1998 Parliamentary Report—*A Voice not a Veto*—and McMurtry's 2007 report. In 2010, Waller examined US and European innovations to address prevention, services, and victims' rights (2010, 154–64). He focused on five key components for comprehensive implementation: an office for victims of crime, standards and training, evaluation and ombudspersons, social science surveys to foster success, and research and development.

In this section we look at four key ways to achieve the shift and reinvestment: model legislation, an independently funded institute, social science surveys, and an amendment to the Charter of Rights and Freedoms. We then discuss the key recommendations from a national symposium in 2011, which were amplified in the federal Ombudsman's Forum in 2013 that looked at ways to help Canada achieve international standards.

Model Legislation

Fourteen international experts met in 2005 to prepare a draft report for a UN Convention that would encourage governments to follow through on the 1985 resolution to prevent victimization and to implement services and rights for victims. Waller has adapted this draft into a model law that could be adopted by a Canadian province (2010, 173–83).

The model law is divided into three major sections: support, justice, and good government. The support section includes subsections on recognition, information, and assistance. The justice section makes provisions for restitution and repayment, protection from the accused, participation, and representation. The good government section covers effective policies to reduce victimization and the all-important issues of implementation.

An Independently Funded Institute

An office for victims of crime responsible for pushing the victims' agenda, as well as a federal ombudsman for victims of crime, is not enough. We need to create a permanently funded institute. Such an institute, while requiring contributions from legal professionals, social researchers, and victim's rights agencies, must be independent of them all. This institute would likely be based out of a Canadian university and would function as a central hub for education, research, and policy observation. It would work in close cooperation with service agencies in the community, the Federal Victim's Ombudsman, and legal practitioners.

One such institute has already been created in Europe and could serve as a best practices model for a Canadian institute. INTERVICT is the International Victimology Institute Tilburg. It was launched by Tilburg University in the Netherlands in 2005, and has continually expanded research on victimization and victim assistance within Europe. It has conducted extensive evaluations of the implementation of victim legislation in the EU and has been leading the world on issues of victimization (identity theft, human trafficking, online victimization, and more).

Social Science Evaluations

The partnership between INTERVICT and the European Forum for Victim Support changed the course of history by demonstrating that the landmark European Framework had not made the difference that was needed in terms of services meeting the needs of victims. As a result, the EU modified its approach to establish the 2012 directive. In the United States, the insistence that the Rights for Victims of Crime Act be evaluated by the GAO has ensured that improvements are being made in how the act is being applied.

An Amendment to Charter of Rights and Freedoms

The Canadian Charter of Rights and Freedoms includes a number of paragraphs protecting the rights of accused and convicted persons against the powers of the state. At this time, it does not include any rights for victims of crime. So the traditional rights of defendants "trump" the basic human rights of victims that have been recognized by the UN but not yet by Canada.

Crime victims need their rights to safety, reparation, and justice to be recognized by an amendment to the Charter of Rights and Freedoms. Such an amendment could include the following wording: "To have the rights of victims of crime to safety, reparation and justice respected" *and* "Balanced fairly, against rights of the accused or convicted offender" *and* "heard through participation and representation equal to that of the accused in all judicial and administrative proceedings" (Waller, 2010, 168–70).

Key Actions

Every year, Justice Canada encourages a Crime Victim Awareness Week in April. In 2011 the Faculty of Social Sciences at the University of Ottawa organized a national symposium titled Crime Victim Rights: Reaching for International Standards. Delegates were invited from the federal, provincial, and municipal governments as well as national associations.

The costs of implementing a national action plan that would include the proposals in this chapter were discussed based on estimates by Waller (2010, 164–68; 2008, 132–34). The reinvestment needed to implement all of the recommendations discussed in this chapter is approximately 10 percent of the expenditures on the traditional criminal justice system. Funding this 10 percent can be done gradually over five years.

The Canadian Resource Centre for Victims of Crime and the International Organization for Victim Assistance were the principal partners for the National Symposium. Following the symposium, they have called for the following:

1. A *national action plan*, including standards such as those in the UK and the model law (see above), that would apply to policing, services, restitution, compensation, prosecution, and courts; that would be sensitive to special needs such as those of women, children, and Aboriginal populations; and that would have leadership offices for victims of crime.
2. A *provincial victim advocate*, supported by *surveys* to provide better data and an *institute* to focus on research and development.
3. *Provincial and municipal prevention strategies* to effectively reduce crime and promote community safety.
4. *Permanent funding* equivalent to at least 10 percent of the current expenditures on criminal justice, to be used for prevention, victim services, and rights.
5. An *amendment* to the Charter of Rights and Freedoms.

In this chapter, we have seen that the needs of victims have been overlooked by the traditional system. Starting with the landmark UN Declaration—the Magna Carta for victims—we have seen that an increase in the awareness of the needs of victims internationally has led to some cautious steps in Canada. These steps have included improvements in policing, victim services and compensation, and courts and restitution, but there is still a long way to go. Rebalancing the justice system to respect victims' human rights requires more than ad hoc solutions. It also requires a national action plan, serious investments in that plan, investments in effective prevention, and possibly an amendment to the Charter of Rights and Freedoms.

One of the most important steps for convincing legislators to make the reinvestments is to get the knowledge out to voters, taxpayers and (potential) victims of crime, while showing how the shift to stopping victimization and implementing victim rights is in the interests of (potential) victims and taxpayers.

QUESTIONS FOR CRITICAL THINKING

1. How can social science help to shift policy from the over-use of punishment to meeting the real needs of most victims of crime.
2. Using federal funding for activities during Crime Victim Awareness Week, it was possible to identify a short list of key actions and their costs to help victims get the services and rights they need. What activities could you plan in your community, university, or college with these federal funds?

● Summary

- About one in four adult Canadians is a victim of some type of crime every year. Though relatively few are victims of serious crime, the cumulative harm to victims was estimated at more than $80 billion for 2008.

- Canada resolved at the UN General Assembly in 1985 to invest in preventing crime and guaranteeing human rights for victims of crime (Declaration of Basic Principles of Justice for Victims), but it has not implemented these promises.

- Canadians paid more than $20 billion in 2010 for a traditional system of police, courts, and corrections that still limits the role of the victim to acting as the complainant and as a witness. Few of these funds have been invested in preventing victimization, assisting victims, and protecting human rights of victims.

- The International Association of Chiefs of Police has developed strategic ways to enhance the police response to victims of crime, but its Canadian members have done little to implement these proven strategies.

- For more than 30 years, surveys have shown that victims of sexual violence rarely report to police, but little has been done to improve this situation.

- The personnel in victim assistance services, sexual assault crisis centres, and shelters for battered women are not paid salaries that are competitive with wages in the traditional criminal justice system. Unlike other criminal justice agencies, victims' organizations often have to reapply for funding every year.

- Compensation to victims for criminal injuries varies from province to province and in most cases is inadequate.

- Restitution and restorative justice are popular discussion points for criminologists but have been losing ground in application in Canada despite the pioneering role played by Canadian groups in the 1970s and 1980s.

- Traditional criminal courts appear to ignore or find ways to overlook sections in the Criminal Code designed to protect victims, such as the victim fine surcharge, restitution, and victim impact statements.

- Canada is at the cutting edge of programs to stop victimization, such as the Alberta Crime Reduction Strategy, the Winnipeg Auto Theft Suppression Strategy, municipal crime prevention strategies, and the 4th R program, but it lacks any overall action plan and funding to shift from over-reliance on the traditional criminal justice system.

- Ways to rebalance the system to meet needs and human rights for victims of crime are well known but have not yet been applied in Canada. These include social science surveys, a research and training institute, national standards, and much more.

NET WORK

1. What practical information exists on the Internet about your home town on
   (a) how to report a crime to the police?
   (b) what services are available in your community for different types of crime victims, including a break-in, an aggravated sexual assault, and a person killed by a drunk driver?
   (c) how to assess harm to victims and apply for compensation from the state if you are injured in a crime, and what the key conditions are, including the maximum award that can be provided?
   (d) how to apply for restitution and get it paid? *and*
   (e) what your right is to a victim impact statement and how you exercise it?
2. Compare your answers to these questions to the following:
   (a) the information on the website of Justice Canada for crime victims (http://www.victimsmatter.gc.ca/index.html)
   (b) help you can get from the Federal Ombudsman for Victims of Crime (http://www.victimsfirst.gc.ca/index.html)
   (c) the British Code of *Practice for Victims of Crime* (http://www.direct.gov.uk/prod_consum_dg/groups/dg_digitalassets/@dg/@en/documents/digital-asset/dg_073647.pdf) and the Criminal Injuries Compensation Authority (http://www.justice.gov.uk/guidance/compensation-schemes/cica/index.htm)
3. (a) Locate the victim services act or the bill of rights for victims of crime for your province, and compare the provisions with those stated in the UN Declaration of Basic Principles of Justice for Victims of Crime and Abuse of Power (http://www.un.org/documents/ga/res/40/a40r034.htm).
   (b) Propose your best action to get them implemented.

Explanations of Crime

The field of criminology is multidisciplinary. Lawyers, sociologists, political scientists, psychologists, biologists, physicians, historians, and philosophers may all consider the study of crime as part of their discipline. Nowhere is this diversity more apparent than in the development of theories of the causes of crime.

Part 2 covers many of the most popular explanations of crime. The debate over which of these explanations is "best" is often heated, and no attempt is made to resolve this issue here. It would be premature to impose such a judgment on a field that has been described as consisting of "a number of fitful leads from one partially examined thesis to another" (Rock, 1980). Instead, each theory is presented by an author who has had experience (and some sympathy) with it and who presents the theory's strengths and weaknesses. Several researchers are now trying to synthesize several of the different approaches, and some of the authors discuss this integrative work.

Part 2 illustrates how theories of crime causation have developed over time. In Chapter 8, several of the earliest approaches to the explanation of crime are discussed. The most important point made in this chapter is that explanations of crime arise from particular historical milieus and reflect the social and intellectual fashions of the day. Chapter 9 presents theories that focus on the traits of individuals. The psychological perspective has been with us for many years and is still popular today. Chapters 10 to 15 are concerned with the sociological explanations of crime. They illustrate the diverse ways in which social structure and social processes may promote or restrain criminal behaviour.

8

Early Theories of Criminology

Tullio Caputo
CARLETON UNIVERSITY

Rick Linden
UNIVERSITY OF MANITOBA

We begin this chapter by exploring the context in which modern criminology developed. Societal beliefs relating crime to superstition and sin were replaced during the Enlightenment by naturalistic explanations based on the idea that people are free and rational beings. This change, which was part of the struggle for individual rights and freedoms during the Enlightenment, reflected the view that the social order was based on a social contract between the individual and the state. This in turn was based on the growing power of the rising merchant classes and the reduced influence of the feudal aristocracy, whose power rested on the ownership of the land and on the loyalty of the peasants who lived and worked on it.

We then discuss the rise of the Classical School of criminology during this era. The principle of "let the punishment fit the crime" represented the core of the philosophy of the Classical School, which maintained a belief in people's ability to reason and to act rationally. Although the Classical School provided the basis for our modern Criminal Code, its principles were too inflexible in practice. The argument of later Positive School criminologists that mitigating circumstances must be considered when dealing with crime and criminals led to further reforms in how society dealt with criminals. The chapter concludes with an examination of early theories that sought the causes of crime in the biological make-up of individual offenders.

Learning Objectives

After reading this chapter, you should be able to

- Discuss the context within which modern explanations of crime and criminality were developed.
- Identify the founders of the Classical School of criminology, the key principles of this approach, and the impact of this school on our legal system.
- Outline the criticisms of the Classical approach and the changes in the legal process that were influenced by the Positive criminologists.
- Describe the basic features of the Positive School of criminology, and outline their approach and key principles.
- Show how the ideas advanced by the Positive School influenced other researchers to search for the biological causes of crime.
- Discuss how biological explanations of criminality influenced the development of this field at the beginning of the 20th century.

Prior to the 18th century, theories about crime were inspired primarily by religious beliefs and superstition:

> From the most primitive beginnings of human history, man [*sic*] believed in the existence of spirits and magic, and ... from the earliest days of his existence on earth, he began to ascribe various unusual phenomena of nature to the activities of evil spirits. This naturally led him to believe that any pathology in human behavior must be due to an evil spirit. (Zilborg, 1969, 11)

The link between evil spirits and wrongdoing is strong in many religions. Judeo-Christian teachings offer two powerful explanations for the role evil spirits play in sinful behaviour: temptation and possession. Ideas about temptation are rooted in the belief that people exercise free will and choose to act in particular ways, even ways they know to be wrong. The Devil is thought to be at work tempting people, but righteous believers can resist the Devil's powerful allure by drawing strength from their faith. They are encouraged to do this by religious leaders, who deploy images of hell-fire and threats of eternal damnation to steel the spines of the faithful who might otherwise waver. These images and beliefs about temptation imply that people who succumb are weak and morally inferior beings. This explains how the poor, the destitute, and other unfortunate members of society have been held responsible for their lot throughout much of history. Their misfortunes are seen as the result of their own moral failures. These beliefs also provide the basis for our ideas about deterrence: most people believe that the threat of severe punishment should be enough to persuade people not to engage in misdeeds.

The second, and equally powerful, Judeo-Christian concept linking sin to evil spirits is that of possession. Wrongdoers were often suspected of being possessed by the Devil or some other malevolent spirit. These unfortunate individuals were thought to have little hope of recovering and were treated quite harshly. A host of horrifying tortures were used to drive the evil spirits from their bodies, and evidence of guilt was determined through a series of trials whose intent was to differentiate between the righteous and the sinner. These included trial by battle, trial by ordeal, trial by fire, and trial by water. In most cases, the accused had little to look forward to, whether innocent or guilty, since these trials were extremely severe and often fatal.

These practices, which reflected a belief in the power of supernatural forces, reached their peak during the Middle Ages with the notorious Inquisition and the witch craze it spawned. This period was marked by tremendous social upheaval, as Western Europe was in the midst of the transition from feudalism to capitalism. Confusion and fear followed the revolution in the material and intellectual worlds of the day. Political and religious elites sought to protect their positions and privileges and to maintain the existing order by any means possible. This included resorting to both religious and civil laws. As Angell (1965) notes, "the development of a common criminal law was aided by the close connection between crime and sin ... Punishment meant expiation. It is only one step from the fear of gods' displeasure to the desire for reassurance concerning the integrity of the moral order" (118).

Medieval society was forced to change because existing social arrangements no longer met the needs of the growing European population. Poverty, misery, wars, and sickness ravaged the masses. All of this led people to question and even to challenge long-standing practices and beliefs, including those related to civil and religious authority. For example, the Protestant Reformation shook the foundations of the Christian world by challenging the power and authority of Rome. Throughout Europe, those in power were increasingly being held to account for deteriorating material conditions and social problems. It is in this context that the Inquisition and the witch craze found fertile ground. The religious and political elites began seeking ways to divert attention from themselves and to silence the rebellious members of society. Blaming existing social problems on the Devil and other evil spirits was a means to achieve both objectives. First, this diverted the public's attention from the elites and helped place blame for social problems on individuals who were identified as possessed by or in league with the Devil. Second, those in power made themselves indispensable by arguing that they alone had the knowledge and power to deal with the threat posed by the Devil (Harris, 1974).

These developments blurred the distinction between sin and crime and provided ideal conditions for the confluence of civil and religious authority. In medieval England, for example, there existed

> an almost paranoid concern for order in society, and a close association between crime and sin. The Reformation and the increased power of the Puritans changed perceptions of crime and justice both in government and in the popular mind. Religion and morality became matters of state law and potential sources of rebellion; although sin and crime were usually dealt with by different courts (crime by the civil court, sin by the ecclesiastical court), they were in some ways almost indistinguishable. (Best, 1998, n.p.)

Drawing and quartering was one of the many horrendous punishments given to individuals during the Middle Ages. This level of cruelty was common across Europe and was lessened only after the Enlightenment in the 18th century.

Chronicle/Alamy

By linking morality to rebellion, the authorities effectively prevented anyone from challenging the status quo. Those who did were likely to be accused of heresy and subjected to extremely harsh punishments, including death. This is precisely what happened to those accused of witchcraft. During the 300 years in which the witch craze flourished, more than half a million people were put to death. The plight of those accused of being witches illustrates how charges of heresy were used to silence critics and quash any rebellious inclinations in the population.

Witches had been active in Western Europe for centuries, although they were never prosecuted. This changed as a result of the growing challenge to religious and civil authorities during the 15th century. Witches served as a convenient scapegoat against whom the masses could vent their anger. Importantly, it was usually the less powerful members of a community who were most in danger of being accused of witchcraft. Although this group included the elderly, the infirm, and children, the witch craze mainly victimized women. Indeed, throughout history, 85 percent of the people executed for witchcraft have been women (Pfohl, 1985). Pfohl suggests "it is hardly surprising that during times in which the great male mastery over nature seemed least secure, times of economic hardship and political instability, the priestly finger of men often found bewitching women to blame" (39). This led to horrific ritual punishments, including "baths in boiling water, crushing by heavy weights, tearing the flesh from the breasts with searing-hot pincers, and torture of the female sex organs" (39).

Economically independent women and women who lived alone and outside the protection of men were most susceptible to charges of witchcraft. Their presence in a community disrupted and threatened the male-dominated power structures. Charges of witchcraft and public executions reasserted the authority of male leaders and reminded community members of their subordinate position in the social hierarchy. At the same time, however, the cruelty and sheer barbarism of the courts and their punishments fuelled cries for reform across western Europe.

Early theorizing about crime and the beginnings of our modern system of criminal justice began to emerge during this tumultuous period of European history. "It was an era of racing industrial revolution, enclosure movements, growing capitalism and growing cities" (Sylvester, 1972, 2). These developments were hastened by a rapidly expanding population and by the growth of trade and manufacturing.

The feudal economy had been based on agriculture, with clearly established relations between the landowning aristocracy and the peasants who worked the land. A system of mutual rights and obligations bound these two classes together, and when this relationship was challenged, the entire system was threatened. Feudalism was unable to meet the needs of the growing population. It is estimated that England's population soared from 2.8 million in 1500 to 8.9 million in 1800. Similar increases were reported for the rest of Europe (Pfohl, 1985). This surge fuelled a period of colonial expansion as European monarchs sought havens for their surplus populations and access to markets and raw materials, which colonies could provide. Europe's merchant classes gained considerable power during this period, for their economic activities offset mounting economic shortfalls (see Chapter 2).

Changes in the economy were mirrored by changes throughout society. Revolutionary developments were taking place in philosophy, art, music, literature, and other intellectual pursuits. Progressive thinkers of the day fought to usher Europe into a new era—"the Age of Reason" emerged during the period known as the Enlightenment. The Enlightenment thinkers argued against fanaticism and religious superstition, advocating "naturalistic" explanations of the world based on people's capacity to reason.

The Enlightenment philosophers believed that people were free and rational beings. This belief led them to call for the establishment of individual rights and freedoms. In their view, society was based on a social contract under which people chose to relinquish a small portion of their individual autonomy in order to ensure their own safety and the well-being of the entire group. These ideas were clearly contrary to the collectivist orientation of feudalism and to notions that rulers held about a privileged nobility. If realized, a system based on rights and freedoms could seriously undermine the bonds of fealty (duty and loyalty) that had long held feudalism together. But those same feudal bonds restricted the availability of labour and hampered the development of manufacturing and industry. Herein lies the essence of the conflict between the aristocracy and the merchants: what was useful for one was detrimental to the other. Each group fought to advance its own interests.

For all their growing economic power, the merchant classes enjoyed little political influence, for only landowners could participate in the legislatures of the day. While they were financially wealthy, the merchants owned little land and were prevented from acquiring any more. Thus, they were barred from gaining political power through landownership. The merchants turned to the legal arena to have their interests served (see Chapter 2).

The merchant classes were able to strengthen their position by financing the costly wars being fought by European monarchs over new colonies. In return for this financial assistance, the merchants gained significant legal concessions. While many of these concessions were aimed specifically at enhancing mercantile activities, they established a number of important legal principles that reflected the ideals of the Enlightenment philosophers. It was in this context that the **Classical School** of criminology made its most significant contributions to the founding of our modern criminal justice system.

> **Classical School**
> Considered to be the first formal school of criminology, Classical criminology is associated with 18th- and early 19th-century reforms to the administration of justice and the prison system. Associated with authors such as Cesare Beccaria (1738–1794), Jeremy Bentham (1748–1832), Samuel Romilly (1757–1818), and others, this school brought the emerging philosophy of liberalism and utilitarianism to the justice system, advocating principles of rights, fairness, and due process in place of retribution, arbitrariness, and brutality.

SEARCH FOR:
"Cesare Beccaria (1738–1794)" *Internet Encyclopedia of Philosophy*

The Classical School

In 1764, Cesare Beccaria published his major work, *An Essay on Crimes and Punishments*. Though this work contained little that was new, it did much to focus the movement for humanitarian reform that was gaining momentum throughout Europe, for Beccaria was criticizing the cruelty and inhumanity that characterized the criminal justice system of his day.

Abuses in the administration of justice were routine. Practices established in the notorious Court of Star Chamber and the institutionalized terror of the Inquisition had become commonplace. Few safeguards existed for the accused, and judicial torture had become a routine method of securing confessions and discovering the identities of accomplices (Langbein, 1976).

The more popular forms of torture for these crimes included the rack, the ducking stool, thumbscrews, and other mechanical devices designed to inflict severe pain. The death penalty was administered in a number of ways, including burning at the stake, hanging, decapitation, and drawing and quartering. Hostettler (2011) describes the savage penalty for high treason under Britain's Bloody Code: "A man found guilty was drawn behind a cart to the place of execution, hanged and cut down whilst still alive, disembowelled and castrated, with his intestines burnt before his eyes and finally decapitated with the remainder of his body cut into quarters" (51).

In 18th-century England, as many as 350 offences were punishable by death. About 70 percent of death sentences were given for robbery and burglary (Newman, 1978). Practices in the colonies were similar in the early 1800s. The first person executed in Toronto was hanged for passing a bad cheque.

Clamour for the reform of such practices had started long before Beccaria's book was published. Humanitarian appeals were heard from jurists, writers, and philosophers of the era, including Hobbes, Locke, Montesquieu, and Voltaire. The criminal law, in particular, embodied practices that directly contradicted many of the principles advocated by the Classical theorists. It was contrary to the ideals of the social contract, for it was administered in such a way that the average citizen was denied fair and impartial treatment by the state. European society was ripe for the liberating ideas of the Classical theorists and their humanitarian reforms. Beccaria's book served as a catalyst for these sentiments. The reform of a barbaric system of justice provided an excellent focus for the ideas of the Classical theorists.

The Classical Theory of Crime

The roots of Classical criminology lie in the philosophy of the Enlightenment. Social contract theory represented a new way of looking at the relationship between people and the state. To avoid living in a state of nature that was, to use Hobbes's famous description, "solitary, poor, nasty, brutish, and short" (1958, 107), people voluntarily entered into a social contract with the state. This involved giving up some of their freedom to the state. In return, the state protected the right of citizens to live in security. The social contract was made with the consent of both parties, and neither had the right to break it. The state was required to provide protection but could not violate the rights of citizens. The citizen was required to obey the rules or face punishment from the state. In the opening chapter of his book, Beccaria wrote:

> Laws are the conditions whereby free and independent men unite to form society. Weary of living in a state of war, and of enjoying a freedom rendered useless by the uncertainty of its perpetuation, men will willingly sacrifice a part of this freedom in order to enjoy that which is left in security and tranquility. (quoted in Monachesi, 1972, 73)

The reforms proposed by the Classical theorists were based on a well-developed theory of the causes of crime, a theory that represented a significant break with earlier ones. The Classical theorists had a simple explanation for crime: people broke the law because they thought that doing so would advance

FOCUS

Box 8.1

WITCHCRAFT AND TORTURE

It is estimated that five hundred thousand people were convicted of witchcraft and burned to death in Europe between the fifteenth and seventeenth centuries. Their crimes: a pact with the Devil; journeys through the air over vast distances mounted on broomsticks; unlawful assembly at sabbats; worship of the Devil; kissing the Devil under the tail; copulation with incubi, male devils equipped with ice-cold penises; copulation with succubi, female devils.

Other more mundane charges were often added: killing the neighbor's cow; causing hailstorms; ruining the crops; stealing and eating babies. But many a witch was executed for no crime other than flying through the air to attend a sabbat ...

Torture was routinely applied until the witch confessed to having made a pact with the Devil and having flown to a sabbat. It was continued until the witch named other people who were present at the sabbat. If a witch attempted to retract a confession, torture was applied even more intensely until the original confession was reconfirmed. This left the person accused of witchcraft with the choice between dying once and for all at the stake or being returned repeatedly to the torture chambers. Most people opted for the stake. As a reward for their cooperative attitude, penitent witches could look forward to being strangled before the fire was lit.

Source: Marvin Harris, (1974). *Cows, Pigs, Wars and Witches*. New York: Vintage Books.

World History Archive/Alamy

Thousands of people were executed for witchcraft between the 15th and 17th centuries.

their own interests. In other words, deviance was the natural result of our rational self-interest. If it suits us, and if we think we can get away with it, we will break the law. Crime was understood to be a rationally calculated activity and not the result of some supernatural force or demonic possession. This was a fundamental shift from earlier explanations of criminality.

Having addressed the causes of crime, the Classical theorists turned to the problem of controlling it. The solution was to set up a system of punishment that would deter people from breaking the law. The Classical theorists believed that humans were rational beings who carefully calculated the consequences of their behaviour. Thus a person who might be tempted to break the law would consider the positive and negative consequences of his or her actions. A well-crafted Criminal Code would ensure that most people would choose to be good rather than evil. One might think that the extremely brutal justice system of the time should have been an effective deterrent, but its excessive harshness was contrary to the Enlightenment view that citizens should not be treated unfairly by the state. Instead, Beccaria proposed that the punishment should fit the crime, that is, it should be proportional to the harm done to society. Beccaria argued this on two grounds: that this amount of punishment would be the most effective deterrent, and that this was the fairest way to punish those who were not deterred and who chose to break the law. Unfair punishment would be a violation of the social contract and would be perceived as unjust by the individual and by other members of society. Beccaria describes how this would affect the social contract and reduce the deterrent effect of law:

> In proportion as torments become more cruel, the spirits of men, which are like fluids that always rise to the level of surrounding objects, become callous, and the ever lively force of the passions brings it to pass that after a hundred years of cruel torments the wheel inspires no greater fear than imprisonment once did … The countries and times most notorious for severity of penalties have always been those in which the bloodiest and most inhumane of deeds were committed, for the same spirit of ferocity that guided the hand of the legislators also ruled that of parricide and assassin. (1963, 43–44)

Crime would be reduced if these reforms were implemented in law because calculating criminals would see that they would not profit from their actions. The punishment would be severe enough that it would cost them more than they could gain from their criminal behaviour. Beccaria also proposed that punishment be swift and certain. If punishment followed too long after the act, or if it was unlikely to happen at all, then the law would not be an effective deterrent to crime. Finally, the law would be most effective in preventing crime if it was clear and simple enough that people could understand it.

With regard to specific reforms, Beccaria felt that the brutality of torture and the practice of executing people for minor offences must be abolished, for they were abuses of state power. Criminal matters should be dealt with in public according to the dictates of the law. Beccaria wanted to restrict the power of judges, which had been exercised in an arbitrary manner, in private, and generally without recourse for the defendant. He sought to restrict this power by separating the lawmaking power of the legislature from the activities of the judges. His view was that the law should be determined by the legislature; it should be accessible to all; trials should be public; and the role of the judiciary should be restricted to the determination of guilt and the administration of punishment as set out in law.

The reforms suggested by Beccaria represented a call for equality and for due-process safeguards. The creation of graded punishments would effectively restrict the arbitrariness and inequality that characterized the existing system. By arguing that the punishment should "fit the crime," Beccaria shifted the focus away from the actor and onto the act. In this way, both noble and peasant would be judged on the basis of what they had done and not on who they were. Moreover, the judiciary would be stripped of its discretion in sentencing, since judges would be bound by punishments fixed by law. This was a powerful directive for equality, since the preferential treatment formerly accorded to those with wealth and power could no longer be granted. However, those with wealth and power had the most influence in shaping the law, so the reforms to the justice system did little to alter the fundamental inequalities based on ownership of property.

Assessing the Contributions of the Classical School

The Classical School and Legal Reform

The ideals of the social contract theorists were translated into progressive criminal justice policy through the reforms promoted by the Classical School. In the process, excesses and injustices were attacked and the foundations of our modern legal system were established. Due-process safeguards (which are taken for granted today), as well as reforms such as the guarantee of individual rights and of equality before the law, the separation of judicial and legislative functions, and the establishment of fixed penalties, remain as the legacy of the Classical School of criminology. Canada's Criminal Code and our modern criminal justice system continue to reflect the work of the Classical theorists.

Limitations of the Classical School

Despite this success, the influence of the Classical School was not all positive. A serious problem with Classical theory was Beccaria's insistence that the degree of punishment must be proportional to the degree of harm that had been done to society. At first glance this proposal seems reasonable, but in practice, it meant that the personal characteristics of the offender and the circumstances of the offence could not be considered when courts determined punishments (Roshier, 1989). Also, by removing the flexibility of judicial discretion, the reforms actually gave more power to the state, which was responsible for passing very specific sentencing laws (Newman and Marongiu, 1990).

Although punishments could be rationally determined on paper, their application in real life often resulted in gross injustices. The courts were bound to follow the letter of the law and could not use discretion to temper the justice being meted out. For example, the hardship that results from having to pay a $1,000 fine varies dramatically depending on whether a person is wealthy or poor. The courts, however, could not take this into account. Furthermore, they were unable to consider mitigating factors such as motive or mental competence, which would alter the responsibility of the convicted person. In this way, attempts to enforce equality resulted in a system that produced a great deal of injustice.

Changing this rigid system was one of the goals of Neoclassical criminologists, including the French magistrate Gabriel Tarde. Tarde rejected the notion of free will and proposed a modification of the system of punishment

Neoclassical theory
Neoclassical theorists sought to allow more flexibility in the justice system such as individualizing sentences to take into account offender characteristics and extenuating circumstances.

to recognize that there must be some individual treatment of offenders. As a result of the work of Tarde and other Neoclassical writers, courts began to take into account factors such as age (children were held less accountable), mental competence, motive, and mitigating circumstances. For example, in France, the Penal Code of 1791, which reflected the views of the Classical School, was revised in 1810 and again in 1819. With each revision, the rigid nature of the code was modified to include more discretion for judges as well as consideration of extenuating circumstances.

The approach the Classical School advocated was based more on a theory of **deterrence** than on a theory of crime, and it can be assessed on these grounds. The issue of deterrence continues to be an important element of this approach. For Classical theorists, penalties need not be severe as long as they are swift and certain. However, for most offences, the likelihood of punishment is so small, and the time between the criminal event and any punishment that is given is so great, that the Classical theorists' hopes of reducing crime by changing the legal codes have not been as successful as they might have been. In Chapter 15 you will learn how crime reduction strategies that follow the Classical principle of certainty of punishment are much more likely to succeed than policies based on severity, but that lawmakers have often focused on "cracking down" rather than on improving the operations of the justice system. Thus the failures of deterrence are due more to the failures of legislators than to Classical theory.

An additional problem with the Classical School is its overly simplified view of human nature and the theory of human behaviour that this supports (Thomas and Hepburn, 1983). The Classical theorists wholly accept the concept of the free and rational human being. This view completely ignores the objective realities faced by different individuals as they make their choices, the inequalities they experience, the state of their knowledge at any given time, and a multitude of other factors that may influence their decisions. This problem was addressed by the Neoclassical theorists.

The ideas of the Classical School have had a strong impact on our modern criminal justice system. Legal principles such as due process and equality before the law are fundamental to our legal system. Beccaria's work had a direct influence on the drafting of the legal code of France following the French Revolution and on the US Bill of Rights, and Classical principles remain part of the legal systems of many countries. For example, in section 15 of our Charter of Rights and Freedoms, Canadians are guaranteed the right to equal treatment before and under the law. We are protected from cruel and unusual punishment by section 12. In sections 7 through 11, a whole array of procedural safeguards guarantee Canadians the right to due process of law. Clearly, modern criminal justice owes a great debt to the Classical theorists and the reforms they introduced. However, our legal system also incorporates many of the changes suggested by the Neoclassical reformers.

SEARCH FOR:
Canadian Charter of Rights and Freedoms, Department of Justice Canada

QUESTIONS FOR CRITICAL THINKING

deterrence
As used in criminal justice, it refers to crime prevention achieved through the fear of punishment.

1. Superstitious and religious explanations of crime had devastating consequences on scapegoated and marginalized people. While most of us no longer believe in these explanations, can you think of ways in which some of

our current explanations of crime have a negative impact on marginalized people?

2. How did the development of the Classical School of criminology reflect the wider changes taking place in European society at the time? Consider how social, economic, and ideological forces influenced the founders of the Classical School.

3. Beccaria recommended that criminal law incorporate punishments that were severe enough to act as a deterrent, but not excessively harsh; certain; applied swiftly; and clear enough to be understood by all citizens. How does our current justice system measure up to these principles?

The Statistical School: Social Structure and Crime

The first half of the 19th century saw the emergence of an approach to criminology that differed markedly from that of the Classical School. This was evident in the work of André-Michel Guerry (1802–1866) in France, Adolphe Quetelet (1796–1874) in Belgium, and Henry Mayhew (1812–1887) in England. These researchers believed that crime, like other human behaviour, was the result of natural causes. Once discovered, these causes could be altered through the application of scientifically derived knowledge. These three men's reliance on objective empirical data, as opposed to philosophical conjecture or speculation, identified them as *Positivists*.

Members of the **Statistical School** did not share the Classical theorists' concept of the rational individual. Instead, they saw behaviour as the product of a host of factors. They systematically analyzed the statistical information available to them and tried to find a relationship between this information and crime. They analyzed such things as population density, education, and poverty (Thomas and Hepburn, 1983). A great deal of their work was based on geographic or cartographic analysis, which involved plotting various crime rates onto maps.

These theorists went far beyond simply describing what they learned from their maps and graphs. Many of their ideas anticipated the work of modern sociologists, in that they addressed issues related to criminal careers, delinquent subcultures, and social learning theory. They provided a critical and insightful perspective as well as a thorough statistical analysis of criminal behaviour.

Perhaps the most significant contribution of these theorists is their discovery of the remarkable regularity of phenomena such as crime. Countries, provinces, cities, and towns all had rates of crime that were remarkably stable from one year to the next. Even the rates of murder—a highly individualistic act—were consistent from one year to the next. They attributed this stability to elements of the social structure. Quetelet, for example, argued that "rather than being the result of our individual free wills, [our behaviour] is the product of many forces that are external to us" (Thomas and Hepburn, 1983). The fact that these forces appeared in regular and recurring patterns prompted these

Statistical School
Associated with early social scientists such as Adolphe Quetelet (1795–1874) and André-Michel Guerry (1802–1866), who began to explore the structure of emerging European societies with the assistance of statistical methods. While their early use of statistics is important, they also developed a structural explanation of crime and other social problems.

theorists to believe that human behaviour was governed by certain laws akin to those found in the natural or physical sciences.

Anticipating much of our contemporary thinking about crime, these theorists focused on inequalities and other structural features of their society. They viewed people in unfavourable social circumstances as having few options open to them. According to Quetelet, "the crimes which are annually committed seem to be a necessary result of our social organization ... The society prepares the crime and the guilty are only the instruments by which it is executed" (in Beirne, 1993, 88).

The influence of the Statistical School was, unfortunately, limited. This was not the result of any shortcomings of the approach; rather, it reflected the wider appeal of the biological theories of Cesare Lombroso and his colleagues. Nevertheless, these early pioneers of statistical criminology provided a uniquely sociological contribution to this emerging field of inquiry and demonstrated the value of testing theoretical formulations with empirical observations. Many contemporary theories have their roots in the work of the Statistical School.

SEARCH FOR:
"Cesare Lombroso" Museo Criminologico

Lombroso and the Positive School

The **Positive School** of criminology is also known as the Italian School because its most influential members were the Italian criminal anthropologist Cesare Lombroso (1836–1909) and his students Enrico Ferri (1856–1929) and Raffaelo Garofolo (1852–1934). Lombroso was influenced by the evolutionary theories of Charles Darwin, by the Positivist sociology of Auguste Comte, and by the work of the sociologist Herbert Spencer, who attempted to adapt Darwin's theory to the social world.

Like the members of the Statistical School, Lombroso brought the methods of controlled observation to the study of criminals, comparing them with noncriminals in order to isolate the factors that caused criminality. His own research was badly flawed, and his work is remembered because of his use of the scientific method rather than because of the specific findings he reported, which have all been discredited. Despite their flaws, Lombroso's ideas were widely accepted at the end of the 19th century. Their popularity was partly due to the growing influence of science, in particular of Darwin's theory of evolution. It was likely also due to the comfort of the ruling classes with the view that criminals were not produced by society's flaws, as Quetelet and his colleagues had shown; rather, criminals were genetic misfits who were born to break the rules that governed the lives of civilized people (Radzinowicz, 1966).

The impact of Darwin's ideas on the Positive School cannot be overstated. As Lilly, Cullen, and Hall (2007) note,

> Darwin's evolutionary thesis represents one of the most profound theories of all times. It not only offered revolutionary new knowledge for the sciences but also helped to shatter many philosophies and practices in other areas. It commanded so much attention and prestige that the entire literate community felt "obligated to bring his world outlook into harmony with their findings" (Hofstadter, 1955b, 3). According to Hofstadter, (1955b) Darwin's impact is comparable in its magnitude to

Positive School
The Italian criminologist Cesare Lombroso and his followers were among the first to study crime scientifically. They believed that crime was caused by biological factors beyond the individual's control, though social factors became more important as this school of thought changed over time.

the work of Nicolaus Copernicus (1473–1543), the European astron-
omer; Isaac Newton (1642–1727), the English mathematician and
physicist; and Freud, the Austrian psychoanalyst. In effect, all of
the Western world had to come to grips with Darwin's evolutionary
scheme. (28)

Fig. 13. Tipo comune - Assassino.

Fig. 16. Tipo comune (a fronte sfuggente) - Omicida-grassatore.

Fig. 14. Tipo comune - Omicida.

Fig. 17. Tipo comune (a fronte sfuggente) - Omicida.

Fig. 15. Tipo comune - Feritore-ladro.

Fig. 18. Tipo comune (a fronte sfuggente) - Omicida-grassatore.

The prison physician Cesare
Lombroso was the founder of the
Positive School of criminology.
These photographs show some
of those who Lombroso felt
should be classified as atavisms.

Chronicle/Alamy

The key ideas in Darwin's theory—"the struggle for survival" and "the survival of the fittest"—found fertile ground in the minds of the Positive School criminologists, who incorporated them into their thinking about criminals and how society should deal with them. Identifying criminals became a matter of searching for those physical and moral traits that differentiated more developed human beings from those who were less advanced in evolutionary terms. Incapacitation of these criminals was necessary, for little could be done to alter their genetic make-up. As you will see, some interpretations of these ideas led to a far more drastic approach called "eugenics," which promoted the sterilization and even elimination of those deemed inferior.

Lombroso worked as an army doctor and as a prison physician. He was interested in psychology and at one stage of his career was a teacher of psychiatry. These diverse interests are reflected in his theory of criminality. Lombroso's interest in physiology led him to note certain distinct physical differences between the criminals and soldiers with whom he worked. His thoughts on the subject came together during an autopsy he was performing on the notorious thief Vilella. He noted that many of the characteristics of Vilella's skull were similar to those of lower animals. In a remarkable description of the moment of discovery, Lombroso recalled:

> This was not merely an idea, but a revelation. At the sight of that skull, I seemed to see all of a sudden, lighted up as a vast plain under a flaming sky, the problem of the nature of the criminal—an atavistic being who reproduces in his person the ferocious instincts of primary humanity and the inferior animals. Thus were explained anatomically the enormous jaws, high cheek-bones, prominent superciliary arches, solitary lines in the palms, extreme size of the orbits, handle-shaped or sessile ears found in criminals, savages, and apes, insensibility to pain, extremely acute sight, tattooing, excessive idleness, love of orgies, and the irresistible craving for evil for its own sake, the desire not only to extinguish life in the victim, but to mutilate the corpse, tear its flesh, and drink its blood. (Quoted in Taylor, Walton, and Young, 1973, 41)

This discovery led Lombroso to believe that criminals were throwbacks to an earlier stage of evolution, or atavisms. His theory has been succinctly described by Gould (1981):

> These people are innately driven to act as a normal ape or savage would but such behaviour is deemed criminal in our civilized society. Fortunately, we may identify born criminals because they bear anatomical signs of their apishness. Their atavism is both physical and mental, but the physical signs, or stigmata as Lombroso called them, are decisive. Criminal behaviour can also arise in normal men, but we know the "born criminal" by his anatomy. Anatomy, indeed, is destiny, and born criminals cannot escape their inherited taint. (153)

The contrast between the primitive criminal and the more completely evolved contemporary man is evident in Lombroso's explanation for the use of professional slang, or argot, by criminals. Born criminals talk differently because they experience the world differently. Their way of speaking is more

atavism
Cesare Lombroso believed that some people were born criminals. These born criminals were throwbacks to an earlier stage of evolution—atavisms—and were morally inferior to the rest of the population. Lombroso's research focused on physical differences (stigmata) that could be used to identify atavisms.

primitive than that of other Europeans because they are throwbacks to an earlier stage of evolution.

To support his theory, Lombroso had to show that organisms lower on the evolutionary ladder were naturally criminal. Thus primitive humans were described as "savages." Even when evidence of their savagery was absent, Lombroso was able to save his theory by speculating that among honourable primitives, the conditions for criminality simply did not yet exist. For example, "it is not possible ... to steal when property does not exist or to swindle when there is no trade" (Lombroso, 1912). Once these supposed savages take on a little civilization, their criminality is inevitable. Lombroso went even further down the evolutionary ladder, finding evidence of criminality in the behaviour of animals, insects, and even insect-eating plants.

Lombroso tested his ideas by observing imprisoned criminals. In one study, he compared the physical characteristics of a group of criminals with those of a group of soldiers and found that the criminals had many more of the atavistic stigmata than did the soldiers. In another piece of research, he found that stigmata were present in 30 to 40 percent of anarchists but in less than 12 percent of members of other extremist movements (Taylor, Walton, and Young, 1973). He also concluded that different types of offenders were characterized by different physiological characteristics. For example, "robbers have ... small, shifting, quick-moving eyes; bushy connecting eyebrows; twisted or snub noses, thin beards ... and foreheads almost receding," while "habitual homicides have glassy, cold, motionless eyes, sometimes bloodshot and injected. The nose is often aquiline, or rather hawklike, and always voluminous" (1972, 70–71). He felt that women had fewer stigmata and lower crime rates than males because women were closer to their primitive origins. He concluded that women were vengeful, deceitful, and jealous, but added that their crime rates were relatively low because these negative traits were neutralized by their maternal instinct, piety, and lack of passion.

Lombroso initially postulated two types of offenders—born criminals and occasional criminals. However, in response to his critics, he later added several more categories, including the following:

1. *Epileptics.* In addition to their disability, epileptics also had the atavistic characteristics of criminals.
2. *Criminal insane.* This was the category of those whose insanity has led to their involvement in crime.
3. *Criminals of passion.* These criminals contrasted completely with born criminals in that they lacked any of the criminal stigmata. They committed crimes for "noble and powerful" motives such as love or politics.
4. *Criminaloids.* This was a grab-bag category, which included anyone who committed a crime but did not fall into one of the other classifications. Lombroso felt that precipitating factors other than biological ones caused criminality among this group.

Some have interpreted this expansion of categories as a softening of Lombroso's commitment to his biological theory. This view seems to be supported by his last major work, *Crime: Its Causes and Remedies*, in which he discussed social and environmental causes of crime along with biological ones. However, this change was more apparent than real. While there were

stigmata
The physical signs that a person is an atavism.

differences between atavistic criminals, the insane, and the epileptics, all three categories had elements of degeneration that stemmed from epilepsy, which he called the "kernel of crime" (Lombroso, 1912). Criminaloids might lack some of the stigmata, but they differed from born criminals only in degree, not in kind. After long periods in prison, criminaloids might even come to resemble born criminals. While those who committed crimes out of passion did not show any of the stigmata, they did show some points of resemblance with epileptics. The only category that had no connection with atavism or epilepsy is that of occasional criminals. Yet even these posed no threat to Lombroso's theory, for he suggested that they should not be called criminals at all.

The Contribution of the Positive School

In its day, Lombroso's work attracted a large following. The stigmata were used as indicators of criminality in many trials, and Lombroso himself appeared as an expert witness on several occasions. In one case, the court had to decide which of two brothers had killed their stepmother. Lombroso's testimony that one of the men had the features of a born criminal helped secure the man's conviction.

Lombroso's theory of criminal anthropology has not stood up to empirical test. His research was poorly conducted by today's standards. His comparison groups were chosen unsystematically, his statistical techniques were crude, his measurements were often sloppy, and he assumed that those in prison were criminals and that those not in prison were noncriminals. Some of the stigmata he mentioned in his research, such as tattoos, could not possibly have been inherited. Yet despite these weaknesses, his work did represent an attempt to provide a scientific explanation of the causes of criminality.

Perhaps Lombroso's most lasting contribution was his discussion of the criminal justice system. Classical theorists felt that crime could be controlled if society could design punishments to fit the crime. Positive theorists, by contrast, believed that the punishment should fit the criminal. Radzinowicz and King have nicely outlined the difference between the two perspectives: "The Classical School exhorts men to study justice, the Positivist School exhorts justice to study men" (1977, 86).

Because Lombroso believed that people became involved in criminality for different reasons, he felt they should be treated differently by the criminal justice system. If a respectable man committed murder because of passion, honour, or political belief, no punishment was needed, for that man would never repeat the crime. For other offenders, indeterminate sentences would best ensure rehabilitation. Born criminals should not be held responsible for their actions, though they needed to be incarcerated for the protection of society. However, this was to be done in a humane way. He recommended that prisoners serving longer sentences be treated better than those serving less time.

Some born criminals could be channelled in a socially useful direction. For example, banishment and transportation to one of the colonies might allow their tendencies to be redirected toward the difficult business of building settlements in a hostile environment. For others, more severe sanctions were required. "There exists, it is true, a group of criminals, born for evil, against whom all social cures break as against a rock—a fact which compels us to eliminate them completely, even by death" (Lombroso, 1912).

indeterminate sentence
A sentence that has no fixed release date. Release is determined by a parole authority based on the individual's behaviour.

A number of features of our current criminal justice system stem from the concern of Lombroso and his followers with individualizing the treatment of offenders. Probation, parole, indeterminate sentences, and the consideration of mitigating circumstances by the courts have all been influenced by Lombroso's work as well as by the work of Neoclassical criminologists. The rational person of Classical theory now had a past and a future.

Biological Theories in the Early 20th Century

Crime and Physical Characteristics

Lombroso's theories came under frequent attack during his lifetime. In 1889, he responded to his critics by challenging them to compare 100 born criminals, 100 people with criminal tendencies, and 100 normal people. He promised to retract his theories if the criminals did not turn out to be different from the other groups. His challenge was ultimately taken up by an English prison medical officer, Dr. G.B. Griffiths, and completed by his successor, Dr. Charles Goring, who succeeded Griffiths in 1903 shortly after the project began.

Goring carefully measured and compared the physical and mental characteristics of 3,000 English convicts with those of diverse samples of "normals," including British university students, schoolboys, university professors, Scots with mental illness, German Army recruits, and British Army soldiers (Goring, 1972). After comparing these groups on 37 physical and six mental traits, Goring concluded that there was no evidence of a distinct physical type of criminal. Lombroso's "anthropological monster," he concluded, "has no existence in fact" (Goring, 1913). Criminals were no more or less likely to possess stigmata than were members of the control groups. Goring did find that criminals were physically inferior to normals, but he attributed this fact to social selection processes.

Goring's most important finding was the high correlation between criminality and low intelligence. This led to his theory that crime was inherited and that the most important constitutional mechanism through which crime was genetically transmitted was mental inferiority. Unlike Lombroso, Goring did feel that hereditary predispositions could be modified by social factors such as education. However, he also supported eugenic measures, which would restrict the reproduction of the constitutional factors leading to crime.

In some respects, Goring's research was a major advance over Lombroso's. His measurement was far more precise, and he had access to statistical tools that were unavailable to Lombroso. But his work also contained a number of serious methodological flaws. Among them was the fact that he was comparing officially labelled criminals, who were not a representative sample of all criminals, with diverse groups of other people who did not represent the noncriminal population. While many of the other criticisms of Goring's research are quite technical, they are serious enough to cast doubt on his own theories as well as on his refutation of Lombroso (Driver, 1972).

The search for individual differences as the cause of crime did not end with Goring. This theme was picked up again in the 1930s by Harvard anthropologist Ernest A. Hooton. He compared more than 13,000 criminals with a sample of noncriminals drawn from college students, firemen, hospital outpatients, militiamen, mental hospital patients, people using the change house at a public beach, and others. On the basis of this comparison, Hooton concluded that criminals were biologically and socially inferior. Among the new stigmata he attributed to criminals were such characteristics as "low foreheads, high pinched nasal roots, nasal bridges and tips varying to both extremes of breadth and narrowness," and "very small ears" (1939, 158).

While Hooton was not as concerned as some of his predecessors with the policy implications of his research, he did not hesitate to draw the obvious conclusion. Since "crime is the resultant of the impact of environment upon low grade human organisms ... it follows that the elimination of crime can be effected only by the expiration of the physically, mentally, and morally unfit, or by their complete segregation in a socially aseptic environment" (175). These ideas formed the basis of the eugenics movement that developed in the United States at the turn of the 20th century (see Box 8.2).

FOCUS

Box 8.2

CRIMINOLOGY AND EUGENICS

The term "eugenics" ... simply means "well born" and it connotes a sense of contributing to or improving the stock of the race or the nation. The term became one of some suspicion when the goal of genetics was embraced by various political regimes and enforced through the state's coercive power as an effective instrument for social engineering. In modern times, the first extended programs in state-sponsored eugenics were developed in the United States in the late nineteenth and early twentieth century. These eugenics programs grew from a constellation of ideas derived from evolutionary theory which embraced Social Darwinism, from contemporaneous criminology encouraged by a scientific hypothesis supported by post-mortem studies of brains of criminals and the findings of the famous Juke Report (1875) on inheritance and criminal behaviour, from demographic concerns about dysgenics—the growth of the criminal population and the growth of the feeble-minded population because of their unrestrained breeding patterns—and from surgical advances, such as vasectomy and salpingectomy [female sterilization], in the practice of medicine. Involuntary sterilization became the instrument of this modern attempt at eugenics. The idea of genetic sterilization, the pursuit of this end as a national goal, and the procurement of means to attain their desired result were pressed by some of the most influential families, by some of the most prestigious societies and foundations, by some powerful lawyers, judges, scientists, and physicians, and by some of the most elite universities in the United States. The central notion and clearest articulation

of the goals of this movement are best recorded in the words of Mr. Justice Oliver Wendell Holmes who, writing for the majority in a 1927 United States Supreme Court decision, Buck v. Bell, found involuntary sterilization to be compatible with the guarantees found in the U.S. Constitution.

Holmes concluded:

We have seen more than once that the public welfare may call upon the best citizens for their lives. It would be strange if it could not call upon those who already sap the strength of the state for lesser sacrifices, often not felt to be such by those concerned, in order to prevent our being swamped with incompetence. It is better for all the world, if instead of waiting to execute degenerative offspring for crime, or to let them starve for their imbecility, society can prevent those who are manifestly unfit from continuing their kind. The principle that sustains compulsory vaccination is broad enough to cover cutting the Fallopian tubes (Jacobson v. Massachusetts, 197 U.S. 11). Three generations of imbeciles are enough. (Buck v. Bell. United States Supreme Court. Report 274, 1927)

(Canada also practiced involuntary sterilization, and the practice remained legal in Alberta until 1972.)

Source: Margaret Monahan Hogan, "Medical Ethics: The New Eugenics: Therapy—Enhancement—Screening—Testing," International Catholic University (n.d.), http://home.comcast.net/~icuweb/c04106.htm.

Hooton's work was controversial, and his findings were challenged on a variety of grounds. He was accused of using poor scientific methods and circular reasoning. For example, he used conviction for a crime as a method of separating criminals from noncriminals; he then examined the convicted groups and concluded they were inferior; finally, he used this finding of inferiority to account for their criminality (Empey, 1982). Only in this way could a trait such as thin lips be turned into an indicator of criminality.

Several other criticisms of Hooton's methods are worth considering. His control group did not represent the general population. Students, firefighters, and mental patients have particular characteristics that distinguish them from the rest of the population. Furthermore, his findings show tremendous differences within the various control groups he used. In fact, the differences between his control groups drawn from Boston and Nashville were actually greater than between prisoners and controls (Pfohl, 1985). As in the case of Lombroso, Hooton's attempt to link criminal behaviour to physical types was thoroughly discredited.

This kind of research has made periodic appearances in a variety of forms since the days of Lombroso and Hooton. In the 1950s, William Sheldon attempted to re-establish the link between body type and criminality in his elaboration of a "somatotype" theory. He described three basic body types, which, he argued, were related to particular personalities and temperaments. These body types were endomorphs (fat, round bodies), who had easygoing personalities; ectomorphs (tall and lean), who had introverted personalities and nervous dispositions; and mesomorphs (well-built and muscular), who had aggressive personalities and were quick to act and insensitive to pain. Sheldon related each of these types to particular kinds of criminal behaviour. He found that the muscular mesomorphs were the type most likely to become involved in delinquent or criminal behaviour.

Sheldon fared no better than his predecessors when his work was subjected to scrutiny. It was found that he had done an extremely poor job of measuring delinquency among the young people he had studied. He had used vague and inconsistent categories that have been described as scientifically meaningless.

These criticisms could not be levelled at Sheldon and Eleanor Glueck, who followed up on William Sheldon's ideas. They applied his somatotype theory to a study of 500 juvenile delinquents. They compared the bodies of 500 adjudicated delinquents with a matched sample of nondelinquents. The Gluecks concluded from their work that delinquents were more likely to be mesomorphs. However, this finding may have raised more questions than it answered. Putting aside a whole host of methodological criticisms levelled at the Gluecks, it may be that mesomorphs actually look more like stereotypical delinquents than either endomorphs or ectomorphs. As a result, people may respond to mesomorphs differently and they may be more likely to be labelled delinquent than those who are nonmesomorphs. Also, other social selection factors may have been involved. Youth who are athletic, muscular, and active may be better candidates for Little League baseball, hockey, or delinquency than their less athletic peers.

Crime and Intelligence

Other biological theories have focused on a variety of factors that have been associated with individual differences. Goring suggested that instead of looking for defective body types, the focus should be on genetic weaknesses demonstrated by low intelligence.

In one famous study of family and heredity, the American psychologist Henry Goddard traced the legitimate and illegitimate offspring of an army lieutenant, Martin Kallikak. Young Martin fathered an illegitimate son with a feeble-minded barmaid before he settled down and married a "respectable" woman. The study compared the descendants of Kallikak's feeble-minded mate to those of his "normal" wife. The offspring of the feeble-minded barmaid produced a collection of deviants and feeble-minded degenerates. By contrast, the family of his wife showed no such weakness (Goddard, 1912).

Even if we ignore the enormous methodological weaknesses of Goddard's study (Gould [1981] has shown that the photographs of the "depraved" Kallikaks had been retouched to make them look like defectives), little is left of scientific consequence. It is hardly surprising that children raised in difficult and impoverished circumstances should be less than model citizens. In fact, life under these conditions may require an individual to learn a great deal of undesirable behaviour simply to survive. The absence of any consideration of the social factors involved in this comparison clearly undermines Goddard's findings.

Goddard continued his work using the Binet-Simon intelligence test, which had recently been developed in France. This IQ test was based on the notion of "mental age." Goddard studied the residents of a New Jersey mental institution and, on the basis of that work, established the mental age of 12 as the cut-off point for determining feeble-mindedness. He then applied this IQ test to the inmates of jails and prisons throughout the New Jersey area. He found that in around half the institutions, 70 percent of the inmates were at or below the mental age of 12. From these findings, he concluded that IQ was an important determinant of criminal behaviour. He also concluded that feeble-mindedness was directly inherited and could only be eliminated by denying those he called "morons" the right to reproduce (1914). Goddard also argued that "criminal imbeciles" should not be held criminally responsible for their actions. His expert testimony helped acquit at least one murderer on the grounds of criminal imbecility (Rafter, 1997).

The acceptance of Goddard's position was short-lived. In 1926, Murchinson published the results of a study in which he compared IQ data from First World War army recruits with those from a group of inmates (Pfohl, 1985). He found that 47 percent of the recruits, but only 30 percent of the prisoners, had IQ scores that fell below the mental age of 12. This startling finding implied that almost half of a very large sample of normal American men could be considered mentally feeble. The absurdity of these findings forced Goddard to lower his cut-off point for feeble-mindedness from 12 years to 9. This reduction resulted in the disappearance of any significant differences between inmates and soldiers, or anyone else for that matter (Pfohl, 1985).

Despite evidence so convincing that even Goddard disavowed his earlier work, governments responded to their fear of those with low IQs by passing legislation controlling their behaviour. These laws resulted in thousands of people with intellectual disabilities in North America being forced into institutions and, in many cases, being involuntarily sterilized.

In Canada, sterilization laws were passed in Alberta in 1929 and in British Columbia in 1933. The Alberta law was not repealed until 1972. As a child growing up in Alberta, Leilani Muir was incorrectly labelled as mentally retarded. She was kept in an institution and was sterilized without her knowledge or consent. In 1995, Muir, who actually had normal intelligence, successfully sued the Alberta government and was awarded substantial damages. This case shows the problems with developing policies based on notions of individual inferiority.

The controversy over IQ tests has continued. A number of serious flaws in the assumptions behind this approach have come to light. For example, it has been suggested that high scores on these tests may have more to say about test-taking ability than they do about intelligence. Furthermore, the composition of these tests has been found to be biased in favour of the cultural locations of those who designed the tests. In a dramatic demonstration, Adrian Dove, a black sociologist, devised an IQ test based on the cultural referents and language of the black ghetto (Pfohl, 1985). Black respondents who were familiar with this culture did well on the tests, but white middle-class respondents did poorly. The validity of IQ tests remains suspect, and their use has often been linked to racist ideology and propaganda.

A number of other recent formulations have sought to re-establish a link between individual characteristics and criminal behaviour. These have focused on such things as chromosomes, unusual EEG results, hypoglycemic disorders, and premenstrual tension. The results in many of these cases are similar. While it would be foolhardy to deny the biological or psychological dimensions of human behaviour, the evidence supporting a link between pathology and criminal behaviour is weak. Moreover, this approach ignores the essentially political nature of social control—what one society praises and rewards, another may condemn. Given this variability in what we define as crime, an assessment of the underlying social and political context is indispensable.

The continued search for individual differences and the erroneous identification of a normal "us" and a criminal "them" has sometimes had political overtones (see Box 8.3 for an extreme example). The emergence of a positive

FOCUS

Box 8.3

BAD SCIENCE OR BAD POLITICS? CRIMINOLOGY IN NAZI GERMANY

Throughout this chapter, we have tried to link the developments in criminology to the wider social, political, and intellectual contexts from which they emerged. For example, we noted the impact of the Enlightenment and humanistic thinking on the development of the Classical School and the reforms that proponents of that school struggled to make to the criminal justice system of the day. We also noted how social Darwinism had a far-ranging influence on the type of thinking that began to gain prominence in a number of fields after Charles Darwin published his famous treatise on evolution. This included the field of criminology and the ideas promoted by the Positive School.

What happens to these ideas and theories once they become popularized depends in large part on how they are used to further particular agendas or views of the world. In the case of the eugenics movement, criminological-biological research was used to justify forced sterilizations, executions of habitual criminals, and even genocide as was the case in Nazi Germany. "Hitler himself, in a speech to the 1929 Nazi Party Congress in Nuremburg, called it outrageous that 'criminals are allowed to procreate' and demanded drastic eugenic measures" (Wetzell, 2000, 180). This pronouncement eerily foreshadowed what was to come. As Rosenhaft (2001) notes,

> from 1935 on, certain categories of criminals were officially treated as racially undesirable. Prostitutes, vagrants, and other so-called asocials, including Roma, or Gypsies, were taken off the streets and sent to prisons or camps indefinitely and without the right to appeal. Homosexuals, whose lifestyle contradicted both criminal law and the racial duty to produce children, were hounded and arrested ... It was from managing these thousands of ordinary captives that the concentration camp system was set up right at the beginning of the regime in 1933.

The unconscionable horrors perpetrated by the Nazis could be attributed to the vicious and racist ideology of the Nazi regime. Their use of science and biological-criminological research to justify their actions, however, should serve as a cautionary tale to us all. The conclusions drawn by Richard Wetzell (2000) after his extensive investigation of German criminology during the Nazi era provide a sobering view on the role of "science":

> A more complex picture of science under the Third Reich also diminishes the distance that we often perceive between "Nazi science" and our own science.

Contemporary scientists as well as the general public often assume that science under Nazism was "bad" or "perverted" science. This view is reassuring because it suggests that our own, more "advanced" science does not have the same dangerous implications that "Nazi science" had. But if science under the Nazis was in fact more sophisticated, the distance between "Nazi science" and science in our own day is diminished, and we are forced to ask ourselves whether the role of science and medicine under the Nazi regime might point to dangers inherent in scientific research in the present. My point here is not to suggest that research on the genetic causes of crime, for instance, is intrinsically evil and dangerous and will necessarily lead to inhumane and murderous state policies. Rather, my point is that much of the scientific research conducted during the Nazi years was not as different from current scientific research as we would like to think. Like science before and after the Third Reich, scientific research in Nazi Germany was characterized by continual tension between the internal dynamics of science and the intellectual and political biases of the scientists and their society. This argument should make us uncomfortable in salutary ways. For it makes us realize that the connection between scientific research and the Nazi regime was more complicated than we might have thought, and it gives us a more critical view of science in our own time.

Source: Wetzell, Richard. (2000). Inventing the Criminal: A History of German Criminology: 1880–1945. Chapel-Hill: The University of North Carolina Press.

TABLE 8.1 Early Theories of Crime

Theory	Theorists	Key Elements
Classical theory	Beccaria	Humans were rational thinkers. Those who contemplated breaking the law considered the positive and negative consequences of their actions. A measured system of punishments was needed to deter crime.
Neo-classical theory	Tarde	Helped develop a more individualized system of criminal justice.
Statistical School	Guerry, Quetelet, Mayhew	Explored the social causes of crime. Related structural factors such as inequality to crime.
Positive School	Lombroso	Criminals were born, not made. They were atavisms who were less evolved than the law-abiding.
Early 20th-century biological	Goring, Hooton, Sheldon, Goddard	Related criminality to several types of theories of biological inferiority, including intelligence and body shape.

science coincided with the rise of a powerful capitalist class and expanded colonial activity. Both of these developments welcomed the ideological justification contained within the Darwinian notion of survival of the fittest. Social Darwinism and positive criminology flourished in this environment.

This biological-criminological approach of the Positive School offered a ready-made and "humane" way of dealing with the problems of social control. This was extremely important at a time when the population was being transformed into a disciplined industrial labour force. Rather than applying the harsh and barbaric punishments of the past, a scientifically designed technology of control could be used to "treat" troublesome individuals. This focus on the pathologies of individuals also serves to conveniently remove one's gaze from the social structure. If it is certain that problems like crime are the result of individual deficiencies, then one needn't be concerned with the social structure. If, on the other hand, the structural sources of inequality, such as racism, sexism, and other social ills, are examined, the very nature of the society may be called into question.

QUESTIONS FOR CRITICAL THINKING

1. What changes did the Positive School of criminology introduce? How did these alter the existing explanations of crime and criminality? What are the implications of the Positive School for the way we treat people who break the law today?
2. What were the major biological explanations of criminality that emerged early in the 20th century? How were these explanations received by social scientists?
3. Discuss the social policy implications of the early biological theories. In other words, if the theories are correct, what should societies do to deal with crime?
4. In general, what have you learned in this chapter about the relationship between theories of criminality and social policy concerning the treatment of criminals?

● Summary

- Early theories of crime were based on superstition and religious beliefs.
- This view of crime changed when the Classical School of criminology became popular. Members of this school argued that people were free and rational actors and proposed that the key to preventing crime was to establish a Criminal Code based on the principle that the punishment should fit the crime.
- The Classical School had a major impact on legal systems in many countries. However, the resulting legal codes were rigid and inflexible. Other scholars proposed a series of Neo-classical reforms, which have since been incorporated into the legal systems of many countries.

- Lombroso and other members of the Positive School brought scientific methods to the study of crime. While Lombroso's biological theory has not stood up to scientific scrutiny, the application of science to criminology represented a major shift in the discipline.

- Lombroso was followed by a number of other researchers who sought to blame crime on the biological inferiority of criminals. As with Lombroso's theory, research has not supported these early 20th-century biological theories. However, they did have a major impact on the legal system, as measures such as involuntary sterilization and lengthy incarceration for "defectives" were passed in many jurisdictions.

- Most of the principles of our current justice system reflect the earlier influence of Classical, Neo-classical, and Positive theories of crime.

NET WORK

In this chapter, you have learned how Classical theory and Positivist theory have influenced the way Western nations such as Canada and the United States address issues like sentencing. The debates over sentencing continue to influence public opinion and criminal justice policy today. Should the punishment fit the crime, or should we take other factors into account when sentencing someone and let the punishment fit the offender? The intensity of this debate is visible in the competing points of view expressed over two sentencing policies: (1) three strikes and (2) mandatory minimum sentences.

To learn more about these debates, follow the links below to some interesting articles and information about other useful sites.

- Three Strikes Policy: http://idebate.org/debatabase/debates/law/house-would-strike-out-three-strikes-laws

- Sentencing in Canada: http://www.lawconnection.ca/content/sentencing-theory-backgrounder

- Mandatory Minimum Sentencing in Canada: http://www.parl.gc.ca/Content/LOP/researchpublications/prb0553-e.htm http://www.justice.gc.ca/eng/rp-pr/csj-sjc/ccs-ajc/rr05_10/rr05_10.pdf

Review the discussion around sentencing in order to answer the following questions:

1. What is the three strikes policy in sentencing?
2. Which theory of criminology is most reflected in the three strikes policy?
3. Summarize the current debates over this criminal justice policy.
4. What is mandatory minimum sentencing?
5. Which theory of criminology is reflected in a mandatory minimum sentencing policy?
6. Summarize the current debate in Canada over this criminal justice policy.

9

Psychological Perspectives on Criminality

Patricia A. Zapf
JOHN JAY COLLEGE OF CRIMINAL JUSTICE

David N. Cox
SIMON FRASER UNIVERSITY

Nathalie C. Gagnon
KWANTLEN UNIVERSITY COLLEGE

Ronald Roesch
SIMON FRASER UNIVERSITY

This chapter reviews different psychological perspectives on criminality. We begin with a discussion of the characteristics of psychological theories and then review various psychological theories that have been proposed to explain criminality. Next, antisocial personality and psychopathy are described, and the differences between the two are illustrated through the use of three case studies—Charles Manson, Vince Li, and Canada's most notorious criminal, Clifford Olson. We conclude with a discussion of crime and mental illness, including a review of research in this area and a discussion of the prevalence of mental illness in jail and prison populations.

After reading this chapter, you should be able to

- Describe and critique the different psychological theories that have been used to explain criminal behaviour, including psychoanalytic theory, moral development theory, Eysenck's theory, social learning theory, and operant conditioning theory.
- Understand what is meant by the term "antisocial personality."
- Describe the difference between Antisocial Personality Disorder and psychopathy.
- Describe the most current theories linking crime and mental illness.

assumption of offender deficit
The view that offenders who break the law have some psychological deficit that distinguishes them from normal, law-abiding citizens.

assumption of discriminating traits
The view that offenders are distinguished from non-offenders by, for example, their high levels of impulsiveness and aggression.

Psychological Theories of Crime

There has been considerable debate over psychological explanations of criminal behaviour. Psychologists typically approach the problem of understanding, explaining, and predicting criminality by developing theories of personality or learning that account for an individual's behaviour in a specific situation. Over 30 years ago, an extensive review of a decade of published research on offenders (Reppucci and Clingempeel, 1978) found that nearly all the research could be characterized as reflecting one of two value assumptions. The first is the **assumption of offender deficit**, which asserts that theories and interventions are premised on the notion that there is something psychologically wrong with offenders. The second is the **assumption of discriminating traits**, which holds that criminals differ from non-criminals, particularly in such traits as impulsivity and aggression. Research based on this assumption involved studies of offender and non-offender populations, utilizing a number of personality tests in an attempt to find traits that differentiate the two groups.

Critics have taken issue with psychology's reliance on these two assumptions. Reppucci and Clingempeel (1978) point to two major omissions in psychological research. One is that there is typically very little emphasis placed on studies of the strengths of offenders. Most of the research and interventions focus on deficits rather than on the positive characteristics of individuals. While the concerns of Reppucci and Clingempeel continue to have validity today, the field has made a considerable shift: research and theory increasingly recognize the importance of offender strengths (Webster et al., 2006; Hoge, Guerra, and Boxer, 2008). A second omission identified by Reppucci and Clingempeel is that psychological research tends to ignore the potential importance of situational and environmental factors for individual behaviour. Again, recent developments have stressed the importance of external factors in both explaining criminal behaviour and developing intervention programs to reduce recidivism (e.g., Haney, 2002; Moretti, Jackson, and Obsuth, 2010).

Others, such as Reid (2003), have been critical of psychological theories of crime that are based on the expectation that it is possible to classify individuals as criminals or non-criminals, arguing that this classification cannot be made reliably. Rather, evidence suggests that criminal behaviour is pervasive, as indicated by studies of self-reported delinquency, white-collar crime, and corporate crime (Thornberry and Krohn, 2000).

Conversely, the work of David Farrington (2002; Loeber and Farrington, 2012) illustrates the importance of understanding individual differences. Farrington views criminal behaviour as the outcome of several different social and psychological factors (see also Loeber, Farrington, and Stouthamer-Loeber, 2001a, 2001b). According to him, the motivation to commit delinquent acts arises primarily out of a desire for material goods or a need for excitement. If these desires cannot be satisfied in a socially approved manner, an illegal act may be chosen. The motivation to commit delinquent acts will be influenced by psychological variables, including the individual's learning history and the beliefs he or she may have internalized regarding criminal behaviour. Eysenck and Gudjonsson (1989) support this position, suggesting that "psychological factors and individual differences related to the personality are of central importance in relation to both the causes of crime and its control." They contend that psychology, with its focus on individual differences, is the central discipline in the study of criminal behaviour and that "no system of criminology has any meaning that disregards this central feature of all criminology: the individual person whom we are trying to influence."

While the individual perspective is clearly the dominant one in psychology, there are other psychological perspectives, such as those of **community psychology** (Roesch, 1988; Wilson, 2004), that are quite closely akin to sociological perspectives. Commonly, such psychologists view social problems from what Rappaport (1977) has termed a "levels of analysis" perspective. Briefly, the four levels are (1) *individual level*, in which social problems are defined in terms of individual deficit; (2) *small-group level*, which suggests that social problems are created by problems in group functioning, essentially problems in

community psychology
A perspective that analyzes social problems, including crime, as largely a product of organizational and institutional characteristics of society. It is closely related to sociology.

interpersonal communication and understanding; (3) *organizational level*, in which the organizations of society have not accomplished what they have been designed to accomplish; and (4) *institutional or community level*, in which it is suggested that social problems are created by institutions rather than by persons, groups, or organizations. At this level the emphasis is on the values and policies underlying institutional functioning.

An example that cuts across these four levels would be the way in which "victimless" crimes, such as drug abuse and prostitution, are defined. If the problem is defined at the first level, individuals would be examined to determine what psychological problems they have. Once this has been determined, direct interventions could be employed in changing these individuals so that they might fit into society better and conform to the existing laws. At the small-group level, the influence of peers, such as drug-abusing friends, could be viewed as influencing the individual's behaviour. At the next level, organizations such as law enforcement agencies would be seen as having insufficient resources to prevent or deter individuals from engaging in criminal behaviour. Finally, if this problem is defined at the institutional level, it might be said that the problems individuals face are caused by the laws their society has created. Therefore, the focus would be on changing the laws so that they do not affect people negatively. If the problem is defined at the institutional level, therapy for an individual would be inappropriate if the cause of the problem was, for example, related to socio-economic factors (Seidman and Rabkin, 1983). Community psychologists tend to define social problems at the organizational and institutional levels and have a theoretical perspective that has much in common with that of sociologists.

Haney (2002) builds on this perspective and makes a strong case for a situational approach to understanding criminal behaviour. He comments that

> a more situation-centered legal system would concentrate less exclusively on defective properties of the person and more on situational pathologies. A modern, psychologically informed criminal law would more carefully weigh the effects of environmental stressors that may have significantly altered a defendant's psychological state, and it would take into explicit account those situational pressures that may have undermined or precluded the "mature reflection" that in the past has been presumed to precede action. (34)

These concerns and alternative perspectives should be kept in mind as various psychological theories of criminal behaviour are considered. These theories focus, for the most part, on individual-level variables and explanations. The remainder of this chapter will review psychological theories that can be directly related to understanding criminal behaviour.

Psychoanalytic Theory

Although psychoanalytic theories as an explanation for criminal behaviour have fallen out of favour in recent decades as the field moves more and more toward a model of evidence-based practice, it is useful to examine the history of psychoanalytic theory, given its importance to the foundations of clinical psychology. Sigmund Freud is the figure most associated with psychoanalytic theory, but he did not make any significant attempts to relate his theory specifically to criminal behaviour. Other psychoanalysts have, however, attempted to explain criminal behaviour with psychoanalytic concepts (Alexander and Healey, 1935; Friedlander, 1947; Polansky, Lippitt, and Redl, 1950; Bowlby, 1953; Redl, 1966).

A basic premise of psychoanalytic theory is that people progress through five overlapping stages of development. These are the oral, anal, phallic, latency, and genital stages. Freud believed that personality is composed of three forces: the **id** (biological drives), the **ego** (which screens, controls, and directs the impulses of the id and acts as a reality tester), and the **superego** (conscience). Psychoanalytic theory holds that the ego and superego are developed through the successful resolution of conflicts presented at each stage of development. It is believed that both biological and social factors are involved in the resolution of each stage (see Figure 9.1).

> **id**
> A psychoanalytical term that denotes the most inaccessible and primitive part of the mind. It is a reservoir of biological urges that strive continually for gratification. The ego mediates between the *id* and the *superego*.

FIGURE 9.1   Freud's Theory of Personality

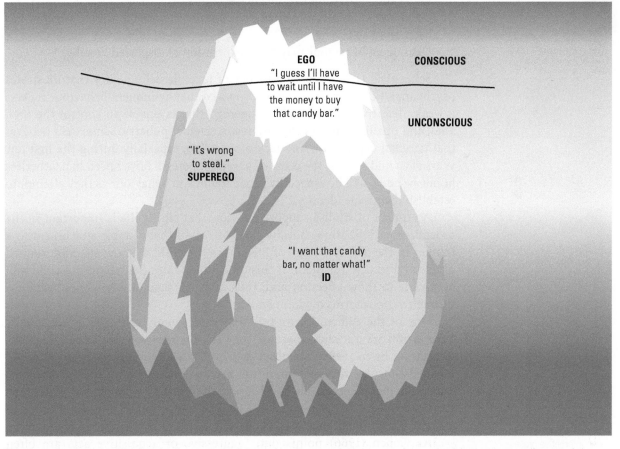

This illustration shows how Freud might picture a person's internal conflict over whether to commit an antisocial act such as stealing a candy bar. Besides dividing personality into three components, Freud theorized that our personalities are largely unconscious—hidden away outside our normal awareness. To dramatize this point, he compared conscious awareness (portions of the ego and superego) to the visible tip of an iceberg. Most of our personality—including the id, with its raw desires and impulses—lies submerged in our subconscious.

Source: From MURRAY/LINDEN/KENDALL. *Sociology in Our Times*, 6E. © 2014 Nelson Education Ltd. Reproduced by permission. www.cengage.com/permissions.

Psychoanalytic theory presents an elaborate, comprehensive view of the psychological functioning of individuals. It deals with all aspects of human behaviour, but the discussion here will be limited to its impact on the study of criminal behaviour. Briefly, this theory suggests that criminal behaviour occurs when "internal (ego and superego) controls are unable to restrain the primitive, aggressive, antisocial instincts of the id" (Nietzel, 1979). Criminal behaviour is the consequence of an individual's failure to progress through the early stages of development; this leaves the superego inadequately developed or deficient. The individual is left susceptible to antisocial behaviour (Martin, Sechrest, and Redner, 1981).

Warren and Hindelang (1979) have summarized five other interpretations of criminal behaviour that can be derived from psychoanalytic theory:

1. Criminal behaviour is a form of neurosis which does not differ in any fundamental way from other forms of neuroses (e.g., while some neurotics work too hard, others set fires).
2. The criminal often suffers from a compulsive need for punishment in order to alleviate guilt feelings and anxiety stemming from unconscious strivings.
3. Criminal activity may be a means of obtaining substitute gratification of needs and desires not met inside the family.
4. Delinquent behaviour is often due to traumatic events whose memory has been repressed.
5. Delinquent behaviour may be an expression of displaced hostility.*

Schoenfeld (1971) offered a theory of juvenile delinquency that illustrates psychoanalytic theory. Schoenfeld proposed that delinquent behaviour reflects a weak, defective, or incomplete superego that is unable to control the oral, anal, and phallic impulses that are resurrected at puberty. Schoenfeld believes that parental deprivation and lack of affection, especially during the first few years of a child's life, is the cause of a weak superego. Boys raised in a fatherless home, he adds, will be especially prone to deviant behaviour as they attempt to establish their male identity.

A number of studies support the view that family life is important in the process of **socialization**. Bowlby (1953) stressed that a stable attachment to a mother in the first few years of life allows the child to show affection toward others and to care for them. If this attachment does not occur, the child will be unable to show affection and, thus, may damage others without remorse through various forms of victimization.

One of the difficulties in assessing psychoanalytic theory is that many aspects of it are untestable because they rely on unobservable underlying constructs. As Ewen (1988) has observed, "psychoanalytic theory presents a formidable difficulty: the most important part of the personality, the unconscious, is also the most inaccessible" (55). It is therefore the psychoanalyst who interprets the offender's behaviours and actions. Any attempt by the offender to refute the interpretation is seen as resistance and further evidence of its truth.

As Cohen (1966) points out, "aggressive or acquisitive acts are often explained by underlying aggressive or acquisitive impulses." This explanation

*Warren, M. Q., and M. J. Hindelang. (1979). "Current Explanations of Offender Behavior." In H. Toch (ed.), *Psychology of Crime and Criminal Justice* (pp. 166–82). New York: Holt, Rinehart and Winston.

is a tautology in that aggressive acts are explained by aggressive impulses, but the only evidence of the aggressive impulses is the occurrence of aggressive acts. Many have suggested that psychoanalytic theory is empirically unverifiable, and verification is a necessary criterion for any scientific theory.

Another criticism of psychoanalytic theory is that studies have failed to demonstrate that criminals desire to be punished or suffer from guilt or anxiety, as one psychoanalyst (Abrahamsen, 1944) suggested. In fact, as Nietzel (1979) asserts, "criminals are very successful in their efforts to prevent detection or if detected, elude official prosecution and conviction. Most offenders do not appear unduly frustrated or further guilt-ridden by the fact that their 'crime pays' at least some of the time." Despite these problems, psychoanalytic theory is regarded by some as a useful conceptual framework for understanding the importance of early development on later behaviour of all types, including criminal behaviour.

Theories of Moral Development

According to moral development theorists, if we wish to understand criminal and delinquent behaviour we need to ask how it is that individuals develop, or fail to develop, a sense of morality and responsibility. One of the first contemporary moral development theorists was the French psychologist Jean Piaget (1932), whose research focused on the moral lives of children. In order to determine how children developed their ideas about right and wrong, Piaget studied how children developed the rules to the games they played. He concluded that moral reasoning develops in stages. The thinking of young children is characterized by egocentrism. That is, they project their own thoughts and wishes onto others because they are unable to take the perspective of those others. Through their interaction with others, by the ages of 11 or 12, children normally have progressed to the stage of cooperation with others. Based on this research, Piaget concluded that schools should teach moral reasoning by allowing students to work out the rules through problem solving in the classroom.

Kohlberg, expanding on Piaget's theory, has hypothesized that there are six stages of moral development (see Table 9.1). The stages are age related, and progression through the stages occurs as "the developing child becomes better able to understand and integrate diverse points of view on a moral-conflict situation and to take more of the relevant situational factors into account" (Jennings et al., 1983). Kohlberg believes that all individuals go through the same sequence of stages, though the pace may vary and some individuals may never progress beyond the first few stages.

TABLE 9.1 Kohlberg's Theory of Moral Development

Level	Stage	Description	
I.	Preconventional	1. Punishment 2. Instrumental hedonism	Egocentric (What happens to me?)
II.	Conventional	3. Approval of others 4. Authority maintaining morality	Social expectations (What do others expect of me?)
III.	Postconventional	5. Democratically accepted law 6. Principles of conscience	Universality (What is best for all?)

Source: Reprinted from *The Psychology of Criminal Conduct*, D.A. Andrews and James Bonta, "The Role of Antisocial Associates and Attitudes in Criminal Conduct," p. 237. Copyright © 2010, with permission from Elsevier.

Kohlberg categorizes the six stages into three levels of moral judgment development, each with two stages of moral reasoning.

The first is the *preconventional* level, characteristic of children under age 11 and of many adolescent and adult offenders. At this level, the morals and values of society are understood as "do's" and "don'ts" and are associated with punishment. The preconventional person is one for whom roles and social expectations are something external to the self.

The *conventional* level reflects the average adolescent and adult in our society and others. He or she understands, accepts, and attempts to uphold the values and rules of society. For a conventional person, the self is identified with or has internalized the rules and expectations of others, especially those of authorities.

The *postconventional* level is the one at which customs are critically examined with regard to universal rights, duties, and moral principles. It is characteristic of a minority of adults after the age of 20. The postconventional person has differentiated his or her self from the rules and expectations of others and has defined his or her value by means of self-chosen principles (Jennings et al., 1983).

Carol Gilligan (1982) has criticized Kohlberg's theory of moral development, stating that it is biased in favour of males. Gilligan argues that there is variation in moral standards by gender, with females taking a more care-oriented approach to morality, while males typically use a more justice-oriented approach. She believes that Kohlberg's theory does not take into consideration the more care-oriented approach of females and that, as a result, females rarely obtain the higher stages of moral development in Kohlberg's theory. To support her argument, she points out that females were not taken into consideration when Kohlberg was developing his theory—the development of moral judgment was based on an empirical study of 84 males whom Kohlberg followed for a 20-year period. Gilligan states that females typically reach only the second level (third stage) in Kohlberg's theory, which is characterized by goodness being equated with helping and pleasing others and is consistent with the care-oriented approach of females to morality. She argues that Kohlberg and Kramer (1969) have looked at this concept of goodness and concluded that this level of moral reasoning would be adequate for women whose lives will take place in the home. They indicate that only when women enter the "traditional arena of male activity" do they realize that this level of moral reasoning is not sufficient, and therefore progress toward the higher stages, as men do. Gilligan (1982) points out that "herein lies a paradox, for the very traits that traditionally have defined the 'goodness' of women, their care for and sensitivity to the needs of others, are those that mark them as deficient in moral development" (18).

Considerable research has been done on the relationship between moral development and delinquency. Kohlberg believes that people with high moral development are more likely to make individual choices and to be less influenced by friends or by consequences of actions. Thus there should be an inverse relationship between moral development and delinquency. Support for this relationship has been found in a number of studies. For example, Kiriakidis (2008) found that delinquents, compared to a non-delinquent sample, scored significantly higher on a moral disengagement scale. Jennings, Kilkenny, and Kohlberg (1983) reviewed a large number of studies on this relationship and concluded that "the overwhelming weight of the empirical data reviewed here supports the notion that juvenile delinquents' moral judgement is at a less advanced level than that of non-delinquent controls matched on a variety of variables." But they were careful to point out that a cause–effect relationship had not been established. Individuals at the same level of moral development may or may not become delinquent. They add that

> these studies lend support to the more modest claims that moral reasoning of increased maturity has an insulating effect against delinquency. Advanced stages of moral judgment cause one's moral orientation to be more integrated, stable and consistent. Higher reasoning makes one a more reliable moral agent and thus better able to withstand some incentives to illegal conduct postulated by a variety of sociological and psychological theories of the etiology of delinquency. (290)

This last statement suggests that moral development theory has considerable relevance for sociological explanations of criminal behaviour. Indeed, Morash (1983) has discussed at length the possible integration of moral development and sociological theories, suggesting that it may be more fruitful to study the interaction of personal and situational variables:

> Most serious delinquency would result from social conditions, primarily those that are enduring, that impinge on youths who possess the personality factors and the pre-conventional reasoning conducive to serious delinquent behavior. An advantage of this explanation is that it allows for the many pre-conventional individuals who do not break the law regularly or not at all, and it accounts for different patterns in delinquency—that is, the repeated serious delinquency and sporadic and/or less serious delinquency. (405)

Research has supported the link between moral development and adult criminality. In a study examining the moral development of 72 adult male sex offenders participating in a community-based treatment program, Buttell (2002) found that sex offenders employed a level of moral reasoning that was two standard deviations lower than the national norm. In addition, theories of moral development have important implications for offender rehabilitation programs (Blasi, 1980). Evidence suggests that education programs that focus on moral development have positive effects on inmates' moral judgments (Power, 2010). Future research will need to examine whether this increased morality leads to lower rates of criminal behaviour and recidivism.

In conclusion, there is evidence that level of moral reasoning is related to delinquent and criminal behaviour. However, the correlations reported in many studies are often quite low. Moral development may affect how an individual behaves in a given context, but it is clear that other characteristics of the individual, as well as the situation, will also be important determinants of behaviour.

SEARCH FOR:
"Hans Eysenck and Other Temperament Theorists," C. George Boeree, Shippensburg University of Pennsylvania

moral development theory
Refers generally to theories of individual psychology that investigate how moral reasoning emerges in the individual and develops as the individual matures.

Eysenck's Theory of Crime and Personality

Hans Eysenck, a noted British psychologist, has developed an elaborate theory of how personality characteristics are related to criminal behaviour (Eysenck, 1977). This theory has generated considerable research, in large part because it lends itself quite readily to the identification of groups of offenders and to predictions about their behaviour.

Eysenck believes that illegal, selfish, or immoral behaviour is simple to explain. These behaviours are inherently reinforcing, and hence it is more fruitful to try to explain why people do *not* commit crimes. Eysenck claims that children will naturally engage in such acts and only refrain from doing so if they are punished. Eysenck's theory is based on **classical conditioning**. Each time a child is punished, he or she may experience pain and fear. This pain and fear may be associated with the act itself. Thus whenever the child contemplates the act, he or she will experience fear, which will tend to inhibit the response. Eysenck equates this conditioned fear with conscience. Delinquents and criminals do not readily develop this conditioned response, either because of lack of exposure to effective conditioning practices by parents and others, or because they are less susceptible to conditioning. Eysenck (1990) states

> Depending on the frequency of pairings between the conditioned and unconditioned stimulus in the field of social behavior, and on the precise content of the conditioning program, children will grow up to develop appropriate types of behavior. Conditionability is a crucial factor on the social or environmental side. In a permissive society where parents, teachers, and magistrates do not take seriously the task of imposing a "conscience" which would lead them to behave in a socialized manner, a large number of individuals with poor or average conditionability will acquire a "conscience" too weak to prevent them from indulging in criminal activities, although had they been subjected to a stricter regime of conditioning, they might have grown up to be perfectly respectable and law-abiding citizens.

As Eysenck points out, the concept of "strictness" is not a function of excessive strength of the conditioning process, but a result of the certainty and frequency of pairings of the conditioned and unconditioned stimuli.

There are three dimensions of personality, according to Eysenck. **Extraversion** is a personality characteristic with highly sociable, impulsive, and aggressive people at one extreme of the continuum. Highly introverted, introspective, and inhibited people are at the other extreme. *Neuroticism* is linked to the psychiatric concept of neurosis. People who are high on this dimension are characterized by such symptoms as anxiety, restlessness, and other emotional responses. The opposite extreme of neuroticism is referred to as stability. The third dimension is *psychoticism*. According to Eysenck and Eysenck (1976, 47), a person who is high on this dimension is "cold, impersonal, hostile, lacking in sympathy, unfriendly, untrustful, odd, unemotional, unhelpful, antisocial, lacking in human feelings, inhumane, generally bloodyminded, lacking in insight, strange, with paranoid ideas that people are against him."

classical conditioning
A basic form of learning whereby a neutral stimulus is paired with another stimulus that naturally elicits a certain response; the neutral stimulus comes to elicit the same response as the stimulus that automatically elicits the response.

extraversion
A personality characteristic associated with sociability, impulsiveness, and aggression.

A number of hypotheses have been generated about the relationship of these dimensions to criminal behaviour. Extraverts, because of their high need for excitement, their impulsivity, and their relatively weak conscience, are believed to be more prone to criminal behaviour. In addition, persons high on both neuroticism and extraversion would be predicted to be delinquents or criminals. Persons high on psychoticism would tend to be more serious offenders, with a propensity for violence. Hare (1982) investigated the relationship between these three dimensions and psychopathy. While neuroticism and extraversion did not correlate with measures of psychopathy, psychoticism did. It is concluded that this may be because each dimension taps a common element of psychopathy (criminal and antisocial tendencies) rather than those psychological features that are assumed in the diagnosis of psychopathy (e.g., lack of remorse, lack of empathy).

Eysenck and others have developed psychological measures of each of these dimensions. Research in testing predictions about offenders has produced mixed results. In their extensive and excellent review of Eysenck's theory, Farrington, Biron, and LeBlanc (1982) summarized data from 16 studies, most of which were conducted in Great Britain, and found that while some studies supported the predictions of Eysenck's theory, other studies did not. Bartol (1980) came to a similar conclusion.

Like other theories, personality theories such as Eysenck's have problems with tautology or circular reasoning. That is, in many measures of personality, the sub-scale that differentiates delinquents from non-delinquents includes items asking about antisocial behaviour (e.g., have you been in trouble with the law)—the very thing it proposes to explain. In addition, some have criticized personality theories for failing to adequately define their terms (Einstadter and Henry, 1995).

Eysenck's theory is important because it shows how psychological and social variables can be interrelated. Individuals who may have a psychological propensity to commit crime may be socialized effectively if they grow up in an environment that provides effective conditioning. Similarly, individuals with a low propensity for criminality may become criminal if their environment is too permissive. Eysenck argues strongly for the importance of individual differences, but he also recognizes the importance of societal influences: "Crime ... is essentially a function of the ethos of the society in which we live; it reflects the practices of positive and negative reinforcement, of reward and punishment, of teaching and conditioning, which are prevalent, and these in turn are mirrored and reflected by the types of films we see, television programs we watch, books and newspapers we read, and teaching and examples we receive at school" (Eysenck and Gudjonsson, 1989, 255). In the next section, it will be seen that social learning theory reflects this perspective more explicitly.

Social Learning Theory

Another theory that lends itself to an integration of sociology and psychology is social learning theory. Though this theory focuses on individual behaviour, it takes into account the environment's influence and the individual's social conditions. Cognitive functioning—the ability to think and make choices—is central to social learning theory.

An important element of social learning theory is **modelling**. Individuals can learn new behaviours through direct experience or by observing the behaviour of others. The latter, also referred to as vicarious learning, can be an effective and efficient way to acquire new behaviours. Albert Bandura, a Stanford University professor of psychology, is a leading social learning theorist. He suggests that virtually all learning phenomena resulting from direct experiences can occur on a vicarious basis through observation of other persons' behaviour and its consequences for them (Bandura, 2000).

Social learning theory has been used to explain how aggression is learned. Since this is of great concern to criminology theory, aggression will be used as an example of an application of social learning theory.

Bandura (1986) suggests that aggressive behaviour can be learned from three sources. The *family* is one source, with a number of studies showing that children of parents who respond aggressively to problems will tend to use similar tactics. Bandura also points to research on child abuse, which shows that many children who have been abused will later become abusers themselves. Another source of aggressive behaviour can be referred to as *subcultural influences*, or the influence of social models and peers. Bandura suggests that the highest incidence of aggression is found in communities in which aggressive models abound and fighting prowess is regarded as a valued attribute. The third source of learned aggressive behaviour is through *symbolic modelling*. An example of this is violence on television, which provides models of aggressive behaviour (Skoler, Bandura, and Ross, 1994).

Bandura's research on the role of film models reinforced existing concerns about the effects of television on aggressive behaviour. Geen (1983) reviewed the research on the relationship between viewing television violence and aggression. He first looked at the vast number of correlational studies, the majority of which support the conclusion that there is a positive relationship between viewing violence and aggressive behaviour. A typical study is the one by Teevan and Hartnagel (1976), which showed that high school students who described their favourite television shows as violent also reported committing more aggressive acts than students whose favourite shows were non-violent. More recently, Anderson and his colleagues (2010) have found evidence for a relationship between playing violent video games and aggressive behaviour.

The problem with correlational research, as Geen points out, is that the direction of causation is unknown. It is possible that people who are more likely to behave aggressively simply prefer more violent television shows. Thus it cannot be concluded through correlational studies alone that viewing violence is the cause of aggressive behaviour. Cook, Kendzierski, and Thomas (1983) reanalyzed data from several large-scale studies of the effects of television violence. They concluded that an association between television viewing and aggression by children can be found regularly but that the level of association is typically quite small and often not statistically significant. Nevertheless, they conclude that the association is most probably a causal one, that watching violence on television does have an effect on children's aggressive behaviour. The same can be said for violence in music videos (Smith and Boyson, 2002).

modelling
A form of learning that occurs as a result of watching and imitating others.

Psychologists have debated the degree to which violent movies and television programs contribute to violent behaviour, but the results of this research are not yet conclusive.

In addition to its direct effect on aggressive behaviour, it is also possible that exposure to television violence increases one's tolerance toward violence and decreases one's sensitivity to acts of violence. Thomas and colleagues (1979) found that both adult and child subjects showed less **autonomic reactivity** to a scene of real-life interpersonal aggression if they had first watched a violent scene from a television show. Malamuth and Check (1981) reported similar results in their study of the effects of film violence on attitudes toward violence. Male and female university students were randomly assigned to view either a violent-sexual or a control feature-length film. The films were shown as part of the regular campus film program, and subjects believed they were viewing the films as a film-rating task. Several days later, unaware of any relationship between the film and the questionnaire, they were asked to respond to a number of attitude measures. Malamuth and Check found that exposure to the film portraying violent sexuality was associated with a greater acceptance of interpersonal violence against women. However, this finding was true only for male subjects. Female subjects had a nonsignificant tendency in the opposite direction: women exposed to violence tended to be less accepting of interpersonal violence than control females. It is important to realize that this study does not provide any data on whether males exposed to violence would actually behave differently toward women. However, the study does demonstrate that such exposure may have a significant effect on attitudes.

In his analysis of antisocial behaviour, Bandura (1986) suggests that the best deterrent to such activity is the provision of more attractive pro-social alternatives. However, he acknowledges that "when inducements to criminal acts are strong, when personal sanctions against such conduct are weak, and when people lack socially acceptable means of getting what they want, fear of

autonomic reactivity
A measurement of the extent to which an individual's physical organism reacts to external stimuli.

punishment serves as a major deterrent to transgressive conduct." Deterrence may take two forms—direct or vicarious. In the former, punishment is used to discourage current transgressors from such activity in the future. In the latter, punishment serves as a general deterrent to others. Bandura identifies three major sources of deterrence against criminal activity: legal sanction, social sanction, and self-sanction. Legal sanctions derive from the belief that there are legal consequences to transgressions, notwithstanding the reality that most crime goes unpunished. Citing research by Clastner (1967), Bandura states that "people who are not in the habit of breaking the law share a distorted perception of legal threats, in which they greatly overestimate the risks of getting caught and punished for unlawful acts. In contrast, offenders judge personal risks to be lower and more in line with the actual probabilities." Social sanctions reflect the negative social consequences that criminal stigmatization can have for an individual and the powerful deterrent effect this risk has. Self-sanctions are self-imposed moral standards; they are viewed as the most effective deterrent, for they operate even when there is no risk of detection. Bandura (1986) states: "In the absence of self-sanctions rooted in societal standards, whenever personal desires conflict with societal codes, external threats in the form of legal and social sanctions, and extensive social surveillance are needed to ensure that the rights and welfare of others are not completely disregarded."

The empirical status of social learning theory has been summarized by Akers and Jensen (2006):

> Indeed, it is reasonable to propose that the theory has been tested in relation to a wider range of forms of deviance, in a wider range of settings and samples, in more different languages, and by more different people, has survived more "crucial tests" against other theories, and is the most strongly and consistently supported by empirical data than any other social psychological explanation of crime and deviance. (37)

Operant Conditioning

Another learning theory is based on the principle of operant conditioning. This involves the use of rewards and punishments to increase the probability or frequency of a given response. B.F. Skinner is the psychologist most identified with this theory, and his research forms the basis for both the theoretical and the applied applications of **operant conditioning**.

One way a response can be learned is through a process referred to as shaping. This involves rewarding approximations of some target behaviour until the behaviour gradually progresses to the desired response. Behaviour can also be learned through punishment, which can involve either the withdrawal of a positive reinforcer or the introduction of a negative stimulus such as an electric shock. There have been a number of attempts to use operant conditioning theory to account for the acquisition of criminal behaviour. Notable among this work is that of Jeffery (1965) and of Burgess and Akers (1966).

Burgess and Akers (1966) and Akers (1990) conceptualize criminal behaviour in terms of operant conditioning and imitation. The main component in Akers's (1990) social learning theory is differential reinforcement. This refers to the balance of rewards and punishments that govern behaviour. In this theory,

operant conditioning
The basic process by which an individual's behaviour is shaped by reinforcement or by punishment.

operant conditioning is the basic process by which an individual's behaviour is shaped, and this can occur through both reinforcement and punishment. Reinforcement refers to any process that strengthens a behaviour; punishment is any process that weakens a behaviour. As applied to deviance and crime, Akers (1990, 655) states that

> social learning is a behavioral approach to socialization which includes individuals' responses to rewards and punishments in the current situation, the learned patterns of responses they bring to that situation, and the anticipated consequences of actions taken now and in the future in the initiation, continuation, and cessation of those actions. It is a "soft behaviorism" that allows for choice and cognitive processes. It views the individual's behavior as responding to and being conditioned by environmental feedback and consequences. It does not view the individual as unreasoning and only passively conditioned.

Considerable research has been conducted on the application of learning theory to the treatment of delinquents. The "teaching family" group home model begun in the late 1960s has been at the centre of group home development. The approach

> rests on the view that an adolescent's behavior patterns, behavior discriminations, and skills are functions of past behavior–environment interactions (learning history), currently ongoing behavior—environment interactions, and genetic organismic variables (Braukman et al., 1980). In this conceptualization, inherited characteristics and environmental features in childhood, particularly parenting practices (relationship development, teaching, supervision, and discipline) affect later development. In adolescence, earlier developed antisocial patterns tend to persevere (indeed, are self-perpetuating) and can be maintained further by ongoing behavior–environment interactions associated with inappropriate parenting, deviant peers, and school failure. (Braukman and Wolf, 1987)

The group home provides a reinforcing environment designed to change existing behavioural interactions in the direction of functional and pro-social skills. The emphasis is on learning social and family life skills. The best known of these programs is Achievement Place, a program first implemented in a cottage-style treatment facility for delinquent youths in Lawrence, Kansas. (The name of the treatment facility was Achievement Place, hence the name of the program.) Youths in Achievement Place programs live in a residence with trained "houseparents." The heart of the program is a **token economy** system in which points can be earned (or lost). For example, residents can earn points for being at class on time, cleaning their bedroom, and engaging in other positive behaviours. Disruptive behaviour in the classroom, making aggressive statements or fighting, and being late for class can result in a loss of points. The points can be used to purchase privileges and material goods. Research on Achievement Place has demonstrated that "contingent token consequences could both establish behaviors basic to participation in lawful, productive intra- and extra-treatment activities, and eliminate behaviors likely to get the

token economy
A behaviour therapy procedure based on operant learning principles. Individuals are rewarded (reinforced) for positive or appropriate behaviour and are disciplined (punished) for negative or inappropriate behaviour.

participants in further trouble" (Braukman and Wolf, 1987). A comprehensive outcome study on the teaching family program (Braukman et al., 1985) indicates that this approach has considerable short-term positive effects. However, the long-term implications are less positive since it is very difficult to control reinforcement following release from the institution. Because of this, increased emphasis has been placed on systematic aftercare to help maintain treatment effects.

QUESTIONS FOR CRITICAL THINKING

1. Describe how each of the major psychological theories would explain criminal behaviour (i.e., psychoanalytic theory, theories of moral development, Eysenck's theory of crime and personality, social learning theory, and operant conditioning).
2. What are the social policy implications of each of these theories?

Antisocial Personality

The study of antisocial personality provides a good example of how psychological theory can be applied to criminal populations. Some confusion has resulted from the variety of terms used to describe basically the same set of behaviours: sociopathy, psychopathy, moral insanity, antisocial personality, and **Antisocial Personality Disorder**. There has also been a tendency for some to use the term very loosely as a "wastebasket" category for antisocial individuals generally. There is, however, strong empirical evidence that the traits underlying this disorder form a valid, clinically meaningful cluster (Hare and Cox, 1978; Skilling et al., 2002). For many, this term is associated with images of violent and sadistic murderers as portrayed countless times on television or, all too often, demonstrated in real life. The brutal murders committed by Clifford Olson (see Box 9.3) and Charles Manson and his followers in California are frequently cited examples of psychopathy. Indeed, while there is some debate over the most appropriate diagnosis for Manson, many would argue that his behaviour best fits the clinical picture of psychopathy. As Nathan and Harris (1975, 361) point out:

> Charles Manson acted upon society in an unbelievable variety of antisocial ways. At one time or another he robbed, deceived, assaulted, exploited, seduced—and murdered. But despite the extraordinary range of antisocial acts for which he had been responsible, perhaps his most surprising characteristic was that at no time did he show guilt or remorse about anything he had done. During his trial for the Tate murders, he said, "I've considered innocence and guilt and I know the difference between them and I have no guilt" (quoted from the *New York Times*, December 25, 1969). A man who could be charming and captivating, brutal and ruthless, Manson could not be guilty, at least in his

Antisocial Personality Disorder
A personality disorder that involves disregard for the rights of others as well as impulsive, irresponsible, and aggressive behaviour.

own eyes. What kind of human being feels no remorse over murder? Why would a person keep committing crimes despite repeated punishment? How can a man charm so many people and yet never relate with genuine feeling to anyone?

These questions are difficult to answer because the crimes Manson and Olson committed seem so senseless to society. However disturbing they may be, it is possible for most people to understand murders motivated by greed or passion, but the murder of Sharon Tate and others by Manson cannot be explained by either of these motivations. A Canadian case highlights the differences between psychopathy or antisocial personality disorder and more severe mental illnesses, such as schizophrenia, which might have a significant impact on one's ability to choose between right and wrong (see Box 9.1).

FOCUS

Box 9.1

VINCE LI: GROTESQUE KILLING ABOARD BUS 1170

Vince Weiguang Li was born in Dandong, China on April 30, 1968. He graduated from University with a Bachelor of Science in 1992. Mr. Li immigrated to Canada in 2001 and became a Canadian citizen in 2005. He was unable to find work in his field and so he worked a number of menial jobs including as a caretaker in a church, a sales assistant in a store, and as a newspaper carrier. His final employer described him as a good worker albeit somewhat unusual. Despite his largely uneventful past with no criminal arrests or convictions, Mr. Li brutally and savagely killed a fellow bus passenger in July 2008 in a fashion that is reminiscent of the gruesome movie *Silence of the Lambs*.

According to witnesses and as documented in the Agreed Statement of Facts, on July 30, 2008, Mr. Li boarded Greyhound Bus #1170 destined for Winnipeg in Erickson, Manitoba at 7 p.m. He sat near the back of the bus. He was described as a tall man in his 40s, with a shaved head and sunglasses. Approximately 90 minutes later, shortly after a rest stop, Mr. Li suddenly produced a large hunting knife and began stabbing his sleeping seatmate in the neck and chest. While most passengers quickly fled out of the bus, the driver and three other male passengers attempted to help the victim. They were chased away by Mr. Li, who slashed wildly at them with a knife.

Mr. Li persisted in brutalizing his victim by decapitating him and displaying his severed head to those gathered outside. Mr. Li continued to dismember the corpse and then proceeded to perform acts of cannibalism.

The rear door was barricaded with a snipe bar to prevent Mr. Li from escaping. In addition, the power to the bus was cut off to render the vehicle inoperable. Several minutes later, the RCMP arrived. They encouraged Mr. Li to drop his weapon out of a small bathroom window, but he refused, while indicating, in addition to some unintelligible words, something to the effect that he had to stay on the bus forever. Two hours later the province's Emergency Response Team took over from the RCMP. Mr. Li refused to give himself up. Instead, he continued pacing the length of the bus, defiling and eating the corpse. At approximately 1:30 a.m., five hours after the attack began, Mr. Li was arrested when he attempted to escape through a broken back bus window. He was tasered several times, handcuffed, and placed in the back of a police cruiser. The victim's nose, tongue, and ear were found in a plastic bag in Mr. Li's pockets. The victim's eyes and parts of his heart were never recovered and are presumed to have been eaten by Mr. Li.

To many, this brutal crime might conjure images of Hannibal Lecter, the psychopath killer played by Anthony Hopkins in the famous movie *Silence of the Lambs*. However, there is one important difference. In *Silence of the Lambs*, Hannibal Lecter was acutely aware of his actions and knew that what he was doing was wrong. As is explained below, this was not the case with Mr. Li. In fact, Mr. Li was suffering from a mental disorder that rendered him unable to appreciate the nature and quality of his actions and to know that they were wrong.

At Mr. Li's second-degree murder trial, which began nearly a year after the crime on March 5, 2009, the Crown and defence attorneys agreed to a number of facts. Among them was that Mr. Li had few friends and that those he did have described him as having had mental problems. In addition, his former wife

(continued)

described him engaging in bizarre behaviours, including sudden and unexplained absences, bus trips to unusual locations, and rambling talk. Despite his unusual behaviour, neither his friends nor his former wife had known him to be violent. One episode of unusual behaviour resulted in the Ontario Provincial Police (OPP) picking him up on a busy highway. He was hospitalized briefly in the fall of 2005 before being released with medication. Both before and after this incident, friends and family were unable to convince him to seek medical help.

At his trial, psychiatric assessments of Mr. Li were put into evidence. In particular, the assessments suggested that Mr. Li was suffering from schizophrenia, a mental illness whose symptoms can include hallucinations, delusions, and paranoia. According to the psychiatrists' assessments, the voice of God had directed Mr. Li to move from Edmonton to Winnipeg. Moreover, the voice had led Mr. Li to believe, under a paranoid delusion, that the deceased victim was a threat to his own life, both before and after the deceased victim's death.

The judge accepted the assessments that Mr. Li was suffering from a mental disorder. In his decision, he said

> These grotesque acts are appalling. However, the acts themselves and the context in which they were committed are strongly suggestive of a mental disorder. He did not appreciate the actions he committed were morally wrong. He believed he was acting in self-defence. (McIntyre, 2009)

Moreover, the judge stated,

> Persons who are profoundly ill do not have the mental capacity to intentionally commit a crime. The goal of criminal law is to punish criminals, not persons who have a mental illness. Moreover, a person who is driven to act by severe psychotic delusions cannot be deterred by the fear of punishment, or public denouncement. In such cases, the only way to change the behaviour of a person who is driven to act by psychotic delusions is through treatment, and where the person poses an ongoing risk to society, through treatment in a secure institution. (Pritchard, 2009)

As a result of these findings, the judge found Mr. Li not criminally responsible on account of mental disorder (NCRMD).

Under Canadian law, no person is criminally responsible for an act committed while suffering from a mental disorder that rendered the person incapable of appreciating the nature and quality of the act or of knowing it was wrong (Criminal Code of Canada, C-46, s. 16(1)). However, not all individuals who are suffering from a mental disorder will be found NCRMD. Rather, an individual will only be found NCRMD if the mental disorder, which is defined in law as a disease of the mind, renders the person unable to differentiate between right and wrong. In *Winko v. British Columbia (Forensic Psychiatric Institute)* the Supreme Court of Canada put it this way:

> [P]eople who commit criminal acts under the influence of mental illnesses should not be held criminally responsible for their acts or omissions in the same way that sane responsible people are. No person should be convicted of a crime if he or she was legally insane at the time of the offence ... Criminal responsibility is appropriate only where the actor is a discerning moral agent, capable of making choices between right and wrong."

In cases where individuals are found NCRMD, they are not admitted to jail or prison. Rather, their disposition depends on a number of considerations, including the protection of the public, the individual's mental condition, the reintegration of the individual into society, and the individual's other needs. Disposition decisions are made by specially constituted Review Boards whose duty it is to weigh these considerations. The disposition of Mr. Li was decided by the Manitoba Review Board on September 15, 2009. His disposition order required him to be detained in a locked ward of a psychiatric hospital in Manitoba. When the order was reviewed on May 31, 2010, the Review Board again ordered him to be detained in a locked ward of a psychiatric hospital in Manitoba. However, this time they allowed for the possibility of escorted access to the hospital grounds (e.g., outside yard). Disposition orders are reviewed by the Review Board at least annually. Mr. Li is currently being held at the Selkirk Mental Health Centre in Manitoba.

Sources: Queen's Bench, Winnipeg Centre, (n.d.), Between Her Majesty the Queen and Vince Weiguang Li—Agreed Statement of Facts. Winnipeg: Queen's Bench; Province of Manitoba Review Board. (2009). A Disposition Hearing held in Winnipeg, Manitoba on Monday, June 1, 2009. Winnipeg: Manitoba Review Board; Province of Manitoba Review Board. (2010). A Disposition Review Hearing held in Winnipeg, Manitoba on Monday, May 31, 2010. Winnipeg: Manitoba Review Board.

Similarly, it is difficult to understand the motivations of "Canada's Ken and Barbie Killers"—Paul Bernardo and Karla Homolka—who were responsible for the grotesque rape and murder of three young women, including Karla Homolka's own sister. Although the prevalence of female psychopaths is lower than that of males, we are especially intrigued by these women. In parole board reports, Karla Homolka has been deemed a psychopath (see Box 9.2), though the motivation for her actions remains unclear.

This section began with a discussion of Charles Manson because it is this image that best fits the common conception of persons with an antisocial personality. It is a misleading picture, however, because many individuals with diagnoses of antisocial personality do not have a history of violence, and even among those who do, very few would exhibit the extreme forms that Manson did. The term *sociopath* was later used instead of the term *psychopath* to convey this less violent picture. More recently, the use of the term *Antisocial Personality Disorder* has become common.

The current edition of the American Psychiatric Association's *Diagnostic and Statistical Manual of Mental Disorder* (DSM-V; APA, 2013) defines Antisocial Personality Disorder as follows: "The essential feature of Antisocial Personality Disorder is a pervasive pattern of disregard for, and violation of, the rights of others that begins in childhood or early adolescence and continues into adulthood" (701).

Lying, stealing, fighting, truancy, and resisting authority are typical early childhood signs. In adolescence, unusually early or aggressive sexual behaviour, excessive drinking, and use of illicit drugs are frequent. In adulthood, those kinds of behaviour continue, with the addition of an inability to sustain consistent work performance or to function as a responsible parent and failure to accept social norms with respect to lawful behaviour. After age 30, the more flagrant aspects may diminish, particularly sexual promiscuity, fighting, criminality, and vagrancy. It is estimated that between 15 and 30 percent of the inmate population in Canadian prisons could be considered psychopathic (Ogloff, Wong, and Greenwood, 1990).

In his book *The Mask of Sanity*, Cleckley (1976) provided a clinical description of the antisocial personality and described the psychopath using the following criteria: unreliability; insincerity; pathological lying and deception; egocentricity; poor judgment; impulsivity; a lack of remorse, guilt, or shame; an inability to experience empathy or concern for others and to maintain warm, affectionate attachments; an impersonal and poorly integrated sex life; and an unstable life plan with no long-term commitments.

Since the 1960s, Hare and his colleagues have devoted considerable attention to the development of a reliable and valid procedure for assessing psychopathy. This program has culminated in the Revised Psychopathy Checklist (PCL-R) (Hare, 1991), a 20-item checklist of traits and behaviours associated with psychopathy (see Table 9.2). Research has continued to support the use of this scale in prison populations. An excellent review of the use, and misuse, of the PCL-R has been provided by Hare. In discussing the PCL-R and its screening version, the PCL-SV (Hart, Cox, and Hare, 1995), he concludes that these checklists:

> provide reliable and valid assessments of the traditional construct of psychopathy. They are used widely for research purposes and for making decisions in the mental health and criminal justice systems. They are strong predictors of violence and recidivism in offenders and psychiatric patients, form a key part of current risk assessment procedures, and play an important role in many judicial decisions. (Hare, 1998c, 99)

| TABLE 9.2 | The 20 Items of the Psychopathy Checklist |

1. Glibness/superficial charm[p]	11. Promiscuous sexual behaviour
2. Grandiose sense of self-worth[p]	12. Early behavioural problems[ab]
3. Need for stimulation / proneness to boredom[ab]	13. Lack of realistic, long-term goals[ab]
4. Pathological lying[p]	14. Impulsivity[ab]
5. Conning/manipulative[p]	15. Irresponsibility[ab]
6. Lack of remorse or guilt[p]	16. Failure to accept responsibility for own actions[ab]
7. Shallow affect[p]	17. Many short-term marital relationships
8. Callous/lack of empathy[p]	18. Juvenile delinquency[ab]
9. Parasitic lifestyle[ab]	19. Revocation of conditional release[ab]
10. Poor behavioural controls[ab]	20. Criminal versatility

Note: The checklist is composed of two factors: [p] identifies the items that define personality traits, and [ab] identifies items descriptive of antisocial behaviour.

Sources: R.D. Hare, "The Hare Psychopathy Checklist—Revised," Multi-Health Systems, Inc. Adapted from R.D. Hare, "A Research Scale for the Assessment of Psychopathy in Criminal Populations," *Personality and Individual Differences* 1: 111–19. Oxford: Pergamon Press, 1991. © 1990 R.D. Hare. Reprinted with permission from Elsevier Science Ltd.

Other commentators and researchers have cautioned against over-reliance on the PCL-R (or any assessment instrument) when making legal determinations and against equating the construct of psychopathy with scores on the PCL-R (see DeMatteo and Edens, 2006; Skeem and Cooke, 2010).

DSM-V estimates that the prevalence of Antisocial Personality Disorder is 3 percent for men and less than 1 percent for women. Estimates of this diagnostic classification in prison populations are, not surprisingly, considerably higher. Indeed, depending on how one interprets the diagnostic criteria, virtually all inmates could be so classified. The differences in interpretation may partly account for the large disparity in prison studies of this disorder, reflecting, in part, changes in diagnostic procedures and criteria. In a Canadian study of the prevalence of Antisocial Personality Disorder, Hare (1983) had two clinicians examine a provincial and a federal prison inmate sample. The clinicians found that approximately one-third of the provincial sample and 42 percent of the federal sample met the criteria for Antisocial Personality Disorder. Overall, 39 percent of the total prison sample received this diagnosis. However, in a previous study described in the same paper, Hare, using the initial criteria proposed in a draft of DSM-III-R, found that 76 percent of a sample of 145 white male criminals met the criteria for Antisocial Personality Disorder. The reason for the difference is that the published version of DSM-III-R required that more stringent criteria be met before a diagnosis of Antisocial Personality Disorder could be made. Hare's work was influential in the decision to change the criteria. The two studies provide a clear illustration of how changes in diagnostic criteria and procedures can influence the perceived prevalence of antisocial personality.

A leading theory about antisocial personality is that these individuals do not learn from negative experiences because they do not become anxious in circumstances that should elicit anxiety. Also, they do not have sufficient fear of the consequences of their behaviour (Hare, 1970; Brodsky, 1977). Applying

FOCUS

Box 9.2

PSYCHOLOGISTS SUGGEST BERNARDO AND HOMOLKA ARE PSYCHOPATHS

TORONTO—Prosecutors painted a picture of a battered woman and a controlling, abusive husband who forced her to take part in unspeakable crimes. But some experts suspect that both Karla Homolka and Paul Bernardo are psychopaths—people who aren't mentally ill but lack any conscience and single-mindedly pursue their own pleasure.

In Bernardo, they suggest, psychopathic qualities combined with sexual sadism to form an explosive mix. Some psychologists who have followed the Bernardo trial say the crimes Homolka and Bernardo admitted to committing, and their almost total lack of emotion in the witness box, suggest psychopathic tendencies.

"What bothers me about him, and her, too, is the casual way these horrific things are described on the witness stand," said psychologist Robert Hare of the University of British Columbia, one of the world's leading experts on psychopaths.

"When a psychopath commits a violent act, they're not doing it because they're malicious or malevolent or evil. They're doing it because they don't give a damn."

Bernardo was "such a good psychopath" that he found a woman who had a penchant for submissive sex that complemented his urge to dominate, said psychologist Marnie Rice of Ontario's Penetanguishene Mental Health Centre. Homolka may not have got into trouble with another man. But hooked up with Bernardo, it's possible she agreed to take part in three-way sex with kidnapped teenage girls as part of a willingly subservient role, said Rice, whose hospital houses some of the province's most dangerous offenders.

"It appears the two found each other."

Homolka testified Bernardo beat her into submission and blackmailed her over her role in the death of her sister, who was drugged and raped by the couple. Two psychologists called by the Crown suggested Homolka suffered from battered women's syndrome. Rendered helpless and hopeless by repeated beatings, someone in her shoes could feel obliged to take part in the most heinous crimes, they said. Hare is skeptical.

"We look for very simple explanations for complex behaviour," he said. "To me, battered women's syndrome does not explain what she did."

Even a psychiatrist retained by the prosecution—but not called as a witness at Bernardo's trial—said Homolka's role in the horrific crimes can't be fully explained by the abuse she suffered.

"Karla Homolka remains something of a diagnostic mystery," Dr. Angus McDonald wrote in his report, which the Bernardo jury never saw.

"Despite her ability to present herself very well, there is a moral vacuity in her which is difficult, if not impossible, to explain."

In Bernardo's case, it appears there were no ethical restraints to hold him back from sex that inflicted pain, terror and humiliation on his partner, psychologists say. Among evidence ruled inadmissible at his trail was a statement the Crown says Bernardo made to two witnesses.

"I have no conscience," prosecutors quoted him as saying. "I could kill anybody."

Experts also say his videotaping of the sexual assaults is typical of many rapists and sex killers, who keep souvenirs of their victims such as jewelry, clothing or hair. Serial killer Harvey Murray Glatman used photographs of the women he murdered in Los Angeles during the 1950s to relive his sexual fantasies.

"They're like stamp collectors," said psychologist Vern Quinsey of Queen's University in Kingston. "They look at them and think about them and try to do better next time."

Psychopaths tend to be egocentric, lack remorse or guilt and constantly seek excitement, said Hare. They're also unable to empathize with others and tend to be deceitful and emotionally shallow. Only a small percentage are physically violent, he said.

"They are predators—emotional and physical and sexual predators."

Bernardo's cool, confident and sometimes condescending demeanor in the witness box was typical, Hare said.

"A psychopath who has committed a crime and is caught is now on stage. He doesn't see himself as any sort of pariah, he sees himself as a victim of the system … He's on stage, he's enjoying it, he's loving it.

"What these people do is confuse fame and infamy."

Source: Tom Blackwell, "Psychologists Suggest Bernardo and Homolka Are Psychopaths" (n.d.). Printed with permission of *The Canadian Press*.

Eysenck's model, reviewed earlier in this chapter, the psychopath can be viewed as an extravert who does not easily acquire conditioned responses or, if he or she does acquire them, extinguishes them very rapidly. Given these characteristics, particularly the inability to learn from punishment or to experience fear or anxiety, it is understandable that Brodsky (1977) concludes that imprisonment is unlikely to have much effect on the post-release behaviour of such individuals. Newman (1998) reviews a position suggesting that psychopaths exhibit deficits in information processing that limit their ability to use contextual cues appropriately in the implementation of goal-directed behaviour and that interfere with effective self-regulation. Hare (1998b) suggests that while a great deal remains to be done, a convergence is developing with regard to etiologic bases of psychopathy, one that forms "a reasonably coherent conceptual/empirical package that helps us understand how and why psychopaths differ from others in the processing and use of semantic and affective information, and in their capacity for callous, predatory behaviour" (131).

Raine and Yang (2006) indicate that there has been surprisingly little brain imaging research done on the neuroanatomical basis of psychopathy. They conclude that this is because the complexity of the clinical construct makes it "highly likely that the neuroanatomical basis to psychopathy is not simple, and that abnormalities to multiple brain mechanisms contribute to the behavioural, cognitive, and emotional characteristics that make up the psychopath" (279). In reviewing the existing literature, they draw two conclusions. One is that the area is very much under-researched and that basic research is still required. The second is that, with regard to psychopathy, questions regarding specific brain impairments and their causes are even further removed from being answered (p. 291). Given these limitations, several possible neuroanatomical impairments have been identified (Raine and Yang, 2006). One is that abnormalities in the prefrontal cortex would support the view that psychopaths are low-arousal, fearless, impulsive, and disinhibited individuals. Impairments in the hippocampus may result in dysregulation in affect and fear conditioning. Dysfunction in the amygdala has also been suggested in psychopaths (Blair, 2006), resulting in a reduction in the individual's "responsiveness to the sadness and fear of potential victims" and "their ability to learn the stimulus–reinforcement associations that are necessary for moral socialization" (307). A concern expressed in the identification of possible pathophysiologies in psychopathy is whether or not they are fundamental to the disorder or are secondary consequences of it (Blair, 2006).

Heilbrun (1979) conducted an interesting study of the influence of intelligence on the relationships between psychopathy, violence, and impulsiveness. His sample of 76 white male prisoners was divided into psychopathic and nonpsychopathic groups ($n = 38$). Two personality measures were used (one of which, incidentally, was validated in a study by Craddick, 1962, using a Canadian prison sample). He further divided the groups into high-intelligence and low-intelligence subgroups. Heilbrun found that intelligence level does indeed have an influence on violence and impulsiveness among psychopaths. The more intelligent psychopaths were neither violent nor impulsive and were more likely to have attained educational goals. This study points to the importance of viewing persons with the label of psychopath, or antisocial personality, in multidimensional ways. Not all such individuals should be expected to be violent or impulsive.

The Heilbrun study should also serve as a reminder that studies of prison populations may present a misleading picture of antisocial personality. Most of the research on antisocial personality has used samples obtained from institutional populations. This may give a distorted view because the impressions one has about people with antisocial personalities are, thus, based on people who committed criminal acts but were unable to avoid apprehension. Furthermore, it is certainly true that not all persons with this label are criminals (Cleckley, 1976). An exception to the focus on institutionalized populations is the work of Cathy Spatz Widom (Widom, 1977; Widom and Newman, 1985). In one study, Widom placed an advertisement in a local newspaper asking for "charming, aggressive, carefree people who are impulsively irresponsible but are good at handling people and at looking after number one." Twenty-nine applicants were interviewed. The demographic and personality test data applied to these people revealed some interesting information about this non-institutionalized population. Only two subjects had not finished high school, and most had some college. Nearly two-thirds had at least one arrest, but the conviction rate was quite low (18%), even though many of the charges were felonies. While 50 percent had been incarcerated, most had been in jail less than two weeks. The subjects scored high on the extraversion and neuroticism scale of Eysenck Personality Inventory, consistent with Eysenck's (1977) notions of psychopathy. Scores on the Minnesota Multiphasic Personality Inventory (MMPI), an objective personality test, fit the classic profile of psychopathy (high scores on the psychopathic deviate and manic scales). Subjects had low scores on the measure of socialization, and most also had low scores on the empathy scale.

While many of the results of Widom's study were similar to those found in institutional populations, it presents a picture of somewhat more successful antisocial persons. That is, they are better educated and more successful at avoiding conviction and lengthy incarceration. These results support the conclusion of Widom and Newman (1985) that research on the antisocial personality must avoid a primary focus on the incarcerated criminal. Her methodology seems to have succeeded in drawing a sample of noninstitutionalized persons who meet the antisocial personality criteria. This is important, for it is vital for us to become more aware of the prevalence of psychopathy within the general population and to begin to understand better the non-criminal manifestations of this personality.

Of direct relevance to this concern is the book by Babiak and Hare (2006), *Snakes in Suits: When Psychopaths Go To Work*, in which the authors examine the impact of the psychopath in the corporate working world. One might initially assume that many of the traits that psychopaths display would make it obvious to potential employers that they would not work well with others and would constitute an employment risk, but this does not appear to be the case. The authors identify four possible reasons for this contradiction. One is that some of the traits associated with psychopathy provide these individuals with skills in social manipulation. Their ability to charm others will often make them initially seem attractive and even charismatic in job interviews. It is only in retrospect that it becomes clear that the decision was not a good one. A second issue is that some of the traits associated with psychopathy may appear on the surface to indicate leadership and management skills though they actually represent a need for dominance and manipulative as well as coercive abilities that are, again, not initially obvious. A third concern reflects the evolution of today's business world, in which large, stable bureaucratic organizations have adopted a faster, more flexible, and somewhat chaotic approach to information processing. This has resulted in a change in hiring policies toward acquiring individuals who can "stir things up" and effect change quickly. As Babiak and Hare note, "the general state of confusion that change brings to a situation can make psychopathic personality traits—the appearance of confidence, strength, and calm—often look like the answer to the organization's problems ... Egocentricity, callousness, and insensitivity suddenly become acceptable trade-offs in order to get the talents and skills needed to survive in an accelerated, dispassionate business world" (2006, xxi). A fourth dilemma is that the decreased constraints and levels of accountability in this new fast-paced business climate create an environment that psychopaths find inviting. The personal gains available are very appealing to the psychopath, who relishes the risks and thrills involved. The relentlessness of this drive is captured in the somewhat chilling comment: "Like all predators, psychopaths go where the action is, which means to them positions, occupations, and organizations that afford them the opportunity to obtain power, control, status, and possessions, and to engage in exploitative interpersonal relationships" (Babiak and Hare, 2006, 97).

Clearly, the implications of corporate psychopathic behaviour for companies and their workers can be disastrous, and the authors provide numerous examples of the devastating impact that such individuals have had in history. Of course, the workplace psychopaths most often cited in the media are the investment bankers and mortgage brokers who brought down the US economy in 2008 and men, such as Bernie Madoff, who created Ponzi schemes that stole billions from investors (see Chapter 17). A concern here is that the extensive forensic research literature on psychopaths needs to be presented in such a manner that those so greatly affected by their behaviour can recognize and better understand them. However, at this time, the fascination with such individuals continues to be mostly a consequence of the overwhelmingly antisocial nature of their acts. In *Without Conscience: The Disturbing World of the Psychopaths Among Us*, Hare (1998a) captures the essence of this in his description of Clifford Olson (see Box 9.3).

As theories of crime, antisocial personality disorder and psychopathy do not completely avoid the tautology that results from failing to distinguish between the criterion (the disorder) and the outcome (crime). However, as previously noted, psychopathy not only identifies those who have committed past offences but also predicts *future* criminality—both general and violent recidivism (Hare, 1998c). The construct of psychopathy has been criticized for being too simple and for disregarding the dynamic nature of human behaviour (Walter, 2004). Even so, many consider psychopathy to be "the single most important clinical construct in the criminal justice system" (Hare, 1998c, 99).

A final note on treatment seems appropriate. Losel (1998) reviews a position taken by Suedfeld and Landon (1978) that no effective treatments exist for this disorder. Losel writes that while our understanding of issues related to assessment, etiology, prediction, and biological, cognitive, emotional, and behavioural correlates has advanced greatly, treatment for such individuals remains an area of uncertainty. Other researchers, however, have recently noted that there appears to be some promise for the treatment of psychopathic characteristics in adolescents (Salekin, Worley, and Grimes, 2010).

FOCUS

Box 9.3

CLIFFORD OLSON—THE PROTOTYPICAL PSYCHOPATH

Canada's most notorious and reviled criminal is Clifford Olson, a serial murderer sentenced in January 1982 to life imprisonment for the torture and killing of eleven boys and girls. These crimes were the latest and most despicable in a string of antisocial and criminal acts extending back to his early childhood. Although some psychopaths are not violent and few are as brutal as he, Olson is the prototypical psychopath.

Consider the following quotation from a newspaper article written around the time of his trial: "He was a braggart and a bully, a liar and thief. He was a violent man with a hairtrigger temper. But he could also be charming and smooth-tongued when trying to impress people … Olson was a compulsive talker … He's a real smooth talker, he has the gift of gab … He was always telling whoppers … The man was just an out-and-out liar … He always wanted to test you to the limits. He wanted to see how far he could go before you had to step on him … He was a manipulator … Olson was a blabbermouth … We learned after a while not to believe anything he said because he told so many lies" (Farrow, 1982). A reporter who talked with Olson said, "He talked fast, staccato … He jumped from topic to topic. He sounded glib, slick, like a con trying to prove he's tough and important" (Ouston, 1982).

These reports by people who knew him are important, for they give us a clue to why he was able to get his young, trusting victims alone with him. They may also help to explain the Crown's decision to pay him $100,000 to tell them where he hid the bodies of seven of the eleven young people he had killed. Not surprisingly, public outrage greeted disclosure of the payment. Some typical headlines were: KILLER WAS PAID TO LOCATE BODIES; MONEY-FOR-GRAVES PAYMENT TO CHILD KILLER GREETED WITH DISGUST.

In the years since his imprisonment Olson has continued to bring grief to the families of his victims by sending them letters with comments about the murders of their children. He has never shown any guilt or remorse for his depredations; on the contrary, he continually complains about his treatment by the press, the prison system, and society. During his trial he preened and postured whenever a camera was present, apparently considering himself an important celebrity rather than a man who had committed a series of atrocities. On January 15, 1983, the *Vancouver Sun* reported, "Mass killer Clifford Olson has written to the *Sun* newsroom to say he does not approve of the picture of him we have been using … and will shortly be sending us newer, more attractive pictures of himself" (Ouston, 1982). [Quotes are from articles by R. Ouston, *Vancouver Sun*, January 15, 1982; and M. Farrow, *Vancouver Sun*, January 14, 1982.]

Olson also wrote to several criminology departments in Canada offering to help them to establish a course devoted to studying him. In 2011, he died of cancer in Archambault prison.

Source: Robert D. Hare, *Without Conscience: The Disturbing World of the Psychopaths Among Us* (New York: Guilford Press, 1998), 132–34. Reprinted with permission of the author.

QUESTIONS FOR CRITICAL THINKING

1. Describe what is meant by Antisocial Personality Disorder and psychopathy.
2. Discuss how these two disorders differ from each other.

Crime and Mental Illness

We begin this discussion of crime and mental illness with a most extreme statement: all crime is symptomatic of mental illness. While this may seem a preposterous statement today, many mental health professionals previously held this belief. Hakeem (1958) has summarized these views:

So powerful is the conviction of some psychiatrists that crime stems from mental disease, that they have held that the commission of crime in itself constitutes evidence of the presence of mental disease. Again, this aspect of the ideology usually draws on the medical analogy. The thesis runs as follows: just as fever is a symptom of physical disease, so crime is a symptom of mental disease.

SEARCH FOR:
"Mental Disorders and Crime: The Connection Is Real," Crime Times

Today, most would disagree with this position. Indeed, the current view is that while many criminals exhibit symptoms of mental illness, many do not (Corrado et al., 2000; Markowitz, 2011). In the remainder of this section, the extent to which persons charged with crimes are in need of mental health intervention will be examined.

There is widespread consensus among researchers, administrators, and front-line staff that the prevalence of mental disorder among those in the criminal justice system is greater than in the general population. So high is the prevalence of mental disorder in jails and prisons that some have referred to them as "the new mental institution[s]" (Arboleda-Florez et al., 1995, 123), the "new psychiatric emergency room[s]" (Lev, 1998, 72), the "new asylum[s]" (Shenson, Dubber, and Michaels, 1990), "America's new mental health hospitals" (Torrey, 1995), or "alternative shelter[s]" for mentally ill individuals who find themselves homeless (Chaiklin, 2001).

SEARCH FOR:
Why Canada's Prisons Can't Cope with Flood of Mentally Ill Inmates

Despite this consensus, there is a lack of agreement with respect to the prevalence of mental disorder in jails, prisons, and other parts of the criminal justice system. This, in part, is because of a lack of consistency with regard to defining mental disorder in the prevalent literature (Hodgins, 1995; Roesch, Ogloff, and Eaves, 1995; Corrado et al., 2000b). In a systematic review of 62 surveys of correctional samples in 12 Western countries, researchers found considerable heterogeneity among studies with regard to how mental disorder was defined (Fazel and Danesh, 2002; see also Andersen, 2004). For example, some studies examined only the most serious disorders such as schizophrenia, bipolar disorder, and major depression (e.g., Teplin, 1989, 1990a), but many others employed broader definitions that included less serious disorders such as dysthymia and anxiety disorders (e.g., Falissard et al., 2006), substance abuse disorders (e.g., Teplin, 1991), and/or personality disorders (e.g., Gunn, Maden, and Swinton, 1991). Other studies have not used disorder-based definitions at all, focusing instead merely on the presence of symptoms (Corrado et al., 2000).

A further consideration when examining prevalence across jurisdictions, both within and between countries, is that the true prevalence may differ markedly from one site to the next as a function of the availability of health care resources and the differing attitudes, practices, and policies of law enforcement agencies and legal institutions (Drewett and Shepperdson, 1995; Harris and Rice, 1997; Corrado et al., 2000). Despite arguably substantial differences in health and criminal justice policies in Canada and the United States, Corrado and his colleagues (2000) found similar rates of serious mental disorder among Canadian and US jails and prisons. Yet even within the same metropolitan centres, rates may reflect the varying characteristics of neighbourhoods. For example, researchers in the Vancouver Metropolitan Area found vastly different prevalence rates for substance misuse across two studies, which were largely attributable to the characteristics of the jails' catchment areas (Ogloff, 1996; Roesch, 1995).

Despite methodological and conceptual challenges, sufficient research exists to estimate the prevalence of mental disorders in various correctional settings. The studies cited most often regarding jail prevalence are those conducted by Teplin in the early 1990s (Teplin, 1990a, 1990b, 1991, 1994; Teplin and Voit, 1996). In her review of jail studies, she found that among jail detainees, the prevalence of *any* mental disorder ranged from 16 to 67 percent and the prevalence of *severe* mental disorder (defined largely as schizophrenia, bipolar disorder, and major depression) ranged from 5 to 12 percent (Teplin, 1991). US surveys and reviews have reported similar estimates (e.g., Ogloff, 2002; Andersen, 2004; James and Glaze, 2006; Scott and McDermott, 2010).

There has been relatively little research in Canada examining the rates of mental disorder in Canadian jails, but the research that does exist suggests that the prevalence of mental disorder in Canadian jails is high. For example, a BC study found that the prevalence of major mental disorders was 15.6 percent (Roesch, 1995). As well, the prevalence of substance use disorders was exceptionally high: over 77 percent of inmates were considered to have alcohol use or dependence disorders, and over 63 percent drug use disorders.

Consistent with the US literature, Canadian research suggests that the prevalence of mental disorder may be lower in prisons than in jails (James and Glaze, 2006; Teplin, 1991). In a 2004 report profiling the health needs of federal prison inmates in Canada, researchers found that 7 percent of inmates at intake had a mental health need that required immediate attention (NA, 2004). A higher proportion of inmates reported mental health problems (31% of females and 15% of males). Moreover, a substantial proportion of incoming inmates (21% of females; 14% of males) had admitted attempting suicide in the preceding five years.

These prevalence rates should not be taken as suggesting that most inmates are healthy (Ogloff, 1996). To the contrary, most inmates in Canadian jails and prisons have substantial mental health needs, particularly with respect to substance use disorders (Hodgins and Coté, 1995; Roesch, 1995; Lamb and Weinberg, 1998). Many of these individuals have co-occurring disorders (e.g., schizophrenia and substance abuse), which compounds the mental health and social problems these individuals experience. The Canadian findings are consistent with US studies, which found considerable overlap between mental disorders and drug or alcohol abuse in jail populations (Abram and Teplin, 1991; Abram, Teplin, and McClelland, 2003).

In a unique study conducted in BC, researchers extracted data from the records of three provincial agencies to get a better understanding of health care and social assistance use among those who were provincially incarcerated (Somers, Cartar, and Russo, 2008). This study included the records of all members of the provincial corrections population in BC from 1997/98 to 2003/04. Over 30 percent of individuals who were incarcerated during the seven-year period had been medically diagnosed with a substance use disorder. An additional 26 percent were diagnosed with a mental disorder unrelated to substance use. Among those who had a substance use disorder, more than 75 percent had a co-occurring disorder. This combination (mental disorder plus substance use disorder) was found to be particularly hazardous, resulting in significantly higher health and service costs as well as greater involvement in corrections.

SEARCH FOR:
"The Prison Careers of
Offenders with Mental
Disorders," Correctional
Service of Canada

The high rate of individuals with co-occurring disorders also suggests the need for treatment programs both within the jail and after release. Abram and Teplin (1991) suggested that these individuals might be particularly appropriate for alternatives to prosecution, such as pretrial diversion programs. Mental health courts are also an option for these individuals (Slinger and Roesch, 1995).

The prevalence of mental disorders in jails has prompted the APA (2000) and the National Commission on Correctional Health Care (2003) to recommend, in their standards and guidelines for the delivery of mental health services in jails, that all institutions adopt a systematic program for screening individuals upon detention. a recommendation echoed by health care providers and researchers (Roesch, 1995; Birmingham et al., 2000; Osher, Steadman, and Barr, 2003; Nicholls et al., 2005). Specialized screening tools devised specifically for mental health screening in jails have started to emerge in the literature. For example, in Canada, Nicholls and her colleagues (2005) have developed the Jail Screening Assessment Tool, a semi-structured interview used to screen inmates for mental health concerns, risk of suicide and self-harm, and risk of violence and victimization. Also in 2005, researchers in the United States created the Brief Jail Mental Health Screen (Steadman et al., 2005), a screening tool for serious mental illness comprising eight yes-or-no questions.

The high prevalence of mental disorders in jails has substantial costs, not only fiscal but also humanitarian both for inmates and for correctional staff. Jail staff perceive mentally disordered offenders as the most disruptive inmates (Kropp et al., 1989; Ruddell, 2006). These inmates are also at an increased risk for suicide and self-harm, victimization, and institutional maladjustments (Ogloff, 2002; Nicholls et al., 2005; James and Glaze, 2006). These adverse events affect not only individuals entering the criminal justice system with mental health difficulties but also those who develop mental health problems during their stay (and perhaps as a result of it) (Andersen, 2004).

There is little question that individuals with mental health problems are increasingly involved with the legal system. The first contact is usually by police officers, and there is evidence that police are increasingly encountering mentally ill individuals. A Vancouver study found that over one-third of calls to police involved a mental health issue (Wilson-Bates, 2008). Police resources are further depleted through the intense efforts involved in working with chronically mentally ill individuals and those who are suicidal. This is exacerbated when gaps in the health care system result in police resources being used in place of health resources to deal with mentally ill individuals (Thompson, 2010).

The training provided to police officers concerning mental-health-related issues varies widely between departments; so does the use of specialized responses for calls involving people with mental illnesses. Hails and Borum (2006) found that some police agencies provided zero hours of training in handling calls involving people with mental illnesses, while others provided as many as 41 hours of training. Most of the agencies provided no post-academy in-service training hours dealing with the topic of mental illness. Hails and Borum also found that only 21 percent of agencies had a special unit or bureau within the department to assist police in handling people with mental illness.

This percentage is disappointing, given findings that in some jurisdictions, specialized teams composed of a police officer and a mental health professional have helped avoid the criminalization of the mentally ill (Lamb et al., 1995). Moreover, in those rare cases where the interaction between a mentally disordered individual and the police has resulted in the need for a coroners' inquest, the recommendation most often made has been for an increase in police training so that they will be better prepared to work with individuals with mental disorder (Cotton and Coleman, 2010).

There is some evidence that the discretionary powers of the police in dealing with the mentally ill have been affected by the deinstitutionalization movement. This movement resulted in the release of large numbers of patients from mental hospitals. At the same time, the civil commitment laws were changed so that commitment had to be based on findings of mental illness and dangerousness. As a consequence, police could no longer use the mental hospital as an alternative disposition to jail and were often forced to arrest a mentally ill person.

If this is true, does it suggest there is a significant relationship between crime and mental disorder? In his study of the rates of mental disorder in prisons, Gunn (1977) answered this question with a note of caution, suggesting that, since other alternatives for the placement of mentally ill persons had been blocked off, it was to be expected that a greater number of persons previously detained in mental hospitals were now ending up in prisons. As Roesch and Golding (1985) point out, the increased rate of mental disorder in prisons has been the result of "institutional and public policy practices that have nothing to do with individual deviance *per se*. In fact, the individual behavior may not have changed at all. What has changed, however, is the manner in which institutions of our society react to that individual behavior."

With these cautions in mind, it will be instructive to review some studies on the extent to which persons considered to be mentally ill are arrested for criminal offences. Most of the research on arrest rates of the mentally ill has relied on police or court records. This research is limited by the availability of information in the files, which are often incomplete and inaccurate. One of the few researchers to actually observe how the police dealt with the mentally ill was Linda Teplin (1984). She was interested in examining the probability of arrest for mentally ill persons compared to persons who were not mentally ill.

Teplin's sample was 1,382 police–citizen encounters involving 2,555 citizens. Overall, the probability of arrest was low, occurring in only 12 percent of 884 encounters (traffic offence and public service incidents were deleted from the total). In individual terms, 506 of the 1,798 citizens involved were considered suspect, but only 29 percent were arrested.

Does the presence of symptoms of mental illness affect the probability of arrest? Teplin's data suggest it does. Of 506 suspects, 30 were considered by observers to be mentally ill. Nearly half (14) were arrested, compared to an arrest percentage of 27.9 percent for those not mentally ill. Furthermore, this difference was not accounted for by differences in type of charge. In other words, mentally ill suspects were not arrested more often because they were suspected of committing more serious crimes. The difference held up across types of crime.

Once arrested, do mentally disordered offenders recidivate at a high level? In a meta-analysis of a large number of empirical studies, Bonta, Law, and Hanson (1998) found that mentally disordered offenders on average showed lower recidivism rates than other offenders. A diagnosis of Antisocial Personality Disorder was found to be a more potent predictor than any other clinical diagnosis. However, with respect to violence after release from custody, Borum (1996) notes that mental disorder is now considered a robust and significant risk factor for predicting violent recidivism, as mentally disordered offenders have a greater probability of committing violent offences after release. But Borum adds that most persons with a mental disorder are not violent, so it is a relative rather than an absolute risk factor. It is important to keep in mind that most mentally disordered offenders are not violent and may have a decreased risk of general recidivism.

In conclusion, it is likely that theories of criminal behaviour that rely on models of mental illness will not account for the behaviour of most criminals. It is certainly true that some people who commit crimes can be considered mentally ill, but these individuals are only a small percentage of the total criminal population. In a legal sense, most criminals are responsible for their actions in that they are aware of their behaviour and can distinguish between right and wrong.

Each of the psychological theories reviewed in this chapter (Table 9.3) makes a contribution to our understanding of criminal behaviour. However, there is a need for greater integration of sociological and psychological perspectives so that both situational determinants and individual differences can be taken into account in attempts to explain criminal behaviour (Monahan and Splane, 1980). A study by Conger (1976) provides an excellent example of an attempt to integrate the two approaches. Conger examined the

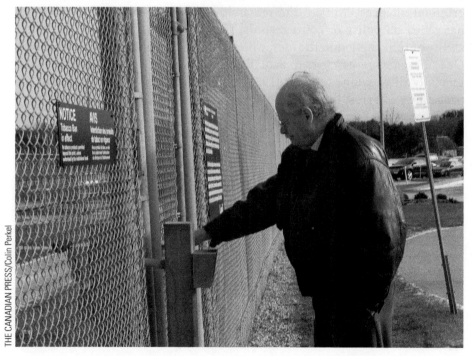

In 2007, 19-year-old Ashley Smith died in Grand Valley Institution for Women of self-inflicted strangulation while guards stood by under orders not to intervene. Originally imprisoned for the minor offence of throwing crabapples at a mailman, Ms. Smith had serious mental health problems and did not receive proper treatment from the prison system. A coroner's jury headed by Dr. John Carlisle called the death a homicide. This photo shows Dr. Carlisle entering the institution.

THE CANADIAN PRESS/Colin Perkel

TABLE 9.3 **Psychological Theories**

Theory	Theorists	Key Elements
Psychoanalytic theory	Freud	Crime results when the ego and superego cannot control the antisocial instincts of the id. This occurs because the individual has not been adequately socialized in early childhood.
Moral development theory	Piaget Kohlberg	Each individual must go through a sequence of moral development. Those with a high level of moral development will be more likely to make responsible choices when faced with the opportunity to get involved in criminal behaviour.
Personality theory	Eysenck	Law-abiding people must develop a conditioned fear of deviance. Those who become delinquents and criminals do not develop this fear because of poor conditioning by parents or because they are less susceptible to conditioning.
Social learning theory	Bandura	Deviant behaviour such as aggression can be learned through direct experience or through modelling the behaviour of others.
Operant conditioning theory	Skinner	Individual behaviour is shaped through both reinforcement and punishment. Behaviour that is rewarded will tend to be continued; behaviour that is punished will cease.
Psychopathy	Cleckley Hare	Psychopaths seem to lack empathy for their victims and do not feel guilty about their crimes. They neither learn from their experience nor fear the consequences of their behaviour.

relationship between two models of delinquent behaviour: the social control model (Chapter 14) and a social learning model. Based on data collected from a sample of Grade 7 boys, Conger demonstrated how social learning theory, particularly the effects of differential reinforcement and punishment, can be used to explain how an individual's bonds to society can be strengthened or weakened. Conger argued that the combination of the two theories can provide a more comprehensive theory of delinquent behaviour than either theory by itself. It is likely that the same arguments can be made for any of the theories reviewed in this chapter.

QUESTIONS FOR CRITICAL THINKING

1. Discuss the relationship between crime and mental illness, and describe the prevalence of mental illness in criminal populations.
2. Is prison the most appropriate place to deal with people with mental illness?

Summary

- Psychological theory is primarily concerned with explanations of behaviour at the level of the individual. Some psychological theories have been criticized for relying too much on trying to explain crime at the level of the individual and for not placing enough emphasis on environmental and situational factors.

- Certain psychological perspectives, such as community psychology, view social problems from a "level of analysis" perspective. Such levels include the individual, small-group, organizational, and institutional or community levels.

- The premise for psychoanalytic theory is a series of five stages of development (oral, anal, phallic, latency, and genital) and three components of personality (id, ego, and superego). Psychoanalytic interpretations of criminality suggest that criminal behaviour occurs when the ego and superego are unable to restrain the id.

- Kohlberg has proposed a six-stage theory of moral development, with two stages occurring at each of three levels (preconventional, conventional, and postconventional). This theory has been criticized from a feminist perspective for not adequately considering the different approaches of males (more justice-oriented) and females (more care-oriented) to morality.

- Eysenck's theory of crime and personality is based on the premise of classical conditioning. He has proposed three dimensions of personality (extraversion, neuroticism, and psychoticism), has developed measures of each of the three dimensions, and has generated a number of hypotheses about the relationship of these dimensions of personality to criminal behaviour. Eysenck's work offers a comprehensive model or theory of criminal behaviour that has yet to be validated.

- Social learning theory integrates sociology and psychology in explaining criminal behaviour. Modelling is an important aspect of social learning theory. Family, subcultural influences, and symbolic modelling are all important sources from which an individual can learn aggressive behaviour. Deterrence, by contrast, can occur through legal sanction, social sanction, and self-sanction.

- Operant conditioning is a subset of learning theory that has been proposed to explain criminal behaviour. Reinforcement and punishment are theorized as playing a large part in strengthening or weakening criminal behaviours. A token economy is one method that has been used to change existing behavioural interactions of individuals.

- Antisocial Personality Disorder is a diagnostic label that refers to a cluster of traits that underlie a pervasive pattern of disregard for the rights of others. Such traits include lying, stealing, fighting, and truancy. Behaviours that may be characteristic of this disorder include excessive drinking or the use of illicit substances, aggressive sexual behaviour, inconsistent work performance, and a failure to accept social norms with respect to lawful behaviour.

- Psychopathy is a term that is often confused with antisocial personality. Psychopathy refers to a pattern of behavioural features that are similar to those associated with Antisocial Personality Disorder. However, in addition to these behavioural features, psychopathic individuals also display certain attitudinal features such as grandiosity, glib and superficial charm, lack of empathy, and a lack of remorse, guilt, or shame.

■ Most criminals do not display any symptoms of mental illness. The prevalence of mental illness in jails and prisons is difficult to assess. However, some studies have estimated it to be between 5 and 12 percent for severe disorders and between 16 and 67 percent for any mental disorder.

NET WORK

In this chapter, you have learned about theories of moral development. You can read more about these theories at http://www.moraledk12.org.

Go to the "Moral Development and Education Overview" section of this website to read more about the work of Piaget, Kohlberg, and Gilligan. Then do the following:

1. Go to the "DBME Classroom Strategies/Guidelines for DBME Classroom Practices" section of the website and read the chapter titled "Using the Academic Curriculum for Moral Development: The Basics," found at the Domain Approach to Values Education link. Describe one of the programs that has been used to teach moral development in schools. How does this differ from the teaching program you experienced when you were in school?

2. In the same chapter, you will see a section titled "Structuring Effective Development Discussions." Can you think of a moral dilemma from fiction or from real life that would be suitable if you were doing a moral development session with first-year university students?

3. Go to the "Articles" section of the website. Using the featured articles, can you find two different contexts to which proponents feel moral development should be applied? Do you think moral development training would be useful in these contexts?

10

Strain Theories

James C. Hackler
UNIVERSITY OF VICTORIA

consensus perspective
Also known as *functionalism*, this perspective assumes that societies have a tendency to maintain themselves in a state of relative equilibrium through mutually adjustive and supportive interaction of their principal institutions. It also assumes that effective maintenance of society is in the common interest of all its members.

conflict perspective
The focus on the inherent divisions of societies based on social inequality and the way these social divisions give rise to different and competing interests, the central assumption being that social structures and cultural ideas tend to reflect the interests of only some members of society rather than society as a whole.

E xplaining the criminality of individuals has been an age-old task. With the growth of sociology, scholars began to look at the wider relationship between crime and social structure. Two broad theoretical perspectives guided this work. The **consensus perspective** maintains that most people share similar values regarding right and wrong. Morality is universal, and important values are shared by all members of society. Customs persist, and the law represents a codification of societal values.

The **conflict perspective** questions these assumptions, arguing that the criminal law reflects the interests of the groups that create and enforce those laws. The character of laws, the kinds of conduct they prohibit, and the types of sanctions depend on powerful groups that influence legislation. The social values that receive the protection of the criminal law are ultimately those treasured by the dominant interest groups. It is not the *majority*, but rather the most *powerful*, whose values and concerns are represented in the justice system. Some of these ideas are discussed in detail in Chapter 11.

This chapter reviews some historical traditions that reflect the consensus perspective. While authors differ in their use of terms, recent discussions of **strain theory** fit this general orientation.

Consensus theorists assume a reasonable degree of agreement on things that matter in society. They also assume that social institutions such as the family, education, government, religion, and the economy normally all contribute to the smooth running of society. Crime occurs when something unusual happens that affects these institutions. This results in strains, stresses, and frustrations that affect behaviour.

Learning Objectives

strain theory
The proposition that people feel strain when they are exposed to cultural goals they are unable to reach because they do not have access to culturally approved means of achieving those goals.

After reading this chapter, you should be able to

- Understand the differences between conflict and consensus perspectives of crime.
- Describe Durkheim's pioneering work on the relationship between crime and social structure, and understand the particular importance of his conception of anomie or normlessness.
- Discuss how Robert Merton modified Durkheim so that anomie theory became a theory of relative deprivation rather than a theory of a lack of social regulation.
- Consider that increasing the threat of punishment for misdeeds of the elite could have an impact on public morality.

- Learn that punishment tends to be used where it has little effect and is rarely used where it has a greater likelihood of changing behaviour.

- Note that strains can arise from features in the society or from situations surrounding individuals.

- Understand the strengths and weaknesses and social policy implications of strain theories.

Durkheim: The Functions of Crime and Anomie

In his book *Division of Labor in Society*, first published in France in 1893, Émile Durkheim argued that social solidarity—social groups working together toward agreed-upon goals—was an essential characteristic of human societies (1933). These agreed-upon goals led to a set of shared norms. Without norms to guide them, societies function poorly. Such "normlessness," or anomie, occurs during periods of rapid change when social solidarity or social cohesion is reduced. The lack of a sense of community and a collective conscience leads to a breakdown in society and increases in suicide and crime.

Although some crime is normal, there must be a balance between the functional and dysfunctional aspects of deviance (see Box 10.1). Excessive crime and deviance would destroy a society, but if there were no crime at all, then society would almost be compelled to create some. According to Durkheim, even in a society of saints, someone would have to be defined as pushing the limits of proper behaviour. Behaviour may be restrained, but someone will violate the rules. Every society needs its quota of deviants.

Anomie and Normlessness

Durkheim popularized the concept of **anomie** to explain crime in more advanced and differentiated urban societies. Heterogeneity and the increased division of labour weakened traditional societal norms, loosened social controls, and encouraged individualism. When social cohesion breaks down in society and social isolation is great, society loses its traditional social control mechanisms and eventually suffers from a high rate of crime.

Anomie is often defined as a "sense of normlessness," but in Durkheim's *Suicide* (1897/1951) he also refers to anomie as a condition in which individual desires, or self-interests, are no longer governed and controlled by society. In other words, self-interest, rather than norms, controls behaviour.

Merton: The Gap Between Aspirations and Means

Merton applied this idea to crime by linking **social structure** and anomie (1938). Too much emphasis on the pursuit of self-interested goals and not enough on "legitimate means" to achieve those goals leaves society "normless" or anomic. People then use illegitimate, or criminal, means to achieve their desires. For Durkheim and Merton, an anomic society places a higher priority on self-interested values such as the acquisition of wealth, status, and power, and a lower priority on collective values such as fairness, equality, and justice.

anomie
A concept developed by Émile Durkheim (1858–1917) to describe an absence of clear societal norms and values. Robert Merton (1910–2003) used the term more narrowly to refer to a situation in which people would adopt deviant means to achieve goals beyond their means.

social structure
The patterned and relatively stable arrangement of roles and statuses found within societies and social institutions.

Crime is a symptom of the gap between **culturally prescribed aspirations** and the socially structured means for realizing them. The culturally prescribed aspirations are the goals held up for all members of society. Merton argues that in America, the accumulation of money and the status that results from material wealth are universal goals.

Socially structured avenues such as schooling are the accepted institutionalized means of reaching such goals. These avenues may not be a problem for some members of the society; for example, if one comes from a family in which the mother or father is a medical doctor it may be realistic for the son or daughter to aspire to the same occupation and social status. The family may live in a nice neighbourhood, the children may attend schools that encourage university education, and the home environment may encourage reading and getting good grades. Although individual characteristics, such as a certain level of intelligence, may also be required, the means to achieve culturally prescribed aspirations are available to many middle-class youths.

By contrast, the child of a poor family, especially a racial minority family, could find things a bit more difficult. If the father has abandoned the family, if an older sibling has already been in trouble with the law, if the mother has been on welfare, and if the local schools are ineffective, then the means to achieve success may not be readily available. A youth coming from such an environment may not respect the school system and may have poor grades and minimal likelihood of entering university or college. However, he or she might still aspire to become a doctor and to have both the material and social rewards that accrue to that occupation.

Thus the gap between goals and means is small for certain portions of the society but large for others. The strain resulting from the gap between goals and the means to achieve those goals may result in some sort of innovation, usually deviant in nature. In simpler terms, when society encourages people to want things but makes it difficult for certain groups to get them, members of these groups are more likely to steal to attain the things they have been encouraged to desire.

Not only is the society anomic but so is the individual. This is the condition known as *micro-anomie*—where an individual places more value on self-interest than on collective values. An individual with these values is then motivated to pursue self-interested desires and not think about or be concerned with the effect that pursuit has on the group. In a study of a sample of college students, Konty (2005) found that those students favouring "**self-enhancing**" values over "**self-transcending**" values were more likely to report having committed criminal and deviant acts. The effect of these values on self-reported behaviour was stronger than the effects of other sociological variables like race and social class. Surprisingly, Konty found that the gap between male and female offending was mostly explained by these different values. Males were more likely than females to have micro-anomic values. But simply having self-enhancing values did not produce crime and deviance if the self-transcending values were also strong. It was when self-transcending, or collective, values were weak that crime and deviance became more likely.

These arguments also fit many forms of lower-class crime, particularly among marginally employed people. Robert Crutchfield (1995) points out that lack of work influences crime. In addition, if these marginally employed people

culturally prescribed aspiration
A rejection of the notion that aspirations are entirely self-created; rather, they are defined by culture and transmitted by other members of the society.

self-enhancing values
Values that emphasize social status, prestige, dominance over others, and personal success.

self-transcending values
Values that emphasize appreciation, tolerance, protection, and the welfare of others.

FOCUS

Box 10.1

DURKHEIM'S GENERAL MODEL OF DEVIANCE

In his classic work on suicide, Durkheim argues that in contrast to community-oriented or collective thinking, individualism leads to a lack of social cohesion. Suicide, crime, and general deviance are inhibited in cohesive communities. His research showed that Protestant communities, which are more individualistic, had higher suicide rates than Catholic communities, which are more oriented toward collective thinking. From this, Durkheim concluded that individualism can cause deviant behaviour by reducing the strength of communities. One can generalize the argument from the specific act of suicide to deviance and crime in general, as illustrated in the sequence below:

An Oversimplified Model of Durkheim's Explanation of Suicide as a General Explanation of Crime

Greater Individualism → Lack of Social Cohesion → Suicide and Crime

reside in concentrations of similarly underemployed people, the propensity to engage in crime is greater. This description fits certain ethnic groups in the United States and Canada.

The argument also fits certain upper-class crimes in which people in business, and others, aspire to great wealth. The legitimate avenues to success may not be sufficient because of severe competition; others may be "cutting corners" in a variety of ways. Thus, one can see that no matter what the situation, if there is a gap between the desired goals and the means, innovation or illegitimate tactics are more likely.

Strain as a Feature of Society (Rather than of Individuals)

Were Merton's ideas intended to explain the behaviour of individuals or, as Thomas Bernard (1987) argued, the behaviour of aggregates or groups? Bernard argued that it was not correct to interpret strain or anomie in psychological or social psychological terms; rather, these were properties of social structures. According to Bernard, Merton's theory would predict that societies whose cultures overemphasized monetary success and underemphasized adherence to legitimate means would have high rates of instrumental crime. If legitimate opportunities to achieve those monetary goals were unevenly distributed, instrumental crime would be unevenly distributed.

One must note the distinction between *cultural* factors and *structural* factors in society. In societies in which structural features create an uneven distribution of legitimate opportunities—that is, in which there are many blocked opportunities—there will be pockets of instrumental crime, regardless of cultural values. When a culture emphasizes the ruthless pursuit of wealth, even if there is equal opportunity, crime will be widespread and such a society will have a high rate of crime. The United States and (to a slightly lesser extent) Canada fit this pattern. Other wealthy countries, like Denmark, Norway, and Sweden, seem to be less concerned with the individual pursuit of wealth. (See Table 10.1 for a summary.)

TABLE 10.1 **Strain Theories (Societal)**

Theory	Theorists	Key Elements
Anomie: weak social regulation	Durkheim	When social cohesion breaks down, society loses its traditional mechanisms of social control and eventually suffers from a high rate of crime.
Anomie: the gap between aspirations and means	Merton	Crime occurs when there is a gap between culturally prescribed aspirations and socially structured means for realizing those aspirations.
Institutional–anomie	Messner, Rosenfeld	Strong pressures to succeed monetarily and weak restraints on the means to succeed in a society that emphasizes economics leads to crime.

Steven Messner and Richard Rosenfeld (2007) extend this argument with their theory of institutional anomie. American culture emphasizes monetary success but places less emphasis on *legitimate* means of achieving that success. This combination of strong pressure to succeed monetarily and *weak restraints on the means* is intrinsic to the "American Dream." It contributes to crime *directly* by encouraging people to use illegal means to achieve culturally approved goals, especially monetary ones. It also exerts an *indirect* effect on crime through its links with and impact on the institutional structure, or "the institutional balance of power." One institution—the economy—dominates all others. This emphasis has created a greater potential for crime.

Modern corporations may increase this tendency toward crime by splitting production aspects from financing ones. In the past, many companies were created by individuals who were primarily concerned with producing a product or service. Of course, they hoped to make a profit. Today, one can make money trading shares while disregarding the productive activities of a company. Shareholders play no part in daily operations, nor are they committed to the product's reputation or the company's long-term success. They are simply entitled to a share of the profits. Investors who "buy low and sell high" are admired. BlackBerry (formerly Research In Motion) illustrates this mentality. A person selling BlackBerry stock at $130 a few years ago was deemed to be clever. However, an investor who bought BlackBerry at its peak only to watch it drop to $9 a few years later might be seen as stupid and greedy. Concern for those who lost their jobs was secondary.

The prison sentence served by Conrad Black (Chapter 1) was unique in that a top corporate leader was actually punished for his criminal behaviour. It is worth noting that Black was tried, convicted, and did prison time in the United States, not Canada. Many have argued that Canadian officials would not have taken action against Black.

People in positions of power are rarely punished in the same way as those without influence. For example, Edgar Bronfman, Jr., heir to the Bronfman fortune, was convicted of insider training in 2011 and given a 15-month suspended prison sentence, meaning he was not incarcerated (McGrath, 2011). These cases illustrate a pattern among those at the top that can be described as a *subculture of power abuse*. Besides being criminogenic, such behaviour is generally antisocial and tears at the social fabric (Hackler, 2006).

The robber barons of the past ruthlessly exploited others to build railways, oil companies, and steel mills; modern entrepreneurs with deviant tendencies have new strategies that offer a faster and less visible way of achieving monetary goals. Stock markets, and the variety of instruments that have been created for "investing," have created a new potential for crime. Vincent Lacroix, president of Norbourg Management, illustrates the rather complex way corporate leaders can cheat. He was convicted in 2007 of 51 fraud charges, sentenced to 12 years in prison, and fined $255,000. In 2008, Lacroix was released from prison, but as a result of further investigations, he almost immediately faced additional charges of fraud. He pleaded guilty in 2009 to 200 criminal charges of fraud, conspiracy to defraud, money laundering, and other illegal acts. His 13-year prison sentence is the longest ever received for white-collar crime in Canada. However, even though he did great social harm in embezzling the life savings of 9,000 people, he was released in January 2011 after serving only a small part of his sentence (Leblanc, 2011).

Lacroix, Black, and Bronfman illustrate the weak restraints on the means to achieve wealth described by Messner and Rosenfeld (2007). Today's white-collar criminals are able to steal much more quickly than Leland Stanford and his railway could pillage California in the 19th century. Enron (Chapter 17) was able to use new strategies to manipulate sales of energy in a manner not previously possible. High-speed computers offer opportunities that threaten the integrity of the stock market itself (El Akkad, 2014).

The corrosive aspects of this system have created unethical incentives for elites.

Occasionally, political leaders vow to crack down on corporate and white-collar crime, but such tasks are often assigned to those who have close ties with the corporate world. After a spurt of publicity, efforts to "crack down on corporate crime" tend to fade. If world leaders and lawmakers are part of a *subculture of power* abuse that condones or at least tolerates these activities, is it likely that corrective action will be taken in Canada or the United States? In this regard, Canada is the only developed country that does not have a national

REUTERS/Mike Cassese/Landov

Nortel was once Canada's most valuable company. Nortel went bankrupt at least in part because its executives were more interested in increasing their bonuses than in the long-term future of the company and its thousands of employees.

securities regulator. Provincial agencies, such as the Ontario Securities Commission, are handicapped in a variety of ways. For example, unlike securities investigators in the United States, Canadian investigators need wiretap approval (McFarland, 2014, B4). One US prosecutor has referred to our enforcement mechanism as "quaint."

Responding to Opportunistic Crimes of the Powerful

Assuming that North America wishes to reduce the crime that results from the abuse of power by corporate leaders, traditional enforcement measures could be used more successfully. Our judicial system may not be particularly effective against crimes such as family violence, but courts and watchdog agencies could deter powerful people who break the law. While long sentences for corporate criminals have become more common in the United States, Canadian investigators have not been nearly as aggressive as their US counterparts, and Canadian sentences remain light.

Prosecution might make corporate leaders rethink certain behaviour. In 2005, the Canadian Imperial Bank of Commerce (CIBC) paid $2.4 billion to resolve a lawsuit in which the University of California alleged that CIBC "participated in an elaborate scheme to defraud investors." Both the Royal Bank of Canada and Toronto Dominion were involved with Enron, but several years after CIBC paid its $2.4 billion in the California lawsuit, the Canadian authorities decided not to proceed with charges against the other banks. This lack of enforcement sends a clear message to potential criminals. Weak restraints on the means to achieve monetary success, and the inability of watchdog agencies and our justice system to respond effectively, together increase the likelihood of white-collar and corporate crime.

So far we have focused on corporate crime, but the *subculture of power abuse* is much broader. Do the same factors that encourage corporate crime increase unethical behaviour in government? According to the *Globe and Mail*, the three independent federal watchdogs created by the Conservative government—Karen Shepherd, Commissioner of Lobbying; Mary Dawson, Conflict of Interest and Ethics Commissioner; and Christiane Ouimet, former Public Sector Integrity Commissioner—have done little to strengthen integrity in government (Galloway, 2010).

Unlike in the past, *economic institutions* dominate North America today. Other important institutions—the family, education, and the political system— are now secondary. Those other institutions traditionally curbed criminal tendencies and imposed controls over the conduct of individuals; today, economic factors have overwhelmed the institutions that once socialized people into prosocial behaviour. In other nations, such as Japan and India, the family appears to rank higher on the hierarchy of institutions and to be more influential relative to economics, than in North America. Thus, North America produces higher levels of serious crime than those countries in which the institutional balance of power leans toward noneconomic institutions.

John Hagan (2010) argues that US government policy has encouraged corporate crime. During what Hagan calls the age of Roosevelt (1933–1973), the Great Depression and the Second World War led politicians to focus more on corporate crime. During the age of Reagan (1974–2008) politics reversed course, demanding harsher treatment of street criminals while reducing scrutiny and enforcement in the financial sector. Financial crimes were seen as of minor importance.

Government policies that believed free enterprise could do no wrong created a criminogenic environment. Merton argued that the gap between aspirations and means would lead to crime by "innovation." New opportunities to "innovate" were certainly created during the Reagan era: financial inventions such as hedge funds and sub-prime mortgages provided even more opportunities for unethical behaviour. The economic crash in 2008–9 owed much to new, sophisticated economic inventions.

Reducing Crime by Changing the Behaviour of the Elite

Would reducing some types of crime lead to a *general* reduction in crime? It is useful to broaden the discussion to unethical, not just criminal, behaviour. I suggest that reductions in the unethical behaviour of corporate executives and other powerful people would lead to a reduction in *all* crime, including street crimes. A wide range of moral and immoral behaviour is woven into the fabric of society. In Figure 10.1, the morality curve lumps all "immoral" acts together. The skewed curve tapers off to the right; that is, minor, nasty acts are more frequent than very serious unethical acts. Shoplifters are much more common than serial killers. Many people think in terms of the broken line with its smaller bump on the right, believing there is a *unique* group of criminals who are different from the rest of us. It is common to think that corporate criminals and income tax evaders are somehow different from those really bad criminals who make up the bump on the right. Many apologists for corporate crime claim that there are only a few rotten apples in the barrel. Not so. Every study since Sutherland's (1949) classic work shows that crime among large corporations is *endemic*.

The dotted line with two humps leads us astray. We deceive ourselves into believing we can punish the few serious offenders, those under the smaller bump, while the rest continue as usual. Actually, the *solid* line represents reality. Furthermore, the shape stays the same. If we wish to create change, we must *move the entire curve to the left*. That is, we must target the *frequent* acts of immorality that make up the bulk of this "morality curve."

Because the social fabric of society is broad, we must think beyond criminal behaviour and consider a broad range of antisocial behaviour. Because of the magnitude of unethical behaviour in commercial activities (e.g., insider trading, unethical mortgage lending, income tax evasion), it is worth considering legislation and enforcement that would diminish these frequent and serious violations. We must also consider the structural conditions that encourage psychopathic behaviour in business.

FIGURE 10.1 **The Morality Curve**

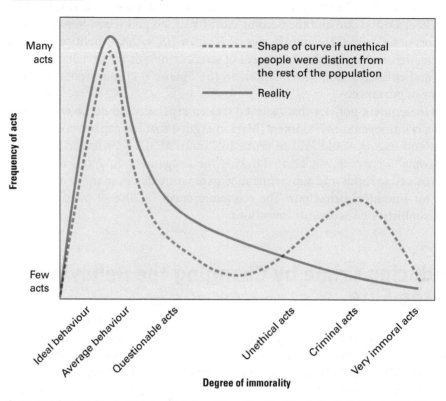

Source: James C. Hackler, *Canadian Criminology: Strategies and Perspectives*, 4th ed. (Toronto: Prentice Hall Canada, 2006), 327. Reprinted with permission by Pearson Canada Inc.

Robert Hare of the University of British Columbia argues that individuals climbing the corporate ladder have higher levels of psychopathic traits (Babiak, Neumann, and Hare, 2010). We should not be surprised, then, that graduate students entering MBA programs have more psychopathic characteristics than those in other disciplines (Heinze et al., 2010).

The 2008–9 recession was fuelled by fraudulent mortgages and irresponsible behaviour by powerful people (Chapter 17). As usual, however, those who are part of *the subculture of power abuse*—those who led us into the recession—have rarely suffered financially.

As Joanna Slater wrote at the time in the *Globe and Mail* (2011): "Fresh revelations emerge about unscrupulous behaviour by bankers in the run-up to the financial crisis. A spasm of outrage follows, along with talk of new investigations. Then, more often than not, nothing happens" (B11).

Could we use punishment more effectively to create a better quality society? Formal punishment does little to produce higher morality. Kindness, honesty, fairness, and so on are more effectively taught in the family. Fear of being sent to jail deters some who are considering materialistic crimes, but it is not particularly effective with crimes of passion. However, a corporate CEO may give more consideration to moving a gas tank on a newly-designed vehicle to a safer place, even if it costs a few dollars, rather than risk arrest and a prison sentence. In other words, if our criminal justice sent a clear message to powerful people—who are often the role models in our society—that some behaviours are simply wrong, it could have an impact. Unfortunately, the powerful have more influence on legislation that makes harmful behaviour criminal.

As a society, we pay much less attention to crimes of the powerful, which hurt citizens the most, than to street crime, which is more widely publicized and feared. Unfortunately, failing to demand ethical behaviour in corporate boardrooms leads to lower ethical standards in the entire society. In other words, a little more punishment (or threat of it) on the elite, and the clear expectation that they follow society's rules, would have an impact on many, and move the morality curve to the left.

Generalizing Merton's Strain Theory to Other Cultures

Hongming Cheng (2011) argues that Chinese academics pursue the "Chinese Dream" in the same way that corporate executives and those who confront blocked opportunities pursue the "American Dream." The concept of "face" is important to the Chinese scholar, but "face" also involves wealth and power. A brilliant scholar who is poor does not receive the respect of a scholar who uses his academic base to earn money. Thus, there is pressure to cheat. Unethical professors then become role models for unethical students and contribute to deviant behaviour to achieve the "Chinese Dream." Academic fraud moves the morality curve to the right. By contrast, honest professors who are content with the real satisfactions of an academic life and who take pride in seeing their students do well as ethical individuals may move the morality curve to the left. This demonstrates that Merton's basic argument fits more than economic institutions; it also provides clues as to how the world can be changed.

Michael Hellenbach (2006) provides a good illustration of how the capitalist economic model, responding as Merton would predict, increased crime in eastern Germany. When the Berlin Wall came down in 1989, many people in the West assumed that capitalism would bring Communist East Germany a better material life. To bring modern industry to East Germany, West German companies were offered incentives; for example, a West German company could purchase a factory for one German Mark provided that it upgraded that factory. Instead, the western companies stripped the factories they had purchased for one Mark and closed them so that they would not compete with their western enterprises.

A decade ago I stayed with a fisherman in a port in eastern Germany that had been purchased by a West German firm that had agreed to revitalize it. Instead, that firm closed the port and stripped it of all usable equipment. The fishermen were all out of work. Today there are fewer jobs in eastern Germany, salaries for the same work are lower, and young people must migrate to the West to find jobs. Unemployment is high, and crime rates are rising. In other words, the unethical—if not downright criminal—behaviour of corporations has led directly to an increase in crime. The aspirations of young eastern Germans are high, but the means to achieve monetary goals are low. The West German corporations had monetary goals, too, but they also had access to unethical means.

Many residents of the former East Germany have not done well economically following the fall of the Berlin Wall in 1989.

AP Photo/FILE/Lionel Cironneau

While corporations offer obvious targets for unethical behaviour, Merton's theory fits many situations. Medical doctors on salaries, when compared to doctors in private practice, may not aspire as much to greater wealth. Those in private practice may also have greater opportunities to "innovate" for profit.

The argument I am making is that just rules, respect for the law, and ethical behaviour by society's leaders all *influence the potential for crime for everyone in that society.* When Jim Shaw stepped down as CEO of Shaw Cable in his early fifties with a pension of $6 million per year, his behaviour was legal, but it was also an abuse of power and privilege. It had moved the morality curve to the right.

By contrast, passing and enforcing laws against white-collar crime, prosecuting income tax violations more vigorously (perhaps publishing the violators' names in the newspaper), and shaming CEOs into linking their bonuses with bonuses to all of their employees would move the morality curve to the left and reduce crime.

When two judges in Luzerne County, Pennsylvania, accepted $2.6 million in kickbacks from the owners of two private juvenile correctional facilities in return for sending children to those places (Schwartz and Levick, 2010), did this reflect a capitalist system in which the profit motive leads to greed that overwhelms other values? Or does a society that tolerates and creates a subculture of power abuse increase the likelihood that those placed in positions of trust will be corrupt? Or are these two ideas connected?

Merton's theories provide us with ideas about how to reduce the harm caused by privileged predators. Figure 10.1 suggests that the successful reduction of crime and unethical behaviour among privileged predators would have far-reaching impacts on the rest of crime.

QUESTIONS FOR CRITICAL THINKING

1. So far in this chapter, you have read about the consensus and conflict perspectives to crime. Think of three different laws that prohibit behaviour most people would agree is wrong. Can you think of any circumstances under which these acts might be permissible? Now think of three different laws that prohibit behaviour that a significant number of Canadians think should be tolerated. Why do these behaviours remain against the law?

2. How would Merton's anomie theory explain the higher rates of deviance and crime among Canada's Aboriginal people? Does the theory help you think of any possible solutions to this problem?

3. The author argues that crime should be viewed as part of a larger morality. Why is he concerned with a *subculture of power abuse*?

Strain as a Feature of Individuals

So far we have emphasized features of society that influence crime. Everyday life leads to strains. Some of these are simply endured. Robert Agnew (2001, 2006, 2010) has written extensively on strain on individuals and the resulting impact on delinquency. Strain can be experienced directly, but it can also be anticipated and vicarious (Agnew 2002). For example, if one anticipates being attacked on the way to school, one may skip school, which could lead to other problems.

Not all strains lead to crime or delinquency. Failing an exam may be stressful, but it may also lead to a greater commitment to study. If more study does not produce the anticipated results, it could have negative consequences and lead to a decision to engage in cheating. But strain alone does not automatically produce delinquency. Strains are more likely to lead to delinquency if they have certain characteristics:

1. Are the strains high in magnitude—for example, a serious rather than a minor assault, or a large rather than a small loss of funds? A juvenile being bullied for a long time, who expects that bullying to continue, may begin to bully others. Does the stress threaten a core identity, such as a masculine self-image? A boy from a lower-class slum may respond to any challenge to his fighting ability, but less to his skill as a good chess player.

2. Are the strains unjust? Did the juvenile have a chance to tell his story? Was he or she treated with disrespect? Did his or her treatment differ from that of others? Was a racial minority student treated differently than a white student for similar behaviour?

3. Strains are more likely to lead to delinquency if they are linked to low social control (Agnew, 2009). Social control comes in different forms. Belief systems, ties to conventional institutions (e.g., school, the family), and group membership (e.g., on a sports team) link one to society and provide restraints from delinquency (Chapter 14). A stake in the community is a stake in conformity.

4. Strains are more likely lead to crime if the crime pays off. If you need money, does stealing or selling drugs or prostitution bring in enough to reduce the strain you feel? If it does not, it loses its attractiveness.

5. Strains that are resolved through contact with people who are involved with crime, such as a group of boys who break into houses, are more likely to persist.

To sum up, we live in a world with many strains. These may make us work harder and spur us to do positive things. In certain circumstances, crime and deviance will be chosen to resolve those strains.

As one applies strain theory to individuals and their situations, one can see a convergence with differential association (Chapter 13) and control theory (Chapter 14). Such thinking lends itself to more universal theories of crime.

The Shift from Control to Opportunity Structures

Durkheim argued that human aspirations had to be regulated and channelled. Human aspirations being boundless, people could not always have what they wanted, so they had to be persuaded to accept what they received. When people were not persuaded, the society became anomic. The moral guidelines were unclear. Social control broke down, and some people violated the norms established by those in power.

Durkheim emphasized the restraints that control crime, whereas Merton focused on **opportunity structures**. He posited that American society had an overriding dominant goal—material success—but that the guidelines for achieving that success were not always clear. But if this type of anomie was so widespread, why wasn't crime distributed evenly throughout society? Merton

opportunity structure
Opportunity is shaped by the way the society or an institution is organized or structured.

accepted the argument that crime was distributed unevenly—that it was higher in urban slums, for instance. To explain this social-class-specific crime, he redefined anomie as the disjuncture between the cultural goal of success and the opportunity structures by which this goal might be achieved. Anomie was shifted from normlessness to **relative deprivation** (as opposed to **absolute deprivation**); thus, it was not the entire community that was anomic but rather specific individuals who were committed to the goal of wealth but who found themselves barred from the means to achieve it.

Richard Cloward: Illegitimate Opportunity Structures

There are differences between legitimate and illegitimate opportunities; there are also different types of illegitimate opportunities. Cullen (1984) pointed out the importance of "structuring variables." Cloward and Ohlin (1960) asserted that simply being subjected to socially generated strain did not enable a person to deviate in any way he or she chose. People can participate in a given adaptation only if they have access to the means to do so (Cullen, 1984, 40). Even though members of the lower class may be under a great deal of strain, they are unlikely to engage in violations of financial trust, political corruption, and other white-collar crimes in order to achieve their goals. In a book he co-wrote with Lloyd Ohlin titled *Delinquency and Opportunity* (1960), Cloward extended Merton's ideas by combining them with themes found in Sutherland's "differential association" (see Chapter 13). Sutherland argued that criminal behaviour is learned through associations with others who define criminal activity favourably. While Merton emphasized legitimate means, Sutherland focused on illegitimate means (Cullen, 1988). People under strain cannot become any kind of criminal they choose; they are limited by the opportunities available to them. Dealing in drugs is not automatically available to a "square" university professor as a means of supplementing her income; she probably lacks the skills and contacts to arrange a source of illegal drugs. In short, illegitimate means are not readily available to people simply because they lack legitimate means. While Durkheim and Merton developed plausible theories of structurally induced pressures, Cloward tried to explain that reasonable opportunities must exist. Illegal opportunities for fraud involving oil wells are more available in Alberta than in Toronto.

Opportunity theory can help explain many types of deviance. Cloward and Ohlin applied their ideas to juvenile delinquency. Juveniles undergoing strain face different barriers to resolving that strain than adults do. Their responses to social barriers for achieving goals could lead to three different types of gangs or **subcultures**: *criminal, conflict,* and *retreatist* gangs.

There are pressures toward conventional goals, such as middle-class respectability. Juveniles who overcome the barriers they face—which most middle-class juveniles do—commit little crime. However, lower-class males may have different goals. Instead of respectability, they may prefer money, or a car or motorcycle. In certain economic conditions, they might achieve these things by working in areas in which their skills are scarce, by working in a hazardous occupation, or possibly by succeeding as a professional athlete. In other words, it is possible to be successful in a working-class style of life. These ideas differ somewhat from Merton's in that aspirations are not universal. Success can mean different things to different people.

relative deprivation Deprivation in relation to others around you, rather than judged against an absolute standard of sustainability.

absolute deprivation The inability to sustain oneself physically and materially.

subculture A group of people who share a distinctive set of cultural beliefs and behaviours that differs in some significant way from that of the larger society.

But there are also barriers to lower-class goals (see Figure 10.2). There is an opportunity structure for those goals as well, and crime has an opportunity structure of its own. If legitimate opportunities are blocked, the next step may be to search for illegal success, but even here there are barriers. Without certain contacts, it may be difficult to get into illegal gambling or learn the skills of credit card fraud. Many juveniles will have difficulty learning the skills necessary to succeed in these areas. One may be able to steal many hubcaps, but there will be barriers to selling them in quantity. However, if there are barriers to profitable property crime, juveniles can still turn to *conflict* as a means of attaining status, at least among their peers.

Juveniles who are unskilled as thieves can show their bravery by fighting for their "turf." This will show others they have "heart"; their courageous behaviour will give them a "rep." But even conflict success has barriers. Not every juvenile is keen on wielding a bicycle chain or a knife or a gun in a gang war. Some may lack strength or courage or both. These juveniles may employ a third delinquent alternative: the use of drugs. In the *drug or retreatist* subculture there are practically no barriers.

Individual characteristics, such as race, will be related to some of these barriers. Thus, Asian youths in Vancouver may have opportunities to work with Asian gangs that extort money from restaurant owners. Blacks who have lived in Nova Scotia since the American Revolution, Jamaican youths in Toronto, and Haitian immigrants in Montreal probably have a realistic view of the barriers to

FIGURE 10.2   **Barriers to Legal and Illegal Opportunities Implicit in the Work of Cloward and Ohlin (1960)**

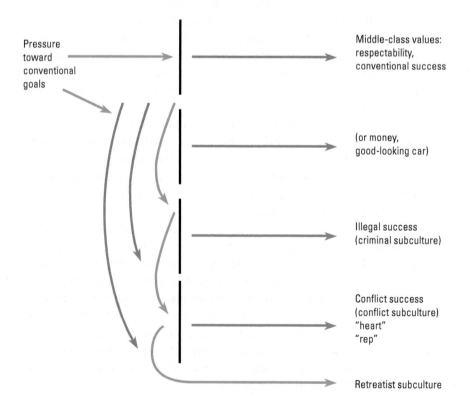

SOCIAL BARRIERS TO ACHIEVING GOALS

Pressure toward conventional goals

Middle-class values: respectability, conventional success

(or money, good-looking car)

Illegal success (criminal subculture)

Conflict success (conflict subculture) "heart" "rep"

Retreatist subculture

legitimate and illegitimate success. Violence and drugs may be the only things left for them. In Canada, the abuse of alcohol by First Nations people may also be influenced by barriers to both legitimate and illegitimate opportunities.

Marginal Opportunity Structures

Francis Cullen (1988) believes that the contributions made by Cloward are underappreciated because they focus primarily on the gap between aspirations and perceived opportunities. Other deviant adaptations to illegitimate opportunities become apparent when one looks beyond traditional types of crime and at different settings. Fred Desroches described the way some men adapt to pressures related to homosexual activity in public restrooms in Ontario (1995). The "tearoom," a public washroom where homosexual activity takes place, provides an opportunity structure for those under certain types of strain. Alternatives do not seem to fill the need; thus, this marginal opportunity structure is used with the risk that police action will create additional problems in their lives.

Street life in Vancouver offers another type of marginal or illegitimate opportunity structure (Hagan and McCarthy, 1997a). Youths in families that are functioning well perform better in school and are more successful in finding work. Negative family experiences increase the likelihood of "hanging out" on the street. The interactions among parental unemployment, weakened marital ties, neglect, and abuse increase the likelihood of crime directly; they also expose such youths to additional new stresses when they leave one negative environment for another. While seeking food and shelter on the street, these vulnerable youths meet seasoned offenders who coach the newcomers in criminal activities. Meanwhile, the police view them as criminally inclined.

Street life increases exposure to networks of seasoned offenders, who offer tutelage in offending as well as a means for acquiring "criminal capital"—that is, information (e.g., where to sell stolen goods) and skills (e.g., how to use burglary tools). Physical and sexual abuse has conditioned youths to respond to police confrontations with defiance and rage. Hagan and McCarthy show how employment, a source of social and **human capital**, in contrast to criminal capital, can reduce involvement in crime and street life.

Cloward's work may also help explain certain marginal activities, such as being an oil company spy. In Alberta, where many oil companies drill wells in the wilderness and try to keep their findings secret, spies from rival companies sometimes pose as hunters or wilderness trekkers to observe drilling operations without being detected. This often hazardous activity highlights the presence of particular opportunities and barriers to potentially profitable tasks.

Opportunity structures, including illegitimate ones, pose an interesting policy question for society. Which is more desirable: having skid row alcoholics with no opportunities, or having drug sellers and gamblers engaging in profitable activities that are seen as deviant by society? While legitimate opportunities are clearly preferable to illegitimate ones, is it possible that the integration of some borderline (or even obvious) deviance would be better than the total breakdown represented by some who have been rejected by society? In a society that must sometimes choose between levels of evils, would policy-makers be wise to consider the nature of different opportunity structures and assess the impact of selected illegitimate opportunities on society? (See Table 10.2 for a summary.)

human capital
The talents and capabilities that individuals contribute to the process of production. Companies, governments, and individuals can invest in human capital, just as they can invest in technology and buildings or in finances.

TABLE 10.2 **Strain Theories (Individual)**

Theory	Theorists	Key Elements
General strain	Agnew	Adolescents in unavoidable unpleasant environments face strain leading to anger and delinquency.
Opportunity structures	Cloward	In addition to strains that create a pressure toward criminal behaviour, there are also different opportunity structures that may facilitate breaking the law. These structures are both legitimate and illegitimate.
Code of the Street	Anderson	Lack of employment opportunities leads to alternative ways of achieving respect: displaying toughness, taking another person's possessions, pulling a trigger. This helps build a reputation that prevents future challenges, but it also creates other problems.

Elijah Anderson: The Code of the Street

Elijah Anderson's *Code of the Street: Decency, Violence, and the Moral Life of the Inner City* (1999) describes the cumulative effects of structural changes on inner cities. During and after the Second World War, manufacturing jobs in the cities recruited many unskilled and semi-skilled workers. Many Blacks, Hispanics, and other ethnic groups benefited from these opportunities. At the same time, more minorities were moving into middle-class jobs. Then, with the exporting of manufacturing to countries paying low wages, the loss of these unionized jobs that paid reasonably well had a serious impact on those at the bottom of the social scale. Barriers to participate in mainstream society persisted for young Blacks. Employers preferred white women and new immigrants to young Blacks.

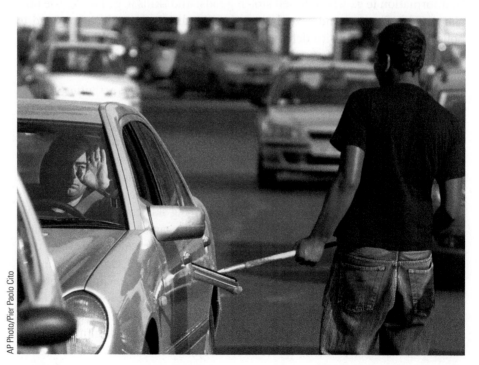

Squeegee kids are among those who have little opportunity to succeed through legitimate opportunity structures.

AP Photo/Pier Paolo Cito

"The Code of the Street," according to Anderson, requires young males, and often females, to let others know how tough they are, how hard it would be for someone else to "roll on" them, how much "mess" they will take before they respond with a fist in the mouth. The most effective way of gaining respect is to manifest nerve. A man shows this by taking another person's possessions, messing with someone's woman, throwing the first punch, "getting in someone's face," or pulling a trigger. These help build a reputation that prevents future challenges (Anderson, 1999, 92).

Many young Blacks actively live their lives in opposition to whites and middle-class Blacks. Lacking trust in mainstream institutions, many turn to "hustling" in the underground economy (1999, 108). To be self-respecting, young men and women must exhibit contempt for a system they are sure has contempt for them.

The drug trade offers economic opportunity. However, it is organized around the code of the street, which employs violence for social control, and thus contributes significantly to the violence of inner-city neighbourhoods. For those with minimal success in the legal job market, illegal activities provide alternatives: the drug trade, prostitution, welfare scams, and other rackets.

Most youths in school are "decent," but even there, the street element dominates. It victimizes those who show weakness. Thus decent kids must take on the code of the street if they are to avoid being victimized. The lack of opportunity for legitimate employment leads to strain. To achieve respect, and the money that enhances respect, young people must display a willingness to use violence.

Assessing Strain Theories

When Durkheim introduced his ideas, scholars were still explaining crime primarily in terms of genetics and psychological forces. Durkheim focused attention on social forces, a radical idea at the time but now the dominant methodology for explaining crime.

Durkheim was less accurate in his description of premodern societies as stable and crime free. In fact, many had high levels of violence. Furthermore, Western countries seem to have experienced a long-term decline in crime over the past few centuries (Pinker, 2011). Setting aside present-day perceptions, during the 17th century the average citizen in most cities in Western Europe would rarely leave the security of a locked home after dark.

Merton's strain theory does not help us explain the lower crime rates of women. He takes into account the differences in opportunity that arise from social class, but he does not apply the same reasoning to blocked opportunities based on gender (Comack, 2009). Women, like disadvantaged lower-class males, might be expected to be more criminal as a means to achieve universal goals. Many conventional theorists have assumed that women experience less strain than men in the struggle to achieve through institutionalized means; however, many feminist scholars reject these statements as assumptions and biases rather than fact (Morris, 1987; Naffine, 1987). Although the strains women experience may differ from those experienced by men, they may be at least as severe. Unless one assumes that women have more modest goals, strain theory does not explain why women are less criminal.

Despite these criticisms, strain theories seem to offer insights into the unethical behaviour of individuals, gangs, and corporations. Recent scholars have even used anomie theory to explain deviance in dictatorship countries that are now moving in the direction of democracy (Zhao and Cao, 2010; Hongming, 2011). Thus the ideas of Durkheim, Merton, and other strain theorists continue to be relevant.

The Convergence of Strain Theory and Other Perspectives

Strain theory, differential association, and control theory are increasingly being seen as complementing one another. Also, the policy implications of these different theories can be similar. For example, enabling the disenfranchised to participate more fully in what society has to offer is probably related to greater social bonding with others and a stronger belief in the rules that guide the larger society. However, when social bonds are primarily with people who condone or rationalize criminal behaviour, and with those who face similar blocked opportunities, criminal behaviour is likely. In such situations, control theory, differential association, and strain theory complement one another.

A vast oversimplification of these ideas might be as follows: (1) learning theories (Chapter 13), such as differential association, explain delinquency by *positive* relations with deviant others; (2) social control theories (Chapter 14) argue that delinquency occurs when juveniles have *little or no* attachment or social bonds to others; (3) Agnew's elaboration of strain theory emphasizes that *negative* relations and experiences in situations beyond their control lead juveniles to delinquency; and (4) all three conditions can reinforce one another and can have a reciprocal impact, increasing the likelihood of criminal behaviour.

Uses of Strain Theory

Modern society has created many new illegitimate opportunities. Credit cards, computers, and the flow of information across borders have made new forms of theft possible. Even the 9/11 terrorist attacks in New York and Washington created opportunities for fraud. More than 200 people have been arrested for defrauding agencies that were trying to help victims and relatives. A morgue manager, for example, was accused of stealing coffins and reselling them. However, most people do not avail themselves of the vast opportunities for theft in complex societies.

Messner and Rosenfeld (2007) argue that the emphasis on material wealth in North America encourages crime. Other countries may have a different value structure. In one informal study conducted by *Reader's Digest*, 1,100 wallets were "lost" in about a dozen countries. Each wallet contained $50 in local currency and the name and phone number of the owner. About 44 percent of the wallets disappeared. However, in Norway and Denmark, every single wallet was returned (Felte, 2001). Do some societies create a climate that produces more good Samaritans and where illegitimate opportunities are ignored?

John Braithwaite: Greater Class Mix and the Reduction of Crime

Braithwaite (1979) argues that one must look at the interaction between the social class of individuals and the social class of the neighbourhood in order to answer the question of whether an increase in class heterogeneity in neighbourhoods would reduce crime. He offers two propositions. The first is that crime is most likely when exposure to illegitimate opportunities is high and exposure to legitimate opportunities is low. The second states that crime is unlikely when legitimate opportunities are high or when illegitimate opportunities are low. In other words, in three out of the four possible combinations, there are factors that inhibit crime. Only when illegitimate opportunities exist *alongside* a lack of legitimate opportunities exist is there a marked increase in crime.

Braithwaite also argues that belonging to the lower class has more effect on delinquency for youth in lower-class areas than for youth in middle-class areas. Consequently, cities with relatively large numbers of lower-class people living in predominantly middle-class areas and relatively large numbers of middle-class people living in predominantly lower-class areas have relatively low crime rates. That is, greater class mix results in less crime.

This implies that the middle classes would be better off if they kept together; on the other hand, if the lower classes stayed together, they would be even worse off. So it may be to the advantage of those with power and influence to keep themselves segregated. The quality of life for the society as a whole, however, would be improved if residential heterogeneity characterized society.

Braithwaite's ideas seem more applicable to property crime. However, another study has shown that the roots of violent crime are also to be found in racial and economic inequality (Blau and Blau, 1982). Spatial mixing in neighbourhoods would be more easily achieved with a reduction of racial and economic inequality. Some observers have suggested that Canada has a lower crime rate than the United States in part because our housing policies have been less likely to "ghettoize" the poor.

Reducing Upper-Class Crime

Braithwaite also argues that "too little power and wealth creates problems of living, and this produces crime of one type; too much power corrupts, and this produces crime of another type" (1979, 200). This does not mean that upper-class people are more criminal than lower-class people. If lower-class people were exposed to the same vast opportunities as white-collar criminals, they, too, would engage in large-scale "power" crimes. Powerful people abuse their occupational power. It makes little sense to ask which social class commits more crime. Rather, opportunities differ by social class. If lower-class people commit crimes because of a lack of power and wealth, increasing their influence and well-being might help. Greater economic equality and a greater distribution of influence among people would modify to some extent those factors that lead to crime.

Lower-class crime may be caused by the failure to achieve success goals. By contrast, upper-class crimes arise from an unprincipled overcommitment to success goals. One study of college students found that those most dedicated to monetary success were those most likely to argue that they "can't afford to be squeamish about the means." Similarly, certain occupational structures can increase commitment to illegitimate success. Quinney (1963) found that pharmacists tended to fall into two divergent categories with different role expectations: professional and business. The "professionals" were bound by guidelines for compounding and dispensing prescriptions. The "business oriented" believed that self-employment carries with it independence and freedom from control. For them, professional norms exercised less control. Prescription violations occurred more frequently among the business-oriented pharmacists. As both Quinney and Braithwaite would argue, the mutual support of like-minded individuals insulated them from the broader society, and from their professional colleagues, increasing the likelihood of crime.

Policy Implications

Five decades ago, crime prevention projects used strain theories to change opportunity structures. In hindsight, the narrow focus of these projects made it difficult for them to make significant impacts, but they illustrate attempts to apply some of the ideas reviewed in this chapter.

Opportunities for Youth (OFY) in Seattle attempted to use work opportunities to reduce delinquency, but the project met with little success (Hackler, 1966). One might argue that temporary job programs do not have a meaningful impact on the larger community. However, this same project had an impact on the attitudes of the adults living in the four communities in which the project was conducted (Hackler and Linden, 1970). Furthermore, parents of black children seemed particularly responsive to the idea of job opportunities for their children. Like so many programs launched during the 1960s, OFY attempted to apply strain theories. Lower-class populations did respond and became involved. Although evidence of crime reduction in the short term is lacking, the opportunity structure was altered for some lower-class families. We should not be overly cynical or skeptical. Early childhood education programs implemented in the 1960s have demonstrated that they can have a significant impact on later school achievement and, eventually, on success in the adult world (Schweinhart, Barnes, and Weikart, 1993).

Unfortunately, opportunities for the lower classes may have decreased in North America over the past decade. While there has been a dramatic increase in the wealth of the upper classes, the frequent display of luxurious lifestyles, especially on television, has created all the more strain for those who aspire to a share of that material wealth.

It may be difficult to alter the structure of society, but governments could support institutions that ease some of the strains that arise from blocked opportunities. Public policies could provide visiting nurses, training and support for disadvantaged mothers, paid family leave, and universal health care. The work done by Richard Tremblay and his colleagues at the Université de Montréal on early childhood development is consistent with preschool Head Start programs that help reduce the strains caused by the challenges of education (Tremblay and Craig, 1995). Young people could be involved in national service programs, such as the Peace Corps, that lead to government funding for higher education or training in skilled occupations. Workplaces could offer ongoing training and upgrading. In other words, some of the strains experienced in the family, school, and workplace do not have to lead to anger and attacks on society if institutions provide alternatives.

A summary of the many successful Nurse–Family Partnership programs that have been offered by David Olds and his colleagues shows how parenting can be more effective than prisons in reducing crime (Hackler, 2011). Disintegrative shaming pervades our current coercive criminal justice operations (Braithwaite, 1989). Social support is the key ingredient in "reintegrative shaming." Andrews and Bonta (1998) have shown that individuals can control their behaviour through rehabilitation programs that make use of cognitive and behavioural therapies. Given the right setting, this can have positive outcomes and lead to legitimate ways of coping. In fact, most current crime control measures increase strain and anger. Unfortunately, moving toward a noncoercive, socially supportive criminal justice system does not seem likely at the present time.

Scholars do not have to be in complete agreement regarding strain theory before applying many of its principles to public policy in the important pursuit of reducing the gap between rich and poor. Nor should we ignore the warning Merton voiced in his 1938 article: "*The ruthless pursuit of profit creates a criminogenic society.*" Increasing opportunities for the less privileged members of society makes a great deal more sense than rewarding the wealthy to encourage them to invest (for a profit, of course). According to strain theory, the self-serving policies advocated by many powerful people in North America in recent years will do little to help reduce crime.

QUESTIONS FOR CRITICAL THINKING

1. Researchers who have studied delinquent gangs have failed to find the three distinct criminal, conflict, and retreatist subcultures predicted by Cloward and Ohlin. Why do you think these distinct types of gangs do not exist?
2. Discuss some of the strengths and weaknesses of strain theory.
3. Merton (and those who followed him) developed strain theory to explain lower-class crime and delinquency. However, some might argue that strain theory actually provides a better explanation for white-collar and corporate crime. Describe how strain theory can be used to explain the crimes of the rich and powerful.

● Summary

- Two broad theoretical perspectives have guided sociological theories of crime. The consensus perspective maintains that the vast majority of the population share similar values regarding right and wrong. The conflict perspective argues that the criminal law does not necessarily represent the moral values of the majority but rather reflects the interests of the groups that are in a position to create and enforce those laws.

■ Strain theory is part of the consensus tradition. Strain theorists assume that social institutions such as the family, education, government, religion, and the economy normally all contribute to the smooth running of society. Crime occurs when something unusual happens that affects some or all of these institutions. This results in strains, stresses, or frustrations that affect people's behaviour.

■ Durkheim saw crime and other deviance as a consequence of modernity. Changes associated with modernity led to a weakening of social controls, and consequently rates of deviance increased.

■ Merton modified Durkheim's theory to account for what he felt were the realities of American society. In Merton's anomie theory, crime resulted from the gap between culturally prescribed aspirations and the socially structured means for realizing those aspirations.

■ Messner and Rosenfeld argued that American culture emphasizes monetary success. When combined with weak restraints on illegitimate means, this encourages economic crimes.

■ To reduce crime, one must respond to a wide range of unethical behaviour, including commercial activities, safety concerns, and income tax evasion.

■ Agnew suggests that adolescents located in unpleasant and stressful environments, such as school, from which they cannot escape become frustrated and angry. If legitimate coping alternatives are not available, violent outbursts and delinquency are likely.

■ Cloward pointed out that illegitimate opportunities were also not equally accessible to all. As a result, he hypothesized that there are three different types of delinquent subcultures: criminal, conflict, and retreatist.

■ Anderson notes that exporting manufacturing jobs overseas has made a bad situation worse in inner cities. Because traditional legitimate work is no longer available, young people have adopted a code of the street. One gains status by being tough and willing to use violence.

■ Early strain theorists focused on lower-class crime, but their work also applies to white-collar and corporate crime. Upper-class crimes can arise from an unprincipled overcommitment to success. Even successful people may feel pressure to make more money and may choose to break the law in order to achieve their financial goals.

NET WORK

Go to this website: http://www.publicsafety.gc.ca/cnt/cntrng-crm/crm-prvntn/tls-rsrcs/vdnc-bsd-eng.aspx. Look at the list of programs designed to prevent crime and delinquency and select a few. Which of these programs address issues raised by strain theorists? How likely do you think it is that these programs will have an impact on crime? Why?

Conflict Theories

Danica Dupont

In this chapter we will explore a number of conflict theories, including cultural conflict theory, group conflict theory, instrumental and structuralist Marxism, and left realism. The conflict perspective assumes that societies are more divided by conflict than they are integrated by consensus. Whereas consensus theorists (see Chapter 10) view the law as the codification of mutually agreed upon societal norms and values, conflict theorists question the assumption that our laws represent the interests of society as a whole. Instead, the conflict perspective argues that the social norms and values codified into law are those endorsed by the more powerful or dominant groups in society.

Learning Objectives

After reading this chapter, you should be able to

- Understand the differences between Sellin's culture group conflict theory and Vold's interest group conflict theory.
- Describe how Quinney's (1970) group conflict theory differs from both Vold's and Sellin's conflict theories.
- Know the basic elements of Marx's mode of production and what is meant by the economic base and superstructure.
- Understand the differences between instrumental Marxism and structural Marxism and the meaning of relative autonomy.
- Describe the basic elements of the left realist position.

Cultural Conflict Theory: Thorsten Sellin

Thorsten Sellin was one of the first criminologists to propose a conflict perspective for the analysis of crime. In *Culture Conflict and Crime* (1938), he presented a criminological theory that focused on the role of "conduct norms" in explaining crime. For Sellin, modern society is composed of diverse cultural groups, each maintaining distinct "conduct norms" or cultural rules that govern appropriate conduct. Sellin suggests that in basic, culturally homogeneous societies the values and norms to which people subscribe will be fairly similar, so the conduct norms of the broader social group will tend to reflect a societal consensus. However, in more complex societies characterized by cultural heterogeneity, urbanization, and industrialization, an overall societal consensus is less likely, and it is more likely that there will be conflict between the **conduct norms** of different cultural groups. In other words, the more complex a society becomes, the greater the probability of culture conflict.

According to Sellin, **cultural conflict** can arise when conduct norms clash on the border areas between distinct cultures; as a result of colonization, migration, or immigration; or when the laws of one cultural group are extended to cover the territory of another. Sellin was particularly interested in how the conduct norms of immigrant cultures could potentially come into conflict with the conduct norms of the established or dominant culture. One sphere where culture conflict appears is in the legal sphere, especially criminal law. Cultural practices in conflict with Canadian law include female genital mutilation, honour killings, marital rape, and forced marriage. While there are various ways in which social groups secure conformity of their members, the criminal law stands out because "its norms are binding upon all who live within the political boundaries of the state and are enforced through the coercive power of the state" (21).

Sellin felt that the criminal law "depends upon the character and interests of those groups in the population which influence legislation" (21). Ultimately, social values that receive the protection of the criminal law are those valued by dominant interest groups. Sellin uses the term *criminal norms* to describe the "conduct norms" embodied in the criminal law that represent the values of the dominant group. The criminal law will generally reflect the social values and conduct norms of the dominant cultural group. According to Sellin, then, crime is an expression of culture conflict when individuals who act based on the conduct norms of their own cultural group find themselves in violation of the conduct norms that the dominant group has enacted into law. Box 11.1 examines the murders of Zainab Shafia, Sahar Shafia, Geeti Shafia, and Rona Amir Mohammed and briefly surveys the Canadian literature on honour killings and honour-related violence, as these crimes provide an example of cultural conflict.

conduct norms
Specific rules or norms of appropriate behaviour generally agreed upon by members of the social group to whom the behavioural norms apply.

cultural conflict
A theory that attempts to explain certain types of criminal behaviour as resulting from a conflict between the conduct norms of divergent cultural groups.

Group Conflict Theory

George Vold

In *Theoretical Criminology* (1958), George Vold views **group conflict theory** as an explanation for certain types of criminal behaviour. Much like Sellin, Vold is interested in examining crime as it relates to conflict between groups. But in contrast to Sellin's explanation of crime as resulting from a conflict between the conduct norms of divergent cultural groups, Vold focuses on crime that occurs as a result of conflict between diverse "interest" groups. Vold begins with the assumption that humans are "group-involved" beings whose lives are oriented toward group associations. Groups form when members have common interests that are best furthered through collective action. Groups will come into contact with one another as their interests begin to overlap and become competitive. Vold sees society as a collection of groups existing in a constantly shifting, but more or less stable, equilibrium of opposing group interests.

group conflict theory
A theory that attempts to explain certain types of criminal behaviour as resulting from a conflict between the interests of divergent groups.

FOCUS

Box 11.1

HONOUR CRIMES IN CANADA: SITUATING HONOUR VIOLENCE

On June 30, 2009, the bodies of Zainab Shafia, 19, Sahar Shafia, 17, Geeti Shafia, 13, and Rona Amir Mohammed, 52, were found underwater, inside a submerged Nissan Sentra at the Kingston Mills Lockstation. After a three week investigation, police arrested the father of the girls, Mohammed Shafia, 58, his second wife Tooba Yahya Shafia, 42, and their son Hamed Shafia, 21, in Montreal.

In January 2012, a jury found each of the defendants guilty of four counts of first-degree murder in the drowning deaths of the Shafias' three teenage daughters and Mohammed Shafia's first wife, Rona Amir Mohammed. The guilty verdict was the culmination of a three-month trial held in Kingston, Ontario, and was the subject of wide media coverage.

The trial opened in October 2011 with Crown attorney Laurie Lacelle's overview of the evidence gathered by police, including physical evidence, forensics, wiretaps, cellphone records, and interviews with police and youth protection workers. The Crown maintained that the three accused were guilty of the planned and premeditated murders of Zainab, Sahar, Geeti, and Rona. Over the next six weeks, the jury heard testimony from detectives, teachers, and child welfare workers that described a disturbing pattern of violence in the Shafia home, including repeated physical abuse, threats, and intimidation.

The Shafia family immigrated from Afghanistan to Canada in 2007. Mohammed Shafia, his second wife Tooba, and their seven children arrived in Montreal in June. Mohammed Shafia's first wife, Rona Amir, followed in November and was admitted to Canada on a visitor's visa as Mohammed Shafia's cousin, as polygamous relationships are not legally recognized in Canada. As is customary in Afghanistan, Shafia had married a second wife because Rona was unable to have children.

By any measure the Shafia household was a troubled one. Zainab, 19, the eldest of the three sisters, suffered violence at the hands of her father and her brother Hamed. Just six weeks before she was killed, she ran away from home and sought refuge at a women's shelter. Sahar, 17, the middle sister, also suffered physical abuse in the home. In 2008, she confided in a teacher that she had tried to commit suicide, that her brother Hamed had assaulted her with a pair of scissors, and that her parents had threatened to pull her out of school. Geeti, 13, was the youngest of the three sisters. There were many warning signs that Geeti was troubled. She skipped class frequently and failed three out of four classes in her final semester at school. She was caught shoplifting. She told police, school staff, and a

youth protection worker that she wanted to be placed in foster care and that her father and her brother Hamed had physically abused her.

On June 1, 2009, 30 days before Rona, Zainab, Sahar, and Geeti were murdered, Hamed travelled to Dubai to meet his father. While father and son were in Dubai, a Google search was entered on a laptop used by Hamed: "Can a prisoner have control over their real estate." Shafia and Hamed returned to Montreal on June 13, 2009. On June 20, there was another Google search: "Where to commit a murder." Other searches were made in June for various bodies of water, boat rentals, bags, and metal boxes. On June 22, 2009, Mohammed Shafia bought a used black Nissan Sentra.

On June 23, the ten-member Shafia family left Montreal, travelling in two cars, the Nissan Sentra and Shafia's Lexus SUV. The children were told they were going on vacation. On June 30, 2009, at about 9 a.m., the bodies of Zainab Shafia, Sahar Shafia, Geeti Shafia, and Rona Amir Mohammed were found in the Nissan Sentra at the bottom of the lock in Kingston Mills.

Twenty days later, Mohammed Shafia was recorded on a police wiretap talking to his second wife Tooba Yahya. Shafia said: "They committed treason from beginning to end. They betrayed humankind, they betrayed Islam, they betrayed our religion and our creed, they betrayed our tradition, they betrayed everything." In a conversation recorded on July 21 between Shafia, Tooba, and Hamed, Shafia said: "Even if they hoist me up onto the gallows [unintelligible] nothing is more dear to me than my honour. Let's leave our destiny to God and may God never make me, you, or your mother honourless … There is nothing more valuable than our honour" (in Friscolanti, 2012).

The UN Population Fund has estimated that 5,000 women and girls are killed each year in honour-related crimes (UNPA 2000), although many women's groups in the Middle East and southwestern Asia believe the number of honour killings to be at least four times that estimate (*The Independent*, 2010). It is almost impossible to assess the true extent of honour killings and honour-related violence because these crimes go unreported in many countries or are disguised as accidents or suicides (Warrick, 2005).

What Are Honour Killings?

What, exactly, is an "honour killing"? According to Korteweg (2012, 136), "the simplest definition of honour related violence, up to and including murder, is a family-initiated, planned,

(continued)

Mohammed Shafia, Tooba Yahya Shafia, and Hamed Shafia were found guilty of first-degree murder for killing the Shafias' three daughters and Mohammed Shafia's first wife.

violent response to the perception that a woman, as wife or daughter, has violated the honour of her family by crossing a boundary of sexual appropriateness."

While definitions of honour killings vary somewhat, certain features appear to be constant. First, honour killings almost always involve the murder of a woman or girl by her male family members. Second, the killer does not normally act alone, but with the approval or encouragement of other members of the family. Third, suspicion or rumour of an alleged impropriety is usually enough to justify an honour crime. Fourth, most experts insist an essential characteristic of an honour killing is that it is premeditated (Terman, 2010, 10).

It's important to note that the term "honour killing" is controversial and that some scholars, activists, and women's organizations in Canada disagree with its use. For example, Yasmin Jiwani and Homa Hoodfar (2012) have argued for the use of "femicide" and maintain there is no material distinction between the murders of intimate partners and honour killing. In a similar vein, the Canadian Council of Muslim Women (CCMW) issued a position paper in January 2012 outlining their opposition to the term, which they argue is "divisive and dangerous," "encourages blatant racism for some," and makes others "defensive or apologetic about their religion or culture." The CCMW urges that murders of women and girls be identified as "femicide."

In contrast, Shahrzad Mojab (2012) argues that honour killing is a distinct phenomenon that cannot be equated with either domestic violence or crimes of passion. First, honour killing is premeditated, "often planned in much detail," whereas passion crimes are normally understood to be spontaneous or unplanned. Second, whereas a passion crime is normally committed by an intimate partner, honour killing is a group action, sanctioned by the family in response to "a female's violation of the codes of honour." In addition, females often participate, "usually as accomplices, in the murder." Third, honour killing is a social relationship and "aims at satisfying a demand or expectation from the community—cleansing shame and restoring honour." Domestic violence, by contrast, is typically not committed in response to pressure from family or community (129–30).

A similar point has been made by Canadian human rights activist Aruna Papp, who has been counselling South Asian immigrants and victims of violence for 30 years. Papp argues that few researchers appreciate the distinction between Western patterns of domestic violence and what Papp identifies as culturally driven abuse of girls and women in some immigrant communities. Among other differences, Western abuse is considered an aberration by kinship groups and by society in general, whereas culturally driven violence "stems from culturally approved codes around collective family honour and shame, and is condoned and even facilitated by kinship groups and the community" (2010, 7).

Ultimately, the way in which we problematize and define honour-based violence, according to Mojab (2012), has critical implications for both preventing honour crimes and protecting the lives of at-risk women and girls. She argues that the framing of honour killing as domestic violence "will make it difficult to prevent, whereas seeing it as a "premeditated, collectively planned and perpetrated crime enables us to detect some early warning signs and save the lives of victims" (121). For example, her research indicates that there are often early warning indicators that a woman or girl's life may be in danger, including physical harm, emotional troubles, and poor school performance. These indicators need to be taken seriously by teachers, social workers, school counsellors, shelter workers, and police. Mojab is convinced that we must "acknowledge honour-based violence [as] a *Canadian* problem, which requires the mobilization of educational, legal, political and social institutions in order to face it boldly and directly" (133).

Imagine that you have been engaged by the Department of Justice to write a position paper on honour-based violence. Should honour violence be viewed as domestic violence, as some have argued? Or is it a contextually specific form of violence that is planned and premeditated, as others have maintained?

Vold is interested in the way the creation of law reflects the activities of antagonistic interest groups in the broader community. One interest group may seek the assistance of the state to enact a new law while an opposing interest group tries to resist the proposed legislation. The interest group marshalling the greater number of votes will have the most influence in determining whether the new law is enacted. Therefore Vold (1958) argues that

the whole political process of law making, law breaking and law enforcement becomes a direct reflection of deep-seated and fundamental conflicts between interest groups and their more general struggles for the control of the police power of the state. Those who produce legislative majorities win control over the police power and dominate the policies that decide who is likely to be involved in violation of the law (209).

For Vold, conflict between interest groups is a normal social process and one of the fundamental principles of organized political society.

Vold describes two general classes of group conflict that can result in criminal behaviour. First, some crimes arise from a conflict between the behaviour of minority groups and the legal norms, rules, and regulations of the dominant majority, which are established in law. For example, Vold argues that the delinquent gang can be understood as a minority group whose interests are in opposition to the rules of the dominant majority—the adult world of regulations established in law and enforced by the police. A further example of a minority group whose interests are in opposition to the dominant majority is that of "conscientious objectors" during wartime, who opt to serve prison sentences rather than participate in any form of compulsory wartime service.

Second, some crimes arise from a conflict between competing interest groups who are vying for power. For example, Vold argues that many crimes are the result of political revolution or protest movements whose aim is direct political reform. "A successful revolution," he contends, "makes criminals out of government officials previously in power, and an unsuccessful revolution makes its leaders into traitors subject to immediate execution" (1958, 215). A further example of intergroup conflict that may result in criminal behaviour is that of the conflict of group interests between management and labour unions. In the case of strikes or lockouts, escalating tensions between management and striking workers may result in violence, property damage, or other crimes.

Vold argues that criminological theories that focus on notions of individual choice and responsibility may not be relevant in understanding criminal behaviour occurring as a result of conflict between interest groups. This is because individual criminal behaviour that results from intergroup conflict represents, for that same individual, a type of "loyal service" to the interest group. Group conflict theory is limited to instances where criminal behaviour arises from the conflict between interest groups and does not try to explain other types of criminal acts.

Conflict theory has been criticized for its narrow scope of explanation. Critics argue that it applies to a narrow range of crimes, where only politically or ideologically motivated crimes can be said to fit the model well. In addition, others argue that most crime is intra-group—that is, committed by one member of a group against another member—rather than the intergroup crime upon which Vold focuses.

Richard Quinney

Although Richard Quinney's theoretical perspective changed significantly in his later work, his 1970 book, The Social Reality of Crime, was widely viewed as an important contribution to group conflict theory. Following Sellin and Vold, Quinney's theory of crime explains criminality as the result of conflict between groups. Whereas Sellin focused on cultural group conflict and Vold on interest group conflict, Quinney's group conflict theory focused on the more broadly defined notion of "segments" of society, which he defined as types of "social groupings." For Quinney, the more powerful segments or social groups are able to secure and protect their own interests by influencing the formulation, enforcement, and administration of criminal law.

SEARCH FOR:
Educational Resource for
Criminology

Although both Sellin and Vold viewed criminal law as generally reflective of the values and norms of dominant groups in society, Quinney placed a much greater emphasis on the unequal distribution of power in society, especially as related to the formation of public policy. While Vold would view society as existing in a relatively stable equilibrium of opposing group interests where all groups are able to make themselves heard in policy decision making, Quinney argues that only some interest groups are sufficiently powerful to influence policy, because power is unequally distributed due to "the structural arrangements of the political state" (1970, 12). Quinney outlines his conflict theory of crime in six propositions:

1. *Crime is a definition of human conduct that is created by authorized agents in a politically organized society.* For Quinney, crime is not inherent in behaviour, but rather is the product of legal definitions; it is a *definition* of behaviour imposed on some persons by others.

2. *Criminal definitions describe behaviours that conflict with the interests of segments of society that have the power to shape public policy.* Quinney argues that the more powerful segments of society can incorporate their interests, values, and norms into the criminal law; thus, these powerful segments can regulate the formulation of criminal definitions. These definitions are formulated because less powerful segments of society are in conflict with other, more powerful segments.

3. *Criminal definitions are applied by the segments of society that have power to shape the enforcement and administration of criminal law.* The interests of powerful segments are represented not only in the formulation of criminal law but also in its application. The enforcement and administration of the law is delegated to legal agents (e.g., police, prosecutors, judges) who represent the interests of these powerful segments.

4. *Behavioural patterns are structured in segmentally organized society in relation to criminal definitions, and within this context persons engage in actions that have relative probabilities of being defined as criminal.* For Quinney, it is not the quality of the behaviour that makes it criminal, but rather the action taken against the behaviour. The decision as to which acts are defined as criminal is made by the more powerful segments of society who formulate and apply criminal definitions. Thus persons in less powerful social segments are more likely to have their behaviours defined as criminal, because their interests are not represented in the formulation and application of criminal definitions.

5. *Conceptions of crime are constructed and diffused in the segments of society by various means of communication.* The mass media play an important role in the diffusion of criminal conceptions throughout society. A particular conception of crime is diffused throughout society and subsequently becomes "the basis for the public's view of reality" (Quinney, 1970, 285). The more powerful segments of society are able to influence the mass media's portrayal of crime.

6. *The social reality of crime is constructed by the formulation and application of criminal definitions, the development of behavioural patterns related to criminal definitions, and the construction of criminal conceptions.* The

sixth proposition is essentially a summation of propositions 2 to 5; thus, Quinney's model posits that the "social reality of crime" is a function of (2) the formulation of criminal definitions, (3) the application of criminal definitions, (4) the development of behaviour patterns in relation to criminal definitions, and (5) the construction of criminal conceptions. Quinney views the first proposition as a definition; thus the body of the theory comprises the middle four propositions.

QUESTIONS FOR CRITICAL THINKING

1. What assumption does Sellin make about society in his theory of cultural conflict?
2. In what way is Quinney's understanding of conflict, in his early work, different from that of Sellin and Vold? In what way is it similar?
3. What assumption does Quinney make about society in his conflict theory of crime?

Marxist Conflict Perspectives in Criminology

In the 1970s, Marxist theories began to gain prominence in the socio-legal and criminological literature. While Marx himself had very little to say about crime, many criminologists believed that aspects of Marx's work could help to analyze the relationship between crime and the broader social world. Similar to the conflict theories of Sellin, Vold, and Quinney, Marxist theories of crime and deviance do not look to the individual offender for explanations of crime. Thus, criminal behaviour is not viewed in isolation as an individual pathology. Marxist criminology takes the position that crime "must be analyzed in the context of its relationship to the character of the society as a whole" (Greenberg, 1993, 17). Marxists believe crime is best understood in relation to the social, political, and economic structures of the society in which it occurs.

You will recall that group conflict theorists, broadly speaking, view conflict as arising from opposing group interests, and crime as resulting from the ability of more powerful or dominant groups to criminalize the behaviour of other less powerful groups, who find themselves in violation of the criminal norms and standards of the dominant majority. Marxist criminologists, on the other hand, view conflict as rooted in the very structure of capitalist society, particularly capitalist economic relations. The political and economic structures under capitalism promote conflict, in turn providing the precipitating conditions (such as unemployment) for crime to occur. Marxist criminologists focus on the relations between crime and the social arrangements of society, especially the way in which societies organize their political, legal, and economic structures (Bohm, 1982). Generally speaking, Marxist criminologists take the position that the organization of capitalist society—both its way of producing material goods and its organization of political, legal, and economic structures—has important implications for the study of the amount and types of crime present in society (Greenberg, 1993).

Marx believed that the history of the development of human societies is best understood through the fundamental role played by production. Through production, we are able to satisfy our basic material needs, such as the need for food, clothing, and shelter. Marx was interested in examining the history of societies from the perspective of how production is organized, or what is described as the *mode of production*. The mode of production refers to the economic system whereby goods are produced, exchanged, and distributed in society. Marx identified several different modes of production throughout history, including the slave economies of ancient Greece and Rome, the agrarian economy of feudalism, and the wage-labour economy of capitalism.

The mode of production, in turn, is composed of the *forces of production* and the *social relations of production*. The forces of production refers to the tools, techniques, raw materials, and labour power used in production, while the social relations of production refers to the relationships that exist among humans with respect to the ownership of the means of production. According to Marx, the social relations of production under capitalism—that is, under the capitalist mode of production—gave rise to two major groups or classes. The bourgeoisie are the economically dominant class who own the means of production (the land, machinery, and factories), and the proletariat are the economically subordinate class who are property-less. Because they neither own nor control the means of production, the proletariat have only their labour power to sell in exchange for their livelihood in the form of wages. It is important to note that class is *not* an attribute or characteristic of an individual or group in Marxist thought; rather it refers to a position in a relationship (Greenberg, 1993). For Marxists, capitalist society, like earlier societies, is based on class exploitation. The relationship between the capitalist class and the working class is inherently exploitative because the capitalist is able to extract the surplus labour of the worker in the form of profits. This surplus is based on the difference between the value the workers produce and what is received by the worker in wages.

Marx argued that because societies are always organized around the dominant mode of production, "the mode of production of material life conditions the social, political, and intellectual life process in general" (Marx, in Cain and Hunt, 1979, 54). Marx made use of the metaphor of a building to describe the relationship between the mode of production and other aspects of society: "The sum total of these relations of production constitutes the economic structure of society, the real foundation, on which rises a legal and political superstructure and to which correspond definite forms of social consciousness" (54).

According to Marx, in Western societies the economic base of capitalism is the foundation upon which the various superstructural institutions of society are built, including political and legal institutions. Another way Marxists put this is that the economic base of capitalism has a *determining influence* on the superstructural institutions of society. Where one class is in a position of dominance over the other class (based on its ownership of the means of production) in the economic sphere, the other social institutions in society will be organized according to the interests of the dominant class (Comack, 1999). The implication for Marxist approaches to law, crime, and criminology is that both the law and crime should not be studied in isolation, but rather in relation to the whole of society and particularly the economic sphere (Greenberg, 1993).

The Marxist approach provides criminologists and legal scholars with a theoretical framework that allows them to study the interrelationships between the capitalist mode of production, the state, law, crime control, and crime (Bohm, 1982). In addition, Marxist analysis typically involves a critical element (see also Chapter 12). It is a critique of the logic of the existing capitalist social order. In critiquing the existing society or social order, Marxian thought often begins with an analysis of the state. While Marx himself did not develop a systematic theory of the state, Marxist theorists have made use of aspects of Marx's writings to attempt to theorize the relationships between the state in capitalist society and class relations, law, crime, and crime control. It has become conventional in the criminological and socio-legal literature to distinguish between *instrumental* and *structural* Marxist theories of the state, law, and crime.

Instrumental Marxism

Instrumental Marxists generally begin with the assumption that the state in capitalist societies broadly serves the interests of the ruling or capitalist class. A well-known passage from Marx and Engels' work, *The Communist Manifesto*, is often cited in support of **instrumental Marxism**: "The executive of the modern State is but a committee for managing the common affairs of the whole bourgeoisie" (1848, 5). For Marx, the economic structure of society determines the nature of that society's political and legal superstructure. Instrumentalist Marxists interpret Marx's statement quite literally and argue that both the state and the legal and political institutions within the state are a direct reflection of the interests of the capitalist class. Law, then, is equated with class rule—the ruling class controls the formation of law, and the focus is on the coercive nature of the law. As Tierney (1996) points out, this approach was based upon an instrumentalist school of thought in political theory (Miliband, 1969; Domhoff, 1970), which argued that those who occupied powerful positions in the state apparatus were either capitalists themselves or they strongly identified with the interests of the capitalist class.

Instrumental Marxists therefore viewed the state and the legal system as instruments that could be directly manipulated by the capitalist class. For example, Miliband (1969, 22) argued that because the ruling class of capitalist society owns and controls the means of production, it is able to "use the state as its instrument for the domination of society." Early Marxist studies tended to focus on how the economic power of the capitalist class provided the opportunity to influence law and law formation. An example of an instrumental Marxist position is found in Richard Quinney's book, *Critique of the Legal Order* (1974). Recall that in Quinney's earlier work, he endorsed a conflict perspective on crime but his views changed over time. In the *Critique of the Legal Order*, Quinney (1974, 16) offers six propositions that summarize his critical Marxist theory of crime control:

1. American society is based on an advanced capitalist economy.
2. The State is organized to serve the interests of the dominant economic class.

instrumental Marxism
The state is viewed as the direct instrument of the ruling or capitalist class. Instrumentalism is based on the notion that the processes of the superstructure are determined by the economic base.

3. Criminal law is an instrument of the state and ruling class to maintain and perpetuate the existing social and economic order.
4. Crime control in capitalist society is accomplished through a variety of institutions and agencies established and administered by a government elite, representing ruling class interests.
5. The contradictions of advanced capitalism … require that the subordinate classes remain oppressed by whatever means necessary, especially through the coercion and violence of the legal system.
6. Only with the collapse of capitalist society and the creation of a new society, based on socialist principles, will there be a solution to the crime problem.*

The instrumentalist Marxist position may be said to offer useful insights into the sociology of the capitalist class, the relationship between class power and state power, and the place of law in capitalist society. Critics, however, point out a number of flaws in the theory. First, instrumental Marxism has been critiqued for portraying the ruling class as a unified and homogeneous group, thus ignoring competing factions that may exist within the capitalist class itself. Second, instrumentalist accounts have been critiqued for ignoring how the actions of ruling-class members are influenced or constrained by structural causes. For example, are there limits to any particular ruling-class member's sphere of influence, such as shifting affiliations with the current party in power in a parliamentary democracy, the deep fluctuations of the stock market, political exigencies, and so on? Third, in its argument that the law represents only the interests of the ruling class, the instrumentalist position is unable to account for legislation that is not in the immediate interest of the ruling class, such as health and safety legislation, employment standards, and so on. Fourth, critics believe that instrumentalism draws upon an overly rigid interpretation of the base/superstructure metaphor. That is, the Marxist argument that the economic base is the foundation of the superstructure is said to be deterministic. By deterministic, we mean there is a form of causality where the superstructure is a necessary consequence of the economic base. In other words, the economic base under capitalism more or less wholly determines the political, economic, ideological, and cultural superstructure. This is why the instrumentalist position argues that the state's legal and political institutions are a direct reflection of the capitalist class.

Structural Marxism

During the 1970s and 1980s, Marxist theorists developed structuralist Marxist accounts of the state, law, and crime. **Structural Marxism** disputes the instrumentalist view that the state can be viewed as the direct servant of the capitalist or ruling class. Whereas the instrumentalist position argues that the institutions of the state are under the direct control of those members of the capitalist class in positions of state power, the structuralist perspective takes the position that the institutions of the state ensure the ongoing viability of capitalism more generally. Another way that Marxists put this is that the institutions of the state must function so as to reproduce capitalist society as a whole (Gold et al., 1975). Structuralists view the state in a capitalist mode of production as taking a specifically capitalist form, not because particular individuals

structural Marxism
The state is viewed as acting in the long-term interests of capitalism as a whole rather than in the short-term interests of the capitalist class.

---

*Quinney, Richard. *Critique of the Legal Order.* Copyright © 1974, CCC Republication.

are in powerful positions, but because the state reproduces the logic of capitalist structure in its economic, legal, and political institutions. We might say that a structuralist perspective would argue that the institutions of the state (including its legal institutions) function in the long-term interests of capital and capitalism, rather than in the short-term interests of members of the capitalist class. Structuralists would thus argue that the state and its institutions have a certain degree of *independence* from specific elites in the capitalist class.

The idea that the state is—to a certain degree—independent of the ruling class is known as **relative autonomy**. Structural Marxists have drawn from the work of Poulantzas (1975) and Althusser (1969) to argue that the relative autonomy of the state functions to preserve the long-term interests of capital, and the long-run stability of the capitalist structure as a whole. To begin with, we cannot assume that the capitalist class is united in its interests and homogeneous in its beliefs. The state must therefore have the relative autonomy to mediate between divergent capitalist class factions in order to preserve the long-term interests of the capitalist class as a whole (Poulantzas, 1975). The relative autonomy of the state, therefore, provides a state structure "capable of transcending the parochial, individualized interests of specific capitalists and capitalist class factions" (Gold et al., 1975, 38). In addition, structural Marxists point to the relative autonomy of the state and its institutions to explain why many laws are enacted that do not represent the immediate interests of the capitalist class. That is, an instrumentalist Marxist position cannot account for the existence of minimum wage laws, laws against discrimination in employment, consumer protection laws, rent control, anti-trust legislation, and welfare legislation, in that these laws are not in the immediate interests of the capitalist class.

An interesting area that Canadian researchers have explored, with respect to law creation that does not seem to represent the immediate interests of the capitalist class as a whole, has been the development of anticombines legislation in Canada (Goff and Reasons, 1978; Snider, 1979; Smandych, 1985). The aim of this legislation was to prevent corporations from monopolizing or cornering the supply of certain commodities or markets, and fixing prices. Goff and Reasons (1978) argue that Canada's first anticombines legislation—the Combines Investigation Act of 1889—came about less from the desire to protect the general populace than from the complaints of small businessmen who "felt their firms were at the mercy of big business interests" (42). For the first decade, this legislation was unenforceable because of the weak wording of the act, which stipulated that combines had to be engaged in behaviour that *unlawfully* as well as *unduly* restricted trade. Snider (1979) examined the later revisions and amendments to the act in 1923, 1935, 1952, and 1960 and concluded that "at each stage proposals were weakened or eliminated in the face of business opposition" (110). Both Snider and Goff and Reasons concluded that while reforms do occur, the state "is susceptible to the interests of powerful economic groups" (Goff and Reasons, 1978, 114), and thus reforms tend to be "resisted for as long as possible by the corporate elite" (Snider, 1979, 118).

Smandych (1985) argued that anticombines legislation in Canada must also be considered in relation to the increasingly vocal trade unions of the late 19th century and the growing confrontations between capital and labour. He

relative autonomy
A term used in the structural Marxist perspective to indicate that the state has a certain amount of independence from the capitalist class and is therefore able to enact laws that are not in the immediate interests of the capitalist class.

points out that the rise of militant trade unions in the late 1800s, such as the Knights of Labour in Toronto, "owed as much to labour's hatred of monopolistic companies as it did to labour's desire to improve working conditions" (45). In addition, the Knights of Labour and other trade unions had a great deal of influence on the working man's vote. Thus Smandych argued that the emergence of Canadian anticombines legislation could be viewed as a pragmatic attempt by the government to find a "symbolic" solution to the confrontation between capital and labour, given the political influence of the more prominent trade unions.

The solution was symbolic because the immense economic and political power of the monopolistic companies of the period influenced the state to enact what was ultimately an "ineffectual law that served only to foster the reproduction of combines activity in the late 19th century" (47). As Chambliss and Siedman (1982) point out, "A great deal of state action concerns not the enhancement of profit for a particular faction of the ruling class, but the maintenance of relations of production that make capitalism possible" (312). Thus the state ensures the reproduction of capitalism as a whole. In some instances the state enacts laws that are ostensibly meant to curb the excesses of capital, yet are ineffective in their design and implementation.

In the structuralist perspective, then, the law cannot be said to exclusively represent the instrumental interests of the dominant capitalist class. Rather, structural Marxists argue that laws that benefit the less powerful reflect an ideological need to develop a widespread *consent* for the existing social order (Einstadter and Henry, 2006). On this view, consensus is generated for the established order by promoting law as an impartial system that protects the public rather than private interests, and where all are equal before the law. Structuralists argue that this notion of "equality before the law," also described as "the rule of law," masks or otherwise obscures the substantive inequalities of class, race, and gender that may exist between individuals who are nevertheless considered equal before the law. Stated differently, the formal equality of each individual in the legal sphere does not extend to the economic sphere (Brickey and Comack, 1989). For example, corporations and labour are treated in collective bargaining law as being on an equal footing, despite the structural inequalities between them, including the corporation's greater material and organizational resources (Bartholomew and Boyd, 1989). Structuralists therefore argue that law functions as an ideological means of reproducing capitalist social and economic relations.

Marxists sometimes use the concept of ideology to analyze legal discourse in ways that go beyond the law's manifest role as an external mechanism of regulation. Hunt (1993) has argued that "the most pervasive ideological effect of law is to be found in the fact that legal rules and their application give effect to existing social relations" (25). Law transforms the human subject into a legal subject and in so doing influences how social relations are lived and experienced. Marxists view law as ideological in the sense that it functions to both legitimate and reproduce the existing social order. In general, the concept of ideology is taken up to explore the linkages between legal discourse and the attitudes, values, and beliefs that support it. Box 11.2 examines Bill C-13, the "Protecting Canadians from Online Crime Act," and explores the often

FOCUS

Box 11.2

LAW, IDEOLOGY, AND BILL C-13

In November 2013, the federal government tabled Bill C-13—the "Protecting Canadians from Online Crime Act"—with the stated goal of combatting cyberbullying, particularly the dissemination of intimate images online without the consent of the subject in the picture. Justice Minister Peter MacKay introduced the legislation during Bullying Awareness Week, describing the bill as a necessary tool in "ensuring that our children are safe from on-line predators and from on-line exploitation" (Meyer, November 27, 2013). Bill C-13 would make it a criminal offence to distribute intimate images of a person online without their explicit consent; it would also give courts the right to seize computers, cellphones, and other devices used in the offence.

The legislation was announced in the wake of recent and deeply tragic suicides of Canadian teenagers who had been subjected to online bullying. BC teenager Amanda Todd (15) took her own life in 2012, after almost two years of being the target of online sexual extortion. Saskatchewan high school student Todd Loik was 15 when he committed suicide in 2013. His mother, Kim Loik, said her son had been cyberbullied nonstop for two years. Perhaps the most widely-publicized case involved a Canadian teenager who committed suicide after photos of her being sexually assaulted were distributed online. This case cannot be described any further because of a court ban on publication of details, but before the ban the tragic details of the case did a great deal to build support for new legislation. Amanda's mother, Carol Todd, has spoken out in favour of Bill C-13, saying "it has been a long time coming, and as parents who have lost our children, it is a necessity" (Todd, November 25, 2013).

During the second reading of Bill C-13, MacKay presented an overview of Bill C-13 and described it as composed of two distinct but related parts. Mackay said the first part addresses "cyberbullying involving the nonconsensual distribution of intimate images," while the second "aims to ensure that the Criminal Code and other federal legislation is keeping pace with technological changes." According to MacKay, the intention of the bill is to propose "updates to offences and to the powers of police to investigate crimes committed using electronic networks or that use electronic evidence" (Parliament of Canada *Hansard*, November 27, 2013).

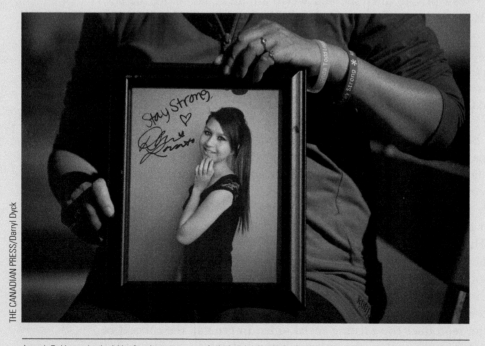

THE CANADIAN PRESS/Darryl Dyck

Amanda Todd committed suicide after almost two years of cyberbullying. Her mother has been a leader in the campaign to pass legislation targeting this behaviour.

Newly proposed laws, such as Bill C-13, that have yet to pass into the Criminal Code offer us a fascinating lens into the process of "law-making" itself and the often conflicting sets of discourses and claims-making activities that underlie the making of law. The tabling and second reading of Bill C-13 has occasioned a great deal of commentary and critique, both in the House of Commons and in the media. Many Canadians have commented on various aspects of C-13, including the Canadian Association of Chiefs of Police (CACP), anti-bullying researchers, legal experts, youth advocates, and privacy activists.

Those who support the legislation, including law enforcement organizations, believe that Bill C-13 addresses many of the evidentiary gaps that exist in the Criminal Code. Chief Constable Jim Chu, President of CACP, said that "the government's new bill to fight cyberbullying and combat illicit sexting has the full support of Canada's police leaders and their organizations" (2014).

In general, the provisions of Bill C-13, which address cyberbullying, have been endorsed in the media and broadly supported from all sides of the House of Commons. However, the second part of the bill has been subject to intense debate. Those who are opposed to the bill allege that it contains troubling legislative and investigative power amendments that will infringe upon the privacy rights of Canadians. There are two major objections to the proposed bill.

First, opponents of Bill C-13 have criticized a new provision that lowers the threshold to obtain warrants for transmission data from "reasonable grounds to believe" to "reasonable grounds to suspect" that an offence has been committed. The argument for lowering the burden of proof to reasonable suspicion is that transmission data is not invasive, and thus a lower threshold is justified. MacKay told the house that these warrants apply to "information with little or no privacy impact" (Parliament of Canada, *Hansard*). However, privacy advocates have warned that noncontent transmission data, commonly referred to as "metadata" is extremely revealing and can "allow police to build a detailed profile of a person by using their digital footprint" (Spratt, 2013a).

Second, critics argue that Bill C-13 contains a troubling new provision that expands the ability of police to obtain Internet data without judicial oversight and encourages disclosure by providing immunity from civil or criminal liability for third parties such as Internet service providers (ISPs), telecom companies, and banks that voluntarily disclose information to police. The proposed amendment removes the requirement that police be engaged in a specific investigation that has to do with the enforcement or administration of the Criminal Code before asking ISPs to voluntarily turn over information to police. Lawyer Michael Spratt (2013b) has argued that "in essence, the police will be able to ask companies to turn over data on anyone, at any time, for any reason." Micheal Geist (2013), Canadian Research Chair of Internet and e-commerce law at the University of Ottawa, has argued that widening the permitted scope of voluntary disclosure in combination with granting legal immunity for intermediaries that disclose is "likely to lead to both increased requests without court oversight and to increased disclosures." Others have pointed out that similar legislation in the United States led to widespread surveillance as revealed by whistle blower Edward Snowden (Meyer 2013).

Rapidly changing technology has created new challenges both for lawmakers and for citizens subject to those laws. Hunt (1993) has argued that "law is ideological in that it conveys or transmits a complex set of attitudes, values, and theories about aspects of society. Its ideological content forms parts of the dominant ideology because these attitudes, values, etc. are ones that reinforce and legitimize the existing social order" (25).

Imagine you are sitting as an independent MP and yours will be the deciding vote on Bill C-13. Unusually, you have been given three choices: (a) accept as is; (b) reject as is; or (c) request a separation of the bill into cyberbullying provisions (clauses 1 to 7) and the investigative power amendments that augment police powers to obtain electronic data (clauses 8 to 47). Which would you choose, and what rationale would you give for your choice? What sorts of tradeoffs might you be prepared to accept? For example, do Canadians who sign contracts with ISPs have a reasonable expectation that their personal data will be safeguarded and not shared without their consent? Or does the need to protect vulnerable Canadians from online exploitation outweigh the privacy concerns some have expressed?

competing sets of claims-making activities that underlie the making of law in a parliamentary democracy such as that of the Canadian State.

By the end of the 1980s, a large body of critical work had been produced by Marxist scholars examining the relationships between the capitalist state, the economy, and the legal and political institutions of the state. Canadian Marxist theorists, in particular, contributed to a rich literature that explored the relationship between the Canadian state, its laws, and its legal institutions, as well as the relationship between the state and the criminal justice system (West and Snider, 1985; Mandel, 1987; Brickey and Comack, 1989; Snider 1989). In addition, Canadian Marxist criminologists have also explored the broader area of corporate crime and social harm (Sargent, 1991; McMullan, 1992; Snider, 1993). We will examine two further areas of Marxist research to illustrate some of the work undertaken in Marxist criminology: first, research that focuses on the crimes of the powerless, and second, research that investigates the crimes of the powerful.

Crimes of the Powerless

Stephen Spitzer

Spitzer (1975) made use of the Marxian notion of "surplus population" to formulate his "Marxian theory of deviance." Spitzer argued that the criminalization of much behaviour is directed toward those problem populations who are surplus to the labour market. These problem populations are created in two ways. First, they are created *directly* through the contradictions in the capitalist mode of production. For example, a surplus population is generated in capitalist economies as new technologies replace workers with machines, or when work is outsourced to other countries. Second, problem populations are created *indirectly* through contradictions in the institutions that help to reproduce capitalism, such as the schools. For example, Spitzer argues that while mass education provides a means of training future wage labourers, this schooling also provides youths with critical insight into the alienating and oppressive character of capitalist institutions. This, in turn, can lead to problem populations in the form of dropouts and student radicals. Problem populations become candidates for deviance processing when they disturb, hinder, or call into question any of the following:

1. Capitalist modes of appropriating the product of human labour (e.g., when the poor "steal" from the rich).
2. The social conditions under which capitalist production takes place (e.g., those who refuse or are unable to perform wage labour).
3. Patterns of distribution and consumption in capitalist society (e.g., those who use drugs for escape and transcendence rather than sociability and adjustment).
4. The process of socialization for productive and nonproductive roles (e.g., youths who refuse to be schooled or those who deny the validity of family life).
5. The ideology that supports the functioning of capitalist society (e.g., proponents of alternative forms of social organization) (1975, 642).*

David Greenberg

Another theorist who makes use of the Marxian notion of surplus population is Greenberg (1993). Greenberg explains juvenile delinquency from a Marxist perspective and argues that juveniles form a "class" of their own because they share a common relationship to the means of production. That is, young people are excluded from economically productive activity in a capitalist society, but

---

*Spitzer, Steven. (1975). "Toward a Marxian Theory of Analysis." *Social Problems* 22(5): 638–51. Copyright (c) 1975, The Society for the Study of Social Problems, Inc. Reprinted by permission of the publisher.

are required to undergo training for their future productive role in the capitalist system. Juveniles can thus be considered a part of the surplus population, because they are excluded from lawful sources of income. This creates motivation toward delinquency, because juveniles' exclusion from the labour market means they cannot finance their leisure and social activities. If their parents are unable or unwilling to finance their social life to the required level, juveniles must seek out other sources of funding. Adolescent theft then occurs because of a conflict between the desire to participate in activities valued by peer culture and the lack of legitimate sources of funding to finance these activities (Greenberg, 1993).

Crimes of the Powerful

Whereas researchers who focus on the Marxian notion of "surplus population" are interested in the relationship between crime and those who are *outside* the sphere of production, Marxist research on corporate crime focuses on the socially harmful conduct of those who are *inside* the sphere of production in capitalist economies. Box 11.3 explores one instance of socially harmful conduct from a Marxist perspective by examining the tainted dog and cat food produced by Menu Foods Income Fund, a pet food manufacturing facility headquartered in southern Ontario. Canadian Marxist scholars argue that the study of corporate crime is important because the losses incurred as a result of corporate malfeasance—whether it is the total dollar amount, or the number of deaths, injuries, and illnesses—are far in excess of the losses incurred as a result of street crime (McMullan, 1992; Snider, 1993). In an early Marxist analysis of illegal activity of US corporations, Pearce (1976) demonstrated that the dollar amount of corporate crime was much greater than the aggregate dollar amount of conventional crime. Similarly, both Snider (1993) and McMullan (1992) drew upon statistical evidence to argue that the total number of workers who died each year from both work-related accidents and occupationally induced diseases was far in excess of death rate statistics for homicide and manslaughter.

This branch of Marxist criminology attempts to situate law, the state, corporate crime, and social harm within the logic of the mode of production under capitalism. Marxist theorists argue that the structure of capitalist economies and the imperative of profit maximization create strong motivation for corporations to engage in criminal activities or other socially harmful behaviours (Henry, 1986; Snider, 1993). Accordingly, Marxist studies attempt to document both the nature and extent of corporate crime, and to analyze the relationship of corporate criminality to the capitalist mode of production (Goff and Reasons, 1978; Glasbeek, 1989). Marxist criminologists are also interested in examining the contradictory role of the state in capitalist economies. That is, the state must create laws and regulate the criminal activities of corporations, but it must also protect the overall interests of the capitalist economy by reproducing the conditions necessary for capitalism to continue (Sargent, 1991; McMullan, 1992; Snider, 1993; Gordon and Coneybeer, 1999).

Structural Marxism criminology has been criticized for its tautological character. This means that critics feel that it presents a circular argument. The theory begins with the assumption of class exploitation under capitalism in order to demonstrate that crime, in turn, is caused by capitalist class exploitation. Structural Marxism has also been critiqued for emphasizing structure at the expense of human agency, that is, at the expense of human action and ability to shape and direct the social world. A further critique has been that the exclusive focus on class relations has precluded other considerations from entering into analysis, such as gender oppression and race oppression. Socialist feminism represents one attempt to incorporate Marxist analysis into a framework that considers the relationship between class exploitation and gender oppression in capitalist societies.

FOCUS

Box 11.3

IS IT A CORPORATE CRIME? THE MENU FOODS PET FOOD RECALL

On March 16, 2007, Menu Foods, a pet food manufacturer headquartered in Mississauga, Ontario, announced a massive recall of 60 million cans and pouches of tainted dog and cat food. Something in its pet food—later identified as wheat flour contaminated with melamine and cyanuric acid—was causing acute kidney failure in dogs and cats. By May 3, 2007, the US Food and Drug Administration (FDA) had received unconfirmed reports of 4,150 cat and dog deaths due to the consumption of tainted food (*USA Today*, May 10, 2007).

The scope of the Menu Foods recall was unprecedented. By May 22, Menu Foods had issued eight separate recall notifications involving 67 brands of cat food and 64 brands of dog food, each sold in multiple varieties, sizes, and packaging formats—over 5,300 products in total (Nestle, 2008). Brands identified in the recall ran the gamut from premium pet foods such as Hill's Prescription Diet, Iams, Eukanuba, and Science Diet, to discount labels such as Walmart's Ol' Roy, Costco/Kirkland Signature dog food, and Price Chopper cat food.

The news for consumers, however, went from bad to worse. The events that followed in the wake of the Menu Foods recall revealed not only how easily melamine contamination could enter the pet food supply, but also how the global sourcing of food ingredients has introduced dangerous vulnerabilities into our human food supply systems. Perhaps two of the most unsettling findings that arose from the pet food recalls were the ubiquity of the global sourcing of pet and human food ingredients and the magnitude of the outsourcing of production of branded pet food to contract manufacturers.

The Menu Foods recall revealed a little-known fact about pet food production—namely, that many pet food companies, including the most trusted premium brands, do not make their own pet food but rather "outsource" this function to third party contractors, known as "co-packers." For example, in 2003 Menu Foods signed a five-year exclusive contract with The Iams Company (purchased by Procter & Gamble in 1999 for $2.3 billion) to manufacture all Iams and Eukanuba canned and pouch pet food in the United States and Canada (2004 Menu Foods Annual Report). At the time of the recall, Menu Foods was the largest co-packer of "wet" pet food—dog and cat food in cans and pouches—in North America (Nestle, 2008).

Pet owners may have been surprised to discover that well over 100 different brands of dog and cat food were made by just one company. A Marxist analysis would point to the structure of capitalist economies and the ongoing pressure on companies to extract ever-increasing amounts of surplus value in the form of profits. Under this economic model, it makes good financial sense for pet food companies such as Iams, Hill's, Purina, and Nutro to seek lower costs of production—and hence greater profits—by outsourcing their pet food requirements to third-party contractors such as Menu Foods. The manufacture of wet pet food is a complicated process, after all, and requires significant investment in plant and machinery. By outsourcing production, pet food companies are able to rationalize their asset base and reduce expenses—for example, by selling off excess manufacturing capacity and eliminating the associated labour costs.

In turn, a giant co-packer like Menu Foods is able to offer significant economies of scale to its pet food clients. More efficiencies can be exploited by a giant contract manufacturer producing 120 brands of pet food than by many individual manufacturing facilities each producing one or a few brands of dog or cat food. One such efficiency Menu Foods ostensibly could offer its clients was its bulk purchasing power and corresponding ability to purchase raw ingredients in the global marketplace for much lower cost than any single pet food company could do on its own. While the extensive global sourcing of lowest-cost raw ingredients is an industry norm for both pet and human food producers (Roth et al., 2008), the Menu Foods recall has helped to demonstrate the risks inherent in the globalization of animal and human food supply chains.

At the centre of the recall was Menu Foods' fateful decision in December 2006 to switch its wheat gluten supplier to Las Vegas importer ChemNutra, which in turn sourced the wheat gluten from an obscure Chinese manufacturer, Xuzhou Anying Biologic Technology Development Co. At the time, wheat gluten from China sold for 20 cents less per pound than that produced by US manufacturers (*Maclean's*, April 30, 2007). Wheat gluten—used in pet food as a protein source and binding agent—is a derivative of wheat flour. FDA investigators were eventually able to determine that the product sold as wheat gluten by Xuzhou Anying was ordinary wheat flour intentionally adulterated with the nitrogen-rich industrial chemicals melamine and cyanuric acid (Kuehn, 2009, 473). Because nitrogen content has long been used as a surrogate for testing the amount of protein in food, the addition of melamine and cyanuric acid allowed unscrupulous suppliers to fraudulently sell the cheaper wheat flour (10 percent protein) as the more expensive wheat gluten (75 percent protein).

As disturbing as it was to discover how a toxic brew of melamine and cyanuric acid could so easily compromise the pet food supply, by the middle of May 2007 a series of announcements revealed surprising vulnerabilities in our human food supply chain. According to the FDA, between 2.7 and 3 million chickens were fed "salvaged" pet food—containing the melamine-adulterated wheat flour—and subsequently sold to consumers. In addition, some 6,000 hogs were fed the contaminated pet food—with the meat from 345 of the hogs entering the human food supply before the remaining hogs could be quarantined (*Washington Post*, May 2, 2007). On May 8, 2007, the FDA announced that the melamine/cyanuric acid contaminated wheat flour had also been purchased by a Canadian manufacturer of fish pellets and subsequently distributed to at least 60 fish farms in Canada and 200 fish farms in the United States (*Washington Post*, May 9, 2007).

It was soon to become tragically clear that melamine adulteration was not limited to pet food or feed for farm animals destined for human consumption. In September 2008, more than 294,000 infants and young children in China were sickened with kidney and urinary tract problems after consuming melamine-contaminated infant formula. By the end of November, the Chinese Ministry of Health reported more than 50,000 hospitalizations and six infant deaths as a result of the consumption of tainted infant formula (Ingelfinger, 2008). Reported symptoms included acute renal failure, kidney and bladder stones, urinary tract infections, and other renal problems (Gossner et al., 2009; Sharma and Paradkar, 2010).

By the end of 2008, the hazards of our increasingly globalized food supply became apparent when an avalanche of food products imported from China were found to contain melamine. The long list of products included yogurts, frozen desserts, cereal products, confectionaries, cakes, biscuits, and protein powders. A variety of nondairy products originating in China were also found to contain melamine—including ammonium bicarbonate,

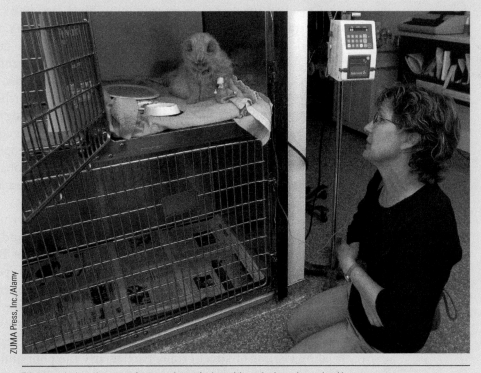

ZUMA Press, Inc./Alamy

This cat required veterinary care after consuming pet food containing melamine and cyanuric acid.

(continued)

powdered eggs, fresh eggs, and nondairy creamer. In total, 47 countries, including Canada, received melamine-contaminated products (Gossner et al., 2009).

A Marxist criminologist might argue that at the same time the benefits of global food production accrue to multinationals, the risks of low-cost global sourcing of products and ingredients are offloaded to individual consumers. This unfair apportioning of surplus and risk is the crux of the Marxist critique of capitalism—that is, capitalism is inherently exploitative unless it is harnessed by the weight of government regulation and a corresponding willingness to detect and prosecute offenders. Currently, there is a lack of scientific data on the long-term health effects of melamine toxicity in humans, making prediction difficult for the health problems that might arise in the future (Ingelfinger, 2008; Sharma and Paradkar, 2010). Preliminary results from animal studies are not encouraging,

however, with carcinogenic effects reported after high exposure to melamine (Gossner et al., 2009; Puschner et al., 2011).

Is melamine adulteration a corporate crime? Marxist theorist Michalowski (1985, 314) defines crimes of capital as "socially injurious acts that arise from the ownership or management of capital or from occupancy of positions of trust in institutions designed to facilitate the accumulation of capital." There were certainly "sins of commission" committed by Chinese manufacturers, who intentionally added melamine and cyanuric acid to pet and human food ingredients to fraudulently boost the apparent protein content. Were there also "sins of omission" committed by contract manufacturers such as Menu Foods and other human food purveyors? Did their collective lack of oversight in the global pursuit of low-cost ingredients—thereby creating the economic vacuum quickly filled by unscrupulous suppliers—constitute criminal negligence? What do you think?

Left Realism

The final conflict perspective we will examine is left realism, which first emerged in Britain in the late 1970s and early 1980s (Young, 1979; Matthews and Young, 1992) and was subsequently taken up as an area of criminological inquiry by Canadian scholars (DeKeseredy, 1991; MacLean, 1991). In Britain, "left realism" was initially developed by Jock Young, John Lea, and Roger Matthews, who advanced a strong critique against what they described as "left idealism." Young (1979) coined the term left idealism to encompass both instrumentalist and structuralist Marxist accounts of the state, law, and crime. Left realists also criticize what they describe as conventional or orthodox criminology, and argue that both Marxist and conventional criminology are superficial accounts of crime. Specifically, left realists maintain that for conventional criminology, crime is "simply antisocial behaviour involving people who lack values," while for Marxist criminology, crime is "proto-revolutionary activity, primitive and individualistic, but praiseworthy all the same" (Lea and Young, 1984, 96).

Left realists emphasize the need to examine the "square of crime," that is, the relationship between the offender, the victim, the police, and the public (Matthews and Young, 1992; Young and Matthews, 1992). In Britain, left realism emerged in response to the perceived failure of other types of criminology, including Marxist criminology, to pay attention to the serious harm generated by street crime, also described as "working-class crime." Left realists such as Young, Lea, and Matthews have argued that Marxist critiques of capitalist society have not paid sufficient attention to the real suffering experienced by victims of street crime, particularly the poor and disadvantaged, who are typically the main victims of street crime. Street crime refers to some form of injury committed directly by one or more specific individuals against the body or property of the victim, such as murder, rape, robbery, theft, vandalism, and burglary. Left realists argue that the victims of most crimes tend to be those from the most vulnerable segments of the community, and that crime is disproportionately distributed among the working class, women, and racial minorities. In addition, the majority of working class crime is intra-class; that is, both the offender and the victim tend to be from the same socio-economic stratum (Lea and Young, 1984; Lowman and MacLean, 1992).

The starting point for left realists is the observation that *crime really is a problem* for the working class and other marginalized groups in the community and that working-class crime must therefore be "taken seriously" (Lea and Young, 1986). Taking crime seriously, for left realists, means developing a working-class criminology that both examines and offers practical solutions to the street crime that marginalized people experience. The strategy employed to examine the problem of crime for the working class is the victimization survey (see Chapter 4). One of the first victimization studies, the Islington Crime Survey (ICS), was conducted in inner-city London in 1985. Employing self-report data, these types of surveys attempt to measure public attitudes, perceptions, and beliefs about the extent and nature of street crime in the community and the effectiveness of police in dealing with it (Jones, MacLean, and Young, 1986). Left realists argue for concrete crime control programs, with the objective of offering nonrepressive crime control policies (Lea and Young, 1986; MacLean, 1991). Crime control policies that have been endorsed by left realists include alternatives to prisons (community service, victim restitution, weekend prison sentences for working offenders); pre-emptive deterrence (encouraging citizens' groups to cooperate with the police); transforming the police force into a police service accountable to the public; and "harnessing the energies of the marginalized" to create a "politics of crime control" (Lea and Young, 1986, 360–63; Young, 1992, 41–42).

Left realism has made some valuable contributions to the criminology literature, including sensitizing us to the amount and kinds of street crime and domestic violence experienced by the most marginalized and vulnerable members of society. In turn, left realism has been subject to a number of critiques. For example, critics have argued that the left realist position is ahistorical; that is, left realism fails to take into consideration the political, economic, and cultural history of the society in which crime occurs. Can the square of crime (the relationship between victims, offenders, police, and the public) really be understood by analyzing responses to local victimization surveys undertaken at a particular point in time and space? O'Reilly-Fleming (1996, 10) suggests that the left realism's advocacy for greater crime control may ultimately have the effect of "widening the net of social control" and thus amount to little more than increasing state powers over the marginalized and disenfranchised groups under study. Finally, Mugford and O'Malley (1991, 23) argue that left realists make use of commonsense notions (crime really is a problem) but neglect to transform these common sense notions into a defensible theoretical account.

TABLE 11.1   **Conflict Theorists**

Theory	Theorists	Key Elements
Cultural conflict	Sellin	Crime occurs when individuals acting on the conduct norms of their own group are in violation of the conduct norms the dominant group has enacted into law.
Group conflict	Vold, Quinney	Interest groups (Vold) or social groupings (Quinney) attempt to protect their own interests by influencing the creation and enforcement of the criminal law.
Instrumental Marxism	Quinney	The state and the legal system are instruments that can be directly manipulated by the capitalist class. The capitalist class can thus directly influence law and law formation.
Structural Marxism	Althusser, Poulantzas	The relative autonomy of the state functions to preserve the long-term interests of the capitalist system. This helps explain why many laws are enacted that do not represent the immediate interests of the capitalist class.
Left realism	Young, MacLean, DeKeseredy	Argues that crime really is a problem for the working class and must be taken seriously. Most working-class crime is intra-class. Major methodological tool is the victimization survey. Argues for a concrete crime control program; endorses crime control policies which are not repressive.

QUESTIONS FOR CRITICAL THINKING

1. How does structural Marxism address the critiques of instrumental Marxism? Describe what is meant by "relative autonomy."
2. In discussing the notion of the "rule of law" and "equality of all before the law," Marxist theorists sometimes make use of the following quote by social critic Anatole France (1894): "The law in its majestic impartiality forbids both the rich and poor alike to sleep under bridges, to beg in the streets or to steal bread." What contradiction is France pointing out? How might this quotation apply to the concept of law and ideology in Marxist thought?
3. Left realists have argued for a concrete crime control program, with the objective of designing crime control policies that are not repressive. Is it possible to engage with the criminal justice system in the area of criminal law reform in a way that is not repressive for the groups that left realists study?

■ Summary

- Conflict theory views societies as more divided by conflict than they are integrated by consensus (see Box 11.1).
- According to Sellin's cultural conflict theory, crime can be viewed as an expression of cultural conflict when individuals who act based on the conduct norms of their own group are in violation of the conduct norms that the dominant group has enacted into law.
- According to Vold's group conflict theory, crime occurs as a result of conflict between diverse interest groups. Vold makes use of group conflict theory to

explain two general classes of group conflict that can result in criminal behaviour: first, crime that arises as a result of minority group behaviour, and second, crime that results from direct contact between groups struggling for the control of power in the political and cultural organization of society.

■ Richard Quinney's group conflict theory explains criminality as arising from conflict between "segments" of society, which he defines as types of social groupings. The more powerful segments or social groups in society are able to secure and to protect their own interests by influencing the formulation, enforcement, and administration of criminal law. Quinney places a greater emphasis than either Sellin or Vold on the unequal distribution of power in society.

■ Instrumental Marxists view the state and the legal system as instruments that can be directly manipulated by the capitalist class. Instrumental Marxists thus maintain that laws are created and enforced in the interests of the ruling or capitalist class.

■ Structural Marxists dispute the instrumentalist view that the state is the direct servant of the ruling or capitalist class and argue that the state and its institutions have a certain degree of independence from specific elites in the capitalist class. Structural Marxists point to the relative autonomy of the state to help explain why many laws are enacted that do not represent the immediate interests of the capitalist class.

■ Left realists emphasize that crime really is a problem for the working class and other marginalized groups in the community, and that working-class crime must be taken seriously. Left realists make use of victimization surveys to examine the problem of crime for the working class, with the objective of offering crime control policies that are not repressive.

NET WORK

Go to the website of the Canadian Encyclopedia at www.thecanadianencyclopedia.com. You can access the articles "Winnipeg General Strike," "Working-Class History," and "Nine-Hour Movement" by entering the name of the article in the search box at the top of the page.

1. As the link on "working class history" points out, "the consolidation of Canadian capitalism in the early 20th century accelerated the growth of the working class." What were some of the issues that the labour unions of the time were concerned about? What argument would structural Marxists make about the Industrial Disputes Investigation Act (1907)?

2. What was the nine-hour movement? Why was this movement considered unsuccessful? What would an instrumental Marxist argument say about the nine-hour movement?

3. When was the Winnipeg General Strike and why is it considered a pivotal event in Canadian history? What was the Citizens' Committee of One Thousand and how did it differ from the Central Strike Committee? What would an instrumental Marxist argument point out about the ensuing events?

12 Contemporary Critical Criminology

Bryan Hogeveen
UNIVERSITY OF ALBERTA

Andrew Woolford
UNIVERSITY OF MANITOBA

The downtrodden, the marginalized, and the impoverished make up the majority of individuals who are arrested by the police; they also represent the greatest number of inmates in our jails and take up the bulk of spaces in the court docket. It seems that we inhabit an unjust world made up of enormous concentrations of wealth and power on one hand and masses of powerless people on the other. This situation raises many questions: Is this the best Canadians can hope for? If so, does this indicate a diminishment of political dreams and the loss of hope for social justice? If it is not, how do we move to a more just state? As you read this chapter, keep in mind the *face* of suffering—whether it be that of the homeless person Canadians hurry by on their way to enjoying a $4 Starbuck's coffee or that of a news story about a starving East African child so easily flipped past on a 60-inch plasma screen television—and ask what you are willing to give up to ameliorate social, economic, and political suffering.

These are the dilemmas that critical criminology forces us to face. As citizens fully socialized into the social order, we rarely critically engage with our world but rather take it for granted. Inspired by promises of "freedom" and "justice," critical criminology draws attention to hidden and overlooked injustices scattered throughout *our* world. Critical criminology attempts to highlight inequalities, discrimination, and suffering and to relate these to the discipline of criminology. Social problems abound but are easily dismissed as someone else's responsibility. Critical criminology attends to the processes through which the social world restricts human freedom and choice. It attempts to assemble and create more "just" worlds with less or no misery: "the possibility daily withheld, overlooked or unbelieved" (Bauman, 2000).

Learning Objectives

After reading this chapter, you should be able to

- Explain what it means to be "critical" in critical criminology.
- Identify the origins of critical criminology in Canada in the New Criminology and the efforts of the Human Justice Collective.
- Understand Michel Foucault's approach to the concept of power and its importance to critical criminology.
- Describe how risk and actuarialism are prevalent in contemporary criminal justice practices and how this relates to the notion of the "risk society."

■ Discuss cultural criminology and its contribution to critical criminology.

■ Explain Pierre Bourdieu's "field theory" and its application to crime in the work of Loïc Wacquant.

■ Define Giorgio Agamben's concept of the "state of exception" and explain its relationship to sovereignty.

■ Describe Jacques Derrida's notion of "deconstruction" and how it is used in critical criminology.

What Is Critical about Critical Criminology?

Contemporary *critical* criminology promises to offer something critical. But what does this mean? To be certain, everyone is critical—at least to a certain extent. We cast judgment on movies (*"Pirates of the Caribbean* was the greatest movie of all time!"), clothing (both our own and, especially, that which belongs to others), and music ("Miley Cyrus does not sing particularly well"). Is this the pursuit in which critical scholars are engaged? Certainly not. However, defining exactly what meets and what fails to meet the "critical" bar is far more difficult than it might seem. If everyone is critical and capable of critique, what sets critical criminology apart?

Some schools of criminology have adopted an administrative approach to the question of crime and have produced policy-oriented knowledge directed toward regulating disruptions and disorders (Young, 1998). The products of this mainstream criminology/criminal justice (programs such as zero tolerance and broken-windows policing) appeal to politicians, who promise an eager electorate that they will be "tough on crime and the causes of crime." Such scholarship is critical to the extent that it challenges existing criminal justice orthodoxy by suggesting that we focus on minimizing criminal opportunities rather than explaining criminal motivations. However, governments and criminal justice organizations can safely adopt this brand of "critical scholarship" within their existing infrastructure without fear that these suggestions and programs will significantly change existing mandates or practices. Government agencies are now promoting and, in some cases, soliciting this type of administrative scrutiny of policy and programming, viewing it as a path toward more efficient governance and control.

By contrast, the promise implied by "critical criminology" ensures a type of critique that prefers "to take the system to task rather than tinker with its parts" (Ratner, 1971, n.p.). Hogeveen and Woolford (2006) maintain that critique should not fall into the trap of conceiving of programs that work well within the existing criminal justice system; instead, critical criminologists should extend critique and thought beyond these limits. Indeed, criminal justice institutions that receive critical criminological scholarship favourably would invite their own destruction (Pavlich, 2005). Critical criminologists, then, practise a transformative brand of critique that confronts inequalities and social suffering with promises of more just outcomes.

So "critical" in critical criminology implies transformation through promises of justice. But what does it mean to be "critical"? That is, if critical criminology is transformative, does this imply that transformation and critique are identical? No. Critique is a means to a transformative (just) end. Thus, while we now know that the goal of critical criminology is justice, we are yet unaware of what "critical" means. When we attempt to understand a *thing*, etymology (the origins of words) is often a productive starting point. George Pavlich (2000, 25), notes that "criticism … crisis and critique relate to the Greek word *Krinein* which is associated with images of judgment (judge, judging), but also with deciding, separating out, discerning, selecting, differentiating, and so on." Interestingly, early medical officials closely associated notions of critique with *Krises*, which involved the art of diagnosing crisis stages in the development of an illness. Traces of this image have survived in common medical diagnoses of patients said to be in critical condition (Pavlich, 2000).

Over many years the broad meaning of the word *critical* has been reduced to such a degree that it is now almost exclusively associated with the act of judging. Take the television program *American Idol* as an example of how Western understandings of *critical* and *critique* have become whittled down to judgment. The program masquerades as a singing competition that features three "experts" who have been tasked with cutting down the hundreds of thousands of applicants to a select few while providing feedback on individual performances. In many ways, Simon Cowell, the curmudgeon among the three judges in the earlier seasons of the show, embodied the modern vision of critique as judgment. His comments have included: "That's atrocious; that's simply not good enough," and "If your lifeguard duties were as good as your singing, a lot of people would be drowning."

Judgmental critique derives its critical ammunition from the veracity of the criterion (or critical standard). Continuing with the *American Idol* example, Cowell held the contestants up to a set of normative criteria for what counts as great singing. It is the *criterion* that allowed him to render judgment ("That was atrocious"). Mainstream criminologists engage in a similar critical enterprise. For instance, many criminologists employ criteria such as recidivism rates as the standard against which to assess programmatic and legislative success or failure. Such judgmental criteria can then be employed to evaluate policing, correctional, and court practices. However, as you learned in Chapter 4, recidivism rates (the criteria) are not as robust and self-evident as once believed. Policing practices and a host of administrative conditions, including how long following their release offenders are tracked, are apt to artificially increase or reduce the criteria—the very foundations of much criminological judgment.

Critique typically implies that we are judging some *thing* against a normative standard held out as the epitome or the ultimate. Thus, when we claimed that Miley Cyrus does not sing particularly well, how did we render this assessment? We arrived at this judgment using Andrea Bocelli as our normative frame. Clearly, we must conclude—even if we prefer pop music to the operatic version—that the latter can sing better than the former. This process and strategy fixes the critic as an expert judge who, because of a certain expertise (in music, in crime, etc.), is "deemed capable of authoritatively judging the true from the false, innocent from guilty, good from bad, progressive from regressive, and so on" (Pavlich, 2000, 74). Critique, as it is currently practised in criminology and elsewhere, is typically judgmental and reactive.

Forms of critique that seek to challenge the criminal justice status quo are not always appreciated. However, Pavlich (2000) claims that there was a time when critical genres in criminology had considerable influence among politicians and policy-makers, especially after the publication and subsequent dissemination of Taylor, Walton, and Young's (1973) highly touted *The New Criminology*. Disenchanted with administrative brands of social science, administrators for a time looked to more radical brands of criminology for inspiration. In the spirit of 1960s radicalism, insight derived from critical questioning of the status quo was evident in governmental discourse and practice. Pleas to abolish prisons, insights into the crime-producing tendencies of the modern criminal justice process, and prisoners' rights discourses were prominent (van Swaaningen, 1997). But the heyday of radical criminology was quite brief. Today, administrative and liberal strains figure most prominently at criminological conferences and in scholarly journals.

The reason why "critical voices beyond the language of pragmatic technocracy are decidedly muted," especially when compared to critical debates from less than three decades ago, is that critics have "failed to address that which distinguishes their radical precepts from proponents of administrative criminology: critique" (Pavlich, 1999, 70). In recent years, drawing on the insights of philosophers such as Michel Foucault, Pierre Bourdieu, Jacques Derrida, and Giorgio Agamben (among others), critical criminologists have called for an approach that goes beyond judgment. Instead of employing one or another yardstick from which to judge the success and failure of criminal justice policies, these scholars employ an art of critique that involves destabilizing seemingly well-anchored relations in an effort to form new patterns of being that do not pander to established social logics or rely on reactive judgments (Hogeveen and Woolford, 2006). A nonjudgmental critical criminology would not render judgments about existing policy, programs, institutions, or societal structures. Rather, it would suggest "other" (just) ways of being in the world. "It would summon them, drag them from their sleep. Perhaps it would invert them sometimes—all the better" (Foucault, 1997).

Critical criminological critique attempts to move beyond complicity in government intrusion into the lives of the least powerful. It does not seek ways to better manage the poor and dangerous classes. Rather, it promises justice to those who are marginalized and discriminated against. Not justice that seeks to punish, however; instead, it promises justice through emancipation. How willing are you to address suffering in your social world?

As we hope you will learn from the rest of this chapter, following the notion of criticism set out in this section, the critical criminologist is not "critical" because he or she is bad-tempered or unconstructive; rather, the negativity of criticism is intended to open your mind to new ways of thinking about and being in the world.

QUESTIONS FOR CRITICAL THINKING

1. Based on what you already know about the criminal justice system, what are you critical of within this system?

2. What purpose is served by being critical? Is there any benefit that comes through criticism?

3. What does it mean to critique the criminal justice system (as critical criminology does) as opposed to simply criticizing the way it currently operates?

Critical Criminology in English Canada

Critical criminology in Canada was invigorated in 1973 with the arrival of *The New Criminology* by British criminologists Ian Taylor, Paul Walton, and Jock Young. In this wide-ranging critique of conventional criminology, Taylor, Walton, and Young identified starting points for a "new" criminology and criticized conventional criminology for supporting the political and economic status quo, for ignoring the structural causes of crime, and for focusing instead on biological and psychological factors. Taylor, Walton, and Young (1973, 270) recommended in contrast a "fully social" criminology that …

1. *understands crime within its wider socio-cultural context.* Crime is not merely an event that occurs between individuals; it takes place within broader social-structural and cultural conditions. Along these lines, a ghetto drug dealer is not just an individual seeking easy money—he may also be the product of a deindustrialized inner city that has been bled of all opportunities other than McJobs because capital investment has fled to the suburbs. He may also be immersed in patriarchal cultural conditions that associate masculinity with money, power, and violence, allowing him to obtain respect and credibility through drug dealing. These are just some of the structures that may influence his decision making.

2. *… examines the structural and political-economic dimensions that produce criminal behaviour.* Crime is not the result of "bad," abnormal, or poorly socialized people; rather, it stems from structural conditions that produce unequal opportunities, stigmatized populations, real and relative deprivation, and other concepts that criminologists often credit as motivations for crime. For example, stigma and labelling occur not only at the micro-level when authorities and significant others impose labels on offenders and contribute to their secondary deviance (see Chapter 13), but also as the result of structural conditions that make certain individuals more likely to choose to commit crime, more likely to be caught, more likely to be punished, and therefore more likely to be labelled. This is all part of what Taylor, Walton, and Young (1973, 274) call a "political economy of social reaction."

3. *… probes the relationship between crime and the prevailing mode of production.* Crime occurs within societies defined by specific systems of economic production. What is defined as a crime, and the way crime is punished, often depends on this mode of production. For example, vagrancy was criminalized in Britain during the 17th century in part because cheap labour was required for the factory system (Chambliss, 1969) to feed the profits of the ruling class and sustain the capitalist mode of production.

4. *… questions the role of power and conflict in shaping crime and criminal justice.* Crime is not simply the reflection of a societal consensus; instead, it is

defined by the powerful and punished in a manner that suits their interests. Therefore, criminologists must not simply accept state-defined crime as a given. They must also question its origins and the ways in which power is implicit in its formation and application.

5. ... *engages in a materialist analysis of the development of law in capitalist societies.* Law is not simply a matter of societal consensus but is a function of the material conditions that define our society. Therefore, the law will contain contradictions because it is a reflection of dominant material interests. For example, gambling is illegal in a private club but not in a government-run casino. Other forms of gambling, such as betting on "futures" in the stock market, may be *encouraged* by the government. Similarly, certain drug habits, such as alcohol and coffee, are tolerated if not encouraged. In contrast, others, such as marijuana, may be viewed as unproductive and criminalized.

6. ... *takes a dialectical approach to analyzing how individuals both influence and are influenced by dominant social structures.* The New Criminology was not simply a shift to an objectivist standpoint holding that human action is fully determined by social structures. Instead, human agency and social structures each affect the other, meaning that though human actions are influenced by their cultural and political-economic conditions, humans can also act to change these conditions.

7. This approach inspired several Canadian criminologists to critically assess the liberal foundations of Canadian criminology. For example, R.S. Ratner (1984) argued that Canadian criminologists had not risen to the challenge of the New Criminology and were guilty of ignoring social structures, failing to challenge state definitions of crime, and naively believing that the institutional apparatus of the criminal justice system could be easily adjusted to address systemic inadequacies and injustices.

Critical criminology soon spread to other venues. In 1985, Thomas O'Reilly-Fleming edited *The New Criminologies in Canada;* this was followed in 1986 by a special edition of the journal *Crime and Social Justice* dedicated to Canadian critical criminology (edited by R.S. Ratner) and a conference in Vancouver on the "Administration of Justice" organized by Brian MacLean and Dawn Currie. By the late 1980s, Canadian critical criminologists had banded together to form the Human Justice Collective, a loose network of scholars assembled around their concerns about the narrow focus of mainstream criminology. These scholars desired a criminology that was more sensitive to the criminogenic impacts of capitalism, patriarchy, racism, and other social structures (Dekeseredy and MacLean, 1993). Out of the Human Justice Collective was born the *Journal of Human Justice.* In the first issue of this journal, R.S. Ratner (1989, 6) defined critical criminology as follows:

> Although varied conceptions abound, we are all united around those premises that underscore the central role of power and conflict in shaping "criminal" outcomes, the range of vested interests that influence "crime," the need for a dialectical analysis of crime and social control that integrates materialist and idealist factors, the crucial importance of the state and the equally important need to debunk state definitions of crime, and the necessity of devising a praxis that is not conditional on the imminent collapse of capitalist society.

This unity, however, was to be short-lived: funding challenges, personality conflicts, and scholarly differences made it difficult to sustain the Human Justice Collective and its journal. Initially, it had been intended that the *Journal of Human Justice* would fund itself through members of the collective adopting it as required reading in their courses. However, classroom use diminished, which placed the journal in a difficult financial position. In addition, personality conflicts had erupted within the collective, leading to disputes among members. In 1995, under these conditions, one of the editors, Brian MacLean, transported the journal to the Division of Critical Criminology at the American Society of Criminology. This move allowed for the journal's continued survival but also marked the end of its Canadian identity.

The growing eclecticism of critical criminology has produced a group of scholars who are difficult to unify under a single label. Initially, a key rift developed between two groups defined as "left realists" and "left idealists" (Young, 1979). Left idealists were said to begin their inquiry into crime from abstract premises (e.g., Marxist theory) rather than empirical work. For this reason, they were criticized by realists for minimizing the harm that crime causes to the working class and for romanticizing criminals as a potentially revolutionary force.

In contrast, left realists worked through local surveys of crime and victimization to try to move beyond partial criminological understandings, which typically focused only on one aspect of crime: the offender, the state, the public, or the victim. Their objective was to take the fear of crime among the working classes seriously and to answer and oppose the work of "right realists," who under the Thatcher, Reagan, and Mulroney governments had spread the popularity of punitive sanctions and administrative approaches. However, left realism did not achieve a sustained following among critical criminologists. Some viewed the reform-based agenda of left realism as compromising the critical thrust of critical criminology by participating in and legitimating the discourses of conventional criminal justice (Pavlich, 1999).

The diversity of critical criminology in Canada would later expand with the popularity of neo-Marxist and post-structuralist theories imported from Continental Europe. The perspectives discussed in the rest of this chapter all derive from these origins and represent a shift in critical criminological theorizing away from distinctly political-economic perspectives. Although the premise remains that state-defined law must be challenged rather than replicated through criminological study, a great diversity of methodology and conceptualization now defines the Canadian critical criminological scene, which has also been significantly shaped by the work of several of the feminist scholars discussed in Chapter 6.

Governmentality and Power: Foucault and Criminology

Foucault did not regard himself as a significant contributor to the discipline of criminology. On the rare occasion when he did comment on

Ian M Butterfield (Ireland)/Alamy

Jeremy Bentham developed a design for a circular Panopticon prison in which the actions of inmates would always be visible so they would behave without the need for direct discipline. Foucault used this idea as a metaphor for the way in which order is maintained by our contemporary social institutions.

criminology, he complained that its "garrulous discourse" and "endless repetitions" only served to relieve judges, police officers, and magistrates of their guilt for delivering pain and suffering on the guilty (Foucault, 1980, 47). Despite Foucault's disdain for the discipline, many scholars have applied his work toward understanding crime and its control. His penological treatise on the "birth of the prison"—*Discipline and Punish*—continues to inspire fresh criminological theorizing. More recently, scholars have used his work on **governmentality**.

Foucault was born in Poitiers, France, in 1926, and died in 1984 from complications of HIV/AIDS. A philosopher and historian who wrote about the history of sexuality, prisons, governance, psychiatry, and knowledge systems, he is heralded for his unique work on **power**. Power, for Foucault, is evident only when it is *exercised*. He did not see it as something that states or individuals can hold, accumulate, possess, or monopolize. In other words, can you show us what power looks like? Some claim often that money or wealth *is* power. Foucault would argue otherwise. For Foucault, money becomes power only when it is used or otherwise put into effect.

A further characteristic of the Foucauldian notion of power is that it is not solely negative or repressive. He instead preferred a more *positive* theory of power: not in terms of good or beneficial, but rather as creative. He argues that "we must cease once and for all to describe the effects of power in negative terms: it 'excludes,' it 'represses,' it 'censures,' it 'abstracts,' it 'masks,' it 'conceals.' In fact power produces; it produces reality; it produces domains of object and rituals of truth" (1979, 194). Thus, rather than viewing power in a manner that exaggerates its negative elements, Foucault urged scholars to focus on what is created when power is exercised. What is the outcome when power is employed?

SEARCH FOR:
Foucault Resources

governmentality
The art of governing. It transcends and is considerably broader than the traditional understanding of government as a state-directed activity. Government, then, encompasses a wide array of techniques, within and outside of the state, intended to (re)shape and (re)direct human actions.

power
Power, for Foucault, extends beyond the state. It is not a quantity to hold or possess. It is, rather, relational, such that power is only ever evident in its exercise.

A third characteristic of the Foucauldian understanding of power is the emphasis he placed on **micro-powers** that are disseminated throughout the social world. Almost everywhere we turn, everywhere we go, power operates on our bodies and souls. It seems that power is perpetually influencing our behaviour, often without our awareness. Consider your daily trip to university or college. Assuming that you are driving a vehicle of some sort, think about all the ways your behaviour is controlled while you drive. Traffic lights, signs, painted lines, photo radar, and the presence or absence of police all affect how we go about our drive.

Foucault was convinced that to intimately understand the operation of power, we must shift our focus from the state to the dispersed spaces in which power operates. This is the essence of what Foucault called discipline. **Discipline** operates at the smallest level of detail and attends to the intricacies of human behaviour through the **surveillance** and observation of individual functioning so as to increase the efficiency and usefulness of human actions. When thinking about discipline, it is the everyday and the mundane that are important. Fully understanding power involves examining it at its main point of application: the body. Remember back to when you were learning how to write using a pencil. Recall the teacher standing over you correcting your finger placement. S/he would watch you (surveillance) and correct your mistakes to make certain you used the implement in the most efficient manner possible (positive power). To maximize the utility of our bodies and to allow hierarchal control and correction, this meticulous exercise of power is infinitely multiplied throughout the social world. As such, discipline requires that individuals be organized in space and time. Consider the timetable from public school. It provided a general framework for activity and organized our days. The timetable structured not only our *use* of time but also the *space* we were to occupy at certain points in the day. The bell organized our behaviour. What happened when the bell sounded? Being conditioned to move according to the sounding of the bell, students would get up to leave while the teacher attempted to quell the mass exodus. Thus time, space, and signals coexisted to discipline not only our minds but also our bodies (Minaker and Hogeveen, 2009).

Foucault's analysis of discipline was criticized (a) for abandoning the state in its analysis and (b) for tending (supposedly) to characterize human subjects as "docile" (inactive) bodies rather than active agents (Garland, 1997). Foucault's later work on governmentality addressed many of these concerns (see Box 12.1). For Foucault (1982), governmentality

> must be allowed the very broad meaning which it had in the 16th century. Government did not refer only to political structures or the management of states; rather it designated the way in which the conduct of individuals or states might be directed; the government of children, of souls, of communities, of families, of the sick. (221)

Therefore, the study of governmentality should cast its gaze widely and address such broad questions as "how to govern oneself, how to be governed, how to govern others, by whom the people will accept to be governed, and how to become the best possible governor" (Foucault, 1991, 45). Government(ality) entails "any attempt to shape with some degree of deliberation aspects of our

micro-powers
Small and mundane relations of governance, with an appreciable effect on human behaviour.

discipline
A meticulous manner or method of training. It intends to ensure constant subjection and obedience. It involves hierarchal observation, normalizing judgment, and examinations.

surveillance
The direct or indirect observation of conduct toward producing a desired outcome (i.e., conformity).

FOCUS

Box 12.1

RESTORATIVE JUSTICE AS GOVERNMENTALITY

Restorative justice is a broad term used to describe a range of justice practices designed to involve victims, offenders, and community members in directly resolving the harms caused by crime. For some of its proponents, restorative justice is intended to empower communities and individuals to creatively solve their own problems, to remove justice control from the hands of the state and professionals, and to allow for a justice tailored specifically to the needs of victims, offenders, and community members. All of this is to occur within informal settings such as community centres, with victims, offenders, and their families and friends as well as community members sitting in a circle to discuss what led to the crime and how its harm might be repaired.

In contrast to this representation of restorative justice as a community-led activity separate from the formal practices of the state, George Pavlich (2005) has given two reasons why restorative justice is a form of governmentality. First, because the participants in restorative justice meetings are encouraged to examine and reshape their conduct in relation to their experiences of crime and justice. Offenders are asked to take responsibility for their actions, victims are asked to express how the crime has affected them and to present reasonable demands for repair, and community members are asked to participate in the reintegration of the offender and the healing of the victim. Moreover, it is hoped that participation in restorative justice will transform the way these participants deal with conflict in the future. All of these aspects of restorative justice encourage individuals to accept and internalize restorative values and practices through which they might better govern themselves and their communities, thus freeing the state of this responsibility.

Second, because restorative justice fashions a way of understanding the world (and crime in particular) that makes the pursuit of "restorative" justice appear more rational and understandable to those involved. If restorative justice is to govern our behaviour, it must first shift how we think about crime and criminal justice. It does this by reframing core components of

criminal justice. For Pavlich, this involves providing different answers to these questions:

1. What is governed? Unlike formal criminal justice, restorative justice claims to govern "harm" rather than "crime" since it is not the violations of the state's law but rather the harms suffered by individuals and communities that are of primary concern.

2. Who is governed? Those who are to be governed are all of those who have a stake in the crime and its effects—victim, offender, and community members—rather than just the offender.

3. Who governs? Whereas judges and lawyers are the individuals empowered through the practice of criminal justice, restorative justice seeks to give greater agency to victims, offenders and community members.

4. What is appropriate governing? Instead of focusing on the past, restorative governance should be directed toward the future. It is therefore less a question of punishing a wrongdoer and more an issue of creating a dialogue among stakeholders so that they can work out how to avoid repetition of the crime.

For Pavlich, the problem with this restorative justice governmentality is that it does not represent a true alternative to the criminal justice system. Instead, restorative justice is fundamentally dependent on the criminal justice system and criminal law. For example, though restorative justice shifts our attention to the harm suffered by victims and community members, it nonetheless relies on criminal law to define the acts that are to be considered harmful. Thus, it restricts itself from addressing harms that are not codified within criminal codes (such as suffering caused by industrial pollution), as well as structural harms (such as the gender inequalities that result from patriarchal systems of domination).

Source: George Pavlich, *Governing Paradoxes of Restorative Justice* (London: Glasshouse Press, 2005).

behaviour according to particular sets of norms and for a variety of ends" (Dean, 1999, 10).

Critical scholars have used Foucault's writings on governmentality to understand a wide range of state and nonstate domains of governance. They have raised important insights about legal change and the centrality of law in the regulation of populations. They have also argued that critical criminology has been limited "by its emphasis on the state, and state-centred constructions of criminality, and by its failure to come to terms with how social injustices are reproduced through private institutions and modes of expertise that operate on the margins of the state and in the shadow of the law" (Lippert and Williams, 2006). For example, Lippert and Williams have looked to the margins of legal governance to explore how the rise of private security affects our social world. These authors maintain that critical scholarship should focus "less on how the machinery of the state is brought to bear on the production and control of individual subjects and offenders, and more on the myriad technologies of governance and their operation across diverse social fields" such as immigration and the policing of financial disorder (706). Governmentality, then, draws scholarly attention to mechanisms *outside* the traditional state governmental machinery that structure and contour human behaviour. Recent years have witnessed the proliferation of private security firms that police a variety of venues, including the local mall, construction sites, and, as the upsurge in alarm companies continues, private dwellings. By attending to the growth of private security, "the governmentality literature presents a unique opportunity to expand the theoretical range and conceptual reach of critical criminology, and to enhance its capacity to reveal and interrogate forms of injustice and domination crafted on the margins of the state" (714–15).

Actuarialism, Risk, and the Risk Society

Perhaps the greatest impact of Foucault's work on critical criminological studies has been on scholars' ability to understand how offenders' lives are increasingly organized around questions of risk. As we have seen already, Foucault was fundamentally concerned with understanding how individuals were normalized through government and discipline—that is, how they were corrected and brought into line with the needs of the larger society (O'Malley, 1996). In the field of crime control, recent years have witnessed the emergence and proliferation of actuarial or "insurance"-based strategies of governance and control. It seems that Western criminal justice systems have become somewhat preoccupied with managing risks as police, probation, prisons, and halfway houses seek to minimize the likelihood of future offending (Bosworth, 2004). Toward this end, many institutions employ a variety of risk prediction tools, all of them part of "actuarial justice" (Feeley and Simon, 1994).

Foucauldian-inspired theorists distinguish the everyday usage of the term *risk* from how it is construed as an actuarial (or insurance-based) technology. When we as citizens refer to risk, it concerns the dangers and perils connected with an objective and often immediate threat—for instance, of being struck by lightning or having our house burglarized. However, this definition and understanding of risk has to be separated from its usage in actuarial terms, where it indicates neither an "event nor a general kind of event occurring in reality, but a specific mode of treatment of certain events capable of occurring to a group of individuals" (Ewald, 1991). Risk, then, is the calculated probability of an eventuality. Think of the last time you purchased car insurance. The agent likely asked you a series of questions: What is your sex? How old are you?

risk
The calculated probability of an eventuality.

actuarial
Refers to statistical calculations of risk across time and groups.

Where do you live? Where do you work? How far do you travel to work/school? These questions were then entered into a computer, which calculated your premium based on these factors. Agents ask these questions to derive a risk score. That is, by employing aggregated data (including accident reports and police statistics) collected over time and then comparing the aggregate to your indicators, insurance companies ascertain the probability of having to pay a claim on your behalf. If you are young, male, and unemployed, your risk and insurance premium will be considerably higher than that of a married 40-year-old female who lives in the suburbs.

Events (car accidents) and populations (males, females, the elderly) are not inherent risks, but become constituted as "actuarial" risks through analyses and calculations of chance. Risk understood from a Foucauldian perspective, then, is constituted in relation to the aggregation of events over time and regulated through techniques such as higher insurance rates designed to contend with individual risk factors. Simon (1988) maintains that risk-based technologies of governance have become dominant largely because of their efficiency and their ability to intensify the effectiveness of disciplinary technologies (O'Malley, 1996). Probabilistic calculation is particularly evident in the youth correctional field, where the Youth Level of Service/Case Management Inventory (YLS/CMI) is employed. Andrews and Bonta (1998, 245) maintain that this tool is premised on the four principles of risk, needs, responsivity, and professional discretion. First, the *risk* principle reflects the contention that criminal behaviour occurs in predictable patterns. Second, the *needs* principle implies that recidivism will be reduced through select targeting of criminogenic need through appropriate treatment programs. Third, given that many juvenile offenders suffer from attention deficit hyperactivity disorder, fetal alcohol spectrum disorder, or oppositional defiant disorder, responsivity is crucial to any "successful" treatment option and refers to the need for service providers to deliver treatment programs in a manner that is consistent with and appropriate to the offender's ability and learning style. Finally, *professional discretion* "strategically reasserts the importance of retaining professional judgment, provided that it is not used irresponsibly and is systematically monitored" (Hannah-Moffat and Maurutto, 2003, 3).

While at first blush actuarial strategies seem efficient and just, several factors raise questions about such assessments. Hannah-Moffat and Maurutto (2003, 7) have found that correctional officials and practitioners fail to conceptualize "the problems intrinsic to this kind of needs assessment and how a failure to distinguish between risk and need can result in increased surveillance of youth." Although blending of risk and need is a problem, the problems of risk-based governance are particularly troubling when applied to female and nonwhite populations (Minaker and Hogeveen, 2008). Notably, "female offenders are more often deemed higher risk because of their risk to themselves, whereas high-risk male offenders are more likely to pose a risk to others" (Hannah-Moffat and Shaw, 2001). Risk assessment tools typically do not account for gender and cultural variation in offending and recidivism. For example, the tests do not adequately capture histories of physical, mental, or sexual abuse prevalent among female youth. Moreover, risk assessment tools do not adequately address the broader socio-cultural and colonial context of Aboriginal youths (Hannah-Moffat and Shaw, 2001).

These Foucauldian notions of risk and actuarialism are occasionally combined with Beck's concept of the "**risk society**." Beck admits that characterizing the present as the "risk society" may seem odd in light of the daily risks and dangers faced by people in pre-industrial societies—such as plagues, famine, and natural disasters. However, there is a qualitative difference between the looming hazards of our industrial present and those of earlier times. Beck suggests that today's hazards are not forces outside of us; rather, they are internal creations, and their danger originates from our own decision making (1992, 98). Our technological development and scientific rationality have provided us with the tools to construct the means of our own destruction—nuclear power, environmental pollution, climate change, and an assortment of life-threatening chemicals, just to name a few dangers. Moreover, Beck does not suggest that we have necessarily witnessed a quantitative increase in risk; rather, we have come to organize our societies more around the *fact* of risk.

This theoretical perspective comes to bear on critical criminology in at least two ways. First, social problems have increasingly come to be understood as "risks" to be *managed* rather than social "problems" to be *solved*. This shift in thinking is noticeable in criminological approaches that take crime to be inevitable and that prescribe various risk reduction strategies to lessen crime's social costs. Along these lines, individuals are encouraged to become responsible for protecting themselves from opportunistic crimes through the techniques of "situational crime prevention" (O'Malley, 1992)—for example, by installing alarm systems in their homes or steering wheel locking mechanisms in their cars (see Chapter 15). As well, "three strikes" laws (see Chapter 15), which impose long-term prison sentences after a third criminal violation, are justified under a risk management logic as a means for warehousing repeat offenders who are perceived to pose too great a threat to the general public. This said, risk management techniques should not be painted solely as oppressive, since they can be used to establish more fair and efficient criminal justice processes under the current system, such as by providing a calculus for justifying the diversion of less risky offenders toward an alternative sentencing or community bail program, and thus away from the formal justice system. But even with such seemingly benign applications of risk, critical criminologists remain skeptical of the individualizing and responsibilizing tendencies of risk-based approaches to crime.

Second, risk thinking transforms criminal justice practices. Risk management strategies infiltrate judicial, correctional, and law enforcement institutions, tasking criminal justice professionals with the collection of aggregated risk data and with administering risk assessments to their charges. For example, Ericson and Haggerty (1997) note how policing practices have been affected by the demands of the risk society. They cite the case of a modern police officer investigating a traffic accident. Today's officer must gather information that is pertinent not only to the courts and police records but also to the insurance companies, the public health system, provincial vehicle registries, and the automobile industry. Ericson and Haggerty report that under these new demands, a simple traffic accident "took one hour to investigate, and three hours to write about it, to account for it, and to bureaucratically process it" (Ericson and Haggerty, 1997, 24).

risk society
An emerging societal form characterized by the production and increased awareness of human-made "risks," such as nuclear destruction and environmental devastation. More importantly, the risk society is organized around the management of such risks.

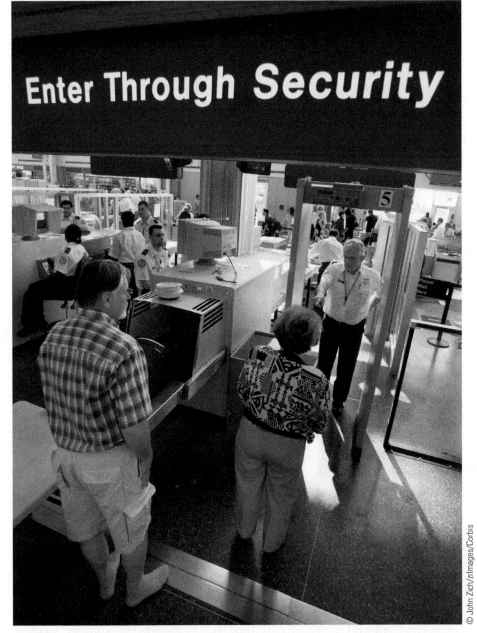

© John Zich/zrImages/Corbis

Airport security screening is one of the ways in which our society is organized around the prevention of risk.

In alerting us to these broader social changes, the "risk society" thesis serves a critical criminological function by demonstrating the effects that broad societal shifts toward increased insecurity have on the ways we think about and react to matters of criminal justice. In this sense, crime and its response are not taken as givens but rather as socially constituted phenomena that can be better understood by locating them in their wider social context. And by identifying this wider social context, we are able to critically assess proposed criminal justice "solutions" through an understanding of their historical contingency.

> ## QUESTIONS FOR CRITICAL THINKING
>
> 1. What does Foucault mean by discipline? Can you think of examples of how discipline operates upon you in your day-to-day life?
> 2. In what sense does Foucault's concept of governmentality suggest a less passive or "docile" form of power than discipline?
> 3. Why have we become so concerned about risk? In what ways has risk come to govern crime control?

Cultural Criminology

SEARCH FOR:
Cultural Criminology

The social reaction perspective (see Chapter 13) brings attention to crime as a process of social interaction involving victim, offender, bystanders, and criminal justice agencies in the construction of deviant meanings and identities. This insight has been absorbed and extended in the work of cultural criminologists, who focus on crime as a cultural rather than a legal construct. These scholars turn their attention away from crime as a "real" phenomenon reflected in police data, victimization surveys, and other quantitative measures, focusing instead on "the debris of everyday life" (Morrison, 2007, 254) through an aesthetic and ethnographic engagement with their subject matter. In this manner, cultural criminologists do not accept crime simply as state-defined illegality; instead, they view it as a culturally negotiated phenomenon through which people create social meaning.

Hayward and Young (2004) identify five "motifs" of cultural criminology. First, cultural criminologists alert us to the importance of "adrenaline" in the commission of crime. In contrast to rational choice theorists, who portray offenders as economic actors engaged in cost–benefit analyses of whether or not to break the law, cultural criminologists acknowledge that crime is *felt*. In other words, crime may be motivated by feelings of anger, insecurity, humiliation, or excitement. Moreover, the act of crime may produce a sensual and visceral rush that incites both panic and pleasure (Katz, 1988; Ferrell, 1998). Thus, though a potential car thief may make a *rational* choice not to steal your car because she or he is afraid it might be a "bait car," the *attraction* of car theft may stem more from the desire to alleviate boredom through risk taking.

Second, cultural criminologists draw our attention to the "soft city" (Raban, 1974). This refers to the "underlife" of the city that hides beneath structured and rationally planned urban space. Whereas urban planning attempts to direct our everyday lives through policing strategies, the design of defensive urban space, and other modalities of social control, the "soft city" bubbles up as a realm of creativity and street-level possibility. While it may seem that we are free to go and do as we please in space, careful design contours our actions in very definite directions. Consider for example the layout of an IKEA store. The interior space has been mapped so that customers are forced to wander through all the showrooms before arriving at what they want to purchase. This is no accident. IKEA designers want us to see all their products on display, hoping this will make us want to purchase more than we intended. The "soft city," by contrast, subverts planners' intentions. It is the space used, for example, by Critical Mass to launch illegal bike rallies to confront our automobile culture and to illustrate how the daily commute is part of the depersonalized and routinized destruction of human sociability (Ferrell, 2004). As Ferrell (2004, 292) notes, "Critical Mass participants define their exuberantly collective bicycle rides not as traditional political protests, but as do-it-yourself celebrations enlivened by music, decoration and play." By resisting the boredom and repetition of the normal "protest march," Critical Mass seeks to reclaim the "soft city" of urban space through theatrical rallies.

Third, cultural criminologists are interested in acts of "transgression" and rule breaking that challenge the justness of laws. In this vein, a cultural criminologist might understand the spectacle of pro-cannabis protesters sparking joints on Parliament Hill not simply as individuals seizing the opportunity for public criminality, but also as a collective act designed to challenge the criminalization of one leisure pursuit while others (e.g., alcohol, tobacco) go uncontested. Similarly, the Critical Mass cycle rallies expose the over-regulated nature of modern urban life and the ways in which this over-regulation denies freedom of movement (as well as dedicated traffic lanes) to slower and less expensive vehicles.

Fourth, cultural criminologists propose a methodology founded on an **attentive gaze**. This requires that researchers do more than sit back in their offices and peruse quantified crime data. They must engage in "an ethnography immersed in culture and interested in lifestyle(s), the symbolic, the aesthetic, and the visual" (Hayward and Young, 2004, 268). This requires that they enter into the world where crime occurs and where it is represented to better comprehend the experiential and interpretive dimensions of crime. For example, O'Neill (2004) employs a methodology she refers to as "ethno-mimesis" that draws on media such as photography, film, performance, theatre, and text to illustrate the complexity of the emotional lives of individuals. In one such study, O'Neill and Campbell encouraged sex workers to use art and writing to represent their "issues, concerns, experiences, and ideas for change" (O'Neill, 2004, 226). The final result was not only a written report but also an art exhibit and information pamphlet, which collectively combined to allow community members to express, reflect on, and relate to pressing local issues in a variety of creative ways.

Finally, the knowledge produced by cultural criminology is argued to be **dangerous knowledge** because its purpose is to question all knowledge, including the status of criminology as an objective science. This might be achieved by drawing on unusual sources of knowledge. For instance, in his exploration of the crime of genocide, Morrison (2007) examines photographs snapped by Nazi police battalions, visits Belgian and Bangladeshi museums, and offers a reading of Joseph Conrad's novel *Heart of Darkness*. He uses these diverse sources to criticize criminology for its dependence on crimes defined and data generated by the state, and thereby its tendency to overlook crimes such as genocide that are perpetrated often by or beyond the state. In this sense, cultural criminology is a critical criminological project intended to relentlessly challenge the taken-for-granted assumptions of criminology and popular understandings of crime in order to expose how they are culturally constructed and delimited by a particular world view.

attentive gaze
A methodological requirement that researchers immerse themselves where crime occurs in the everyday world in order to better understand the ways in which crime is experienced and interpreted by individuals.

dangerous knowledge
A form of knowledge that leaves no concept, notion, or idea untouched by criticism. To achieve this relentlessly critical stance, cultural criminologists often turn to diverse sources of information (e.g., novels and street-level observation) as means to reveal alternative perspectives that might shake the foundations of our taken-for-granted assumptions about crime.

"Field Theory" of Criminology

The sociology of Pierre Bourdieu also provides insight into the cultural and economic conditions in which crime and our understanding of crime are produced, although on a much broader scale. The grounding concept of Bourdieu's theoretical work is that of the **field** (DiMaggio, 1979). Bourdieu's notion of the field can be likened to a battlefield or sports field (Bourdieu, 1992). It is a space of conflict and competition wherein competitors, who each possess varying levels of social and economic power, vie for control. But the field is not level, nor is it without pre-existing rules. Rather, participants encounter a field that is tilted to favour the already powerful (they will play downhill) and structured by predetermined rules that all must follow.

It is within a field of social activity, such as art, politics, or law, that a market defined by its own measures of value is established, and it is in accordance with a field that actors seek the "profit of distinction"—in other words, the awards associated with a display of competence (Bourdieu, 1991, 1990a, 1984). An actor's ability to display competence within a particular field depends in part on his or her **habitus**. This is one's "feel for the game"—that is, it refers to a set of "dispositions acquired through experience" (Bourdieu, 1990b, 9) that allow one to react to situations that arise within a particular field without the need to actively plot one's moves. Keeping with our sports analogy, imagine that in a game of hockey the skilled power forward Hogeveen finds a loose puck in a scrum in front of the net. In that instance, he automatically shifts the puck to his backhand and lifts it over the sprawling goalie, Woolford. Here, Hogeveen's dedication to his sport, and his practised experience of it, provide him the embodied knowledge necessary to succeed on the ice without needing to "overthink" his game (whereas Woolford's coach might advise him to work more on his hockey habitus).

The actor's "feel for the game" within the market relations of a specific field will vary, with those endowed with greater quantities of the forms of **capital** valuable within the field (e.g., economic, symbolic, cultural, or linguistic capital) more capable of transmitting an aura of competence (Brubaker, 1985). Thus, within a specific "game" or market situation, actors come pre-equipped with differing amounts of capital, depending on their position(s) in the structural arrangements of society (e.g., level of education, occupation, age), and based on these factors are predisposed toward certain behaviours or practices. The valuational rules of the market ascribe to these practices and behaviours differing levels of profitability within the field, allowing some actors to feel more at home on their appointed terrain. To put this in simpler terms, if you are currently seeking a criminology degree, this may be motivated by your desire to obtain employment in the legal or juridical field (e.g., as a police officer, lawyer, or probation worker). However, success in this field will depend on more than your possession of a criminology degree or your ability to extol Merton's strain theory. You will require possession of the forms of capital most valued within this field of activity. You will acquire some of this capital through your increased knowledge about the field of law, but you might also profit from the symbolic, linguistic, and cultural capital you have obtained through the

field
A basic unit of social activity. The social world is divided into many fields (e.g., the "artistic" field, the "academic" field, or the "economic" field). Each field of activity is defined by its own market through which certain practices or dispositions are valued more than others.

habitus
A set of durable dispositions acquired through experience that allow one to achieve a "feel for the game" within a specific field of activity. These are internalized practices that serve as a "second nature" responsive to the immediate demands of everyday life.

capital
The primary field of activity for state or government actors, as well as those who are funded by the government, and where these actors compete to define and shape government resources and responsibilities.

practice of writing essays, making public presentations, and reading "classic" works of literature and philosophy. These latter forms of capital equip you with an aura of competence that communicates to your future employer that you are a "capable" person (see—essays, presentations, and readings *are* important!). However, it should be noted that due to our inequitable social structures, some people enter university already in possession of a great deal of the capital needed to get a job within the juridical field and therefore are at an advantage. For example, an individual who was raised by a father/lawyer and mother/judge, who habitually thinks of the world in terms of law and adversarial justice, and who models his parents' ways of speaking and carrying themselves, is armed with a habitus that invests them with the capital needed to more easily navigate the legal profession.

In criminological analysis, Bourdieu's field theory has been most influentially used by Wacquant, who has expanded Bourdieu's notion of the "bureaucratic field" to foster better understanding of the space in which state-sponsored crime control and welfare policy are performed and intersect (see Wacquant 2009, 2010).

The bureaucratic field is "a splintered space of forces vying over the definition and distribution of public goods" (Wacquant, 2010, 200). It is thus the primary field of activity for state or government actors, as well as those who are funded by the government, and it is where these actors compete to define and shape government resources and responsibilities. Those who are better positioned in this field may, for example, be able to determine which government outlays ought to be defined as "welfare" (e.g., monetary support for the poor) and which as investments (e.g., tax relief for businesses).

According to Bourdieu (1994, 1998), the bureaucratic field is characterized by two intersecting axes. On the vertical axis, at its top, rests the higher state nobility of the political elite—those governmental actors in powerful ministries such as finance and justice, who are often committed to implementing the interest-driven policies of socially dominant groups. At the bottom of this vertical axis sits the lower state nobility of government agents whose positions require them to deal more directly with the everyday needs of citizens in areas such as health, education, and housing. Across the horizontal axis, the "left hand" and the "right hand" of the state stand in opposition to one another. The left hand refers to government departments and government-sponsored social service agencies that offer social protection and support (e.g., welfare, housing, and employment); the right hand consists of state and state-supported institutions that represent the might or force of the state, such as state departments of finance that possess the power to impose austerity measures on all other areas of government. The various actors (i.e., upper and lower state nobilities) and institutions (i.e., left and right hands) that occupy the bureaucratic field compete with one another for control over public goods and the ability to define the terms and values that will guide state actions. To this extent, the bureaucratic field is often a fractious setting; however, there also are periods when these actors and institutions achieve coherence around a dominant set of ideas and practices, such as those that characterize neoliberalism.

Wacquant's extension of Bourdieu's work on the bureaucratic field comes primarily through his inclusion of police, courts, and prisons as part of the right hand of the state. This move allows him to map how the neoliberal era of increased flexibility, state rollbacks, and deregulation is also characterized by increases in the punitive and disciplinary might of the state. Wacquant locates the simultaneous disappearance of traditional welfare protections and expansion of punitive and surveillant workfare policies on the left hand next to the growing network of prisons designed to warehouse the risky "fractions of postindustrial proletariat" and contend with the fallout of vicious neoliberal economic policies on the right hand (Wacquant, 2010, 210). Together, these processes impose a "double regulation" or "carceral-assistential mesh" that is the peculiar product of the neoliberal state (Wacquant, 2009, xviii), under which the left hand of the state begins to function in a manner eerily similar to the right hand.

It is under these conditions that Wacquant observes a "deadly symbiosis" between the prison and the ghetto (Wacquant, 2001). Whereas the right hand of the state transforms prisons into spaces where the recidivist poor are warehoused rather than reformed, the ghetto becomes a space where the risky poor are contained and disciplined through the government-sponsored services of the state's left hand. Consider, for example, the amount of work involved in being poor. For those welfare recipients deemed capable of work, the attitude of the state is that they should "take a job, any job." And their continued social assistance support is often dependent on them participating in government-funded employment programs, their engagement in weekly job searches, and regular meetings with their income assistance workers. On top of this, these individuals face the challenge of finding child care for children, the search for safe and affordable housing, and access to health care services. In their search for all of these supports, which itself can be a full-time job, the poor find themselves unable to move from certain stigmatized neighbourhoods, while their behaviour is increasingly observed and regulated through a battery of forms, training courses, meetings, and other requirements attached to their ongoing access to government and not-for-profit social service agency assistance.

Wacquant's Bourdieusian approach fits the label of "critical criminology" because it does not simply accept "criminalized" identities as constructed through the criminal law and its application. Instead, it seeks to identify the symbolic, cultural, and economic factors (e.g., the conditions of the bureaucratic field) that empower dominant actors to create and apply criminal categories while simultaneously disempowering subordinate groups from resisting this criminalization because they lack the necessary "capital" to achieve "profit" within various arenas of social action (or "fields").

carceral-assistential mesh
Under neoliberalism, this is a mode of "double regulation" whereby the right (e.g., prisons) and left (e.g., social welfare) jointly function to punish and discipline the poor rather than offering rehabilitation and care.

QUESTIONS FOR CRITICAL THINKING

1. Can you think of examples of how welfare and punishment interact in your city to form a carceral-assistential mesh?
2. Wacquant's approach shifts the focus from "criminals" to the strategies and manoeuvres of the bureaucratic field. Explain why this is in keeping with the notions of "critique" and critical criminology.

Agamben: Sovereignty and the State of Exception

In political theory and public discourse, the West is generally viewed as an asylum of human rights enmeshed within robust democracy (Ek, 2006). But this image has begun to erode in the wake of the "exceptional" and seemingly extreme measures introduced after the 9/11 attacks in New York and Washington on September 11, 2001. What are we to think about the massive numbers of suspected terrorists being detained in Guantánamo Bay without ever being charged with an offence? North American governments maintain that such practices are necessary to protect the public from similar future attacks. In 2013, US whistle blower Edward Snowden released thousands of secret documents he had obtained while working as a contractor for the National Security Agency. Many of these documents revealed programs under which the United States and other countries collected information about their own citizens as well as about friendly countries. Critics have complained that many of these surveillance programs are illegal. In the United States, the government's Privacy and Civil Liberties Oversight Board has concluded that the collection of mass telephone records is a violation of privacy law and that the program has never resulted in any successful terrorism investigations (Ackerman and Roberts, 2014). Snowden's leaked information was one factor that led Canada's Interim Privacy Commissioner to recommend that the federal government tighten privacy regulations and that Community Security Establishment Canada (CSEC) be required to report its activities annually to Parliament in order to improve public oversight of that agency (Office of the Privacy Commissioner of Canada, 2014).

The Snowden leaks seem to have finally awakened some public concern. For more than a decade, citizens rarely protested these intrusions into their private lives. It seems that citizens had become stoic; that is, any measures the government implemented in the name of national security (and, perhaps more important, the prevention of future terrorist attacks) had come to be perceived as appropriate—indeed, they were welcomed. North American governments' actions since 9/11 have typically been carried out in the name of protecting the nation and have been passively accepted by the citizenry.

It seems that anything and everything (including torture?) is now permitted so long as the goal is to protect the state and the public. Such a policy has lethal implications. For example, after four terrorist attacks left 52 dead and many wounded in the heart of London, England, an innocent man (Jean Charles de Menezes) was shot dead by police officers. Police Chief Sir Iain Blair, while disturbed by this tragedy, later admitted that more guiltless Londoners could lose their lives as police scoured the city for the suspected bombers. In effect, the police chief was admitting that a mistake had been made and that it could likely be made again in the future. How are we to make sense of this? Giorgio Agamben, in an extension of Foucault's work, has perhaps done more to assist scholars, activists, and the public in coming to terms with the post-9/11 world than any other academic.

Agamben's work is complex and not easily classifiable. He has been heavily influenced by Foucault, Carl Schmitt, Walter Benjamin, and Saint Paul. He tends to extract the most "useful" conclusions from prominent and influential scholars and assemble them in a meaningful way, so it might be best to read him as an eclectic scholar—that is, one who does not rigidly hold to a single philosophical tradition but instead integrates many ideas, concepts, and styles into his work.

Much of Agamben's work is grounded in his concerns about the modern conditions of sovereignty. He takes his lead from Schmitt, who defines political sovereignty in his now classic work *Political Theology*. For both Schmitt and Agamben, the **sovereign** is the one who holds the power to declare a **state of exception** during which civil liberties (among other precautions) are suspended in the interest of defending the nation. That is, the sovereign is the one whom the juridical order grants the power to proclaim a state of exception. Declarations of this sort are typically issued after natural disasters, during wartime, and, especially, when the state is confronted by civil unrest. According to Schmitt (1985), a state of exception or emergency (as it is sometimes referred to) is declared when the sovereign deems suspension of the existing social order necessary in order that social order be restored. Typically, the state of exception is lifted once stability is returned.

Under Canada's National Emergencies Act (1988), which replaced the War Measures Act (1914), any national, provincial, or municipal government can declare a state of emergency. The act defines an emergency as "an urgent and critical situation" that threatens Canadian citizens and the government's capacity to preserve Canadian "sovereignty, security and territorial integrity." Declaring a state of emergency empowers the government to, among other things, prohibit travel and remove people from their homes. Perhaps the most egregious invocation of such powers was the imprisonment of German and Ukrainian Canadians during the First World War and of Japanese Canadians during the Second World War. (In both cases, their property was confiscated as

sovereign
One who holds supreme power in a territory or space. Agamben, following Carl Schmitt, claims that the sovereign is the one who is empowered to declare a state of exception.

state of exception
A period of time where the sovereign declares civil liberties suspended: typically in a time of national crisis.

During the Second World War, over 20,000 Japanese-Canadians (most of whom were Canadian-born) were forcibly relocated to internment camps.

C-046350, Library and Archives Canada

well.) But a world war is not a necessary condition for a state of emergency to be declared. During the October Crisis of 1970, in the hunt for terrorists from the Front de libération du Québec (FLQ), soldiers in full battle attire raided the homes of Quebecers while tanks patrolled city streets. In response to a seven-year campaign of bombings that culminated in the kidnapping of a Quebec cabinet minister and a British diplomat, Prime Minister Pierre Elliott Trudeau had invoked the War Measures Act, which effectively suspended civil rights and extended the police wide-ranging powers of arrest and detention. By the time the dust had settled, nearly 500 people had been arrested and detained; of these, only 62 were ever formally charged.

How does this make sense? How can a government simply suspend your rights? For Agamben, the answer lies in the fact that it is only by virtue of citizenship that modern states offer protections via human rights. At the same time, the nation's citizens are subordinated to the sovereign, who can decide at any time to suspend those rights (Ek, 2006). That is, human rights are afforded by specific geopolitical orders (e.g., Canada) and can be suspended only by the de facto sovereign. In this way, in the name of protection or defence of society and nation, the sovereign establishes the conditions under which he or she can abandon his or her subjects and return them to a state of **naked life**—that is, life unprotected by law and rights. When a state of emergency is declared, rights-bearing citizens can be deemed enemies of the state and subjected to exceptional and extreme measures.

We should "ask ourselves if we are today witnessing a definitive paradigmatic break in conceptions of the relationship between countries and their citizens" (Minca, 2006)—that is, whether we are facing the creation of an enormous space of exception within which each and every one of us, through the temporary suspension of law and rights, might be whisked away to a secret prison. Do you think this cannot happen in Canada? That it is a horror tale confined to the United States or Britain? In Canada, the Department of Citizenship and Immigration can remove persons deemed threatening to the security and well-being of Canadians by issuing a Security Certificate under the Immigration and Refugee Act. Under this scheme, both foreign nationals and permanent residents may be detained indefinitely without charge and without having full access to any evidence against them. In 2004, the Federal Court of Appeal ruled that both detention and the withholding of evidence are justified in the interests of national security. Human rights are violated under this legislation, including the right to a speedy trial and the right to be presumed innocent until proven guilty.

Maher Arar's arrest as a suspected terrorist attests to the "paradigmatic break" described by Minca. Arar was born in Syria and immigrated to Canada in 1987. After earning a master's degree in computer engineering, he took a job as a telecommunications engineer in Ottawa. In 2002, during a stopover in New York while he was returning from a vacation in Tunisia, US officials detained him, accusing him of links to al-Qaeda. After intense questioning, during which he was denied legal representation and phone calls, his wrists and ankles were shackled and he was taken to a nearby building, where he was detained in a cell. The next morning he faced more intense interrogation before being put on a flight to Zurich, where he was once again grilled about his

naked life
For Agamben, naked life is akin to *Homo Sacer*—an individual who is excluded from possessing human rights and can be killed by anyone but cannot be sacrificed during a religious ceremony.

suspected terrorist ties. After three months of this, Arar was deported to Syria, where he was detained and tortured (O'Connor, 2006). Arar was eventually released, but only after spending a year in custody under very difficult conditions (see Box 12.2). For much of Arar's stay in Syria, the Canadian government made few efforts to help him.

An egregious tragedy in all of this is that Arar was *not* working with al-Qaeda or any other terrorist group (O'Connor, 2006). But under a state of exception, such considerations—the juridical order and human rights—are of little importance compared to national security interests. It seems that the evidence linking him to terrorism and resulting in an innocent man being imprisoned and tortured was provided by the RCMP—in other words, by his own country's national police force! After months of public outcry and media scrutiny, former RCMP Commissioner Giuliano Zaccardelli appeared before the House of Commons Committee on Public Safety and National Security to admit that he knew his officers had passed on false information about Arar to US authorities in 2002. Previously, he had given misleading testimony that he had only been made aware of this information in the fall of 2006! Zaccardelli subsequently resigned from the RCMP.

Maher Arar's handling by Canadian and US officials prompted a commission of inquiry headed by Justice Dennis O'Connor (O'Connor, 2006). Faced

FOCUS

Box 12.2

STATEMENTS FROM MAHER ARAR'S INTERVIEW WITH AMNESTY INTERNATIONAL

"I remember one of the immigration officers on the second day at the airport he asked me to voluntarily go to Syria—of course I refused—I explained to him why. And in one of the interviews at the embassy I explained at length that I would be tortured in Syria if I am sent back. They did not seem to care …

"I could not believe what I saw. I saw a cell almost the size of a grave. Three feet wide 6 feet deep and 7 feet high. And when I looked at him and said what is this he just did not say anything—he did this with his hands—so basically 'I have nothing to with that.' So I entered the cell and he locked the door. The cell had no light in it; it only had two thin mattresses [two thin blankets] on the ground. And I first thought they would keep me in that place, which I now call the grave, for a short period so that they could put pressure on me. But I was kept in that dark and filthy cell for about 10 months and 10 days. That was torture …

"The worst beating happened on the third day and they were trying to, you know, they were asking the same set of questions some times, some times more questions and they would beat me 3 or 4 times. They would stop, they would beat me again. They would ask questions; they would sometimes take me to another room where I could hear the other people being tortured. They would keep me there for a while. They would bring me back they would beat me again ask questions sometimes they would take me to the hallway and make me stand for a couple of hours blindfolded. That third day they wanted me, they kept telling me I had been to Afghanistan and I kept telling them no. And at the end of the day I could not take the pain any more and I falsely confessed of having been to Afghanistan …

"In fighting this so-called war on terror what do we do with basic human rights? Do we throw them in the garbage and forget about our values that we pride ourselves with? Those are really the main points. And as I'm talking now, there are people, human beings being tortured …

"I think we have reached a point where we can confirm that these abuses, or this kind of torture is happening at different parts of the world at the behest of the CIA and the Bush Administration in general. So, there needs to be an action. Unless we do something about, it if we keep silent, if governments keep silent—in a way they are complicit."

Source: © Amnesty International, 1 Easton Street, London WC1X 0DW, UK, http://www.amnesty.org.

with nagging allegations of corruption and dereliction of duty on the part of various government and police officials, in January 2007 Prime Minister Stephen Harper offered an official apology to Arar along with $10.5 million (plus legal fees) in compensation.

Jacques Derrida: Deconstruction Is Justice

> Deconstruction, if such a thing exists, should open up. (Derrida, 1987, 261)

For Agamben and most others, sovereignty refers to a singular entity: to a head of state or some similar figure who can decide on the state of exception. Jacques Derrida (2005), in one of his last writings before his death in 2004, argued for a more open and wide-ranging definition. In keeping with the deconstructive ethic in which he worked throughout his life, Derrida attempted to open the concept of sovereignty to other ways of thinking and relating. For him, sovereignty was intrinsic to each and all of us, insofar as the sovereign function is "anchored in a certain ability to do something" (Balke, 2005). Derrida was intent on undoing language and, in the process, peering behind discourse to reveal how it does not have a determinable meaning. He wanted to show that all language exceeds the boundaries of the taken for granted (e.g., sovereignty). Deconstruction attempts to reveal what is *really* going on in and through language. According to Derrida, we always say more than the surface of our language reveals.

But what is deconstruction? Derrida often defined deconstruction in negative terms by referring to what it *is not* rather than what it *is*. For example, he argued, "deconstruction is not a method or some tool that you apply to something from the outside" (Derrida, in Caputo, 1997, 9). But what is it? We might say that deconstruction has to do with opening up given linguistic arrangements to the mostly silent, background suppositions that give words and phrases their meaning. Given Derrida's reticence, perhaps showing deconstruction at work would aid us here. As an example, let us consider the word "promise." What does this mean to you? When you promise your mother you will be home tonight for dinner, what are you doing? On the face of things, you are giving her an assurance that you will sit down with her to eat this evening. Unless you are truly irresponsible, there is no reason to doubt the truth of your assurance. Humans typically relate to presence, to what is uttered. Nevertheless, what is unspoken in language (the perversion of the promise) is as important to determining meaning as what we hear from another. What would happen if you did not show up? Your mother would be upset that you broke your promise, and others would certainly feel let down by your absence. Such perversions of the promise are as fundamental to its meaning as carrying through with the promised event. For a promise to be such, the statement must have the potential of falling through. If it does not, if what is assured is already guaranteed, there is no promise, only perfect conjugation of the assertion ("I will be home for supper") and the event. Again using the above example, when you promise your mum you will come to dinner while sitting at the table with fork and knife in hand, you have not promised anything.

deconstruction
An opening up of seemingly closed "things." It intends to encounter the hidden and excluded elements of language, meaning, and experience.

If we had only to consider the presence of speech, we could take everyone at their word and there would be no need for contracts, warranties, or oaths. Typically, however, when we hear language we do not attempt to read its hidden meaning; instead, we relate to what is laid out before us. However, and this is the important part, when speaking and writing we say much more than what is present on the page or in conversation. Deconstruction, then, attends closely to the unspoken elements that enable the central, or privileged, structure of a given meaning formation (Pavlich, 2007).

Underlying all language is a **trace**: the silent or absent element of language that provides words with an essential part of their meaning (i.e., perversion in the promise). The trace can be likened to a footprint or a comet. That is, when we observe a comet in the sky we are struck by the *presence* of the comet and/or tail. However, what is absent here is the comet's nucleus and essence, which is composed of rock and ice. When we observe a comet we are not privy to its essence—the nucleus remains hidden. The same can be said of language. No element, no idiom, can function as a sign without at the same moment referring to another that is simply not present but that gives meaning to it (Derrida, 1981). While we are at liberty to separate out presence and trace for the purposes of reducing the promise to its constituents, we (obviously) do not typically perform this operation.

Opening language up to its silent constituents (the trace) is at deconstruction's core. However, before we pass such analysis off as banal wordplay of little utility to *real* social problems, let us consider the implications of "community" under the Youth Criminal Justice Act. Community-based sanctioning and interventions occupy pride of place in the act. The preamble, for example, states:

> WHEREAS members of society share a responsibility to address the developmental challenges and the needs of young persons and to guide them into adulthood; WHEREAS communities, families, parents and others concerned with the development of young persons should, through multi-disciplinary approaches, take reasonable steps to prevent youth crime by addressing its underlying causes, to respond to the needs of young persons, and to provide guidance and support to those at risk of committing crimes. (YCJA, preamble)

Without the insights of deconstruction, we are apt to quickly read over the term *community* and be off to the next of the Act's many sections. Calls for community responsibility for youth crime may be laudable. However, given that the very essence of community is exclusionary, perhaps such enthusiasm should be tempered. That is, we cannot have a community—a school, a neighbourhood, a class, a town, or whatever other configuration—without exclusion. Those who belong define themselves in opposition to the excluded. If everyone were included under this or that community rubric, the term *community* would cease to hold meaning. "Community" designates divisions between and among people. Under the YCJA it is the young offenders—their deviance and criminality—who provide impetus for the creation of community in the first instance. For example, Youth Justice Committees, which are made up of community members who hear and adjudicate relatively minor crimes

trace
The mark of absence in words that is the necessary condition of thought and experience (Derrida, 1976).

committed by youths, find their meaning and definition in the wrongdoings of young people. A crime committed by a young offender brings this community together. Because of his or her contravention, the young person becomes not only the rationale for the formation of community but also, by virtue of the offence, its antithesis. Pavlich (2005) maintains that this is the very essence of community: "communities are identified—implicitly or explicitly—by exclusion." Before declaring this a meaningless play of words, let us remember the repulsive consequences that may accrue when exuberance for and devotion to community has spilled over its limits: ethnic wars of annihilation have been waged, genocide has been carried out, and prisons have become overcrowded with the residues of such intolerance (Hogeveen, 2006).

Communities may derive their *raison d'être* in relation to a particularly deviant and troubling other. A string of car thefts or a proliferation of graffiti in a geographical space may inspire previously disorganized citizens to band together against this provocation. Writes Hogeveen (2005): "Recent efforts to rid (affluent) neighbourhoods of prostitutes, the use of CCTV on busy city streets, broken windows policing, and gated neighbourhoods are poignant examples of community inspired attempts to exclude the 'other' while shoring up a privileged lifestyle. This regulation of the 'other' may contribute to and assist in shoring up the creation of community, but it also holds the insidious possibility of contributing to exclusionary practices which limit, rather than encourage, wider and more inclusive patterns of harmony" (295; see also Pavlich, 2005).

Through the examples of promises and community, we can see that deconstructive critique involves "opening up" things to examine what lies behind and beyond presence. However, there is one word that cannot be deconstructed: justice. In common parlance, we use the term *justice* in a variety of ways: we have a justice system; there are Justices of the Peace; Canada boasts a federal Department of Justice; "justice" is used in law and legislation to imply the impartiality of the system (e.g., the Youth Criminal *Justice* Act); and there is even a village in Manitoba called Justice (northwest of Brandon). But by far the most commonplace understanding of justice (see Box 12.3) is *vengeance*. Here, justice refers to an ethic of punishment that delivers obvious signs of unpleasantness to offenders. We live in an era during which war, prison overcrowding, and vigilantism are justified in the name of justice. For example, the US government constructed Osama bin Laden as a moral monster and a lunatic for crimes perpetrated on the United States. All the while, the civilian and military death toll from the American campaign for "justice" continued to mount. The costs in dollars and human life are spiralling out of control, while domestic atrocities and oppressions are glossed over by a nation seeking justice.

If these are all instances of "justice," how can Derrida say it does not exist? It is because Derrida seeks a different kind of justice, one that goes beyond "right, a justice finally removed from the fatality of vengeance" (1994, 21). One of Derrida's most faithful followers, John Caputo (1997), puts the situation this way: "Justice is not a present entity or order, not an existing reality or regime; nor is it even an ideal *eidos* towards which we earthlings down below heave and sigh while contemplating its heavenly form. Justice is the absolutely unforeseeable prospect (a paralyzing paradox) in virtue in which the things that get

broken windows policing
Just as houses with broken windows indicate that nobody cares about the neighbourhood, proponents of this policing style feel that tolerating minor misbehaviour will mean that residents will be afraid to use their streets. They feel that police should quickly deal with minor incivilities such as panhandling, vandalism, and other behaviours that contribute to fear of crime. Critics feel this policing style potentially discriminates against the poor.

justice
For Derrida, since it is perpetually deferred, justice cannot be defined adequately. It is not contained in or constrained by law. It is infinite. It is "to come."

deconstructed are deconstructed" (131). For Derrida, then, "justice appears as a promise, beyond law, and is itself incalculable, infinite and undeconstructable" (Pavlich, 2007, 989). It is not a thing or a person that we can hold up as exemplary, nor is it a criterion for future generations. To maintain that Canada is a just nation or that we ourselves are just would be to conclude that our work is done. It would be the height of injustice to think that justice exists here in tolerant Canada in the midst of the unimaginable suffering of Indigenous people, the tragic abuse of female partners, and the expanding extremes of poverty and wealth ... and we could go on (Caputo, 1997). But, you may conclude, the law is just ... right? On the contrary, there are situations in which the application of law was legal but unjust (e.g., Arar, Menezes). This is not to say that law is unnecessary or that it is wrong in its conception. Only that law can be unjust in its application and in its fundamental opposition to justice.

QUESTIONS FOR CRITICAL THINKING

1. In 2012, the government of Canada passed the Safe Streets and Communities Act. Ignoring for now the content of this act, deconstruct its title. What is present in the title? What "trace" can you identify that makes the notion of "safe streets" meaningful to those who hear it?
2. What assumptions about the nature of justice are built into the title of the Safe Streets and Communities Act?

FOCUS

Box 12.3

CRIME PAYS OFF IN CANADA

Consider the assumptions made about "justice" in the following article: What are the sources of the reporter's dissatisfaction with the Canadian criminal justice system? What expectations does she have about justice, and in what ways are they not being met? Also, note how she speaks as though her views represent taken-for-granted values that we all share and how she compares us (the "good" law-abiding and deserving) with youth offenders (the "bad," dangerous, and undeserving).

Maybe this holiday weekend you're putting in another shift to help pay for your child's college tuition.

Maybe you are that student, worried about how you're going to put the cash together for school and your first apartment.

Or maybe you're a victim of crime, and you can't afford the counselling you so desperately need.

Too bad you're not a teen killer, because then you'd be showered—thanks to the Canadian government—with more than $100,000 a year.

It's called the Intensive Rehabilitative Custody and Supervision program or IRCS and for 24 of this country's worst youth offenders, the little-known federal justice program is akin to hitting the jackpot.

In return for accepting treatment for their mental issues, serious violent offenders can escape adult prison and do easy time instead in a youth facility, like Ontario's Sprucedale, while taxpayers spend $100,375 per inmate for academic courses, counselling, "life skills" and reintegration.

The theory is that these heavily damaged "kids" need intensive help if they are ever to find their way back into society.

What kind of help, you may ask?

Well, there was the $700 piece of wood we purchased for a killer who brutally beat and sexually assaulted 15-year-old Elisha Mercer under the Lorne Bridge in Brantford in 2001. According to a Sprucedale insider, the young murderer was given the lumber to fashion his very own homemade guitar.

"It makes us all want to vomit," says the employee, who doesn't want to be named. "The victims should be getting this money, not them."

When told by the *Sun*, Elisha's mom was outraged to learn what constitutes therapy for the killer of her only child. "It's ridiculous, absolutely ridiculous," Wilma Martin says. "These have been very hard years. My husband and I split up because of what happened, he took off and I was left to pay the mortgage and the bills. I came close to losing my home.

"I could have used $100,000."

Instead, Ottawa last year earmarked $3.4 million for the country's worst of the worst young murderers and rapists with psychological disorders.

In 2004, one of the first accepted into the new program was the 18-year-old Hamilton youth who had killed Jonathan Romero the year before. Romero, 18, had gone to Lime Ridge Mall to buy a Christmas present for his mom. Standing on the sidelines when his friend got involved in a fight, Romero was sucker punched by the youth and after falling to the ground, was savagely punched four more times in the head and neck. He died hours later in hospital.

A judge turned down the Crown's request for a 6½-year adult sentence for manslaughter and instead agreed to just 30 months in custody at Sprucedale. The young offender was deemed eligible for IRCS because—wait for it—he was diagnosed with attention deficit and hyperactivity disorder, post traumatic stress disorder and mood disorder.

If only every kid with ADD could get free one-on-one counselling and government-sponsored perks.

The Hamilton youth was assigned a "life coach" and various IRCS counselling programs. He was released four weeks ago to a six-month reintegration period, but according to the Sprucedale worker, none of the expensive rehabilitation seemed to have any impact at all. "He felt no remorse whatsoever for his crime and anyone who worked with him over the last three years will tell you the same thing," he says. "He was a poster child for everything that was wrong with the system."

"Do I think he still poses a danger to society? You bet I do. At that summer camp, he didn't learn a thing."

The youth, stung by a previous article slamming easy time at Sprucedale, insists he's a changed man in a letter published in the *Sun*. "Every achievement that I completed here is to the memory of that boy."

According to his former worker, the letter is just another demonstration of how he's learned to talk the talk as well as how to use the IRCS program to his advantage.

Now 20, the Hamilton killer was boasting to everyone that the federal government will now be paying for his college tuition, laptop computer and his living expenses. On his $16,000 IRCS wish list, he also requested a plasma screen TV and new designer clothing. The insider says he doesn't know if those goodies were granted as well.

"All of this stuff," says the angry youth worker, "an average family can't afford and these kids are getting it for murdering other kids? It's unbelievable. The public needs to know."

Oh Canada, why are we such gullible souls?

Source: Michele Mandel, "Crime Pays off in Canada," *Toronto Sun*, July 1, 2007. http://torontosun.com/News/Columnists/Mandel_Michele/2007/07/01/4304140.html. Reprinted by permission of QMI Agency, A Quebecor Media Division.

Criticisms of Contemporary Critical Criminology

Given the diversity of contemporary critical criminological theorization, criticisms tend to be more specific to particular critical criminological approaches, rather than general and applicable to all forms of critical criminology. Nonetheless, there are a few complaints that are often heard with respect to critical criminology. The first, and the one possibly most glaringly felt by readers of this chapter, has to do with the sometimes obscure and abstract nature of critical criminological theorizing. Does critical criminology fetishize theory and disguise meaning behind difficult language? Critical criminologists would argue

TABLE 12.1   **Contemporary Critical Criminology**

Theory	Theorist(s)	Key Elements
Governmentality	Michel Foucault	Understandings of power and governance should be broadly conceived. Power creates subjects in dispersed locations in accordance with preconceived and useful ends.
Actuarialism, risk, and the risk society	Foucault, Beck	Social problems are no longer considered issues requiring solutions, but risks to be managed. In the "risk society" eventualities can be calculated and thus managed. Risk of victimization can be mitigated in accordance with risk factors.
Cultural criminology	Ferrell, Hayward, Young	"Crime" is culturally negotiated. The importance of adrenaline in the commission of crime is emphasized. These theorists attend to how rule breaking challenges the justness of law. It produces dangerous knowledge through critical engagement with knowledge (including criminology).
Field theory	Bourdieu, Wacquant	Society is divided into fields, which are basic areas of social activity. In the contemporary bureaucratic field, social support is increasingly disciplinary and punitive. It is taking on characteristics of the "right hand" of the state.
Sovereignty and the state of exception	Agamben	Inspired by Schmitt, Foucault, and Benjamin, Agamben has constructed a nuanced understanding of sovereignty and its exceptions. During times of crisis, emergency, or exception, subject's rights and the rule of law are suspended in the name of the sovereign.
Deconstruction	Derrida	Language is infinitely complex. Deconstruction attempts to uncover silences in discourse. Justice is an infinite promise.

that such terminology is necessary to push criminological thought in new and transgressive directions, beyond the mundane, taken-for-granted meanings of regular language. A second criticism follows from the first and is perhaps the more serious one for critical criminologists: What are the practical implications of critical criminology? If critical criminology is to be more than ivory tower navel-gazing, it must have implications for the real world of crime, crime control, and social justice. And some find it difficult to discern a call to action in the theoretical language of contemporary critical criminology. Yet all of the critical criminologists with whom we are familiar aspire toward such real-world change. Their dedication is not to theory for the sake of theory, but rather to using theory to think about the worlds of crime and victimization in new, more just terms.

QUESTIONS FOR CRITICAL THINKING

1. Is it enough to criticize, to expose the limits placed on our thinking about crime, or is it incumbent on the critical criminologist to devise a "solution" to the "problem" of crime?
2. Some have criticized critical criminologists for using a complex, academic discourse. In your view, is it the responsibility of scholars to place their thoughts in terms that everyone can understand? Are there ever situations where complex ideas demand complex language?

Summary

- Critical criminology attempts to draw attention to hidden and overlooked injustices scattered throughout our world. It seeks to highlight and genuinely grasp inequalities, discrimination, and suffering.

- Early critical criminology in Canada, inspired by Taylor, Walton, and Young's *The New Criminology*, maintained a focus on how economic power is implicated in the operations of criminal justice. Efforts to create a unified collective among Canadian critical criminologists were, however, cut short by several factors, including the growing diversity of critical criminology.

- Today's critical criminology does not maintain this dedication to a political economic approach to crime. Critique is less and less understood as a form of judgment gauged upon a fixed standard of evaluation and more as a means for disrupting and destabilizing taken-for-granted assumptions about and approaches to crime. The goal is not to prescribe a new social order but rather to create opportunities for unencumbered ideas and practices to arise and take form.

- Foucault contributed to critical criminology through his work on power. For Foucault, power is not solely repressive—it is also productive. Through the tactics of discipline, surveillance, and governmentality, power shapes individuals so that they are transformed (or transform themselves) into more governable subjects.

- Actuarialism, risk, and the risk society are all terms used to understand the growing fixation on insurance-like evaluations of risk and harm in contemporary criminal justice practices. Through an understanding of the larger social context producing the "risk society," critical criminologists are able to challenge the logic of various risk management approaches to criminal justice.

- Cultural criminology revives the ethnographic tradition in criminology and directs it toward discovering crime as a lived experience. Cultural criminologists investigate the cultural production of crime and our understandings of crime and thereby question popular notions about crime and criminal justice.

- Bourdieu's "field theory" alerts critical criminologists to the many forms of power that are amassed and the role they play in the domination over and definition of excluded and criminalized classes. Crime, therefore, is understood as a consequence not only of economic domination but also of symbolic, cultural, and social domination.

- Giorgio Agamben points us to the power of the sovereign to define individuals as being outside of law. Thus built into law is the state of exception—that is, the sovereign's ability to suspend rights and protections. And through this concept criminal law is vividly revealed as a source of exclusion.

- Jacques Derrida's concept of deconstruction provides critical criminologists with a tool for evaluating what is hidden or unspoken within social life and, in particular, criminal justice practices. It is a particularly powerful tool for unpacking the meanings hidden in fashionable criminal justice jargon, such as "community," "safety," and "security."

NET WORK

Visit the American Society of Criminology Divisions page at http://www.asc41.com/divisions.htm. Compare and contrast the description of the Critical Criminology Division to other divisions of the ASC. What makes it "critical" in contrast to the other divisions?

Interactionist Theories

Robert A. Stebbins
UNIVERSITY OF CALGARY

13

S train and conflict theories deal with causes of crime at the level of social structure. *Strain theorists* relate crime to variables such as cultural goals and the access to opportunities provided by society. For *conflict theorists*, cleavages between different groups in society and the power relationships among these groups are critical in explaining criminality. *Interactionist theories*, for their part, turn our attention to the smaller details of social life. They consider crime to be a consequence of interpersonal relationships and of what those relationships mean.

A central concept in interactionist theories of crime is the *deviant career*, or the passage of an individual through the stages of one or more related deviant identities. This idea is at the heart of labelling theory, which explains how the social response to initial, tentative acts of deviance can move a person toward a deviant identity and a deviant career. The other important interactionist theory discussed in this chapter—differential association—sets out how people learn to be criminals through interaction with other criminals and how they acquire a criminal identity.

Learning Objectives

After reading this chapter, you should be able to

- Describe primary and secondary deviation and explain how primary deviation leads to secondary deviation.
- Understand the process of drift among juvenile delinquents.
- Explain how moral entrepreneurs create and enforce the law.
- Discuss the various contingencies that criminals encounter in their deviant careers.
- Understand how people are socialized into a life of crime.
- Outline the strengths and limitations of interactionist theories of deviance.

Interactionist theory in criminology focuses on the interchanges people have with one another and on the meanings of these interchanges in the past, present, and future. Blumer (1986) notes that **symbolic interactionism**, the broader theory from which the interactionist theories of crime are derived, rests on three premises. First, people act toward the human and nonhuman

symbolic interactionism
A sociological perspective that focuses on the dynamics of how people interpret social situations and negotiate the meaning of these situations with others. It differs from more structurally focused perspectives in seeing individuals as actively creating the social world rather than just acting within the constraints of culture and social structure.

objects in their lives according to the meanings those objects have for them. Second, these meanings emerge from interactions among people. Third, the meanings of objects learned in this manner are applied and occasionally modified as individuals interpret how objects and their meanings fit particular social situations, the people in them, and their reasons for being there.

Much of this chapter is about criminal interactions, meanings, interpretations, and situations. Before turning to these processes, however, let us set the stage for discussion with a brief illustration of the three premises operating on the scene of a crime. The following interview with Allen, about 20 years old, shows how the meaning of a situation changed through social interaction with other people present in an all-night drugstore:

> From what I understand from them, they didn't go in there with the intent to rob or beat anybody up or anything. I think they only really wanted to buy some gum and cigarettes, but by being drunk, they was talking pretty tough, and so the lady behind the counter automatically got scared … The druggist … got a little pushy or ordered them out of the store, and by them being all fired up, naturally the next thing they did was jump on him.
>
> So now what do you have? You've got a drugstore. You've got a scared lady in the corner somewhere with her hands over her face. You've got a beat-up druggist laying on the floor. You've got three dudes that came in for chewing gum and cigarettes, but now they got two cash registers. So what do they do? They take the cash. Wasn't nothing to stop them, and it was there. Why would they leave it? They're thieves anyway and supposed to be hustlers … There wasn't nothing to stop them, so they just took the money. (Katz, 1990)

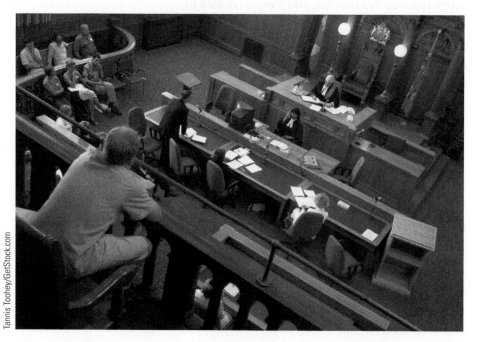

Labelling theorists believe that being found guilty in a criminal court can force a person drastically change his or her lifestyle.

Tannis Toohey/GetStock.com

The Deviant Career

Interactionism centres chiefly on what happens to criminals once their deviant activities commence. Interactionists have observed, for example, that some groups or individuals have enough power to force the label of deviant on less powerful groups or individuals. The **labelling** process, however, is not always accurate. It is not even always fair. Some deviants escape public detection of their behaviour. Some who have not deviated are nonetheless labelled as having done so, despite their protests to the contrary. The application of the deviant label is sometimes subject to considerable negotiation between possibly deviant people and those in a position to label them as deviant.

Thus, interactionist theory in criminology helps explain the establishment of moral rules, their application through labelling, and the long-term consequences of these two processes for deviants and for society. In interactionist theory, labelling and its consequences are viewed as unfolding within the deviant career.

A **career**, be it in deviance or in a legitimate occupation, is the passage of an individual through recognized stages in one or more related identities. Careers are further composed of adjustments to, and interpretations of, the contingencies and turning points encountered at each stage. For example, Short (1990) notes that careers in youth crime are likely to be prolonged after certain turning points have been reached. One of these turning points is an early interest in delinquent activities; another is an interest in drugs. The inability to find legitimate employment, a career contingency, also contributes to continued criminality. Type of offence, however, has been found to be unrelated to length of career in youth crime and even to the rate at which it is perpetrated. During the careers of young offenders and other deviants, there is a sense of continuity. This sense is fostered by perceptions of increasing opportunities, sophistication, and perhaps recognition among one's associates for skill in, or at least commitment to, the special endeavour.

Primary Deviation

Lemert (1972) contributed two important concepts to the study of deviant careers: **primary deviation** and **secondary deviation**. Primary deviation produces little change in one's everyday routine or lifestyle. The individual engages in deviance infrequently, has few compunctions about it, and encounters few practical problems when performing it. A person who occasionally smokes marijuana supplied by someone else exemplifies primary deviation.

Primary deviation occurs in the early stages of the deviant career, between the first deviant act and some indefinite point at which deviance becomes a way of life. Subsequently, at a still more advanced stage, secondary deviation (discussed later) sets in. According to Matza (2010), one precondition of deviance is a willingness to engage in it. That is, the individual must have an affinity—innate or acquired—for the intended act (e.g., theft, homicide, drug use). This affinity helps him or her choose among existing options. By way of illustration, imagine someone who believes the rich cheat others to get their money. This person has an affinity for stealing from the rich. That affinity could lead

labelling
According to labelling theory, deviance is not a quality of the act but of the label that others attach to it. This raises the question of who applies the label and who is labelled. The application of a label and the response of others to the label may result in a person becoming committed to a deviant identity.

career
In common use, this refers to the sequence of stages through which people in a particular occupational sector move during the course of their employment. It has also been applied to the various stages of personal involvement with criminal activity.

primary deviation
Occurs when an individual commits deviant acts but fails adopt a primary self-identity as a deviant.

secondary deviation
Occurs when an individual accepts the label of deviant. The result is adoption of a deviant self-identity that confirms and stabilizes the deviant lifestyle.

the individual into crimes against the rich when faced with such unpleasant alternatives as poverty, unemployment, or tedious manual labour.

Underlying the willingness to engage in deviance lies a weak commitment to conventional norms and identities. Few young people have a strong value commitment to deviant norms and identities; instead, they **drift** between the world of respectability and that of deviance. They are "neither compelled to deeds nor freely choosing them; neither different in any simple or fundamental sense from the law abiding, nor the same; conforming to certain traditions in ... life while partially unreceptive to other more conventional traditions" (Matza, 1990, 28).

Matza was writing about American males who were young offenders. He found these youths firmly attached to certain marginal, masculine, *subterranean traditions* or ways of life. They found satisfaction in drinking, smoking, renouncing work, being tough, and enjoying the hedonistic pleasures of "real" men. Matza's subjects saw themselves as grown and mature, but their behaviour was hardly a true picture of adult life in general in the United States.

Lemert (1972) explains how this peculiar orientation can set one adrift toward deviance:

> While some fortunate individuals by insightful endowment or by virtue of the stabilizing nature of their situation can foresee more distant social consequences of their actions and behave accordingly, not so for most people. Much human behaviour is situationally oriented and geared to meeting the many and shifting claims which others make upon them. The loose structuring and swiftly changing facade and content of modern social situations frequently make it difficult to decide which means will insure the ends sought. Often choice is a compromise between what is sought and what can be sought ... All this makes me believe that most people drift into deviance by specific actions rather than by informed choices of social roles and statuses. (79–80)

For young offenders and young adults, social control has failed. This failure occurs because it is important for deviant individuals to enjoy good standing with their friends in the group. Good standing is attained by honouring and practising the marginal, or subterranean, traditions that Matza describes. The quest for honour among peers helps explain how entire groups of youth can drift toward deviance (Hirschi, 2001).

It appears that much, if not all, of this is applicable to Canada. For instance, a comparative study conducted in California and Alberta found that ties to peers were important in the sample of delinquent youth; being in touch with home and school were valued much less (Linden and Fillmore, 1981).

The young offender subculture (see Chapter 11) is composed of many elements, one of the most important being the **moral rhetorics** (Schwendinger and Schwendinger, 1985) used to justify deviant behaviour. Each rhetoric consists of a set of largely taken-for-granted guiding principles, sometimes logically inconsistent and always selectively applied according to the social situations in which youths find themselves. The rhetoric of *egoism* is most often used by those who still feel guilty about their deviant acts. Typically, these are early offenders, who have learned various ways to neutralize the **stigma** that

drift
A psychological state of weak normative attachment to either deviant or conventional ways.

moral rhetoric
In the study of crime, this is the set of claims and assertions deviants make to justify their deviant behaviour. The moral rhetoric of a group is an important component of socialization into a deviant identity.

stigma
As used by Erving Goffman (1922–1982), a personal characteristic that is negatively evaluated by others and thus distorts and discredits the public identity of the individual. For example, a prison record may become a stigmatized attribute. The stigma may lead to the adoption of a self-identity that incorporates the negative social evaluation.

comes with their behaviour—for example, by claiming they steal in response to the greed and immorality of shopkeepers whose prices are unfair. Later, young offenders are more likely to use *instrumental* rhetoric when justifying their acts. Here they stress the cunning and power they bring to bear against people who are otherwise more powerful and uncontrollable. Fraud, deceit, and violence are used to pursue deviant aims whenever they appear to pay off, whenever these youths can benefit from a weak moment in the lives of such people. The main point here is that young offenders, like people in many other walks of life, justify what they do. Though the law-abiding world sees them otherwise, offenders have their ways of defending their deviant acts as morally right.

During the primary deviation stages of a deviant career, young offenders and young adults drift, in part because they lack *value commitment* to either conventional or deviant values. Value commitment is an attitude toward an identity, one that develops when a person gains exceptional rewards from assuming that identity (Stebbins, 1970). Young men and women drifting between criminal and respectable pursuits have found few, if any, enduring benefits in either type of activity. This pattern, however, begins to change with more contact with agents of social control.

Agents of Social Control

Those members of society who help check deviant behaviour are known as agents of social control. They include the police, judges, lawmakers, prison personnel, probation and parole officers, and ordinary citizens with an active interest in maintaining law and order as they define it. Groups of ordinary citizens and lawmakers sometimes join hands as **moral entrepreneurs**: "Rules are the products of someone's initiative, and we can think of the people who exhibit such enterprise as *moral entrepreneurs*. Two related species—rule creators and rule enforcers—will occupy our attention" (Becker, 1963, 147).

The prototype of the rule creator, Becker observes, is the crusading reformer, whose dissatisfaction with existing rules is acute and who, therefore, campaigns for legal change (i.e., for adding new laws or procedures and rescinding old ones) and sometimes for attitudinal change intended to lead to "proper" behaviour. Canadian society is replete with crusades, both past and present, such as those which seek to eliminate drug abuse, discourage use of alcohol, reduce the availability of pornography, and stop the exploitation of women in the workplace. Moral entrepreneurs are currently working to curb Internet crime (for a further example involving marijuana legalization, see Box 13.1).

To conduct an effective crusade, moral entrepreneurs must construct an argument capable of convincing the community that a deep and genuine internal threat exists. This process of collective definition (Hewitt and Hall, 1973; Spector and Kitsuse, 2000) centres largely on the "claims-making activities" of entrepreneurs, which include these:

moral entrepreneur
Someone who defines new rules and laws or who advocates stricter enforcement of existing laws. Often such entrepreneurs have a financial or organizational interest in particular definitions or applications of law.

1. They assert the existence of a particular condition, situation, or state of affairs in which human action is implicated as a cause.
2. They define the asserted condition as offensive, harmful, undesirable, or otherwise problematic to the society but as nonetheless amenable to correction by humans.
3. They stimulate public scrutiny of the condition as the claims makers see it.

The claims are explained by quasi-theories. Unlike scientific theories, quasi-theories are selectively constructed to square with the claims makers' views, are seldom responsive to empirical evidence, and contain simple explanations of complex, ill-defined problems.

Moral entrepreneurs also enforce legislated rules, applying them to people who misbehave. Such rules provide enforcers (police, security personnel) with jobs as well as with justifications for them. Since the enforcers want to keep their jobs, they are eager to demonstrate that enforcement is effective. Yet they also realize there are more infractions than they can possibly prevent or respond to. Therefore, they must establish priorities. Thus,

> whether a person who commits a deviant act is in fact labelled a deviant depends on many things extraneous to his actual behaviour: whether the enforcement official feels that at this time he must make some show of doing his job in order to justify his position, whether the misbehaver shows proper deference to the enforcer, whether the "fix" has been put in, and where the kind of act he has committed stands on the enforcer's list of priorities. (Becker, 1963)

empirical evidence
Evidence as observed through the senses; it can be seen, touched, heard, smelled, tasted, and, to some extent, measured. This is the only form of scientifically acceptable evidence.

FOCUS   Box 13.1

MORAL ENTREPRENEURSHIP FOR LEGALIZING MARIJUANA IN CANADA

Canadians have been regularly consuming marijuana and other cannabis products for nearly a century, despite their prohibition. This has been a costly practice, for the measures taken to enforce this prohibition have squandered billions of dollars on ineffective or incomplete law enforcement. These efforts have also clogged our judicial system. Various policies calling for decriminalization or legalization of the drug were recommended by the 1969–72 Commission of Enquiry into the Non-Medical Use of Drugs, the 2002 Canadian Senate Special Committee on Illegal Drugs, and the 2002 House of Commons Special Committee on the Non-Medical Use of Drugs. Today we continue to legally regulate marijuana by means of the criminal law. This endangers Canadians because it spawns gang-related crime and the smuggling of weapons. This menace could be very easily overcome through the regulation and legitimization of Canada's marijuana industry.

At the 2012 Liberal Party of Canada Convention, the Young Liberals put forward a resolution calling for a new Liberal government to legalize marijuana. This would include the regulation and taxation of the drug's production, distribution, and use. The resolution proposes strict penalties for illegal trafficking, importation, and exportation of marijuana as well as for driving impaired by its consumption. According to the resolution, a new Liberal government would "invest significant resources" in programs designed to prevent, and educate about, the health risks and consequences of using marijuana and the dependency it can create. Youth will be especially targeted by these programs. A new Liberal government would extend amnesty to all Canadians previously convicted of simple and minimal possession of the drug. It would also eliminate all criminal records related to such possession. Lastly, the Young Liberals called for a new Liberal government to work with the provinces and local governments of Canada to fashion a "coordinated regulatory approach" to marijuana. However, the new government would maintain "significant federal responsibility" for controlling the drug, always doing so in consideration of provincial health jurisdictions and regional concerns and practices.

Could MADD (Mothers against Drunk Driving) become a counter moral entrepreneur to legalization of marijuana use in Canada? They reprinted this newspaper story on their website:

> Smoking marijuana within three hours of driving doubles the chances of being involved in a collision, a recently published study shows.
>
> That, combined with the reality auto collisions are the leading cause of death for Canadian teens, drives home the need to see youth taught to take a pass on weed in same way they should nix mixing booze with driving, MADD Canada said.

"People think smoking pot is not as bad as alcohol," national president, Denise Dubyk said.

"They all impaired individuals, the crashes still happen.

"It's about awareness … it's not just alcohol."

The study published in the British Medical Journal last week showed teens who drove within three hours of smoking pot are twice as likely to be in a collision.

The Canadian Centre on Substance Abuse findings showed 10.6% of Grade 12 students in Alberta admit they have driven within one hour of smoking up at least once in the last year (Moharib, 2012).

What do you think about this issue? Should the government legalize marijuana or do its potential harms outweigh the benefits of legalization?

It is no accident, then, that the least influential members of society (e.g., the poor or certain **ethnic groups**) are often caught in the web of social control and labelled deviant out of proportion to their numbers. In other words, deviance is created in part by people in society. Moral entrepreneurs make certain laws, the infraction of which constitutes deviance. Moral entrepreneurs also apply these laws to particular people, labelling them as some kind of deviant. As Becker (1963) points out, "deviance is not a quality of the act … The deviant is one to whom that label has successfully been applied; deviant behaviour is behaviour that people so label."

But rules are applied to some people and not to others; application is sometimes biased. Hence, some people remain at large as secret but potentially identifiable deviants. Others go through life falsely accused of antisocial acts. To discover why only certain people are labelled deviant, labelling theorists also study those who make the laws that deviants violate and how those laws are applied.

Those publicly labelled "deviant" generally face some sort of community or societal reaction to their misdeeds (Lemert, 1951). Depending on the nature of the deviance, the deviant may experience one or more of the following: imprisonment, ostracism, fines, torture, surveillance, and ridicule. All labelled deviants soon learn they must cope with stigma.

A *stigma* is a black mark, or disgrace, associated with a deviant identity. It is part of the societal reaction—that is, a collective construction by agents of social control, and by ordinary members of the community, of the supposed nature of the unlawful act and the person perpetrating it. As Goffman (1986) and Link and Phelan (2001) note, the collective image of stigma is constructed from social, physical, or psychological attributes the deviant is believed to possess. Here *imputed* possession of the attributes is far more important than *actual* possession.

After years of participant observation of outlaw motorcycle gangs, Watson (1984) and Wolf (1991) concluded that their members had a mentality and background noticeably different from that imputed to them by the general public. They were not especially hostile to most social institutions, including government, education, and the family. Most members had finished high school and had occasionally held jobs. Some had gone to college, some were military veterans. Nearly every member had been married at least once. They were, to be sure, not particularly successful in these areas of life, which accounted for their tendency to live for the moment. And though they were basically not violent men, they thought it important to be seen as "manly" in the most traditional sense of the term.

ethnic group
A group of individuals having a common, distinctive subculture. Ethnic groups differ from races; the term implies that values, norms, behaviour, and language, not necessarily physical appearance, are important distinguishing characteristics.

Secondary Deviation

The existence of moral rules and the stigma that arises when society believes those rules have been violated sets the stage for secondary deviation. Deviation becomes secondary when deviants see that their behaviour has substantially modified their ways of living. A strong desire to deviate can foster this redefinition of one's deviant activities; so can extreme feelings of guilt. But accusations of deviance are typically the most influential factor behind the redefinition. Being labelled by the authorities as a murderer, rapist, prostitute, or cheque forger and being sanctioned for such behaviour forces the deviant to change his or her lifestyle drastically. As Lemert (1972) puts it, "This secondary deviant … is a person whose life and identity are organized around the facts of deviance."

What does a lifestyle of secondary deviation actually consist of? Stebbins (1997) defines lifestyle as

> a distinctive set of shared patterns of tangible behaviour that is organized around a set of coherent interests or social conditions or both, that is explained and justified by a set of related values, attitudes, and orientations and that, under certain conditions, becomes the basis for a separate, common social identity for its participants. (350)

For example, drug addicts regularly buy or produce their drugs, habitually follow certain practices designed to prevent discovery by the authorities, and routinely consume the illicit substances thereby acquired. Some addicts, prostitutes among them, justify this lifestyle as an escape from intolerable working conditions. The identity of addict is pejorative, however, as the label "junkie" clearly indicates. The links between primary deviance, societal reaction, and secondary deviance are illustrated in Figure 13.1.

Among the factors leading to secondary deviation is society's tendency to treat someone's criminality as a **master status** (Becker, 1963). This status overrides all other statuses in perceived importance. Whatever laudable achievements the deviant might claim, such as a good job or a successful marriage, this person is judged in the community primarily by the fact of deviance (see Box 13.2). Liberman, Kirk, and Kideuk (2014) found that first arrests increased the likelihood of both subsequent offending and subsequent arrest. These two were discovered to be separate processes, however, suggesting that deviant labels trigger what the authors call "secondary sanctioning,"

Lack of success in attaining respectability among nondeviants, or a perceived low probability of achieving it, may lead to interaction with other deviants. Here we consider a unique aspect of the interaction between the labelled deviant and the organized deviant group. There are several characteristics of

master status
A status overriding all others in perceived importance. Whatever other personal or social qualities individuals possess, they are judged primarily by this one attribute. *Criminal* exemplifies a master status that influences the community's identification of an individual.

FIGURE 13.1   **Links Between Primary Deviance, Societal Reaction, and Secondary Deviance**

this type of group life that stimulate or maintain such behaviour. These characteristics are effective partly because the wider community has rejected the deviant.

As Becker (1963) observed, individuals who gain entrance to a deviant group often learn from that group how to cope with the problems associated with their deviance. This makes being a deviant easier. Furthermore, the deviant acquires rationalizations for his or her values, attitudes, and behaviour, which come to full bloom in the organized group. While these rationalizations vary greatly, note that the very existence of rationalizations seems to point to the fact that some deviants feel a need to deal with certain conventional attitudes and values they have also internalized.

Prus and Sharper (1991) quote one of their respondents, who was explaining how he developed the callous attitude prized by professional card hustlers:

> When I first got involved in hustling, my attitudes were less calloused [*sic*]. I might be at a stag of some sort and say some fellow is losing a little money. Through the course of the evening, talking back and forth, you find out that maybe he just got married, or that he has some kids and here he's writing cheques and I would slow down. If you pull something like this with a crew [of hustlers], the other guys will want to know what the hell you are doing! They're waiting for you to take him, and you're saying, "Well gee, the guy doesn't have much money." You would get the worst tongue lashing! The position they take is that "You can't have feelings on the road." And it's true, if you start saying to yourself, "Well, maybe I better not beat this guy or that guy," you would soon be out of business or at least you would really cut down on your profits."

FOCUS

Box 13.2

THE PRISON-MADE TATTOO AS MASTER STATUS

Prison-made tattoos serve as master statuses both inside and outside the walls. For anyone who knows their meaning, particular tattoos communicate particular attitudes and memberships. These identifiers tend to override all others.

"Marked Men: The Art and Meaning of Prison Tatoos" by Peter Wollheim and Christine Brady

Prison-made tattoos are a form of communication for inmates who live in a situation that bans most other means of self-expression. These messages, which are easily "read" by other inmates, tell a lot about the wearer, including gang membership, status in prison, family relationships, special life events, spiritual beliefs and personal values.

Reciprocal influences exist between prison and professional tattooing. For many years, prison tattoos emulated the techniques of professional tattoo artists. While the professional shops had access to tattoo machines as early as the 1890s, prison tattoo artists relied on a similar hand-held method that used a bundle of sewing needles affixed to a handle. Using this crude set-up, a strong line could be worked that was very similar to that created by the electric machine, which also used several needles.

Tattoos made in this style have a heavy outline with little or no interior shading.

In the 1970s, prison tattoo artists began to use a single needle (often affixed to simple electric motor); this method

(continued)

Chris Leschinsky/Photolibrary/Getty Images

spawned a distinct style of tattooing labeled "fineline" for the characteristic subtle details of shading that result in an almost photo-realistic product. This new look was noted by "outside" professional tattoo artists, who adopted and popularized the all-black fineline style in the mid- to late-1970s. It remains an important prison and mainstream tattoo style today.

Source: From Peter Wollheim and Christine Brady (2013). "Marked Men: The Art and Meaning of Prison Tattoos," *The Blue Review*, March 7, http://www.thebluereview.org/prison-tattos/. Reprinted with permission.

Just because group forces operate to maintain and even promote deviance, we should not assume—as Goffman (1986) apparently does—that full-fledged deviants are always members of groups. There are those who reject the label of deviant during certain phases of their career, though they may be forced into that status. Some of these individuals spend part of their career trying to re-enter conventional life, often without success. Yet the fact that they refuse to identify themselves as deviant leads them to avoid others labelled thus (e.g., shoplifters and embezzlers). There are, moreover, some forms of deviant behaviour that for whatever reason are enacted alone (e.g., rape, some cheque forging). Nevertheless, it is probably true that deviance has collective support in most instances.

The amount of interaction between individuals suspected of deviant behaviour and agents of social control, and the forms these interactions take, are extremely important for the future course of deviant careers. In fact, such interactions constitute a major set of deviant career contingencies. A **career contingency** is an unintended event, process, or situation that occurs by chance; that is, it lies beyond the control of the individual pursuing the career. Career contingencies emanate from changes in the deviant's environment or personal circumstances, or both. Movement through the career is affected by the contingencies the deviant meets along the way.

Cohen (1965) has presented this process most clearly: Alter (the agents of social control) responds to the action of ego (the deviant). Ego, in turn, responds to alter's reaction. Alter then responds to his perception of ego's reaction to him; and so forth. As a result, ego's opportunity structure is in some way modified, permitting either more or fewer legitimate or illegitimate opportunities.

When opportunities for a deviant career are expanding, the steady growing apart of the deviant and the control agents spawns open conflict. Some proportion of these encounters lead in the opposite direction, however, resulting in some kind of accommodation and a decrease in opportunities for a deviant career (West, 1980).

This process of agent–deviant interaction is illustrated in the following circumstances associated with a shooting in downtown Toronto:

> CTV News had managed to obtain in late September 2013 an amateur video showing a Toronto police officer repeatedly striking a suspect. The suspect was at the time on the ground in a backyard of a residence near Yonge St. and St. Clair Ave. He was apparently wanted for his alleged role in a shooting in the city's center. "A witness told CTV Toronto that the suspect appeared to have been resisting arrest." The witness said that "the police warned the suspect several times not to resist. The suspect continued to resist, the police then suppressed the suspect and in the process the suspect was injured." The president of the Toronto Police Association said he had "no issue" with what the video contained. He pointed out that a gunman had attempted to murder somebody in downtown Toronto, and that the police had to take action. From what he saw in the video, he believed that the officers had acted professionally. (CTV News, 2013)

Another prominent contingency in secondary deviation is **continuance commitment**. Continuance commitment is "the awareness of the impossibility of choosing a different social identity ... because of the imminence of penalties involved in making the switch" (Stebbins, 1976). Like value commitment (mentioned earlier in this chapter), continuance commitment helps explain a person's involvement in a deviant identity. Unlike value commitment, which

career contingency
An unintended event, process, or situation that occurs by chance, beyond the control of the person pursuing the career.

continuance commitment
Adherence to a criminal or other identity arising from the unattractiveness or unavailability of alternative lifestyles.

explains this involvement by stressing the rewards of the identity, continuance commitment explains it by describing the penalties accrued from renouncing the deviant identity and trying to adopt a conventional identity.

As Ulmer (1994) notes, such penalties may be structural (i.e., they flow from the social structure of the community) or personal (i.e., they flow from the person's attitudes and sense of self). Stebbins's (1976) study of male, nonprofessional property offenders in Newfoundland revealed a number of commitment-related penalties of both types. Being ex-offenders with prison records, the men in the study had difficulty finding jobs within their range of personally acceptable alternatives. The work they found was onerous, low in pay, and low in prestige. Many of the men had amassed sizable debts before going to prison, which upon release tended to discourage return to a conventional livelihood. Also penalizing were questions from casual acquaintances about the nature of criminal life and the insulting remarks these people occasionally made about those who had done jail time. Even where their records were unknown, these nonprofessional offenders often heard people express unflattering opinions about men like them.

For these reasons and others, the man with a criminal record was often inclined to seek the company of those who understood him best—namely, other criminals—and to seek the way of life that afforded him at least some money and excitement—namely, crime. The police knew all this, and they would question local ex-offenders to determine whether they were possibly guilty of certain crimes. The ex-offenders, who were trying to "go straight," saw this as an additional penalty.

What the ex-offender experiences as a string of penalties is, from another perspective, a set of expressions of the societal reaction. These expressions, when ex-offenders define them as penalizing, affect their deviant careers. Such expressions force many of them into the company of other deviants. Here they find greater understanding for their situation. Here, too, is at least the possibility of a better living than they believe exists in the conventional world.

What is the significance of all this to the process of drift? Teenagers and young adults who fail to drift *out of* crime into a more or less conventional way of life drift *into* a more or less solid commitment to crime. Once a prison record has been acquired, after several years of secondary deviation, continuance commitment develops. Most deviants in this stage of their moral careers appear to be trapped in a self-degrading form of continuance commitment. The image they have of themselves is unflattering. They would gladly abandon the world of crime if only they could find a palatable way to do so (see also Schwendinger and Schwendinger, 1985).

But some criminals, including professional offenders, are quite attached to their deviant activities. Because they find leaving crime for a conventional way of life no easier than it is for the nonprofessional offender, they are also committed to deviance. Theirs, however, is a self-enhancing commitment. For these professional criminals, continuance commitment is of little consequence; they enjoy what they do and are disinclined to abandon it.

Reactions to Commitment

self-enhancing commitment
Commitment leading to a better opinion of oneself.

Generally speaking, **self-enhancing commitment** presents no problem for deviants, setting aside that they are more or less compelled to retain their nonconformist role. There is little motivation for them to leave it for reasons of self-conception. Self-degrading commitment, however, presents a dramatically different situation. An individual committed to an identity in this manner has numerous alternatives.

People motivated by **self-degrading commitment** have the objective alternative of redefining the values and penalties associated with their committed identity, such that they become attached to them. Basically, this alters their perception of the balance of penalties. This psychological leap from self-degrading to self-enhancing commitment in the same deviant identity is exemplified by some of the repeat offenders in Shover's (1983) study. They wrestled with the frustrating gap between their legitimate aspirations and what they could actually achieve in life. Since conventional work offered little, they turned to living from day to day, with crime being one of their more enjoyable activities.

Without really switching to a form of self-enhancing commitment, it is possible for some deviants to adjust psychologically to self-degrading commitment. This depends, of course, on how strong a motivating force the current state of self-degrading commitment actually is for them. Certain types of mildly rejected deviants seem to manage this form of adaptation. Lemert (1972) refers to them as "adjusted pathological deviants." The subsequent development of character disorders is another possibility under these circumstances (Griffiths and Verdun-Jones, 1994). Successful adjustment apparently depends in part on the availability of a role for them to play in the community.

Lemert also considers "self-defeating and self-perpetuating deviance." He cites alcoholism, drug addiction, and systematic cheque forgery as examples of this sort of vicious circle of cause and effect, characterized by an almost complete absence of durable pleasure for those involved. Finally, if the desire to escape self-degrading commitment is exceptionally strong, and none of the alternatives mentioned so far appeals to the committed individual, suicide becomes a prominent alternative.

Undoubtedly, there are many other alternatives to self-degrading commitment besides those discussed here. Much, it seems, depends on the nature of the identity to which the deviant is committed. There are different ways in which commitment can manifest itself. Extensive research is still needed to isolate the kinds and circumstances of commitment and the diverse reactions to it.

For many deviants, however, commitment is not a lasting contingency in their careers once they are aware of being trapped in their identity. In fact, this is one reason for stating the case for commitment in subjective terms. That the deviant feels a certain way does not always correspond to the objective state of affairs. Criminological theory and research support this observation. For instance, Matza (1990) holds that delinquents generally end their deviant careers at maturation, with few continuing on to adult crime (see Shannon, 1988). West (1980) and Wolfgang, Thornberry, and Figlio (1987) found that many adult criminals mature out of their antisocial ways: they take up a serious romantic relationship, find a legitimate job they like better than crime, or simply decide "to settle down" (see Chapter 14). Even deviants who are attached to their way of life often experience disillusionment and shifts of interest (Sommers, 2001), which is what "maturation" means in everyday terms in the

self-degrading commitment
Commitment leading to a poorer opinion of oneself.

world of crime (Jankowski, 1991). There is always the possibility of therapy for alcoholics, gamblers, and drug addicts. And, of course, some deviance requires youthful vigour, a quality lost with increasing years (Inciardi, 1974).

It is possible that self-enhancing commitment lasts longer than the self-degrading variety. Underlying this suggestion is the assumption that self-degrading commitment, while preferable to certain alternatives in the conventional world, is still undesirable in itself. A mortifying self-conception is a special penalty. It furnishes a significant part of the pressure to deal with an unpleasant state of affairs. Commitment to an identity or expectation leading to a negative self-image is a lesser-evil choice when initially compared with certain alternatives, and a greater-evil choice when subsequently compared with certain others. The strength of the individual's desire to abandon an unpleasant status is an important consideration in determining whether the transition will be made.

criminal identity
This social category, imposed by the community, correctly or incorrectly defines an individual as a particular type of criminal. The identity pervasively shapes his or her social interactions with others. This concept is similar to master status.

QUESTIONS FOR CRITICAL THINKING

1. Identify and describe a recent change in existing criminal law or a recent passing of a new criminal law initiated by moral entrepreneurs.
2. Select a vulnerable category (e.g., lower-class male youths, Aboriginal peoples) and describe how they could be falsely accused of certain crimes. How does such an explanation relate to deviant identity?
3. Identify some factors contributing to secondary deviation among heroin users.

Socialization into Crime

Most of the theories of criminality discussed elsewhere in this book help explain why people start a life of crime. By contrast, interactionism has been interested chiefly in what happens to criminals once their deviant activities commence. Still, two areas of interactionist theory, though not causal, can be properly seen as contributions to the study of socialization into crime. They are the processes of differential association and acquisition of a **criminal identity**.

differential association
Developed by Edwin Sutherland in the 1930s, this theory argues that crime, like any social behaviour, is learned in association with others. If individuals regularly associate with criminals in relative isolation from law-abiding citizens, they are more likely to engage in crime. They learn relevant skills for committing crime and ideas for justifying and normalizing it.

Differential Association

Sutherland set out his theory of differential association in 1939 in *Principles of Criminology*. The statement there differs little from the most recent edition written by Sutherland and Cressey (1978). The theory consists of nine propositions describing the complicated pattern of interaction that Sutherland called **differential association**:

1. people learn how to engage in crime;
2. this learning comes about through interaction with others who have already learned criminal ways;
3. the learning occurs in small, face-to-face groups;

4. what is learned is criminal technique (e.g., how to open a safe), motives, attitudes, and rationalizations;

5. among criminals, one important learned attitude is disregard for the community's legal code;

6. one acquires this attitude by differentially associating with those who hold it and failing to associate with those who do not;

7. differential associations with criminals and noncriminals vary in frequency, duration, priority, and intensity;

8. learning criminal behaviour through differential association rests on the same principles as learning any other kind of behaviour; and,

9. criminal behaviour is a response to the same cultural needs and values as noncriminal behaviour. For instance, one individual steals to acquire money for a new suit of clothes, while another works as a carpenter to reach the same goal. Consequently, tying societal needs and values to crime fails to explain it (Sutherland and Cressy, 1978, 80–82).*

Based on what is known about the antecedents of crime, Sutherland's theory offers a valuable albeit partial explanation of theft, burglary, prostitution, and marijuana use. Also, differential association is often a major antecedent in the use of addictive drugs and dependence on alcohol. It may even play an explanatory role in some mental disorders.

However, many other factors, which dilute the importance of differential association, must be considered when explaining such behaviour. For example, two processes discussed earlier in this chapter—drift, and primary deviance—indicate that deviant motives and meanings are often gradually learned and tentatively applied and modified over time in interactions with both deviants and nondeviants (see Figure 13.2). The motives and meanings are not mere causal antecedents of criminal acts and memberships in criminal groups (Davis, 1980).

Birkbeck and LaFree (1993) reviewed another set of factors. Symbolic interactionism, they note, further aids our understanding of crime by directing attention to the motives and meanings operating in the situations in which crimes are committed. In this connection, Katz (1990) found that the expressive reasons behind many criminal acts (e.g., thrill, enjoyment) are as important as the instrumental reasons (e.g., money, status). Additionally, precisely how a crime is committed and even which crimes are committed depend, in part, on decisions made on the spot by the criminal. These decisions may relate to the possibility of being apprehended, serving a longer or shorter sentence, or enduring a hostile reaction from the community to the deviance being considered.

Although the theory of differential association has been widely tested, convincing support for it has always been blocked by the difficulty of operationalizing some of Sutherland's key concepts (e.g., frequency, intensity, and duration of criminal and noncriminal associations). Nonetheless, in Matsueda's (2001) words,

> differential association theory represents one of the most important theoretical traditions in criminology. Historically, the theory brought a sociological perspective to the forefront of criminology and, with his

*Sutherland, Edwin H., and David R. Cressey. (1978). *Principles of Criminology* (10th ed.). Philadelphia: Lippincott.

FIGURE 13.2 Commitment

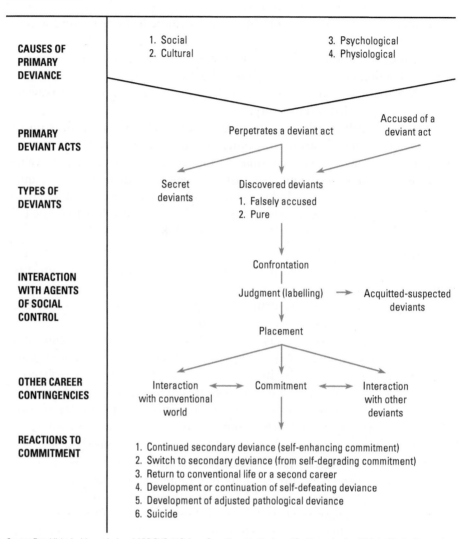

path-breaking work on white-collar crime, established Edwin Sutherland as perhaps the most important criminologist of his generation ... Over 50 years later, differential association theory continues to stimulate revisions, extensions, and original research into the causes of crime.

The major contribution of differential association is that it has highlighted the importance during the criminal career of ties to deviant peers. Daniel Wolf, an anthropologist who rode with the Rebels (an Edmonton biker gang), observed that the willingness of peers to stand up for one another can be crucial for maintaining power when faced with violent opposition from competitors:

For an outlaw biker, the greatest fear is not of the police; rather, it is of a slight variation of his own mirror image: the patch holder of another club. Under slightly different circumstances those men would call each other "brother." But when turf is at stake, inter-club rivalry and warfare completely override any considerations of the common bonds of being a biker—and brother kills brother. None of the outlaws that I rode with enjoyed the prospect of having to break the bones of another biker. Nor did they look forward to having to live with the hate–fear syndrome that dominates a conflict in which there are no rules. I came to realize that the willingness of an outlaw to lay down his life in these conflicts goes beyond a belligerent masculinity that brooks no challenge. When a patch holder defends his colours, he defends his personal identity, his community, his lifestyle. When a war is on, loyalty to the club and one another arises out of the midst of danger, out of apprehension of possible injury, mutilation, or worse. (1991, 11)

There is a great deal of research evidence showing that having young offenders as friends is one of the strongest correlates of deviant behaviour. Researchers have also found that among at-risk youth, gang membership contributes to delinquency above and beyond the influence of associating with deviant peers. Sutherland's work helps us understand why this is true. Differential association theory also points to the need to learn the skills for committing certain crimes. These range from very simple techniques such as hitting a man over the head and stealing his watch, to taking an unlocked bicycle, to sophisticated computer crimes. According to Sutherland, people learn necessary techniques and motives, drives, rationalizations, and attitudes of deviant behaviour from others with whom they associate.

Letkemann (1973), for example, described how a former penitentiary resident learned the now-obsolete art of safecracking:

Prior to doing his first "can" [safe] [he] bugged an older safecracker in prison "until he finally divulged how to do it." This instruction, he added was "not like a teacher–student, it was just a matter of discussion during work."

When he left the prison he went back to his regular partner and described to him what he had learned about safes. His partner said this was ridiculous but [he] persuaded him to come along: "I followed the instructions to the letter. It opened—we were both overcome with it all—the ease of it all!"

This first job had been a punch job [breaking into a safe without explosives]—technically the simplest. Following this [he] and his partner "opened many doors by trial and error" ... This went on for four years; they had not yet used explosives, nor had they ever been caught punching safes. They became increasingly eager to try explosives since they found so many safes that couldn't be opened any other way.

During this time, [he] was associating with other safecrackers ... He eventually asked another safecracker whether he could borrow some grease [nitroglycerine]. "I wouldn't admit that I knew nothing about it." He obtained the grease and chose a small safe, but was unsuccessful. The next day, he discussed his problem with some more experienced safecrackers. He found he had used too long a fuse and was advised to use electric knockers [detonators]. This he did with success. (Letkemann, 1973, 136)

Criminal Identities

A *criminal identity* is a social category into which deviants are placed by others in the community and into which, eventually, they may place themselves. That is, the process of identification of an individual as deviant has two sides. Based on a variety of criteria (e.g., appearance, actions, associates, location), members of the community come to view someone as a particular kind of criminal. The woman wearing garish, suggestive clothing who frequents a street corner in the red-light district is identified as a prostitute. The man with long, unkempt hair, dirty jeans, and a black leather jacket who rides a Harley-Davidson motorcycle is identified, as we saw earlier, as a member of a gang bent on rape, violence, and drunkenness.

Moreover—and this is the second side—community identification of people tends to be highly persuasive, even for deviants. That is, with officials, neighbours, relatives, and others asserting that these people are outlaws, it becomes increasingly difficult for them to deny the charge. At the very least, the alleged prostitute must accommodate her everyday life to such opinion, whether or not she is selling sex. The biker has the same problem.

Acquiring a community reputation, or identity, for unsavoury behaviour often furthers individual criminality. This is especially likely when the reputed criminal is forced into association with others of similar status and away from those who are "respectable." Once deviant ties are forged and nondeviant ties are sufficiently weakened, the socializing potential of differential association begins to take effect.

Limitations

Like all theories of crime and deviance, interactionist theory has its limitations. It is not itself a complete explanation for crime. It falls well short of explaining all crime under all the conditions in which it is committed. Throughout this chapter, we have discussed the strengths of the theory (summarized in Table 13.1). We now examine its limitations in terms of three critiques: neo-Marxist, empiricist, and ethno-methodological (taken from Glassner, 1982). Each critique is also the nucleus of still another approach to the study of crime.

The Neo-Marxist Critique

The principal neo-Marxist objection to interactionist theory is that it fails to relate crime and other forms of deviance to the larger society. It fails to account

TABLE 13.1   **Interactionist Theories**

Theory	Theorists	Key Elements
Labelling	Lemert, Becker	Primary deviance is infrequent deviance that involves little change in routine or lifestyle. Secondary deviance occurs when deviance becomes a way of life and a part of the deviant's self-image.
Differential association	Sutherland	Crime and delinquency are primarily learned in interaction with others in small, face-to-face groups. This involves learning techniques of deviance and justifications for it.

for historical and contemporary political and economic interests. After all, deviant acts and careers do occur in such contexts.

It is further charged that in explaining deviance, labelling theorists overlook the division between the powerful and the powerless. Powerful members of society also violate laws and other norms even while establishing some of their own as moral entrepreneurs. Consider an internal investigation of the Toronto Police Service in 2004 that recommended 218 criminal charges be laid against a dozen officers for offences such as paying informants with drugs seized in other cases, stealing drugs and weapons from suspects and selling them, and extorting money from bar owners (CBC News Toronto, 2007). Charges were laid against six officers. In 2012, five were convicted of obstruction of justice and three were also convicted of perjury (Small, 2012). All were sentenced to 45 days of house arrest.

The concept of moral entrepreneur and the categories of secret and falsely accused deviants suggest, however, that interactionists have some understanding of power differences in society. Perhaps the fairest criticism is that they have failed to go as far as they might in linking power to concepts such as *labelling, deviant career,* and *agent of social control.* Still, the observation that labelling theory overlooks the larger social context of deviance is a fair one. The perspective is predominantly social-psychological.

The Empiricist Critique

The empiricists have found several research weaknesses in labelling theory. Glassner (1982) discusses three of these. First, interactionists are said by empiricists to examine only, or chiefly, labelled deviants—those who have been officially identified as having deviated (charged and convicted, examined, and hospitalized). It is true that labelling theorists have often followed this narrow conception of the labelling process. Some deviants—for example, religious fanatics or occultists—are deviant and are labelled by the community as such, even though they rarely if ever gain official recognition. This exposes interactionists to the criticism that community labelling makes no practical difference to the individual.

Second, the empiricists argue that labelling as a cause of deviance is inadequately conceptualized. This is a misunderstanding. As this chapter shows, interactionists view labels as interpretations, not causes. The label of deviant is a career contingency, an event, a process, or a situation interpreted by deviants as having a significant impact on their moral careers.

Third, the empiricists claim that labelling theory lacks testable propositions. Consequently, data in this area can be explained in many different ways. They hold that quantitative statistical testing is the only definitive way to confirm propositions. Interactionists defend their approach by pointing out that qualitative methods—especially participant observation—are more appropriate for studies of interaction, labelling, career, and self-conception. These phenomena rest on definitions of the situation, images of self and others, negotiations of reality, and similar processes that are difficult to measure and are therefore largely unquantifiable. Even so, qualitative research often proceeds from the intense examination of individual groups and cases. Such studies are complicated and time-consuming, so there are relatively few of them. They tend to be exploratory rather than confirmatory.

The Ethno-Methodological Critique

The **ethno-methodologists** and conversational analysts are the modern-day inheritors of the phenomenology of Alfred Schutz. (In fact, Glassner refers to them as "phenomenologists" in his review.) Phenomenology is the study of how we perceive and understand the objects and events of reality. Reality, the phenomenologists hold, is not independent of human perception, of human consciousness. The chief concern of the ethno-methodologists with labelling theory is its tendency to neglect this question: How do people make sense of their social world?

According to Keel (2000), the perspective of ethno-methodology suggests that deviance and the deviant are not independent of the ways people socially construct the meaning of the situations in which they find themselves in daily life. The work of ethno-methodologists has led to an understanding of how deviant labels and categories are created and applied through three key processes: interpretation, typification, and negotiation. Thus the qualities and attributes of particular individuals become lost or distorted as they are located by other people (e.g., bystanders, agents of social control) in the context of a certain category of deviance. Their behaviour and identity come to represent that category of deviance, and that category in turn becomes an explanation for the behaviour or identity in question.

However, the people of interest to the ethno-methodologist are not always deviant. Rather, ethno-methodologists study how agents of social control and ordinary citizens make sense of deviants and deviant acts. Interactionists are accused of ignoring the ways in which the conventional world identifies and classifies morally offensive individuals and their behaviour. The important data for ethno-methodologists are the clues people use to identify kinds of deviants and deviant acts. People use this knowledge to reach such conclusions as "guilty" or "innocent."

To some extent, interactionists are guilty as charged. Although there are occasional hints of ethno-methodological thinking in the interactionist literature on deviance, there has been until recently a tendency to rely heavily on official definitions, or labels, of what and who is deviant. But even official definitions and their applications are informed by common sense. They, too, warrant ethno-methodological analysis.

ethno-methodology
Ethnomethodological theory was pioneered by Harold Garfinkel. Roughly translated, the term means the study of people's practices or methods. The perspective does not see the social world as an objective reality, but as something people constantly build and rebuild through their thoughts and actions. Ethnomethodologists try to uncover the methods and practices people use to create their taken-for-granted world.

Implications

The most profound implication of interactionist theory is that it offers a unique perspective on deviance, one that enhances understanding of this phenomenon. For instance, observations on moral enterprise underscore the arbitrariness of criminal law and call attention to patterns of local and national power (though rarely to the extent that neo-Marxists would like). Practically speaking, little can be done to counteract most moral enterprise. But interactionist research, at least, exposes its existence.

On a more practical level, interactionist theory stresses the damaging effects of the deviant label. These effects are of at least two types. First, the label (to the extent that the wider community is aware of it) makes re-entry into the community problematic. Nondeviants are inclined to avoid known deviants. Why? Because their own reputations could be damaged if they associated with deviants, and, possibly, because they are revolted by the deviant's lifestyle and moral behaviour. Deviants are more than rule violators. They are also outcasts.

Second, labels colour the judgments many people make of those who are labelled. Labels are names for stereotyped images. Both the images and the labels help nondeviants, including practitioners, define situations involving deviants. These two effects of the deviant label have led Empey, Stafford, and Hay (1999), among others, to argue that the juvenile courts should be used for only the most serious cases. Juvenile diversion and decriminalization programs, including Canada's Youth Criminal Justice Act, are practical responses to this implication of interactionist theory.

QUESTIONS FOR CRITICAL THINKING

1. Identify some legitimate "side bets" people make that help them avoid criminal acts and criminals make that help them avoid further criminality.
2. Because of the influence of labelling theory, society has become more sensitive to the costs of deviant labels. List some measures taken in our youth and adult courts to reduce the number of people officially labelled by those institutions.
3. According to Katz, some criminal activities are fun—a leisure activity that produces thrill and enjoyment. Identify one of these activities and explain how their criminal participants might find them thrilling and/or enjoyable.

Interactionist theory calls attention to the deviant career as a process that helps explain deviance beyond its initial causes. One practical implication of this career is that over time, people often become committed to certain lifestyles. But to the extent that they make substantial "side bets" (Becker, 1963) in one or more conventional identities, they are unlikely to deviate. Their possible deviance, if discovered and labelled, could ruin their reputation in the conventional world (e.g., the politician exposed in the press for patronizing a prostitute).

One antidote to initial or continued deviance, then, is to give people every possible opportunity to build strong side bets in "respectable" pursuits. By this reasoning, juveniles and adult ex-offenders should be encouraged to drift toward conventional interests. The interactionist concept of career is also useful here, albeit the career in mind is one of serious leisure (Stebbins, 2007). This is the leisure of amateurs, hobbyists, and skilled and knowledgeable volunteers, where participants find a career in activities such as music, woodworking, or outdoor pastimes, leading to personal development realized through the acquisition of new skills, knowledge, and experiences related to a leisure activity. Two outcomes of this process are positive change in sense of self-worth as well as production of a respectable social identity.

■ Summary

- Interactionist theory centres on the deviant interchanges among people and the meanings of these interchanges in the present, past, and future.

- A deviant career is the passage of an individual through the stages of one or more related deviant identities.

- Primary deviation occurs in the early stages of the deviant career. Here, deviance is enacted with little change in the person's everyday routine or lifestyle.

- The deviant drifts between two moral worlds. In youth offender subcultures, deviance is facilitated by certain moral rhetorics and by other aspects of the subterranean tradition.

- Agents of social control help check deviant behaviour. Moral entrepreneurs create and enforce rules, violation of which constitutes deviance. Thus, only some people get labelled deviant.

- When deviants see their lives as substantially modified by deviance, they have moved into secondary deviation. The rules are applied to some people and not others. Those publicly labelled deviant generally face some sort of societal reaction to their misdeeds. Labelled deviants may have to cope with stigma.

- Continuance commitment, or forcing a person to remain in an identity, sometimes results from these encounters. When self-degrading commitment sets in, those affected are inclined to redefine continuance penalties or otherwise adjust to this unsettling situation.

- Although the theory of criminal socialization is not central in the interactionist perspective, interactionists have contributed to the theory in two major ways. First, people learn crime through differential association with others who are already criminal. Second, they are further socialized into it by being placed in and coming to accept (often grudgingly) a criminal identity.

- Limitations to the interactionist theories have been noted by neo-Marxists, empiricists, and ethnomethodologists. At the moment, however, none of these approaches have progressed beyond finding weaknesses in the interactionist perspective.

- Interactionist theory has certain theoretical and practical implications. One is that, wherever possible, continuance commitment to deviance among juveniles should be eschewed by avoiding the official label of criminal.

NET WORK

Gun control is an issue that has seen groups of moral entrepreneurs with different viewpoints trying to influence lawmakers. Bill C-68, the Firearms Act, was particularly controversial, with both sides working hard to have their views accepted. On one side of the issue was the National Firearms Association (NFA), which strongly objected to restricting ownership and use of firearms as set out in Bill C-68 (see www.nfa.ca).

On the other side was the Coalition for Gun Control. Arguments favouring gun control can be found at their website (www.guncontrol.ca).

1. What claims are these two sets of moral entrepreneurs making?
2. What reasons lie behind their conflicting views?
3. What strategies did the National Firearms Association use to fight implementation of Bill C-68? What arguments did the Coalition for Gun Control use in its successful fight to persuade the government to pass Bill C-68?

Social Control Theory

Rick Linden
UNIVERSITY OF MANITOBA

We begin by examining some of the early social disorganization theories exploring the relationship between social structure and deviance. These theories were important, because along with Merton's work (Chapter 10) they challenged the view that the sources of crime lay within the individual. Instead, they proposed that the structure and culture of the American city was responsible for deviant behaviour. Social disorganization theorists contended that disorganized communities did not provide meaningful employment to residents and did not have strong families, schools, and churches. This lack of effective social controls led to high rates of crime and other types of deviance. While the early theorists looked at the relationship between community characteristics and crime, later theorists focused more on the way the social bonds of individuals help constrain crime and delinquency. Final sections of this chapter deal with some of the issues surrounding control theory and with the policy implications of the theory.

Learning Objectives

After reading this chapter, you should be able to

- Understand the early social disorganization theories that sought to explain why crime rates were highest in neighbourhoods characterized by poverty, physical deterioration, and ethnic conflict.
- Know the importance of the social bonds of attachment, involvement, commitment, and belief in the causation of delinquency and crime.
- Explain the role of the family, the school, and the church in the causation of delinquency and crime.
- Describe the criticisms that have been made of social control theory and understand the validity of these criticisms.
- Understand the social policy implications of social control theory.

social control theory
The theory proposes that people refrain from committing criminal acts because they do not want to jeopardize their bonds to conventional society.

Social control theory assumes that human beings are neither good nor evil. However, we are born with the capacity to do wrong. Unlike most theories of criminality, control theory requires no special motivation for people to deviate. Given that humans naturally try to gratify themselves with no concern for right and wrong, and that the "wrong" way may be the quickest and most efficient way of achieving that gratification, it is conformity rather than deviance that must be explained. Where other theorists ask, "Why do they do it?", the control theorist is concerned with the question, "Why don't we *all* do it?" The answer given by control theory is, "We all would, if only we dared, but many of us dare not because we have loved ones we fear to hurt and physical possessions and social reputations we fear to lose" (Box, 1971, 140). All societies have developed ways of making people conform, and the control theorist is concerned with the processes that bind people to the social order.

Theories of Social Disorganization— Durkheim, Thrasher, and Shaw and McKay

Durkheim and Social Integration

The earliest social control theories explained how some types of social structure led to high rates of crime and deviance. Communities characterized by poverty, physical deterioration, and racial or ethnic conflict were too disorganized to exert effective control over the behaviour of residents. These early social disorganization theorists included Durkheim, Thrasher, and Shaw and McKay.

In his monograph *Suicide* (1951), Durkheim pointed out the importance of social bonds to our understanding of deviant behaviour. Egoistic suicide results from a situation in which a person's social ties are so weak that he or she is freed from social constraints and acts only on the basis of private interests. Anomic suicide occurs when a lack of social integration, caused by factors such as rapid economic change, leaves a society without a clear system of moral beliefs and sentiments. In each case, social organization is weak and the individual lacks moral guidance. If the rules are strong and if there is consensus about their validity, there will be little deviance. If the rules are weak and if there is minimal agreement about their applicability, society will be unable to regulate morality effectively, and deviance will be common. Without socially regulated goals, deviance is more likely, as people pursue their aspirations without check.

We saw in Chapter 10 that in Merton's reformulation of anomie theory, he shifted from Durkheim's emphasis on a society's failure to define appropriate goals to an emphasis on the failure to define the appropriate means of reaching common culture goals, and on the unequal distribution of legitimate means of reaching these goals. The social disorganization theorists—among them Thrasher, and Shaw and McKay—were more faithful to Durkheim's view of the effects of social bonds on deviance.

Thrasher and *The Gang*

In his classic study *The Gang*, Thrasher located gangs both geographically and socially where there are breaks in the structure of social organization. They occur "in city slums characterized by physical deterioration, rapid succession of inhabitants, mobility, and disorganization; along economic and ecological boundaries; along political frontiers; ... and during adolescence, an interstitial period between childhood and maturity" (Kornhauser, 1978, 51). Gangs arise spontaneously in areas where social controls are weak. Gangs are not necessarily delinquent, though delinquency will often be the natural result of the

social bonds
The degree to which an individual has ties to his or her society. In Hirschi's theory, social bonds include attachment, commitment, involvement, and belief.

Vancouver's Downtown Eastside is a very poor, high-crime neighbourhood where social controls are weak.

activities of groups of adolescents in communities with weak social controls (Thrasher, 1963). In a slum setting, delinquency was often the most exciting and interesting thing for these youths to do.

Shaw and McKay—Ecological Analysis

Shaw and McKay saw deviance originating not in the pathology of individuals but rather in the social disorganization of communities. They found that some Chicago neighbourhoods had disproportionately high rates of officially recorded crime and delinquency. Rates were highest in slum areas near the city centre and generally declined as one moved outward. In many of these neighbourhoods, crime rates remained high over a long period of time, even though the racial and ethnic characteristics of the residents changed as new waves of immigrants moved into the city. Shaw and McKay attributed these high rates of crime to the failure of neighbourhood institutions and organizations such as families, schools, and churches to provide adequate social controls. Like Thrasher, they emphasized the importance of exposure to the criminal subculture that developed in these areas and attracted young people to deviant behaviour.

Control theory was not fully developed in the work of Thrasher and Shaw and McKay. From the 1930s to the 1960s, subcultural and strain theories dominated the field of criminology and very few changes were made to the social disorganization model (Kornhauser, 1978). There were several reasons why control theory all but disappeared from the scene despite this promising beginning. The most important reason was that the early research was methodologically flawed. The relationships among **independent variables** such as social class, mobility, and community diversity and crime and other forms of deviance consistent with social control theory, but they also were consistent with other perspectives such as strain theory, and Shaw and McKay never directly measured the degree of social control that existed in a particular community. They inferred, but did

independent variable
A presumed cause of a dependent variable. If unemployment is thought to cause crime to increase, unemployment is the independent variable, and crime the dependent variable.

not demonstrate, that higher income communities were better organized than were lower-class slums. The research done by Shaw and McKay was also subject to the problem of the **ecological fallacy**. Consider the finding that official crime rates are higher in lower-class than in middle-class areas. The conclusion usually drawn from this finding is that being a member of the lower class makes one more likely to become involved with crime. However, this inference is not necessarily true. Perhaps most crimes in lower-class areas are committed by middle-class residents of those census tracts. Perhaps the resident population is not responsible for crime at all. Engstad (1975) showed that some businesses in Edmonton, such as bars and shopping centres, attract people from other parts of the city and provide opportunities for crime. Chambliss (1973) found that middle-class adolescents migrated to other parts of the city to commit their delinquencies. Eventually, the vague and often value-laden term "social disorganization" fell into disrepute among sociologists.

Despite these problems, Thrasher and Shaw and McKay did lay the foundations for a control theory of crime and delinquency. They found that delinquents come from poorly organized communities whose institutions are not well integrated. Families are unable to adequately socialize their children, and the local schools are poor. These elements all reappear in the work of later theorists. Unfortunately, most of the later work focused on individuals rather than on neighbourhood variables. However, recent research from Statistics Canada has focused attention again on the correlation between neighbourhood conditions and crime in several Canadian cities. This research shows that crime is heavily concentrated in economically disadvantaged neighbourhoods (Savoie, 2008), just as it was in Chicago during the time of Shaw and McKay.

Early Social Control Theories—Reiss and Nye

Albert Reiss

The social disorganization theorists had been concerned with community and family controls. Reiss (1951) was the first to distinguish between *social* controls, which include ties to primary groups such as the family and community institutions, and *personal* controls, which have been internalized by an individual. If these controls are absent, if they break down, if they are in conflict, or if they cannot be enforced, delinquency will result. Using information from the files of male juvenile probationers, Reiss found that success or failure on probation was associated with the absence of social *and* personal controls.

Ivan Nye

In terms of theory, the work of Nye (1958) simply expanded on that of Reiss, but in terms of method, it was a great advance. Reiss had relied on court records of "official" delinquents; Nye developed a technique for measuring self-reported delinquency and gathered his data from a random sample of high school students in three small American cities. His work was one of the first attempts at unravelling the causes of delinquency using the self-report approach.

ecological fallacy
An error made when information is gathered at a group level (the unemployment rate of a neighbourhoods) and conclusions are drawn about individuals (unemployed persons). Areas with high unemployment may have high crime rates, but this does not tell us that those crimes are necessarily committed by unemployed persons.

Reiss did not elaborate on the theory underlying personal and social controls, whereas Nye explicitly stated his theoretical perspective: "Control theory assumes delinquency is not *caused* in a positive sense (motivated by the gains to be derived from it) but *prevented* (determined by the relative costs of alternative benefits) … Weak controls free the person to commit delinquent acts by lowering their cost relative to available alternatives" (Kornhauser, 1978, 140–41, emphasis added). Individuals are motivated to achieve certain goals as quickly as possible, but most are prevented from doing so by the laws and customs that societies have established to protect their members.

Nye believed the family was the most significant group in the development of social controls. The extent to which the family enforced controls and the degree to which family members got along determined the extent to which a child would develop internal controls. His research supported these hypotheses. Children from close families in which there was agreement on basic values were unlikely to be delinquent.

Reiss and Nye provided a promising beginning for contemporary control theory, and subsequent research received much more empirical support than did the theories of Merton, Cohen, Cloward and Ohlin, Miller, and Sutherland, which dominated the field. However, it took a number of years before control theory became widely accepted by criminologists.

Hirschi and the Social Bond

Control theory received renewed attention in 1969 with the publication of Travis Hirschi's *Causes of Delinquency*. Hirschi developed a concise version of control theory and demonstrated that it explained delinquency better than did competing theories. Like earlier control theorists, Hirschi postulates that individuals are more likely to turn to illegitimate means if their bonds to society are weak or broken. For Hirschi, four linked aspects of social bonds constrain our behaviour: attachment, commitment, involvement, and belief.

Attachment

Attachment refers to the degree to which an individual has affective ties to other persons, particularly those in his or her primary group. Individuals who are sensitive to the feelings of others and close to those others will constrain their behaviour because they will not want to hurt or embarrass the people they like. Those lacking such ties will not have to consider the feelings of others and will be free to deviate. Thus, youth who do not get along with their parents will be more free to commit acts of delinquency than those who are close to their families.

Commitment

The essence of commitment is the pursuit of conventional goals. "The idea, then, is that the person invests time, energy, himself, in a certain line of activity—say, getting an education, building up a business, acquiring a reputation for virtue" (Hirschi, 1969, 20). A person who decides to engage in deviance

attachment
The degree to which an individual has affective ties to other persons. One of the social bonds in Hirschi's theory.

commitment
The degree to which an individual pursues conventional goals. One of the social bonds in Hirschi's theory.

will be putting that investment at risk. The student who has worked hard in school and who aspires to become a professional may reject the temptations of delinquency for fear of jeopardizing this future career. However, the youth who is failing in school and who has no career aspirations may not feel as constrained. For the second youth, the immediate rewards of delinquency may outweigh the potential long-term costs. Both commitments and attachments can change over time. For example, the phenomenon of maturational reform—as we get older, we behave better—can be at least partly explained by the fact that adults typically have a greater investment in conventional lines of activity than do adolescents, so deviance may have higher costs.

Involvement

Hirschi hypothesized that level of **involvement** has an impact on delinquency. If people are busy with conventional activities, they will not have time to engage in deviant behaviour. For example, a student who is busy at school and is involved in extracurricular activities will not have as much opportunity to commit delinquencies as do peers who are not as involved.

Belief

Our **belief** in conventional values, morality, and the legitimacy of the law will constrain our behaviour. Some conflict theorists (Chapter 11) contend that deviants are tied to value systems that are different from those of the rest of the population; Hirschi, by contrast, claims that society does have a common value system. However, individuals vary in the degree to which they believe they should obey the rules. Conflict theorists tell us that acts that are deviant from the perspective of those who have the power to make and enforce the rules are *required* by the beliefs of members of certain subcultures; the control theorist says that deviant acts are made possible by the *absence* of beliefs forbidding them.

Research has largely supported Hirschi's theory, particularly for the variables of attachment and commitment. Belief in the law has also been found to be inversely related to delinquency (Gomme, 1985). But some of the evidence is mixed: involvement in school activities is related to lower involvement in delinquency, while participation in sports, hobbies, and part-time jobs is not (Hirschi, 1969).

Self-Control—The General Theory of Crime

Hirschi's early work focused on external sources of social control such as family, friends, and school. In 1990, Gottfredson and Hirschi published *A General Theory of Crime*, in which they proposed that individuals with low self-control have a greater propensity to commit crimes when they have the opportunity to do so. They will also be more likely to engage in other risky behaviour such as smoking, drinking, and dangerous driving. Gottfredson and Hirschi believe their theory applies to all types of crime.

Individuals who lack self-control are impulsive and focus on the moment instead of planning for the future. They also have unstable personal relationships and are less likely to feel shame or remorse when their actions hurt others. When "desires conflict with long-term interests, those lacking self-control opt

involvement
The degree to which an individual is active in conventional activities. One of the social bonds in Hirschi's theory.

belief
The degree to which an individual believes in conventional values, morality, and the legitimacy of law. One of Hirschi's social bonds.

for the desires of the moment, whereas those with greater self-control are governed by the restraints imposed by the consequences of acts displeasing to family, friends, and the law" (Gottfredson and Hirschi, 1990, xvi).

Why do some people lack self-control? For Gottfredson and Hirschi, the answer lies in early childhood socialization. Children will have low self-control if they have poor relationships with their parents or if their parents do not have good parenting skills. Those who fail to develop self-control in childhood will be more likely to be involved in crime throughout their lives; thus, the impact of poor early socialization may persist for many years.

Several Canadian researchers have studied the relationship between self-control and criminal behaviour. Using data collected during a night-time roadside survey of Ontario drivers, Keane, Maxim, and Teevan (1993) found that men and women with lower self-control had higher blood alcohol levels than other drivers. Also, Sorenson and Brownfield (1995) found a correlation between self-control and drug use. However, they found that ties to delinquent friends were correlated more strongly with drug use than any of their self-control variables. LeBlanc (1997) suggested that low self-control is just one of several psychological traits that should be a part of a comprehensive social control theory of offending. He found that Quebec youth with "egocentric personalities"—a construct similar to Gottfredson and Hirschi's notion of low self-control—have weaker social bonds and higher levels of delinquency than their peers (LeBlanc, Ouimet, and Tremblay, 1988). LaGrange and Silverman (1999) found that self-control explained part of the difference in delinquency involvement between males and females in Edmonton.

While some research does support this theory, other evidence suggests it will not replace more traditional versions of control theory. In the general theory of crime, Gottfredson and Hirschi turned away from Hirschi's earlier view that ongoing social bonds make involvement in crime and delinquency less likely. Instead, they proposed that early childhood experiences can produce low levels of self-control that result in higher levels of deviance throughout the life course.

Sampson and Laub (2003) have cast doubt on this hypothesis. They obtained access to data collected by Sheldon and Eleanor Glueck (1950) involving interviews with delinquent and nondelinquent males beginning in the 1940s. Sampson and Laub were able to track these males until age 70 and even to complete interviews with many of them. Their initial analysis (1993) followed the boys from ages 17 to 25 and showed that those who developed adult social bonds, including stable jobs and cohesive marriages, were less likely to be involved in criminality than peers who did not develop these ties. Their later work (Laub and Sampson, 2003, 249) looked at the men's entire lives and found that some men who had been involved in criminality encountered *turning points* that marked a transition in their lives:

> Men who desist from crime do so when they, on the one hand, experience structural turning points (for example marriage, the military) that lead to a strengthening of their social support systems and, on the

other hand, make an inner resolve to change their lives. They are thus better positioned situationally to respond to the monitoring and control and the love and social support around them—turning points are not deterministic … Men who did not change referred to their lack of turning points and/or their own inability (often due to immaturity) to take advantage of turning points when they presented themselves … Finally, in a painful and tragic way, these narratives point to the destructive power of alcohol, brutal institutional confinement, anger, racial and ethnic division, domestic conflict, and horrific war experiences in shaping an individual's life course and in reciprocally inducing further negative turning points.

Thus, rather than remaining stable over the life course, the propensity to deviate appears to be variable. Childhood patterns of deviance are not necessarily carried into adulthood. These findings are consistent with social control theory, in that turning points typically involved the men developing conventional social bonds.

In the remainder of this chapter, we will look in detail at some of the research evidence bearing on control theory, discuss some issues with the theory, suggest ways in which it might be revised, and consider its social policy implications.

FOCUS

Box 14.1

CAN MARSHMALLOWS PREDICT BEHAVIOUR?

Walter Mischel has conducted a fascinating study of self-control. Mischel's daughters attended a nursery school at Stanford University, where he taught psychology. He set up a simple study to examine why some people were able to delay gratification while others were not. He asked children to sit at a small desk in a room at the nursery school. Each child chose a treat, such as a marshmallow, from a tray and then was told that they could eat the treat immediately. However, if they were willing to wait, they would get a second treat. The researcher left the room and the children were filmed while they tried to avoid eating the treat until the researcher returned.

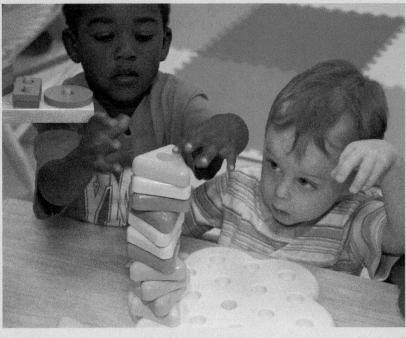

Jim West/Alamy

(continued)

In the years following this research, Mischel's daughters occasionally discussed their friends and he noticed that the children who were able to delay eating the treat seemed to be doing better in school than those who could not wait. He followed up as many of the children as he could and found that those who had been able to delay gratification were doing better than the others in many dimensions of their lives (Shoda, Mischel, and Peake, 1990). They had fewer behavioural problems, better coping skills in adolescence, higher college entrance test scores, and less illicit drug use (Mischel et al., 2011). The ability to delay gratification is also associated with lower levels of aggression, higher self-esteem, and less involvement in bullying (Mischel et al., 2011). Mischel concluded: "If you can deal with hot emotions, then you can study … instead of watching television … and you can save money for retirement. It's not just about marshmallows" (Lehrer, 2009, 29).

Mischel and his colleagues have found evidence that there is a neurobiological component to the ability to delay gratification and have also found that this ability can be improved through training.

This work represents an interesting dimension of self-control theory and is potentially helpful because researchers in this area have suggested strategies for improving children's abilities to control their behaviour through measures such as reframing the situation to make the stimulus (in this case, the marshmallow) less immediately appealing.

For an amusing look at children confronted by a marshmallow, go to https://www.youtube.com/watch?v=QX_oy9614HQ.

Family Relationships

Social control theory emphasizes family relationships since these provide children with the attachments that restrain their deviance. Several aspects of family relationships, including strength of family ties, parental supervision and discipline, and the role modelling provided by parents, are related to delinquency.

Strength of Family Ties

Strong family ties are important for the development of social bonds. If parents are close to their children and provide a congenial atmosphere in the home, this should deter delinquency. Children who care about what their parents think of them should be less likely to become involved in delinquency.

Warm, affectionate family relationships are associated with low rates of delinquency, while mutual rejection and hostility are typical of the families of delinquents (Glueck and Glueck, 1950; Nye, 1958). Conflict between the parents also characterizes the families of delinquents.

Parental Supervision and Discipline

Children who are adequately supervised by their parents and who are disciplined appropriately have lower delinquency rates than their peers who are not. Researchers have demonstrated the importance of parents' knowing what their children are doing and ensuring they play with friends whom the parents consider suitable (Hirschi, 1969; West and Farrington, 1973; Wilson, 1980). Studies in Montreal and Edmonton have found that supervision was more strongly related to delinquency than any other family variable (Kupfer, 1966; Caplan, 1977; Biron and LeBlanc, n.d.).

Closely related to supervision is parental discipline. While critics of control theory have complained that the theory advocates the harsh treatment of children, control theorists do not view physical punishment as the best way to control behaviour. Rather, they believe that "disapproval by people one cares about is the most powerful of sanctions. Effective punishment by the parent or major caretaker therefore usually entails nothing more than explicit disapproval of unwanted behaviour" (Gottfredson and Hirschi, 1990, 99–100). Studies have consistently found the disciplinary practices of delinquent families to be different from those of nondelinquent families. Families with inconsistent or lax discipline were much more likely to have delinquent children (West and Farrington, 1973). Children learn best from discipline that is administered in a clear, consistent manner.

Strict discipline results in higher rates of delinquency, particularly if it is associated with harsh physical punishment (Fischer, 1980) and if parental warmth and supportiveness is lacking (Simons et al., 2000). Very strict discipline is seen as unfair and may lead to frustration and resentment on the part of the child. Harsh punishment may gain immediate compliance, but moderate discipline is more effective in encouraging children to internalize a set of values that will ensure long-term compliance (Aronson, 1984).

In his study of a poor inner-city community, Anderson described how "street-oriented" parents—his term for those who do not try to emulate the "decent-family model"—discipline their children:

> In these circumstances, a woman—or a man, although men are less consistently present in children's lives—can be quite aggressive with children, yelling at them and striking at them for the least little infraction of the rules she has set down. Often little, if any, serious explanation follows the verbal and physical punishment. This response teaches children a particular lesson. They learn that to solve any kind of interpersonal problem, one must quickly resort to hitting or other violent behaviour. (Anderson, 1994, 83)

The importance of parenting style is clear from an analysis of Canada's National Longitudinal Survey of Children and Youth (NLSCY), which is following the lives of more than 23,000 children (Statistics Canada, 1998). The researchers asked the children's parents about their parenting styles—for example, in terms of punitiveness, hostility, consistency, and the amount of positive interaction. Parenting style was strongly correlated with relationship and behavioural problems in children. Children exposed to hostile or ineffective parenting were *nine* times more likely to have behavioural problems than were children who were not exposed to these parenting styles. Parenting style—particularly hostile parenting and parental harshness (Ho, Bluestein, and Jenkins, 2008)—was more strongly related to behavioural problems than other factors, including income and family structure. The most aggressive children at ages 10 and 11 were much more likely than their peers to report having negative relations with their family and to feeling rejected by their parents (Sprott and Doob, 2000).

Parental Role Model

Hirschi argued that strong ties to parents will act as a deterrent to delinquency regardless of the criminality of the parents. However, there does appear to be a relationship between the criminality of the parent and that of the child. West and Farrington (1973) found that boys with at least one parent convicted of a criminal offence were more than twice as likely to become delinquent as those whose parents had no convictions. "Youthful crime often seems to be part of a family tradition" (West, 1982, 44). West does not feel that parents deliberately transmit criminal values to their offspring, for few of the children were involved in their parents' criminality and the parents expressed disapproval of their children's involvement in delinquency. The relationship is partly explained by the fact that parents with criminal records were lax in applying rules and did not supervise their children effectively. Consider this comment from a high-risk auto theft offender in Winnipeg who was required to wear an electronic monitoring bracelet that would notify officials if he left home after his curfew time (Pearson, 2012, 104).

> My friends would come over and we would party at my house, my mom didn't like that. We partied every day and she would get mad, trip out and bitch at me to turn the music down. When she was in my face I would feed her pieces [crack] until she left me alone.

In light of West's finding that criminal fathers were likely to be on social assistance and unemployment benefits and that this dependency was repeated among their sons, it would appear that families with criminal parents face a variety of problems that manifest themselves in both parental criminality and poor family relationships. West and Farrington (1977) suggest that labelling may also be a factor, in that an arrest was more likely to result in a conviction if a boy came from a criminal family.

Direct modelling of parental behaviour does not appear to be a major cause of delinquency, but it may be a factor in some types of offences. Rutter and Giller suggest that "criminal parents may provide a model of aggression and antisocial attitudes, if not of criminal activities as such" (1984, 183). The fact that a high proportion of abusive parents were themselves abused as children supports the view that family violence is learned in the home (Steinmetz and Straus, 1980). And abusive parents contribute to delinquency in another way. In a study of homeless youths in Toronto, Hagan and McCarthy (1997) found that some of their respondents were living on the streets in order to escape abuse at home. Once on the street, their need for food, shelter, and money led to delinquency.

Schooling

The school plays a primary role in socialization and is an important determinant of delinquency. Schools are pervasive in young peoples' lives. Children spend all day in classes and return to school after hours for other activities such as sports and dances. The school is an arena in which an adolescent's performance is constantly being judged. Those who are successful enjoy the prestige conferred by teachers, classmates, and parents. Those who fail may feel they have been rejected by the adult world as well as by their peers. For those who are successful and who enjoy their educational experience, school provides a stake in conformity. Those who fail do not have this stake and hence are more likely to become involved in delinquency. The correlation between school failure and delinquency is relatively strong and has been replicated in Canada (Gomme, 1985), Britain (Hargreaves, 1967), and the United States (Polk and Schafer, 1972).

The school affects delinquency in two interrelated ways. First, the school has taken over many of the occupational socialization functions formerly performed by the family. Formal educational qualifications have become the basis for entry into most occupations. A child's school experiences will have a profound impact on that child's future life chances. Second, the school is related to delinquency through its effects on children's daily lives. For some, the experience is interesting, pleasant, and enriching. For others, it is irrelevant, degrading, and humiliating.

Both types of impact have an effect on a student's stake in conformity. Those whose school experiences will clearly not qualify them for a meaningful occupation may not have the same degree of commitment as their peers whose expectations are higher. The daily consequences of failure and the resulting lack of attachment to the school also affect the child. In fact, research suggests that the daily problems of coping with school failure may be more strongly related to delinquency than are concerns about the future. Linden (1974) found that measures reflecting present school status (whether the child liked school, finished homework, skipped school, valued good grades, and got along with teachers) were more highly correlated with delinquency than were measures of educational aspirations and expectations. Arum and Beattie (1999) showed that students who enjoyed a school environment with small class sizes and course materials relevant to their lives had lower rates of adult incarceration than those with less positive school experiences, even when their education did not provide any labour market benefit. Using data from Canada's National Longitudinal Study, Sprott (2004) found that the classroom environment had an impact on later delinquency. Children who attended an emotionally supportive classroom between the ages of 10 and 13 had lower rates of violence two years later. Those with an academically supportive classroom environment committed fewer property crimes over the same period.

Some criminologists see a broader relationship between schools and delinquency. From a structural perspective, the school "cuts adolescents off from participating in the social and economic life of the community: it reduces their commitments and attachments" (West, 1984, 169). Even within the school, the educational process involves the student in only a passive way. Polk and Schafer (1972) illustrate the irrelevance of the student role by asking what happens when a student dies. The student disappears without leaving a social ripple aside from family bereavement. The student's role is not one that has to be filled by someone else. This marginality may contribute to delinquency by leaving the adolescent relatively free of the commitments that constrain deviance.

Religion

Conventional wisdom has long held that people with strong religious commitment are not likely to become criminals. In the early penitentiaries that were the predecessors of our current prison system, Bible study was a major rehabilitative tool (Rothman, 1971). Early prison education programs were intended to provide inmates with the basic literacy skills needed to read the Bible and other religious literature; this was expected to motivate the offender to mend his ways.

This view was supported by early studies that showed a modest negative relationship between religious involvement and criminality. However, in 1969, Hirschi and Stark reported that religiosity was *not* related to delinquency. Neither church attendance, nor a belief in supernatural sanctions for rule breakers, nor the religiosity of parents, was associated with delinquency. Because the work of Hirschi and Stark was methodologically superior to that of earlier researchers (and perhaps because of a secular bias among criminologists), the results of this study were commonly accepted as definitive. Most contemporary theories of the causes of crime do not include religion as a key variable.

However, several subsequent studies have found strong negative correlations between church attendance and delinquency. How are we to reconcile these conflicting findings? Stark, Doyle, and Kent (1982) concluded that the key to resolving the contradiction was to look at differences in the communities being studied. The studies that found *no* relationship between religiosity and delinquency had been conducted in communities where religious participation was low, while the studies that *did* find a relationship between religiosity and delinquency had been conducted in communities that had high religious participation.

Stark, Doyle, and Kent provided evidence to support this view. They compared boys from Provo, Utah, where the church membership rate is very high, with boys from Seattle, where church membership rates are among the lowest in the United States. The relationship between attending church and not being involved in delinquency was much stronger in Provo than in Seattle. The relationship also holds for adult crime. In another study, Stark, Doyle, and Kent (1980) found a negative relationship between church membership and crime rates in 193 US cities. These researchers concluded that religiosity is related to reduced levels of involvement in crime and delinquency in communities where religion is important, but not in highly secularized communities.

Their explanation of this finding has broader implications for social control theory. Stark and colleagues contend that an **individualistic**, psychological view of the manner in which religion constrains behaviour has led researchers astray. Rather than assuming that religion affects deviance through an individual's fear of religious sanctions, they suggest that "religion only serves to bind people to the moral order if religious influences permeate the culture and the social interactions of the individuals in question" (1982, 19). Religion has its greatest impact where it binds its adherents into a moral community in which religious teachings are salient and consistently reinforced. In these circumstances, an individual is less likely to consider deviant behaviour, for the costs of violating community norms may be high, and the likelihood of finding reference groups that support such violations will be relatively low. Religion has a greater impact where it is part of the community's institutional order rather than a private matter.

It seems clear that religion constrains involvement in delinquent and criminal behaviour. However, this relationship is complex: it is greatest where there

individualistic
A theory that focuses on explaining the behaviour of individuals and using factors or features of the individual in explaining this behaviour.

is a strong religious community; it is mediated by relationships with family and friends (Elifson, Petersen, and Hadaway, 1983); and it has the most impact on behaviour (such as marijuana use) that may not be universally condemned by other segments of society (Linden and Currie, 1977).

The studies discussed in this section were carried out several decades ago, but recent research reviews have confirmed the findings. Johnson and colleagues (2000) reviewed 40 studies and found that 75 percent of them showed that young people who were committed to religious values and beliefs were less likely to be involved in delinquent behaviour than nonreligious youth. Baier and Wright (2000) reviewed 60 studies and found support for the hypothesis that religion was negatively associated with crime and that its impact was greater for minor crimes than for more serious ones. Most recently, Salas-Wright, Vaughn, and Maynard (2014) have found that religion has as strong an impact on young adults (18 to 25) as it does on adolescents (12 to 17) and is an important deterrent for both males and females.

One of the most interesting illustrations of the influence of religion on offenders comes from a study of offenders who had lengthy criminal careers despite having religious beliefs (Topalli, Brezina, and Bernhardt, 2013). Some dealt with the conflict between religion and criminality by misunderstanding religious principles:

> I mean anything can be forgiven. We live in Hell now and you can do anything [transgression] in Hell. When it all end … We go up there [to heaven] and the Devil comes down here. Only the Devil lives in Hell forever man all by his self. God has to forgive everyone, even if they don't believe in him. (2013, 59)

Others had a very selective view of religious doctrine:

> The way it works is this. You go out and do some bad and then you ask for forgiveness and Jesus have to give it to you, and you know wipe the slate clean. So, I always do a quick little prayer right before and then I'm cool with Jesus. Also another thing is this: if you doing some wrong to another bad person, like if I go and rob a dope dealer or a molester or something, then it don't count against me because it's like I'm giving punishment to them for Jesus. That's God's will. Oh you molested some kids? Well now I'm [God] sending Cool over to your house to get your ass. (2013, 60)

This research suggests that religious belief is a possible deterrent to crime but that some offenders are able to rationalize their behaviour so that they can continue with their chosen lifestyles.

QUESTIONS FOR CRITICAL THINKING

1. What assumption underlies social control theories? How does this differ from the underlying assumption of most other theories of crime and deviance?

2. Discuss the role of turning points in determining whether people might continue deviant behaviour or desist from it. Can you think of any examples of such a turning point in either real life or in a fictional account of desisting from crime?

3. Religious attendance in Canada has been declining for many decades. Can you think of what impact this might have on rates of crime and delinquency?

Issues with Social Control Theory

Many criminologists believe that empirical research provides more support for control theory than for its competitors. However, a number of issues have been raised about the theory that will be addressed in this section.

How Does Control Theory Explain Upper-World Crime?

Control theory has focused on street crime and delinquency, not on occupational crime committed by high-status adults. In fact, upper-world crime would appear to contradict control theory's emphasis on the role of commitment in preventing crime because high-status people have a great stake in conformity. However, control theory can be used to understand such crime.

In his analysis of the Watergate cover-up in the United States, Hagan (1985) provided a control theory of upper-world crime. The Watergate affair took place over a two-year period from 1972 to 1974. It involved efforts by highly placed US government officials to conceal their involvement in an unsuccessful plot to break into the offices of the Democratic National Committee. Ultimately, these events led to the resignation of President Richard Nixon and to the imprisonment of several of his senior advisors.

From a control perspective, such illegal events might have been prevented by the belief that such acts were wrong. However, our society has not clearly defined upper-world morality. Politicians and business leaders rarely receive more than token punishments for illegal activities and are more likely to see their behaviour as only technically wrong than to see it as criminal. Transcripts of tapes made by Nixon reveal no concern with morality or ethics. In the absence of moral constraints, "the occurrence of such behaviors will depend largely on the risk and rewards … associated with violating public and financial trust" (1985, 173). As you will see in Chapter 17, the rewards of upper-world crime are often very great. What, then, about the risks?

The situational controls operative at the time of the initial Watergate offences were inadequate. White House aides were able to manipulate funds and personnel for criminal political reasons with little expectation of detection. One reason why there was so little expectation of detection, of course, was that the criminals here were people who controlled the institutions of legal control. (Who could have been better positioned to deviate than those who controlled the FBI, the Justice Department, and so on?) Furthermore, once "caught," punishment became problematic in an atmosphere confused by discussions of pardons. The uncertainties surrounding these events emphasize the porous nature

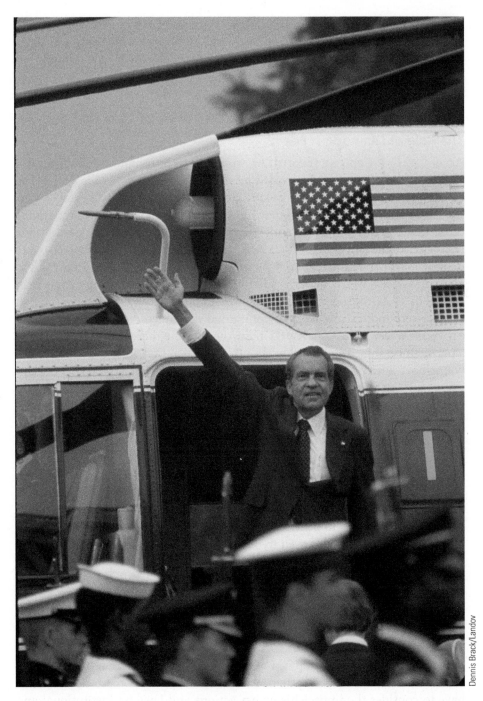

Former President Nixon leaves the White House in the presidential helicopter following his impeachment over his role in the Watergate cover-up.

Dennis Brack/Landov

of the controls that were operating in one upper-world setting (1985, 173). You will learn in Chapter 17 that even for upper-world offenders who are not part of the political process, the likelihood of sanctions is very low.

Later in this chapter, you will learn that control theory has a message for those who wish to control deviance: monitor behaviour, recognize deviance, and punish deviant behaviour. While these principles are intended as advice for parents raising children, they are also applicable to upper-world crime. As Hagan tells us: "If there is a message to the policy-minded in the Watergate experience … it is that checks and balances on power are crucial. Upperworld vocations, particularly politics and business, often carry with them a freedom to deviate unparalleled in the underworld. As control theory reminds us, unchecked freedom is a criminogenic condition" (1985, 173).

Does Everyone Have the Same Motivation to Deviate?

The Role of Delinquent Peers

According to the control theorist, we would *all* be criminal or delinquent if it were not for the restraints provided by social controls, so there is no need to account for the motivation to deviate. However, this appears to be only a partial explanation. Several factors may increase the likelihood of deviance among those who lack ties to the conventional order. We will consider just one of these here—ties to deviant peers, which have been found to be strongly correlated to delinquency. For example, Sorenson and Brownfield (1995) found that ties to delinquent peers were a better predictor of drug use among young people than several measures of social control. Thornberry and colleagues (1993) found that youths were more likely to have committed delinquent acts while they were active members of juvenile gangs than they were either before or after their gang membership. In the study discussed earlier that followed the lives of young boys until they turned 70, Laub and Sampson (2003) found that deviant peers had a strong influence on the lives of those men who became persistent offenders. The researchers believed this was because these peers provided the personal contacts and criminal opportunities that made ongoing criminality attractive to these offenders.

One way to address control theory's failure to account for the influence of deviant peers is to integrate the differential association (see Chapter 13) and control theories. These two theories present conflicting notions about the causes of crime and delinquency. For the differential association theorist, the crucial concept is ties to others; for the pure control theorist, it is individuals with *no* ties to others—not even to deviant others—who are the most likely to become deviant.

Control theory conceives of an individual's social bonds as having only a single dimension, weak to strong. When we fold into that theory differential association's emphasis on the importance of ties to deviant peers, however, we should see social bonds as multidimensional: conventional—weak to strong; unconventional—weak to strong. In bringing the two perspectives together, it is proposed that the first step is a weakness in the controls that bind an individual to the conventional system. An individual without these ties does not have to consider the impact his or her actions will have on institutional and personal relationships. With the person "adrift" in this way (Matza, 1964), delinquency is a possible alternative. We are then faced with the problem of accounting for the motivation to commit acts of crime and delinquency (if we wish to go beyond the control theorists' reliance on natural motivation) and with explaining how one learns the techniques and rationalizations that facilitate deviance.

At least part of the answer to this can be found in differential association theory. We can postulate that the adolescent's lack of ties to the conventional order will increase the likelihood of association with deviant peers since the adolescent no longer has anything to lose by such affiliation. These ties will, in turn, increase the probability that the adolescent will be involved in deviance (see Figure 14.1).

This extension of control theory explains more of the variation in delinquency than either of its parent theories alone (Linden and Hackler, 1973; Linden and Fillmore, 1981). However, both these studies used cross-sectional data rather than longitudinal data, which are more appropriate to the sequential theory we have proposed. Maume, Ousey, and Beaver (2005) used longitudinal data to examine the relationship between marriage, delinquent peer attachment, and marijuana use; their findings support the integrated theory: desistance from marijuana was influenced by marriage and, to a lesser extent, by a reduction in ties to deviant peers following a person's marriage.

The sequential model proposed here is more consistent with control theory than with Sutherland's differential association. The control–differential association model does not necessarily entail the strong element of normative approval required by Sutherland's cultural deviance perspective. Even if this normative approval is not a factor, delinquency may be fun and profitable and is not disapproved of by delinquent peers. The internal dynamics of the group are such that it would be difficult for a reluctant member not to go along. Several researchers (Short and Strodtbeck, 1965; Velarde, 1978) have found that delinquent boys may try to look "bad" or "tough" in front of the group, even though they may express different views privately, because each believes the others are committed to such values. "An individual delinquent may wonder if or even think that his/her friends are not committed to delinquencies, but he/

FIGURE 14.1 **Control-Differential Association Theory**

Source: Rick Linden and Cathy Fillmore, "A Comparative Study of Delinquency Involvement," *Canadian Review of Sociology and Anthropology* 18 (1981): 343–61. Copyright © 2008, John Wiley and Sons. Reprinted with permission.

she can never confront the others to be sure of the degree of commitment they have" (Velarde, 1978). Several of the Winnipeg high-risk auto thieves who were on electronic monitoring said that they welcomed the bracelets because they gave them an excuse to avoid going out with their friends to steal cars.

Other criminologists have integrated control theory with competing perspectives. Marc LeBlanc and several colleagues at the University of Montreal (Caplan and LeBlanc, 1985; Fréchette and LeBlanc, 1985; LeBlanc, 1997) have folded together the variables of external social control, personality traits, and the structural conditions of sex and social status. Hardwick (2002) has shown that personality variables such as childhood temperament and self-control interact with social bonding variables and other social variables to produce delinquent and criminal behaviour. Because none of the theories you have studied in this text provide a complete explanation of crime and delinquency, this integrative work will continue.

Is Control Theory a Conservative Theory of Crime?

Many different perspectives have been used to explain crime. In the absence of consensus, some criminologists have taken an ideological approach in which theories are accepted or rejected on the basis of whether they are sufficiently conservative or radical. Robert Bohm has observed that "political and value preferences, ideology, empiricism, and positivism ... stand in the way of any unity between traditional and radical criminologists" (1987, 327). For example, some conflict criminologists have been critical of theories of crime (such as control theory) that do not focus on the political and economic structures that produce crime.

To some degree, this critique is a fair one. Control theorists have emphasized people's immediate environment, and from the time of Shaw and McKay until recently, they have not considered the political and economic structures of their communities. However, the critics mistakenly reject the theory rather than recognize that control variables can be incorporated into a structural perspective. For example, Shaw and McKay (1942) pointed out the importance of community variables in the development of social bonds. Control theory explains individual differences in criminal involvement in ways that are compatible with any number of structural theories, including conflict theories; it also provides the link between society and individual that structural theories lack.

Control theory focuses on an individual's relationships with social institutions; structural factors condition those relationships. Crime involves the behaviour of individuals, but it has its origins in the social structure in which these individuals live. Lynch and Groves (1989) point out that "persons are more likely to conform when they stand to gain by doing so. But to make conformity attractive, society must do something for the individual; it must provide minimal satisfaction for both human and culturally defined needs. Social structures that provide for these needs are more likely to encourage conformity" (78).

When social institutions work together to support conforming behaviour, rates of deviance should be low. However, if these institutions do not work together and if individuals and groups are alienated from social institutions, rates of deviance will be high. Consider the problems faced by Canada's Aboriginal people. They have far less power and fewer resources than other Canadians. They must cope with systems of education and religion imposed from outside that are not compatible with Aboriginal customs and traditions. Forced attendance at residential schools and forced adoption outside the community have destroyed family ties, and crippling rates of unemployment mean no job ties. School curricula that are irrelevant to Aboriginal students weaken children's attachment to their schools. Many Aboriginal Canadians face daily encounters with racism. They must submit to government policies that have not allowed Aboriginal communities to achieve effective institutional integration. Under these conditions, strong social bonds are very difficult to develop, and the high rates of crime described in Chapter 5 can be expected. Recent work by Fitzgerald and Carrington (2008) has supported this view by showing the relationship between the structural characteristics of Winnipeg's disadvantaged neighbourhoods and Aboriginal involvement in crime.

SEARCH FOR:
"Manitoba Aboriginal Justice Inquiry"

Manitoba's Aboriginal Justice Inquiry concluded: "From our review of the information available to us, including the nature of the crimes committed by aboriginal people, and after hearing the hundreds of submissions presented to us in the course of our hearings, we believe that the relatively high rates of crime among aboriginal people are a result of the despair, dependency, anger, frustration, and sense of injustice prevalent in aboriginal communities, stemming from the cultural and community breakdown that has occurred over the past century" (Hamilton and Sinclair, 1991, 91). The impact of structural conditions on social bonds and on rates of crime and other deviance is illustrated in the discussion of life in Davis Inlet, Labrador, in Box 14.2. By incorporating control elements within a structural perspective, the example demonstrates the complementarity of the control and conflict approaches.

FOCUS

Box 14.2

THE MUSHUAU INNU OF DAVIS INLET

On several occasions over the past 25 years, Canadians were saddened by television images of young children sniffing gas in Davis Inlet in Labrador. The first incident was described by a team of researchers who studied the Mushuau Innu of Davis Inlet:

> One day in February 1992, six children in the Innu community of Davis Inlet in Labrador burned to death in a house fire. Almost a year later, six of their friends, depressed at the approaching anniversary of the tragedy and convinced that the ghost of a young Innu was telling them that they should end their own lives, barricaded themselves in an unheated shack in temperatures of −40 and tried to kill themselves by sniffing petrol. The

local Innu policeman reached them in time and, with great presence of mind, videotaped their responses as they were removed to safety. Then, to show the world the horrors of life in Utshimassits (as the Innu call Davis Inlet), he passed the tape on to a television station.

Over the next few days, his graphic pictures of wild-eyed children hurling themselves against the wall and screaming "Leave me alone! I want to die!" shocked Canada and made Utshimassits, after years of official neglect, the focus of national and international media attention. Journalists and television crews suddenly converged on Davis Inlet from all over North American and Europe to try to discover how a supposedly "modern" and enlightened country like Canada could produce such

(continued)

a vision of desolation and despair. They were scandalized by what they found.

Utshimassits is a community living in almost unimaginable squalor and disarray. Rows of battered wooden shacks, looking more like a Third World refugee camp than a "western" village, line unmade roads that for most of the year are no more than sheets of dirty ice. Virtually none of the houses—except for a handful belonging to non-Innu professionals like the priest, schoolteachers and nurses—have running water or mains drainage. Sewage is simply thrown onto the ground, where it is eaten by dogs or trampled by the gangs who roam the settlement … These conditions are reflected in the appalling health and mortality statistics for Davis Inlet, where family breakdown, sexual abuse, drunkenness and alcohol-related disease, violence, accidents and self-harm have become endemic. (Samson, Wilson, and Mazower, 1999, 6)

These problems did not exist prior to European colonization. Thus Samson and his colleagues conclude that the cultural and social disintegration of the Mushuau Innu has been caused by their past and current relationship with Canadian society. While many Aboriginal communities in Canada are healthy and thriving, particularly those that own valuable land and resources, many others share at least some of the problems of the Innu.

How did colonialism cause the decline of a healthy people? The Mushuau Innu were successful nomadic hunters. However, colonial governments did not consider hunting to be an economically viable way of life and forced the Innu to give up their centuries-old way of life and settle in sedentary communities:

After Newfoundland and Labrador joined Confederation in 1949, the federal government began to build new houses for the Innu. The houses were small (750 square feet) and built close together and had few amenities. While equipped with tubs, toilets, and sinks, the houses had no water or sewage services, few pieces of furniture, and a single power outlet. Many families used hot plates or diesel fuel to start fires to warm their homes. Gradually, the residents of Davis Inlet found themselves slipping out of touch with their traditional migratory way of life while having difficulty fully embracing a "modern" sedentary lifestyle. (Burns, 2006, 68)

After their initial settlement, the entire community was moved three times. The first move, in 1948, was a forced migration from Davis Inlet to Nutak, over 300 kilometres away (Denov and Campbell, 2002). The Innu were moved without their consent to a location far from their traditional hunting grounds, ostensibly to improve their economic prospects. The band did not accept the move and walked back to their former location. In 1967, they were moved to an island on Davis Inlet, again for economic reasons. However, as with the earlier move, there were no economic opportunities on the island and they were isolated during the spring thaw and fall freeze-up, during which the island was accessible only by air. Their new houses lacked running water and sewer systems and quickly degenerated to Third World standards (Denov and Campbell, 2002). The move was intended to help the Innu become more economically self-sufficient, yet there were few jobs in the area.

In addition to the shift from a nomadic to a sedentary life, the horrible living conditions, and the disruption caused by the moves, other factors have contributed to the problems of the Innu. Missionaries tried to replace traditional spiritual practices with Christianity. Massive hydroelectric projects, mining, and logging have destroyed part of the traditional territory of the Innu without their approval and without compensation. The government required the traditional family-based governance structure to be replaced by a single leader. All of these changes have disrupted the cultural continuity of the people of Davis Inlet by altering their relationship with their traditional lands:

Land is of central importance to aboriginal culture, identity and well-being. Aboriginal people have a unique relationship with the land that guides their daily life and provides them with great meaning … Isolating people from their traditional habitat, therefore, breaks the spiritual relationship with the land that exists within many aboriginal communities. (Denov and Campbell, 2002, 24)

The Innu have been cut off from their ties to the land, and their knowledge of how to survive on the land is not relevant to their sedentary lifestyle: "Displacement among the Innu can thus be seen as part of a painful process of dispossession and alienation of their society from the land and from the cultural and spiritual roots it nurtures, ultimately leading to a sense of powerlessness" (Denov and Campbell, 2002, 24).

This discontinuity (what Durkheim would call anomie) is particularly acute among young people. The school system is a major source of their problems. Schooling interfered with learning traditional skills yet did not prepare them for mainstream jobs. Because the schools did not use the Innu language, many young people could not communicate with their Innu-speaking elders. Several generations of Innu have been cast adrift between two cultures and prepared for what Samson has called "a way of life that does not exist … Many Innu have gradually become neither hunters nor 'modern' Canadians" (2003, 13). As a result, they face strikingly high rates of suicide, gas sniffing, alcoholism, interpersonal violence, and vandalism. In the words of one young Innu:

We were taught in school to be doctors, nurses, store managers, teachers, that's what we were taught in school, to be one of those people. I was never taught to be a hunter or to learn about my culture, I was never taught like that, it was always the white culture that was focused in the school … I see a lot of kids that have failed in school … They feel so ashamed about not learning to speak English and then they will start drinking, they will drink and drink, and a lot of those people are still drinking because they are ashamed, they don't know how to write, how to speak the language. (Samson et al., 1999, 22)

In looking at the tragic story of the Mushuau Innu, we can see the complementarity of the control and conflict approaches. At one level, members of groups with high rates of crime and other deviance typically lack the social bonds that might tie them to the social order. However, if we ask why the strength of social bonds is less among those who, like many Aboriginal people, are forced to live on the margins of society, we must turn to the work of conflict theorists and their analyses of the political and economic forces that have created the poverty, powerlessness, and inequality that shape their lives.

As a postscript to this tragedy, for many years the Innu had asked to be allowed to move from Davis Inlet back to the mainland. The federal and provincial governments spent $280 million building a new community at Natuashish (Burns, 2006), about 15 kilometres from Davis Inlet, and in 2003 the move this community was completed. While this led to a major improvement in housing and other physical conditions, it did not end the problems of the Innu; gas sniffing and other social problems continue (CBC News, 2013). The reasons why these problems persist are complex (Burns, 2006), but without question, unwinding the legacy of colonialism is a very difficult process, particularly with groups as isolated as the Innu.

Source: Samson, Colin, James Wilson, and Jonathan Mazower. (1999). *Canada's Tibet: The Killing of the Innu*. London: Survival. Reprinted by permission of the publisher.

Policy Implications of Control Theory

Early control theorists were concerned about social policy. For example, Shaw established and worked for many years with the Chicago Area Project, trying to strengthen community ties in a slum area. To illustrate some of the possible uses to which the findings of research done from a social control perspective might be put, let us consider the role of the family and the school in delinquency prevention.

Policy Implications—The Family

Research has shown the importance of family relationships in the causation of delinquency. How can we strengthen families and make sure that parents love and care for their children?

SEARCH FOR:
Oregon Social Learning
Center

While many of the family relationship problems of delinquents may require structural solutions, some small beginnings have been made in re-establishing bonds between parents and children. One of the best examples of this is the work of Gerald Patterson and his colleagues at the Oregon Social Learning Center.

Based on his experiences treating several hundred families of antisocial children and on detailed observation of interaction patterns within these families (see Box 14.3), Patterson concluded that since "antisocial acts that are not punished tend to persist" (1980, 89), the key to changing the behaviour of these troublesome children was to punish their misdeeds. Hirschi observed that "this conclusion may come as no surprise to those millions of parents who have spent years talking firmly to their children, yelling and screaming at them, spanking them, grounding them, cutting off their allowances, and in general doing whatever they could think of to get the little bastards to behave; but it is exceedingly rare among social scientists, especially those who deal with crime and delinquency" (1983, 53).

While this approach might seem disturbingly authoritarian to some, Patterson is, in fact, merely advocating techniques used by families that are successful in avoiding delinquency. You will recall that parental supervision and disciplinary practices were strongly related to delinquent behaviour. Patterson concluded that this process involves three key steps: "(1) monitor the child's behavior; (2) recognize deviant behavior when it occurs; and (3) punish such behavior" (in Hirschi, 1983, 55). In a properly functioning family, the parents understand this process, and the system is activated by the bonds of affection and caring between parent and child. The key is not simply punishment—many parents of problem children punished them more often and more harshly than the parents of normal children. However, the parents of problem children did not know *how* to punish their children, and punishment actually made things worse. Discipline was used, but it was erratic and unpredictable and was not directed specifically at the child's misbehaviour. "The failure of parents to use reasonable reinforcements contingent on steadily monitored behaviour places the child in a situation in which he comes to understand that he cannot control by his own actions what happens to him" (Wilson, 1983, 53). As a result, the children in effect train their parents (and others, such as teachers) to accept their misbehaviour.

Working with the families of pre-adolescent problem children, Patterson taught parents to shape their children's behaviour by using nonphysical punishments (such as time-outs), by rewarding good conduct, and by interacting more positively as a family. This training process was often long and difficult. Many of the parents did not like their children, did not identify with the role of parent, and refused to recognize that their children were deviant (Patterson, 1980). Many were trying to cope with difficult economic and family situations as well as with the problems created by their antisocial children, and they resisted help.

Despite these problems, the program had positive results. One evaluation showed that stealing had been reduced from an average of 0.83 incidents per week to 0.07 incidents per week after the parent training program. The treatment effects persisted for six months, but within one year, stealing rates had gone back to pre-treatment levels (Moore, Chamberlain, and Mukai, 1979). This suggests that parental retraining may be necessary. Longer-term results were obtained with children diagnosed as aggressive; with them, program effects lasted longer than 12 months. The program also had a positive impact on siblings, indicating that the parenting skills of the parents had improved.

Tremblay and colleagues (1991) evaluated a similar program in which preventive treatment was provided for disruptive kindergarten boys in a low-income community in Montreal. The treatment taught social skills to the boys and trained their parents to be consistent and constructive toward their children. Two years after the treatment, the treated boys reported less fighting and less theft than comparison groups of boys who did not receive the treatment. The classroom behaviour of the treated boys also showed improvement.

More recently, the Parent–Child Interaction Therapy (PCIT) program, which is similar in many ways to the Oregon program, has shown significant impacts on parents (whose parenting skills improved and who were more satisfied with their parental roles) and children (whose behaviour improved) (Nixon

et al., 2003). Another type of parenting program that has proven to be successful in improving parenting and reducing criminal and antisocial behaviour
of children has been home visiting programs, in which nurses make frequent
visits to at-risk mothers during their pregnancies and for two years after the
child is born (Olds et al., 1998).

Programs like these may be too expensive to be broadly implemented,
though many communities do have nurse visiting programs. However, given
the high concentration of criminality in a relatively small proportion of families, they do have some potential for reducing crime rates. The demonstration that improved parenting can have an impact on misbehaviour should
encourage those who are advocating structural changes aimed at least in part
at providing more family stability (e.g., improved foster care).

A potential drawback to this approach is that it can lead to blaming parents
for their children's behaviour when the parents themselves have been victimized by their social and economic circumstances. For example, there has been
considerable documentation of the impact of the residential school system,
which forcibly removed Aboriginal children from their parents and placed
them in residential schools where attempts were made to destroy their cultures and where many, in addition, were physically and sexually abused (Miller,
1996). As a result, many victims of the residential school system never learned
how to raise their own children.

FOCUS

Box 14.3

PARENTING DELINQUENT YOUTH

"When I met him, he was six and a half years of age. There was nothing about his appearance that identified him as the boy who had set the record."

These words are those of Gerald R. Patterson, a family therapist at the Oregon Social Learning Center in Eugene. The "record" to which he referred was the frequency—measured with painstaking care by the Learning Center's staff—with which Don, a small boy, displayed rotten behavior. Nearly four times a *minute* while in his home, Don would whine, yell, dis-obey, hit, or shove. When he was not at home, telephone calls from teachers and merchants would mark his progress through the neighborhood: "He left school two hours early, stole candy from a store, and appropriated a toy from a neighborhood child."

Don had "a sleazy look about him," Patterson wrote, "like a postcard carried too long in a hip pocket." His violent out-bursts were frightening; any simple request or minor provoca-tion would trigger obscene shouts, attacks on other children, or assaults on the furniture. His mother was tired, depressed, and nearly desperate as a result of coping unaided with this monster—no baby-sitter would take on the job of minding Don, whatever the pay. She nevertheless persevered, changing his wet sheets, bathing and dressing him, even feeding him, all the while talking to him in tones that vacillated between cajolery and scolding, murmurs and shouts. When her seemingly bot-tomless patience was at last at an end, she would threaten or hit him with a stick. That produced only temporary compliance. When the father was home, things were not much different. The shouting and fighting between Don and his younger brother continued, occasionally punctuated by the father slapping both children.

Children like Don are the youthful precursors not only of difficult teenagers, but sometimes of delinquents and adult criminals. The progression from violent, dishonest young-ster to violent, dishonest teenager is not automatic, but it is common.

Source: James Q. Wilson, "Raising Kids," *The Atlantic*, October 1983, 45.

The Schools and Social Policy

In assessing the role of schools in delinquency, Schafer and Polk (1967) suggest that schools fail youth in two ways: "The school not only fails to offset initial handicaps of lower-income and minority group children, but actively contributes to education failure and deterioration. If this is true, the school itself becomes an important active force in the generation of delinquency insofar as it is linked to failure" (236).

Some schools and some teachers are better than others in helping children function both academically and behaviourally. Rutter and Giller (1984) have suggested a number of factors differentiating good from bad schools. These include the standards and values set and maintained by the school, the degree to which students are allowed to participate in decision making, school and class size, staff turnover, and the degree of concentration of intellectually and socially disadvantaged pupils. Each of these factors has rather obvious policy implications.

Several studies have looked at the impact of the teacher–student relationship on students' behaviour. Some teachers provoked deviance, while others were able to get students to cooperate (Hargreaves et al., 1975). Failure to get along with teachers may weaken an adolescent's commitment to school. It may also affect grades by leading teachers to make negative judgments about a youth's abilities and character. Thus the classroom process may help weaken an adolescent's attachment and commitment to the school.

Incredible Years is a program that has succeeded in changing teachers' methods so that they are better able to teach youth with behaviour problems. It involves programs for parents, teachers, and youth, with the focus on training teachers in techniques for building positive relationships with their students. The techniques include using praise and incentives to encourage desired behaviours, giving clear instructions, using positive discipline, and helping students with problem solving. Hutchings and colleagues (2013) conducted a

TABLE 14.1   **Social Control Theories**

Theory	Theorists	Key Elements
Social disorganization theories	Durkheim, Thrasher, Shaw and McKay	Deviance will be highest in disorganized communities that lack social controls.
Early social control theories	Reiss, Nye	Stress the importance of personal controls, particularly those provided by the family.
Social bond theory	Hirschi	The four elements of the social bond: attachment, commitment, involvement, and belief.
General theory of crime	Gottfredson, Hirschi	Individuals with low self-control have a greater propensity to commit crimes when they have the opportunity to do so.
Control-differential association theory	Linden	Lack of ties to the conventional order will increase the likelihood of association with deviant peers. These ties will in turn increase the probability of delinquency involvement.

randomized clinical trial of the program in Wales. They found that the teachers reduced their negative behaviour toward the children, and that the children engaged in less off-task behaviour and showed less negative behaviour toward the teachers. Programs such as this one hold potential for improving the educational outcomes of high-risk youth.

Schools must also ensure that their curriculum is relevant to the lives of their students. This is not being achieved in Canada's North. A child who has grown up in a small settlement on the Arctic coast will be flown south to Yellowknife or another southern point for high school. Besides being cut off from family and community, the student is educated into a way of life that is very different from that which exists in their home settlement. As a result, students may no longer fit into their home communities; but at the same time, they are not completely acculturated into southern ways (Brody, 1975). The consequences of this system can be increasing rates of crime and other deviance among people who lack strong community ties.

QUESTIONS FOR CRITICAL THINKING

1. How could you apply the principles of social control theory to reduce the amount of white-collar and corporate crime in Canada?
2. This chapter has discussed the relationship between the community and crime. Starting with the example of the tragic situation in Davis Inlet, discuss some of the government policies that have led to high rates of crime and other types of deviance among Canada's Aboriginal people.
3. Based on your knowledge of social control theory, what changes would you make to the public school system to help reduce delinquency?

Summary

- Rather than asking, "Why do some people break the law?" social control theorists ask, "Why don't we all do it?" The answer to this question lies in the processes that bind people to conventional society.

- Early theorists, including Thrasher and Shaw and McKay, looked at community-level controls. Disorganized communities that did not provide meaningful employment to residents and did not have strong families, schools, and churches could not provide adequate social controls and would have high rates of crime and other types of deviance.

- Later social control theories focused on the social bonds of individuals. Hirschi described four interrelated aspects of the social bond that constrain our behaviour: attachment, commitment, involvement, and belief.

- Research on social control theory has pointed to the importance of the family and the school in restraining involvement in delinquency. While less research has been done with adults, it suggests that stable employment and a cohesive marriage are important factors.

- Among the criticisms of social control theory are these: it does not adequately explain white-collar crime; it does not account for the motivation to deviate; it is too individualistic; and it is too conservative.

- Recent theoretical work has returned to the social disorganization tradition and has once again linked societal and community factors to individual-level bonds.

NET WORK

For over two decades, the Canadian government has supported the Aboriginal Head Start program. This program is intended to help reserve communities meet the educational, emotional, social, health, and nutritional needs of children under the age of six. Some early childhood education programs have proven very successful in reducing rates of crime and delinquency. This program is based on the US Head Start program. You can find out more about Head Start at http://www.acf.hhs.gov/programs/opre/research/topic/overview/head-star.

Using some of the evaluations you will find on this link, do the following exercises:

1. What do you think would be the impact of Head Start programs on delinquency and crime? Do you think they are a cost-effective way of reducing crime?

2. The most effective early childhood education program is the Perry Preschool program, which you can read about at http://www.highscope.org/Content.asp?ContentId=219. What lessons can those running Head Start programs learn from the Perry Preschool program?

3. How important do you think it is to involve parents in Head Start programs? Does the research show that programs involving parents are more effective than those based only in the schools?

Deterrence, Routine Activity, and Rational Choice Theories

15

Rick Linden
UNIVERSITY OF MANITOBA

Daniel J. Koenig
FORMERLY OF UNIVERSITY OF VICTORIA

This chapter introduces you to several perspectives on crime with roots in the Classical theory of crime discussed in Chapter 8. Most sociological and psychological theories of crime seek to explain why people break the law and focus on the backgrounds, character, and motivation of offenders. In contrast, *deterrence theories* such as Beccaria's Classical theory focus on the factors influencing an individual's decision whether to commit an offence and assert that the legal system can be used to affect that decision.

The other theories discussed in this chapter—*rational choice theory* and *routine activities theory*—also examine the decision to commit specific criminal acts, so they also focus more on the crimes than on the background of the people committing these crimes. *Rational choice theory* postulates that people break the law because they believe crime will provide them with a reward: a burglar steals money to pay living expenses, an addict smokes crack to get high and to avoid withdrawal, a gang member shoots a rival to protect his drug business. The criminal's decision may or may not appear rational to the rest of us, but it does meet a goal for the offender. *Routine activities theory* tells us that crime will not occur unless there is a motivated offender, a suitable target, and ineffective guardianship of that target. As you will learn later in this chapter, the routine activities approach has been particularly useful for developing ways to prevent crime because it moves beyond the mere consideration of penalties advocated by proponents of deterrence theory.

Learning Objectives

After reading this chapter, you should be able to

- Understand the role of law as a deterrent to crime and recognize the limits of deterrence.

- Discuss how offenders make choices whether or not to commit offences, and understand the assumptions of rational choice theory.

- Discuss the routine activities approach to crime, and understand the role of the motivated offender, suitable target, and ineffective guardianship in any criminal event.

- Know the rationale underlying situational crime prevention and be familiar with the research demonstrating its effectiveness.

- Understand the need for comprehensive crime prevention initiatives, including crime prevention through social development.

Deterrence Theory

You will recall from Chapter 8 that Beccaria's Classical theory was based on rational choice—people will break the law if they think that doing so will advance their own interests. If it is to our advantage, and if we think we can get away with it, we will break the law. This implies that the best way to control crime is to set up a system of punishment that will ensure people do not find lawbreaking to be in their best interests. Beccaria posited that punishments should be severe enough to deter people from breaking the law but should also be proportionate to the nature of the crime. Also, punishment should be swift and certain. A well-crafted justice system would ensure that most people chose good over evil.

At the heart of Classical theory was the belief that humans were rational beings who carefully calculated the consequences of their behaviour. Crime would be prevented if the potential criminal realized that the costs of committing the crime were greater than the rewards. Classical theorists had great faith in the ability of a well-designed criminal code to deter criminal behaviour.

How effective is the law as a deterrent? This is a critical question, because our legal system is based heavily on deterrence. We know that at one level, deterrence is effective: most people do not deliberately park where they know their car will be towed away, and they do not normally speed when they see a police car behind them. On the rare occasions when the police have gone on strike, crime has risen dramatically. During one notable police strike in Montreal in 1969, armed robberies began to occur within minutes of the strike and huge mobs of people ran through the shopping district, breaking windows and stealing whatever they could get their hands on. Many people were injured, and a police officer was shot to death.

While the law clearly does deter, the more important policy question is whether we can change our current system to make it more effective as a deterrent. Many people, including "law and order" politicians, believe that the best way to reduce crime is to hand down longer prison sentences. Since the Conservatives were elected in 2006, Canada's Parliament has passed several pieces of legislation designed to put more people in jail for longer periods of time. Prisons are expensive—the cost of keeping someone in a federal penitentiary is $118,000 per year (Public Safety Canada, 2013). This means it is very important to know whether sending more people to jail for longer periods has an impact on crime rates or whether other crime reduction strategies would keep Canadians safer.

Research suggests that *certainty* of punishment is more important than *severity* of punishment—a finding Classical theorists might have predicted. The impact of increased certainty is illustrated by the dramatic decline in obscene and harassing telephone calls after the introduction of caller ID services. Penalties did not increase, but the new technology increased the certainty that the offending caller could be identified and charged. This was much more effective than increasing penalties for the rare offenders who eventually got convicted.

Unfortunately, it has been easier for governments to pass tougher sentencing laws than to increase the certainty of punishment. Tougher laws led to a 500 percent increase in rates of imprisonment in the United States between 1972 and 2009 (Bureau of Justice Statistics, 2009). The United States now has the world's highest imprisonment rates. Much of this increase was because of harsher penalties for drug offenders even though there is no evidence that mass incarceration has had an impact on the sale and use of illegal drugs.

Does Imprisonment Deter Crime?

Steven Durlauf and Daniel Nagin (2011b) conducted a thorough review of the evidence on the deterrent effect of imprisonment. Most of the research they reviewed was conducted in the United States, much of it in response to the massive increases in imprisonment in that country. Durlauf and Nagin conclude that long prison sentences "are difficult to justify on a deterrence-based, crime prevention basis" (38). Some of the research they reviewed suggests that imprisonment may actually *increase* an individual's likelihood of future criminal behaviour. Labelling theorists (see Chapter 13) would suggest this is because punishment may stigmatize people and reduce their opportunities for a life in the non-criminal world. Also, offenders may adjust to prison life so that the threat of prison does not deter them; they may learn criminal values and skills in prison; or imprisonment may create feelings of resentment against society that result in increased criminality when they are released.

One of the most interesting studies in their review examined whether young people reduced their offending when they reached the age of 18, when they began to be treated as adults in court. Many people believe that youth courts coddle offenders and that the more serious penalties prescribed for adults will deter criminal behaviour. However, Florida research by Lee and McCrary cited by Durlauf and Nagin showed that there was only a slight reduction in offending when youth turned 18, so apparently the threat of adult penalties did not act as a deterrent.

Do Mandatory Minimum Sentences Deter Crime?

The most definitive work on the deterrent effect of imprisonment looks at the impact of mandatory minimum prison sentences for particular offences and for offenders with significant prior records. Mandatory sentences are widely used, but there has been much debate about their effectiveness.

What are mandatory minimum sentences? The Criminal Code provides a broad range of penalties for many offences. For example, breaking into someone's home can result in penalties ranging from an absolute discharge to life imprisonment. Judges have a great deal of discretion, though appeal courts set limits on this discretion. When complaints from the public follow a particularly light sentence or when a paroled offender commits a serious crime, politicians may try to limit judicial discretion by legislating mandatory minimum penalties for certain offences. Between 2006 and 2014, through legislation such as the Safe Streets and Communities Act, the Conservative government imposed or increased mandatory minimum sentences for many crimes, including marijuana-related offences.

The harshest mandatory sentencing law in any Western country is California's three strikes law. While the law is complicated, one of its components is a mandatory sentence of 25 years in prison for a third felony conviction following two earlier convictions for serious felonies (a category that includes residential burglary). This has resulted in some bizarre sentences, including cases where two men will spend much of the rest of their lives in prison, one for stealing a slice of pizza and the other for shoplifting a small package of meat. This punishment seems far too harsh, at least for minor felonies like shoplifting and other forms of petty theft. However, in 2003 the US Supreme Court ruled that it did not violate the constitutional protection against cruel and unusual punishment. This decision covered two cases, one involving a defendant who received a sentence of 25 years without parole for stealing three golf clubs, and the other a defendant who was given two consecutive 25-year sentences (50 years in all) for stealing nine videotapes in two separate incidents.

This law has been very costly. According to the California State Auditor (2010), one-quarter of California's prison inmates were serving time under the three strikes law. The auditor estimated that the cost of "three strikes" sentencing was $20 billion more than if the convicted had been sentenced for the actual crimes they had committed rather than for the "strikes" against them. Partly as a result of three strikes laws, California cannot afford its prison system, and in 2011, the US Supreme Court ordered the state to release 32,000 inmates because of severe overcrowding. Mandatory minimum sentences also significantly increase court costs because individuals facing long mandatory penalties are more likely to insist on a trial instead of pleading guilty. The law is also very hard on the offenders and their families.

California's three strikes sentencing laws led to massive overcrowding of prisons but had no impact on crime rates.

AP Photo/California Department of Corrections, File

The high social and financial costs of mandatory minimum sentences might be worthwhile if they reduced crime rates. However, they do not. Michael Tonry (2009), after reviewing the research on mandatory minimum sentences, has concluded that "mandatory penalties are a bad idea. They often result in injustice to individual offenders ... And the clear weight of the evidence is, and for nearly 40 years has been, that there is insufficient credible evidence to conclude that mandatory penalties have significant deterrent effects" (100).

Tonry bases this conclusion in part on several evaluations of California's three strikes laws. California's crime rate has declined since the passage of three strikes in 1994, but this decline has not been a result of the three strikes laws. Only one of 15 studies reviewed by Tonry concluded that the legislation reduced crime rates. Several studies, including those by Marvell and Moody (2001) and Chen (2008), found that crime rates in California did not decline faster than in other states even though the penalties in California were far more severe than in any other state. Kovandzic, Sloan, and Vieraitis (2004) arrived at similar findings, using cities rather than states as the unit of analysis. Other studies compared the California counties that made the most use of three strikes with the counties that made the least use of the law and found no differences in reductions in total crime or in violent crime following the three strikes law (Legislative Analyst's Office, 2005). Several of these comparative studies also found that three strikes laws produced *increases* in homicide rates, possibly because offenders facing a third strike conviction wanted to eliminate people who could identify them.

Why don't these severe penalties deter crime? One reason is that offenders may not feel they are at risk of getting caught. Potential offenders are actually correct in believing that their next crime is unlikely to lead to punishment.

Crime statistics show that most criminal offences are not reported, that most reported offences do not result in an arrest, that most arrests do not lead to a conviction, and that most convictions do not result in imprisonment. Nearly 2 million crimes were reported to Canadian police in 2009 (Perreault, 2013). Victimization surveys have shown that less than one-third of all crimes are reported to the police, so there are likely over 6 million crimes each year in Canada. Despite this huge number of offences, only about 5,000 people were sentenced to the federal penitentiary system (which includes all sentences of two years or more) and 74,000 to provincial custody (Public Safety Canada, 2013). Thus, the likelihood of being arrested, convicted, and punished for any offence is so low that tinkering with the level of punishment makes no difference. Governments promise to "crack down" on crime, but if the promise of a tougher response is rarely kept by the justice system, it is ignored by potential offenders, who know from their own experience (and from that of their peers) that the odds of getting away with a crime are in their favour. This means that a harsh system like California's is really one of randomized severity in which some offenders receive very harsh sentences while many others with similar patterns of offending remain on the streets.

Deterrence is also affected by the fact that many offenders have alcohol, drug, or mental health issues that may lead them to make bad decisions (see Box 15.1). Furthermore, some offenders are unaware of the sentence they face if convicted. A study of serious firearms offenders came up with a striking finding: "even felons who had been *prosecuted, sentenced, and were interviewed while incarcerated* dramatically underestimated the magnitude of their *current sentence*" (Kennedy, 2009, 26). An inmate who was the first person sentenced under a new US federal three strikes law said that

> I ain't never heard anything about the law until they applied it on me. I never thought anything like this would happen to me, man … It is going to make a few guys think, but some other guys don't even watch TV or care; they don't know nothing about the law. (Kennedy, 2009, 26)

One of the biggest failures of mandatory sentencing and other deterrence policies relates to the war on drugs. Billions of dollars have been spent combating drug trafficking and consumption without reducing the problem. More than 30,000 people were killed in Mexico's drug wars between 2006 and 2010 (CNN, 2010). Even the risk to Mexican drug dealers of being murdered by other traffickers or of being killed by the police has not deterred new recruits to the drug business, which is so lucrative that when one distributor is killed or arrested, another will very quickly take his place. The failure of this costly war on drugs was demonstrated recently by a study showing that while drug seizures have increased over the past two decades, the price of drugs has gone down and their potency has gone up (Werb et al., 2013). Declining prices and increased quality indicate that supply has increased despite the increase in drug seizures by enforcement agencies.

Another possible reason why harsh sentences have little impact is that prosecutors and judges find ways to evade penalties such as mandatory minimum sentences that they feel are too severe. Cases may be plea-bargained to lesser charges, or prosecutors may lay related charges that do not carry a mandatory minimum penalty. A study of the use of section 85 of Canada's Criminal Code, which imposed mandatory minimum sentences for certain firearms offences, found that many of the charges laid under this section were dealt with through plea bargaining and that about two-thirds of the charges were stayed, withdrawn, or dismissed (Roberts, 2005). The Canadian government recently passed legislation requiring a mandatory sentence of at least six months in prison for growing as few as six marijuana plants if the grower was involved in marijuana trafficking. It is very likely that some prosecutors and judges will work around the law in cases where they don't feel a jail term is desirable. However, other similar offenders who face less sympathetic prosecutors and judges will go to jail.

In 2014 the Supreme Court of Canada overturned parts of the Harper government's "tough on crime" legislation on the grounds that the laws were contrary to the Charter of Rights and Freedoms. In 2013 and 2014, judges in several provinces refused to impose the mandatory minimum sentences passed by the government, but these cases had not reached the Supreme Court of Canada when this chapter was written, so the constitutional status of these laws is not yet clear.

Finally, it is likely that the existing level of punishment is severe enough for most of us. To give just one example, there is no evidence that capital punishment is a greater deterrent to crime than a lengthy term of imprisonment. In fact, one international study found that homicide rates actually went *down* after capital punishment was abolished (Archer et al., 1983).

FOCUS

Box 15.1

THE LIMITS OF DETERRENCE

Not all people can be deterred. Jacobs (2010) describes an incident in which

> an offender stabbed a victim after a traffic dispute in a fully lit Taco Bell drive-thru window. The ... stabbing took place in view of at least ten potential eyewitnesses. The entire encounter was captured on surveillance video and (subsequently) broadcast worldwide on YouTube. The offender began the altercation with the victim *while the victim was on the phone with the police* (to report the traffic accident) *and under the reasonable presumption that the police were on their way.* The offender did not attempt to conceal or disguise

his identity in any way. The offender attacked the victim despite the fact that he (the offender) had $6,000 worth of marihuana packaged for sale under the front seat of his car—a quantity that would trigger a charge of intent to distribute (as opposed to simple possession) if the police were to discover it (recall that the police were on their way). The offender attacked the victim despite the presence and direct intervention of two peacemakers (a cousin of the offender and an unrelated customer). Following the stabbing, the offender made no attempt to flee, despite the fact that he knew the police were coming. (428)

The Impact of Increasing the Certainty of Punishment

Increasing the *severity* of punishment beyond current levels does not seem to have a deterrent effect. Even the minority of studies that have found that longer sentences help reduce crime do not show a sufficient impact to justify the enormous costs of growing prison populations. However, you will recall that Beccaria also discussed the need for *certainty* of punishment if the law was to be an effective deterrent. There is now a substantial body of research showing that efforts to increase certainty can have a strong deterrent effect (Durlauf and Nagin, 2011b). Two of these measures are **hot spots policing** and *individualized deterrence*.

Hot Spots Policing

Most studies of the impact of increased certainty have focused on the police because their actions can increase or decrease the certainty of punishment. One promising strategy is "hot spots" policing. This strategy is based on the fact that a small number of addresses produce a high percentage of calls to the police. For example, half the calls to the Minneapolis police came from just 3 percent of the city's addresses (Sherman, Gartin, and Buerger, 1989), and half the commercial robberies in Boston took place at 1 percent of the addresses (Braga, Hureau, and Papachristo, 2011). Several studies have shown that focusing police resources on these high-crime areas can significantly reduce crime by increasing the certainty of apprehension (Braga, 2008).

Individualized Deterrence

The most dramatic results demonstrating the importance of certainty of punishment have come from the new strategy of **individualized deterrence**. This

SEARCH FOR:
Smart Policing Initiative

hot spots policing
Most crimes occur at a small number of addresses in any community. Hot spots policing concentrates police resources on these high-crime locations.

individualized deterrence
Offenders who are heavily involved in criminal activity are individually warned that their actions are being monitored and that future violations of the law will be dealt with immediately. Extra police and/or probation resources are added to ensure that the legal system does keep its promises.

involves directly informing individuals about the consequences that will result from future misbehaviour and then ensuring that those promises are kept.

Boston's Operation Ceasefire

The best-known example of the individualized deterrence strategy is the gang violence reduction program called Operation Ceasefire. The program was developed in response to high homicide rates among young, African-American males in Boston.

The project involved a significant number of agencies and groups. Police, probation workers, and gang outreach workers sought to deter violence by telling gang members that violence would not be tolerated and that gangs that continued to use violence would be targeted for intensive enforcement. Operation Ceasefire was not just a police effort; it involved other law enforcement and criminal justice agencies as well as academics from Harvard University. The planning team also recruited social service agencies and local churches and community groups to work with youth in their communities. These community groups made it clear to the gang members that their violent behaviour was not going to be tolerated by the community; they also used whatever formal and informal sanctions they could to enhance the certainty of deterrence. Suppression was a major component of the project, but it also offered gang members training, counselling, mentoring, and remedial education to help them get out of the gang lifestyle. Community organizations, including faith-based agencies, were involved in providing these services.

The impact of the project was dramatic. Operation Ceasefire was responsible for a 63 percent decline in youth homicide over nearly three years (Kennedy et al., 2001). Many of the gang members said they actually welcomed the intervention because it gave them an excuse to avoid being pressured into violence by peers and because they felt safer themselves because rival gangs were also constrained. However, when the Boston Police Department dropped the program and several community groups ended their involvement, rates of youth homicide returned to previous levels and continued to climb until at least 2006 (Pollack, 2006).

The US government further tested the individualized deterrence model through the Strategic Approach to Community Safety Initiative, which sponsored programs in 10 cities (Roehl et al., 2006). The results of this were also very positive. For example, in Indianapolis there was a 32 percent reduction in homicide, in New Haven there was a 32 percent reduction in gun crime, and in Portland there was a 42 percent reduction in homicide and a 25 percent decrease in other violent crime. The model is now being promoted nationally in the United States through Project Safe Neighborhoods.

Project HOPE

Another project based on individualized deterrence is Hawaii's Project HOPE. This project was designed by Judge Steven Alm to reduce high rates of non-compliance with probation conditions requiring abstinence from drugs. He was concerned that probationers were being allowed to commit many violations before any action was taken. When sanctions were imposed, they often involved revocation of probation, which could result in a lengthy period of reincarceration. Judge Alm believed that short, certain penalties might work better than the uncertain threat of lengthy prison sentences.

In Project HOPE, probationers are first given a clear warning that if they fail to show up for drug testing, if they fail a drug test, or if they violate any other probation condition, they will immediately be brought before a judge, who will send them to jail for a brief period of time if they are found to have violated the terms of their probation. However, their probation is not revoked and after a few days in jail they are released and placed back on probation. Each probationer must call HOPE staff every morning and receive random drug testing at least once a week. Treatment is provided for some offenders, particularly those who have committed several probation violations. This program is much more intensive than normal probation supervision, which consists of monthly meetings with probation officers, with no random drug testing.

An evaluation showed a major improvement in drug-testing outcomes among the group assigned to HOPE (Hawken and Kleiman, 2009). Over a six-month period, rates of drug test failures among the HOPE participants dropped from 53 percent to only 4 percent, a decline of 93 percent. Over the same period, failure rates for the probationers in the comparison group who received normal probation declined by only 14 percent (from 22% to 19%). Thus, HOPE participants had a rate of probation revocation only one-third that of the comparison group. Despite the automatic use of custody for violators in the HOPE program, the total number of days spent in prison was over 50 percent less for the HOPE probationers. This demonstrates that intensive community supervision can lead both to less crime and to lower prison costs.

In Canada, the Winnipeg Auto Theft Suppression Strategy is an award-winning crime reduction program that includes an individualized deterrence component. This program, which has reduced auto theft by over 80 percent, is discussed in detail at the end of this chapter.

The evidence demonstrates that the legal system can deter crime. Even though many politicians promise us that harsher sentences will reduce crime rates, there is compelling evidence that policies that increase certainty of punishment are both more effective and less costly than policies that increase the severity of punishment.

QUESTIONS FOR CRITICAL THINKING

1. Many of our politicians suggest that the best way to deal with crime is to toughen up the Youth Criminal Justice Act and to increase the penalties for crime. After reading this chapter, do you think these politicians are correct? What evidence supports your position on this question?
2. The evidence presented in this chapter suggests that longer prison sentences are not an effective way of reducing crime. Despite this evidence, many Canadians strongly support these "get tough" campaigns. Why do you think people support the "get tough" approach?

Rational Choice Theory

Rational choice theory was developed by researchers at Britain's Home Office who were trying to develop better crime prevention programs. While similar in some respects to deterrence theory, rational choice theory incorporates an extensive body of research on how offenders actually make their choices about whether to commit crimes. Instead of simply assuming that potential offenders will be deterred by the threat of legal sanctions, rational choice theory took a research-based view of offenders' decision making. Offenders told researchers they selected targets based on their perception of risks and rewards; they also described characteristics of desirable and undesirable targets, and they gave detailed descriptions of their criminal actions. The research showed that while criminal behaviour was goal-oriented, there was little planning involved in most crimes. That is, offenders did not carefully calculate the benefits and costs of their criminal behaviour.

This work was the basis of **rational choice theory** (Cornish and Clarke, 1986), which postulated that crime was the result of deliberate choices made by offenders based on their calculation of the risks and rewards of those choices. The basic assumption of rational choice theory was that "crime is purposive behaviour designed to meet the offender's commonplace needs for such things as money, status, sex, and excitement, and that meeting these needs involves the making of (sometimes quite rudimentary) decisions and choices, constrained as these are by limits of time and ability and the availability of relevant information" (Clarke, 1995, 98).

Rational choice theory did not focus on the potential offender's background, but rather on the situational dynamics involved in the decision whether to commit a crime. Rational choice theorists do not believe that all crimes result from the same social processes. Thus the analysis of particular crime problems is the key to understanding the dynamics of offences and to planning prevention programs. The factors involved in the decision to commit crime can vary even within the same crime category—the decision-making process is very different for professional thieves who steal cars to sell abroad than for a 14-year-old who sees a car running in front of a convenience store and takes it for a joyride before deliberately crashing it. One of the most important findings of this research was that offenders' behaviour was typically based more on short-term costs and benefits than on long-term considerations such as possible penalties (Felson and Clarke, 1998). The immediate rewards of a heroin injection are more important than the eventual possibility of a jail term or the long-term health risks, and the approval of peers for assaulting a member of a rival gang outweighs the possible costs of an assault conviction or of potential retaliation for the assault.

Environmental Criminology

The work of Patricia and Paul Brantingham on *environmental criminology* is an extension of rational choice theory. Their work examines the target search process that precedes involvement in a crime. Like everyone else, criminals have activity patterns, and the environmental opportunities they encounter in the course of these activities influence their decisions to commit particular

rational choice theory
Rational choice theory posits that crime is the result of deliberate choices made by offenders based on their calculation of the risks and rewards of these choices.

criminal acts (Beavon, Brantingham, and Brantingham, 1994). Criminals are more likely to commit their offences along the paths they travel in the course of their daily activities; it follows that criminal opportunities are shaped by road networks and other factors that shape potential criminals' daily routines. Even if these actors are not actively seeking criminal opportunities, they may take advantage of vulnerabilities they encounter in the course of their daily affairs. Brantingham and Brantingham (1995) analyzed crime patterns in terms of nodes, paths, and edges. Nodes are important places to would-be offenders—the places where they live, work, and socialize—and they frequently commit crimes in the areas around these nodes. Paths are routes between nodes, and these routes are vulnerable to crime. For example, a convenience store on the route from junior high school students' homes to their school is vulnerable to shoplifting, and homes that are on the route from a large bar to the area where patrons have parked their cars may be vulnerable to vandalism and other types of minor disorder as well as to burglary (Engstad, 1975). Edges are boundaries or barriers between different types land use. An example is a street that separates an industrial area from an adjoining residential neighbourhood. Crime rates are often high in these areas because neighbourhood social control may be weaker and because they may contain properties that attract or generate criminal activity. Beavon, Brantingham, and Brantingham (1994) studied the influence of street networks on patterns of property crime in Maple Ridge and Pitt Meadows, British Columbia. They found that property crimes are most likely to occur on street segments that are readily accessible, have high flows of traffic or people, and include attractive targets.

Planners can use this knowledge to help prevent crime when designing roads and accessibility routes in new communities. Police are also using knowledge of crime patterns as the basis of new tactics, such as hot spot policing, that have been shown to reduce crime.

Routine Activities Theory

Routine activities theory is closely linked to rational choice theory. Both theories focus on the circumstances of the criminal event. Routine activities theory was developed from research on patterns of crime, such as when and where it occurs, the immediate circumstances of crime, the relationship between victims and offenders, and the reasons why some people are more likely than others to be victimized by crime.

Hindelang, Gottfredson, and Garofalo (1978) used this approach to develop the lifestyle/exposure theory to account for personal victimization. This theory posits that the lifestyle and routine activities of people place them in social settings with higher or lower risks of being victimized. For example, people who spend a lot of time in public places at night have a higher risk of being robbed than people who spend their evenings at home. According to 2009 Canadian General Social Survey (GSS), those who reported engaging in 30 or more of these evening activities a month had violent victimization rates four times higher than those who engaged in 10 or fewer of these activities a

lifestyle/exposure theory
A theory of crime victimization that acknowledges that not everyone has the same lifestyle and that some lifestyles expose people to more risks than others do.

month (Perreault and Brennan, 2010). Similarly, people whose lifestyles put them in frequent contact with people who commit crimes are more likely to be victimized than those whose time is spent with law-abiding companions. For example, members of organized crime gangs have higher rates of homicide victimization than most other Canadians. They have chosen a lifestyle in which violence is used as a means of settling disputes and in which factors like the competition for the exclusive right to sell drugs in particular areas ensure that there will be many disputes to settle. While much of gang violence has been between competing gangs, it is also used as a means of settling accounts within gangs. The homicide rate among sex workers is also very high. Robert Pickton was convicted of killing six sex workers in Vancouver (and is likely responsible for the deaths of at least 20 more), and investigations into similar serial killings are under way in several other Canadian cities. The working conditions of street prostitutes, and their association with the drug culture, place them at very high risk of victimization.

Additional confirmation of lifestyle/exposure theory comes from studies of repeat victimization. If victimization is more likely among people with risky lifestyles, then we would expect that people who have been victimized once should have a higher probability of being victimized a second time than people who have not been victimized. This is, in fact, the case. Repeated victimization of the same victim (or victim's household), by both the same type of crime and different crimes, has been observed frequently in surveys both in the United States (US Department of Justice, 1974a, 1974b; Sparks, 1981) and in Canada (Koenig, 1977; Sacco and Johnson, 1990). In the 2004 Canadian General Social Survey, of those who stated that they had been victimized by a crime during the preceding 12 months, 40 percent reported that they had been victimized more than once (Gannon and Mihorean, 2005).

Cohen and Felson (1979) made the assumptions of lifestyle exposure theory more explicit when they formulated the **routine activities approach** to crime (Figure 15.1). This approach begins with the observation that three factors must be present at the same time and space for a crime to occur:

routine activities approach
An extension of the lifestyle/exposure theory, this approach assumes that crimes are the expected outcomes of routine activities and changing social patterns.

FIGURE 15.1   **The Routine Activities Approach**

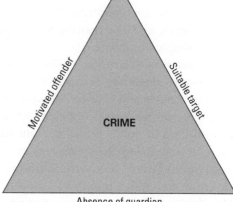

1. *A motivated offender.* Unless someone wants to commit a crime, it will not take place. Most of the theories of criminal behaviour discussed in this book try to explain why some people are motivated to commit crimes.
2. *A suitable target.* A theft will not take place unless there is property to steal, and an assault cannot happen unless there is someone to attack.
3. *A lack of guardianship of that target.* If a target is well-guarded, it will be much less likely to be victimized.

Changes in any of these factors can lead to increases or decreases in crime.

Suitable Targets

Even without additional motivated offenders, an increase in the number, the value, or the accessibility of suitable targets can result in increases in crime. For example, 30 years ago electronic equipment was bulky, heavy, and difficult to carry. Today, potential criminals have the opportunity to steal laptop computers, expensive phones, and other valuable electronics that weigh very little and that are easy to conceal. Cohen and Felson predicted that unless small, attractive items were carefully protected, theft rates would increase as these items became more common, and their data supported this view. Less suitable targets were less frequently stolen. For example, Cohen and Felson observed that not many people stole refrigerators and washing machines because these were worth far less per pound than electronic equipment and because they were much harder to carry away.

Besides providing better protection, there are other ways of making small, expensive theft targets such as smartphones less attractive. The Federal Communications Commission (2014) has reported that smartphones are the targets of 30 to 40 percent of robberies in American cities. A kill switch to make the phone inoperable if it is stolen would help reduce these thefts, but the industry has been reluctant to implement this solution because service providers and manufacturers make billions of dollars selling insurance on phones and providing replacements. However, politicians in several jurisdictions, most notably California, have passed legislation requiring these features by July 2015, so the robbery problem may eventually be greatly diminished as it is likely that this will become a universal standard.

Another example of the importance of suitable targets was the discovery by young people in Winnipeg and Regina that some models of Chrysler vehicles built in the 1990s were very easy to steal. This discovery helped fuel a boom in joyriding that saw rates of motor vehicle theft soar in both cities (Anderson and Linden, 2014). On the other hand, vehicles protected by electronic ignition immobilizers, which are almost impossible to start without a key, are very rarely stolen unless the owners leave their keys in the car.

As a final example, as the value of all types of metal rose dramatically in the middle of the last decade, thieves started stealing metal items such as manhole covers, aluminum billboards and road signs, and stainless steel tanker trailers. In Prince George, BC, thieves even tried to steal the head of a bronze statue of Terry Fox in order to recover the metal. Several people in Canada have died because they cut into live power lines in an attempt to steal the copper wire. In 2014, the city of Surrey, BC, decided to spend $9 million replacing all the copper wire in its streetlights because of the cost of repairing the lines after thefts and the inconvenience caused by power blackouts. The copper wire is being replaced with a much less valuable alloy that will be less attractive to thieves.

Effective guardianship refers to actions such as having neighbours watch your home when you are on vacation, drawing a steel mesh curtain overnight across glass display windows of jewellery, and taking evening walks on busy, well-lit streets rather than walking alone in an isolated park or down a dark alley. Changes in guardianship affect crime rates. Cohen and Felson showed that as daytime occupancy of homes (guardianship) decreased because of factors such as the increased employment of women outside the home and increases in the length of vacations, there was a substantial increase in daytime residential burglaries while the proportion of commercial burglaries declined.

This perspective is consistent with the results of interviews with offenders. Bennett and Wright (1984a) concluded that risk factors were the major consideration in target selection or **target suitability**. Burglars would be deterred if they believed that someone was home or if possible entrances were visible from nearby buildings or by passersby. When Wright and Decker asked their respondents to describe unsuitable targets, most said they would avoid targets in areas where it looked like neighbours would look out for one another. Older people were considered to be especially likely to report suspicious behaviour to the police:

> The thing is if you got a lot of elderly people on one block, that'll get you killed mostly ... I wanted to do [a burglary] over here by the bakery shop, but that's a retired area. Almost everybody that live on that block is retired and they constantly lookin' out windows and watchin' [out] for each other. Ain't nothin' you can do about that. (Wright and Decker, 1992, 87)

The routine activities perspective has been extended to incorporate two additional variables—*intimate handlers* and *crime facilitators*. Felson (1986) has described "the 'handled offender,' the individual susceptible to informal social control by virtue of his or her bonds to society, and the 'intimate handler,' someone with sufficient knowledge of the potential offender to [control the offender]" (119). This variable incorporates into routine activities theory social bonds such as ties to parents and other community members, which have been shown to reduce involvement in delinquency and crime (see Chapter 14). Clarke and Eck (2003) have proposed that the decision to commit a crime can also depend on the presence of physical, social, or chemical crime facilitators. *Physical* facilitators are objects such as guns to be used in an armed robbery or scanning devices that enable restaurant employees to steal debit card numbers along with their associated PINs. *Social* facilitators can be peers who teach the individual the techniques of committing crime and who provide social support during the criminal event. *Chemical* facilitators include drugs and alcohol, which reduce inhibitions and lead to acts that might not be committed if the individual was not under their influence. These substances can also make potential victims more vulnerable.

The importance of chemical facilitators is illustrated by the results of the 2009 GSS victimization survey, which found that alcohol consumption and illicit

effective guardianship
An aspect of the routine activities approach to understanding crime victimization that argues that three key factors are required for crime to happen: a motivated offender, a suitable target, and ineffective guardianship of that target. Effective guardianship would include having locks on bikes, or security lights in the backyard, or putting goods in the trunk of the car.

target suitability
Because of their vulnerability, some potential crime targets are more attractive than others. A home that is unlit, has shrubs blocking a view of the front door, and has no alarm system will be seen as a more suitable target than a well-protected home.

drug use increase one's likelihood of being a victim of crime. Those who reported consuming more than four alcoholic drinks in one sitting in the past month had experienced about three times as many incidents of violent victimization during the preceding 12 months as did non-drinkers (Perreault and Brennan, 2010). Those who reported using illicit drugs every day had violent victimization rates eight times higher than those who did not use illicit substances. Regular drug users also had much higher rates of property victimization. Most victims of physical assault reported that the crime was due to the offender's alcohol or drug use. These findings are consistent with the fact that the western provinces, which have the highest rates of crime in Canada (see Chapter 5), also have the highest rates of alcohol and drug use problems (Veidhuizen et al., 2007).

QUESTIONS FOR CRITICAL THINKING

1. Understanding patterns of crime means that you can reduce your chances of becoming a victim of crime if you change certain aspects of your lifestyle. Some people argue that they should not have to change the way they dress, work, or play to avoid being victimized. What do you think?

2. As a student at a university or college, how do you assess your risk of victimization? What changes could you or others make that might reduce your chances of being a crime victim? Does this approach involve blaming the victim, or is it just a realistic way to adapt to the realities of the situation?

The Diverse Attractions of Crime

Critics of rational choice and routine activities theories suggest that they may account for financially motivated crimes but that they do not account for expressive crimes that involve strong emotions (Hayward, 2007). Proponents of rational choice and routine activities theories do take the view that "opportunity causes crime" (Felson and Clarke, 1998, 9). This notion is easy to understand when we think of situations such as a person leaving an expensive bike unlocked and unattended in a high-crime neighbourhood or when managers of a convenience store near a junior high school do not take precautions against shoplifting. However, these theorists have also realized that the attractions of crime are very diverse and that motivations for criminal behaviour can be quite complex.

Consider the reasons armed robbers give for committing their offences in the interviews quoted below. Most of us can understand the financial motives of the first robber, but the other three quotes show that robberies are not just committed for economic reasons. These might seem like bad decisions to most of us, and few of the robberies had much advance planning. However, it is clear that for the offenders, robbery is the result of a rational choice that satisfies certain needs and desires:

It's the fastest and most direct way to get money. There's no thrill in getting it. It's for the cash, the money that I do it. (Gabor et al., 1987, 63)

When I have a gun in my hands, nothing can stop me. It makes me feel important and strong. With a revolver you're somebody. It's funny to see the expression of people when they have a .38 in their face. Sometimes when I went home at night I thought of it and laughed. I know that it's bad to say that. Maybe I was just fascinated. (63)

I was mad and I had to do something to get it out of my system. I was mad at my cousins and my girlfriend. I was mad at my mom at the time. (Feeney, 1986, 58)

Just to cause some trouble. Well, we just wanted to try that, you know. Goof around, you know, have some fun—jack up somebody … We thought we were really big and stuff like that. (58)

Some of the motivations for homicide are discussed in Box 15.2.

FOCUS

Box 15.2

THE DYNAMICS OF HOMICIDE

Researchers following the interactionist approach (see Chapter 13) have interviewed violent offenders and analyzed the accounts of homicides contained in police files to better understand the dynamics of homicide events. Luckenbill (1977) examined the typical roles played by offenders, victims, and bystanders in situations that resulted in homicide. He looked at the social context in which homicides occurred and concluded that many of them were confrontations that escalated into "character contests"—that is, violence became a means of saving face for the individuals. While their choice to use violence may not make sense to most of us, from their perspective it was a rational decision.

In most cases, the individuals involved were with family, friends, or acquaintances. Often the victim and the offender had a previous history of disputes that led them to anticipate or even to seek out confrontation. In some cases, one of the parties insulted the other either intentionally or inadvertently; in others, there was a refusal to carry out some requested action. This was interpreted as being offensive, and rather than ignoring the insult or leaving the scene, the offended individual responded aggressively in order to save face. In some cases, other people at the scene either encouraged a violent response or did nothing to try to defuse the situation. These points are illustrated in one of Luckenbill's (1977) examples:

The offender, victim, and three friends were driving in the country drinking beer and wine. At one point the victim started laughing at the offender's car which he, the victim, scratched a week earlier. The offender asked the victim why he was laughing. The victim responded that the offender's car looked like junk. The offender stopped the car and all got out. The offender asked the victim

to repeat his statement. When the victim reiterated his characterization of the car, the offender struck the victim, knocking him to the ground. (181)

What is striking about this incident is just how trivial it was. A joking remark made among friends led to the death of one young man and a long prison sentence for another. This case is not like most of those you see on television or in movies or read about in the headlines, but it is more representative of the "typical" homicide than are the cases of Paul Bernardo, Clifford Olson, or Robert Pickton, which get so much of the media's attention.

Can you think of some reasons why "respect" was so important to the young men involved in this case or in the following account of a Toronto murder trial:

When prosecutor Laura Bird began speaking yesterday, it sounded for all the world as though she had borrowed her story line from a violent video game or, in another age, a Bugs Bunny and Road Runner cartoon.

Hers was a tale of characters with childish nicknames who seethed with preening masculinity, nourished ridiculous grievances over months and whose ludicrous code of behaviour is redolent with more ritual gestures than a formal audience with royalty.

It would have been comic, but Ms. Bird was describing the real lives of real people and the terrible and senseless death of one of them.

Wayne Anthony Reid, a young black man, died in a hail of bullets on June 15 last year and, Ms. Bird said, he died because the friend he was with that night had, almost a full year earlier, either not nodded in respect, or not nodded vigorously enough, or not been seen to nod, in deference to a friend of the man now alleged to have killed him.

The prosecutor was delivering her opening address, designed to give jurors an overview of her case, in the second-degree murder trial of Leon Patrick Boswell ...

The victim, the alleged killer and their two friends either lived or grew up in the notorious housing complexes of the Jamestown area of northwest Toronto, a neighbourhood where territory is so clearly marked that, Ms. Bird said, "When you walked through the turf of someone else you were expected to acknowledge the other person in order to show your respect for them.

Failure to nod, or otherwise hail them up, could be considered to be extremely disrespectful."

And, she said, "Disrespect was taken seriously and could be expected to result in violent retaliation" such that a code of silence envelops the whole community, "preventing citizens from coming forward to report crimes for fear that they may be next in line at the morgue."*
(Blatchford, 2002)

*Adapted from Christie Blatchford. (November 27, 2002). "Doesn't Take a Lot to Get You Killed," in *National Post*. Material reprinted with the express permission of National Post, a division of Postmedia Network Inc.

Policy Implications—Preventing Crime

Most of the criminologists who developed rational choice and routine activities theories were looking for ways to reduce crime. Their work led to situational crime prevention, which has been very successful in reducing crime. In this section, we will focus mainly on situational prevention but will also discuss the social development approach to crime reduction, which you learned about in Chapter 7. The chapter will conclude with a discussion of a successful auto theft reduction program that combines several approaches to crime prevention into one comprehensive program.

Situational Crime Prevention

Over three decades ago, robberies of city bus drivers declined dramatically when transit systems installed sturdy fare boxes and implemented exact change systems so that drivers did not have to carry cash. Most models of new cars have very low theft rates because they have electronic immobilizers that make them virtually impossible to steal without using the keys or towing them. Researchers in England found that break-in victims were often victimized again within a

TABLE 15.1 **Deterrence, Routine Activity, and Rational Choice Theories**

Theory	Theorists	Key Elements
Classical/deterrence theory	Beccaria	Humans are rational thinkers. Those who contemplate breaking the law consider the positive and negative consequences of their actions
Rational choice theory	Clarke, Cornish	Crime is the result of deliberate choices made by offenders based on their calculation of the risks and rewards of those choices
Environmental theory	Paul and Pat Brantingham	The activity patterns of offenders and environmental opportunities influence decisions to commit particular criminal acts
Lifestyle/exposure theory	Hindelang	Some lifestyles expose people to more risks than others do
Routine activities theory	Cohen and Felson	Crimes are the expected outcomes of routine activities and changing social patterns

These photos from the Peel Regional Police Force shows how pruning trees can increase the level of surveillance for several housing units.

Courtesy of the Toronto Housing Authority.

BEFORE   AFTER

few weeks of the initial crime. Based on this knowledge, they worked with the victims to improve physical home security measures (such as better locks), and they established "cocoon" Neighbourhood Watch programs that enlisted the help of the victims' immediate neighbours. Subsequent break-and-enter rates declined dramatically relative to similar areas that did not have this follow-up. These are all examples of **situational crime prevention**.

Situational crime prevention assumes that much crime is opportunistic and contextual rather than that offenders are driven to commit a crime no matter what. You will recall that Cohen and Felson stated that three factors—target suitability, ineffective guardianship, and a motivated offender—must converge in space and time for a crime to occur. Efforts to reduce crime can focus on any or all of these components. Clarke (2005) has identified five categories of situational crime prevention techniques and has provided examples of strategies that have been used for each category (see Table 15.1):

1. Increasing the *effort* required to commit a crime by target hardening or by controlling access to targets or the tools required to commit a crime.
2. Increasing the *risks* by increasing levels of formal or informal surveillance or guardianship.
3. Reducing the *rewards* by identifying property in order to facilitate recovery, by removing targets, or by denying the benefits of crime.
4. Reducing *provocations* by controlling for peer pressure or by reducing frustration or conflict.
5. Removing *excuses* by setting clear rules and limits.

Hundreds of studies have shown the effectiveness of situational crime prevention programs. Some of the research cited by Clarke (2005) illustrates the potential of the approach:

- In the UK, suicide rates declined when natural gas was detoxified, making it impossible for people to commit suicide by putting their heads in a gas oven.
- Graffiti was almost eliminated in the New York subway system when graffiti was removed from cars immediately so that the "artists" could not see their work on display.
- Electronic tagging of library books reduced theft from libraries.
- Better inventory control reduced employee thefts from an electronics retailer.
- Tighter procedures for mailing credit cards helped reduce rates of credit card fraud.

situational crime prevention
Premised on the belief that most crime is opportunistic rather than the outcome of those driven to commit a crime no matter what the circumstances. This form of prevention attempts to reduce the opportunities for crime rather than just relying on the police after the crime has occurred.

TABLE 15.2 **Ronald Clarke's 25 Techniques of Situational Prevention**

Increase the Effort	Increase the Risks	Reduce the Rewards	Reduce Provocations	Remove Excuses
1. Target harden • Steering column locks and immobilizers • Anti-robbery screens • Tamper-proof packaging	6. Extend guardianship • Take routine precautions: go out in group at night, leave signs of occupancy, carry phone • "Cocoon" neighbourhood watch	11. Conceal targets • Off-street parking • Gender-neutral phone directories • Unmarked bullion trucks	16. Reduce frustrations and stress • Efficient queues and polite service • Expanded seating • Soothing music/muted lights	21. Set rules • Rental agreements • Harassment codes • Hotel registration
2. Control access to facilities • Entry phones • Electronic card access • Baggage screening	7. Assist natural surveillance • Improved street lighting • Defensible space design • Support whistle blowers	12. Remove targets • Removable car radio • Women's refuges • Pre-paid cards for pay phones	17. Avoid disputes • Separate -enclosures for rival soccer fans • Reduce crowding in pubs • Fixed cab fares	22. Post instructions • "No Parking" • "Private Property" • "Extinguish camp fires"
3. Screen exits • Ticket needed for exit • Export documents • Electronic merchandise tags	8. Reduce anonymity • Taxi driver IDs • "How's my driving?" decals • School uniforms	13. Identify property • Property marking • Vehicle licensing and parts marking • Cattle branding	18. Reduce emotional arousal • Controls on violent pornography • Enforce good behavior on soccer field • Prohibit racial slurs	23. Alert conscience • Roadside speed display boards • Signatures for customs declarations • "Shoplifting is stealing"
4. Deflect offenders • Street closures • Separate bathrooms for women • Disperse pubs	9. Utilize place managers • CCTV for double-deck buses • Two clerks for convenience stores • Reward vigilance	14. Disrupt markets • Monitor pawn shops • Controls on classified ads • License street vendors	19. Neutralize peer pressure. • "Idiots drink and drive" • "It's OK to say NO" • Disperse troublemakers at school	24. Assist compliance • Easy library checkout • Public lavatories • Litter bins
5. Control tools/weapons • "Smart" guns • Disable stolen cellphones • Restrict spray paint sales to juveniles	10. Strengthen formal surveillance • Red light cameras • Burglar alarms • Security guards	15. Deny benefits • Ink merchandise tags • Graffiti cleaning • Speed humps	20. Discourage imitation • Rapid repair of vandalism • V-chips in TVs • Censor details of modus operandi	25. Control drugs and alcohol • Breathalyzers in pubs • Server intervention • Alcohol-free events

Source: "Twenty Five Techniques of Situational Prevention," POP Center, http://www.popcenter.org/25techniques.

Table 15.2 shows the broad variety of situational techniques that can be used to reduce crime. These and other situational techniques have been very effective in reducing crime. However, some critics have pointed out that it is also important to reduce the number of motivated offenders:

The control of crime involves interventions on all levels: on the social causes of crime, on social control exercised by the community and the formal agencies, and on the situation of the victim. Furthermore, that social causation is given the highest priority, whereas formal agencies, such as the police, have a vital role, yet one which has in the conventional literature been greatly exaggerated. It is not the "Thin Blue Line," but the social bricks and mortar of civil society which are the major bulwark against crime. Good jobs with a discernable future, housing [projects] that tenants can be proud of, community facilities which enhance a sense of cohesion and belonging, a reduction in unfair income inequalities, all create a society which is more cohesive and less criminogenic. (Young, 1997, n.p.)

Stephen Romilly/Alamy

Transit officials in many cities have found that immediately removing graffiti from subway cars is the best way to prevent it.

Reducing Motivated Offenders

Crime Prevention Through Social Development

crime prevention through social development
An approach to crime prevention that focuses on reducing the number of motivated offenders by changing the social environment.

The initiatives that Young describes are called **crime prevention through social development** programs. Stephen Schneider studied crime prevention in Vancouver's Downtown Eastside, one of Canada's most crime-ridden neighbourhoods. His experience in this community led him to a conclusion similar to Young's—that crime problems eventually must be addressed through "a comprehensive strategy that ultimately is based upon a reinvigoration of civil society, the centrality of the local community in social problem solving,

FOCUS

Box 15.3

LESS CASH, LESS CRIME?

For many of us, credit cards, debit cards, and gift cards have replaced cash. This has had an impact on crime because cash—a very attractive target—is less available to potential thieves. The loss of this potential target is one reason for the crime decline over the past two decades. Bank robberies have declined in most countries, and robberies—once common on paydays and days when government cheques arrived—have dropped now that governments and employers have replaced cheques with direct bank deposit. Street crimes such as robbery and pickpocketing will be much less profitable in a cashless society.

Of course the move to electronic funds has also led to criminal opportunities. Credit card and debit card fraud are now commonplace. To deal with this problem, credit and debit cards in Canada now use a chip and PIN system that is more difficult to counterfeit than the older magnetic stripe cards. With the older cards, criminals could attach devices to the payment terminals that would scan the customer's information from the magnetic stripes. This information could then be used on fraudulent duplicate cards. A spokesman for Interac—the network that processes debit card transactions—reported that debit card fraud in Canada dropped by 45 percent from 2011 to 2012 (Shaw, 2014) because of the chip technology.

---

and the empowerment and participation of those who are in the most need. This means that a greater share of public resources and power be allocated to the local level and to the poorest communities in particular" (2007, 306). The work of Young and Schneider has led them to conclusions that are very different from those of politicians who promise us that a bit of tinkering with the justice system will quickly end most of our crime problems. Their work helps place the solutions suggested by routine activities theory in a broader perspective. Situational measures are an important way of reducing crime, but we must also consider other methods that will help overcome the serious social problems that breed motivated offenders.

Social development programs are intended to reduce the pool of motivated offenders by altering the conditions that breed crime. These programs (several of which were described in Chapter 7) focus on factors such as family problems, peer issues, poverty, and a range of school and community factors. Some have tried to improve the parenting skills of high-risk parents; others have provided job training and employment for young people who are cut off from the labour market because they live in poor communities. Social development strategies are often targeted at young people, who appear to be the most amenable to intervention and who make up the next generation of offenders.

One of the most promising areas involves providing preschool programs for children from deprived backgrounds. One of the few social development programs that has undergone a long-term evaluation is a Michigan program called the Perry Preschool Project. The students were 123 African American children from poor families. Children aged three and four attended a preschool with an active learning curriculum five mornings a week, and teachers visited the children's homes once a week. The program lasted 30 weeks each year. A control group did not receive these services. Like the earlier Head Start program, this project sought to remedy the impact of the children's impoverished backgrounds on their later school success.

SEARCH FOR:
Institute for the Prevention of Crime

SEARCH FOR:
Perry Preschool Program

The most recent follow-up of the Perry Preschool project looked at the participants at age 40 (Schweinhart et al., 2005). Far fewer of the program participants than controls had been arrested five or more times (36% versus 55%), and they had less than half the arrest rate for drug offences (14% versus 34%). The program group had higher incomes, were more likely to own their own homes, and were less likely to have been on welfare. They had greater educational achievement and lower rates of illiteracy. Program group members were more likely to have had stable marriages, and females had lower rates of out-of-wedlock births. The costs of the program had been more than recovered through reduced welfare costs and increased earnings of the graduates. Schweinhart and colleagues estimate that the saving was more than $17 for every dollar invested in the program. Those responsible for this program maintain that the intervention must be made while the children are young and must be thorough enough to overcome the range of disadvantages faced by the participants. The Canadian government has responded to this research by establishing early childhood education programs in a number of communities and by establishing a national Aboriginal Head Start program.

The Need for Comprehensive Crime Reduction Initiatives

Some critics have expressed fears that situational techniques may lead to a fortress society or to a "big brother" state where our actions are always subject to scrutiny through technology such as surveillance cameras. Other practitioners and academics have viewed social development as the only acceptable way of preventing crime. They have gone from the reasonable position that society needs to do something about the root causes of crime to the not so reasonable position that social development programs are the only ones that are acceptable.

In fact, developmental and situational approaches are complementary. We can distinguish between "criminal involvement" and "criminal events" (Clarke, 1995). Criminal involvement relates to criminal careers and is appropriately addressed by social development approaches. Criminal events are short-term acts that may be more appropriately addressed by situational prevention.

The most sensible strategy to pursue is one that recognizes that all crime prevention strategies have their strengths and weaknesses. A comprehensive strategy should include prevention programs that involve cooperation among different levels of government and other agencies and groups that can contribute to solutions (see Chapter 7), that are targeted to areas where they are most needed, that use a broad range of prevention approaches tailored to the specific needs of communities, and that draw upon programs that have been shown to be effective in other places.

To illustrate the potential of this approach as a guide to preventing crime, consider a Winnipeg program that one of this chapter's authors help plan and implement.

The Winnipeg Auto Theft Suppression Strategy (WATSS)

From 2003 to 2008, Winnipeg had North America's highest rate of auto theft. Nearly one in five Criminal Code offences in the city was an auto theft, and the 2006 rate was 67 percent higher than the next highest Canadian city. In addition to the property loss involved in these thefts, there was significant physical violence. In 2007, two people were killed by drivers of stolen vehicles, and an early morning jogger was seriously injured after being deliberately run down by a youth driving a stolen car. In one 16-month period in 2007–8, eight drivers deliberately tried to run down police officers with stolen vehicles. Vehicle thieves also frequently attempted to ram police cars. Some youth engaged in other dangerous behaviour, such as jamming down vehicle accelerators and launching driverless vehicles down city streets and into parking garages.

Research done by the Manitoba Auto Theft Task Force found that auto theft rates were so high because auto theft had become an important part of youth culture in parts of Winnipeg. Virtually all the stolen vehicles were used for joyriding or as temporary transportation and were eventually recovered, often with major damage. Interviews with young offenders found that they stole cars for excitement and to show off for their peers and that they were very committed to auto theft. For example, one of the respondents said he stole cars "for a joyride ... for the rush!", and another reported that "[stealing cars] is addicting. When you find something you're good at, you want to keep doing it" (Anderson and Linden, 2014, 254).

This auto theft culture developed after a few young people learned how easy it was to steal some models of cars and realized that the probability of arrest was very low. These offenders told their friends and schoolmates about this new pastime, and the number of people willing and able to steal cars grew quickly. Children in some neighbourhoods learned to steal cars at a very early age (a number of young people were able to steal dozens of cars before they were 12 years old), and a peer culture developed that focused on car theft. Cars were often stolen by groups of friends, and over half the respondents reported that they had taken part in contests to see who could steal the most cars in a given period of time. This culture was reinforced by the mass media as well as by peer groups. Most of the youth who were interviewed played video games such as *Grand Theft Auto*, which glamorizes stealing cars and using them to create mayhem on the streets. Several also said that movies such as *Gone in 60 Seconds* had helped teach them some of the techniques for stealing cars.

For almost a decade, the favourite targets were Chrysler products manufactured in the early 1990s, which were particularly easy to steal. Although recent models are much more difficult to steal, older model Chrysler vehicles can be entered and started in a few seconds using only an ordinary screwdriver.

The solution to this problem focused on all three components of routine activities theory:

1. *Effective Guardianship.* Earlier in this chapter we discussed the notion of individualized deterrence. In the language of routine activities theory, increasing certainty is a way of making guardianship more effective. The most serious auto theft offenders were typically in the community under conditions of release such as curfews. The WATSS program provided

intensive supervision to enforce these conditions. Youth were contacted in person every day by youth probation workers or the police Stolen Auto Unit and were contacted by phone every three hours. Youth who violated their conditions of release were immediately apprehended by the police so that they did not have the opportunity to reoffend.

2. *Target Suitability.* The vulnerability of certain models of vehicles was a major reason why young people were able to learn to steal vehicles. Thus a major part of the prevention strategy was a mandatory program requiring electronic vehicle immobilizers for the 100,000 most at-risk vehicles in Winnipeg. These immobilizers were immediately effective: five years after the program began, none of the immobilizers approved by the program's sponsor, Manitoba Public Insurance, had yet been defeated by vehicle thieves.

3. *Motivated Offenders.* The third component of WATSS involved addressing the social causes of auto theft by working with young people and their families to try to reduce the number of young people who found auto theft an appealing form of recreation. Much of this work was done by youth probation staff. Support programs for high-risk offenders and their families were run with community partners, including the Winnipeg School Division, Big Brothers and Big Sisters, and New Directions for Children, Youth, Adults and Families. The goals were to move current offenders away from auto theft and to end the flow of new recruits to this dangerous and costly pastime.

This program was highly effective in reducing crime. As shown in Figure 15.2, rates declined dramatically after WATSS was fully implemented. Between 2006 and July 2011, auto thefts declined by 83 percent. There was no displacement to other crimes; indeed, offences such as break and enter, robbery, and theft from vehicles also declined over this period. Because of this reduction in vehicle thefts, Winnipeg drivers are paying about $40 million less each year in vehicle insurance premiums.

 FIGURE 15.2 **Rates of Auto Theft**

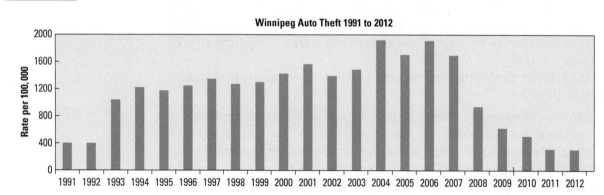

The success of WATSS and other programs based on rational choice and routine activities theories of crime demonstrate the need for governments to invest in evidence-based approaches to crime reduction rather than simply building more jails. The deterrent effects of increased certainty are demonstrably more likely to reduce crime than increasing severity by legislating longer sentences. Furthermore, many situational prevention programs have been more successful than those that rely on the justice system to reduce crime, particularly when these programs are part of broad, comprehensive initiatives.

QUESTIONS FOR CRITICAL THINKING

1. What are the most significant crime problems in your community? Can you think of some strategies that might help reduce these problems?
2. Can you find any examples of comprehensive crime prevention programs in your community? Why do you think these programs are not more widely used?

Summary

- Deterrence theories focus on the factors influencing an individual's decision whether or not to commit an offence and assert that the legal system can be used to affect that decision. Research on the deterrent effects of imprisonment shows that increasing the severity of our current laws is not likely to have an impact on crime rates. However, several studies show that increasing the certainty of punishment can reduce crime, particularly through programs targeted at frequent offenders.

- Rational choice theory assumes that people commit crimes because they believe this will provide them with some reward. A person's decision to commit a crime may or may not appear rational to the rest of us, but it does meet a goal for the offender.

- Routine activities theory is based on the observation that crime results from the simultaneous presence of a motivated offender, a suitable target, and ineffective guardianship of that target. This approach was used to develop lifestyle/exposure theory, which is based on the idea that the lifestyle and activities of some people place them at higher risk for crime victimization

- The routine activities approach leads to a number of crime reduction strategies. These include situational measures, crime prevention through social development, and incapacitation of high-rate offenders.

- The most effective way to reduce crime is to implement comprehensive crime prevention programs that focus on reducing the number of motivated offenders, increasing guardianship, and reducing target suitability.

NET WORK

In this chapter, you have learned about the routine activities approach to crime. This approach has had an impact on crime prevention programs in North America and Europe by drawing attention to the role of the attractiveness of the target and the importance of effective guardianship. To see how these insights are used in crime prevention, look at Chapter 7 of the report *Preventing Crime: What Works, What Doesn't, What's Promising*, https://www.ncjrs.gov/works. In that chapter, by John Eck, find three projects that are intended to reduce the attractiveness of the target and three projects that increase effective guardianship. Have these projects been successful in reducing crime?

Patterns of Criminal Behaviour

Many behaviours are illegal, but they vary widely in seriousness. Murder, for instance, is in a very different category from not putting enough change in a parking meter. In Part 3, we look at some of the kinds of misconduct that frequently occur in Canada.

When the average citizen thinks of crime, the images that most commonly come to mind are the so-called street crimes—robbery, assault, break and enter, and so on. These offences have been discussed throughout most of this text because they occupy most of the time and attention of the criminal justice system, are the focus of the media, and have been the concern of most criminologists.

This section of the text examines three other types of crime. Chapter 16 looks at the "organized" criminals, who are in the business of providing access to illegal goods and services. Chapter 17 looks at crimes committed by "respectable" people: many of our leading citizens are white-collar criminals, and many of our largest businesses are corporate offenders. This chapter makes the important point that the power we give to those in positions of authority and ownership in modern corporations may encourage them to become involved in illegal activities that cause a great deal of social harm. Finally, Chapter 18 covers cybercrime, which will almost certainly become much more of a threat in the future as we live more of our lives online.

16

Organized Crime

Stephen Schneider
SAINT MARY'S UNIVERSITY

Organized crime can be distinguished by *how* crimes are carried out and by the ultimate *goal* of these crimes—financial profit. Broadly speaking, criminal activity is "organized" if it is perpetrated by a group of people who conspire together on a continuing and secretive basis with the goal of obtaining a financial or other material benefit. Scale is also an important factor in determining the extent to which criminal activity is organized; the broader the scope of the criminal activities, the greater the need for a high level of organization and, often, for the involvement of people in several different jurisdictions.

Learning Objectives

After reading this chapter you should be able to

- Define a criminal organization according to the Criminal Code of Canada.
- Understand the characteristics, complexity, and diversity of organized crime.
- Identify the dominant organized crime "genres" operating in Canada.
- Analyze the competing theories on the causes of organized crime and the social, economic, and political factors that give rise to organized crime in North America, and specifically in Canada.
- Compare competing theories on the structure of organized crime.
- Understand the role Canada plays in global organized crime.

Defining Organized Crime

Different countries have different legal definitions of organized crime. Section 467.1 of the Criminal Code defines a criminal organization as a group, however organized, that

> (a) is composed of three or more persons in or outside Canada; and
> (b) has as one of its main purposes or main activities the facilitation or commission of one or more serious offences that, if committed, would likely result in the direct or indirect receipt of a material benefit, including a financial benefit, by the group or by any of the persons who constitute the group.

The legislation goes on to state that a criminal organization "does not include a group of persons that forms randomly for the immediate commission of a single offence." While this caveat does provide some conceptual precision, the legal definition in Canada of a criminal organization remains exceptionally broad and provides little help in understanding the complexity of organized crime.

The Commission of the European Communities and EUROPOL define a criminal organization as "a structured association, established over a period of time, of more than two persons, acting in concert with a view to committing offences which are punishable by deprivation of liberty of a maximum of at least four years or a more serious penalty; whether such offences are an end in themselves or a means of obtaining material benefits and, where appropriate, of improperly influencing the operation of public authorities" (2001, 42). To clarify this definition for legal purposes, the Commission and EUROPOL set out the 11 fundamental traits of a criminal organization:

1. collaboration of more than two people
2. each with own appointed tasks
3. for a prolonged or indefinite period of time (refers to the stability and potential durability)
4. using some form of discipline and control
5. suspected of the commission of serious criminal offences
6. operating at an international level
7. using violence or other means suitable for intimidation
8. using commercial or businesslike structures
9. engaged in money laundering
10. exerting influence on politics, the media, public administration, judicial authorities, or the economy
11. determined by the pursuit of profit and/or power.*

To be deemed a criminal organization for law enforcement and prosecution purposes, an identified conspiracy need only exhibit six of the 11 traits, which is constructive because it reflects the reality that not every organized crime group encompasses all of these traits. Yet the European Union (EU) also recognizes the need to identify core characteristics (#1, 3, 5, and 11) that are present in all types of criminal organizations: the collaboration of more than two people, for a prolonged or indefinite period of time, who are engaged in the commission of serious criminal offences, for the pursuit of profit and/or power.

SEARCH FOR:
EUROPOL

Characteristics of Organized Crime

This section builds on the preceding definition by elaborating on the core characteristics of organized crime (summarized in Table 16.1). These characteristics can be divided into four categories: structural/organizational, institutional, commercial, and behavioural. Not all of these characteristics are present in every organized criminal conspiracy.

---

*Mark Haller (1990) "Illegal enterprises: A theoretical and historical interpretation," *Criminology*, 28 (2): 207

TABLE 16.1   **A Comprehensive Classification of Organized Crime**

Structural/Organizational	Institutional	Commercial	Behavioural
Two or more people involved	Continuing enterprise	Illegal activities committed for financial or other material benefit	Rationality
Conspire together to commit (serious) illegal acts	Sophistication	Consensual and predatory crimes	Contempt for civil society
A systematic pattern to the relationship of the offenders	Motivation	Legal commercial activities	Rules, regulations, and codes
Assigned tasks/specialization/division of labour	Career criminals	Goods and services	Discipline
Insulation against law enforcement and prosecution	Limited or exclusive membership	Tactics to support commercial activities: corruption, violence, money laundering	
Specialized channels and modes of communication	Recruitment	Multiple enterprises	
Multi-jurisdictional/transnational in scope	Secrecy	Constant demand for goods and services	

Structural/Organizational Characteristics

Two or More People Involved

One of the core traits of organized crime is that it involves multiple individuals. The more offenders involved in a criminal conspiracy, the greater the likelihood it will constitute an organized criminal conspiracy.

Conspire to Commit (Serious) Illegal Acts

A distinguishing characteristic of organized crime is that the individuals involved have come together with the express purpose of committing illegal acts for financial gain. This distinguishes organized criminal conspiracies from other organizations, such as corporations or governments, which are legitimately formed but may commit illegal acts in the course of their otherwise legitimate affairs. Furthermore, to constitute a criminal organization, the illegal acts should be "serious" in nature (e.g., drug trafficking, extortion, human trafficking, etc.). This aspect distinguishes it from rudimentary groups of offenders that limit their illegal activities to less serious crimes such as thefts from homes and vehicles.

A Systematic Pattern to the Relationship of the Offenders

For a group to constitute an organized criminal conspiracy, there must be multiple offenders, and there must also be a systematic pattern to the relationship among these offenders. This systematic pattern separates organized crime from other forms of collective criminal action such as riotous mobs.

A major controversy in the study of organized crime concerns the nature of the relationships among the offenders and how these relationships are structured. There is no single pattern to such relationships, just as there is no single type of organizational structure. The pattern of relationships may be based on kinship, friendship, or business ties, while the structure of an organized criminal conspiracy may be hierarchical (based on power relations among the offenders involved) or more symmetrical (based on the specialized tasks of or resources available to the conspirators).

In his seminal study of criminal groups in New York City, Ianni (1974) identified two basic forms of relationships among individuals involved in organized crime. The first are "associational networks," which are held together by close personal relationships among members. Examples of these personal relationships are kinship and shared ethnicity, as embodied by the Italian mafia "family." The second follows an "entrepreneurial model," where the bond among the offenders is less personal and determined more by business interests. The historical trend in organized crime has seen business relationships replacing associational networks as the principal binding force among the offenders involved.

Specialization/Division of Labour

Many organized crime conspiracies have a division of labour whereby the individuals involved are assigned certain functions (Abadinsky, 2012). In a hierarchical criminal organization, this division of labour often corresponds to the member's position in the power structure. In the more symmetrical network model, individuals play different roles based on their particular skills or resources. A prime example is Colombia's Medellin and Cali cocaine cartels, which established intricate divisions of labour, with different cells specialized in one specific function, such as refining the raw coca into cocaine, transportation, bribing government officials, laundering money, distributing drugs wholesale, providing security, and managing "stash" houses in destination countries (President's Commission on Organized Crime, 1986b; US Senate Committee on Governmental Affairs, 1989).

Insulation against Enforcement and Prosecution

A hierarchical organizational structure helps insulate the upper echelons of a criminal group against law enforcement actions. This is done by ensuring that the hands-on execution of illegal activities is carried out by those at the lowest level of the organization or even by "associates" who are not official members of the organization (the Italian Mafia in Montreal is well known for delegating criminal tasks to "associates," while outlaw motorcycle gangs often use "prospects," (probationary members of a biker club chapter) "hangers-on" (associates of a biker club) and "**puppet clubs**" to carry out their dirty work). The more buffers between those who physically carry out crimes and those in the upper echelons of the organization, the more the latter will be insulated from prosecution. The Cali Cartel used an innovative network structure that was specifically designed to protect the organization and its members from law enforcement. This was accomplished by ensuring that the identities of offenders working within one "cell" of the network were unknown to those working in other cells. If one should be compromised, the operations of the other cells (and the larger organization) would not be endangered (President's Commission on Organized Crime, 1984, 562; Constantine, 1994). Insulation against enforcement actions is also helped by a code of silence. For example, central to the Italian Mafia is a code of *omertà*. At the most practical level, *omertà* is about secrecy; members are expected to keep the operations of the family secret from nonmembers and, ultimately, protect its leaders and the organization itself

puppet club
A motorcycle club that is subsidiary to a more dominant outlaw motorcycle gang and that is often expected to carry out the dirty work of the latter.

from law enforcement. For decades, members of the Italian mafia in the United States escaped prosecution because of their commitment to this sacrosanct code. The once-powerful Italian mafia has been decimated in the United States, in part because members increasingly turned their back on the code of *omertà* by becoming witnesses for the state (Reppetto, 2007).

Specialized Modes and Channels of Communication

Because of the danger of electronic eavesdropping by police, those taking part in organized criminal conspiracies must often be very guarded about how they communicate and what they say to avoid providing law enforcement with evidence that can be used in court.

Communication can be protected in one of two ways. First, offenders can structure their communication so it cannot be interpreted by police; this is most often accomplished by talking in abstract codes. Second, criminal groups will undertake measures to ensure that their conversations are not intercepted by police—for example, by physically "patting down" people to guard against surreptitious recording, using electronic devices that can detect recording bugs, encrypting digital communication, and using multiple disposable cellular telephones.

Transnational in Scope

SEARCH FOR:
UN Transnational Organized
Crime Threat Assessment

transnational organized crime
Organized crime that is coordinated and conducted across national borders.

One of the most significant trends in organized crime has been the internationalization of criminal groups and their illegal activities. Despite the historical prevalence of organized international smuggling, until the 1970s most criminal groups operated in specific local territories and usually did not attempt to function to any great extent outside their immediate sphere of influence. Organized crime is now international. The unprecedented frequency with which criminal groups and activities cross national boundaries, combined with the global structure and reach of some crime groups, has led to the emerging spectre of what is referred to as "transnational organized crime" (TOC).

FOCUS

Box 16.1

STRUCTURAL AND ORGANIZATIONAL CHARACTERISTICS OF OUTLAW MOTORCYCLE GANGS (OMGS)

To outsiders, a biker gang may represent the epitome of wild, unrestrained anarchism. Yet organizations like Hells Angels are actually highly structured, tightly knit, and quite hierarchical. There is an organizational hierarchy to each chapter, complete with management positions, a division of labour, and skills-based advancement. There is general uniformity in style of dress, colours, and motorcycles (large, modified Harley-Davidsons). Most clubs have a written constitution and bylaws. Minutes of meetings are recorded, dues and other revenues collected, and accounting records maintained.

The organizational structure of an outlaw motorcycle gang (OMG) chapter is relatively consistent. Most have a president, vice president, secretary-treasurer, enforcer, sergeant-at-arms, road captain, rank-and-file members, and prospects. The chapter president is often elected and has final say over all the business of the chapter. In addition, the president may receive all sorts of booty and monetary tribute from members. The secretary-treasurer collects dues on behalf of the chapter, acts as book-keeper and secretary (e.g., keeps the minutes of meetings), and keeps track of who owes what and to whom. The sergeant-at-arms maintains order at meetings and on the chapter's "biker runs." This position is usually filled by the toughest member of the chapter. He may also serve as an enforcer and has the power to discipline a club member. The road captain organizes the logistics and security for the time-honoured biker run.

Only members of the OMG are allowed to wear its "colours." A chapter will have no less than six and no more than 25 members. Each chapter has prospective members ("strikers" or "prospects"), who spend from one month to one year on probation. To become a member, one must first be sponsored by an existing member, who is responsible for his prospect. During this time, the prospect must prove himself worthy of membership by following orders and committing crimes. A vote is ultimately taken by chapter members to determine whether the prospect will become a full, patch-wearing member.

The OMG and its leader are insulated from law enforcement through the chapter's organizational hierarchy and through a strict code, which strives to ensure that the ultimate loyalty of each member is to the club. Prospects, hangers-on, puppet club members, and external associates will often take the fall for particular crimes involving OMG members, especially those members who occupy management positions in the chapter.

Many of the larger OMGs have developed specialized units to carry out important functions, such as enforcement, violence, and even murder. Hells Angels enforcers used to be adorned with Nazi storm-trooper-like lightning bolts tattooed below the words "Filthy Few." The Outlaws have their "SS Death Squad," and the Pagans have the "Black T-Shirt Squad." The Hells Angels' former puppet gang in Quebec—the Rockers—had a special assassination squad called the "football team"; it also operated a "baseball team," which "was made up of members and associates who were responsible for carrying out brutal beatings of rivals" (*Canadian Press*, 2002).

While OMG chapters exhibit a formal organizational structure, individual members often maintain networks of associates and connections through which they carry out their criminal rackets. For business purposes, each member is at the centre of a network that operates independently of the chapter. In other words, the OMG chapter's formal structure is not necessarily the same as its revenue-generating commercial structure, which is broader than the gang. But "members can call upon the muscle of the club in the event of conflict, making them formidable entrepreneurs" (Abadinsky, 2000, 238). Lavigne (1996, 246) adds: "The Hells Angels are truthful when they say they are not a criminal organization. Rather, they are an organization of criminals." Indeed, "belonging to the Hells Angels guarantees to each member the possibility of running an illicit activity" (Nicaso, 2001).

Wayne Leidenfrost/The Vancouver Sun

Institutional Characteristics

Continuity/Continuing Enterprise

Some organized crime groups are designed to last beyond the life of the current membership (Abadinsky, 2012, 4). The interests of individuals are subordinate to those of the organization, and personnel can be replaced as a matter of course. There is a line of succession to leadership, and as a rule, there are no indispensable members (Salerno, 1967, 7). The Hells Angels have officially existed since the 1950s, with roots stretching back to the immediate postwar period (see Box 16.1). Each of the five major New York mafia families has survived for more than 75 years; so has the Montreal-based mafia. Canada's Criminal Code recognizes organized crime as a continuing enterprise by emphasizing that a criminal organization "does not include a group of persons that forms randomly for the immediate commission of a single offence."

Career Criminals

One reason why some organized crime groups persist over time is that the offenders involved are usually career criminals. In some crime groups, a criminal record is a prerequisite for "official" membership. Once initiated, many criminal groups require their members to undertake a wide range of illegal activities. Members of criminal organizations often do not have legitimate jobs (though some will hide behind artificially created jobs or businesses), and even after accumulating considerable wealth or spending long periods of time in jail, many continue with their illegal activities.

Motivation

Organized crime groups are not motivated by political ideology, religious dogma, or a desire to change society. Their goal is to accumulate financial and other material benefits. Corruption for these groups is merely a tactic for gaining protection from the state and/or immunity to continue their illegal operations. This distinguishes criminal organizations from terrorist groups, whose illegal activities have social and political change as their goal.

Sophistication

To maximize profits and to avoid incarceration, some organized crime groups have become quite sophisticated. The level of sophistication with which they carry out their activities separates them from unorganized criminals; it also separates the larger transnational criminal groups from smaller local gangs or networks. According to CISC (2007):

> Only a small number of organized crime groups are capable of operating elaborate criminal operations. These groups are engaged in diverse and complex activities. For the most part, they operate out of the largest urban areas but have secondary operations or criminal influence in other cities or rural areas. These groups are distinguished by sophisticated operations, often involving importation, manufacture or distribution of a wide range of illicit commodities as well as the ability to commit complex frauds, money laundering or financial schemes. In addition, many of these groups

display the capability to target, coerce or employ individuals in legitimate business, professionals, such as lawyers and accountants, and other community members in order to facilitate their criminal activities. Many of these groups are difficult to target as they strategically insulate themselves from law enforcement. (CISC, *2007 Annual Report*)*

Another indication of sophistication is the expanding use of technology by organized crime. Police have uncovered criminal conspiracies that have produced exact replicas of credit cards, passports, currency, and consumer goods. Some crime groups possess the computer technology to steal personal identification directly from bank cards or through the Internet. Computer hackers who are able to decode complex security systems and breach the firewalls of corporations have increasingly been linked to organized criminals whose intentions are theft for financial gain (Brown, 2007; Verizon Business Risk Team, 2009). "Cybercrime groups" even develop and market "crimeware"—malicious software specifically designed to steal confidential personal and financial information (CISC, 2010, 12). Some crime groups have engineered intricate encryption codes and software to communicate surreptitiously online; others have the technology to conduct radar sweeps of drug surveillance planes to map out gaps in coverage. Some groups have even used submarines to smuggle contraband (*New York Times*, 2012).

SEARCH FOR:
Criminal Intelligence Service Canada

Limited or Exclusive Membership

Most traditional organized crime groups place restrictions on membership. Group membership is based on factors such as ethnicity, race, nationality, kinship, or criminal record. Ethnicity and/or nationality has long been a major binding tie for members of organized crime groups, which explains why most of the dominant organized crime groups are referred to by the ethnic backgrounds of their members (the Sicilian mafia, Chinese triads, Japanese Yakuza, Colombian cartels, Jamaican posses, etc.).

Membership in traditional organized crime groups is more than symbolic. Having been made a member of a mafia family, the "made guy," "wiseguy," or "goodfellow" can oversee his own crew and/or have jurisdiction over a neighbourhood to carry out his criminal activities. He also has greater access to criminal markets, to government, private sector, and/or union officials, and to other resources that cannot be accessed by most ordinary criminals. More importantly, criminal organizations such as the mafia and the Hells Angels provide members with intimidating power, affluence, and credibility within the criminal underworld.

An important recent change in the world of organized crime has been the emergence of criminal networks that have abandoned all traditional restrictions on membership, such as ethnicity or nationality. Instead, the only criterion for an individual who wants to join the criminal network is the ability to contribute to the accumulation of profits (see Figure 16.3).

Recruitment

Traditional organized crime groups like the Italian mafia, outlaw motorcycle gangs, and Chinese triads use "an institutionalized process for inducting new

cybercrime
Illegal acts in which a computer and a network are central to committing a crime and are also the targets of the crime.

2007 Annual Report on Organized Crime in Canada, p. 14, Criminal Intelligence Service Canada, 2007. Reproduced with the permission of the RCMP.

members and inculcating them with the values and ways of behaving" (Cressey, 1969, 36). Recruitment is increasingly important to modern criminal organizations because of their need for specialized skills and resources. According to the CISC (2009), "where critical skills necessary to facilitate criminal activities are absent within a criminal group, skilled outsiders are recruited or exploited to provide this service. The individual may be considered an outside contractor or part of the criminal network" (13).

Secrecy

Organized crime groups protect the secrecy of their operations through violence, intimidation, insulation, bribery, rules, and codes of conduct. Secrecy is vital for organized crime groups. Thus, the mafia's code of *omertà* defines a mafioso in part by his ability to conceal the existence and operations of *the family*, especially from the law.

Commercial Characteristics

Profit-Oriented Criminal Activities

The business of organized crime is making money. This distinguishes organized crime from crimes of passion, vandalism, and terrorism. Organized crime groups generate money through myriad activities, both illegal and legal (see Table 16.2). Drug trafficking is the biggest moneymaker for most organized crime groups. The CISC estimates that 80 percent of all identified criminal organizations in Canada are involved in the illegal drug trade (2007, 13; 2009, 9). Human trafficking comes second (according to many observers) in terms of geographic scope, the number of people victimized, and the amount of revenue generated for criminal entrepreneurs (ILO, 2012; UN, 2012). Many criminal groups will involve themselves in almost any activity that will make them money.

TABLE 16.2   Common Organized Criminal Activities

Consensual	Predatory/Consensual (Includes Both a Victim and a Consumer)	Predatory
Drug smuggling/trafficking	Automobile theft	Extortion ("protection rackets") Human trafficking (indentured slavery and forced prostitution)
Smuggling and marketing of legal consumer products (tobacco, liquor, fuel, digital products, clothing)	Environmental crimes (illegal dumping of waste)	Business and labour racketeering
Gambling	Counterfeiting and product piracy (bank cards, government documents, currency, consumer products)	Murder, grievous bodily injury
Migrant smuggling	Corruption (of government officials, labour racketeering)	Kidnapping
Loansharking	Illegal trade in wildlife	Consumer fraud (Ponzi schemes, telemarketing)
Prostitution	Illegal trade in organs and tissue (human and animal)	Government fraud (tax, health care, employment insurance, social insurance and assistance)
Money laundering	Illegal trafficking in arms, ammunition and explosives	Corporate fraud (credit card, insurance, mortgage)
	Trafficking in nuclear and radioactive substances	Stock market manipulation
	Illegal trade in stolen artifacts, art, jewellery, precious gems	Theft (including robbery, burglary, hijacking)
	Trafficking in endangered plant species	Computer crime (computer hacking)

Consensual and Predatory Criminal Activities

Organized criminals are involved in both consensual and predatory crimes. A consensual crime is one where no "victim" exists; that is, two or more individuals voluntarily engage in an illegal transaction. The business of organized crime has been described as providing goods and services that are in demand by the public but that have been made illegal by the state or are tightly regulated.

Predatory crimes are those in which a victim suffers a direct physical, emotional, or financial loss. Predatory crimes carried out by organized criminal groups include extortion (protection rackets), theft, human trafficking, currency counterfeiting, and various types of fraud.

A clear distinction between consensual and predatory crimes is often difficult to draw, given that even consensual crimes can harm the individual consuming the good or service (e.g., a drug addict or compulsive gambler) as well as society at large. Table 16.2 summarizes the wide range of illegal activities associated with organized crime and categorizes each according to whether it is a consensual crime, a predatory crime, or both.

Goods and Services

Organized illegal enterprises provide both goods and services. Popular illegal goods include drugs, legal contraband (such as cigarettes or liquor), stolen goods, weapons, counterfeit currency, pirated commercial products, and even human or animal organs. Common illegal consensual services include gambling, prostitution, loansharking, migrant smuggling, and illegal waste dumping (which is provided to legitimate businesses seeking to avoid the high costs of obeying environmental laws).

Supply of Legal and Illegal Goods

Most products supplied by organized crime groups are illegal. However, they also supply goods and services that are legal but whose distribution is controlled by the state. For example, while cigarettes and liquor are legal products, they are also distributed through black markets. Most black markets for legal consumer products exist due to high government taxes. The United States has lower taxes on cigarettes and alcohol than Canada, so organized groups smuggle large quantities of these products across the border, where they are sold to Canadians well below their retail price. Other legal products are stolen and then fenced through underground markets or through legal businesses such as bars or pawnshops. Besides selling legal products illegally in underground markets, organized crime groups have become involved in legitimate and legal businesses for the purposes of generating revenue, legitimizing the offender, or laundering money.

extortion
An offender unlawfully obtains money, property or services from an individual or entity through coercion and intimidation.

human trafficking
The illegal trade in people for the purposes of commercial sexual exploitation and other forms of forced labour.

loansharking
Lending money at very high interest rates, often enforced through the use of physical force.

Constant Demand for Goods and Services

Organized crime groups are able to stay in business largely because of a loyal customer base that voluntarily consumes its products and services. Without drug users, gamblers, "johns," or people wanting to immigrate, organized crime would be much less profitable. Indeed, one reason it is so difficult to eradicate organized crime is that its goods and services are in high demand.

Monopolistic Goals

Organized crime groups often seek a monopoly over the sale of a particular good or service in a particular geographic area. Typically, these monopolies are sought and maintained through violence, the threat of violence, or corrupt relationships with government, businesses, or union officials (Abadinsky, 2012, 4). Competition for market share often leads to serious violence, as demonstrated by the biker war that erupted in Quebec in the 1990s. More than 160 people were killed when the Hells Angels tried to monopolize the lucrative cocaine trade in that province (Sher and Marsden, 2003).

Tactics to Support Commercial Activities

Many organized crime activities generate revenues directly; other activities, though, are carried out to facilitate the criminal organization's profit-making enterprises. Like legitimate corporations, criminal groups must undertake certain activities to support the production, distribution, and marketing of their products and services. One factor that separates organized crime from unorganized crime is their resort to tactical illegal activities, in particular corruption, violence, intimidation, money laundering, intelligence gathering, and surveillance.

Corruption—of public officials, labour unions, political parties, and the judiciary—has long been key to organized crime tactics. In recent years, police in Canada have uncovered many conspiracies to corrupt officials working in marine ports and airports, to facilitate the international movement of drugs, contraband, and the cash proceeds of crime (CISC, 2004, 10–14; Schneider, 2009, 366–67). Tobacco companies have knowingly cooperated with criminal groups to smuggle cigarettes into the country (*National Post*, 2003), and Canadian financial institutions have been complicit in money-laundering schemes (Beare and Schneider, 1990; Schneider, 2003). Recently, a Quebec

The enormous profits made by those involved in organized crime mean that these groups have significant amounts of cash that must be laundered in order to disguise the illegal sources of these funds.

Ian Kucerak/QMI Agency

public commission investigating corruption in Montreal's public works sector uncovered evidence pointing to the Rizzuto family's influence in determining the successful bidders on public contracts; the Rizzutos, a mafia family, received a cut from the winning companies. Among those alleged to be implicated in the mafia-related graft were politicians, municipal civil servants, labour union officials, and the owners of private construction firms, (Canadian Press, 2012, 2013; *Montreal Gazette*, 2012).

Gangland violence may seem indiscriminate, but it is often applied "rationally" to ensure that certain individuals—usually victims, witnesses, informants, or competing gangsters, and sometimes government officials—do not obstruct the activities of the criminal organization. Violence is also used to maintain internal discipline within crime groups and to enhance the group's reputation. As in other countries, violence is a constant in Canada's criminal underworld. According to police-reported crime statistics, in 2011 there were 95 "gang-related" homicides in Canada—roughly 16 percent of all murders in Canada that year (Perrault, 2012, 8). Outlaw motorcycle gangs have carried out some of the worst mass killings in Canadian criminal history. This includes the murder of five Quebec Hells Angels members on March 24, 1985, and the killing of eight members of the Bandidos motorcycle club in Ontario on April 8, 2006. Both mass executions were "internal cleansings"—that is, they were carried out by fellow club members. More recently, violence erupted in Quebec after Vito Rizzuto, the head of the Montreal mafia, was imprisoned. During his imprisonment, different factions tried to fill the void in the Montreal's criminal underworld that Rizzuto's departure had created; others manoeuvred to take over his mafia family. Many of those loyal to Rizzuto were murdered, including his son, who was shot to death in 2009; the following year, his father was murdered in his Montreal home. Vito Rizzuto himself died (of natural causes) in 2013.

One tactic for protecting the profits of organized crime is money laundering, referring to the process of legitimizing illegally earned revenue. Cash is the universally accepted mode of payment in the underground economy. Thus, organized criminals—drug traffickers, in particular—accumulate large amounts of cash, often in small denominations. This can make them targets for law enforcement and taxation officials. That is why organized criminals must devise creative methods for converting large amounts of cash into less suspicious assets while concealing the criminal source of the funds. A typical money laundering technique involves opening a cash-based business, such as a restaurant or bar, and then depositing the cash proceeds of crime in that business's bank account, thereby masking it as revenue from the legitimate business. A 2003 survey of RCMP proceeds of crime cases found that in Canada, banks are the most frequently used sector of the economy for laundering money (Schneider, 2003).

A final tactic, used by more sophisticated criminals, is intelligence gathering and counter-surveillance. This includes the use of eavesdropping technology as well as placing gang associates inside enforcement agencies to gather information. In Canada, some outlaw motorcycle gangs have become well known for their intelligence gathering and surveillance activities, which they use against both rival gangs and law enforcement agencies.

Police raids on biker clubhouses have turned up electronic surveillance equipment, confidential police radio frequency lists, and scanners. Some chapters even have a designated intelligence officer, who is responsible for compiling dossiers, including photographs, physical descriptions, home addresses, and licence plate numbers of rival gang members, police, journalists, and witnesses (Schneider, 2009, 385).

Behavioural Characteristics

Rationality

Rational choice theory (see Chapter 15) posits that many offenders are self-maximizing decision makers who calculate the advantages and disadvantages associated with specific criminal acts (Clarke and Cornish, 1985). Arguably, organized crime is one of the most rational forms of criminality because it responds to the laws of supply and demand in the same way as legitimate businesses. This rationality is reflected in the criminal organization itself. Criminal groups "selling illicit goods and services must, if they are to capitalize on the great demand for their wares, expand by establishing a division of labour … The next rational move is consolidation and integration of separate divisions of labor into a cartel designed to minimize competition and maximize profits" (Cressey, 1969, 34–35). Even violence is used rationally by criminal groups in that it is meant to support the goals of the group.

Contempt for Civil Society

Members of traditional organized crime groups, such as the Italian mafia, the Japanese Yakuza, the Russian vory v zakone, and outlaw motorcycle gangs, openly rebel against the social rules and values that govern civil society; instead, they organize their behaviour according to the norms of their criminal group. This particular trait of organized crime is associated with subcultural theories of criminality and violence, which argue that serious and chronic offenders adhere to values and norms that are at odds with the dominant law-abiding culture and that they learn through their immersion in a deviant subculture (Ferracuti and Wolfgang, 1967). The organized crime subculture is exemplified by the term "wiseguy," which is used to refer to members of Italian-American mafia groups. A wiseguy believes that anybody who follows the commonly accepted rules and laws of civil society is a sucker and deserves to be victimized. Pileggi adeptly captures the wiseguy's attitude toward society: "They lived in an environment awash in crime, and those who did not partake were simply viewed as prey. To live otherwise was foolish. Anyone who stood in line was beneath contempt" (1985, 36). Subcultural theories of crime and deviance are also epitomized by the original norms of outlaw motorcycle gangs, which initially cultivated their own anti-establishment attitudes. Revelling in their image as social outcasts, they deliberately cut themselves off from the majority culture through their label "one percenter" – the "one percent who has given up on society" (Bandidos MC Randers, n.d.). Motorcycle gangs are particularly attractive to individuals who are involved in deviant behaviour because these gangs are mutually supportive of many types of deviant acts, including murder, drug dealing, and rape (RCMP, 1987, 9).

vory v zakone
A "thief in law." That is, a high-ranking, well-respected organized crime figure in the old Soviet underworld and the new Republic of Russia. Akin to the Italian Mafia. The code of the "Thieves World" emphasizes a rejection of government authority and traditional social norms. The "vor" predate the Soviet Union, but many were inmates interned in Soviet prison camps who organized themselves in an attempt to rule the criminal underworld.

Rules, Regulations, and Codes

Like legitimate organizations, traditional organized crime groups have established rules and regulations that members are expected to follow (Abadinsky, 2012, 5). In some groups, these rules are implicit; in others, they are explicit and may actually be written out. The most important rules focus on secrecy and loyalty, because those are the rules that protect illegal organizations from the threats posed by law enforcement officials and by other organized crime groups.

Discipline

To ensure that the rules and regulations are obeyed, most criminal groups have strict forms of discipline based on loyalty, a code of honour, and most importantly, the fear of reprisal (death).

QUESTIONS FOR CRITICAL THINKING

1. Compare and contrast the Criminal Code of Canada definition of a criminal organization with other definitions of organized crime. From an enforcement point of view, what are the strengths and weaknesses of this definition?
2. How is organized crime distinguished from other types of criminal conspiracies carried out by groups of people and organizations, such as terrorism, corporate crime, and state crime? In particular, compare and contrast corporate crime with organized crime. Do you believe there are forms of corporate crime or state crime that should be classified and prosecuted as organized crime?
3. Are the organized crime characteristics presented in this chapter complete? Can you think of any characteristics that may have been missed?

Dominant Organized Crime Genres and Groups

This section provides an overview of some of the organized crime groups currently active in Canada. These groups can be placed in the following categories: Italian, Chinese/Asian, Russian/Eastern European, Aboriginal, and outlaw motorcycle gangs. The specific criminal groups that fall within each of these are powerful, widespread, and highly sophisticated and embody many of the characteristics already described in this chapter. According to the CISC, organized crime groups have different levels of capabilities. The most sophisticated groups include some Hells Angels chapters, Asian gangs and networks in BC, the Italian mafia in Quebec, and the 'ngrangheta in Ontario. These groups, which have survived threats from the police and from competing gangs, are "distinguished by their large-scale, sophisticated operations involving the importation, manufacture or distribution of a wide variety of contraband, as well as through financial crimes such as fraud and money laundering" (CISC, 2006, 6).

FOCUS

Box 16.2

RULES, RITES, AND RITUALS OF THE 'NDRANGHETA

In 1971, while Toronto police were searching the home of a suspected member of the Canadian cell of an Italian organized crime network, they found 27-page document, handwritten in an antiquated Italian script, in his kitchen cupboard.

Experts from Canada and Italy would later conclude that the papers outlined the rules, rites, rituals, and structure of the *Honorata Società* (known as the 'ndrangheta). This was the first time such an authentic document had fallen into the hands of police in North America. The heading on the first page was *Come Formare una Società* ("How to Form a Society"), and the preamble read in part: "My stomach is a tomb, my mouth a bleated work of humility." Another section dictates the initiation rites of an inductee, who symbolically vows to take "a bloody dagger in my hand and a serpent in my mouth" should he betray the Honoured Society.

A 1972 *Globe and Mail* article described the remainder of the document as a "a tangle of centuries old archaic Italian, the phrases laced with flowery, mystic imagery dealing with such matters as collecting opinions from society members,

punishing members who don't surrender their guns at meetings, catechism-like initiation rituals and the proper words to be used when separating a member from the group."

The papers also outlined the basic structure of an 'ndrangheta cell, which includes three levels or ranks. There were also references to the pledges and obligations of members, the most important being a vow of silence. The document uses the term *mastro di sgarru*, the obligation of members to exact vendettas against enemies of the Society. Another common term was *baciletta*, which can be defined as "extorted money" collected by Society members, which should be "given to the ones who need it, the ones who have been arrested, for the defence lawyers, to help the people the police are looking for."

The discovery of this document was a significant breakthrough in efforts by police to prove the existence of a secret criminal society in North America with roots in Southern Italy.

Source: Based on Globe and Mail (1972). "Metro Police Raid Turned Up Copy of Mafia Linked Society's Secret Rituals, Court is Told," *Globe and Mail*, June 2.

Italian

Italian organized crime in Canada falls into three subcategories: the Sicilian "mafia," the 'ndrangheta, and the Canadian wings of the Italian-American crime families, often referred to collectively as *la cosa nostra* (LCN) (CISC, 2002, 16). Since the late 1940s, Italian-Canadian organized crime has been influenced most heavily by the 'ndrangheta, which traces its roots to the southern Italian region of Calabria (see Box 16.2). Most of the founders, leaders, and members of Italian-Canadian crime groups immigrated from Calabria or at least can trace their roots to that region. Despite this lineage, Italian-Canadian criminal organizations operated for many years as wings of the Italian-American mafia families: the Montreal mafia was controlled by New York's Bonanno family, while many of the Italian-Canadian crime groups in Ontario were answerable to the Magaddino family in Buffalo. But in the 1950s, Italian-Canadian crime groups were established in Toronto that had direct ties to the 'ndrangheta in Calabria.

Italian prosecutors allege today that in Toronto there are seven dominant Calabrian mafia families—including both Italian and Canadian nationals—all of which are part of an international network of 'ndrangheta cells (*National Post*, 2010b, 2010c). Since the late 1970s, the Montreal-based mafia has been dominated by made members of Sicilian heritage. Under the command of the Rizzuto family, the Montreal group is run independently of other crime groups in either Italy or the United States; it is involved in drug trafficking, illegal gambling (bookmaking), and extortion (protection rackets), and it has been accused of rigging bids related to commercial construction and public works contracts (discussed earlier in this chapter). Once considered the most powerful mafia group in this country, in recent years it has experienced a decline because of strong law enforcement crackdowns, the jailing of its leader Vito Rizzuto in the United States (and his subsequent death in 2013), competition from rival crime groups, and the 2010 murder of the family patriarch, 86-year-old Nicolo Rizzuto (Lamothe and Humphreys, 2006; Schneider, 2009, *Gazette*, 2011).

Chinese/Asian

Contemporary Asian organized crime in Canada can be broken down into six categories: (1) local street gangs made up of both youth and adults; (2) Chinese triads, which evolved from gangs in Toronto's Chinatown in the 1970s into sophisticated transnational criminal syndicates with links to Hong Kong, Taiwan, and Mainland China; (3) non-triad Chinese criminal networks, which tend to specialize in one particular criminal activity, such as drug trafficking or migrant smuggling; (4) a loose network of criminals from Mainland China (originally referred to as the Big Circle Boys), who commit a wide variety of crimes; (5) Vietnamese crime groups, which include violent street gangs in Toronto and Vancouver and now include some of the biggest marijuana producers and traffickers in Canada; and (6) Indo-Canadian crime groups, which are confined largely to BC and are involved in cocaine, marijuana, and synthetic drug trafficking and smuggling (Schneider, 2009, 443–44).

The most dominant and deeply entrenched of the Asian organized crime gangs are Chinese criminal groups. During the first half of the twentieth century, Chinese merchants in Vancouver were behind some of the largest opium smuggling and trafficking rings in the country. Canada's first Chinatown in Victoria was home to illegal gambling halls, brothels, and opium dens, most of which were controlled by leading Chinese merchants. In the 1950s, the RCMP uncovered illegal Chinese immigrant smuggling operations from Hong Kong. In the 1970s, Southeast Asian heroin began to supplant the Turkish variety in North America, and before long, Chinese drug trafficking syndicates were some of the world's biggest heroin suppliers. In the mid-1970s, a plague of extortion within Toronto's Chinese community exposed the presence of Canada's first modern triad, the Kung Lok. Around the same time, Chinese street gangs emerged in Vancouver. A few years later, aggressive Vietnamese gangs began to challenge the Chinese triads for supremacy in the Asian underworld in Toronto and Vancouver. By the end of the 1980s, the Big Circle Boys, former soldiers from Mainland China, were being blamed for a series of violent robberies, home invasions, and other crimes in the two cities. Within 10 years, this loose network would evolve into one of Canada's largest and most sophisticated criminal conspiracies, committing a wide range of highly profitable crimes, including drug trafficking (production, smuggling, and/ or wholesale distribution of marijuana, heroin, cocaine, and synthetic drugs), bank card fraud, product piracy, people smuggling, human trafficking, contraband tobacco manufacturing and distribution, and currency counterfeiting (Schneider, 2009; Dubro, 1992; CISC, 2004).

Outlaw Motorcycle Gangs

Outlaw motorcycle gangs (OMGs) emerged in the United States after the Second World War. They were originally formed for camaraderie and excitement. Biker gangs gradually moved into for-profit criminal pursuits, initially working as muscle-for-hire and as street-level drug distributors. The Hells Angels is the world's largest OMG, with almost 200 chapters worldwide. Canada once had many competing biker gangs; today, the Hells Angels predominate. Its first Canadian chapter was founded in Montreal in 1976, and over the next 40 years, it became the first truly national criminal organization, with chapters, puppet clubs, and/or associates in every province. Indeed, Canada has become an international stronghold for the motorcycle club; at one time, there were more Hells Angels members per capita in Canada than any other country. While drug trafficking remains a significant source of income for the Hells Angels, it is also involved in the illegal trafficking of firearms and explosives, protection rackets, automobile theft and export, fraud, and prostitution. To facilitate its international smuggling operations, the Hells Angels relies on corruption and internal conspiracies at international ports of entry. It is believed to have infiltrated shipping lines, port corporations, and longshoreman's unions in Canada and abroad (Sher and Marsden, 2004; Schneider, 2009).

Russia/Eastern European

Organized crime factions from Russia, Ukraine, and other former republics of the Soviet Union are active throughout the former Communist Bloc as well as in Western Europe, North America, Israel, and Australia. Russian criminal organizations that trace their roots back for decades, like the *vory v zakone*, have been joined by younger career offenders, street criminals, businessmen, and former Soviet intelligence officers and government officials. Other Eastern European crime groups originated in Albania, Croatia, and Serbia; most of these are involved in smuggling drugs, guns, and weapons in the Balkans and Europe. While Russian and Eastern European organized crime exploded in the chaotic atmosphere that followed the fall of the Soviet Union in the early 1990s, they had been operating on a small scale in North America since the 1970s. These loosely networked groups operated mostly in New York, Los Angeles, and Toronto.

In Toronto during the 1970s and 1980s, Eastern European criminals were involved in extortion, gambling, loansharking, and drug trafficking, much of this in conjunction with the Ontario arm of the American Cosa Nostra (Lamothe and Nicaso, 1994, 45; FBI, 1995; *Toronto Star*, 1996; Rawlinson, 1997). Russian and other Eastern European crime groups are most active in large cities in Ontario, Quebec, and BC. They have varying degrees of organization and sophistication and engage in a wide array of crime, from petty theft to sophisticated fraud schemes. Financial frauds, in particular **debit card fraud** schemes, are major activities for these groups. They are also involved in human trafficking, contraband smuggling, illegal drug importation, and the theft and illegal export of vehicles to Eastern Europe (*Globe and Mail*, 1998; CASC, 2002, 14–15; 2004, 7–9). In recent years, large-scale high-profile cases involving human trafficking and "distraction theft" have been linked to Hungarian and Romanian crime groups operating in Canada (*Globe and Mail*, 2012; *Ottawa Sun*, 2012; *Windsor Star*, 2012).

debit card fraud
Debit card fraud entails a four-step process: (1) create fake debit cards, (2) steal personal identification and banking information from legitimate cards, (3) emboss the stolen information on the fake cards, and (4) use the illegal debit cards for purchases or cash advances.

Aboriginal

Aboriginal organized crime in Canada can be categorized as follows: (1) criminal groups and activities in central Canada (Ontario and Quebec) that revolve around smuggling and contraband cigarette production, and (2) criminal gangs in the prairie provinces. The former groups play a central role in smuggling, due primarily to geopolitical factors that facilitate the movement of contraband across the Canada–US border. In 1994, RCMP Commissioner Norman Inkster said that as much as 70 percent of the contraband tobacco entering Canada was coming in through the Akwesasne reserve. Populated by the Mohawk Nation, this 5,600-hectare reserve has the unique distinction of straddling the US–Canada border, making it ideally suited for smuggling. The reserve's territory actually falls within five jurisdictions—Canada, the United States, Ontario, Quebec, and New York State—and agreements have been negotiated with federal, state, and provincial governments in both countries that uphold the right of the Mohawk people to freely cross the borders that cut through the reserve. These factors, combined with a well-honed smuggling infrastructure, have meant that a variety of contraband, drugs, and weapons pass through the reserve, with resident smugglers constantly shifting products based on demand and profitability. Aboriginal groups are active in the smuggling of alcohol, tobacco, drugs, firearms, explosives, jewellery, vehicles, electronic equipment, and people (*Montreal Gazette*, 1996; US Congress, 2000; Schneider, 2009). Aboriginal crime groups in central Canada are also involved in the distribution of contraband goods at the wholesale and retail levels. In recent years, cigarette manufacturing plants and retail outlets have been established on several Aboriginal reserves in Ontario and Quebec. These outlets, combined with cigarette smuggling from the United States, have been blamed for a flood of contraband cigarettes on the streets of Quebec, Ontario, and other parts of Canada (RCMP, 2008; CCSA, 2009; *National Post*, 2010a).

Aboriginal criminal groups in the prairie provinces mostly operate as street gangs. According to the CISC, they "are generally involved in opportunistic, spontaneous and disorganized street-level criminal activities, primarily low-level trafficking of marihuana, cocaine and crack cocaine and, to a lesser extent, methamphetamine. The gangs are also involved in prostitution, break-and-enters, robberies, assaults, intimidation, vehicle theft and illicit drug debt collection" (2004, 20–21). These Aboriginal gangs have connections to Asian and outlaw motorcycle criminal groups, from which they purchase drugs at the wholesale level.

While the organized crime categories discussed above include some of the largest and most sophisticated criminal groups and networks, they do not have a monopoly on organized criminal activities. Today, organized crime is represented by a diverse number of "genres" that have emerged from a multitude of ethno-cultural and national backgrounds. Moreover, while a defining characteristic of these dominant organized crime genres has been a shared nationality, ethnicity, and/or language, in recent years it has become apparent that these factors are no longer the most important criteria in determining who participates in a particular organized criminal conspiracy. Three BC-based gangs—the Red Scorpions, the United Nations, and the Independent Soldiers—are prominent examples of the multi-ethnic criminal groups that emerged in the 1990s (CFSEU BC, 2013, 3). Thousands of individual criminal entrepreneurs work together on an ad hoc or ongoing basis in the pursuit of illegal revenues, regardless of ethnicity, nationality, or language. In this sense, modern organized crime can best be characterized as a fluid network of many autonomous buyers, brokers, financiers, middlemen, and distributors from different groups, ethnicities, nationalities, and countries that come together to make deals by capitalizing on one another's specialties and strengths. The proliferation and increasing diversity of criminal groups in Canada began in the early 1970s and gathered speed in subsequent decades. By 2009, the CISC estimated there were 750 criminal gangs in Canada (CISC, 2009, 9).

Theories of Organized Crime

Theories that help explain organized crime can be placed in two categories: those that try to identify and analyze the causes of organized crime (etiological theories), and those that attempt to understand the structure of organized criminal conspiracies.

Etiological Theories

Several theories have tried to explain the causes and existence of organized crime in North America. Some of these theories are specific to organized crime; others are based on the theories of criminality you have read about in this textbook, which have been adapted to organized crime. This chapter will focus on theories that explain the causes of organized crime. These can be grouped into the following categories: (1) alien conspiracy theory, (2) ethnic succession theory, (3) economic theories, and (4) public policy impetus.

Alien Conspiracy Theory

One of earliest theories of the origins and causes of organized crime in America is alien conspiracy theory. Originally developed to explain the origins and scope of Italian organized crime in the United States, it has also been applied to other ethnic-based organized crime genres, including Chinese triads, Colombian cocaine cartels, Jamaican posses, Nigerian crime groups, and Russian/Eastern European crime groups.

Proponents of alien conspiracy theory believe that organized crime in America is the result of the importation of secret criminal societies rooted in foreign cultures. Thus, organized crime does not emerge from American culture; rather, it has been thrust upon the United States by specific immigrant groups. When used to explain Italian-American crime groups, the theory also contends that a nationwide criminal network exists, made up of two dozen or so "families" of Italian lineage, all of which are governed by a national commission collectively known as the "mafia" or "la cosa nostra."

The theory, which was not developed by scholars, was most forcefully promoted in the early 1950s by a US Senate committee chaired by Estes Kefauver (US Congress, 1951). The committee's report alleged that a sinister secret

la cosa nostra
Term used to denote Italian-American organized crime. It was originally applied by the FBI in an attempt to make this criminal fraternity sound ominous and threatening. Members of the so-called LCN never used this label themselves, though they have often referred to their secret society as "this thing of ours," which roughly translates into Italian as "la cosa nostra."

organization originating in Sicily had made its way to the United States during the period of massive Italian immigration in the late 19th and early 20th centuries (Kelly, 1987, 13). This secret society grew into a monolithic nationwide criminal conspiracy, under "centralized direction and control," that was subverting and eroding the fundamental law-abiding values of American society (Smith, 1975, 138). Similar allegations were made by several later commissions, including the President's Commission on Law Enforcement and Administration of Justice (1967). Criminologist Donald Cressey lent scholarly credence to this theory in his work as a consultant to the President's Commission and in a subsequent book, *Theft of a Nation*, which overestimated the scope and power of the Italian mafia in America and implied that American values and institutions were being subverted by an invading alien force.

Like many conspiracy theories, alien conspiracy theory has some tenuous roots in reality. However, when applied to North America it has been widely criticized as xenophobic and racist. Subsequent scholarly research, and evidence gathered by criminal justice agencies, has refuted the two main pillars of this theory as an almost fictional exaggeration of the roots and scope of Italian organized crime in North America.

Regarding the first pillar: The origins and perpetuation of the Cosa Nostra in America cannot simply be blamed on the importation of a secret society from Sicily. The American LCN can trace part of its family tree to the Sicilian mafia, and the early secret societies in North America were made up of Italian immigrants, some of whom brought with them the traditions and criminal activities of the Sicilian mafia (or the Calabrian 'ndrangheta). However, the LCN—and indeed, modern organized crime—is overwhelmingly an American (and to a lesser extent Canadian) creation. It is a product of North American culture, profitably fuelled by popular vices and the spirit of capitalism and facilitated by private and public corruption (Bell, 1953).

Regarding the second pillar: There is little evidence that there was ever a truly nationwide mafia criminal conspiracy with centralized control. There were a number of Italian organized crime groups spread across North America, and these were linked through ideology, ethnicity, methods, illegal networks, and criminal activities. In addition, some influential Italian organized crime figures attempted to create a "commission" that would coordinate and regulate the competing interests of the various Italian crime groups. But a *national* commission never fully materialized, and most groups worked independently in their own cities, with sporadic cooperation (and conflict) (Albini, 1971; Smith, 1975). The so-called "Commission" was largely confined to New York and had only limited power over the five mafia families in that city. During the 1970s and 1980s, the Commission was respected among certain mafia groups in Quebec and Ontario and often dictated the activities of its Canadian mafia cells; it was called in to help settle internal disputes, and it had to be consulted if a made mafia member in Canada was to be killed as a result of an internal dispute.

In his 1975 book *The Mafia Mystique*, Dwight Smith argues that the alien conspiracy theory arose in the United States in part because self-serving government commissions, politicians, and law enforcement officials were fabricating or exaggerating stories to help secure greater enforcement and prosecutorial resources.

The notion of a national organized crime conspiracy generally did not resonate among Canadian scholars or government and law enforcement officials. In fact, until the early 1960s, police, politicians, and judicial inquiries typically denied that the mafia existed in Canada (*Toronto Star*, 1948; *Toronto Telegram*, 1961; Roach, 1962). Thus, Canadian officials erred in the opposite direction of their American counterparts. While many of the early ethnic Italian criminal societies in this country were made up of immigrants who brought with them some basic ideologies and criminal methods from Sicily and Calabria, organized crime evolved and prospered in this country as a result of the same conditions that existed in United States. While there was never any nationwide confederation of Italian crime groups in Canada with a centralized command and control, law enforcement evidence and scholarly research has indicated that some ethnic Italian crime groups in Quebec and Ontario operated as cells of American mafia families and were also linked through international criminal conspiracies that included drug trafficking, immigrant smuggling, and bookmaking. Cells of the 'ndrangheta clans based in Italy have existed in Toronto since at least the 1950s (*National Post*, 2010b, 2010c).

Ethnic Succession Theory

Other etiological theories of organized crime in North America place greater emphasis on local conditions. This perspective can be condensed into the adage that "societies get the crime they deserve." These theories situate the root causes of organized criminality in the broader social, political, cultural, and economic environment of North America. Several general theories of crime and criminality, detailed in previous chapters, have informed this school of thought.

Strain theory (see Chapter 10) forms the basis of the ethnic succession theory, which posits that many immigrant ethnic groups are disproportionately involved in organized crime in the United States because of the barriers they encounter in their pursuit of the American Dream (Bell, 1953; Ianni, 1974). Thus, the ethnic basis of many organized crime groups in North America is not tied to the importation of foreign criminal cultures or secret societies; rather, it is the result of minority groups struggling for prosperity and a place in mainstream society. Each successive immigrant group experiences strains such as discrimination, unemployment, poverty, lack of political power, and social exclusion, and some members of these groups respond by involving themselves in criminal activities. As time passes, and as legitimate and socially acceptable avenues of mobility open up to these ethnic groups, the strain subsides and members of the particular ethnic group rely less and less on crime to realize the American Dream. Ethnic succession occurs when subsequent immigrant groups fill this criminal void as they attempt to climb the ladder of success. According to this thesis, persons or entire ethnic groups that are implicated in organized crime are not committed to a deviant subculture; they are merely using available, albeit illegal, opportunities to achieve economic and social success (see Box 16.3). Thus, involvement in organized crime is a rational response to blocked opportunities (Abadinsky, 2012, 46).

Critics of ethnic succession theory point out that many people of Italian or Chinese heritage remained active in organized crime long after these groups were assimilated into mainstream society and found success through

FOCUS

Box 16.3

CAN ETHNIC SUCCESSION THEORY BE APPLIED TO CANADA?

The history of organized crime in Canada provides some evidence supporting ethnic succession theory. In the mid- to late nineteenth century, Irish immigrants were disproportionately represented in violent criminal gangs in Upper and Lower Canada, in part because they were discriminated against by the English and Scots, who held most positions of power.

During the first half of the twentieth century, Irish gangs were eclipsed by more sophisticated Jewish criminals, who dominated such organized rackets as gambling and drug trafficking, particularly in Montreal, where anti-Semitism was rife. Samuel Bronfman is a good illustration of ethnic succession theory. Bronfman was born in Canada to immigrant Jewish parents, made his fortune supplying American bootleggers during Prohibition, and eventually headed Seagram's distilleries, one of the largest corporate empires in Canadian history.

During the early twentieth century, Chinese merchants in British Columbia were involved in gambling, prostitution, and selling opium. Their clientele were Chinese immigrant labourers, who found refuge in such vices in the face of constant racial hatred, violence, and legislative disenfranchisement by the white population.

The Prohibition era in the 1920s witnessed the rise of the Italian racketeers, many of whom emerged from the poverty-stricken tenements of southern Ontario and Montreal and were unable to find legitimate employment because of discrimination.

By the 1970s, Italian-Canadian crime groups outside of Montreal were in decline, with the void being filled by other groups that had immigrated to Canada more recently, from China, Vietnam, the West Indies, Colombia, and Russia (Carrigan, 1991; Schneider, 2009).

legitimate means (Abadinsky, 2012, 94). Potter (1994) concludes that members of immigrant ethnic and racial groups may turn to organized crime, but they do not necessarily replace existing ethnically and racially based criminal groups. Moreover, this theory does not explain why those from the middle class become involved in organized crime, nor does it account for the organized economic crimes committed by the wealthy and powerful. Finally, this theory fails to explain how criminal organizations that are made up primarily of White Anglo-Saxon Protestants—such as outlaw motorcycle gangs—emerge in North American society.

Economic Theories

An economic analysis views organized crime not as pathological but rather as a rational system that operates according to the laws of supply and demand. In fact, basic economic concepts such as supply, demand, and price elasticity are quite applicable to underground markets. For example, research has shown that the price of illegal or contraband commodities is related to supply and demand (Caulkins and Reuter, 1998; Office of National Drug Control Policy, 2004; RCMP, 2007). Thus, if the local cocaine supply is plentiful, the price will be low, but if the local supply is limited, the price will usually rise.

An economic approach focuses on how criminal organizations make money supplying goods and services that are in demand but that have been declared illegal by the state. Underground markets also profit by providing the public with a cheaper supply of certain legal goods (e.g., contraband tobacco and liquor), primarily by evading taxes or by supplying stolen or counterfeit goods. One significant implication of this economic analysis is that organized crime is not viewed as alien to the societies in which it operates, but as part of its commercial markets. In short, organized crime fulfills certain commercial functions, thereby creating a symbiotic relationship between criminal organizations (as suppliers) and segments of society (as consumers) (Martens and Miller-Longfellow, 1982, 4; Dickie and Wilson, 1993, 216).

One criticism of this economic perspective is that underground markets are highly distorted relative to legitimate markets. Naylor (2004) contends that "the facile analogy between legal and illegal firms is at best a serious oversimplification, at worst simply wrong. In illegal markets that are highly segmented, decisions are personalized, information flows constricted, capital supplies short term and unreliable, objective price data lacking, and the time horizons (indeed the very existence) of enterprises coterminous with those of the entrepreneurs" (21). Moreover, the application of traditional economic theory to organized crime only captures consensual crimes, ignoring predatory criminal activities such as theft, hijacking, kidnapping, extortion, and fraud.

Public Policy Impetus

Governments decide whether particular goods or services that people desire will be made available in legal markets. A product or service only becomes illegal when the government passes laws prohibiting its sale and consumption. Generally, the state criminalizes or restricts products or services—drugs, prostitution, ganbling, alcohol, cigarettes, and so on—that it views as immoral vices and as personally and/or socially harmful.

When a government outlaws a particular product or service that the public wants, it drives supply to the "underground market." This creates an opportunity for criminal entrepreneurs to monopolize that product or service. A fundamental reason why organized crime exists is that governments have criminalized certain vices. The best-known historical example of how government policies create illegal markets and fuel the rise of organized crime was the outlawing of liquor in the United States and Canada in the 1920s and early 1930s. Prohibition catapulted organized crime into a new level of profitability, power, and sophistication and set the stage for today's large, profitable drug trafficking organizations and networks.

Goods and services do not have to be criminalized to fuel organized crime. Taxation policies have been the impetus for the involvement of organized crime in the trafficking of legal goods such as alcohol, fuel, and tobacco. The international and domestic smuggling of legal products is usually the result of a disparity in the level of taxes that have been applied to a product by different jurisdictions (see Box 16.4).

Theories of the Structure of Organized Criminal Conspiracies

As noted earlier, a defining characteristic of organized crime is a systematic pattern to the relations among offenders; this in turn helps define the structure of a particular ongoing criminal conspiracy. In general, four theoretical models capture the different types of relationships and structures of organized crime: (1) the bureaucratic/hierarchical model, where there is a vertical power structure with at least three permanent ranks; (2) the kinship model, structured around blood relationships; (3) the patron–client model, where influential

FOCUS

Box 16.4

GOVERNMENT CIGARETTE TAXATION POLICIES, SMUGGLING, AND ORGANIZED CRIME

Since the end of the American Revolution, legitimate consumer goods have been illegally smuggled into Canada from the United States due to much lower prices south of the border. This is largely because of the import duties or high taxes imposed on similar products in Canada.

Historically, tobacco products have been the most popular contraband smuggled between the two countries. In the 1890s, the Canadian government imposed an import duty to protect domestic cigarette manufacturers from foreign competition. This duty raised the cost of a small package of cigarettes imported into Canada to 10 cents; in the United States they could be purchased at half that price. The result, according to an 1895 *Toronto Star* article titled "Smuggle the Vile Cigarette," was that tobacco smugglers were now "doing business on a tremendously large scale, bringing the goods both to Toronto and to Montreal." Cigarette smuggling persisted over the following century but increased dramatically in the 1990s.

In 1991, the Canadian government increased the excise tax on the domestic sale of cigarettes by almost 140 percent. However, no similar tax hikes were imposed on Canadian tobacco products destined for export. This resulted in a substantial difference between the retail price of exported Canadian cigarettes and those sold domestically. This price difference initiated a wave of smuggling that involved the lawful export of tax-exempt Canadian cigarettes to the United States and the smuggling of these cigarettes back into Canada. In less than two years following the tax hike, cigarette exports to the United States rose from 1.7 billion to 15.7 billion cigarettes (Canadian Tobacco Manufacturers Council, n.d.). This increase can be attributed almost exclusively to the burgeoning Canadian black market. According to a report on smuggling by the Canadian Association of Chiefs of Police (1994, 7), most of the contraband tobacco products in Canada during this period were supplied by well-organized smuggling groups and networks.

Today, legitimately produced cigarettes are being smuggled into Canada from the United States, counterfeit cigarettes are being surreptitiously imported from China, and cigarette factories are springing up on First Nations reserves in Ontario and Quebec. In 2010, the RCMP estimated the number of criminal groups involved in the illicit tobacco trade in Canada to be 175 (*Canadian Press*, 2010; *National Post*, 2010a).

---

professional criminals become "patrons" to others; and (4) the network model, characterized by a fluid association of like-minded criminal offenders connected through complementary specializations or resources.

The Bureaucratic/Hierarchical Model

The bureaucratic/hierarchical model views criminal groups as tightly structured and controlled. This model was first applied to Italian-American organized crime groups, which have been viewed by some as structured hierarchically, with a deliberate and rational arrangement of positions and roles based on a well-defined vertical power structure and division of labour (President's Commission, 1967; Cressey, 1969). In Canada, the ethnic Italian criminal organizations that predominated from the 1950s to the early 1980s did appear to be hierarchical, though their structure was somewhat simpler and flatter than the one detailed by Cressey in his work for the President's Commission. For example, during the late 1960s and early 1970s, Montreal's Cotroni mafia group, a wing of New York City's Bonanno family, was headed by Vic Cotroni. Below him at any one time were four or five senior lieutenants. Each lieutenant was in charge of a particular district of Montreal and had his own crew of several "soldiers," who were in charge of, or had business ties with, a number of other people outside the Cotroni group (Charbonneau, 1975; Quebec Police Commission, 1977; Edwards, 1990).

But many experts would *not* apply the bureaucratic/hierarchical model to the Italian mafia in North America. According to Ianni and Reuss-Ianni (1972), the bureaucratic analogy arose as "honest attempts to explain syndicate organization in terms that are familiar to the public" (110). They added there was "another, more suspect motivation" behind this model, which was, that it helped buttress the government-promoted theory that the mafia was a national conspiracy, which in turn "demand[ed] the existence of a national organization." Critics of this model also contend that many aspects of a bureaucracy, such as lengthy chains of command, rigidity, and a well-defined division of labour, may not apply to Italian mafia families in the United States and Canada.

Setting aside the criticisms, this model may be applied to other criminal organizations such as the Medellin and Cali cartels. Many analysts have concluded that these cartels emulated multinational corporations and were structured to control each step required in the processing, exporting, and wholesaling of cocaine. To facilitate this vertical integration, "each of the trafficking groups in Medellin, Bogota, and Cali contain various sections, each with a separate function, such as manufacturing, transportation, distribution, finance and security" (President's Commission, 1984, 562). The exact structure of a Colombian cartel varied from group to group and was quite fluid over time; Figure 16.1 provides a generic version.

Kinship Model

Ianni and Reuss-Ianni (1972) suggest that the Italian-American mafia family has nothing to do with modern bureaucratic or corporate principles; instead, it is primarily a social grouping shaped by culture, patterned by tradition, and structured around kin relations. Italian-American crime families are just that: families interconnected by blood or marriage (and in some cases, simply a shared ethnicity). There is no real vertical hierarchy; instead this social unit is built around a symbiotic relationship between a "patron" and a "client"—a pattern of relationships first proposed by Joseph Albini (1971).

In their study of one Italian-American organized crime family, Ianni and Reuss-Ianni (1972) found that members of the Lupollo family (a pseudonym) were sustained by kinship, not criminal activities or a secret society. The Lupollo family operated as a "social unit with social organization and business functions merged. [All] leadership positions, down to 'middle management' level," were assigned on the basis of kinship (106).

Ianni and Reuss-Ianni outlined some of the differences between mafia families and formal organizations. The latter are composed of positions, not personalities, which means that the duties and rights of a corporate executive, for instance, are clearly delineated so that the organization can swiftly replace an incumbent for whatever reason. In some mafia families, by contrast, particular members are indispensable because they possess special skills or have established highly personal contacts. The death of a member who acts as a "corrupter" may significantly disrupt the family's criminal operations because no immediate substitute has the same level of political connections. Also, formal organizations are supposed to be rationally organized, with individuals rising to leadership because of their demonstrated skill, intelligence, dedication, and expertise. Ianni and Reuss-Ianni argue

FIGURE 16.1 **Generic Organizational Structure of the Cali Cartel**

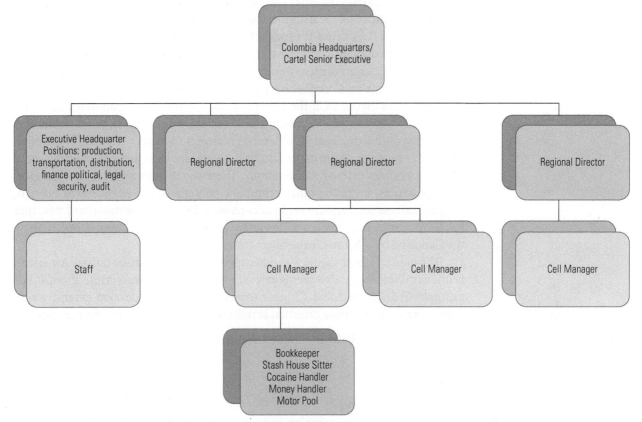

Source: United States. Comptroller General. (1989). *Nontraditional Organized Crime: Law Enforcement Officials Perspectives on Five Criminal Groups.* Washington, DC: U.S. Government Printing Office; United States Drug Enforcement Administration. (n.d.). *Major Traffickers and Their Organizations.* Washington, DC: U.S. Drug Enforcement Administration; Thomas Constantine. (1994). "Statement before the U.S. Senate Drug Caucus." February 24. Washington, DC: United States Drug Enforcement Administration; Howard Abadinsky. (2000). *Organized Crime.* New York: Wadsworth Publishing, p. 149.

that family standing and tradition are equally important—perhaps more important than merit—in determining which family members will assume leadership roles. In the Lupollo mafia family, power accrued to an individual not because he was the best qualified but because kinship or tradition demanded it.

Patron–Client Model

For Ianni and Reuss-Ianni (1972), the ongoing criminal operations of the Italian-American mafia family involve a loose system of power and "business" relationships and thus require a middleman, who becomes a patron to others by providing contacts, influence, and criminal opportunities. Over time, the patron comes to dominate a network of individuals in a geographic area (Ianni and Reuss-Ianni, 1983). At the centre of this patron–client model is the Capo. The Capo is less a CEO than a patron to his family and associates; he is the centre of a network of family and business relationships. In this role, he provides services, especially for those who can't or won't turn to the government— from the peasantry in southern Italy, where the government presence is weak, to the Italian immigrant unfamiliar with or suspicious of the government in the new land, all the way to the thief or murderer who cannot approach the government for help. The Capo helps ensure the welfare and security of his family, friends, and associates. For example, he puts up start-up capital to assist new enterprises, handles the flow of graft to politicians, regulates the use of violence, and resolves disputes among members (Albini, 1971; Hess, 1973; Gambetta, 1993). A Capo is especially important as an intermediary, whether as a commercial agent bringing legitimate businessmen or criminals together to make a deal, as a political power broker helping friends get elected, or as a mediator arbitrating a conflict between two parties.

As seen in Figure 16.2, the Capo is at the centre of this patron–client structure, immediately surrounded by members of the crime family, to whom he acts as a patron (and from each of whom he receives a monetary tribute). In addition, each made member of the mafia family cultivates his own network of clients, who include associates external to the family. These clients may represent a wide spectrum of society, including other criminals, politicians, law enforcement officials, judges, businessmen, and union leaders (Albini, 1971). The patron–client structure has the potential to generate a wide variety of money-making connections, both by the Capo and by other made members of the mafia family.

The patron–client model was developed mainly to describe Italian-American crime families, but it also seems relevant to other organized crime groups. For example, Hells Angels and Chinese triads are known to develop extensive network of associates, whose criminal activities revolve around specific members.

FIGURE 16.2   **The Patron–Client Organization Model**

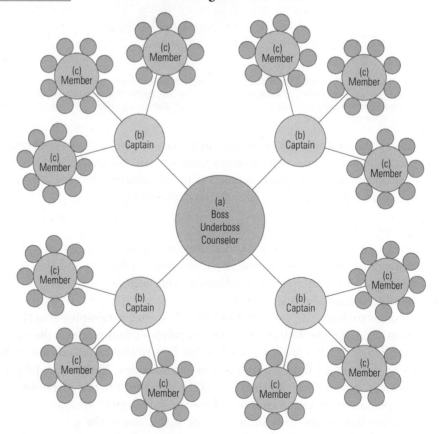

Source: From ABADINSKY. *Organized Crime*, 8E. © 2007 South-Western, a part of Cengage Learning, Inc. Reproduced by permission. www.cengage.com/permissions.

Network Model

The network model views organized crime not as a monolithic, self-contained organization but as a fluid and loosely knit network of like-minded criminal entrepreneurs, none of whom has any long-term authority over the others. A network model of organized crime views the patterns of relationships not as hierarchical but as symmetrical; business partnerships are based on complementary areas of specialization that contribute to one particular deal or a series of ongoing criminal conspiracies. In a network, relations among criminals are defined not by power but by the particular functions that individuals perform in the criminal conspiracy and/or by the financial investment that a "business partner" has made in the venture.

Criminologist James Finckenauer (2005) wrote that most contemporary organized crime conspiracies are "loosely affiliated networks of criminals who coalesce around certain criminal opportunities. The structure of these groups is much more amorphous, free floating and flatter, and thus lacking in a rigid hierarchy" (65). In her analysis of Chicago crime groups, Anderson (1979) concluded that the network model may be viewed as a combination of the bureaucratic/hierarchical model and the kinship/patron–client model. She argued that well-defined criminal organizations do exist and that some entail a hierarchical structure. She found that traditional organized crime groups do have layers of positions, such as boss, underboss, lieutenant, and so on, but that they also include various associates who are not themselves true members. These associates—who may include small-time crooks, sophisticated criminal entrepreneurs, legitimate businessmen, politicians, and even other criminal organizations—carry out many activities (both legal and illegal) necessary for the success of the group and enter into patron–client type arrangements with the members of this criminal group.

In their research into organized crime in Canada, Morselli (2005, 2009) and Morselli and Roy (2008) identified a number of "networked" aspects of contemporary organized criminal conspiracies. For example, such conspiracies arise through personal contacts and social networking among offenders. Also, criminal conspiracies have a "flexible order" that makes them resistant to law enforcement targeting and enforcement, and "brokers" play an important centralizing role within loosely structured criminal group ventures. In its 2006 annual report, the CISC elaborated on the relationships among criminal entrepreneurs that make up modern organized criminal conspiracies:

> Law enforcement is identifying crime groups that are based on temporary alliances of individual criminals who merge their particular skills to better achieve success in specific criminal enterprises. Once a specific criminal venture is completed, these individuals may continue to collaborate on further criminal activities, or the group may dissolve. Although the individuals may go their separate ways, they sometimes reform into new groups based upon the skill requirements of new criminal opportunities. The nature and success of such networks are largely determined by individual characteristics and skills among those who act as their component parts. (6)[*]

---

[*] *2006 Annual Report on Organized Crime in Canada*, p. 6, Criminal Intelligence Service Canada, 2006. Reproduced with the permission of the RCMP.

The network model is perhaps most applicable to large-scale drug import-ation and trafficking conspiracies, which rarely are carried out by a single organized group. Heroin finds its way onto the streets of Toronto through the efforts of many individuals and groups, each of which operates independently. These include the farmers who grow the opium, the chemists who turn the opium into heroin, the transportation brokers who arrange safe passage of the product, the shippers who physically transport the product, and the wholesalers who arrange for the heroin to be cut and then distributed to street dealers, who sell it at the "retail" level. A good example of the network model for large-scale international drug trafficking was the legendary "French Connection," which began in the 1940s. It brought together Turkish farmers, who cultivated the opium; Instanbul-based brokers, who trafficked the morphine; French Corsican gangsters, who processed the morphine into heroin in France and then moved the final product across the Atlantic; American and Canadian mafia groups, who coordinated its importation and wholesale distribution in North America; and diverse individuals and groups who sold the drugs at the retail level (Charbonneau, 1975; Naylor, 2004; Schneider, 2009).

To summarize, the traditional bureaucratic/hierarchical model of organized crime emphasizes hierarchy and centralized control, while the network model envisions greater decentralization, with separate enterprises that pool resources and expertise. According to Haller, (1990), such decentralization renders a business less vulnerable to law enforcement. By spreading the risks, entrepreneurs minimize their losses from police raids. Decentralization also makes sense for another important reason: "Criminal entrepreneurs generally have had neither the skills nor the personalities for the detailed, bureaucratic oversight of large organizations. They are, instead, hustlers and dealers, for whom partnership arrangements are ideally suited. They enjoy the give and take of personal negotiations, risk-taking, and moving from deal to deal" (222). To corroborate his arguments, Haller used Al Capone's criminal empire as a historical case study, arguing that Capone was at the centre of an expansive network of associates and entities (see Figure 16.3).

Conclusion: Canadian Organized Crime

Organized crime in Canada spans more than 400 years, from pirates who pillaged ships and towns off the Atlantic coast during the seventeenth and eighteenth centuries, to bank robbers, smugglers, horse thieves, cattle rustlers, and currency counterfeiters in the nineteenth century, to opium traffickers, white slave traders, and professional gamblers of the early twentieth century, to bootleggers during the era of Prohibition, to the Italian mafia, outlaw motorcycle gangs, Chinese triads, and other criminal groups that have predominated in recent times.

The past 40 years have seen a proliferation of criminal groups, networks, and organized conspiracies in Canada and worldwide. As the number of crime groups has multiplied, so have the scope, diversity, and profitability of organized criminal activities. In 2012 the UN Office on Drugs and Crime estimated

FIGURE 16.3   **Al Capone's Crime Network**

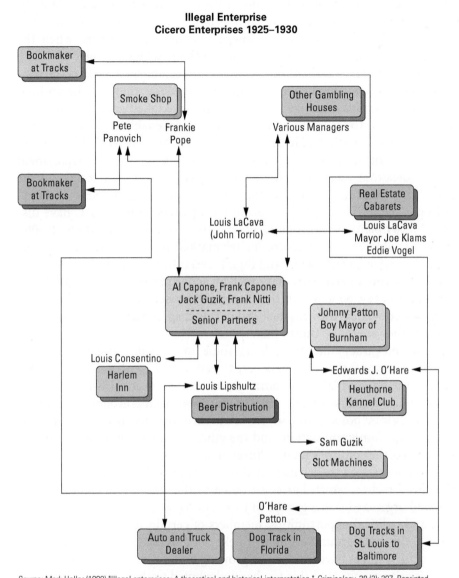

Illegal Enterprise
Cicero Enterprises 1925–1930

Source: Mark Haller (1990) "Illegal enterprises: A theoretical and historical interpretation," *Criminology*, 28 (2): 207. Reprinted with permission from the American Society of Criminology.

that "the annual turnover of transnational organized criminal activities such as drug trafficking, counterfeiting, illegal arms trade and the smuggling of immigrants is … around $870 billion" (UN News Centre, 2012).

Canada continues to serve as a branch plant for transnational crime groups and as a transit point for the international movement of illegal drugs. According to the US Department of State (2002) "heroin, cocaine, and MDMA (ecstasy) are trafficked through Canada, as international drug traffickers take advantage of Canada's proximity to the United States, less stringent criminal penalties as compared to the U.S., and the constant flow of goods across the U.S.-Canada border" (V6). Canada is also a conduit for undocumented immigrants, primarily from Asia, who illegally enter the United States. Canada supplies an embarrassingly rich assortment of illegal and contraband goods, a tradition that began when British Columbia became a major producer of smokable opium in the early part of the 20th century. This tradition continued through Prohibition, when Canada was America's main source of illegal liquor, and found new life in the 1970s, when the country surfaced as a major producer of synthetic drugs (Schneider, 2009). By the start of the new millennium, Canada had established itself as the continent's pre-eminent supplier of high-grade marijuana, methamphetamines, and ecstasy: "various organized crime groups have taken great advantage of opportunities to diversify their criminal activities, enabling them to swiftly advance from domestic trafficking to global distribution" (RCMP, 2007, 1). In its 2013 report on international narcotics trafficking, the US Department of State notes that Canada is "the primary foreign source of ecstasy to the United States" and that it "also supplies Japan, Australia and New Zealand" (US Department of State, 2013, 118). In recent years, police in BC have discovered fields planted with opium poppies (*Globe and Mail*, 2010a; 2010b). Canada has also become a centre for telemarketing fraud and the counterfeiting of currency, bank cards, and digital entertainment products.

Why does organized crime have such an active presence in Canada? Many of the answers can be found in the theories discussed earlier in this chapter. Indeed, the etiological theories included in this chapter may be as applicable to Canada as they are to the United States.

Alien conspiracy theory explains some of Canada's organized crime problem. Many of the dominant organized crime genres active in this country—the Italian mafia and 'ndrangheta, Chinese triads, US-based outlaw motorcycle gangs, Russian and Eastern European crime groups, Colombian cartels, Jamaican posses, and so on—find their origins in other countries. Canada is an immigrant nation, and the ethnic composition of its organized crime reflects the country's multicultural make-up.

Ethnic succession theory may shed some light on historically rooted institutionalized racism, which has contributed to the "ethnic" basis of criminal gangs and organized crime groups in this country. Shut out of legitimate economic and political opportunities, members of certain minority groups have turned to the underground economy to eke out a living. Similar social factors and structural forces have produced a growing underclass of young men, often from minority groups, and this too has contributed to the recent proliferation of gangs and criminal organizations in Canada. The postwar political economy has helped create the structural preconditions for spatial concentrations of crime in many larger urban centres by fuelling socio-economic disparities and the amalgamation of poverty and other social problems within certain neighbourhoods and/or racial groups. The wealth of Canada and other Western nations is being held by a shrinking number of individual and corporate elites, the gap between the rich and the poor has been widening, urban centres have become segregated along socio-economic lines, and poverty has become more concentrated in certain neighbourhoods, communities, and racial groups. These trends and developments, according to critical criminologist Jock Young (2001), are leading developed nations like Canada toward a "dystopia of exclusion," where "the poor are isolated in inner-city ghettos, in orbital estates, and in ghost towns" (20).

Another indigenous factor that is contributing to organized crime in this country is the symbiotic relationship between crime groups and the Canadian public. There is a strong demand for illegal goods and services in this country, and this has created an economic foundation for organized crime to prosper. Canada's public policies have also contributed to the proliferation of organized crime by creating contraband markets through the criminalization of heroin, marijuana, and other substances in demand by the public. In addition, high taxes have bolstered the smuggling trade and underground markets and, it follows, organized crime (in particular the contraband cigarettes and liquor trade).

Geopolitics in another factor in Canadian organized crime. There is probably no country in the world that has as many factors conducive to a vibrant smuggling trade: an enormous land mass and airspace, three ocean coastlines that are impossible to adequately monitor and protect, the longest unguarded border in the world (with the United States), and a relatively small tax base for funding adequate enforcement. Most unique, perhaps, is the large concentration of Canadians living within a short distance of the US border, given that the United States is a convenient market for the contraband and offers a skilled labour pool from which to draw smugglers and distributors.

Globalization is also generating opportunities for criminal groups in Canada. Those groups now export drugs and other contraband overseas as well as to the United States. The strong demand for premium Canadian illicit products, such as highly coveted "BC Bud" marijuana, has nurtured organized crime in this country. The influx of sophisticated international criminal groups into Canada has strengthened this country's position as a global hotbed of illegal drug production, currency and credit card counterfeiting, product piracy, and telemarketing fraud.

The historical and contemporary narrative of organized crime in Canada helps shed light on the character of the country and its people. Though influenced by global forces, modernization, and the United States, organized crime in Canada is reflects our own society. (See Box 16.5 for a discussion of new legislative measures implemented in Canada to combat organized crime.)

QUESTIONS FOR CRITICAL THINKING

1. When thinking about organized crime, what are the parallels between the prohibition of alcohol during the 1920s and the current prohibition of marijuana? In 2013, the Liberal Party of Canada instituted as policy the legalization of marijuana. In contrast, the official policy of the NDP is to decriminalize marijuana, while the Conservative Party continues to adhere to a policy of prohibition through criminalization. Do you think it would be in the best interests of Canadian society to decriminalize or even legalize the personal use of marijuana? Why? How would legalization affect organized crime?

2. We often distinguish organized crime genres through nationality (Italian, Nigerian, Russian, etc.). Do you believe there is a distinctive "Canadian organized crime"? If so, how would you characterize it? What is there in

Canadian history, norms, values, and institutions that might contribute to the formation of Canadian organized crime?

3. How does the information presented in this chapter compare with the depictions of organized crime in the entertainment media (television, movies, games, etc.)? Are there any myths and misconceptions popularized by the entertainment industry regarding organized crime that appear to have been refuted in this chapter?

FOCUS

Box 16.5

NEW LEGISLATIVE MEASURES TO COMBAT ORGANIZED CRIME

In the past, offenders involved in organized criminal conspiracies in Canada were charged with individual illegal offences, most of laid them out in the Criminal Code or federal drug statutes. Relevant sections of the Criminal Code included illegal gaming and betting (ss. 201 to 209), extortion (s. 346), criminal interest rate (s. 347), forgery (ss. 366 to 378), and fraud (ss. 380 to 396). There were no substantive criminal offences specifically related to organized crime.

This began to change in the mid-1990s. As Freedman notes, "Canada and a host of other countries have created new forms of individual criminal liability through targeted organized crime legislation ... These new laws specify culpability for individual conduct but place the act within the context of group activity, rationalizing more onerous individual punishment as deterrence of group-oriented criminality" (2006, 172). This new breed of organized crime legislation has created new offences and penalties for committing crimes in the context of an ongoing organized criminal conspiracy.

The United States was the first country to introduce such laws through the Racketeer Influenced and Corrupt Organizations (RICO) statute of 1970, which makes it unlawful to acquire, operate, or receive income from an enterprise through a pattern of racketeering activity.

For decades, Canada resisted legislation that created specific organized crime offences. It was not until 1997, when Bill C-95—officially called *An Act to Amend the Criminal Code (Criminal Organizations) and to Amend Other Acts in Consequence*—became law. It was enacted in the wake of the violent events associated with the turf war between outlaw biker gangs in Quebec. For the first time, the Criminal Code defined a "criminal organization," included a "criminal organization offence" and a "participation in a criminal organization offence," and prescribed specific penalties for conviction under these sections.

After further amendments that took effect in 2002, section 476 of the Criminal Code now defines "criminal organization" and designates three criminal organization offences:

467.11: knowingly participating in or contributing to any activity of a criminal organization for the purpose of enhancing the ability of said organization to facilitate or commit an indictable offence under a federal statute (with a maximum penalty of five years in prison)

467.12: committing an indictable offence under a federal statute for the benefit of, at the direction of, or in association with, a criminal organization (with a maximum penalty of 14 years in prison)

467.13: being a member of a criminal organization, and instructing another person to commit an offence under a federal statute for the benefit of, at the direction of, or in association with, a criminal organization (with a maximum penalty of life in prison).

In July 2005, Madam Justice Michele Fuerst found two members of an Ontario chapter of the Hells Angels guilty of extortion and of committing that crime "in association" with a criminal organization. The ruling was viewed as a significant victory for the government, because it upheld section 467.12 and because it ruled that Hells Angels were a criminal organization. On January 23, 2002, two men wearing motorcycle club colours arrived at the home of a Barrie, Ontario, businessman who had allegedly sold them faulty equipment for stealing satellite television signals. By wearing their Hells Angels colours, the two men "presented themselves not as individuals, but as members of a group with a reputation for violence and intimidation," Justice Fuerst wrote in her decision. "They committed extortion with the intention to do so in association with a criminal organization, the HAMC (Hells Angels Motorcycle Club) to which they belonged" (*Toronto Star*, 2005).

Summary

- Organized crime can be broadly defined by *how* crimes are carried out and by the ultimate *goal* of the criminal activity; it is perpetrated by a group of people who conspire together on a continuing and secretive basis with the goal of obtaining a financial or other material benefit.

- Dominant organized crime genres in Canada include Italian, Chinese/Asian, outlaw motorcycle gangs, Russian/Eastern European, Aboriginal.

- A defining characteristic of these organized crime genres has long been a shared nationality, ethnicity, and/or language. In recent years, however, these factors are no longer the most important criteria determining who participates in a particular organized criminal conspiracy. There are thousands of individual criminal entrepreneurs who work together, on an ad hoc or ongoing basis, in the pursuit of illegal revenues, regardless of the ethnicity, nationality, or language of the participants.

- Two competing and diametrically opposed theories regarding the origins of organized crime in North America are (1) alien conspiracy theory, which holds that organized crime in North America is the result of the importation of secret criminal societies rooted in foreign cultures; and (2) ethnic succession theory, which emphasizes how conditions indigenous to North America have contributed to the growth of organized criminality on this continent.

- The past 40 years have seen a proliferation of criminal groups, networks, and organized criminal conspiracies in Canada and worldwide. Canada continues to serve as a branch plant for transnational crime groups and as a transit point for the international movement of illegal drugs. The country is also a major producer of illegal drugs, including marijuana, methamphetamines, and ecstasy. Canada has also become an international centre for telemarketing fraud and for the counterfeiting of currency, bank cards, and digital entertainment products.

NET WORK

Using resources available through the Internet, examine a particular organized crime genre (e.g., outlaw motorcycle gangs) and group (e.g., the Hells Angels) by applying what you have learned in this chapter. In particular, apply the following frameworks: (1) characteristics of organized crime (2) etiological theories of organized crime, and (3) theories of the Structure of Organized Criminal Conspiracies.

For many years, the CISC has published an annual report examining organized crime in Canada. Recent reports can be found on their website at http://www.cisc.gc.ca. Based on an analysis of recent reports, describe the impact that organized crime has on Canada.

One can play various interactive games on the Internet (or through smart phone apps) that centre on organized crime. Join one of these games and assess the extent to which the game reflects the information presented in this chapter.

17

Corporate and White-Collar Crime

John Hagan
NORTHWESTERN UNIVERSITY

Rick Linden
UNIVERSITY OF MANITOBA

W e know far more about street crime and organized crime than we do about corporate and white-collar crime. While cases such as the Conrad Black trial (see Chapter 1) have raised the profile of these crimes, few Canadians are aware of the harm that is done by corporate and white-collar criminals. These crimes are much more costly in dollar terms than street crime. The $6 billion lost to investors in the Bre-X fraud discussed in this chapter is far more than the money lost in all the robberies in Canadian history. Few bank robbers get away with more than a few thousand dollars, but Julius Melnitzer, an Ontario lawyer, defrauded banks and friends of $90 million to support his lavish lifestyle. Corporate and white-collar crimes are also dangerous; many occupational deaths and injuries are the result of unsafe and illegal working conditions.

The term "white-collar crime" was introduced by Sutherland (1940) more than a half-century ago. While there is disagreement about the precise meaning of the term, the concept of white-collar crime has forced a reconsideration of some very basic criminological assumptions.

No longer is it possible to take definitions of crime for granted. No longer can the official data collected on crime by agencies of crime control be accepted uncritically. No longer can we assume that the poor are necessarily more criminal than the rich. The criminological enterprise took on new form and substance when the concept of white-collar crime became central to the discipline.

Learning Objectives

After reading this chapter, you should be able to

- Describe the concept of white-collar crime and explain the impact the notion of white-collar crime had on the discipline of criminology.
- Understand the occupational and organizational components of white-collar crime.
- Explain the physical and social harm caused by white-collar crime in Canada.
- Analyze how the structure of the modern corporation facilitates criminal activity.
- Understand the nature and extent of occupational crime.
- Understand the causes and consequences of our weak laws concerning corporate and white-collar crime.

The Extent and Nature of Corporate and White-Collar Crime

The Extent of Corporate and White-Collar Crime

The business section in your daily paper normally deals with stories involving company profits, corporate mergers, and economic forecasts. But in recent years, criminal matters have become a routine part of business reporting. To give you some idea of the extent of corporate and white-collar crime and deviance, consider these recent stories:

- Calgary lawyer David Blott has been disbarred for his handling of settlements given to residential school survivors. His firm represented 4600 survivors, and he was accused of providing minimal service (taking an average of 8 minutes per case) and of arranging cash advances for his clients at very high rates of interest. His firm stands to collect over $16 million for work done for the 1,168 cases completed up to Mr. Blott's disabarment (*Vancouver Sun*, 2014).

- SNC-Lavalin, one of the world's largest construction companies, has been implicated in a number of scandals, particularly for bribing foreign officials to secure construction contracts. Most notably, they have been accused of paying $160 million in bribes to secure Libyan contracts from dictator Moammar Gadhafi's regime. According to the RCMP, the Montreal-based company offered one of Gadhafi's sons a job as a vice president in order to help them secure further contracts in northern Africa. Several executives have been criminally charged, but the board of directors led by Gwyn Morgan, one of Canada's most experienced business executives, has not been held responsible for its lack of effective oversight.

- Victoria mutual fund salesman David Michaels defrauded 484 clients out of $65 million. Michaels attracted his clients through a radio infomercial and encouraged them to make very risky investments by misrepresenting the nature of these investment products (Duffy, 2014).

- A Chinese man resident in Vancouver was charged in the United States for conspiring with hackers in China to access the computers of Boeing and other aviation firms for the purpose of stealing secrets involving planes such as the F-35 fighter and the C-17 transport in order to benefit Chinese aircraft manufacturers (Freeze and Posadzki, 2014).

- A leading US bank, Citigroup, agreed to pay a settlement of $7 billion to settle an inquiry into its sale of defective mortgages to investors despite knowledge that clients would default on many of these mortgages (Corkery, 2014). These practices were endemic in the US banking system and led to the stock market crash in 2008.

- Haruko Obokata, a researcher at Japan's Riken Center for Developmental Biology, was found guilty of falsifying data in a paper on stem cell research that was published in the prestigious journal *Nature*. The leader of the research group, who was a co-author of the paper, committed suicide after the fraud was exposed (Hu, 2014).

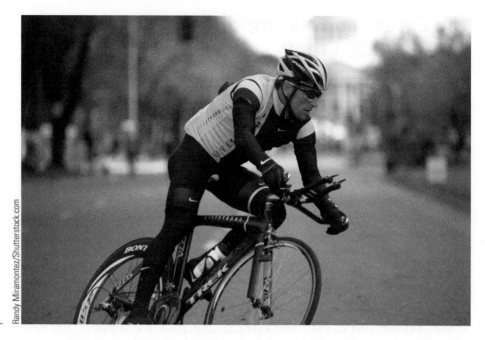

Cyclist Lance Armstrong is one of many world-class athletes who have tried to win by using performance enhancing drugs. Armstrong was stripped of the seven Tour de France titles he had won.

Randy Miramontez/Shutterstock.com

- WorkSafe BC levied a fine of over $1 million against Babine Forest Products after the company's negligence led to a sawmill explosion in Burns Lake that killed two men and injured 20 more (Morton, 2014).
- Several members of Canada's Senate, including Conservative Senators Mike Duffy and Patrick Brazeau and Liberal Senator Mac Harb, have been charged with fraud over expenses they claimed from the government.

Even the sports pages are full of stories about athletes and officials who have broken serious rules or violated the law. Some of the world's best athletes, including cyclist Lance Armstrong and baseball players Alex Rodriquez, Roger Clemens, and Barry Bonds, have been accused of using performance-enhancing drugs. Several American universities, most notably the University of North Carolina, have set up fake courses to enable student athletes to receive grades high enough to stay eligible in the sports program. In 2014, members of FIFA, the governing body of soccer, were accused of accepting millions of dollars in bribes to support Qatar's successful bid for the 2022 World Cup.

Clearly, corporate and white-collar crime is a major problem. Most stories about it remain on the business pages, but many have become front page news. The public is finally becoming aware of the harm being done by corporate and white-collar criminals.

The Nature of Corporate and White-Collar Crime

Corporate and white-collar offenders have many ways of making money. Table 17.1 shows the range of offences committed by corporations and by individuals in the course of their legitimate occupations. In this chapter you will learn something about both types of offences.

TABLE 17.1   **Types of Corporate and White-Collar Crime**

Crimes against the Public
Corporate and Business Crime
Price-fixing (conspiring on contract bids or on prices for selling to the public)
Manipulation of stocks and securities
Commercial and political bribery and rebates
Patent and trademark infringements
Misrepresentation and false advertising
Fraudulent grading, packaging, and labelling
Tax fraud
Adulteration of food and drugs
Illegal pollution of the environment
Crimes by Individual and Professional Practitioners
Obtaining fees, payments, or charges through fraud and deception
Deceiving or defrauding patients, clients, customers
Immoral practices in relations with clients
Unprofessional conduct and malpractice
Falsification of statements on vital documents
Crimes within the Organization
Offences against the Organization
Theft of funds by employees
Theft of inventory by employees
Offences against Employees
Violation of workplace health and safety laws
Violation of labour laws
Discriminatory employment practices
Harassment

Source: Stone, Christopher. (1975). Where the Law Ends: The Social Control of Corporate Behavior. New York: Harper and Row.

Class, Crime, and the Corporations

Occupation, Organization, and Crime

White-collar crimes are often committed through and on behalf of corporations. Corporate involvement in crime has been recognized for over 100 years. In 1907, Ross wrote of a new type of criminal "who picks pockets with a 'rake-off' instead of a jimmy, cheats with a company prospectus instead of a deck of cards, or scuttles his town instead of his ship." Some actions of corporations have been criminal offences in Canada since 1889 (Casey, 1985). However, it was not until 1940 that Edwin Sutherland attached a permanent name to these offenders. He proposed that **white-collar crime** be defined "as a crime committed by a person of respectability and high social status in the course of his occupation."

Since Sutherland defined the term, there has been confusion regarding the concepts of *occupation* and *organization* in the study of white-collar crime. Wheeler and Rothman (1982) note that two influential works—Clinard's (1952) and Hartung's (1950) studies of black market activities during the Second World

SEARCH FOR:
Scams and Frauds RCMP Site

white-collar crime
Sutherland defined white-collar crime "as a crime committed by a person of respectability and high social status in the course of his occupation."

War—defined white-collar crime in rather different ways. Clinard defined it occupationally, as "illegal activities among business and professional men," while Hartung included an organizational component, defining such crimes as "a violation of law regulating business, which is committed for a firm by the firm or its agents in the conduct of its business." A distinction is still often drawn today between "occupational crime—that is, white collar crime committed by an individual or group of individuals exclusively for personal gain," and "organizational crime—white collar crimes committed with the support and encouragement of a formal organization and intended at least in part to advance the goals of that organization" (Coleman, 1985, 8). Organizational crime is also known as corporate crime.

In some cases the occupational and organizational components of white-collar crimes cannot be easily separated. Clinard and Yeager (1980) give the example of a Firestone Tire official who helped his corporation secure and administer illegal political contributions benefiting the company but then embezzled a large part of the funds for himself. Note, however, that locating white-collar offenders in their ownership and authority positions in occupational and organizational structures is a key part of the class analysis of white-collar crime (Geis, 1984; Hagan and Parker, 1985; Weisburd, Waring, and Wheeler, 1990). Sutherland's emphasis on "respect" and "status" in defining white-collar crime opens up the issue of class position and the role it plays in any understanding of white-collar crime. A key element of social class is the power to commit major white-collar crimes that only people in ownership and authority positions can carry out.

Sutherland (1945) insisted that if there is a "legal description of acts as socially injurious and legal provision of a penalty for the act," criminologists should consider such acts as crimes. Despite this, many such acts go undetected and unprosecuted. For example, many stock and securities frauds can be prosecuted under provincial securities legislation *or* under the Criminal Code of Canada. Securities laws are considered "quasi-criminal" statutes. Yet the behaviours prosecuted under either body of law may be identical. Prosecutorial discretion determines whether these behaviours are officially defined as crimes. Sutherland insisted that in either case, the behaviours were to be regarded as criminal. This can make a major difference in the relationship observed between class and crime.

Consider the issue of deaths and accidents that result from workplace events. Occupational deaths outnumber deaths resulting from murder (Sharpe and Hardt, 2006). It cannot be assumed that most of these deaths result from the illegal actions of employers; even so, there is good reason to believe that many are not simply the result of employee carelessness.

One rather dated estimate (Reasons, Ross, and Paterson, 1981) holds that more than one-third of all on-the-job injuries are due to illegal working conditions and that another quarter are due to legal but unsafe conditions. At most, one-third of all such accidents are attributed to unsafe acts on the part of employees. There are many well-documented examples of employers intentionally, knowingly, or negligently creating hazards. These include failing to follow administrative orders to alter dangerous situations and covering up the creation and existence of such hazards. The penalties for these offences

SEARCH FOR:
"Get Tough on Corporate Crime," Aaron Freeman and Craig Forcese, Democracy Watch Online

occupational crime
Refers to violations of the law in the course of practising a legitimate occupation.

organizational or corporate crime
White-collar crime committed with the support and encouragement of a formal organization and intended, at least in part, to advance the goals of that organization.

are very light. For example, a 2007 vehicle accident took the lives of three BC farm workers and injured 14 others. The workers had been packed into a 10-passenger van and were sitting on wooden benches without seatbelts. The RCMP recommended 33 criminal charges in this case, but none were laid. The driver was fined $2,000 but the labour contracting company that owned the van and employed the workers was not penalized (Sandborn, 2010).

The failure of the Johns-Manville Corporation to protect workers from asbestos poisoning is one of the best-known examples of employer liability. Asbestos has been recognized as a serious health hazard since the turn of the century, but asbestos workers were not informed, and governments and the medical community ignored the hazard. At the Johns-Manville plant in Toronto, company doctors regularly diagnosed lung diseases among the asbestos workers, but they never told the workers their lung problems were related to asbestos. Many of the workers subsequently died of asbestos-related illnesses. In 2005, asbestos-related deaths accounted for nearly one-third of workplace fatalities in Canada (Sharpe and Hardt, 2006).

The construction industry has high rates of death and injury because of failure to implement workplace health and safety regulations. For example, one Manitoba company was fined $75,000 because of the death of a bridge painter who was working on a platform with no guard rails, and another was fined $27,500 for its role in the death of a young worker who was electrocuted when he was allowed to work on a high-voltage light fixture while the wires were live (McIntyre, 2001). According to Swartz (1978), these deaths should be recognized as a form of murder—what is sometimes called "corporate homicide." However, as with the Westray mine disaster (see Box 17.1), corporate executives are almost never held personally responsible for their negligence. At most, their companies are ordered to pay small fines.

Several incidents have highlighted the particular vulnerability to workplace injury of people admitted to Canada under the government's Temporary Foreign Workers program. The program came to the public's attention in 2014 when several fast food restaurant chains were accused of replacing Canadian workers with temporary foreign workers. The foreign workers were paid very low wages and were also exploited by their employers in other ways. Sargeant and Tucker (2010) have found that such workers are vulnerable because they can be sent back to their home countries if their employers are not happy with them. Many are employed as farm workers—a very dangerous occupation. Migrant workers can be forced to work long hours and are vulnerable to injuries caused by overwork. And because they are reluctant to object to unsafe working conditions, they face a high risk of workplace accidents. They are also not likely to have been well-trained in the use of dangerous substances such as agricultural chemicals or in the safe use of farm or factory machinery.

Social Class and Crime

There is evidence that a small number of offenders account for a large proportion of serious street crimes (see Chapter 15). The same may be true of white-collar crime. For example, crimes such as corporate homicide may be much more frequent among particular employers in particular kinds of industries. The mining, asbestos, and construction industries have already been noted.

It may be difficult to pinpoint such employers in conventional research designs, and this may obscure the relationship between class position and this type of criminality.

Implicit in the discussion of street crimes and corporate homicide is the strong likelihood that different kinds of crime likely have different connections to the concept of class. Among adults, class is negatively related to street crimes of violence and is likely positively related to causing harms less directly through criminal acts involving the use of corporate resources. Similarly, among juveniles, it may be that some common acts of delinquency (e.g., forms of theft that include illegal copying of computer software and music and the unauthorized use of credit and bank cards) are related positively to class (Hagan and Kay, 1990), while serious forms of violent delinquency are negatively related to class (Chapter 5). The study of white-collar crime and delinquency provides increasing reason to believe that measures of class are connected to crime and delinquency in complicated ways.

Why do higher status people get involved in criminal behaviour? Shover and Hochstetler (2006) suggest three cultural components of middle- and upper-class life that may shape these people's criminality: a competitive spirit, arrogance, and a sense of entitlement. Many of the sports figures mentioned earlier carried out unethical acts to help them win. Athletes are told that "winning is the only thing," and some respond to this pressure by cheating. According to Shover and Hochstetler, employees at Enron (see below) were continuously evaluated and 15 percent were always rated unacceptable. The resulting competitive pressure and the insecurity it generated among employees fostered a culture that encouraged misconduct. The fact that success in business is often measured by the size of one's salary helps explain why executives who are already making huge salaries will break the rules so that they can make even more money.

FOCUS

Box 17.1

WESTRAY: A DISASTER OF CRIMINAL PROPORTIONS

"In the early morning of 9 May 1992 a violent explosion rocked the tiny community of Plymouth, just east of Stellarton, in Pictou County, Nova Scotia. The explosion occurred in the depths of the Westray coal mine, instantly killing the 26 miners working there at the time" (Richard, 1997, vii). These words begin the report of a judicial inquiry into the Westray mine explosion that tells a shocking story of corporate and government misconduct that resulted in one of the largest occupational disasters in Canadian history.

Glasbeek and Tucker (1994) point out that the Westray explosion was not an accident; rather, it resulted from conscious decisions by those responsible for the miners' safety. This conclusion was reinforced by the title of Justice Richard's inquiry: *The Westray Story: A Predictable Path to Disaster*.

The explosion was not an accident, but nobody intended to kill the miners. Rather, their deaths were the result of "a complex mosaic of actions, omissions, mistakes, incompetence, apathy, cynicism, stupidity, and neglect" (Richard, 1997, viii). The inquiry concluded that Westray managers "displayed a certain disdain for safety and appeared to regard safety-conscious workers as the wimps in the organization" (ix).

The mine was built in an area that was known to be treacherous because of geological faults and high levels of methane gas. However, only minimal safety precautions were taken. The mine owners and governments were more concerned about the economic impact of mining than about protecting the workers. The government relied on the company to meet safety standards and provided very limited compliance inspections.

The company, Curragh Corporation, was having financial difficulties and put pressure on Westray to increase production levels in order to increase company revenues. Safety violations were common, and some miners quit; others stayed because of the lack of alternative employment in the province. The mine's safety conditions were summed up by Justice Richard:

> I find that the source of ignition was sparks struck by the cutting bits of the continuous miner working in the Southwest 2 section of the mine. But it became apparent as the Inquiry proceeded that conditions at Westray were of greater significance to what happened than was the source of the ignition. Had there been adequate ventilation, had there been adequate treatment of coal dust, and had there been adequate training and an appreciation by management for a safety ethic, those sparks would have faded harmlessly. (3)

Despite clear evidence of these violations, the government did not exercise its responsibility to shut down the mine until it was safe.

Five employees of the Nova Scotia Natural Resources Department and the Department of Labour were fired for their role in the explosion, but nobody from the mining company was ever held legally responsible for the tragedy. Clifford Frame, president of Curragh Corporation, refused to testify at the inquiry and was never charged with any offence. Mine managers Gerald Philips and Roger Parry were charged with manslaughter and criminal negligence, but these charges were stayed by the Crown because a conviction was unlikely. This is but one of many cases that illustrate the inability of our laws to control corporate crime. The weakness of the law was addressed by Justice Richard:

> The government of Canada … should institute a study of the accountability of corporate executives and directors for the wrongful or negligent acts of the corporation and should introduce in the Parliament of Canada such amendments to legislation as are necessary to ensure that corporate executives and directors are held properly accountable for workplace safety. (57)

Six years after the inquiry, the government passed Bill C-45 (known as the Westray Act), which introduced the obligation to protect workers into the Criminal Code. However, the legislation has had little impact on worker safety; few charges have been laid, and there have been only three convictions. And the only people convicted have been small business owners; major corporations have not been affected by the legislation. Bittle and Snider (2014) found that the government did not want to make the legislation so onerous that it would affect the ability of businesses to make a profit and that prosecutors did not target large corporations with this law. Many of those responsible for enforcing the new law have preferred to use provincial workplace safety legislation to deal with these issues (Giesbrecht, 2012). These provincial laws do not have criminal penalties but are easier to use and offer a higher likelihood of conviction.

Shover and Hochstetler (2006) proposed that people who are used to power and authority can develop an arrogance that convinces them that the rules do not apply to them. Conrad Black explicitly contrasted his abilities with those of people who were not among the rich and powerful. Recall from Chapter 1 that Black was expelled from Upper Canada College for several offences, including selling copies of final examinations. In his memoirs he justified his actions by describing his contempt for the school staff:

> All those who, by their docility or obsequiousness, legitimized the excesses of the school's penal system, the several sadists and few aggressively fondling homosexuals on the faculty, and the numerous swaggering boobies who had obviously failed in the real world and retreated to Lilliput where they could maintain their exalted status by contract threat of battery: all that gradually produced in me a profound revulsion. (Olive, 2007, 1)

SEARCH FOR:
2002 Fraud and Misconduct
Survey KPMG

A sense of entitlement may also play a role in white-collar crime. Shover and Hochstetler cite research showing that doctors who had been convicted of defrauding the US Medicare system felt they were entitled to the money they took illegally because of their status as doctors. Many executives who have been accused of criminality have long histories of using their rank in the corporation to benefit themselves in ways that would not be allowed for their subordinates. Another quote from Conrad Black illustrates this sense of entitlement. In the 1980s, Black tried to take funds that were in his employees' pension plan; he accused them of stealing from him and used this accusation to support his claim on the money (a battle Black later lost in court):

> It's sometimes difficult to work myself into an absolute lachrymose [tearful] fit about a work force that steals on that scale … We are not running a welfare agency for corrupt union leaders and a slovenly work force. (Olive, 2007, 1)

White-Collar Crime and the Social Organization of Work

Not all white-collar crimes are committed by high-status persons. Much embezzlement is committed by relatively low-status employees (Daly, 1989), and blue-collar workers also commit crimes in the course of their legal occupations. However, if white-collar crime is positively related to class position, it is reasonable to ask why. The answer may lie in the power derived from ownership and authority positions in modern corporations. These positions of power carry with them a freedom from control that may be criminogenic. That is, to have power is to be free from the kinds of constraints that may normally inhibit crime. The modern corporation facilitates this kind of freedom.

Crime and the Corporation: Executive Disengagement

The organization of the corporation is crucial to understanding most corporate crime (Reiss, 1980; Ermann and Lundman, 1982; Hagan, 1982). As Wheeler and Rothman (1982) noted, the corporation "is for white-collar criminals what the gun or knife is for the common criminal—a tool to obtain money from victims."

The corporation itself is a "legal fiction," with, as H.L. Mencken aptly observed, "no pants to kick or soul to damn." The law chooses to treat corporations as **juristic persons**, thus making them formally liable to the same laws as "natural persons." Some of the obvious faults in this legal analogy become clear when we consider that it is impossible to imprison or execute corporations. However, there are more subtle differences between corporate and individual actors that have equally significant consequences:

> When individuals are placed in an organizational structure, some of the ordinary internalized restraints seem to lose their hold. And if we decide to look beyond the individual employees and find an organizational "mind" to work with, a "corporate conscience" distinct from the consciences of particular individuals, it is not readily apparent where we would begin—much less what we would be talking about. (Stone 1975)*

Stone goes on to suggest some interesting ways in which the corporate conscience and corporate responsibility could be increased. However, these

juristic person
The legal concept that corporations are liable to the same laws as natural persons. Treating corporations as individuals raises practical difficulties for legal enforcement and punishment.

---

*Stone, Christopher. (1975). *Where the Law Ends: The Social Control of Corporate Behavior.* New York: Harper and Row.

mechanisms have not been put in place. Corporate power in this sense remains unchecked and thus is criminogenic.

The problem is in part the absence of cultural beliefs that discourage corporate criminality (Geis, 1962). There is some evidence that cultural climates vary across time and political regimes. However, even when condemnatory beliefs about corporate crime have been strong, there have been too few controlling mechanisms in place to deal effectively with white-collar crime.

Modern global corporations are huge, with hundreds of thousands of employees and many layers of bureaucracy. It is difficult for the boards of directors that are responsible for corporate governance to know the details of their corporation's daily operations. Top officers and directors can be sued by the corporation itself (through a shareholders' action) if they allow a law violation to occur through negligence. However, the courts have not imposed a duty on directors to uncover corporate wrongdoing. This provides an incentive for senior managers and directors to remain uninformed about illegal activities.

The bankruptcy of Britain's Barings Bank provides an example of **executive disengagement**. Barings, which had been controlled by the same family since 1762, was brought down by the actions of a 28-year-old trader. Nicholas Leeson lost almost $1 billion of the company's money on financial derivatives, which were essentially bets on the future performance of the Tokyo stock market. When the Tokyo market fell, Barings collapsed when it could not cover the losses. The size of this gamble was in violation of British banking laws. While bank officials were quick to blame Leeson, it is very likely that senior bank officials at least tacitly approved of Leeson's trading activities. Several financial experts have suggested that the profits Leeson had previously made for Barings led bank officials to allow him to risk their shareholders' money by making illegal trades (Drohan, 1995).

Canadian law in this area was tested in the case of YBM Magnex, a company that ostensibly sold a variety of products, including industrial magnets and bicycles, primarily to Eastern European markets. Starting its Canadian life as a shell corporation on the Alberta Stock Exchange, YBM Magnex stock rose in value from 85 cents to $20 in less than three years and had a total share value of about $1 billion. Several eminent Canadians served on its board of directors, including former Ontario premier David Peterson. Notwithstanding these eminent directors, the company had a very shady background. It was controlled by Semion Mogilevich, one of Russia's most powerful organized criminals (Howlett, 2002). YBM Magnex had been investigated in Britain for a variety of offences, including money laundering. The RCMP had been investigating the company since it was established in 1995 (Rubin, 1999). Stockholders' money disappeared in 1998 when the Ontario Securities Commission (OSC) stopped all trading in the company's shares. Auditors had refused to accept the company's financial statements, and US law enforcement officials had raided the company's Pennsylvania headquarters while investigating charges of fraud and money laundering. The company's directors and auditors were sued for $635 million and were charged by the OSC with withholding information from the public concerning the fact that the company was under investigation for its ties to organized crime. In 2003 the OSC prohibited five of the former directors of YBM Magnex from becoming directors or officers of any companies

executive disengagement
The custom by which lower-level employees assume that executives are best left uninformed of certain decisions and actions of employees, or the assumption that executives cannot be legally expected to have complete control over their individual staff.

for periods ranging from five years to life. Other directors, including former premier Peterson, were not punished. Shareholders recovered some money through lawsuits against company executives. While these penalties were not nearly as harsh as those in similar US cases, boards of directors are now taking their responsibilities more seriously and programs have been set up to train directors in how to perform their supervisory roles more effectively.

The Criminogenic Market Structure

Corporate crime research suggests not only a freedom at the top of organizations from the need to accept responsibility for criminal activity below, but also a growing pressure from managers that is also criminogenic. Farberman (1975) has referred to such pressures in the automotive industry and in other highly concentrated corporate sectors as constituting a **criminogenic market structure**. The crime-generating feature of these markets is their domination by a relatively small number of manufacturers who insist that their dealers sell in high volume at a small per-unit profit. Dealers who fail to perform risk losing their franchises. The result is strong pressure to maximize sales and minimize service. Farberman suggests that car dealers may be induced by the small profit margins on new cars to compensate through fraudulent warranty work and repair rackets. Thus, auto executives can distance themselves from the criminal consequences of the "forcing model" (high volume/low per-unit profit) they impose. The result is an absence of control over repair and warranty frauds at the dealership level.

The Large Scale of Corporations

Access to corporate resources makes it possible to commit very large-scale crimes. Wheeler and Rothman (1982) placed white-collar offenders into three groups: individual offenders, occupational offenders, and those who committed offences in which both organization and occupation were ingredients (organizational offenders). The study demonstrated the enormous advantages accruing to those who use formal organizations in their crimes. For example, across a subset of four offences, the median "take" for individual offenders was $5,279, for occupational offenders $17,106, and for organizational offenders $117,392. In a parallel Canadian study, Hagan and Parker (1985) reported that securities violators who made use of organizational resources committed crimes that involved larger numbers of victims and that were broader in geopolitical scope.

The organizational form has facilitated economic and technological development on a scale far beyond that achieved by individuals; it has also allowed criminal gains of a magnitude that individuals acting alone would find hard to attain.

The structure of the modern corporation has created a power imbalance in which individuals at the top experience relative freedom, while those at the bottom often experience pressure applied from the top that encourages various kinds of white-collar crime. The corporate form itself can be used to perpetrate bigger crimes than can be achieved by individuals acting alone. Access to these corporate resources is a unique advantage of class positions involving ownership and authority in business organizations. In this sense, it can be said that in the world of the modern corporation, the social organization of work itself is criminogenic.

criminogenic market structure
An economic market that is structured in such a way that it tends to produce criminal behaviour.

Corporate Accounting Scandals

While corporate crime has always been a major problem in North America, the new millennium saw scandals that shocked even the most avid supporters of free enterprise. Several of America's largest corporations, including the energy company Enron and the telecommunications company WorldCom, went bankrupt, stock markets crashed, and the economy declined. Several years later, in 2008, corporate misconduct dealt the world economy another severe blow as a mortgage financing scandal in the United States and high-risk lending policies in several other countries led to another major financial crisis. Why do we keep facing these crises, which are caused by what one observer has called a "scandalous rot" (DeCloet, 2002)?

While these crises have many causes, an explanation can start with how corporate executives are paid. Many companies provide senior executives with stock options that allow them to purchase shares in the company at a later date for a price guaranteed at the time the options were issued. If the stock goes up in the future, the executive can buy it at the guaranteed price and keep the difference between the issue price and the value of the stock at the time it was purchased. If the stock goes down, the executive will not use the option and so will not lose money. The purpose of stock options is to provide executives with an incentive to work hard and raise the company's value. This will ensure that the company's shareholders benefit from the company's growth. Many companies also pay their senior employees very large bonuses if the company meets specified profit targets.

Some executives take a long-term perspective and work to build up the value of their companies; others, though, take a short-term approach that can prove disastrous for shareholders. They use a variety of short-term measures to raise both company profits and the stock price so that they can make enormous profits on their stock options and bonuses very quickly. For example, "Chainsaw Al" Dunlap (named for his willingness to reduce costs by firing employees) was the CEO of the household appliance company Sunbeam. Dunlap's aggressive methods included artificially inflating sales figures so that the company's profits appeared higher than they actually were. Sunbeam eventually went bankrupt. Dunlap was fired and fined $15 million, which was only a part of the illegal gains he had made from Sunbeam stock.

In the late 1990s, the stock market rose dramatically and CEOs became corporate superstars. Many paid themselves enormous sums of money—in large companies, as much as $50 to $100 million per year. Executives convinced themselves that they deserved this high pay even when their companies were losing money. The greed of senior executives led directly to two of the largest bankruptcies in US history: Enron and WorldCom.

The Collapse of Enron

How did senior managers at Enron cost their investors $63 billion? Enron was a pipeline company that delivered natural gas. This business was very profitable, but to CEO Kenneth Lay, it was a boring business that lacked the potential for quick profit growth. Enron developed a business model that involved trading futures contracts, which are bets on the future prices of commodities such as natural gas, electricity, and pulp and paper. This new focus proved very profitable, and the stock's price climbed. Enron became the seventh most valuable company in the United States. However, the company took greater risks, and the new business model broke down. To keep the company growing, Enron executives resorted to illegal financial measures to make it appear as if profits were still increasing. Some of these complex measures involved the company selling its own assets to itself and showing the "profits" from these sales in its revenues. The company also tried to hide its debts by transferring them to outside "partnerships" that had actually been established by Enron.

Enron developed a culture of greed. Senior Enron employees acted like children in a candy store, taking massive personal profits from the financial schemes the company had organized. Several finance department employees invested $125,000 of their own funds in one of Enron's illegal financial transactions and made $30 million in a few months (Butler, 2002). As the illegal schemes began to unravel and the company began to slide into bankruptcy, Enron paid bonuses of $681 million to 140 top executives, including $67 million to CEO Kenneth Lay, who continued to encourage employees and members of the public to buy Enron stock even as he and his executives stripped the company of its remaining value (Kranhold and Pacelle, 2002). Ultimately, creditors, stockholders, and other Enron employees suffered huge losses when the financial arrangements fell apart.

Enron executives must take most of the blame for the company's demise, and several have received lengthy jail terms. However, they had help from the managers of other large corporations. The Arthur Andersen accounting firm, one of the world's largest, allowed Enron's many lapses of legal and ethical standards to slip by its auditors to help it obtain lucrative consulting contracts with Enron. Many of Wall Street's largest banks and brokerage firms collaborated with Enron in order to profit from stock commissions, consulting contracts, and interest from loans. One of Canada's largest banks, CIBC, was accused of helping Enron with its fraudulent financial dealings. While not admitting any wrongdoing, in 2005 CIBC paid $2.4 billion to settle a lawsuit over its Enron dealings.

WorldCom

The Enron debacle was quickly followed by an even larger bankruptcy. The failure of WorldCom, the largest long-distance telephone service provider in the United States, cost investors a massive $175 billion (Kadlec, 2002). WorldCom, led by CEO Bernard Ebbers, a former Edmonton milkman, admitted it overstated earnings by $3.8 billion over a period of 15 months. That is, the company reported earning $3.8 billion more than it actually made. While the Enron fraud was very complex, WorldCom used a simple method of inflating its nonexistent profits. It simply treated its everyday expenses (mainly payments to local phone companies for using their services to complete calls) as capital investments that could be written off over several years. This made its profits look higher than they really were because it did not have to deduct these expenses from the money it took in from its customers. This would be like you pretending that you are paying your current tuition over a period of four years instead of in the current academic year. This pretence makes your accounts look better than they really are, but eventually you are going to have to account for the missing money. These revelations led to a collapse in the company's stock. Ebbers, the company's CEO, is now serving a 25-year prison sentence and has lost most of the fortune he made from his company.

Arthur Andersen, the global company that was responsible for auditing Enron, WorldCom, and several other companies accused of misleading accounting, was found guilty of a felony count of obstructing the SEC's investigation into Enron. Andersen employees had shredded documents and tried to persuade others to cover up the scandal. After the verdict, the company announced that it was going out of business. It was victim of a corporate culture in which generating revenue for the company became a greater concern than protecting the public by doing its job competently.

Canada's Nortel

In 2000, Nortel, a Canadian-based telecommunications company, was the most valuable company in Canada. Unfortunately for investors, its financial statements greatly overstated the company's revenues. At a time when the market for technology stocks was collapsing, revelations that Nortel was not as profitable as it had claimed to be, along with a realization that the company had greatly overpaid for smaller companies it had purchased, drove its shares from $124 to less than $1. Some shareholders lost 99 percent of their investments, but John Roth, Nortel's CEO, retired after cashing in most of his shares at the top of the market. Executives who followed Roth were given bonuses if they could return Nortel to profitability. Nortel did report a profit in 2003, and the executives were given nearly $300 million in bonus payments. However, in 2004 the company revealed that most of the profits had been due to faulty accounting, and company shareholders again suffered a devastating loss. In 2008, the RCMP charged three officials, including former CEO Frank Dunn, with several fraud-related charges relating to these false reports. In 2009, the company filed for bankruptcy protection and Canada lost one of the world's pre-eminent technology companies. In 2013, Dunn and his colleagues were acquitted.

The Financial Collapse of 2008

The collapse of Enron and WorldCom and an earlier wave of crimes involving US savings and loan institutions led to economic crises involving stock market crashes and increased unemployment. You might have expected governments to respond to these financial disasters by increasing regulation and making financial institutions more accountable for their activities. But they did not, at least in part because financial institutions strongly resisted increased regulation, claiming that free market forces would ensure that businesses operated properly. Thus US financial institutions were allowed to engage in extremely risky investments. The collapse of these institutions in 2008 caused a financial catastrophe that cost trillions of dollars, led to the loss of hundreds of thousands of jobs in North America and Europe, and bankrupted several countries.

This massive financial collapse was very complex, but a major cause was that prominent financial institutions in the United States and several other countries took on excessive risk and engaged in reckless lending practices. Christine Lagarde, the head of the International Monetary Fund, has described the situation as extractive capitalism, by which she means that corporations were more focused on making profits than on their social responsibilities: "We can trace the problems to the evolution of the financial sector before the crisis. Financial actors were allowed to take excessive risks, leading to a situation whereby the profits on the upside went to the industry—and the losses on the downside were picked up by the public" (2014, n.p.).

What risks did the banks take that precipitated the crisis? Some US mortgage companies issued what were called NINJA mortgages. NINJA is the acronym for No Income, No Job or Assets. Normally, people in those circumstances are not issued mortgages because they are likely to default, thereby costing the bank its money. But in the United States, the institutions issuing these mortgages would repackage them with other mortgages and sell them to other financial institutions and to individual investors. Many banks and mortgage companies were involved in this, and few have been punished. One exception was Wells Fargo bank, which was fined $85 million for falsifying loan documents and for pushing homeowners into more costly types of mortgages during the housing boom (Rugaber and Kravitz, 2011). This fine represented an insignificant amount for one of the largest mortgage lenders in the United States. J.P. Morgan, another large US bank, settled its charges for the much larger sum of $13 billion. However, even a fine that large had no impact on the bank's stock price; indeed, it may have been less than the company made selling its bad mortgages.

The greed of many of those responsible for the US banking system led to a financial catastrophe. Even those whose behaviour was at least technically legal failed to do their jobs in assessing risk, so purchasers of the toxic mortgages did not know what they were buying. When mortgage holders defaulted in large numbers, the impact spread quickly through the financial system. Yet Goldman Sachs, one of the companies that sold the repackaged mortgages, actually profited from the defaults because in separate transactions, the company had made market bets *against* the mortgages it was selling to others. This is part of the reason why Taibbi (2010) described Goldman Sachs as "a great vampire squid wrapped around the face of humanity, relentlessly jamming its blood funnel into anything that smells like money" (n.p.).

Several senior officials of Enron and WorldCom were charged and sentenced for their misconduct, as were some of the people responsible for the earlier savings and loan scandal. However, while hundreds of charges have been laid against minor players in the mortgage industry, no high-ranking officials from the companies involved in precipitating the latest financial crisis have been prosecuted (Morgenson and Story, 2011). Instead, US taxpayers have been forced to bail out many of these companies because letting them go bankrupt could have destroyed the economy. And the citizens of many countries around the world have paid the price in unemployment, lost pension funds, and massive government cutbacks, while those responsible have gone unpunished. Pontell and Geis (2013) have concluded that even with the passage of tougher legislation following the economic meltdown, "regulatory gaps and continued lack of adequate oversight as a result of intense lobbying by the financial industry, as well as a nonunderstanding of the role of fraud in major financial debacles by policy makers, virtually guarantee that future financial crises will occur due to fraud, even in the most elite firms" (70).

An interesting footnote to this story is that Canadian financial institutions were relatively unaffected by the crisis, and our mortgage market is very stable. This is because Canadian politicians and regulators did a much better job of ensuring that financial institutions did not become reckless in their search for profits. In this, and in many other types of corporate and white-collar crime, aggressive regulation and enforcement can do a great deal to reduce misconduct. Unfortunately, this is often lacking.

QUESTIONS FOR CRITICAL THINKING

1. A number of online sites such as unemployedprofessors.com (Slogan: "Paper? PARTY? The choice is all yours") sell term papers to students. Do you think that students who use these services should be considered white-collar criminals? Why or why not?
2. Some judges give light sentences to white-collar offenders because they feel that these offenders have already suffered from the publicity surrounding their convictions and because their employment prospects have suffered. Do you feel that these are appropriate sentencing criteria?
3. Do you think that boards of directors of companies should be held individually responsible for corporate misconduct? What do you think would be the advantages and disadvantages of such a policy?

Consumer-Safety Issues

In the 1960s the consumer movement began to hold manufacturers accountable for the safety of their products. Ralph Nader's book *Unsafe at Any Speed*, which described the deaths and injuries caused by the faulty design of the GM Corvair automobile, helped focus public attention on consumer safety. Widely publicized cases like the calculation by Ford executives that it would be cheaper to pay for lawsuits brought by the families of Ford Pinto drivers who had been burned to death in accidents than to fix the fuel tank design flaw that caused the fires, and the production of Firestone tires that came apart at high speed, led to tougher safety regulations and convinced companies that it was good business to manufacture safe products.

Over the next 40 years, governments have become more active in regulating consumer goods and products have become much safer. However, safety issues continue to cause injury and death. In 2014, General Motors recalled about 15 million cars because of a faulty ignition switch that caused engines to shut down, leading to a loss of power steering and power brakes. General Motors knew about the problem many years ago but did not warn car owners or rectify the problem, showing that the automobile industry's culture and practices still have not completely changed. By October, 2014, General Motors had attributed 23 deaths to this problem but many claims had yet to be processed so the actual number will almost certainly be larger.

In 2007, people who took product safety for granted were surprised to learn of several incidents in which unsafe products manufactured in China were being sold in the North American market. The first was the melamine-contaminated pet food that you read about in Chapter 11. The second was the sale of counterfeit Colgate toothpaste in discount stores throughout Canada.

The toothpaste contained potentially harmful chemicals. The third scandal involved children's toys, including Elmo, Big Bird, and Dora, that were recalled by manufacturers because of safety concerns. A few months later, Mattel, the maker of Fisher-Price toys, was forced to issue three recalls involving millions of toys. Some of the toys had lead paint, which can be poisonous; others had design flaws, including loose magnets that children could swallow.

The toy recall is an example of a criminogenic market structure that has resulted from globalization. Mattel manufactures most of its toys in China because low wage levels and an absence of environmental and workplace health and safety regulations make it much cheaper to manufacture toys there. However, in China the toy companies contract out their production to local companies, which makes quality control difficult to maintain. The president of Mattel blamed Chinese manufacturers for the safety problems, but in fact the responsibility must be shared more broadly.

Some of the blame does fall on China, where regulation is lax, corruption and bribery are common, and the government tacitly approves of a wide range of illegal practices. But Mattel is also at fault. Quality control is not nearly as effective in China as it is in North American factories. Thus the toy companies must be responsible for doing sufficient testing of their Chinese-made products to ensure that they are safe. And what about the Canadian and US governments? There are toy safety regulations, but we know that unless regulations are actively enforced, some businesses will ignore them. Neither country does routine testing of toys, leaving that task to the toy companies. Unfortunately, even when safety violations are found, neither country is likely to impose any sanctions against the violators. Ultimately, the consumer must enforce safety regulations. If Mattel and other companies have to keep issuing safety-related recalls, customers will stop putting their children at risk by buying these companies' products and will turn to more reliable suppliers.

White-Collar Crime and Legal Sanctions

We can ask how effective legal sanctions are in combating white-collar crime. White-collar offences are often dealt with through the civil courts rather than as criminal matters. However, this may have limited impact. "We have arranged things," writes Christopher Stone (1975), "so that the people who call the shots do not have to bear the full risks." This is a consequence of the limited liabilities borne by modern corporate actors:

> Take, for example, a small corporation involved in shipping dynamite. The shareholders of such a company, who are typically also the managers, do not *want* their dynamite-laden truck to blow up. But if it does, they know that those injured cannot, except in rare cases, sue them as individuals to recover their full damages if the amount left in the corporations' bank account is inadequate to make full compensation … What this means is that in deciding how much money to spend on safety devices, and whether or not to allow trucks to drive through major cities, the calculations are skewed toward higher risks than suggested by the "rational economic corporation/free market" model that is dreamily put forth in textbooks. If

no accident results, the shareholders will reap the profits of skimping on safety measures. If a truck blows up, the underlying human interests will be shielded from fully bearing the harm that they have caused. And then, there is nothing to prevent the same men from setting up a new dynamite shipping corporation the next day; all it takes is the imagination to think up a new name, and some $50 in filing fees. (462–63)*

Large corporations are not quite as free as this small corporation to dissolve and reconstitute their operations. Also, the separation of shareholder and management interests creates a related problem of liability. Damage judgments against corporations are taken from the companies' revenues and rarely affect the salaries of the managers who made the decisions leading to the penalties. Thus the shareholders suffer for the misdeeds of corporate managers while the managers are shielded by the corporate structure.

So civil remedies are not very effective. What about the impact of criminal sanctions? Earlier we discussed how the legal system has done a poor job of holding white-collar offenders to account. What about the few white-collar offenders who *have* been held criminally liable and processed through the criminal justice system? Notions of "equality before the law" are perhaps nowhere more subjective than when they are being applied to the sentencing of white-collar offenders (Hagan and Albonetti, 1982). This is reflected in at least two kinds of comments made by judges about the sentences they impose for white-collar crimes: first, in the suggestion that white-collar offenders experience sanctions in a different way than other kinds of offenders, and second, in the assertion that different kinds of sanctions are appropriate in white-collar cases.

The view, common among judges, that white-collar offenders experience sanctions differently is summarized in Mann, Wheeler, and Sarat's (1980) study of a sample of judges who tried such cases: "Most judges have a widespread belief that the suffering experienced by a white-collar person as a result of apprehension, public indictment and conviction, and the collateral disabilities incident to conviction—loss of job, professional licenses, and status in the community—completely satisfies the need to punish the individual" (479). This belief persists in the face of Benson's (1989) finding that "although they commit the most serious offences, employers and managers are least likely to lose their jobs after conviction for a white-collar crime" (474).

The use of fines in sentencing white-collar offenders is controversial. Some judges feel that fines are the only penalties that should be given to white-collar offenders. Posner (1980) argues that if fines are suitably large, they are an equally effective deterrent and cheaper to administer and thus socially preferable to imprisonment and other punishments. It has already been noted that corporate entities are liable to little else than fines. However, Mann and colleagues (1980) found judges to be skeptical of fines. The sense that emerges from this research is that judges are acutely aware of the issues of deterrence, disparity, and discrimination in the sentencing of white-collar offenders and that they try to compromise by fashioning sentences that combine sanctions.

---

*Adapted from Ronald Akers. (1973). *Deviant Behaviour: A Social Learning Approach.* Belmont, Wadsworth, p 180-181. Reprinted with permission of the author.

Consistent with this view, Hagan and Nagel (1982) found in a sentencing study covering the years 1963 to 1976 in the Southern District of New York that judges attempted to compensate for the shorter prison terms given to white-collar offenders by adding probation or fines to their sentences. Similarly, fines were most frequently used in conjunction with prison and probation. In any case, all of these findings suggest that white-collar offenders are advantaged by the specific types and combinations of legal sanctions that are imposed on them.

In both Canada and the United States, there is some evidence that the mid-1970s brought a new and somewhat harsher attitude toward white-collar crime. Katz (1980) speaks of a "social movement against white-collar crime" that began in the United States in the late 1960s, and public opinion polls have found that concerns about white-collar crimes are increasing (Cullen et al., 1982). These concerns seem at least in part to be a response to events such as the Watergate Scandal in the United States and a major Canadian scandal involving dredging contracts. They are also visible in the proactive prosecutorial policies of several US attorneys (Hagan and Nagel, 1982) and in the increased prosecution of large-scale securities violations in Ontario (Hagan and Parker, 1985).

So there *appears* to be a move toward tougher legal sanctions for white-collar offences. Of course, charges must be laid before sanctions can be imposed, and the power of corporations and of persons in higher class positions makes decisions to prosecute problematic (see Benson et al., 1988). Hagan and Palloni (1983) reported an increased use of imprisonment for white-collar offenders after Watergate, but they also found that the length of these prison sentences was unusually short. A study of the enforcement of securities laws in Ontario (Hagan and Parker, 1985) found a similar pattern of tradeoffs in the severity with which white-collar offenders were treated. Overall, the treatment of white-collar offenders seems to have been lenient in the past, and despite some examples of harsher sentences, there is no clear evidence that this situation has changed markedly. And even when white-collar offenders receive prison sentences, they typically obtain parole very early.

In recent years, the huge Enron and WorldCom scandals (see above) have led to harsher treatment of corporate criminals in the United States. These crimes led to a serious loss of confidence in the stock market—why would anyone want to invest money in companies whose earnings reports could not be trusted? The scandals were so pervasive that it became obvious that major changes were needed in regulation and corporate governance. While corporate lobbying has limited regulatory changes, governments in the United States have made their laws tougher and have put more resources into investigating and prosecuting corporate crime. Many senior executives have been publicly arrested and taken into custody in front of the media in the so-called "perp walks," designed to show the public that politicians have acted. The jail sentences received by high-profile offenders in cases such as Enron and WorldCom have been very harsh—two executives received sentences of over 20 years—so there is at least anecdotal evidence that the new guidelines are having an impact.

But there is no evidence that Canadian courts have become more punitive toward corporate criminals, and the police and securities regulators have not made much effort to clean up the business world. The fact that Conrad Black was prosecuted in the United States rather than in Canada reflects the fact that the US justice system is now much tougher on corporate malfeasance than the Canadian system. Even Jim Flaherty, the former federal Minister of Finance, has said that Canada's securities regulations are ineffective.

Why does the justice system not deal with white-collar crimes more effectively? The public is usually more concerned about violent crime and neighbourhood safety issues, so police chiefs are under pressure to invest their resources in those offences. Thus, local police typically do little white-collar crime enforcement, and federal and provincial governments have not invested sufficient resources in these investigations, which can be extremely lengthy and expensive. The Nortel investigation (see above) took four years and required 50 people to go through 20 million documents (*Toronto Star*, June 20, 2008). The amount of information collected in these complex cases results in lengthy delays in going to trial. It is difficult to keep good investigators because they are attracted away by much higher salaries in private industry. Also, many white-collar offences involve multiple jurisdictions, which can further complicate investigations. And even when a white-collar prosecution is successful, the offenders are seen as good parole risks and are usually soon back in the community.

In response to these problems, in 2004 Canada passed legislation intended to make it easier to prosecute fraud-related offences. Maximum penalties for stock fraud were increased, new insider trading rules were introduced, protection was provided for employees who reported corporate misconduct, and new rules made it easier for investigators to gather evidence concerning fraud. Also, the federal government established interdisciplinary Integrated Market Enforcement Teams (IMETs) to investigate stock market frauds. Since that time, several other pieces of white-collar crime legislation have been passed.

Despite these measures, the conviction record has been abysmal (Le Pan, 2007). Bittle and Snider (2014) report that from 2003 to 2012, IMETs charged 52 individuals, of whom only 11 were convicted. They attribute this lack of success to several factors: large corporations can hire the best experts to advise them on how to get around new legislation and to defend them if charges are laid; the IMETs are limited to major cases even though it may be easier to obtain convictions in less complex ones; and corporations swamp prosecutors with huge volumes of paperwork and use other methods of delaying and obstructing investigations. Bittle and Snider also conclude that, as with workplace safety legislation, governments struggle to control corporate fraud because of their reluctance to impose tough regulations on businesses that provide jobs and that have the ear of legislators. This ensures that the interests of corporations will be reflected in any legislation that is passed and in the way in which this legislation is enforced.

Occupational Crime

In the rest of this chapter you will learn about crimes committed by individuals who violate the law in the course of practising a legitimate occupation.

As with corporate crime, at the heart of occupational crime is the violation of trust (Shapiro, 1990).

Unprofessional Conduct and Malpractice

In the past, malpractice and unprofessional conduct among groups such as lawyers and doctors was dealt with privately by the governing bodies of professional associations. However, society has become less tolerant of professional deviance. Complainants have become more vocal, and more violations have come to the attention of the public. Also, governments have become more willing to prosecute in cases that involve violations of the criminal law.

In every occupation there are people who violate legal or ethical codes for their own benefit. The problem is made worse when those responsible for regulating the conduct of individual practitioners fail to do their job. Cases of sexual abuse by clergy and malpractice by doctors illustrate how the failure of governing bodies to respond to complaints against members of their professions has led to greater harm being done.

The most widely publicized cases of unprofessional conduct over the past two decades have involved sexual abuse by members of the clergy. The Anglican Church has been named as a co-defendant in more than 1,200 complaints from former students of Indian residential schools, and several Catholic priests have been convicted of sexual assault charges in which the victims were former residential school students. Aboriginal children who attended residential schools have not been the only victims of abuse. The first major case to come to the attention of the Canadian public involved the Mount Cashel Orphanage in St. John's, Newfoundland, which was run by members of the Christian Brothers order. Abuse at the orphanage was hidden for many years. In 1975 a police investigation heard testimony that included this statement from a former resident:

> I am 11 years old … I have been at Mount Cashel Orphanage for about five years. I am happy at the orphanage except for Brother Burke, Brother Ralph and Brother English. I don't like Brother Burke because he beats me across my bare backside with a stick about three days ago Brother Burke took me into a closet and made me pull down my pants he hit me five or six times across my backside with a stick. He beat me because I threw a after shave tin into the garbage and it made a noise and Brother Burke was watching T.V. Both Brother Ralph and Brother English on seven or eight times have caught a hold of me and have felt my legs and felt my bird. Sometimes this has happened when I have been in bed. Brother Ralph would sit down on the bed and feel my bird inside my pyjama pants. Most times Brother English would feel my bird when I was in the dining Hall he would do it sometimes when I was in bed. (Law Commission of Canada, 2000, 28)

When the investigating officers recommended laying charges against members of the Christian Brothers, the chief of the Royal Newfoundland Constabulary refused to allow charges. No further action was taken until a Royal Commission was established in 1989 following a series of public complaints from former residents of the orphanage. The commission found that

Many of the Aboriginal children who lived in residential schools were physically and sexually abused by school staff. A report on these abuses will be released by the Truth and Reconciliation Commission of Canada in 2015.

Janice Longboat/Aboriginal Healing Foundation/OMI Agency

senior Catholic Church officials covered up accusations of sexual and physical abuse, as did the police chief and a provincial deputy minister. As a result, 15 members of the Christian Brothers were charged, and both the Newfoundland government and the Christian Brothers order were forced to make multimillion-dollar payments to the abused victims.

This failure of church officials to deal with abusive clergy is by no means unique. In Boston, Cardinal Bernard Law resigned his post in 2002 after facing criticism that he had failed to act in many cases of sexual misconduct by priests. Not only did he fail to take action, but he covered up many instances of misconduct and reassigned several priests who had been accused of abusing children to positions where they continued to work with children. A number of these priests reoffended, including Father John Geoghan, who was accused of fondling or raping 150 children. Geoghan received a sentence of 9 to 10 years for one case, and by 2002 the Catholic Church had paid out over $10 million in settlements to 86 of his victims. Geoghan had been moved to a number of parishes in the Boston area in response to complaints, but the Church otherwise took no action until after the case had received wide publicity.

The scandal has not been limited to North America. In 2011, after the release of a government report on child abuse by Catholic priests, Irish Prime Minister Enda Kenny expressed his anger at the failure of the Church hierarchy to protect Irish children:

> The Cloyne report excavates the dysfunction, disconnection, elitism, the narcissism that dominate the culture of the Vatican to this day ... The rape and torture of children were downplayed or "managed" to uphold instead, the primacy of the institution, its power, standing

and "reputation." Far from listening to evidence of humiliation and betrayal with St Benedict's "ear of the heart" … the Vatican's reaction was to parse and analyse it with the gimlet eye of a canon lawyer." (Fitzgerald, 2011)

Medical doctors have been accused of many types of violations, ranging from false billing to ethical lapses in the treatment of patients to sexual misconduct with patients. Perhaps the most serious violations by doctors involve malpractice. Most doctors are competent professionals, but accusations of malpractice are not uncommon. In 2012, patients began 869 legal actions against physicians. Typically, only about one-third of actions against doctors are successful (CMPA, 2013). Some of the cases that resulted in action against doctors included a Manitoba doctor who was sanctioned for sewing beads into the stitches of an Aboriginal woman and an American doctor who was convicted of assault for carving his initials into a patient (Henderson, 2000). One tragic case of malpractice involved a Winnipeg surgeon who specialized in pediatric cardiac surgery. In 1994, 12 young children died while undergoing surgery at the Health Sciences Centre. A judicial inquiry found that at least five of the deaths were likely preventable (Sinclair, 2000). The inquiry determined that the surgeon was at fault but also blamed the hospital, which failed to ensure that the surgeon was qualified, and his supervisors, who failed to take action even when there were complaints about his performance. There was a culture of secrecy surrounding the work of the doctor, and nurses who complained about the program were ignored by hospital officials.

The failure by professional licensing and regulatory bodies to hold their members accountable has seriously harmed clients and patients. For example, Dr. Richard Neale lost his surgical privileges in BC after a series of complaints. He was allowed to retrain for six months and then to return to his surgical duties. In 1981, an Ontario patient died as a result of Dr. Neale's incompetence, but he continued to operate and to injure patients until he was finally banned from practice in 1985 as a result of the 1981 case. He left Canada for England, where he continued to practice, and had a complication rate five times higher than that of his colleagues (Wente, 2000). British authorities had been warned about Neale, yet they did not remove him from practice until 2000.

In 2007, Toronto real estate agent Krista Stryland died of complications following liposuction surgery at the Toronto Cosmetic Clinic. Her condition deteriorated after surgery that removed more than the standard amount of fat and liquids from her body. The doctor who treated her did not respond appropriately to her complications.

The surgery had been carried out by Dr. Behnaz Yazdanfar, a family physician who was not a qualified plastic surgeon. However, Dr. Yazdanfar was permitted to perform cosmetic surgery in Ontario without formal surgical training. The year before Ms. Stryland's death, another doctor had complained about Dr. Yazdanfar's lack of qualifications and about her advertising, but the College of Physicians and Surgeons of Ontario determined that she was qualified to conduct cosmetic surgery procedures and allowed her to continue doing liposuction and breast augmentations.

In 2009 the College of Physicians and Surgeons conducted hearings into a number of complaints against Dr. Yazdanfar, including the Stryland case. The Discipline Committee determined that Dr. Yazdanfar had committed professional misconduct by failing to meet the standard of practice, that she had violated advertising regulations, and that she had acted in a manner that was "disgraceful, dishonourable or unprofessional" (College of Physicians and Surgeons of Ontario, 2009, 1). The committee concluded that Dr. Yazdanfar was incompetent and prohibited her from performing further surgery.

SEARCH FOR:
College of Physicians and Surgeons Judgment in Yazdanfar case:

Investment and Securities Fraud

Many people rely on financial advisors to help them prepare for retirement. This is usually a good idea, but unfortunately, not all advisors can be trusted. For example, Earl Jones, a Montreal investment advisor, defrauded clients of over $50 million in order to support his lavish lifestyle. Many investors had trusted Jones with their life savings and were financially destroyed by his actions (Sutherland, 2009). But Jones's crimes pale by comparison with those of Bernie Madoff, who victimized thousands of people and cost them close to $20 billion. Both Jones and Madoff used **Ponzi schemes** to defraud their clients. In a Ponzi or pyramid scheme (Evola and O'Grady, 2009), investors are promised high returns on their investments. They are initially paid dividends on those investments; however, the funds paid out are not generated from actual investments. Indeed, their money has generally not been invested. Instead, the payouts come from the contributions of new investors. That is why the "returns" for earlier investors are often quite high—those high returns are meant to attract more investors to generate investment funding that can be spent by the organizers and/or paid out to earlier investors. Eventually the new money runs out and the scheme collapses.

Madoff, once a highly respected Wall Street financier, is now serving a prison term of 150 years in the United States. Jones was sentenced to 11 years in prison but was released in 2014 after serving four years.

Another type of securities fraud is insider trading, which occurs when someone—usually an owner or employee of the company—receives information about the company that is not available to the general public. It is illegal to buy or sell stock using this information because this would give the insider an advantage over other investors. In 2000, Glen Harvey, former president of Alberta-based Golden Rule Resources, was sentenced to one year in jail and fined $3.95 million for trading $4 million worth of company stock while withholding assay results showing that the company had almost no gold on one of its properties. When the news was finally released, the company shares dropped by over half. Harper was only the second person to be sentenced to jail in Canada for insider trading (Canadian Press, 2000). Successful prosecutions for this offence are rare.

A third type of investment fraud is the "pump and dump." In this scam, stock promoters take a worthless company, invent a story about that company, then tell that story in order to get people to buy the stock. If they succeed, the stock price rises; the promoters can then sell their shares for a profit, leaving the other investors with worthless shares. The story of Bre-X, the most expensive stock fraud in Canadian history, is described in Box 17.2.

> **Ponzi scheme**
> A fraud in which old investors are paid with the funds invested by new investors. When the scheme runs out of new investors, the scheme collapses.

FOCUS

Box 17.2

BRE-X: THE ANATOMY OF A STOCK FRAUD

The speculative segment of the Canadian stock market has had a very bad reputation. *Forbes* magazine once called Vancouver the "scam capital of the world" because of the fraudulent stocks being sold on the Vancouver Stock Exchange. Until recently, governments failed to regulate some of the more aggressive stock promoters. This neglect led to one of the world's largest stock swindles, involving Bre-X, a company that claimed to have discovered a gold mine in Indonesia.

Mines have been "salted" for hundreds of years. Owners of a worthless property can attract investors by scattering gold at the mine site or by adding it to rock samples after they have been collected. Despite this long history of fraud and deception, investors around the world fell for the story of Bre-X. Many of these investors lost their life savings, and at least one killed himself after Bre-X stock collapsed. The fraud came to light after the company's chief geologist, Michael de Guzman, jumped to his death from a helicopter. Shortly after the geologist's death, assay reports revealed that there was no gold and that the Bre-X property was worthless. Investors lost $6 billion when Bre-X stock collapsed.

Bre-X had been built on a flimsy structure of lies. However, greed led many to ignore the risks and warning signs and to believe the story spun by the Bre-X principals and by their supporters in the financial world. Jennifer Wells describes the press release by company president David Walsh, a man whose stock-promoting career had been, up until Bre-X, a disaster:

> The Walsh press release described the prospect as a "deposit," which it was not, the presumed gold resource as "reserves," which they were not, and said that drilling on the property by the previous tenant had yielded numerous intersections of more than two grams of gold per tonne, which was a lie. (1998, 122)

To raise exploration money, Walsh essentially announced that he had a producing gold mine, even though the company had not even begun to explore the property.

After initial samples showed no signs of gold, somebody—most likely de Guzman—began salting the samples. Not surprisingly, tests of these samples were more successful, and Bre-X officials used the results to regularly increase their estimates of the amount of gold. As the mythical gold reserves increased, the stock began to soar. Shares that once sold for six cents per share were soon worth hundreds of dollars.

In addition to the problems with the mine, Bre-X had to contend with the corrupt Indonesian government, which eventually took nearly half the project. When this happened, company officials simply doubled their estimates of the amount of gold. Investors were comfortable even though over half their investment had been assigned to the Indonesians and to a large mining company selected by the Indonesian government (Wells, 1998).

The involvement of this company, Freeport McMoRan, spelled the beginning of the end for Bre-X and its investors. When Freeport carried out its own testing program, assay results showed there was no gold on the Bre-X property. The last nail was hammered into the Bre-X coffin by Graham Farquharson, an independent analyst whose report concluded:

> The magnitude of the tampering with core samples that we believe has occurred and resulting falsification of assay values at Busang, is of a scale and over a period of time and with a precision that, to our knowledge, is without precedent in the history of mining anywhere in the world. (Wells, 1998, 368)

Nobody will ever be punished for the Bre-X fiasco. De Guzman committed suicide, and David Walsh died of natural causes in 1998. John Felderhof, the company's chief geologist, was acquitted of fraud charges in 2007. The company is bankrupt, and nobody associated with Bre-X has the resources to replace the billions of dollars lost by investors.

The Justice System: Wrongful Convictions

People who work in the justice system sometimes break the rules or exhibit incompetence. One consequence of this can be the imprisonment of innocent people. Besides the cases involving Dr. Smith (Box 17.3), there have been a number of wrongful convictions in Canada, including those of Guy Paul Morin, Thomas Sophonow, David Milgaard, and Donald Marshall. One factor these cases have in common is that justice system personnel had "tunnel vision"—that is, they focused on only one suspect and thus failed to properly investigate the crime or to adequately assess evidence that might have cleared the suspect during the investigation or at trial. In some of these cases, police and prosecutors deliberately withheld evidence from the defence that might have resulted in an acquittal of the accused.

Tax Fraud

No current estimates are available, but many billions of dollars are lost to tax fraud. In 1997, the Auditor General estimated the loss to be $12 billion (Auditor General of Canada, 1999), a sum greater than the budget of the Department of National Defence. Canada's income tax system requires all taxpayers to report their incomes honestly. Clearly, not all do, and there is evidence that in some occupations, the rate of noncompliance is as high as 90 percent (Gabor, 1994). On a global level, tax evasion is massive. French economist Gabriel Zucman has estimated that $7.6 trillion are illegally hidden in tax havens by corporations and very wealthy individuals (Leslie, 2014).

How do so many people avoid taxes? People who are working at jobs where all their income is paid by an employer have little opportunity to avoid tax because the employer deducts the tax and reports salary information to the government. However, a large number of Canadians work at jobs that enable them to hide income. Many of you have likely worked as servers in the restaurant industry or have friends who do. Much of servers' income is from tips, and the employer usually does not keep a record of this income. As a result, many servers do not pay tax on this portion of their earnings. Also, restaurants and other businesses have purchased electronic sales suppression software for their cash registers that allows them to hide some of their sales so that the owners do not have to pay tax (CRA, 2008). Some unscrupulous contractors offer a reduced price if the customer pays in cash so that they will not have records of income that could be uncovered through an audit. These workers are part of the "underground economy," whose size in 2008 was estimated at $36 billion (Statistics Canada, 2011).

FOCUS   Box 17.3

DR. CHARLES SMITH: WRONGFUL CONVICTIONS

Dr. Smith was a forensic child pathologist who gave crucial testimony in many child fatality cases. He worked at Toronto's Hospital for Sick Children and was recognized as an authority in his field despite a lack of training in forensic pathology. He was heavily involved testifying in court from 1990 to 2005, when criticism finally led to a review of his work. This review concluded that Smith had made serious errors in almost half the 45 child autopsies reviewed and that there was serious doubt about 13 cases that had resulted in convictions. Among those convicted and later released after Smith's evidence was refuted by other experts were the following: Louise Reynolds, who served 22 months for fatally stabbing her daughter, who had actually been mauled by dogs; William Mullins-Johnson, who served 12 years after being convicted of raping and murdering his niece; and Tammy Marquardt, who was freed in 2011 after serving 14 years for murdering her son. As with many others responsible for wrongful convictions, Dr. Smith was overly zealous in trying to secure convictions. The proper role of an independent expert is to provide objective evidence to the court, not to support the Crown's case. However, Smith began his investigations with the idea that a child had died as the result of a crime, and he saw his job as helping the Crown

(continued)

prosecutor prove that an accused was guilty. His technique was sloppy, he lacked knowledge of forensic pathology, and he behaved in an unprofessional manner. Smith's approach to his job led to many miscarriages of justice (Goudge, 2008).

According to a judicial inquiry, Dr. Smith's competence should have been questioned much earlier, but his supervisors ignored complaints about the accuracy of his work. Judges, prosecutors, and his supervisors all failed to ensure that his work was competent and fair:

> As this review demonstrates, for over a decade, while the danger signals about Dr. Smith kept coming, those in charge at the [Office of the Chief Coroner for Ontario] who ultimately might have done something about the mounting problem did far too little.

It is a graphic demonstration of how the oversight of pediatric forensic pathology could and did fail, almost completely. In large measure, responsibility for this failure lies in three areas: the grave weaknesses that existed in the oversight and accountability mechanisms, the inadequate quality control measures, and the flawed institutional arrangements of pediatric forensic pathology in particular, and forensic pathology as a whole. (Goudge, 2007, 31)

> As in so many other instances of corporate and white-collar wrongdoing, much of the harm done by Dr. Smith could have been avoided if governments had provided adequate regulatory frameworks and if those responsible for supervision had actually done their jobs competently.

People often justify tax fraud by contending that taxes are too high and that governments are taking money that rightfully belongs to the taxpayer. Many Canadians were particularly upset when the GST was implemented, and there is some evidence that people in businesses such as contracting turned to the underground economy as a way of avoiding the GST.

Other types of tax fraud have involved exaggerating income tax deductions. According to Donovan (2007), more than 100,000 Canadians had their claims for charitable deductions rejected by the CRA because they were grossly inflated. People who donated funds to phony charities would receive tax receipts for many times the value of their donation. About $1.4 billion in tax revenue has been lost because of this scam, and it was unlikely that any of the donated money actually reached people in need. Also, large numbers of Canadians circumvent the tax system by purchasing smuggled cigarettes, alcohol, and other forms of contraband.

Political Corruption

Canadian politicians are more honest than their counterparts in many other countries; that said, we have had our share of political scandals. In 1873, just six years after Confederation, John A. Macdonald's government was forced to resign over allegations of bribery involving the selection of a contractor to build and operate the Canadian Pacific Railway. Perhaps the most corrupt political regime in Canada was that of Maurice Duplessis, the Quebec premier for most of the period between 1936 and 1959. He created a powerful political machine that routinely violated election rules and violated many of Quebeckers' basic rights, such as the right to freedom of political expression. In addition, his supporters used inside information to make money on the stock market and accepted financial kickbacks from people who wanted to do business with the Quebec government (Corrado, 1996).

Corruption has marked more recent Quebec governments. In 2015, Justice France Charbonneau will deliver the results of her inquiry into corruption in the province. In 2014, the inquiry spent much of its time looking into the construction industry, including the links between construction unions and organized crime groups such as the mafia and Hells Angels. It also heard testimony concerning the illegal financing of political parties. Gerald Tremblay, mayor of Montreal, Gilles Vaillancourt, mayor of Laval, and Michael Applebaum, interim mayor of Montreal, all resigned after testimony implicated them in various forms of corruption. Arthur Porter, the former head of the McGill University Health Centre, who was appointed by Prime Minister Stephen Harper to head the Security Intelligence Review Committee, has been charged with taking kickbacks from the engineering firm SNC-Lavalin for the construction of a massive new hospital complex.

At the federal level, a major scandal helped defeat the Liberal government in 2006. In 2002 a newspaper reported that a Montreal advertising company had received over half a million dollars for a report that was never completed. The Auditor General investigated and concluded there had been massive misspending in a government program that provided federal funding for the sponsorship of events, most of which were in Quebec. In many cases, money was given to companies that

Quebec Superior Court Justice France Charbonneau heads the inquiry into corruption in Quebec's construction industry. Judge Charbonneau is a former prosecutor who heard many high-profile cases, including the murder trial at which Hells Angels leader Maurice (Mom) Boucher was convicted of murder and sentenced to life in prison.

REUTERS/OLIVIER JEAN/LANDOV

had not actually done any work for the government. The Auditor General concluded: "I think this is such a blatant abuse of public funds that it is shocking. I am actually appalled by what we've found" (CBC, 2004, n.p.).

Justice John Gomery headed an inquiry to further investigate what had by then become known as the Sponsorship Scandal. His report, released in 2005, concluded that over $150 million of taxpayers' money had been given by the Liberal government to five advertising and communications companies in Quebec with ties to the federal Liberal Party. In many cases, these companies had done nothing to earn the money. Several of the executives who received this money subsequently made large donations to the Liberal Party and paid the salaries of party workers. Justice Gomery concluded that "whether legal or illicit, there was at least an implicit link between the contributions [to the Liberal party] and the expectation that the government contracts would be awarded" (2005, 79). Thus government money appears to have been returned to the party to use for its own purposes.

The report laid some of the blame for the scandal on Prime Minister Jean Chrétien, his chief of staff Jean Pelletier, and Public Works Minister Alfonso Gagliano, all of whom had failed to ensure that government funds were spent properly. While no elected officials were charged, one government official and several marketing executives were convicted and sentenced to jail for their part in this affair.

In 2006, Stephen Harper's Conservatives were elected on a platform that included bringing greater honesty and accountability to government. However, they have also become involved in a number of scandals, many of them involving election campaigns. These included violating campaign spending rules by spending more than they were allowed to, which allowed them to buy more advertising than the other parties who obeyed the limits.Conservative campaign worker Michael Sona was convicted in 2014 for arranging robocalls to potential Liberal voters that told these voters that the location of the polling stations had been changed. This was an attempt to discourage opposition supporters from voting. Harper himself has been found in contempt of Parliament for refusing to provide members of Parliament with cost information, and his government has defied court orders to release information on a number of issues—for example, documents relating to the residential school experience of Aboriginal people. Several military veterans who have been critical of government policies found that Veteran's Affairs had leaked their medical information in an attempt to silence them.

Despite these problems, Canada is relatively well governed. Many countries are governed by politicians who abuse their citizens by repressing dissent and denying people their basic human rights. These problems are most prevalent in dictatorial regimes such as Zimbabwe and China, but even democratic societies are not immune. During US President George Bush's post-9/11 "War on Terror," the government placed a series of restrictions on civil liberties. Legislation such as the Patriot Act and the Protect America Act allowed the government to open people's mail and to carry out wiretaps and other types of electronic surveillance without the judicial supervision required by the American Constitution. Suspected terrorists were held at a US military base in Guantánamo Bay, Cuba, rather than in the United States so that American laws would not apply, and prisoners were tortured and humiliated by the US soldiers at the Abu Ghraib prison in Iraq.

Blue-Collar Crime

The concept of white-collar crime also fits many people who wear blue collars. Because of this, some have suggested that the term *occupational crime* may be a better one. Many tradespeople defraud the government by doing work "off the books" to avoid provincial sales tax and the GST. Some blue-collar businesses have very bad records of consumer fraud. For example, Robert Sikorsky (1990) documented an appalling degree of misconduct in the auto repair business. Travelling across Canada, he visited 152 repair shops. Before each visit, he disconnected the idle air control in his car, triggering a warning light on the instrument panel. The repair was obvious and very simple—reinsert the connector. Over half the shops Sikorsky visited performed unnecessary work, overcharged him for work, or lied about the work that had been done. In one case he was presented with an estimate of $570. A similar study was conducted by Menzies (2000). In this case, a mechanic disabled one of the spark plugs on a car that was otherwise in good working order. In each case, Menzies requested and paid for an engine diagnosis that ranged in price from $69 to $103, so there was ample information available to do the repair, which should have cost about $20. Menzies visited only four Toronto repair shops, but his study reinforced Sikorsky's findings. Only one shop, a Honda dealership, repaired the problem without recommending any further work. Of the other three, Goodyear estimated that the repair would cost $234, Speedy Auto Service estimated $300, and Canadian Tire estimated $648 would be required to return the car to working order.

Employee Fraud

Corporations are also often the *victims* of crime. A 2001 survey sponsored by the accounting company Ernst & Young found that about 25 percent of the Canadian workforce reported either having committed fraud against their employer or witnessing someone committing fraud during the previous year. An earlier survey of employers found that 80 percent reported having been victimized by employee fraud (CBC, 2001). Examples of frauds reported to Ernst & Young included taking kickbacks from suppliers in exchange for contracts, creating phony invoices and collecting the money, stealing company property, and stealing cash from the company. Canadian retailers estimated that in 2012 they lost $1.3 billion to employee theft, almost as much as their losses from shoplifting and other types of customer theft ($1.7 billion) (PWC, 2012). To put this figure in perspective, the Canadian Bankers Association reported that in 2013, losses from credit card fraud were $465 million (2013). Corporations of all sizes are victimized, but often the toll is greatest on small companies. For example, many small restaurants have been forced out of business because of theft of money and food by staff. Lisa Leduc interviewed Ottawa restaurant employees about ways of "scamming" their employers. One of the interviewees described some of these methods:

> A manager would bring in his friends, a table of, let's say, eight, and [they would have] wings and beer, and he would go into the cooler

where the beer was and grab it when the bartender wouldn't even notice, and [there would be] free dinner and beer for this person's friends ... Also, people weren't punching in drinks and [were] pocketing the money. Cooks [were] taking food home, all staff [were] taking dishes and cutlery. (qtd. in Gabor, 1994, 78–79)

In recent years, new technology and changes in financial practices have made larger corporations more vulnerable to the actions of individual employees. Earlier in this chapter you read about the illegal trades by Nicholas Leeson that drove Barings Bank into bankruptcy. Since the Leeson case, there have been several others where an individual trader has done significant harm to his company. Toronto's Stephen Duthie lost $182 million through unauthorized trading that was essentially gambling with his company's money. Duthie would have received a huge bonus if his gamble had succeeded in making large profits for his company. But the trades *lost* money, and Duthie's employer, Phoenix Trading and Research, was forced to close. These cases have become so common that the term *rogue trader* has been invented to describe the actions of people like Leeson and Duthie.

QUESTIONS FOR CRITICAL THINKING

1. Why do you think the government has refused to implement laws that would hold corporate officials more responsible for their actions?
2. In previous chapters of this text, you have studied a number of theories of criminal behaviour. Select one of these theories and assess how well it explains white-collar and corporate crime.
3. Can you think of three different actions that might be taken by governments and/or corporations to reduce the amount of white-collar and corporate crime in Canada?

● Summary

- The study of white-collar crime has demonstrated that the relationship between class and crime is more complicated than early criminologists had believed. Theories of crime must account for the crimes of the privileged as well as for the crimes of the poor.
- Even when they are reported to the authorities, white-collar crimes are often not reported in official crime statistics because they are dealt with under quasi-criminal statutes.
- Corporations are instruments that enable people to commit crimes that are vast in scope. The financial and physical costs of corporate crimes are very high.
- The structure of the modern corporation provides managers with a great deal of freedom from control. This has the unintended consequence of

encouraging crime. In some industries, high-level managers demand such unreasonably high levels of profit that their subordinates feel pressured to break the law.

■ Corporations are subject to legal regulation, but the laws that govern them are weak. Even when punishment is administered, it is often so light that it is regarded as an accepted cost of doing business.

■ There is some evidence that penalties for white-collar offenders are increasing in the United States, but this does not appear to be the case in Canada.

■ One of the major contributors to many types of occupational crime is the failure of professional organizations to adequately control the behaviour of their members. Another is the fact that many people do not strongly condemn crimes such as tax fraud.

NET WORK

There are several websites dealing with fraud. Two of the best are www.scambusters.com and www.fraud.org.

1. Go to these websites and briefly describe three different types of fraud. How can each of these frauds best be prevented?
2. How have the white-collar criminals who carry out these frauds adapted to new communications technology?

18 Cybercrime and Cyberdeviance

Michael Arntfield
WESTERN UNIVERSITY

This chapter provides an overview of electronic and computer-mediated crime in Canada, including its implications for traditional criminology. Specifically, we examine the difference between crime and deviance (Chapter 1) while applying the routine activities theory of crime (Chapter 15) to offender–victim interactions in digital environments. We also address some of the determinants of victimization (Chapter 7) as they exist in virtual spaces, where contact between offender and victim tends to be asynchronous (not happening at the same time). This differentiates online offences from most other types of offending studied by criminologists.

Web 2.0, the second generation of the Internet, includes social media, wiki sites, public comment boards, and other computing environments that bring together people from disparate backgrounds. Even though Web 2.0 has existed for well over a decade, there is no consensus on how to apply existing theoretical models of crime to these spaces. Suffice it to say that the intersection of cybercrime, cyberdeviance, and criminology is a field ripe for discussion, especially in terms of how technology and legislation influence each other.

This chapter also examines how criminologists, policy-makers, and law enforcement officials might develop a consensus on how to define criminality in a self-contained digital environment and how the social norms of that environment are expected to mirror the values of the conventional, offline world. Defining and legislating cyberbullying, trolling, and other forms of electronic harassment remains problematic, so this chapter straddles both established and experimental methods of inquiry while also looking to criminology's future role in helping define the different forms of online misconduct. Understanding the origins and causes of this misconduct will in turn help us better understand the very real and often very damaging effects of cybercrime and cyberdeviance beyond the digital spaces where offending begins—but does not necessarily end.

Learning Objectives

After reading this chapter, you should be able to:

- Differentiate between cybercrime and cyberdeviance and understand why it is often difficult to separate one from the other both legally and theoretically.
- Understand how recurring or habitual computing behaviours constitute routine activities that enable offenders by placing certain users at increased risk of being victims of cybercrime.

- Discuss the connection between traditional offline physical bullying and online cyberbullying, including derivatives of cyberbullying such as Internet trolling, cybermobbing, and other forms of electronic harassment.

- Define the different forms of identified paraphilia, both criminal and noncriminal, and understand how they manifest themselves in virtual environments as predictors of offline offending.

- Understand that cybercrime is a very dynamic and changeable area of offending that requires improved training initiatives for law enforcement, as well as clarified legislation in order to hold offenders accountable and ensure the cooperation of technology providers in cybercrime prevention and investigation.

What Is Cybercrime?

The Internet continues to change how people communicate, connect with one another, and cultivate personal relationships. Digital technologies and Internet-enabled "smart" devices have changed the dynamics of work, travel, and the economy. These technologies have also changed the landscape of criminality to the extent that we might now look beyond traditional approaches to understanding offenders and their decision making.

Because the term "**cyberactivities**" can describe any number of computing activities that rely on Internet connectivity such as e-mail, online research, streaming media, and interactive gaming, cybercrime must be a broad concept (Miller and Morris, 2012, 75). Over the past decade, police services have begun establishing specialized cybercrime units within their criminal investigation bureaus. However, no two agencies seem to have the same vision with respect to what should be investigated by these units or how cybercrime should be defined.

Despite the lack of a consistent definition of cybercrime, we can specify some activities that most people would consider to fit this category:

- *Phishing.* The use of misleading or counterfeit electronic transmissions, such as e-mails purportedly from credit card companies or other financial institutions, requesting sensitive personal information or password data with the intention of compromising the victim's banking or credit accounts.

- *Ripping.* The use of specially designed software or other methods of circumventing copyright protection for the purposes of downloading or copying original material from a protected media source (DVD, online video, etc.) to a hard disk, usually for the purposes of resale or redistribution.

- *Hacking.* The attempt to remotely circumvent the security or privacy measures initiated by an Internet website, server, or database, for the purposes of either stealing information or interfering with operations and compromising data through **distributed denial-of-service attacks**, deployment of viruses, or other malicious actions.

- *Luring.* The act of using an Internet connection to access social media, chat rooms, or other places of electronic assembly to make contact with a child or

cyberactivities
Any number of tasks carried out through the use of a computer and a network connection, including but not limited to Internet browsing, e-mail correspondence, online banking, interactive gaming, media downloading or uploading, the use of file transfer protocols, and accessing social media platforms.

distributed denial-of-service attack (DDoS)
A term that describes any number of methods of varying sophistication, usually carried out by a group of hackers or by a series of bot attacks, for infiltrating and sabotaging a host server, thereby denying access to a website or online service or otherwise disrupting the operations of business, industry, or government.

person under 16 for the purposes of counselling them to commit a sexual act or to meet at a physical location for sexual purposes. This is typically accomplished by the offender posing online as an underage person himself in order to conceal his real identity and intentions.

■ *Stalking.* The use of a computer or other network-enabled device to repeatedly make unwanted contact with a person using any number of means (e-mails, text messages, etc.), and doing so knowing that this behaviour is likely to cause fear or annoyance.

■ *Spamming.* The use of one or more computer networks and servers to send unsolicited and unwanted bulk messages to other users, often consisting of vexatious advertisements or pornographic content delivered either by e-mail or by pop-up windows in Internet browsers.

■ *Skimming.* The use of specific software *and* hardware to intercept e-transmissions containing sensitive financial data, usually related to credit card purchases. The stolen data enable the cloning or counterfeiting of specific financial instruments (credit cards, bank cards, etc.) for the purposes of theft and fraud.

■ *Trafficking.* Any use of a computer network to move illicit images (or other media), controlled substances, or people. In the context of cybercrime, trafficking can include distributing child pornography; selling or distributing drugs via the "Deep Web"; or making contact with victims to "groom" them for human trafficking operations—essentially another version of luring but with different objectives and victims.

Most police cybercrime units are tasked mainly with investigating and interdicting criminal offences involving the exploitation of children through computers. These offences typically involve child pornography or child luring. However, a number of other offences that constitute cybercrime fall outside the relatively limited scope of typical cybercrime enforcement strategies. Moore (2005) has defined cybercrime as any criminal offence or series of offences committed through the use of a computer and a computer network, including an Internet connection. This definition would add to the previous list offences that fall under the umbrella of "cyberterrorism" (a term just as vague as cybercrime), which usually involve using a computer to orchestrate large-scale "attacks on information," including government or critical infrastructure servers or any database of interest to national security (Baranetsky, 2009). While there are law enforcement units, as well as divisions of the federal government such as the Communication Security Establishment Canada (CSEC) and the Canadian Security and Intelligence Service (CSIS), that address and investigate these types of offences, they are normally distinguished by the use of operational titles such as "technological crimes" or "e-crimes." Limited police resources have meant that in many departments, the policing of cybercrime has been limited to those computer offences that have human victims and that cause physical harm in the offline world beyond financial losses or service disruptions. Offences such as Internet child exploitation and cyberbullying are akin to cyberviolence, and like all forms of violent offending, they often involve targeted victims.

Deep Web
Sometimes called the "invisible Web," it is the parallel Internet that exists beneath the surface of conventional browsers. It features sites not indexed by search engines. It is essentially unregulated and is rife with criminal activity and illegal transactions.

E-crime and Cybercrime

Cybercrime has come to denote online crimes that are largely analogous to offline crimes of violence and sexual offending. Computer offences committed against financial institutions or the state tend to fall under blanket terms such as electronic crime (e-crime), cyberespionage, cyberterrorism, and any number of other terms that differentiate institutional targets from human ones. These crimes are being reported more frequently in the media. In April 2014, the Canada Revenue Agency (CRA) had its website compromised at the height of the annual tax-filing season after the Heartbleed security bug was deployed by a hacker and roughly 900 social insurance numbers belonging to Canadian taxpayers were stolen. A 19-year-old university student in London, Ontario, was arrested and charged with unauthorized use of a computer and mischief (Bogart, 2014). Had the incident occurred in the United States, the charges laid might have been more serious, reflecting more recently enacted laws to protect business, industry, and government from the escalating threat of complete electronic shutdown.

Despite tougher laws, these crimes continue to make news in the United States. One of the most significant cases was the December 2013 breach of Target's database at the height of the holiday shopping season. Hackers were able to access the credit card information of roughly 40 million customers of the US retail giant, which made the attack one of the worst data security breaches ever recorded (Harris and Perlroth, 2014). Several arrests were made in relation to the breach, but the full extent of the organization behind the attack may never be known. The scale of the Target breach changed the social and political climate surrounding e-crime.

The Target case was soon followed by the revelation that five Chinese military officers had been added to the FBI's Most Wanted List in May 2014. US officials alleged that the Chinese had engaged in cyberactivities designed to infiltrate and compromise the servers of several US corporations in order to steal industrial secrets. The charges faced by this group include conspiring to commit computer fraud, damaging computers through the transmission of code commands, and theft of trade secrets, along with a host of other indictments carrying potential life sentences. All of this reflects the vulnerability of records in this digital age and points to the potentially disastrous consequences of a full cyberattack aimed at disrupting state interests (Schmidt and Sanger, 2014). With each new attack becoming increasingly sophisticated and organized in its methodology, the line between e-crime, organized crime, and cyberterrorism is becoming increasing blurred.

Cyberterrorism has the potential to permanently disrupt the economic or environmental stability of entire nations or regions. Traditional, comparatively narrow definitions of cyberterrorism have included network attacks against **critical infrastructure sites** (telecommunications, nuclear or water treatment facilities, etc.) through distributed denial of service (DDoS) attacks and other forms of electronic sabotage. But cyberterrorism no longer needs to be tied to geopolitical or ideological motives as in the case of offline terrorist activities. It can take the form of any attempt to damage data or cause a large-scale disruption that compromises the state's ability to carry on as usual or that affects

SEARCH FOR:
FBI Most Wanted List

critical infrastructure site
Any location or asset, either physical or virtual, that is vital to the socio-economic and physical security of a nation or region, including but not limited to water treatment facilities, telecommunications centres, hospitals and health care facilities, nuclear and other power-generating facilities, airports and railway stations, and centres of major economic activity, such as stock and security exchanges.

a population's ability to obtain the necessities of life. Given our modern dependence on electronic banking and other networked systems that control everything from traffic signals to aircraft controls to life support systems in hospitals, cyberterrorism is one of the most pressing issues facing government and law enforcement today. Because national security is increasingly dependent on network systems, it is difficult to know where to draw the line between e-crime and more deliberate attempts at cyberterrorism, particularly since these network systems are increasingly being contracted out to private companies. This issue also illustrates how computer crime is difficult to classify into black-and-white categories and why 20th-century laws are often inadequate when dealing with increasingly complex and constantly changing 21st-century crimes.

Lawmakers and legal analysts, including criminologists, are tasked with defining and legislating cybercrime as a more personalized and typically less organized form of cyberterrorism. Cybercrime includes attacks that are not directed against the state or institutions for the purposes of causing large-scale harm; instead, these attacks are against individuals, who may be targeted for a variety of reasons. Like e-crime and cyberterrorism, cybercrime, as the online version of similar types of violent, intimidating, and predatory offences that exist offline, can lead to financial and personal disruption and even threaten human life. Some well-publicized suicides in Canada have brought this issue to the forefront of public consciousness and raised its importance to legislators.

One of the main advantages that researchers studying cybercrime have over those studying e-crime or cyberterrorism is access to data. Hacking and phishing activities tend to occur sporadically and employ any number of methods of covert delivery; cybercrime tends to be more conspicuous and is comparatively public in its methodology. Indeed, many forms of cybercrime, including cyberbullying, are harmful *because* they are carried out in the public eye. So to understand what brings victims and offenders together and what motivates cybercrime offenders is to understand how social media function as the new public sphere of the 21st century.

When Social Media Become Antisocial

Criminology has changed to reflect changes in society and culture. For example, green criminology (Chapter 1) has emerged as a subfield that studies environmental crime, even when the offences committed do not always reflect violations of criminal law. Cybercriminology has also emerged as a subfield of criminology, one that concerns itself with the study of crime in the context of computing and network technologies, even when these "crimes" are not necessarily codified or spelled out in the Criminal Code but instead amount to acts of deviance that clearly violate social norms. Cybercriminology may present a new opportunity for academics to apply the consensus model of crime in determining where the line between crime and deviance is drawn in online communities, which are interactive environments that tend to otherwise be comparatively permissive and informal. Specific operating systems (Windows, Mac OS, Linux, etc.) and social networks (Facebook, Instagram, Twitter, etc.) have their own distinct cultures and social norms, and this complicates blanket assumptions about computing habits and online behaviours as a whole. These differences underscore why determinations of which cyberactivities deserve to be criminalized need to look beyond the online environments themselves and begin with a broader understanding of computer technologies as being inherently criminogenic. Specifically, a more thorough understanding of the role of **technological determinism** in online offending is required when discussing cybercrime and cyberdeviance.

The term technological determinism (Ellul, 1964) helps us understand how specific technologies drive changes in culture. When the mass production of the Model T on Henry Ford's moving assembly line made cars an everyday commodity rather than a luxury, we soon saw a rise in crimes such as kidnapping and bank robbery, both of which relied on automobiles (Arntfield, 2012). Today, understanding changes in computing technologies and the rise of a networked society can help us better understand cybercrime as a response to the culture surrounding those technological changes.

The architecture of a given digital environment, and the dominant culture of that environment, both play a major role in offending. Raskauskas and Stoltz (2007) found that the most common form of electronic victimization among adolescents was text messaging via mobile device, reflecting 32.1 percent of reported cases; social media came a distant second at 15.5 percent of documented incidents. The same study found that females are more likely to be cybervictims or at least were more likely to report an incident of cybercrime—a finding replicated by Hinduja and Patchin (2009). The vast majority of publicized cases of extreme cybercrime (including cyberbullying, cyberstalking, and exploitation-related offences) seem to involve malevolent uses of social media networks. Once again, as technology evolves and cyberactivities change, the patterns and locations of offending also change. This means that timely and relevant research is needed to help advance effective legislation.

Another issue faced by criminologists studying cybercrime and also by law enforcement officials tasked with trying to enforce laws originally created for an offline, physical world is how to separate criminal behaviour that clearly violates the law from generally antisocial behaviour that is not legally prohibited. Much of the behaviour exhibited during deviant cyberactivities, including cyberbullying, has no codified definition and is more accurately defined as what Holt and Bossler (2009) broadly classify as cyberdeviance. Access to a computer and a network seems to have enabled individuals who might not otherwise show a propensity for offending to engage in behaviours that demonstrate a consistent disregard for the rights and feelings of others, as well as a general disrespect for property and the rule of law.

Social media networks are therefore prone to antisocial behaviour. In many cases this behaviour is deviant but not necessarily *criminal*. For instance, even something as harmful as cyberbullying is not necessarily illegal, and responses by authorities—if any—vary greatly by jurisdiction. Child luring, unlawfully recording and distributing copyrighted motion pictures, causing mischief to data, and electronic voyeurism are all legislated offences whose statutory wordings in the Criminal Code reflect their status as computer-mediated crimes. Cyberbullying, like cyberstalking, is more difficult to immediately link to codified offences. Similarly, in the United States, the 2009 federal case of *United States v. Lori Drew* for offences alleged to have been committed under the Computer Fraud and Abuse Act confirmed that violating a

technological determinism
The theory that technological innovation is the key driving force behind changes in society and that new technologies shape culture and human behaviour, not vice versa.

private website's terms of use, now matter how egregious, is cyberdeviance and does not in itself constitute criminal culpability (Zetter, 2009). In that case, Lori Drew created a fictitious MySpace account to infiltrate the online profile of a 13-year-old female named Megan Meier. Drew's own teenaged daughter and Meier had been friends and had attended school together in St. Charles County, Missouri. By the fall of 2006, Drew was concerned that Meier was spreading rumours about her daughter. Using the screen name Josh Evans, Drew posed as a teenaged boy and sent flirtatious messages to Meier's MySpace account in order to get her attention and earn her trust. When the interactions failed to turn up any real evidence that Meier was slandering Drew's daughter, a message was nonetheless sent to Meier from the Josh Evans account telling her the world would be better off without her. Other MySpace users saw this message and followed suit, engaging in what is now identified as **cybermobbing**, or the mass cyberbullying of a single victim by large numbers of users who may or may not know one another. After Meier received a flurry of these spiteful messages, she hanged herself in her bedroom closet. She was found dead by her mother. At a trial in November 2008, the prosecution was only able to secure a misdemeanour conviction against Drew for violating the Computer Fraud and Abuse Act by creating the fake MySpace account. This conviction was later vacated in August 2009. Drew was acquitted when it was ruled that violating MySpace's terms of use in creating the account did not meet the standard required to justify a criminal prosecution, regardless of how serious the eventual outcome of that violation—in this case, the counselled suicide of a young girl. Do the international implications of the *Lori Drew* case coupled with the ongoing lack of a specific statute criminalizing cyberbullying mean that cyberbullying is therefore not cybercrime by definition? Does the phenomenon of cyberbullying merit analysis by criminologists, or is it instead a social problem that is better addressed by schools and families in terms of prevention and awareness? What do you think?

SEARCH FOR:
CyberSCAN

cybermobbing
A group activity that in effect merges cyberdeviance with learning theories of crime and interactional models of offending. That is, many disparate users (a mob) within a virtual space follow the lead of a cyberbully and publicly gang up on a single victim by sending harassing and humiliating communications.

FOCUS

Box 18.1

A SNAPSHOT OF CYBERBULLYING IN CANADA

Following a tragic incident in early 2013, the province of Nova Scotia introduced a new Cyber Safety Act in August 2013. As the first legislation of its kind in Canada, the Cyber Safety Act mandated the formation of the CyberSCAN Unit as its provincial investigative arm. The CyberSCAN Unit has no authority to lay charges but can refer files to the police for criminal sanctions. The unit is staffed by civilians, but it has broad search and seizure powers relating to personal electronic information and devices. Most importantly, the unit has made the first attempt to provide a legislative definition of cyberbullying in Canada. The operating definition of cyberbullying used by CyberSCAN when initiating their investigations is as follows:

Any electronic communication through the use of technology including, without limiting the generality of the foregoing, computers, other electronic devices, social networks, text messaging, instant messaging, websites and electronic mail, typically repeated or with continuing effect, that is intended or ought reasonably [be] expected to cause fear, intimidation, humiliation, distress or other damage or harm to another person's health, emotional wellbeing, self-esteem or reputation, and includes assisting or encouraging such communication in any way. (CyberSCAN, 2014)

This definition of cyberbullying does not change the law in Canada, nor does it expand the powers of police to lay charges or of judges to hand down sentences. In fact, it changes things very little except to provide a guideline for other jurisdictions in terms of establishing investigative standards and mandates. Whether a federal cyberbullying law will ultimately stem from this definition will depend in part on the perceived successes of the CyberSCAN Unit. It will also depend on whether the use of this interpretative definition to obtain personal information on suspected cyberbullies without a court order—including both Internet protocol (IP) and home address information—will withstand challenges under the Charter of Rights and Freedoms. A unanimous Supreme Court ruling in June 2014 declared that police will henceforth require a search warrant under section 487 of the Criminal Code merely to obtain subscriber names from IP addresses associated with trafficking in child pornography and with other serious criminal offences online. This decision suggests that the pendulum is actually swinging toward protecting privacy interests rather than violating privacy rights in order to make it easier to apprehend offenders. Cyberbullying is becoming a major public concern, but at the same time, demands for increased privacy measures are impeding efforts to identify predators. Thus the coming few years are likely to see further wrangling in the courts in the search for a middle ground between safety and privacy.

Thinkstock

QUESTIONS FOR CRITICAL THINKING

1. Many crimes are never reported to police—in Chapter 4 you learned about the dark figure of crime. Most cases of cyberbullying also go unreported, and many other cybercrimes are going undetected online. What other types of cybercrimes do you think are most likely to be unreported? Is the dark figure of crime even more prevalent in digital environments?

2. The 2009 Ontario Superior Court case *R. v. Polius* ruled that smartphones and other digital devices are more than just communication technologies, likening them to the modern equivalent of personal diaries. If this is the case, why do some users feel compelled to share so much personal information with strangers using these devices and through online forums? Is there a link between exercising common sense and informational self-restraint and avoiding being a victim of cyberbullying?

3. In keeping with the routine activities theory of crime, are Canadian critical infrastructure sites—as evidenced by the 2014 Canada Revenue Agency security breach—the equivalent of "soft targets" for cyberterrorists, given the lack of consolidated enforcement resources and lack of codified cyber-terrorism and cybercrime laws (as seen in the United States)?

Cyberdeviance & Digital Paraphilia

The relationship between social media and cyberdeviance suggests that a number of social networking sites taken for granted as extensions of the public sphere may actually conform to what Durkin (2009) and Roberts and Hunt (2012, 757) have called "deviant cybercommunities." This is facilitated by the fact that social media can be accessed instantaneously, asynchronously, and in many cases anonymously. **Deviant cybercommunities** consist of subcultural networks made up of people who seek to circumvent the customary user experiences of these sites, and who seek to exploit weaknesses and vulnerabilities, or what are sometimes called "soft targets." Deviant cybercommunities can in turn be identified by their paradoxical architecture. They serve a "social" purpose but they also intensify deviant and anti-social impulses among some users (Durkin, 2007; Quayle and Taylor, 2002; Quinn and Forsyth 2005).

A traditional approach to identifying specific typologies of deviance, whether criminal or noncriminal, is through the categorization of what are known as **paraphilias**. Paraphilias are deep-seated psychological or sexual drives that are reflected in unusual or bizarre relationships to objects or circumstances. Over 500 paraphilia types and subtypes have been identified, and have been itemized by severity, based on the threat to public safety posed by these deviant behaviours (Aggrawal, 2008). While not all acts of cyberdeviance explicitly involve a sexual motivation, a review of some of the more common paraphilias suggests that cyberdeviance often encompasses one or more of the traditional offline paraphilias. We can compare offline paraphilias with similar online behaviours that range from noncriminal acts of cyberdeviance to cybercrimes:

Erotomania

Erotomania is the phenomenon of a person developing an unfounded infatuation or imagined relationship with a person unknown or barely known to them (Hickey, 2010, 178).

Offline

Erotomania is commonly associated with stranger-obsessional stalking, and typically involves behaviour such as sending letters, gifts, and flowers or making hang-up phone calls. Generally considered more of a nuisance and an annoyance than a genuine threat to safety, and generally noncriminal in nature.

Online

The vast majority of cyberstalking incidents involve strangers or casual or passing acquaintances (Freiberger, 2008). This is because the Internet is not

deviant cybercommunity An online community whose culture and customs would be classified as deviant and delinquent if exported to the offline world, but in which socially abnormal behaviour is accepted and even endorsed in the context of the given digital environment.

paraphilia The use of unusual objects, situations, processes, or people to obtain sexual excitement and channel obsessions or fantasies that are inherently deviant and either prohibited by law (criminal paraphilia) or deemed taboo and forbidden by conventional society.

limited to any particular geographic location and because erotomania is stranger-obsessional in nature. It can include the compulsive viewing of social media profiles and images (known as "creeping" in the parlance of Web 2.0), creating fake social media accounts in order to gain a target's trust and initiate a dialogue, and repeatedly performing search engine queries of a target to find personal information or to view photographs. In some cases it may also include sending e-mails, text messages, or social media messages to a mobile device, often anonymously.

Exhibitionism

The unsolicited practice of exposing one's body in explicit or suggestive fashion to captive audiences or nonconsenting observers for attention, personal gratification, arousal, or excitement or to project power is referred to as *exhibitionism*. (Hickey, 2010, 178).

Offline

Exhibitionism is commonly associated with crimes such as committing an indecent act or causing a disturbance by indecent exhibition. Acts of exhibitionism can also be more subtle and noncriminal, such as undressing in front of open windows or dressing inappropriately for certain social contexts.

Online

The practice of taking digital self-portraits (selfies), is now commonplace. However, it is sexting (the sending of sexual images sent by text message) that is currently at the forefront of debates about cybercrime and cyberdeviance. Typically, sexting consists of sending inappropriate images of oneself to others, often without prompting and without consent (Rufo, 2012). As in its offline version, this can be done for attention, personal gratification, arousal, excitement, to project power, or to frighten. In 2014, the federal Justice Minister introduced legislation that would make nonconsensual trafficking in intimate images a criminal offence (Department of Justice, 2014a).

Scopophilia or Voyeurism

The terms *scopophilia* and *voyeurism* refer to a paraphilia that involves the sense of arousal, excitement, and power that a person obtains by secretly watching others without their consent, usually in a private or intimate setting (Hickey, 2010, 179). The discreet observation of people in nonintimate, day-to-day settings is a paraphilic subtype known as cryptoscopophilia (Aggrawal, 2008).

Offline

This paraphilia was made infamous through films like *Psycho* (1960) and the lesser-known *Peeping Tom* (1960), but has only recently come to be understood as extremely dangerous behaviour if left to escalate. Voyeurs of a criminal nature have historically been prosecuted under prowling and trespass-by-night sections of the Criminal Code, but these sections were treated as minor (summary) offences until 2013, when they were changed to hybrid offences, reflecting the fact that the potential seriousness of this paraphilia was for many years not taken seriously (Kaplan and Krueger, 1997).

Online

Since 2002, voyeurism—now recognized as symptomatic of one or more paraphilias and as a serious forms of offending—has become a codified offence specifically in the context of cybercrime (Department of Justice, 2014b). The offence of voyeurism includes the use of electronic devices for the surreptitious and sexually motivated recording or photographing of unknown and nonconsenting individuals, whether or not the there is a reasonable expectation of privacy.

Scatologia

The paraphilia referred to as *scatologia* involves an individual making obscene, threatening, or otherwise menacing (open-line heavy breathing, etc.) phone calls to either random or specific victims as means of self-gratification and to project power and dominance by causing fear and anxiety (Hickey, 2010, 179). Historically known as telephone scatologia, this paraphilia is directly linked to technology and is a good example of the connection between paraphilia and technological determinism.

Offline

In the days when people had only landline telephones, Dalby (1988) and Saunders and Awad (1991) postulated that scatologia was simply a technologically mediated variant of exhibitionism. As a form of offending made possible by the instantaneity and anonymity of calls placed to unsuspecting victims, the offences of harassing telephone calls and obscene telephone calls have long been prohibited by the Criminal Code, though they are now much less common because of the development of new technologies, including call tracing and the Internet.

Online

Few paraphilias underscore the role of technology in offending more than scatologia. Now that the telephone has been largely replaced by electronic or other preferred and virtual forms of communication—including communication between smartphones, which more closely approximates the interface of a computer than a traditional landline telephone—cyberbullying, cybermobbing, and Internet trolling might all be said to constitute the *new* scatologia. In telephone scatologia, specific legislation has historically reflected that the telephone is an instrument for offending; no such laws exist with respect to analogous cyberactivities even though the underlying motives and methods are largely identical. In fact, three of the historically identified "classes" of telephone scatologists—the ingratiating seducer, the annoyance creator, and the panic creator (Aggrawal, 2008, 339)—are ideally suited for online forums, where it seems that activities like trolling and cyberbullying can satisfy the offender's compulsions much more effortlessly, engaging multiple victims at one time and with essentially guaranteed anonymity.

New Media, New Crimes: A Changing Technological Landscape

Some cyberactivities that simultaneously qualify as both cyberdeviance and cybercrime reflect identified paraphilias more than others, and also suggest more obvious correlations between offline and online offending. Pedophilia as both a paraphilia and a precipitator of child luring and child pornography is an obvious example. Another is necrophilia, or an attraction to corpses. A notorious case of the latter involved New York Police Department patrol officer Gilberto Valle, the so-called "Cannibal Cop," who in March 2013 was convicted of using chat rooms on fetish Internet sites to conspire to kidnap, torture, and commit necrophilic and cannibalistic acts against women, including his own wife and a teenaged neighbour. In 2014, Valle's conviction was overturned by a judge, who accepted the argument that Valle's actions online only represented role playing rather than an actual attempt to commit a crime.

In looking at scatologia as the progenitor of what now amounts to an electronic version of anonymous telephonic harassment, we find that the connections are not as well understood. This is less a criminological or psychopathological concern than a legal one relating to how best to codify terms like "trolling" and "bullying" as types of scatologia, especially given that these terms are highly interpretative and often mean different things to different people.

The lack of progress in combating, legislating, or even reaching a national consensus on cyberbullying is partly due the fact that most cyberbullying almost certainly goes unreported (Hinduja and Patchin, 2008). Perhaps this is because of the stigma attached to being a victim of cyberbullying, in much the same way that stigma is attached to victims of offline, physical bullying. To date, the identification and classification of cyberbullying has relied by default on now-dated criminological research on the causes and consequences of physical or "corporeal" bullying as first defined by Olweus (1993). By this definition, such bullying is a frequently adolescent phenomenon that manifests itself as the causing of unprovoked and sadistic physical harm and the repeated assertion of real or perceived physical and social power differentials.

To gain a better understanding of cyberbullying and the motives of online offenders, we may need to step outside traditional criminology and draw from terminologies used in other fields such as digital media and communications, which also lay claim to the study of cybercrime and cyberdeviance (Arntfield, 2014). One term often used to describe post-Web 2.0 spaces is *new media*. Note, however, that the "new" in new media is not a temporal distinction for denoting the vintage of a particular technology or media product; rather, new media describes any traditional, tactile media that now exist in newly computer-compatible forms and that rely on digitization processes for their creation, manipulation, or dissemination (Manovich, 2001). The shift from the telephone to Internet or networked-mobile devices is one such example.

The relationship between new media and earlier, long-established offences is sometimes straightforward (e.g., possessing digital versions of prohibited analogue images such as child pornography). But other offences, including electronic manifestations of identified paraphilias, have no clear offline referent. They are therefore much more difficult to define and even more difficult to legislate. Because technology changes at a rate far faster than bills can be pushed through Parliament and laws enacted or changed, the relationship between cybercrime and new media remains poorly understood. As the technological landscape continues to evolve and as new devices and operating systems are deployed and become popularized, the law is bound to be in a perpetual state of playing catch-up.

FOCUS

Box 18.2

CORPUS LINGUISTICS &CYBERDEVIANCE: INDEXING THE CYBERBULLY'S VOCABULARY

In the winter of 2014, the *Cyberbullying Reporter,* an open-access site created to collect samples of text appearing in cases of electronic harassment, was launched at Western University as part of a national research initiative on forensic linguistics and cyberbullying. The purpose of collecting these samples was to build a sizable list of terms (known as a corpus) and investigate the recurrence of specific keywords and word groupings with respect to cyberbullying. Unlike traditional bullying, cyberbullying requires no direct or real-time contact and is carried out largely through written content. This written content includes both words and characters, such as numerals and emoticons used to complement or aggravate those words. The study is concerned with applying **critical discourse analysis** (CDA) to aggressive or antisocial online exchanges to try to identify a bullying lexicon (word stock) common to cases of electronic harassment. Because cyberbullying relies predominantly on words to victimize, each act of cyberbullying requires that perpetrators select particular words as mechanisms of offending. These words reflect specific social symbols that have meaning beyond the digital space in which they appear (Mautner, 2009, 33). The result is a written transcript of delinquent social actions that allows researchers to identify points in common among different sets of victims connected by common bullying terms online. Unlike in cases of scatologia, where victims might be bullied, harassed, or intimidated via telephone for the gratification of the offender, the fact that these statements are now in written form enables a large-scale analysis of the relationship between word distinctions and cyberdeviance using a methodology known as **corpus linguistics**.

Corpus linguistics was first employed as a research method by Kucera (1967) at Brown University in Providence, Rhode Island. Kucera conducted a computer-based analysis of the state of everyday English as gleaned from years' worth of media articles and other field texts—an archive ultimately known as the Brown Corpus. The Brown Corpus was a compilation of millions of pieces of written text drawn from a wide array of public sources. It enabled the identification of patterns in language and of how society reserved certain words for certain situations, or paired certain words in specific contexts. Since that time, no known study has applied corpus linguistics to the study of language as it exists in purely digital environments, where nearly all forms of communication necessitate putting words into writing. This includes cases of cyberbullying, cybermobbing, trolling, and other forms of electronic harassment that rely purely on word choices to commit symbolic acts of violence.

The preliminary stages of this research are focused on collecting text samples in known or suspected cases of cyberbullying; the ultimate goal is to identify how specific digital environments shape the harmfulness of bullying content. For instance, how do personal and discreet inbox messages yield a corpus of terms that is distinct from more public acts of cyberbullying, which are intended to also be read by third parties (such as on a public message board) and thereby intensify victimization? The cyberbullying lexicon (the working vocabulary employed by offenders) being generated from this corpus should help develop legislation on cyberbullying prevention and enforcement.

The study is also expected to help identify a baseline vernacular to cyberbullying that reflects the "average" degree of aggression in terms of content. This will help generate a consensus on where to draw the line between deviance and criminality when it comes to harassing or scatologic cyberactivities. While the medium and the method may be new, the reality is that Canadian lawmakers and courts have long had to determine thresholds for criminality with respect to written content that falls outside the scope of freedom of expression as guaranteed by section 2(b) of the Charter of Rights and Freedoms. In fact, section 163.1(1)(b) of the Criminal Code specifies that child pornography need not consist solely of images; it can also consist of prohibited written materials (stories, poems, diaries, etc.) that contain words and phrases that sexualize children and are thus obscene. Similarly, courts long had to weigh at what point spoken content delivered through unwanted and repetitive telephone calls crosses the line between deviant and criminal. To this point, the linguistic content of cyberbullying and its various secondary forms of cyberdeviance has not yet been closely scrutinized.

The preliminary data suggest there may be a strong paraphilic component to cyberbullying. This can include scatologia, as well as other paraphilias not yet identified but for which—at least in a digital forum—the use of the written word is integral to the commission of any offence. It is probably not coincidental that some of the best-known and most tragic cases of cyberbullying in Canada in recent years have been closely associated with pedophilic activities. These include the case of Rehtaeh Parsons (cited earlier in this chapter) as well as that of Amanda Todd, whose suicide in October 2012 touched off an international debate about the damage caused by cyberbullying. In April 2014, nearly two years after Todd's death, a 35-year-old Dutchman named Aydin Coban was arrested and charged

(continued)

with a number of crimes, including child pornography offences related to his harassment and blackmailing of the B.C. teen as well as other victims around the world, whom he targeted through Internet chat rooms (Hootsen and Rovers, 2014). Will an examination of Coban's writings to his victims help identify a common method or pattern among cyberdeviants and help identify harmful material before more victims are targeted? Do new media and cases like those of Todd and Parsons allow us to identify the link between language and paraphilia for the first time? What do you think?

Cybercrime and Routine Activities Theory Online

Digitization provides a permanent electronic transcript of deviant cyberactivities and allows for new insights into both online and offline offending as well as the relationship between the two. Yet while changes in technology and in the way harmful content is delivered explain *how* acts of cyberbullying are carried out, they do not explain *why*. Drawing on Cohen and Felson's (1979) routine activities theory (Chapter 15), certain correlates among victims can be identified with respect to how much time they spend engaged in cyberactivities and to the nature of the virtual environments they choose to visit. For instance, an Australian study suggested that an excessive number of Facebook "likes" associated with singular profiles and other forms of oversharing is inversely related to happiness and confidence. Also, users who post excessive personal details are likely struggling to find personal connections and are trying to initiate conversations because of their social alienation (Sankin, 2014). This is an important predictor of victimization using the routine activities approach, in that users already predisposed to self-esteem issues and emotional distress tend to have fewer privacy safeguards in place and may thus reveal themselves as soft targets to online predators looking to exploit the personal information being disclosed by the potential victim. Knowledge of these types of online behaviours might help us determine why certain victims are selected for cyberbullying and also why victim responses vary so widely, ranging from indifference in cases where victims are also bullied offline (Olweus, 2012), to extreme responses such as self-harm, emotional despair, and even suicide.

Research on cyberbullying and cybervictimology must therefore initiate a critical reassessment of social media as a routine activity. This needs to include the assessment of risk. Victims might then be classified according to a continuum of risk tolerance, ranging from infrequent users to frequent users whose communications tend to occur in or near real-time. These frequent users will have a social media and digital experience defined by negligible lapses between the delivery and the reception of aggressive or harassing communication, compared to less frequent users who only sporadically and sparingly access these same digital environments and who are less invested in what occurs in them. In this context, the duration and frequency of use—or more accurately, the inability or unwillingness to disengage from these environments—might be seen as an increased tolerance for risk among cybervictims. It therefore stands to reason that opting into a digital lifestyle where social media pervade everyday functioning, allowing all digital communications to push to a mobile device that is always present versus limiting cyberactivities to the home or workplace, creates a disproportionate risk based on frequency of routine use alone.

critical discourse analysis
A method used in linguistic analysis in which the totality of communicative exchanges (discourse) is examined in the context of the social, political, or cultural power held between sender and receiver.

corpus linguistics
The study of a language or dialect by collecting everyday samples of text, which comprise a body of keywords (a corpora), which can then be used to gauge long-term trends and patterns in communication.

SEARCH FOR:
Cyberbullying Reporter

Digital media offer cyberbullies access to users who would normally not have direct face-to-face contact with them. As Hayward (2012) has noted, the Internet—and by extension digital culture generally—has broken down traditional barriers between life stages and led to generational and demographic confusion, thus bringing about unforeseen online collisions between groups of people with different value systems. Social media, from their earliest versions (ICQ, MSN Messenger, MySpace, etc.) to the current menu of customizable and multiplatform networks, inevitably entail a certain degree of risk-taking by all users that elevates a baseline *assumed* risk. These are risks not normally seen in offline contexts, where offenders are much less anonymous and where it would be largely impossible for a 50-year-old male pedophile, for instance, to masquerade as a teenaged girl to win over the trust of his victim. Such deceptions are, unfortunately, rather common online.

Victims are targeted by online offenders in various ways, but bullying is facilitated by digital environments that offer little in the way of suitable guardianship. These environments allow cyberbullies, trollers, and other cyberdeviants to identify victims who can predictably be found operating there, and in circumstances where they are both vulnerable and accessible. A bully will wait at the edge of an unlit and isolated footpath that serves as a customary route home from school for suitable offline targets; in much the same way, certain digital environments enable predatory violators to watch, wait, and take advantage of specific routines as they target victims online. As with the perilous but more direct or convenient route home that may bring them in contact with a predator, victims ultimately weigh the risks versus the rewards of certain routes and routines and then make decisions based on their individual tolerance for those risks. This generates the question: Who should be the guardians? As the legal and philosophical debate rages on with respect to whose responsibility it is to police and regulate these virtual spaces—and ultimately who has the authority to do so—it seems there are no clear answers.

In late 2012, Canadians generally rejected the idea that the suitable guardian in the Wild West of the Internet should be police officers or other law enforcement agents. Offline, people apparently want a police officer on every street corner to deter motivated offenders; online, it seems quite the opposite is true. Following the Council of Europe Convention on Cybercrime in 2001, the Canadian government tabled Bill C-30, which would have significantly expanded the powers of police to conduct online surveillance and ostensibly act as guardians of virtual spaces. The same bill included a requirement that technology providers relinquish Internet Protocol (IP) addresses and other personal information without a search warrant, production order, or other court order during the early stages of criminal or regulatory investigations (Press, 2012). By February 2013, Bill C-30 in its original form had been scrapped, much to the delight of the federal Privacy Commissioner and many Canadians. With some aspects of the original bill being preserved in a subsequent rewriting, the future of guardianship on the Internet is now difficult to predict, and so is what that guardianship might look like and how cyberdeviance will be defined and monitored—if at all. In moving forward, criminologists may have an increasing role to play in helping moderate this socio-legal debate amid an ever-changing technological and cultural landscape ripe with risks.

SEARCH FOR:
Bill C-30 Canada

QUESTIONS FOR CRITICAL THINKING

1. Does the culture of social media and the emergence of deviant cybercommunities as mainstream places of online assembly lead to experimentation with delinquent behaviours and paraphilias that might not otherwise occur offline? If so, are social media sites, despite some of their redeeming qualities, criminogenic by design?

2. Why is there so much disparity between citizens' expectations of a public police presence in the offline world, and extensions of those same public spaces in the online world, where it seems that Canadians want to police themselves and exercise their own informal social controls? What is it about virtual environments and peoples' activities there that make them so wary of monitoring initiatives, even if such initiatives might help protect potential victims and prevent crime? Should privacy concerns outweigh concerns about harmful online behaviour?

3. If acts of cyberbullying and Internet trolling often have paraphilic and scatologic elements, should these deviant cyberactivities be made a priority with respect to Criminal Code amendments, much like voyeurism was codified as a new offence?

● Summary

- Cybercrime is a diverse area of study that remains in its adolescence. There is a long way to go before lawmakers and criminologists reach a middle ground. As technologies change and technology providers become increasingly invested as stakeholders in the investigative and legislative process, the courts will be tasked with drawing the line between cyberdeviance and cybercrime. They will need to find ways to balance privacy interests and freedom of expression with the rights of victims and protection of the public.

- Cyberbullying as a derivative of both cybercrime and cyberdeviance is a socially and politically charged issue but has proven difficult to define and legislate, in part because it is so open to interpretation. While there is a move afoot to amend laws to prohibit trafficking in "intimate images" (sexting), little has been done to address the fact that all documented cases of cyberbullying also involve the exchange of words and written communications that are nearly impossible to police consistently.

- Beyond the linguistic elements in cyberbullying that equate it with other criminal offences encompassing obscene or offensive written content (child pornography), there appears to be a paraphilic element or etiology to cybercrime in its various forms. This suggests that offences like cyberbullying and Internet trolling may represent a new medium or electronic extension of scatologia, a paraphilia that previously relied on the anonymity and distance afforded by the landline telephone.

- Applying the routine activities model of crime to virtual environments, specifically in relation to the cyberactivities of both online predators and victims, a useful starting point might be to gain a better understanding of how specific activities and environments pose greater risks than others, and how and why certain victims are targeted in those environments.

- Despite the high-profile and tragic suicides in the wake of prolonged instances of cyberbullying, cybermobbing, and other forms of electronic harassment that blur the line between cyberdeviance and cybercrime, Canadians remain conflicted in their opinions regarding the role of the police and lawmakers in regulating online behaviour. Cyberbullying in particular is bound to be a conduit for ongoing debates about how to balance privacy with public safety in a digital world.

NET WORK

Are you interested in how the cyberbullying and Internet trolling study at Western University works? Do you perhaps want to participate? Are you curious about how samples of online text are collected and how a corpus is assembled? Do you want to learn more about cyberbullying prevention and what resources are available to victims, parents, educators, and prevention advocates? Visit http://cyberbullyingreporter.com.

Using the Google search terms found throughout this chapter, see if you can answer the following questions:

1. How should the federal government approach redrafting Bill C-30, and how should lawmakers determine the best method for balancing privacy with pubic safety as cyberactivities continue to pervade all elements of life? Do cybercrime, cyberbullying, and Internet policing merit a national referendum?

2. Describe the advantages and disadvantages of having a cyberbullying task force comprised of civilian investigators as opposed to sworn police officers. Does this reflect the fact that because cyberbullying is not a codified cybercrime, it doesn't merit police resources?

Glossary

absolute deprivation
The inability to sustain oneself physically and materially. *p. 293*

actuarial
Refers to statistical calculations of risk across time and groups. *p. 336*

actus reus
All the elements contained in the definition of a criminal offence, other than the mental elements (*mens rea*). *p. 63*

administrative record
A collection of information about individual cases. *p. 94*

advisor system
An extension of the self- or kin-based redress system of dispute settlement. It involves—albeit in a relatively passive way—a third-party decision maker (or makers). *p. 36*

anomie
A concept developed by Émile Durkheim (1858–1917) to describe an absence of clear societal norms and values. Robert Merton (1910–2003) used the term more narrowly to refer to a situation in which people would adopt deviant means to achieve goals beyond their means. *p. 281*

Antisocial Personality Disorder
A personality disorder that involves disregard for the rights of others as well as impulsive, irresponsible, and aggressive behaviour. *p. 262*

assumption of discriminating traits
The view that offenders are distinguished from non-offenders by, for example, their high levels of impulsiveness and aggression. *p. 248*

assumption of offender deficit
The view that offenders who break the law have some psychological deficit that distinguishes them from normal, law-abiding citizens. *p. 248*

atavism
Cesare Lombroso believed that some people were born criminals. These born criminals were throwbacks to an earlier stage of evolution—atavisms—and were morally inferior to the rest of the population. Lombroso's research focused on physical differences (stigmata) that could be used to identify atavisms. *p. 237*

attachment
The degree to which an individual has affective ties to other persons. One of the social bonds in Hirschi's theory. *p. 384*

attentive gaze
A methodological requirement that researchers immerse themselves where crime occurs in the everyday world in order to better understand the ways in which crime is experienced and interpreted by individuals. *p. 341*

autonomic reactivity
A measurement of the extent to which an individual's physical organism reacts to external stimuli. *p. 259*

belief
The degree to which an individual believes in conventional values, morality, and the legitimacy of law. One of Hirschi's social bonds. *p. 385*

bourgeois class
The term bourgeois class, or bourgeoisie, was used by Marx to refer to the capitalist or ruling class in modern societies. *p. 41*

broken windows policing
Just as houses with broken windows indicate that nobody cares about the neighbourhood, proponents of this policing style feel that tolerating minor misbehaviour will mean that residents will be afraid to use their streets. They feel that police should quickly deal with minor incivilities such as panhandling, vandalism, and other behaviours that contribute to fear of crime. Critics feel this policing style potentially discriminates against the poor. *p. 351*

capital
The primary field of activity for state or government actors, as well as those who are funded by the government, and where these actors compete to define and shape government resources and responsibilities. *p. 342*

Canadian Centre for Justice Statistics
A division of Statistics Canada, formed in 1981, with a mandate to collect national data on crime and justice. *p. 96*

carceral-assistential mesh
Under neoliberalism, this is a mode of "double regulation" whereby the right (e.g., prisons) and left (e.g., social welfare) jointly function to punish and discipline the poor rather than offering rehabilitation and care. *p. 344*

career
In common use, this refers to the sequence of stages through which people in a particular occupational sector move during the course of their employment. It has also been applied to the various stages of personal involvement with criminal activity. *p. 359*

career contingency
An unintended event, process, or situation that occurs by chance, beyond the control of the person pursuing the career. *p. 367*

Charter
The Canadian Charter of Rights and Freedoms, enacted by the Canada Act 1982 (UK) c. 11 *p. 61*

chiefdoms
Geopolitical communities ruled by a chief. A chief was the highest political authority in the community and was recognized as having the ultimate power in settling disputes. The chief's decisions were binding, though others may have been required to enforce them. Chieftainships tended to be based on heredity or supernatural knowledge and, chiefs were usually rich men from influential families. *p. 38*

class conflict theory
Laws are passed by members of the ruling class in order to maintain their privileged position by keeping the common people under control. *p. 19*

classical conditioning
A basic form of learning whereby a neutral stimulus is paired with another stimulus that naturally elicits a certain response; the neutral stimulus comes to elicit the same response as the stimulus that automatically elicits the response. *p. 256*

Classical School
Considered to be the first formal school of criminology, Classical criminology is associated with 18th- and early 19th-century reforms to the administration of justice and the prison system. Associated with authors such as Cesare Beccaria (1738–1794), Jeremy Bentham (1748–1832), Samuel Romilly (1757–1818), and others, this school brought the emerging philosophy of liberalism and utilitarianism to the justice system, advocating principles of rights, fairness, and due process in place of retribution, arbitrariness, and brutality. *p. 228*

collective solidarity
A state of social bonding or interdependency that rests on similarity of beliefs and values, shared activities, and ties of kinship and cooperation among members of a community. *p. 33*

commitment
The degree to which an individual pursues conventional goals. One of the social bonds in Hirschi's theory. *p. 384*

common law
The common law tradition found in English Canada derives from feudal England, where it had become the practice for the king to resolve disputes in accordance with local custom. Customs that were recognized throughout the country were called common custom, and decisions made by the king and by subsequent courts set up to settle disputes became known as *common law*. Common law is the body of judge-made law that has evolved in areas not covered by legislation. *pp. 40, 60*

community psychology
A perspective that analyzes social problems, including crime, as largely a product of orga-

nizational and institutional characteristics of society. It is closely related to sociology. *p. 249*

compensation from the state
Victims of crimes who suffered physical or other injuries may apply to an agency in most provinces to receive lump sum or monthly payments according to provincial legislation. *p. 192*

conduct norms
Specific rules or norms of appropriate behaviour generally agreed upon by members of the social group to whom the behavioural norms apply. *p. 304*

conflict perspective
The focus on the inherent divisions of societies based on social inequality and the way these social divisions give rise to different and competing interests, the central assumption being that social structures and cultural ideas tend to reflect the interests of only some members of society rather than society as a whole. *p. 280*

consensus perspective
Also known as functionalism, this perspective assumes that societies have a tendency to maintain themselves in a state of relative equilibrium through mutually adjustive and supportive interaction of their principal institutions. It also assumes that effective maintenance of society is in the common interest of all its members. *p. 280*

consensus theory
Laws represent the agreement of most of the people in society that certain acts should be prohibited by the criminal law. *p. 19*

conservative approach
An approach that understands "difference" between men and women as biologically based sex differences. Women are viewed as "naturally" inferior or unequal to men. *p. 156*

conspiracy
An agreement by two or more persons to commit a criminal offence. *p. 75*

continuance commitment
Adherence to a criminal or other identity arising from the unattractiveness or unavailability of alternative lifestyles. *p. 367*

corpus linguistics
The study of a language or dialect by collecting everyday samples of text, which comprise a body of keywords (a corpora), which can then be used to gauge long-term trends and patterns in communication. *p. 511*

correlate
A phenomenon that accompanies another phenomenon and is related in some way to it. *p. 119*

counselling
Procuring, soliciting, or inciting another person to commit a crime. *p. 73*

counting procedure
A consensus on how to count units and data elements. *p. 94*

crime
Conduct that is prohibited by law and that is subject to a penal sanction (such as imprisonment or a fine). *p. 55*

crime prevention through social development
An approach to crime prevention that focuses on reducing the number of motivated offenders by changing the social environment. *p. 426*

crime rate
Criminologists calculate crime rates (or rates of incarceration, conviction, or recidivism) by dividing the amount of crime by the population size and multiplying by 100,000. This produces the standard rate per 100,000; occasionally it is useful to calculate a rate per million or some other figure when looking at less frequently occurring offences. *p. 91*

criminal attempt
A criminal attempt occurs when an individual does—or omits to do—anything for the purpose of carrying out a previously formed intention to commit a crime. The conduct in question must constitute a substantial step towards the completion of the crime that is intended. *p. 75*

criminal identity
This social category, imposed by the community, correctly or incorrectly defines an individual as a particular type of criminal. The identity pervasively shapes his or her

social interactions with others. This concept is similar to master status. *p. 370*

criminal law

A body of jurisprudence that includes the definition of various crimes, the specification of various penalties, a set of general principles concerning criminal responsibility, and a series of defences to a criminal charge. *p. 57*

criminal procedure

A body of legislation that specifies the procedures to be followed in the prosecution of a criminal case and that defines the nature and scope of the powers of criminal justice officials. *p. 59*

criminogenic market structure

An economic market that is structured in such a way that it tends to produce criminal behaviour. *p. 478*

criminology

The body of knowledge regarding crime as a social phenomenon. It includes the processes of making laws, breaking laws, and reacting to the breaking of laws. Its objective is the development of a body of general and verified principles and of other types of knowledge regarding this process of law, crime, and treatment. *p. 9*

crisis of legitimacy

A situation where the state no longer maintains the authority to govern. Sometimes referred to as a legitimation crisis. A number of factors can contribute to such a crisis, for which there are only two possible resolutions: (a) the state regains legitimacy, or (b) a new governing body is instated. *p. 47*

critical discourse analysis

A method used in linguistic analysis in which the totality of communicative exchanges (discourse) is examined in the context of the social, political, or cultural power held between sender and receiver. *p. 511*

critical infrastructure site

Any location or asset, either physical or virtual, that is vital to the socio-economic and physical security of a nation or region, including but not limited to water treatment facilities, telecommunications centres, hospitals and health care facilities, nuclear and other power-generating facilities, airports and railway stations, and centres of major economic activity, such as stock and security exchanges. *p. 503*

cultural conflict

A theory that attempts to explain certain types of criminal behaviour as resulting from a conflict between the conduct norms of divergent cultural groups. *p. 304*

cultural construction

A perspective on a subject that is shaped by cultural assumptions rather than having a natural or objective basis. *p. 167*

culturally prescribed aspiration

A rejection of the notion that aspirations are entirely self-created; rather, they are defined by culture and transmitted by other members of the society. *p. 282*

cyberactivities

Any number of tasks carried out through the use of a computer and a network connection, including but not limited to Internet browsing, e-mail correspondence, online banking, interactive gaming, media downloading or uploading, the use of file transfer protocols, and accessing social media platforms. *p. 501*

cybercrime

Illegal acts in which a computer and a network are central to committing a crime and are also the targets of the crime. *p. 441*

cybermobbing

A group activity that in effect merges cyberdeviance with learning theories of crime and interactional models of offending. That is, many disparate users (a mob) within a virtual space follow the lead of a cyberbully and publicly gang up on a single victim by sending harassing and humiliating communications. *p. 506*

dangerous knowledge

A form of knowledge that leaves no concept, notion, or idea untouched by criticism. To achieve this relentlessly critical stance, cultural criminologists often turn to diverse sources of information (e.g., novels and street-level observation) as means to reveal alternative perspectives that might shake the foundations of our taken-for-granted assumptions about crime. *p. 341*

dark figure of crime

The amount of crime that is unreported or unknown. *p. 99*

data element

Specification about what, exactly is to be collected. *p. 94*

debit card fraud

Debit card fraud entails a four-step process: (1) create fake debit cards, (2) steal personal identification and banking information from legitimate cards, (3) emboss the stolen information on the fake cards, and (4) use the illegal debit cards for purchases or cash advances. *p. 450*

deconstruction

An opening up of seemingly closed "things." It intends to encounter the hidden and excluded elements of language, meaning, and experience. *p. 349*

Deep Web

Sometimes called the "Invisible Web," it is the parallel Internet that exists beneath the surface of conventional browsers. It features sites not indexed by search engines. It is essentially unregulated and is rife with criminal activity and illegal transactions. *p. 502*

deterrence

As used in criminal justice, it refers to crime prevention achieved through the fear of punishment. *p. 233*

deviant cybercommunity

An online community whose culture and customs would be classified as deviant and delinquent if exported to the offline world, but in which socially abnormal behaviour is accepted and even endorsed in the context of the given digital environment. *p. 508*

differential association

Developed by Edwin Sutherland in the 1930s, this theory argues that crime, like any social behaviour, is learned in association with others. If individuals regularly associate with criminals in relative isolation from law-abiding citizens, they are more likely to engage in crime. They learn relevant skills for committing crime and ideas for justifying and normalizing it. *p. 370*

differential offending hypothesis

There are actual differences between racial groups in terms of the incidence, level of seriousness, and persistence of offending patterns. *p. 132*

differential treatment hypothesis
Structural inequality in the administration of justice (from police patrols to courtrooms to correctional services) is responsible for the overrepresentation of minority groups in the criminal justice process. *p. 132*

discipline
A meticulous manner or method of training. It intends to ensure constant subjection and obedience. It involves hierarchal observation, normalizing judgment, and examinations. *p. 334*

denial-of-service attack (DDoS)
A term that describes any number of methods of varying sophistication, usually carried out by a group of hackers or by a series of bot attacks, for infiltrating and sabotaging a host server, thereby denying access to a website or online service or otherwise disrupting the operations of business, industry, or government. *p. 501*

drift
A psychological state of weak normative attachment to either deviant or conventional ways. *p. 360*

duress
Duress may be a defence to a criminal charge when the accused was forced to commit a crime as a consequence of threats of death or serious bodily harm made by another person. *p. 83*

ecological fallacy
An error made when information is gathered at a group level (the unemployment rate of a neighbourhood) and conclusions are drawn about individuals (unemployed persons). Areas with high unemployment may have high crime rates, but this does not tell us that those crimes are necessarily committed by unemployed persons. *p. 383*

effective guardianship
An aspect of the routine activities approach to understanding crime victimization that argues that three key factors are required for crime to happen: a motivated offender, a suitable target, and ineffective guardianship of that target. Effective guardianship would include having locks on bikes, or security lights in the backyard, or putting goods in the trunk of the car. *p. 420*

ego
A psychoanalytical term denoting the rational part of the personality. It mediates between the id and the superego and is responsible for dealing with reality and making decisions. *p. 252*

elder councils
Small groups of respected community members, usually men, who are sought after to determine the best possible outcome of disputes between community members. *p. 38*

empirical evidence
Evidence as observed through the senses; it can be seen, touched, heard, smelled, tasted, and, to some extent, measured. This is the only form of scientifically acceptable evidence. *p. 362*

ethnic group
A group of individuals having a common, distinctive subculture. Ethnic groups differ from races; the term implies that values, norms, behaviour, and language, not necessarily physical appearance, are important distinguishing characteristics. *p. 363*

ethno-methodology
Ethno-methodological theory was pioneered by Harold Garfinkel. Roughly translated, the term means the study of people's practices or methods. The perspective does not see the social world as an objective reality, but as something people constantly build and rebuild through their thoughts and actions. Ethno-methodologists try to uncover the methods and practices people use to create their taken-for-granted world. *p. 376*

executive disengagement
The custom by which lower-level employees assume that executives are best left uninformed of certain decisions and actions of employees, or the assumption that executives cannot be legally expected to have complete control over their individual staff. *p. 477*

extortion
An offender unlawfully obtains money, property or services from an individual or entity through coercion and intimidation. *p. 443*

extraversion
A personality characteristic associated with sociability, impulsiveness, and aggression. *p. 256*

feminist approach
Understands "difference" between men and women as structurally produced by inequalities of class, race, and gender that condition and constrain women's lives. *p. 164*

feudalism
A system of economic and social organization found historically in several areas of the world. In Western Europe, feudalism was at its height between about 1000 and 1500. The economic foundation of the system was the feudal manor, which included a central farm owned by a landlord and small landholdings for a class of bonded farm labourers (serfs). The serfs were required to work the central manorial farm and to provide the lord with produce and/or money payments in return for their right to use the land. The system declined as cities and towns grew and power became centralized in nation-states under monarchies. *p. 40*

field
A basic unit of social activity. The social world is divided into many fields (e.g., the "artistic" field, the "academic" field, or the "economic" field). Each field of activity is defined by its own market through which certain practices or dispositions are valued more than others. *p. 342*

free trade zone
A specially designated geographical area within a nation that is exempt from the regulations and taxation normally imposed on business. These zones are intended to facilitate cross-border production and trade. Zones like these are found along the US–Mexico border, where they are referred to as maquilladoras. *p. 46*

gender-ratio problem
Poses the question of why there are sex differences in rates of arrest and types of criminal activity between men and women. *p. 162*

generalizability problem
Raises the issue of whether mainstream theories of crime—which have largely been developed with men in mind—can be made to "fit" women. *p. 162*

governmentality
The art of governing. It transcends and is considerably broader than the traditional

understanding of government as a state-directed activity. Government, then, encompasses a wide array of techniques, within and outside of the state, intended to (re)shape and (re)direct human actions. *p. 333*

gross counts of crime

A count of the total amount of crime in a given community, making no distinction between crime categories. *p. 102*

group conflict theory

A theory that attempts to explain certain types of criminal behaviour as resulting from a conflict between the interests of divergent groups. *p. 304*

habitus

A set of durable dispositions acquired through experience that allow one to achieve a "feel for the game" within a specific field of activity. These are internalized practices that serve as a "second nature" responsive to the immediate demands of everyday life. *p. 342*

harm to victims

The direct impact of crime on victims includes harm, such as loss, injury, pain, and emotional trauma. These can be exacerbated by the experience with the police, courts, corrections, and others. *p. 189*

hegemonic masculinity

A particular idealized form of masculinity that is culturally glorified, honoured, and exalted. For example, associating "the masculine" with physical strength, aggression, independence, ambition, lack of emotion, and heterosexuality. *p. 184*

hot spots policing

Most crimes occur at a small number of addresses in any community. Hot spots policing concentrates police resources on these high-crime locations. *p. 413*

human capital

The talents and capabilities that individuals contribute to the process of production. Companies, governments, and individuals can invest in human capital, just as they can invest in technology and buildings or in finances. *p. 295*

human rights

The minimum conditions required for a person to live a dignified life. Among the rights set out by the Universal Declaration of Human Rights are the right to life, liberty, and security of the person; the right to be free of torture and other forms of cruel and degrading punishment; the right to equality before the law; and the right to the basic necessities of life. *p. 15*

human trafficking

The illegal trade in people for the purposes of commercial sexual exploitation and other forms of forced labour. *p. 443*

id

A psychoanalytical term that denotes the most inaccessible and primitive part of the mind. It is a reservoir of biological urges that strive continually for gratification. The ego mediates between the id and the superego. *p. 251*

ideal type

A theoretical construct abstracted from experience that brings together observed characteristics of real social relationships. Observed empirical instances are combined to create a social form that has conceptual coherence that is never entirely observed in any actual community but that can be used as a standard against which to compare any real community. *p. 33*

ideology

A linked set of ideas and beliefs that act to uphold and justify an existing or desired situation in society. *p. 93*

inchoate crime

A criminal offence that is committed when the accused person seeks to bring about the commission of a particular crime but is not successful in doing so. The three inchoate offences in the Criminal Code are attempt, conspiracy, and counselling. *p. 73*

independent variable

A presumed cause of a dependent variable. If unemployment is thought to cause crime to increase, unemployment is the independent variable, and crime the dependent variable. *p. 382*

indeterminate sentence

A sentence that has no fixed release date. Release is determined by a parole authority based on the individual's behaviour. *p. 239*

individualistic

A theory that focuses on explaining the behaviour of individuals and using factors or features of the individual in explaining this behaviour. *p. 392*

individualized deterrence

Offenders who are heavily involved in criminal activity are individually warned that their actions are being monitored and that future violations of the law will be dealt with immediately. Extra police and/or probation resources are added to ensure that the legal system does keep its promises. *p. 413*

Industrial Revolution

A period of social transformation from the mid-1700s until the mid-1800s, marked primarily by new manufacturing technologies and a harnessing of new forms of energy, such as coal and steam. *p. 42*

instrumental Marxism

The state is viewed as the direct instrument of the ruling or capitalist class. Instrumentalism is based on the notion that the processes of the superstructure are determined by the economic base. *p. 312*

intoxication defence

Intoxication caused by alcohol and/or other drugs may be a defence if it prevents the accused from forming the intent required for a specific intent offence, such as murder or robbery. *p. 82*

involvement

The degree to which an individual is active in conventional activities. One of the social bonds in Hirschi's theory. *p. 385*

juristic person

The legal concept that corporations are liable to the same laws as natural persons. Treating corporations as individuals raises practical difficulties for legal enforcement and punishment. *p. 476*

justice

For Derrida, since it is perpetually deferred, justice cannot be defined adequately. It is not contained in or constrained by law. It is infinite. It is "to come." *p. 351*

la cosa nostra

Term used to denote Italian-American organized crime. It was originally applied by the FBI in an attempt to make this criminal fraternity sound ominous and threatening. Members of the so-called LCN never used this label themselves, though they have often referred to their secret society as "this thing of ours," which roughly translates into Italian as "la cosa nostra." *p. 452*

labelling
According to labelling theory, deviance is not a quality of the act but of the label that others attach to it. This raises the question of who applies the label and who is labelled. The application of a label and the response of others to the label may result in a person becoming committed to a deviant identity. *p. 359*

legal definition of crime
A crime is an act that violates the criminal law and is punishable with a jail term, a fine, and/or some other sanction. *p. 14*

levels of aggregation
Refers to how data are to be combined. Do we want city-level, provincial, or national data? *p. 94*

liberal approach
Distinguishes sex (biological) from gender (cultural) and sees differences between men and women as resulting from gender roles and socialization patterns. *p. 159*

lifestyle/exposure theory
A theory of crime victimization that acknowledges that not everyone has the same lifestyle and that some lifestyles expose people to more risks than others do. *p. 417*

loansharking
Lending money at very high interest rates, often enforced through the use of physical force. *p. 443*

master status
A status overriding all others in perceived importance. Whatever other personal or social qualities individuals possess, they are judged primarily by this one attribute. Criminal exemplifies a master status that influences the community's identification of an individual. *p. 364*

maturational reform
The fact that people are less likely to commit crime as they grow older. *p. 121*

mens rea
The mental elements (other than voluntariness) contained in the definition of a criminal offence. *p. 65*

methodology
Refers to the study or critique of methods. *p. 91*

micro-powers
Small and mundane relations of governance, with an appreciable effect on human behaviour. *p. 334*

mistake of fact
Mistake of fact may be a defence where the accused person acts under the influence of an honest mistake in relation to any of the elements of the *actus reus* of the offence charged. *p. 79*

mode of production
The dominant form of social and technical organization of economic production in a society. Historically, a variety of modes of production can be distinguished based on both technology and the structure of social relationships. *p. 32*

modelling
A form of learning that occurs as a result of watching and imitating others. *p. 258*

moral development theory
Refers generally to theories of individual psychology that investigate how moral reasoning emerges in the individual and develops as the individual matures. *p. 255*

moral entrepreneur
Someone who defines new rules and laws or who advocates stricter enforcement of existing laws. Often such entrepreneurs have a financial or organizational interest in particular definitions or applications of law. *p. 361*

moral rhetoric
In the study of crime, this is the set of claims and assertions deviants make to justify their deviant behaviour. The moral rhetoric of a group is an important component of socialization into a deviant identity. *p. 360*

naked life
For Agamben, naked life is akin to Homo Sacer—an individual who is excluded from possessing human rights and can be killed by anyone but cannot be sacrificed during a religious ceremony. *p. 347*

NCRMD
The special verdict of "not criminally responsible on account of mental disorder." In order to be found NCRMD, it must be proved on the balance of probabilities that, because of mental disorder, the accused lacked the capacity to appreciate the nature and quality of the act or omission in question or to know it would be considered morally wrong by the average Canadian. *p. 77*

necessity
Necessity may be a defence to a criminal charge when the accused person commits the lesser evil of a crime in order to avoid the occurrence of a greater evil. *p. 83*

Neoclassical theory
Neo-classical theorists sought to allow more flexibility in the justice system such as individualizing sentences to take into account offender characteristics and extenuating circumstances. *p. 232*

norms
Established rules of behaviour or standards of conduct. *p. 13*

objective *mens rea*
The *mens rea* elements of a criminal offence are considered to be objective if they are based on a determination of whether a reasonable person, in the same circumstances and with the same knowledge as the accused, would have appreciated the risk involved in the accused's conduct and would have taken steps to avoid the commission of the *actus reus* elements of the crime in question. *p. 66*

occupational crime
Refers to violations of the law in the course of practising a legitimate occupation. *p. 472*

operant conditioning
The basic process by which an individual's behaviour is shaped by reinforcement or by punishment. *p. 260*

opportunity structure
Opportunity is shaped by the way the society or an institution is organized or structured. *p. 292*

organizational or corporate crime
White-collar crime committed with the support and encouragement of a formal organization and intended, at least in part, to advance the goals of that organization. *p. 472*

paramount chieftainship
A political system similar to a kingdom that brings together the leaders of a number of partly autonomous villages or communities under the hierarchical rule of a grand chief. *p. 38*

paraphilia
The use of unusual objects, situations, processes, or people to obtain sexual excitement and channel obsessions or fantasies that are inherently deviant and either prohibited by law (criminal paraphilia) or deemed taboo and forbidden by conventional society. *p. 508*

party to a crime
The Criminal Code specifies that one is a party to—and liable to conviction of—a criminal offence if one actually commits it, aids and/or abets it, becomes a party to it by virtue of having formed a common intention with others to commit a crime, or counsels the commission of an offence that is actually committed by another person. *p. 72*

patriarchy
A system of male domination that includes both a structure and an ideology that privileges men over women. *p. 167*

Ponzi scheme
A fraud in which old investors are paid with the funds invested by new investors. When the scheme runs out of new investors, the scheme collapses. *p. 491*

population
Refers to all members of a given class or set. For example, adult Canadians, teenagers, Canadian inmates, and criminal offenders can each be thought of as a population. *p. 92*

Positive School
The Italian criminologist Cesare Lombroso and his followers were among the first to study crime scientifically. They believed that crime was caused by biological factors beyond the individual's control, though social factors became more important as this school of thought changed over time. *p. 236*

power
Weber saw power as the ability to realize one's goals despite resistance from others. In small-scale societies, the power to make decisions and affect group life was not institutionalized in social structures, and it was shared by the members of the group. In modern societies, power has become formally encoded in law, and authority (the legitimate use of power) is bestowed by social institutions. Also, for Foucault, power extends beyond the state. It is not a quantity to hold or possess. It is, rather, relational, such that power is only ever evident in its exercise. *pp. 37, 333*

primary deviation
Occurs when an individual commits deviant acts but fails adopt a primary self-identity as a deviant. *p. 359*

provocation
Provocation may be a partial defence to a charge of murder (if successful, it reduces the offence from murder to manslaughter). The required elements of provocation are (1) that the accused responded to a wrongful act or insult that was of such a nature that an ordinary person would have been likely to lose the power of self-control, and (2) that the accused acted "on the sudden and before there was time for his (or her) passion to cool." *p. 85*

puppet club
A motorcycle club that is subsidiary to a more dominant outlaw motorcycle gang and that is often expected to carry out the dirty work of the latter. *p. 437*

racialization
A process in which categories of the population are constructed, differentiated, inferiorized, and excluded. *p. 140*

rational choice theory
Rational choice theory posits that crime is the result of deliberate choices made by offenders based on their calculation of the risks and rewards of these choices. *p. 416*

regulatory offences
Regulatory offences arise under legislation (either federal, provincial, or territorial) that regulates inherently legitimate activities connected with trade, commerce, and industry or with everyday living (driving, fishing, etc.). These offences are not considered to be serious and usually carry only a relatively minor penalty upon conviction. Indeed, many regulatory offences are sanctioned by means of a ticketing system, and the fines may often be paid online. *p. 59*

relative autonomy
A term used in the structural Marxist perspective to indicate that the state has a certain amount of independence from the capitalist class and is therefore able to enact laws that are not in the immediate interests of the capitalist class. *p. 314*

relative deprivation
Deprivation in relation to others around you, rather than judged against an absolute standard of sustainability. *p. 293*

reliability
Identifies one of the standards (another being validity) against which the tools used to measure concepts are judged. Reliability refers to consistency of results over time. *p. 91*

repeat victimization
The phenomenon of a person being a victim of a crime more than once. *p. 189*

restitution from the offender
Victims of any type of crime may request that the offender pay the victim money as reparation for financial or other losses caused by the crime. *p. 192*

rights of crime victims
Legislators in different countries and intergovernmental agencies such as UN have recognized various fundamental principles of justice and rights for victims of crime, such as the right to be informed, to receive restitution, and to be present when decisions such as bail or sentencing are being decided in court. *p. 191*

risk society
An emerging societal form characterized by the production and increased awareness of human-made "risks," such as nuclear destruction and environmental devastation. More importantly, the risk society is organized around the management of such risks. *p. 338*

role convergence hypothesis
The hypothesis that as the work roles of women become similar to those of men, so will their involvement in crime. *p. 128*

routine activities approach
An extension of the lifestyle/exposure theory, this approach assumes that crimes

are the expected outcomes of routine activities and changing social patterns. *p. 418*

sample
A group of elements (people, offenders, inmates) selected in a systematic manner from the population of interest. *p. 109*

secondary deviation
Occurs when an individual accepts the label of deviant. The result is adoption of a deviant self-identity that confirms and stabilizes the deviant lifestyle. *p. 359*

self-defence
Section 34 of the Criminal Code states that a person may use a reasonable amount of force in self-defence if she or he reasonably believes that they or another individual are the target of actual force or that a threat of force is being made against them. *p. 86*

self- or kin-based redress
Self-based redress exists where the society allows the harmed party to take matters into his or her own hands in order to seek a settlement. This could be revenge or a successful negotiation of some kind of compensation. Some societies resort to kin-based redress, which involves a member of a kin group seeking a settlement on the harmed party's behalf. *p. 35*

self-degrading commitment
Commitment leading to a poorer opinion of oneself. *p. 369*

self-enhancing commitment
Commitment leading to a better opinion of oneself. *p. 368*

self-enhancing values
Values that emphasize social status, prestige, dominance over others, and personal success. *p. 282*

self-report study
A method for measuring crime involving the distribution of a detailed questionnaire to a sample of people, asking them whether they have committed a crime in a particular period of time. This has been a good method for criminologists to determine the social characteristics of offenders. *p. 113*

self-transcending values
Values that emphasize appreciation, tolerance, protection, and the welfare of others. *p. 282*

seriousness rule
If there are several crimes committed in one incident, only the most serious crime is counted. UCR 1.0 uses the seriousness rule. *p. 100*

sexism
Attributing to women socially undesirable characteristics that are assumed to be intrinsic characteristics of that sex. *p. 156*

situational crime prevention
Premised on the belief that most crime is opportunistic rather than the outcome of those driven to commit a crime no matter what the circumstances. This form of prevention attempts to reduce the opportunities for crime rather than just relying on the police after the crime has occurred. *p. 424*

social bonds
The degree to which an individual has ties to his or her society. In Hirschi's theory, social bonds include attachment, commitment, involvement, and belief. *p. 381*

social constructionist approach to crime
This approach questions the idea that there is an observable or measurable social reality, but rather proposes that a crime is whatever a particular society defines it to be. *p. 139*

social control theory
The theory proposes that people refrain from committing criminal acts because they do not want to jeopardize their bonds to conventional society. *p. 380*

social structure
The patterned and relatively stable arrangement of roles and statuses found within societies and social institutions. *p. 281*

socialization
The interactive process whereby individuals come to learn and internalize the culture of their society or group. *p. 252*

sovereign
One who holds supreme power in a territory or space. Agamben, following Carl Schmitt, claims that the sovereign is the one who is empowered to declare a state of exception. *p. 346*

state
As defined by Max Weber (1864–1920), the state is an institution that claims the exclusive right to the legitimate exercise of force in a given territory through the use of police to enforce laws or the army to maintain civil stability. While there have been stateless societies, most complex societies have state systems of formal government and administrative bureaucracies. *p. 32*

state of exception
A period of time where the sovereign declares civil liberties suspended: typically in a time of national crisis. *p. 346*

Statistical School
Associated with early social scientists such as Adolphe Quetelet (1795–1874) and André-Michel Guerry (1802–1866), who began to explore the structure of emerging European societies with the assistance of statistical methods. While their early use of statistics is important, they also developed a structural explanation of crime and other social problems. *p. 234*

strain theory
The proposition that people feel strain when they are exposed to cultural goals they are unable to reach because they do not have access to culturally approved means of achieving those goals. *p. 280*

stigma
As used by Erving Goffman (1922–1982), a personal characteristic that is negatively evaluated by others and thus distorts and discredits the public identity of the individual. For example, a prison record may become a stigmatized attribute. The stigma may lead to the adoption of a self-identity that incorporates the negative social evaluation. *p. 360*

stigmata
The physical signs that a person is an atavism. *p. 238*

structural Marxism
The state is viewed as acting in the long-term interests of capitalism as a whole rather than in the short-term interests of the capitalist class. *p. 313*

subculture
A group of people who share a distinctive set of cultural beliefs and behaviours that differs in some significant way from that of the larger society. *p. 293*

subjective *mens rea*

The *mens rea* elements of a criminal offence are considered to be subjective if they are based on a determination of "what actually went on in the accused person's mind." The forms of subjective *mens rea* are intention and knowledge; recklessness; and willful blindness. *p. 66*

superego

A psychoanalytical term denoting the ethical and moral dimensions of personality; an individual's conscience. The ego mediates between the superego and the id. *p. 252*

surplus

The excess of production over the human and material resources used up in the process of production. In simple societies, there was often little if any surplus since the production from hunting and gathering was entirely used up in subsistence. With the development of animal herding and settled agriculture, production exceeded immediate subsistence needs, and social inequality and class division became possible when particular individuals or groups were able to take control of this surplus. *p. 33*

surveillance

The direct or indirect observation of conduct toward producing a desired outcome (i.e., conformity). *p. 334*

symbolic interactionism

A sociological perspective that focuses on the dynamics of how people interpret social situations and negotiate the meaning of these situations with others. It differs from more structurally focused perspectives in seeing individuals as actively creating the social world rather than just acting within the constraints of culture and social structure. *p. 357*

target suitability

Because of their vulnerability, some potential crime targets are more attractive than others. A home that is unlit, has shrubs blocking a view of the front door, and has no alarm system will be seen as a more suitable target than a well-protected home. *p. 420*

technological determinism

The theory that technological innovation is the key driving force behind changes in society and that new technologies shape culture and human behaviour, not vice versa. *p. 505*

terrorism

The illegitimate use of force to achieve a political objective by targeting innocent people. *p. 24*

theory

A set of concepts and their nominal definitions or assertions about the relationships between these concepts, assumptions, and knowledge claims. *p. 93*

token economy

A behaviour therapy procedure based on operant learning principles. Individuals are rewarded (reinforced) for positive or appropriate behaviour and are disciplined (punished) for negative or inappropriate behaviour. *p. 261*

tort law

The branch of law concerning non-contractual wrongs against individuals. Examples include negligence, trespassing, nuisance, and defamation. Tort lawsuits are filed by a plaintiff who seeks compensation for damages purportedly caused by some defendant. *p. 46*

trace

The mark of absence in words that is the necessary condition of thought and experience. *p. 350*

transnational corporation

A corporation that has sales and production in many different nations. Because of their multinational reach, these corporations are often thought to be beyond the political control of any individual nation-state. *p. 44*

transnational organized crime

Organized crime that is coordinated and conducted across national borders. *p. 438*

"true crime"

A "true crime" occurs when an individual engages in conduct that is not only prohibited but also constitutes a serious breach of community values; as such, it is perceived by Canadians as inherently wrong and deserving of punishment. Only the Parliament of Canada, using its criminal law power under the Constitution Act, 1867, may enact a "true crime." *p. 59*

Uniform Crime Reports (UCR)

Since 1962, Statistics Canada has published the Uniform Crime Reports based on a standardized set of procedures for collecting and reporting crime information. *p. 100*

validity

The extent to which a tool or instrument (questionnaire, experiment) actually measures the concept the researcher claims to be interested in and not something else. *p. 91*

value

A collective idea about what is right or wrong, good or bad, and desirable or undesirable in a particular culture. *p. 19*

victim fine surcharge

A monetary penalty similar to a fine, which can be assessed at sentence or added to a fine such as in a traffic violation, but can only be used by the government to fund services for victims. *p. 196*

victimization survey

A survey of a random sample of the population in which people are asked to recall and describe their own experience of being a victim of crime. *p. 109*

vory v zakone

A "thief in law." That is, a high-ranking, well-respected organized crime figure in the old Soviet underworld and the new Republic of Russia. Akin to the Italian Mafia. The code of the "Thieves World" emphasizes a rejection of government authority and traditional social norms. The "vor" pre-date the Soviet Union, but many were inmates interned in Soviet prison camps who organized themselves in an attempt to rule the criminal underworld. *p. 446*

white-collar crime

Crime that is committed by middle- and upper-class people in the course of their legitimate business activities. Sutherland defined white-collar crime "as a crime committed by a person of respectability and high social status in the course of his occupation." *pp. 14, 471*

Bibliography

CHAPTER 1

Akman, D.D., A. Normandeau, and S. Turner. 1967. "The Measurement of Delinquency in Canada." Journal of Criminal Law, Criminology and Police Science 58: 330–37.

Alberici, E. (2007). What Causes People to Become Multiple Killers? Australian Broadcasting Corporation. Web.

Beirne, Piers, and Nigel South. 2007. Issues in Green Criminology: Confronting Harms Against Environments, Humanity, and Other Animals. Portland: Willan.

Bennett, Colin, Kevin Haggerty, David Lyon, and Valeries Steeves. 2014. Transparent Lives: Surveillance in Canada. Edmonton: Athabasca University Press.

Black, Conrad. 1993. A Life in Progress. Toronto: Key Porter Books.

Blumstein, Alfred. 2003. "The Kid Whiz: Richard Tremblay." Time, May 26: 54.

Boyd, Susan, and Connie Carter. 2014. Killer Weed: Marijuana Grow Ops, Media, and Justice. Toronto: University of Toronto Press.

Brayne, Sarah. 2014. "Surveillance and System Avoidance: Criminal Justice Contact and Institutional Attachment." American Sociological Review 79: 367–91.

Carter, Sarah. 1990. Lost Harvests. Montreal and Kingston: McGill–Queen's University Press.

Christakis, Dimitri, Michelle Garrison, Todd Herrenkohl, Kevin Haggerty, Frederick Rivara, Chuan Zhou, and Kimberley Liekweg. 2013. "Modifying Media Content for Preschool Children: A Randomized Control Trial." Pediatrics 131: 431–38.

Chunn, Dorothy, Susan Boyd, and Robert Menzies. 2002. "'We All Live in Bhopal': -Criminology Discovers Environmental Crime." In Toxic Criminology: Environment, Law and the State in Canada, ed. Susan Boyd, Dorothy Chunn, and Robert Menzies. 7–24. Halifax: Fernwood.

Commission of Inquiry into the Actions of Canadian Officials in Relation to Maher Arar. 2006. Report of the Events Relating to Maher Arar: Analysis and Recommendations. Ottawa: Public Works and Government Services Canada.

Cook, Shirley. 1969. "Canadian Narcotics Legislation, 1908–1923: A Conflict Model Interpretation." Canadian Review of Sociology and Anthropology 6: 36–46.

Croall, Hazel. 2007. "Food Crime." In Issues in Green Criminology: Confronting Harms Against Environments, Humanity and Other Animals, ed. Piers Beirne and Nigel South. 206–29. Portland: Willan.

CSIA (Canadian Sportfishing Industry Association). 2007. "Federal Animal Cruelty Legisltion." Web.

Dowler, Ken, Thomas Fleming, and Stephen Muzzatti. 2006. "Constructing Crime: Media, Crime and Popular Culture." Canadian Journal of Criminology and Criminal Justice 48: 837–50.

Ericson, Richard. 2007. Crime in an Insecure World. Cambridge: Polity Press.

Gabor, Thomas. 1994. Everybody Does It: Crime by the Public. Toronto: University of Toronto Press.

Galloway, Gloria. 2003. "Parents Sentenced for Exorcism Gone Wrong." Globeandmail.com.

Ganor, Boas. 2002. "Defining Terrorism: Is One Man's Terrorist Another Man's Freedom Fighter?" Police Practice and Research 3: 287–304.

Gibbs, Carole, Meredith Gore, Edmund McGarrell, and Louie Rivers III. 2010. "Introducing Conservation Criminology: Towards Interdisciplinary Scholarship on Environ-mental Crimes and Risks." British Journal of Criminology 50: 124–44.

Hagan, John. 1985. Modern Criminology: Crime, Criminal Behaviour, and Its Control. New York: McGraw-Hill.

Haskins, George Lee. 1969. "A Rule to Walk By." In Crime and Justice in Society, ed. Richard Quinney. 33–54. Boston: Little, Brown.

Hennessey, Karen. 2014. Response from independent counsel for the Canadian Wireless Telecommunications Association Regarding Information Requests from Government Authorities. Ottawa: Office of the Privacy Commissioner of Canada.

Hugill, David. 2010. Missing Women, Missing News: Covering Crisis in Vancouver's Downtown Eastside. Halifax and Winnipeg: Fernwood.

Jackman, Tom. 2003. "Murder Defendants Claim Connection with Hit Movie." HoustonChronicle.com. Web.

Kellett, Anthony. 2004. "Terrorism in Canada: 1960–1992." In Violence in Canada: Sociopolitical Perspectives, 2nd ed. ed. Jeffrey Ian Ross. 284–312. New Brunswick: Transaction Press.

Knoll, James. 2010. "The 'Psuedocommando' Mass Murderer: Part II, The Language of Revenge." Journal of the American Academy of Psychiatry and the Law Online 38: 263–72.

Laqueur, Walter. 1987. The Age of Terrorism. Boston: Little, Brown.

Lynch, Michael J., and Paul Stretesky. "Green Criminology in the United States." In Issues in Green Criminology: Confronting Harms Against Environments, Humanity and Other Animals, ed. Piers Beirne and Nigel South. 248–69. Portland: Willan.

McCormick, Chris. 1995. Constructing Danger: The Misrepresentation of Crime in the News. Halifax: Fernwood Publishing.

McIntyre, Mike. 2003. Nowhere to Run: The Killing of Constable Dennis Strongquill. Winnipeg: Great Plains.

McNish, Jacquie, and Sinclair Stewart. 2004. Wrong Way: The Fall of Conrad Black. Toronto: Viking Canada.

Media Index. 1999. "South Park Gets Nasty at Record-Setting Pace." Austin American-Statesman, July 16, E1.

Murphy, Christopher. 2007. "'Securitizing' Canadian Policing: A New Paradigm for the Post 9/11 Security State?" Canadian Journal of Sociology 32: 449–75.

Murray, Jane Lothian, Rick Linden, and Diana Kendall. 2011. Sociology in Our Times, 5th ed. Toronto: Nelson Education.

Normandeau, Andre. 1966. "The Measurement of Delinquency in Montreal." Journal of Criminal Law, Criminology, and Police Science 57: 172–77.

O'Connor, The Honourable Dennis R. 2002. Report of the Walkerton Inquiry: Part One: Summary. Toronto: Queen's Printer for Ontario.

Ottawa Citizen. 2007. "Arar on Time's '100 Most Influential' List, But He's Still Not elcome in U.S." Ottawa Citizen, May 4. Web.

Plotz, David. 2001. "Conrad Black." Slate, August 31.

Rodgers, R.S. 1962. Sex and Law in Canada: Text, Cases and Comment. Ottawa: Policy Press.

Schwendinger, Herman, and Julia Schwendinger. 1970. "Defenders of Order or Guardians of Human Rights." Issues in Criminology 5: 123–57.

Senate Committee on Legal and Constitutional Affairs. 2006. "Evidence." December 4.

Shuqin, Yang. 2010. "The Polluting Behaviour of the Multinational Corporations in China." In Global Environmental Harm: Criminological Perspectives, ed. Rob White. 150–58. Cullompton: Willan.

Smandych, Russell, and Rodney Kueneman. 2010. "The Canadian–Alberta Tar Sands: A Case Study of State-Corporate Environmental Crime." In Global Environmental Harm: Criminological Perspectives, ed. Rob White. 87–109. Cullompton: Willan.

South, Nigel. 2010. "The Ecocidal Tendencies of Late Modernity." In Global Environmental Harm: Criminological Perspectives, ed. Rob White. 228–47. Cullompton: Willan.

Staples, David. 2002. "Fearless, Painless, Senseless: The Sand Brothers." Edmonton Journal, March 31, D1.

Statistics Canada. 2010. "Police Personnel and Expenditures 2010." Ottawa: Statistics Canada. Web.

Statistics Canada. 2013. "Police Resources in Canada." Ottawa.

Stern, Mark. 2014. "103 Gang Members Indicted Thanks to Their Incriminating Facebook Messages." Slate, 5 June. Web.

Sutherland, Edwin. 1940. "White-Collar Criminality." American Sociological Review 5: 1–12.

Sutherland, Edwin, and Donald Cressey. 1960. Principles of Criminology, 6th ed. Philadelphia: J.B. Lippincott.

Turk, Austin. 2004. "Sociology of Terrorism." Annual Review of Sociology 30: 271–86.

White, Rob. 2007. "Green Criminology and the Pursuit of Social and Ecological Justice." In Issues in Green Criminology: Confronting Harms Against Environments, Humanity, and Other Animals, ed. Piers Beirne and Nigel South. 32–54. Portland: Willan.

White, Rob. 2011. Transnational Environmental Crime. Routledge: London.

Winnipeg Free Press. 1993. "Law, Religion Clash over Child Marriage." September 24.

Wortley, Scot. 2009. "Introduction: The Immigration–Crime Connection: Competing Theoretical Perspectives." Journal of International Migration & Integration 10, no. 4: 349–58.

Woolford, Andrew. 2010. "Criminological Nightmares: A Canadian Criminology of Genocide." In Critical Criminology in Canada: New Voices, New Directions, ed. Aaron Doyle and Dawn Moore. 136–61. Vancouver: UBC Press.

CHAPTER 2

Becker, Howard. 1963. "Moral Entrepreneurs." In The Outsiders, ed. Becker. New York: Free Press.

Braithwaite, John, and S. Mugford. 1994. "Conditions of Successful Reintegration Ceremonies." British Journal of Criminology 34, no. 2: 139–71.

Brodeur, Paul. 1985. Outrageous Misconduct: The Asbestos Industry on Trial. New York: Pantheon Books

Broswimmer, Franz. 2002. Ecocide: A Short History of the Mass Extinction of Species. London: Pluto Press.

Brownmiller, Susan. 1975. Against Our Will: Men, Women, and Rape. New York: Simon and Schuster.

Carroll, Stephen J., Deborah Hensler, Allan Abrahamse, Jennifer Gross, Michelle White, Scott Ashwood, and Elizabeth Sloss. 2002. "Asbestos Litigation Costs and Compensation: An Interim Report." Santa Monica: RAND Corporation, DB-397-ICJ. Web.

Carroll, Stephen J., Deborah R. Hensler, Jennifer Gross, Elizabeth M. Sloss, Matthias Schonlau, Allan Abrahamse, and J. Scott Ashwood. 2005. "Asbestos Litigation Costs, Compensation, and Alternatives. Research Brief." Santa Monica: RAND Corporation, RB-9155-ICJ. Web.

Chambliss, William. 1969. "The Law of Vagrancy." In Crime and the Legal Process, ed. Chambliss. 51–63. New York: McGraw-Hill.

Clark, Lorenne, and Debra Lewis. 1977. Rape: The Price of Coercive Sexuality. Toronto: Women's Press.

Colson, Elizabeth. 1974. Tradition and Contract: The Problem of Order. Chicago: Aldine.

Comack, Elizabeth. 1985. "The Origins of Canadian Drug Legislation: Labelling versus Class Analysis." In The New Criminologies in Canada: State, Crime and Control, ed. Thomas Fleming. 65–86. Toronto: Oxford University Press.

Dowie, Mark. 1977. "Pinto Madness." Mother Jones, September–October.

Graham, James. 1976. "Amphetamine Politics on Capital Hill." In Whose Law, What Order?, ed. William Chambliss. 107–22. New York: Wiley.

Gray, Barbara, and Pat Lauderdale. 2007. "The Great Circle of Justice: North American Indigenous Justice and Contemporary Restoration Programs." Contemporary Justice Review 10, no. 2 (June): 215–25.

Grossman, Richard L., and Frank T. Adams. 1993. Taking Care of Business: Citizenship and the Charter of Incorporation. Web.

Gulliver, P.H. 1979. Disputes and Negotiations: A Cross-Cultural Perspective. New York: Academic Press.

Hall, Jerome. 1952. Theft, Law, and Society, 2nd ed. Indianapolis: Bobbs-Merrill.

———. 1969a. "Theft, Law, and Society: The Carrier's Case." In Crime and the Legal Process, ed. William Chambliss. 32–51. New York: McGraw-Hill.

———. 1969b. "Crime and the Commercial Revolution." In Delinquency, Crime, and Social Process, ed. Donald Cressey and David Ward. 100–10. New York: Harper and Row.

Hoebel, E. Adamson. 1973. The Law of Primitive Man. New York: Atheneum.

Jeffery, Clarence Ray. 1969. "The Development of Crime in Early English Society." In Crime and the Legal Process, ed. William Chambliss. New York: McGraw-Hill.

Kinnon, Dianne. 1981. Report on Sexual Assault in Canada. Report to the Canadian Advisory Council on the Status of Women.

Lenski, Gerhard. 1966. Power and Privilege: A Theory of Social Stratification. New York: McGraw-Hill.

Mallea, Paula. 2011. Fearmonger: Will Stephen Harper's Billions for His Tough-on-Crime Agenda Make Our Streets and Safer? Toronto: James Lorimer.

Marchak, Patricia. 1991. The Integrated Circus: The New Right and the Restructuring of Global Markets. Montreal and Kingston: McGill–Queen's University Press.

Miliband, Ralph. 1969. The State in Capitalist Society. London: Quarter Books.

Newman, Katherine. 1983. Law and Economic Organization: A Comparative Study of Preindustrial Societies. London: Cambridge University Press.

Oxfam. 2014. "Working for the Few: Political Capture and Economic Inequality." Oxfam International. Web.

Reasons, Charles, Lois Ross, and Craig Paterson. 1981. Assault on the Worker. Toronto: Butterworths.

Ross, Rupert. 1989. "Leaving Our White Eyes Behind: The Sentencing of Native Accused." 3 Canadian Native Law Reporter 1 at 4.

Small, Shirley. 1978. "Canadian Narcotics Legislation, 1908–1923: A Conflict Model Interpretation." In Law and Social Control in Canada, ed. W. Greenaway and S. Brickey. 28–42. Scarborough: Prentice Hall.

Snider, Laureen. 2000. "The Sociology of Corporate Crime: An Obituary." Theoretical Criminology 4, no. 2:169–206.

Thompson, Edward P. 1976. Whigs and Hunters: The Origin of the Black Act. New York: Pantheon.

Tigar, Michael, and Madeleine Levy. 1977. Law and the Rise of Capitalism. New York: Monthly Review Press.

Tonnies, Ferdinand. 1957. Community and Society. Newton Abbot: Courier Dover.

Weitekamp, Elmar G.M. 2002. "Restorative Justice: Present Prospects and Future Directions." In Restorative Justice: Theoretical Foundations, ed. Elmar G.M. Weitekamp and Hans-Jürgen Kerner. Portland: Willan.

WHO. 2010. "Asbestos: Elimination of Asbestos-Related Diseases." Fact sheet #343. Web.

CHAPTER 3

CASES CITED

Canada (Attorney General) v. Bedford, [2013] 3 SCR 1101. Online at: http://www.canlii.org/en/ca/scc/doc/2013/2013scc72/2013scc72.html

R. v. Beatty, [2008] 1 S.C.R. 49. Available at http://www.canlii.org/en/ca/scc/doc/2008/2008scc5/2008scc5.html

R. v. Bouchard-Lebrun, [2011] 3 S.C.R. 575. Available at http://www.canlii.org/en/ca/scc/doc/2011/2011scc58/2011scc58.html

R. v. Boudreault, [2012] 3 SCR 157. Available at: http://www.canlii.org/en/ca/scc/doc/2012/2012scc56/2012scc56.html

R. v. Briscoe, [2010] 1 S.C.R. 411. Available at http://www.canlii.org/en/ca/scc/doc/2010/2010scc13/2010scc13.html

R. v. Chaulk, [1990] 3 S.C.R. 1303. Available at http://canlii.org/en/ca/scc/doc/1990/1990canlii34/1990canlii34.html

R. v. Crangle (2010), 256 C.C.C. (3d) 254 (Ont.C.A). Available at http://www.canlii.org/en/on/onca/doc/2010/2010onca451/2010onca451.html

R. v. Creighton, [1993] 3 S.C.R. 3. Available at http://canlii.org/en/ca/scc/doc/1993/1993canlii61/1993canlii61.html

R. v. Daviault, [1994] 3 S.C.R. 63. Available at http://canlii.org/en/ca/scc/doc/1994/1994canlii61/1994canlii61.html

R. v. Gauthier [2013] 2 SCR 403. Available at http://www.canlii.org/en/ca/scc/doc/2013/2013scc32/2013scc32.html

R. v. Hamilton, [2005] 2 S.C.R. 432. Available at http://www.canlii.org/en/ca/scc/doc/2005/2005scc47/2005scc47.html

R. v. Hibbert, [1995] 2 S.C.R. 973. Available at http://www.canlii.org/en/ca/scc/doc/1995/1995canlii110/1995canlii110.html

R. v. Hydro-Québec, [1997] 3 S.C.R. 213. Available at http://canlii.org/en/ca/scc/doc/1997/1997canlii318/1997canlii318.html

R. v. Landry, [1991] 1 SCR 99. Available at http://www.canlii.org/en/ca/scc/doc/1991/1991canlii114/1991canlii114.html

R. v. Lavallee, [1990] 1 S.C.R. 852. Available at http://canlii.org/en/ca/scc/doc/1990/1990canlii95/1990canlii95.html

R. v. Mabior, [2012] 2 SCR 584. Available at: http://www.canlii.org/en/ca/scc/doc/2012/2012scc47/2012scc47.html

R. v. Malmo-Levine; R. v. Caine, [2003] 3 S.C.R. 571. Available at http://www.canlii.org/en/ca/scc/doc/2003/2003scc74/2003scc74.html

R. v. Malott, [1998] 1 S.C.R. 123. Available at http://www.canlii.org/en/ca/scc/doc/1998/1998canlii845/1998canlii845.html

R. v. Martineau, [1990] 2 S.C.R. 633. Available at http://canlii.org/en/ca/scc/doc/1990/1990canlii80/1990canlii80.html

R. v. Molodowic, [2000] 1 S.C.R. 420. Available at http://www.canlii.org/en/ca/scc/doc/2000/2000scc16/2000scc16.html

R. v. Olan, Hudson and Hartnett, [1978] 2 S.C.R. 1175. Available at http://canlii.org/en/ca/scc/doc/1978/1978canlii9/1978canlii9.html

R. v. Perka, [1984] 2 S.C.R. 232. Available at http://canlii.org/en/ca/scc/doc/1984/1984canlii23/1984canlii23.html

R. v. Pétel, [1994] 1 S.C.R. 3. Available at http://canlii.org/en/ca/scc/doc/1994/1994canlii133/1994canlii133.html

R. v. Pickton, [2010] 2 S.C.R. 198. Available at http://canlii.org/en/ca/scc/doc/2010/2010scc32/2010scc32.html

R. v. Roy, [2012] 2 SCR 60. Available at: http://www.canlii.org/en/ca/scc/doc/2012/2012scc26/2012scc26.html

R. v. Ruzic, [2001] 1 S.C.R. 687. Available at http://www.canlii.org/en/ca/scc/doc/2001/2001scc24/2001scc24.html

R. v. Ryan, [2013] 1 SCR 14. Available at http://www.canlii.org/en/ca/scc/doc/2013/2013scc3/2013scc3.html

R. v. Sharpe, [2001] 1 S.C.R. 45. Available at http://canlii.org/en/ca/scc/doc/2001/2001scc2/2001scc2.html

R. v. Stone, [1999] 2 S.C.R. 290. Available at http://canlii.org/en/ca/scc/doc/1999/1999canlii688/1999canlii688.html

R. v. Théroux, [1993] 2 S.C.R. 5. Available at http://canlii.org/en/ca/scc/doc/1993/1993canlii134/1993canlii134.html

R. v. Thibert, [1996] 1 S.C.R. 37. Available at http://www.canlii.org/en/ca/scc/doc/1996/1996canlii249/1996canlii249.html

R. v. Tran, [2010] 3 SCR 350. Available at http://www.canlii.org/en/ca/scc/doc/2010/2010scc58/2010scc58.html

R. v. Wholesale Travel Group Inc., [1991] 3 S.C.R. 154. Available at http://canlii.org/en/ca/scc/doc/1991/1991canlii39/1991canlii39.html

Rodriguez v. British Columbia (Attorney-General), [1993] 3 SCR 519. Available at: http://www.canlii.org/en/ca/scc/doc/1993/1993canlii75/1993canlii75.html

Winko v. British Columbia (Forensic Psychiatric Institute), [1999] 2 S.C.R. 625. Available at http://canlii.org/en/ca/scc/doc/1999/1999canlii694/1999canlii694.html

CHAPTER 4

Boak, A., H.A. Hamilton, E.M. Adluf, and R.E. Mann. 2013. "Drug Use Among Ontario Students, 1999–2013." CAMH Document Series no. 36. Toronto: Centre for Addiction and Mental Health.

Brennan, Shannon, and Mia Dauvergne. 2011. "Police-Reported Crime Statistics in Canada, 2010." Juristat 30, no. 4. Web.

Bureau of Justice Statistics. 2012. Prison Statistics. Washington: Department of Justice. Web.

Catlin, G., and S. Murray. 1979. Report on Canadian Victimization Survey Methodological Pretests. Ottawa: Statistics Canada.

Chicago Magazine. 2014. "The Truth About Chicago's Crime Rates." May.

Dauvergne, M., and J. Turner. 2010. "Police-Reported Crime Statistics in Canada, 2009." Juristat 30, no. 2. Web.

de Silva, S., and R.A. Silverman. 1985. "New Approaches to Uniform Crime Reporting in Canada." Paper presented at the annual meeting of the American Society of Criminology, San Diego, November.

Engstad, Peter, and John L. Evans 1980. "Responsibility, Competence, and Police Effectiveness in Crime Control." In Effectiveness of Policing, ed. R.V.G. Clarke and J.M. Hough. Aldershot: Ashgate.

Evans, J., and G. Leger. 1978. "The Development of Victimization Surveys in Canada." Public Data Use 6 (November).

Fréchette, M., and Marc LeBlanc. 1979. "La délinquance cachée à l'adolescence." Inadaptation juvénile Cahier 1. Montréal: Université de Montréal.

———. 1980. "Pour une pratique de la criminologie: configurations de conduites délinquantes et portraits de délinquants." Inadaptation juvénile Cahier 5. Montréal: Université de Montréal.

Gannon, Maire. 2006. "Crime Statistics in Canada, 2005." Juristat 26, no. 4. Web.

Hindelang, M.J., T. Hirschi, and J.G. Weis. 1981. Measuring Delinquency. Beverly Hills: Sage.

Hirschi, Travis. 1969. Causes of Delinquency. Berkeley: University of California Press.

"LAPD Misclassified Nearly 1,200 Violent Crimes as Minor Offenses." LA Times, August 2014

Nettler, G. 1974. Explaining Crime. New York: McGraw-Hill.

Ogrodnick, Lucie. 2007. Seniors as Victims of Crime, 2004 and 2005. Ottawa: Statistics Canada.

Perreault, Samuel, and Shannon Brennan. 2010. "Criminal Victimization in Canada, 2009." Juristat 30, no. 2. Web.

Piquero, Alex, Carol A. Schubert, and Robert Brame. 2014. "Comparing Official and Self-Report Records of Offending Across Gender and Race/Ethnicity in a Longitudinal Study of Serious Youthful Offenders." Journal of Research in Crime and Delinquency 51: 526–56.

Polsky, Ned. 1967. Hustlers, Beats, and Others. Chicago: Aldine.

Savoie, J. 2006. "Youth Self-Reported Delinquency, Toronto, 2006." Juristat 27, no. 6. Web.

Shearing, Clifford D. 1984. "Dial-A-Cop: A Study of Police Mobilization." Report for the Centre of Criminology, University of Toronto.

Silverman, R.A. 1980. "Measuring Crime: More Problems." Journal of Police Science and Administration 8, no. 3: 265–74.

Silverman, R.A., and J. Teevan. 1975. Crime in Canadian Society. Toronto: Butterworths.

Skogan, W. 1978. "Review of Surveying Crime." Journal of Criminal Law and Criminology 69: 139–40.

———. (1981). Issues in the Measurement of Victimization. Washington: US Department of Justice, Bureau of Justice Statistics.

Statistics Canada. 2003. Canadian Crime Statistics. Ottawa: Canadian Centre for Justice Statistics, Chapter 6. Catalogue no. 85-205-XIE.

———. 2010. Uniform Crime Reporting Survey (UCR). Ottawa: Statistics Canada.

Thornberry, Terence P., and Marvin D. Krohn. 2000. "The Self-Report Method for Measuring Delinquency and Crime." Criminal Justice 2000 4. National Institute of Justice, Washington.

UK Statistical Authority. 2014. Assessment of Compliance with the Code of Practice for Official Statistics, Statistics on Crime in England and Wales. London: Office for National Statistics.

CHAPTER 5

Aaltonen, Mikko, John MacDonald, Pekka Martikainen, and Janne Kivivuori. 2013. "Examining the Generality of the Unemployment–Crime Association." Criminology 51, no. 3: 561–94.

Aaltonen, Mikko, Janne Kivivuori, Pekka Martikainen, and Venla Salmi. 2012. "Socio-Economic Status and Crimi-

nality as Predictors of Male Violence: Does Victim's Gender or Place of Occurrence Matter?" British Journal of Criminology 52: 1192–211.

Agozino B. 2003. Counter Colonial Criminology: A Critique of Imperialist Reasoning. London: Pluto Press.

Abramsky, T., C. Watts, C. Garcia-Moreno, K. Devries, L. Kriss, M. Ellsberg, H. Jansen, and L. Heise. 2011. "What Factors Are Associated with Recent Intimate Partner Violence? Findings from the WHO Multi-Country Study on Women's Health and Domestic Violence." BMC Public Health 11: 1–17.

Anderson, Elijah. 1999. Code of the Street: Decency, Violence, and the Moral Life of the Inner City. New York and London: W.W. Norton.

Ansara, Donna, and Michelle Hindin. 2010. "Exploring Gender Differences in the Patterns of Intimate Partner Violence in Canada: A Latent Class Approach." Journal of Epidemiology and Community Health 64: 849–54.

Anthias, F. 1998. "Rethinking Social Divisions: Some Notes Towards a Theoretical Framework." Sociological Review 46, no. 3: 505–35.

APA (American Psychological Association). 2014. "Socioeconomic Status." http://www.apa.org/topics/socioeconomic-status.

Arnavites, T., and R. Davina. 2006. "Business Cycles and Street Crime." Criminology 44: 139–64.

Barrett, Jessica. 2013. "Covert Racism Behind Increased Numbers of Aboriginals and Other Visible Minorities in Prisons, Watchdog Says." Web.

Boritch, H., and J. Hagan. 1987. "Crime and the Changing Forms of Class Control: Policing Public Order in 'Toronto the Good,' 1859–1955." Social Forces 66: 307–35.

Boyce, Jillian, and Adam Cotter. 2013. "Homicide in Canada, 2012." Centre for Canadian Justice Statistics. Web.

British Columbia Vital Statistics Agency. 2005. Selected Vital Statistics and Health Status Indicators. Annual Report 2005. Web.

Brownridge, Douglas A. 2010. "Intimate Partner Violence Against Aboriginal Men in Canada." Australian and New Zealand Journal of Criminology 43, no. 2: 223–37.

Buxton, Jane A., Andrew W. Tu, and Tim Stockwell. 2009. "Tracking Trends in Alcohol, Illicit Drugs, and Tobacco Through Morbidity Data." Contemporary Drug Problems 36: 485–97.

Buxton, Jane A., Azar Mehrabadi, Emma Preston, Andrew Tu, and the Canadian Community Epidemiology Network on Drug Use (CCENDU) Vancouver Site Committee. 2009. "Local Drug Use Epidemiology: Lessons Learned and Implications for Broader Comparisons." Contemporary Drug Problems 36: 447–58.

Cao, Liqun. 2011. "Visible Minorities and Confidence in the Police." Canadian Journal of Criminology and Criminal Justice 53, no. 1: 1–26.

Carlson, Kathryn B. 2013. "Mother 'Elated' as Ashley Smith's Jail Death Is Ruled a Homicide." Globe and Mail. Web.

Charles, Grant, and Mike DeGagné. 2013. "Student-to-Student Abuse in the Indian Residential Schools in Canada: Setting the Stage for Further Understanding." Child & Youth Services 34, no. 4: 343–59.

Chongatera, Godfrey. 2013. "Hate-Crime Victimization and Fear of Hate Crime Among Racially Visible People in Canada: The Role of Income as a Mediating Factor." Journal of Immigrant and Refugee Studies 11: 44–64.

Clark, Heather. 2009. "A Coordinated Approach to Student Drug Use Surveys in Canada." Contemporary Drug Problems 36: 409–25.

Clelland, D., and T.J. Carter. 1980. "The New Myth of Crime." Criminology 18, no. 3: 319–36.

Cohen, G.B., and R.J. Smith. 2010. "The Racial Geography of the Federal Death Penalty." Washington Law Review 85: 425–92.

Collin-Vezina, Delphine, Jacinthe Dion, and Nico Trocme. 2009. "Sexual Abuse in Canadian Aboriginal

Communities: A Broad Review of Conflicting Evidence." Pimatisiwin: A Journal of Aboriginal and Indigenous Community Health 7, no. 1: 27–47.

Comack, Elizabeth, and Jim Silver. 2008. "A Canadian Exception to the Punitive Turn? Community Responses to Policing Practices in Winnipeg's Inner City." Canadian Journal of Sociology 33, no. 4: 815–43.

Commission on Systemic Racism in the Ontario Criminal Justice System. 1995. Report of the Commission on Systemic Racism in the Ontario Criminal Justice System. Toronto: Queen's Printer.

Cotter, David, Joan Hermsen, and Reeve Vaneman. 2011. "The End of Gender Revolution? Gender Role Attitudes from 1977–2008," American Journal of Sociology 117, no. 1: 259–89.

Daly, Kathleen. 1992. "Women's Pathway to Felony Court: Feminist Theories of Lawbreaking and Problems of Representation." Southern California Review of Law and Women's Studies 2: 11–52.

———. 1989. "Gender and Varieties of White Collar Crime." Criminology 27, no. 4: 769–94.

Dauvergne, Mia. 2009. "Trends in Police-Reported Serious Assaults." Web.

———. 2002. "Homicide in Canada, 2001." Juristat: Statistics Canada 22: 1–20.

Delgado, Richard, and Jean Stefancic. 2012. Critical Race Theory: An Introduction. New York: NYU Press.

De Souza, Elenice, and Joel Miller. 2012. "Homicide in the Brazilian Favela: Does Opportunity Make the Killer?" British Journal of Criminology 52, no. 4: 786–807.

Doan, B., and B. Snook. 2008. "A Failure to Find Empirical Support for the Homology Assumption in Criminal Profiling." Journal of Police and Criminal Psychology 23: 61–70.

Duff, Cameron, Warren Muchelow, Clifton Chow, Andrew Ivsins, and Tim Stockwell. 2009. "The Canadian Recreational Drug Use Survey: Aims, Methods and First Results." Contemporary Drug Problems 36: 517–39.

Dumont, J. 1993. "Justice and Aboriginal People." In Royal Commission on Aboriginal Peoples and the Justice System, 42–85. Ottawa: Supply and Services Canada.

Edin, Kathryn, and Maria Kafalas. 2005. Promises I Can Keep: Why Poor Women Put Motherhood Before Marriage. Berkeley: University of California Press.

Elias, Brenda, Javier Mignone, Madelyn Hall, Say P. Hong, Lyna Hart, and Jitender Sareen. 2012. "Trauma and Suicide Behaviour Histories Among a Canadian Indigenous Population: An Empirical Exploration of the Potential Role of Canada's Residential School System." Social Science & Medicine 74, no. 10: 1560–69.

Fanon, F. 1967. Black Skin, White Masks, trans. C.L. Markmann. New York: Grove Press.

———. 1963. The Wretched of the Earth, trans. Constance Farrington. New York: Grove Press.

Farmer, P. 2005. Pathologies of Power: Health, Human Rights, and the New War on the Poor. Berkeley: University of California Press.

Feld, B.C. 2009. "Violent Girls or Relabeled Status Offenders? An Alternative Interpretation of the Data." Crime and Delinquency 55: 241–65.

Fife, Robert, and Philip Ling. 2012. "Feds Studying Private Prisons as Way to Save Money." Web.

Fischer, Benedikt, Joseph Anthony De Leo, Christine Allard, Michelle Firestone-Cruz, Jayadeep Patra, and Rehm. 2009. "Exploring Drug Sourcing Among Rregular Prescription Opioid Users in Canada: Data from Toronto and Victoria." Canadian Journal of Criminology and Criminal Justice 51, no. 1: 55–72.

Fitzgerald, Robin T., and Peter J. Carrington. 2008. "The Neighbourhood Context of Urban Aboriginal Crime." Canadian Journal of Criminology and Criminal Justice 50, no. 5: 523–57.

Fitzgerald, Robin T., and Peter J. Carrington. 2011. "Disproportionate Minority Contact: Police and Visible

Minority Youth." Canadian Journal of Criminology and Criminal Justice 53: 449–86.

Fox, J.. and Timothy F. Hartnagel. 1979. "Changing Social Roles and Female Crime in Canada." Canadian Review of Sociology and Anthropology 16, no. 1: 96–104.

Francisco, Joycelyn, and Christian Chenier. 2007. "A Comparison of Large Uurban, Small Urban, and Rural Crime Rates, 2005." Juristat 27, no. 3.

Freud, Sigmund. 1933. New Introductory Lectures on Psychoanalysis. New York: W.W. Norton.

Furman, Wyndol and Laura S. Hand. 2006. "The Slippery Nature of Romantic Relationships: Issues in Definition and Differentiation," In Romance and Sex in Adolescence and Emerging Adulthood: Risks and Opportunities, ed. Ann C. Couter and Alan Booth. Mahwah: Lawrence Erlbaum.

Gabbidon, Shaun. 2010. Race, Ethnicity, Crime, and Justice: An International Dilemma. Los Angeles: Sage.

Gartner, Rosemary, Cheryl Marie Webster, and Anthony Doob. 2009. "Trends in the Imprisonment of Women in Canada." Canadian Journal of Criminology and Criminal Justice 51, no. 2: 169–98.

Gaylord, Mark, and John Galliher. 1988. The Criminology of Edwin Sutherland. New Brunswick: Transaction Books.

Gilchrist, Kristen. 2010. "Newsworthy Victims? Exploring Differences in Canadian Local Press Coverage of Missing/Murdered Aboriginal and White Women." Feminist Media Studies 10, no. 4: 373–90.

Gliksman, Louis, and Margaret Rylett. 2009. "The World Health Organization's Global Alcohol Disease Database: Opportunities for Research and Support for Policy." Contemporary Drug Problems 36: 589–605.

Goldstein, PJ. 1985. "The Drugs–Violence Nexus: A Tripartite Conceptual Framework." Journal of Drug Issues 15: 493–506.

Gouldner, Alvin. 1973. For Sociology: Renewal and Critique in Sociology Today. Harmondsworth: Penguin.

Greenburg, D. 1979. "Delinquency and the Age Structure of Society." In Criminology Review Yearbook, ed. S.L. Messinger and E. Bittner. 586–620. Beverley Hills: Sage.

Greenberg, Hirch, Jana Grekul, and Rhonda Nelson. 2012. "Aboriginal Youth Crime in Canada." In Youth at Risk and Youth Justice: A Canadian Overview, ed. J. Winterdyk and R. Smandych. 228–244. Toronto: Oxford University Press.

Gutierrez, Leticia, Holly A. Wisdom, Tanya Rugge, and James Bonta. 2013. "The Prediction of Recidivism with Aboriginal Offenders: A Theoretically Informed Meta-Analysis." Canadian Journal of Criminology and Criminal Justice 55, no. 1: 55–99.

Hagan, John. 1992. "The Poverty of a Classless Criminology—The American Society of Criminology 1991 Presidential Address. Criminology 30, no. 1: 1–19.

Hagan, J., A.R. Gillis, and John Simpson. 1985. "The Class Structure of Gender and Delinquency: Toward a Power–Control Theory of Common Delinquent Behavior." American Journal of Sociology 90, no. 6: 1151–78.

———. 1987. "Class in the Household: A Power–Control Theory of Gender and Delinquency." American Journal of Sociology 92, no. 4: 788–816.

Hagan, John, and Fiona Kay. 1990. "Gender and Delinquency in White-Collar Families: A Power–Control Perspective. Crime and Delinquency 36: 391–407.

Hagan, J., C. Shedd, and M.R. Payne. 2005. "Race Ethnicity, and Youth Perceptions of Criminal Injustice." American Sociological Review 70: 381–407.

Hansen, K. 2003. "Education and the Crime-Age Profile. British Journal of Criminology 43: 141–68.

Hartnagel, Timothy F. 2012. "Correlates of Criminal Behaviour." In Criminology: A Canadian Perspective, 7th ed., ed. R. Linden. Toronto: Nelson Education.

Health Canada. 2014. "Canadian Alcohol and Drug Use Monitoring Survey: Summary of Results for 2012." Web.

Heimer, Karen, and Stacey De Coster. 1999. "The Gendering of Violent Delinquency." Criminology 37, no. 2: 277–318.

Henry, Frances, and Carol Tator. 2005. The Colour of Democracy: Racism in Canadian Society. Toronto: Nelson Education.

Henry, F., C. Tator, W. Mattis, and T. Rees. 2000. The Colour of Democracy: Racism in Canadian Society, 2nd ed. Toronto: Harcourt Brace Canada.

Hingson, R.W., T. Heeren, and M.R. Winter. 2006. "Age at Drinking Onset and Alcohol Dependence: Age at Onset, Duration, and Severity." Archives of Pediatrics and Adolescent Mecidine 160: 739–46.

Hirtenlehner, Hulmut, Brenda S. Blackwell, Heinz Leitgoeb, and Johann Bacher. 2014. "Explaining the Gender Gap in Juvenile Shoplifting: A Power–Control Theoretical Analysis." Deviant Behavior 35: 41–65.

Hooghe, Marc, Bram Vanhoutte, Wim Hardyns, and Tuba Bircan. 2011. "Unemployment, Inequality, Poverty, and Crime: Spatial Distribution Patterns of Criminal Acts in Belgium, 2001–6." British Journal of Criminology 51, no. 1: 1–20.

Jackson, J., and B. Bradford. 2010. "What Is Trust and Confidence in the Police?" Policing 4, no. 3: 241–48.

Johnston, P. 1994. "Academic Approaches to Race—Race Statistics Do Not Justify Their Collection." Canadian Journal of Criminology 36: 166–73.

Kelly, Nora, and William Kelly. 1973. The Royal Canadian Mounted Police: A Century of History, 1873–1973. Edmonton: Hurtig.

Kiecolt-Glaser, Janice, and Tamara L. Newton. 2001. Marriage and Health: His and Hers. Psychological Bulletin 127: 472–503.

Kirk, David S. 2012. "Residential Change as a Turning Point in the Life Course of Crime: Desistance or Temporary Cessation?" Criminology 50, no. 2: 329–58.

———. 2009. "A Natural Experiment on Residential Change and Recidivism: Lessons from Hurricane Katrina." American Sociological Review 74: 484–505.

Klein, Dorie. 1973. "The Etiology of Female Crime." Issues in Criminology 8, no. 2: 3–30.

Kreager, Derek, Ross L. Matsueda, and Elena A. Erosheva. 2010. "Motherhood and Criminal Desistance in Disadvantaged Neighbourhoods." Criminology 48, no. 1: 221–58.

Kruttschnitt, Candace. 2013. "Gender and Crime." Annual Review of Sociology 39: 291–308.

Kubrin, Charis, and Eric Stewart. 2006. "Predicting Who Reoffends: The Neglected Role of Neighbourhood Context in Recidivism Studies." Criminology 44, no. 1: 165–97.

La Prairie, Carol. 2002. "Aboriginal Over-Representation in the Criminal Justice System: A Tale of Nine Cities." Canadian Journal of Criminology 44: 181–208.

Larson, Matthew, and Gary Sweeten. 2012. "Breaking Up Is Hard to Do: Romantic Dissolution, Offending, and Substance Use During the Transition to Adulthood." Criminology 50, no. 3: 605–36.

Laub, J., and R. Sampson. 2001. "Understanding Desistance from Crime." Crime and Justice 28: 1–69.

Lauritsen, Janet L., Karen Heimer, and James P. Lynch. 2009. "Trends in the Gender Gap in Violent Offending: New Evidence from the National Crime Victimization Survey." Criminology 47, no. 2: 361–99.

Lavery, B., A.W. Siegel, J.H. Cousins, and D.S. Rubovitts. 1993. "Adolescent Risk-Taking: An Analysis of Problem Behavior in Problem Children." Journal of Experimental Child Psychology 55: 277–94.

Levitt, S.D., and L. Lochner. 2000. "The Determinants of Juvenile Crime." In Risky Behaviour by Youths, ed. J. Gruber. Chicago: University of Chicago Press.

Li, G. 2008. "Homicide in Canada, 2007." Juristat: Statistics Canada 28: 1–26.

Lianping, Ti, Evan Wood, Kate Shannon, Cindy Feng, and Thomas Kerr. 2013. "Police Confrontations Among Street-Involved Youth in a Canadian Setting." International Journal of Drug Policy 24: 46–51.

Lin, M.J. 2008. "Does Unemployment Increase Crime? Evidence from US Data 1974–2000." Journal of Human Resources 43: 413–36.

Lochner, L. 2004. "Education, Work, and Crime: A Human Capital Approach." International Economic Review 45: 811–43.

Lochner, L., and E. Moretti. 2004. "The Effects of Education on Crime: Evidence from Prison Inmates, Arrest, and Self-Reports." American Economic Review 94: 155–89.

Lofland, Lyn H. 1973. A World of Strangers: Order and Action in Urban Public Space. New York: Basic Books.

Lombroso, Caesar, and William Ferrero. 1895. The Female Offender. New York: D. Appleton and Company.

Ludwig, J., G.J. Duncan, and P. Hirschfield. 2001. "Urban Poverty and Juvenile Crime: Evidence from a Randomized Housing-Mobility Experiment," Quarterly Journal of Economics 116: 655–79.

MacDonald, Scott, Jinhui Zhao, Basia Pakula, Tim Stockwell, and Lorissa Martens. 2009. "Unlocking Patterns of Alcohol Consumption in British Columbia Using Alcohol Sale Data: A Foundation for Public Health Monitoring." Contemporary Drug Problems 36: 499–516.

MacMillan, R., and R. Gartner. 1999. 'When She Brings Home the Bacon: Labor Force Participation and the Risk of Spousal Violence Against Women." Journal of Marriage and Family 61: 947–58.

MacMillan, R., and C. Kruttschnitt. 2005. Patterns of Violence Against Women: Risk Factors and Consequences. Rockville: National Institute of Justice.

Mahony, T.H. 2011a. "Homicide in Canada, 2010." Juristat. Web..

———. 2011b. "Women and the Criminal Justice System." Juristat. Web.

Manzoni, Patrik, Benedikt Fischer, and Jurgen Rehm. 2007. "Local Drug-Crime Dynamics in a Canadian Multi-Site Sample of Untreated Opioid Users." 341–73. Canadian Journal of Criminology and Criminal Justice.

Martin, D.F. 1992. "Aboriginal and Non-Aboriginal Homicide Homicide: Same but Different. In Homicide: Patterns, Prevention, and Control, ed. H. Strang and S. Gerull. 167–76. Camberra: Australian Institute of Criminology.

Mascoll, Philip, and Jim Rankin. 2005. "Racial profiling exists." Toronto Star, March 31, A1.

Matza, D. 1964. Delinquency and Drift. New York: Wiley.

McGill, Jena. 2008. "An Institutional Suicide Machine: Discrimination Against Federally Sentenced Aboriginal Women in Canada." Race and Ethnicity 2, no. 1: 89–119.

Merton, Robert. 1938. "Social Structure and Anomie." American Sociological Review 3: 672–82.

Miles, R. 1989. Racism. London: Routledge.

Millar P., and A. Owusu-Benpah. 2011. "Whitewashing Criminal Justice in Canada: Preventing Research Through Data Suppression." Canadian Journal of Law and Society 26, no. 3: 653–61.

Mirchandani, K., and W Chan. 2002. "From Race and Crime to Racialization and Criminalization." In W. Chan, Crimes of Colour: Racialization and the Criminal Justice System in Canada. Peterborough: Broadview.

Moffitt, T., and A. Caspi. 1999. "Findings About Partner Violence from the Dunedin Multidisciplinary Health Development Study." National Institute of Justice, Research in Brief. Washington: US Department of Justice.

Moral, Paulina G. 2011. "Representation as a Technology of Violence: On the Representation of the Murders and Disappearances of Aboriginal Women in Canada and Women in Ciudad Juarez." Canadian Journal

of Latin American and Caribbean Studies 36, no. 72: 33–62.

Morenoff, Jeffrey D., Robert J. Sampson, and Stephen W. Raudenbush. 2001. "Neighborhood Inequality, Collective Efficacy, and the Spatial Dynamics of Urban Violence." Criminology 39, no. 1: 517–58.

Morris, Patrice K., and Adam Graycar. 2011. "Homicide Through a Different Lens." British Journal of Criminology 51, no. 5: 823–38.

Munch, Christopher. 2012. "Youth Correctional Statistics in Canada, 2010–2011." Web.

Myrdal, G. 1962. An American Dilemma: The Negro Problem and Modern Democracy. Volume 1. New York: Harper & Row.

———. 1963. Challenge to Affluence. New York: Pantheon.

National Immigration Forum. 2013. The Math of Immigrations Detention: Runaway Costs for Immigration Detention Do Not Add Up to Sensible Policy. Web.

Nivette, A. 2011. "Cross-National Predictors of Crime: A Meta-Analysis." Homicide Studies 15, no. 2: 103–31.

Nye, F. Ivan, and James F. Short. 1957. "Scaling Delinquent Behavior." American Sociological Review 22: 326–31.

Nye, F. Ivan, James F. Short, and Virgil Olson. 1958. "Socioeconomic Status and Delinquent Behavior." American Sociological Review 63: 381–89.

Office of the Correctional Investigator. 2012. "Spirit Matters: Aboriginal People and the Corrections and Conditional Release Act." Web.

O'Grady, William, Patrick Parnaby, and Justin Schikschneit. 2010. "Guns, Gangs, and the Underclass: A Constructionist Analysis of Gun Violence in a Toronto High School." Canadian Journal of Criminology and Criminal Justice 52, no. 1: 55–77.

Owusu-Benpah, A., and P. Millar. 2010. "Revisiting the Collection of 'Justice Statistics by Race' in Canada."

Canadian Journal of Law and Society 25, no. 1: 97–104.

Pederson, Jeanette S., Lorraine H. Malcoe, and Jane Pulkingham. 2013. "Explaining Aboriginal/Non-Aboriginal Inequalities in Postseparation Violence Against Canadian Women: Application of Structural Violence Approach." Violence Against Women 19, no. 8: 1034–58.

Pernanen, K., M.M. Cousineau, S. Brochu, and F Sun. 2002. "Proportions of Crimes Associated with Alcohol and Other Drugs in Canada. Ottawa: Canadian Centre on Substance Abuse.

Perreault, Samuel. 2014. "Admissions to Adult Correctional Services in Canada, 2011/2012." Web.

Perreault, Samuel. 2013. Police-Reported Crime Statistics in Canada, 2012. Juristat. Ottawa: Statistics Canada.

Perry, Barbara. 2009. "'There's Just Places Ya' Don't Wanna Go': The Segregating Impact of Hate Crime Against Native Americans." Contemporary Justice Review 12, no. 4: 401–18.

Peterson, Ruth. 2012. "The Central Place of Race in Crime and Justice—the American Society of Criminology's 2011 Sutherland Address." Criminology 50, no. 2: 303–27.

Peterson, Ruth, and Lauren J. Krivo. 2010. Divergent Social Worlds: Neighborhood Crime and the Racial–Spatial Divide. New York: Russell Sage Foundation.

Pollak, Otto. 1950. The Criminality of Women. Philadelphia: University of Pennsylvania Press.

Poynter, Bilbo. 2012. "Private Prison Firms Look to Cash in on Canada Asylum Crackdown." The Guardian. Web.

Pridemore, William Alex. 2011. "Poverty Matters: A Reassessment of the Inequality–Homicide Relationship in Cross-National Studies." British Journal of Criminology 51, no. 5: 739–72.

Public Safety Canada. 2014. "Substance Abuse." Web.

Rand, Julia. 2011. "Residential Schools: Creating and Continuing Institution-alization Among Aboriginal Peoples in Canada." First Peoples' Child and Family Review 6, no. 1: 56–65.

Rehm, Jurgen, and Robin Room. 2009. "Monitoring of Alcohol Use and Attributable Harm from an International Perspective." Contemporary Drug Problems 36: 575–87.

Reiman, Jeffrey H., and Paul Leighton. 2013. The Rich Get Richer and the Poor Get Prison: Ideology, Class, and Criminal Justice, 10th ed. Boston: Pearson.

Rennison, C.M. 2009. "A New Look at the Gender Gap in Offending." Women and Criminal Justice 19: 171–90.

Roberts, J. 1994. "Crime and Race Statistics: Toward a Canadian Solution." Canadian Journal of Criminology 36: 175–85.

Roy, Elise, Isabelle Richer, Nelson Arruda, Jill Vandermeerschen, and Julie Bruneau. 2013. "Patterns of Cocaine and Opioid Co-use and Polyroutes of Administration Among Street-Based Cocaine Users in Montreal, Canada." International Journal of Drug Policy 24: 142–49.

Sabates, Ricardo. 2008. "Educational attainment and juvenile crime", British Journal of Criminology, 48: 395-409.

———. 2007. "Education and Juvenile Crime: Understanding the Links and Measuring the Effects." In Youths and Social Capital, ed. J. Bynner and H. Helve. London: Tufnell.

Sacks, H. 1972. "Notes on Police Assessment of Moral Character." In Studies in Social Interaction, ed. D. Sudnow. New York: Free Press.

Salvatore, Christopher, and Michael W. Markowitz. 2014. "Do Life Course Transitions and Social Bonds Influence Male and Female Offending Differently? Gender Contrasts and Criminality." Deviant Behavior 35: 628–53.

Sampson, R.J. 2012. "Moving and the Neighborhood Glass Ceiling." Science 337: 1464–65.

Sampson, R.J., Stephen Raudenbush, and Felton Earls. 1997. "Neighborhoods and Violent Crime: A Multilevel Study of Collective Efficacy." Science 277: 918–24.

Sampson, Robert, and John Laub. 2005. "A Life Course View of the Development of Crime." Annals of the American Academy of Political and Social Science 602: 12–45.

Schaefer, David, Nancy Rodriguez, and Scotte H. Decker. 2014. "The Role of Neighbourhood Context in Youth Co-offending." Criminology 52, no. 1: 117–39.

Shaw, C.R., and H.D. McKay. 1942. Juvenile Delinquency and Urban Areas. Chicago: University of Chicago Press.

Schissel, Bernard. 1992. "The Influence of Economic Factors and Social Control Policy on Crime Rate Changes in Canada." Canadian Journal of Sociology 17, no. 4: 405–28.

Schneider, Stephen. 2013. "Violence, Organized Crime, and Illicit Drug Markets: A Canadian Case Study." Sociologia 71: 125–43.

Sharkey, Patrick, and Robert J. Sampson. 2010. "Destination Effects: Residential Mobility and Trajectories of Adolescent Violence in Stratified Metropolis." Criminology 48: 639–82.

Shedd, C., and J. Hagan. 2006. "Toward a Developmental and Comparative Conflict Theory of Race, Ethnicity, and Perceptions of Criminal Injustice." In The Many Colors of Crime, ed. R.D. Peterson, L.J. Krivo, and J. Hagan, 313–33. New York: NYU Press.

Silver, A. 1967. "The Demand for Order in Civil Society: A Review of Some Themes in the History of Urban Crime, Police, and Riot." In The Police: Six Sociological Essays, ed. David J. Bordua. New York: Wiley.

Simon, Rita. 1975. Women and Crime. Lexington: D.C. Heath.

Skardhamar, Torbjørn, and Jukka Savolainen. 2014. "Changes in Criminal Offending Around the Time of Job Entry: A Study of Employment and Desistance." Criminology 52, no. 2: 263–91.

Snowball, Lucy, and Don Weather-burn. 2008. "Theories of Indigenous

Violence: A Preliminary Empirical Assessment." Australian and New Zealand Journal of Criminology 41, no. 2: 216–35.

Sprott J.B., and A.N. Doob. 2014. "Confidence in the Police: Variation Across Groups Classified as Visible Minorities." Canadian Journal of Criminology and Criminal Justice 56, no. 3: 367–78.

Statistics Canada. 2011. "Immigration and Ethnocultural Diversity in Canada." National Household Survey 2011, Cat. no. 99-010-X2011001. Web.

Steenbeek, Wouter, and John Hipp. 2011. "A Longitudinal Test of Social Disorganization Theory: Feeback Effects Among Cohesion, Control, and Disorder." Criminology 49, no. 3: 833–71.

Steffensmeier, Darrell, and Dana Haynie. 2000. "Gender, Structural Disadvantage, and Urban Crime: Do Macrosocial Variables Also Explain Female Offending Rates." Criminology 38, no. 2: 403–38.

Steffensmeier, Darrell, Jennifer Schwartz, and Michael Roche. 2013. "Gender and Twenty-First Century Corporate: Female Involvement and the Gender Gap in Enron-Era Corporate frauds." American Sociological Review 78, no. 3: 448–76.

Steffensmeier, Darrell, Jennifer Schwartz, H. Zhong, and J. Ackerman. 2005. "An Assessment of Recent Trend in Girls' Violence Using Diverse Longitudinal Sources: Is the Gender Gap Closing?" Criminology 38: 403–38.

Steffensmeier, D., and C. Streifel. 1992. "Time-Series Analysis of the Female Percentage of Arrests for Property Crimes, 1960–1985." Justice Quarterly 9, no. 1: 77–103.

Stevens, T., M. Morash, and M. Chesney-Lind. 2011. "Are Girls Getting Tougher, or Are We Tougher on Girls? Probability of Arrest and Juvenile Court Oversight in 1980 and 2000." Justice Quarterly 28: 719–44.

Stockwell, Tim, et al. 2009. "The British Columbia Alcohol and Other Drug Monitoring System: Overview and

Early Progress," Contemporary Drug Problems 36: 459–84.

Sutherland, Edwin. 1940. "White Collar Criminality." American Sociological Review 5: 1–12.

Tanovich, D.M. 2006. The Colour of Justice: Policing Race in Canada. Toronto: Irvin Law.

Tator, C., and F. Henry. 2006. Racial Profiling in Canada: Challenging the Myth of a Few Bad Apples. Toronto: University of Toronto Press.

Tatum, B.L. 1994. "The Colonial Model as a Theoretical Explanation of Crime and Delinquency." In African American Perspectives: On Crime Causation, Criminal Justice Administration, and Prevention, ed. A.T. Sulton. 33-52. Englewood: Sulton Books.

Taylor-Butts, A., and A. Bressan. 2006. "Youth Crime in Canada, 2006." Juristat 28: 1–16.

The Sentencing Project. 2014. "Racial Disparity," http://www.sentencingproject.org/template/page.cfm?id=122. Accessed June 12, 2014.

Thomas, W.I. 1923. The Unadjusted Girl. New York: Harper and Row.

Thompson, R., and J.K. Tabone. 2010. "The Impact of Early Alleged Maltreatment on Behavioural Trajectories." Child Abuse and Neglect 34: 907–16.

Thompson, Sara K., and Rosemary Gartner. 2014. "The Spatial Distribution and Social Context of Homicide in Toronto's Neighbourhoods." Journal of Research in Crime and Delinquency 51, no. 1: 88–118.

Thornhill, Esmeralda. 2008. "So Seldom for Us. So Often Against Us: Blacks and Law in Canada." Journal of Black Studies 38, no. 3: 321–37.

Ti, Lianping, Evan Woo, Kate Shannon, Cindy Feng, and Thomas Kerr. 2013. "Police Confrontations Among Street-Involved Youth in a Canadian Setting." International Journal of Drug Policy 24: 46–51.

Tittle, C.R., and Robert Meier. 1990. "Specifying the SES/Delinquency Relationship." Criminology 28, no. 2: 271–99.

Tittle, C.R., W.J. Villemez, and D.A. Smith. 1978. "The Myth of Social Class and Criminality." Social Forces 56, no. 2: 474–502.

Tittle, C.R., W.J. Villemez, and Douglas Smith. 1978. "The Myth of Social Class and Criminality: An Empirical Assessment of the Empirical Evidence." American Sociological Review 43: 643–56.

Tonry, M. 1997. "Ethnicity, Crime, and Immigration." Crime and Justice 21: 1–29.

Truth and Reconciliation Commission of Canada. 2014. "Residential Schools," http://www.trc.ca/websites/trcinstitution/index.php?p=4. Accessed June 11, 2014.

Tyler, T. 1990. Why People Obey the Law. New Haven: Yale University Press.

UN Office on Drugs and Crime. 2011. 2011 Global Study on Homicide: Trends, Context, Data. Vienna.

Wacquant, Loïc. 2008. Urban Outcasts: A Comparative Sociology of Advanced Marginality. Cambridge: Polity.

———. 2004. Body and Soul: Ethnographic Notebooks of An Apprentice-Boxer. New York: Oxford University Press.

———. 2001. "The Penalization of Poverty and the Rise of Neo-Liberalism." European Journal on Criminal Policy and Research 9: 401–12.

Walklate, Sandra, ed. 2012. "Introduction." In Gender and Crime: Critical Concepts on Criminology, 1–5. London and New York: Routledge.

Warren, P., D. Tomaskovic-Devey, W. Smith, M. Zingraff, and M. Mason. 2006. "Driving While Black: Bias Processes and Racial Disparity in Police Stops." Criminology 44, no. 3: 709–38.

Weekes, J.R., W.A. Milson, F.J. Porporino, and D. Robinson. 1994. The Offender Substance Abuse Pre-Release Outcomes. Ottawa: Research and Statistics Branch, Correctional Service of Canada.

Weinrath, Michael, Janna Young, and Steven Kohn. 2012. "Attitudes

Towards the Criminal Justice System in a High Crime Canadian Community." Canadian Journal of Urban Research 21, no. 2: 112–31.

Werb, Dan, Bohdan Nosyk, Thomas Kerr, Benedikt Fischer, Julio Montaner, and Evan Wood. 2012. "Estimating the Economic Value of British Columbia's Domestic Cannabis Market: Implications for Provincial Cannabis Policy." International Journal of Drug Policy 23, no. 6: 436–41.

Wesley-Esquimau, Cynthia, and Magdalena Smolewski. 2004. Historic Trauma and Aboriginal Healing. Aboriginal Healing Foundation Research Series. Web.

Wolfgang, Marvin E., and F. Ferracuti. 1967. The Structure of Violence: Towards an Integrated Theory in Criminology. London: Tavistock.

Woodworth, Michael, Ava D. Agar, and Richard B.A. Coupland. 2013. "Characteristics of Canadian Youth-Perpetrated Homicides." Criminal Justice and Behavior, 40, no. 9: 1009–26.

Wortley, Scott. 1999. "A Northern Taboo: Research on Race, Crime, and Criminal Justice in Canada." Canadian Journal of Criminology 41, no. 2: 261–74.

Wortley, Scot, and Andrea McCalla. 2007. "Racial Discrimination in the Ontario Criminal Justice System: 1994–2007." In Criminal Justice in Canada: A Reader, 3rd ed., ed. Julian Roberts and Michelle Grossman. Toronto: Thomson Nelson.

Wortley, Scot, and Akwasi Owusu-Bempah. 2011. "The Usual Suspects: Police Stop and Search Practices in Canada." Policing and Society 21, no. 4: 395–407.

Wortley, S., and J. Tanner. 2003. "Data, Denials, and Confusion: The Racial Profiling Debate in Toronto." Canadian Journal of Criminology and Criminal Justice 45, no. 3: 367–89.

———. 2005. "Inflammatory Rhetoric? Baseless Accusations? Responding to Gabor's Critique of Racial Profiling Research in Canada." Canadian Journal of Criminology and Criminal Justice 47, no. 3: 581–609.

Wright, B.E. 1994 [1984]. The Psychopathic Racial Personality and Other Essays. Chicago: Third World.

Wright, Bradley, Avshalom Caspi, Richard Miech, and Phil A. Silva. 1999. "Reconsidering the Relationship Between SES and Delinquency: Causation But Not Correlation." Criminology 37, no. 1: 175–94.

Young, Jock. 1999. The Exclusive Society: Social Exclusion, Crime, and Difference in Late Modernity. London: Sage.

Yun I., J.D. Ball, and H. Lim. 2011. "Disentangling the Relationship Between Child Maltreatment and Violent Delinquency: Using a Nationally Representative Sample." Journal of Interpersonal Violence 26: 88–110.

CHAPTER 6

Adelberg, Ellen, and Claudia Currie. 1993. "In Their Own Words: Seven Women's Stories." In In Conflict with the Law: Women and the Canadian Justice System, ed. E. Adelberg and C. Currie. Vancouver: Press Gang.

Adler, Freda. 1975. Sisters in Crime. New York: McGraw-Hill.

Amir, Menachem. 1967. "Victim Precipitated Forcible Rape." Journal of Criminal Law and Criminology 58, no. 4: 493–502.

———. 1971. The Patterns of Forcible Rape. Chicago: University of Chicago Press.

Amnesty International. 2004. Stolen Sisters: A Human Rights Response to Discrimination and Violence Against Indigenous Women in Canada. Web.

Anderssen, Erin. 2011. "Toronto Police Officer Offers Inappropriate Safety Tip." Globe and Mail, February 17.

Arnold, Regina. 1995. "The Processes of Victimization and Criminalization of Black Women." In The Criminal Justice System and Women, ed. B.R. Price and N. Sokoloff. New York: McGraw-Hill.

Bertrand, Marie-Andrée. 1967. "The Myth of Sexual Equality Before the Law." Fifth Research Conference on Delinquency and Criminality. Montreal, Centre de Psychologies et de Pédagogie.

Boritch, Helen. 1997. Fallen Women: Female Crime and Criminal Justice in Canada. Toronto: Nelson.

Boyle, Christine. 1994. "The Judicial Construction of Sexual Assault Offences." In Confronting Sexual Assault: A Decade of Social and Legal Change, ed. J. Roberts and R. Mohr. Toronto: University of Toronto Press.

Brennan, Shannon. 2012. "Police-Reported Crime Statistics in Canada, 2011." Juristat, July 24.

Brinkerhoff, Merlin, and Eugen Lupri. 1988. "Interspousal Violence." Canadian Journal of Sociology 13, no. 4: 407–34.

Brock, Deborah. 1998. Making Work, Making Trouble: Prostitution as a Social Problem. Toronto: University of Toronto Press.

Bronson, Diana. 1989. "A Time for Grief and Pain." Globe and Mail, December 8, A7.

Browne, Angela. 1987. When Battered Women Kill. New York: Free Press.

Brownmiller, Susan. 1975. Against Our Will: Men, Women, and Rape. New York: Bantam Books.

Bruckert, Chris, and Colette Parent. 2014. "The In-Call Sex Industry: Reflections on Classed and Gendered Labour on the Margins." In Criminalizing Women: Gender and (In)justice in Neo-liberal Times, 2nd ed., ed. G. Balfour and E. Comack. Halifax: Fernwood.

Busby, Karen. 1997. "Discriminatory Uses of Personal Records in Sexual Violence Cases." Canadian Journal of Women and the Law 9, no. 1: 149–77.

———. 2014. "'Sex Was in the Air': Pernicious Myths and Other Problems with Sexual Violence Prosecutions." In Locating Law: Race/Class/Gender/Sexuality—Connections, 3rd ed., ed. E. Comack. Halifax and Winnipeg: Fernwood.

Cain, Maureen. 1990. "Towards Transgression: New Directions in Feminist Criminology." International Journal of the Sociology of Law 18: 1–18.

Carlen, Pat, ed. 1985. Criminal Women. Cambridge: Polity.

_____. (1988). Women, Crime and Poverty. Milton Keynes: Open University Press.

Chan, Wendy. 2001. Women, Murder and Justice. London: Palgrave.

Chesney-Lind, Meda, and Noelie Rodriguez. 1983. "Women Under Lock and Key." Prison Journal 63: 47–65.

Chesney-Lind, Meda, and Randall Sheldon. 1998. Girls, Delinquency, and Juvenile Justice. California: Wadsworth.

Chunn, Dorothy E., and Shelley A.M. Gavigan. 2014. "From Welfare Fraud to Welfare as Fraud: The Criminalization of Poverty." In Criminalizing Women: Gender and (In)justice in Neo-liberal Times, 2nd ed., ed. G. Balfour and E. Comack. Halifax: Fernwood.

Cohen, Albert. 1955. Delinquent Boys. Glencoe: The Free Press.

Comack, Elizabeth. 1993. "Women Offenders' Experiences with Physical and Sexual Abuse: A Preliminary Report." Criminology Research Centre, University of Manitoba.

_____. 1996. Women in Trouble: Connecting Women's Law Violations to Their Histories of Abuse. Halifax: Fernwood.

Comack, Elizabeth, and Gillian Balfour. 2004. The Power to Criminalize: Violence, Inequality and the Law. Halifax and Winnipeg: Fernwood.

Comack, Elizabeth, and Salena Brickey. 2007. "Constituting the Violence of Criminalized Women." Canadian Journal of Criminology and Criminal Justice 49, no. 1: 1–36.

Comack, Elizabeth, Vanessa Chopyk, and Linda Wood. 2000. "Mean Streets? The Social Locations, Gender Dynamics, and Patterns of Violent Crime in Winnipeg." Winnipeg: Canadian Centre for Policy Alternatives.

_____. 2008. "Aren't Women Violent Too? The Gendered Nature of Violence." In Marginality and Condemnation: An Introduction to Critical Criminology, 2nd ed., ed. B. Schissel and C. Brooks. Halifax and Winnipeg: Fernwood.

Connell, R.W. 1987. Gender and Power. Cambridge: Polity.

_____. 1995. Masculinities. Cambridge: Polity.

_____. 2000. The Men and the Boys. Berkeley: University of California Press.

Connell, R.W., and James Messerschmidt. 2005. "Hegemonic Masculinity: Rethinking the Concept." Gender & Society 19, no. 6: 829–59.

Cowie, John, Valerie Cowie, and Eliot Slater. 1968. Delinquency in Girls. London: Heinemann.

Crocker, Diane, and Val Marie Johnson. 2010. Poverty, Regulation, and Social Justice: Readings on the Criminalization of Poverty. Halifax and Winnipeg: Fernwood.

Daly, Kathleen. 1987. "Discrimination in the Criminal Courts: Family, Gender, and the Problem of Equal Treatment." Social Forces 66, no. 1: 152–75.

_____. 1989. "Rethinking Judicial Paternalism: Gender, Work-Family Relations, and Sentencing." Gender and Society 3, no. 1: 9–36.

Daly, Kathleen, and Meda Chesney-Lind. 1988. "Feminism and Criminology." Justice Quarterly 5, no. 4: 101–43.

Dauvergne, Mia. 2012. "Adult Correctional Statistics in Canada, 2010/2011." Juristat (October 11).

DeKeseredy, Walter, and Ronald Hinch. 1991. Woman Abuse: Sociological Perspectives. Toronto: Thompson.

Dobash, R. Emerson, and Russell Dobash. 1979. Violence Against Wives: A Case Against Patriarchy. New York: Free Press.

_____. 1992. Women, Violence, and Social Change. London: Routledge.

Dobash, Russell, R. Emerson Dobash, Margo Wilson, and Martin Daly. 1992. "The Myth of Sexual Symmetry in Marital Violence." Social Problems 39, no. 1: 71–91.

Dutton, Donald. 1994. "Patriarchy and Wife Assault: The Ecological Fallacy." Violence and Victims 9.

Edwards, Susan. 1985. "Gender Justice? Defending Defendants and Mitigating Sentence." In Gender, Sex and the Law, ed. S. Edwards. Kent: Croom Helm.

Faith, Karlene. 1993. Unruly Women: The Politics of Confinement and Resistance. Vancouver: Press Gang.

Frenschkowski, Joanne. 2002. "We've Learned Little from Kimberly Rogers's Death." Globe and Mail, August 9, A13.

Gelsthorpe, Lorraine, and Allison Morris. 1988. "Feminism and Criminology in Britain." British Journal of Criminology 23: 93–110.

Gilfus, Mary. 1992. "From Victims to Survivors to Offenders: Women's Routes of Entry and Immersion into Street Crime." Women and Criminal Justice 4, no. 1: 63–89.

Glueck, Eleanor, and Sheldon Glueck. 1934. Five Hundred Delinquent Women. New York: Alfred A. Knopf.

Gotell, Lise. 2001. "Colonization Through Disclosure: Confidential Records, Sexual Assault Complainants, and Canadian Law." Social and Legal Studies 10, no. 3: 315–46.

Hagan, John, A.R. Gillis, and John Simpson. 1985. "The Class Structure of Gender and Delinquency: Toward a Power-Control Theory of Common Delinquent Behavior." American Journal of Sociology 90: 1151–78.

Hagan, John, John Simpson, and A.R. Gillis. 1979. "The Sexual Stratification of Social Control: A Gender-Based Perspective on Crime and Delinquency." British Journal of Sociology 30: 25–38.

_____. 1987. "Class in the Household: A Power-Control Theory of Gender and Delinquency." American Journal of Sociology 92, no. 4 (January): 788–816.

Hamilton, Alvin C., and C. Murray Sinclair. 1991. The Justice System and Aboriginal People: Report of the Aboriginal Justice Inquiry of Manitoba. Vol. 1. Winnipeg: Queen's Printer.

Hannah-Moffat, Kelly. 2001. Punishment in Disguise: Penal Governance and Federal Imprisonment of Women in Canada. Toronto: University of Toronto Press.

Hannah-Moffat, Kelly, and Margaret Shaw, eds.. 2000. An Ideal Prison? Critical Essays on Women's Imprisonment in Canada. Halifax: Fernwood.

Harries, Kate. 2002. "Inquest to Probe House-Arrest Death," Toronto Star, October 15.

Hayman, Stephanie. 2006. Imprisoning Our Sisters: The New Federal Women's Prisons in Canada. Montreal and Kingston: McGill–Queen's University Press.

Hazelwood, Roy, Janet Warren, and Park Elliot Dietz. 1993. "Compliant Victims of the Sexual Sadist." Australian Family Physician 22, no. 4: 474–79.

Heidensohn, Frances. 1968. "The Deviance of Women: A Critique and an Enquiry." British Journal of Sociology 19, no. 2: 160–75.

_____. 1985. Women and Crime. London: Macmillan.

Heimer, Karen. 1995. "Gender, Race and Pathways to Delinquency." In Crime and Inequality, ed. J. Hagan and R. Peterson. Stanford: Stanford University Press.

Hoffman-Bustamante, Dale. 1973. "The Nature of Female Criminality." Issues in Criminology 8: 117–36.

Hugill, David. 2010. Missing Women, Missing News: Covering Crisis in Vancouver's Downtown Eastside. Halifax and Winnipeg: Fernwood.

Johnson, Holly. 1996. Dangerous Domains. Toronto: Nelson Education.

Johnson, Holly, and Karen Rodgers. 1993. "A Statistical Overview of Women in Crime in Canada." In In Conflict with the Law: Women and the Canadian Justice System, ed. Ellen Adelberg and Claudia Currie. 95–116. Vancouver: Press Gang.

Jones, Anne. 1994. Next Time She'll Be Dead: Battering and How to Stop It. Boston: Beacon.

Kelly, Liz. 1988. Surviving Sexual Violence. Minneapolis: University of Minnesota Press.

Kendall, Kathleen. 1991. "The Politics of Premenstrual Syndrome: Implica-

tions for Feminist Justice." Journal of Human Justice 2, no. 2 (Spring): 77–98.

_____. 1992. "Dangerous Bodies." In D. Farrington and S. Walklate (eds.), Offenders and Victims: Theory and Policy. London: British Society of Criminology.

_____. 1993. Program Evaluation of Therapeutic Services at the Prison for Women. Ottawa: Correctional Services Canada.

Kennedy, Leslie, and Donald Dutton. 1989. "The Incidence of Wife Assault in Alberta." Canadian Journal of Behavioural Science 21: 40–54.

Kinnon, Dianne. 1981. Report on Sexual Assault in Canada. Ottawa: CACSW.

Klein, Dorie 1973. "The Etiology of Female Crime: A Review of the Literature." Issues in Criminology 8, no. 3: 3–30.

Konopka, Gisella. 1966. The Adolescent Girl in Conflict. Englewood Cliffs: Prentice Hall.

Kruttschnitt, Candace. 1980–81. "Social Status and Sentences of Female Offenders." Law and Society Review 15, no. 2: 247–65.

_____. 1982. "Women, Crime, and Dependency." Criminology 195: 495–513.

Laberge, Danielle. 1991. "Women's Criminality, Criminal Women, Criminalized Women? Questions in and for a Feminist Perspective." Journal of Human Justice 2, no. 2: 37–56.

Laframboise, Donna. 1996. "Men and Women Are Equals in Violence." National Post, July 10.

La Prairie, Carol. 1993. "Aboriginal Women and Crime in Canada: Identifying the Issues." In In Conflict with the Law: Women and the Canadian Justice System, ed. Ellen Adelberg and Claudia Currie. Vancouver: Press Gang.

Leonard, Eileen. 1982. Women, Crime, and Society: A Critique of Theoretical Criminology. New York: Longman.

Lombroso, Cesare, and William Ferrero. 1895. The Female Offender. London: Fischer Unwin.

Luckhaus, Linda. 1985. "A Plea for PMT in the Criminal Law." In Gender, Sex, and the Law, ed. S. Edwards. Kent: Croom Helm.

MacLeod, Linda. 1980. Wife Battering in Canada: The Vicious Circle. Ottawa: CACSW.

Mahony, Tina Hotton. 2011. Women and the Criminal Justice System. Ottawa: Statistics Canada. http://statcan.gc.ca/pub/89-503-x/2010001/article/11416-eng.pdf.

Mann, Ruth. 2003. "Violence Against Women or Family Violence? The 'Problem' of Female Perpetration in Domestic Violence." In Power and Resistance: Critical Thinking about Canadian Social Issues, ed. L. Samuelson and W. Antony. Halifax: Fernwood.

Martin, Dianne L. 1999. "Punishing Female Offenders and Perpetuating Gender Stereotypes." In Making Sense of Sentencing, ed. J. Roberts and D. Cole. Toronto: University of Toronto Press.

Martin, Dianne L., and Janet E. Mosher. 1995. "Unkept Promises: Experiences of Immigrant Women with the Neo-Criminalization of Wife Abuse." Canadian Journal of Women and the Law 8: 3–44.

McGillivray, Anne. 1998. "'A Moral Vacuity in Her Which Is Difficult If Not Impossible to Explain': Law, Psychiatry, and the Remaking of Karla Homolka." International Journal of the Legal Profession 5, ns. 2/3: 255–88.

Messerschmidt, James. 1993. Masculinities and Crime: A Critique and Reconceptualization of Theory. Landham: Rowman and Littlefield.

_____. 1997. Crime as Structured Action: Gender, Race, Class, and Crime in the Making. Thousand Oaks: Sage.

_____. 2004. Flesh and Blood: Adolescent Gender Diversity and Violence. Landham: Rowman and Littlefield.

_____. 2012. Gender, Sexuality, and Youth Violence: The Struggle for Recognition. Landham: Rowman and Littlefield.

Miller, Eleanor M. 1986. Street Woman. Philadelphia: Temple University Press.

Monture Angus, Patricia. 1999. "Women and Risk: Aboriginal Women, Colonialism, and Correctional Practice." Canadian Women's Studies 19, no. 1: 24–29.

Morris, Allison. 1987. Women, Crime, and Criminal Justice. Oxford: Basil Blackwell.

Morrissey, Belinda. 2003. When Women Kill: Questions of Agency and Subjectivity. London: Routledge.

Mosher, Janet E. 2014. "The Construction of 'Welfare Fraud' and the Wielding of the State's Iron Fist." In Locating Law: Race/Class/Gender/Sexuality Connections, 3rd ed., ed. E. Comack. Halifax and Winnipeg: Fernwood.

Naffine, Ngaire. 1987. Female Crime: The Construction of Women in Criminology. Sydney: Allen and Unwin.

_____. 1997. Feminism and Criminology. Sydney: Allen and Unwin.

NWAC (Native Women's Association of Canada). 2010. What Their Stories Tell Us: Research Findings from the Sisters in Spirit Initiative. Ottawa. Web.

Osborne, Judith. 1989. "Perspectives on Premenstrual Syndrome: Women, Law and Medicine." Canadian Journal of Family Law 8: 165–84.

Pearson, Patricia. 1997. When She Was Bad: Violent Women and the Myth of Innocence. Toronto: Random House.

Perreault, Samuel. 2009. "The Incarceration of Aboriginal People in Adult Correctional Services." Juristat 29, no. 3.

Pollak, Otto. 1961. The Criminality of Women. New York: A.S. Barnes.

R v Ewanchuk, (1999) 1 SCR 330, reversing (1998) 57 AR 235.

R v Mills, (1998) 3 S.C.R. 688.

R v O'Connor, (1995) 4 SCR 411.

R v Rhodes, (2010), Man.CR08-15-00316(QB); [2011], MJ (Q/L) No. 67 (QB) (Sentencing Transcript), overturned [2011], 281 CCC (3d) 29 (CA), retried 2013 MBQB 166 (CanLII), sentencing 2013 MBQB 251.

R v Seaboyer, (1991) 2 SCR 577.

Rafter, Nicole H., and Elena M. Natalizia. 1981. "Marxist Feminism: Implications for Criminal Justice." Crime and Delinquency 27 (January): 81–98.

RCAP (Royal Commission on Aboriginal Peoples). 1996. Report. Ottawa: Department of Indian and Northern Affairs.

RCMP. 2014. Missing and Murdered Aboriginal Women: A National Operational Overview. Ottawa. Web.

Ritchie, Beth. 1996. Compelled to Crime: The Gender Entrapment of Battered Black Women. New York: Routledge.

Sapers, Howard. 2013. Annual Report of the Office of the Correctional Investigator, 2012–2013. Ottawa: Correctional Investigator Canada. Web.

Schwartz, Martin, and Walter DeKeseredy. 1993. "The Return of the 'Battered Husband Syndrome' Through the Typification of Women as Violent." Crime, Law, and Social Change 20: 249–65.

Scully, Diana, and Joseph Marolla. 1984. "Convicted Rapists' Vocabulary of Motive: Excuses and Justifications." Social Problems 31, no. 5: 530–44.

Scutt, Jocelyn. 1979. "The Myth of the 'Chivalry Factor' in Female Crime." Australian Journal of Social Issues 14, no. 1: 3–20.

Seshia, Maya. 2005. The Unheard Speak Out. Winnipeg: Canadian Centre for Policy Alternatives.

Shaw, Margaret. 1993. "Reforming Federal Women's Imprisonment." In In Conflict with the Law: Women and the Canadian Justice System, ed. E. Adelberg and C. Currie. Vancouver: Press Gang.

Shaw, Margaret, Karen Rogers, Johannes Blanchette, Tina Hattem, Lee Seto Thomas, and Lada Tamarack. 1991. Survey of Federally Sentenced Women: Report on the Task Force on Federally Sentenced Women: The Prison Survey. Ottawa: Ministry of the Solicitor General of Canada. User Report No. 1991-4.

Simon, Rita. 1975. Women and Crime. Lexington: D.C. Heath.

Smart, Carol. 1976. Women, Crime, and Criminology: A Feminist Critique. London: Routledge and Kegan Paul.

_____. 1977. "Criminological Theory: Its Ideology and Implications Concerning Women." British Journal of Sociology 28, no. 1: 89–100.

_____. 1989. Feminism and the Power of Law. London: Routledge.

Snider, Laureen. 1991. "The Potential of the Criminal Justice System to Promote Feminist Concerns." In The Social Bias of Law: Critical Readings in the Sociology of Law, 2nd ed., ed. E. Comack and S. Brickey. Halifax: Fernwood.

_____. 1994. "Feminism, Punishment, and the Potential of Empowerment." Canadian Journal of Law and Society 9, no. 1: 74–104.

_____. 2003. "Constituting the Punishable Woman: Atavistic Man Incarcerates Postmodern Woman." British Journal of Criminology 43, no. 2: 354–78.

Sommers, Evelyn. 1995. Voices from Within: Women Who Have Broken the Law. Toronto: University of Toronto Press.

Statistics Canada. 1993. "The Violence against Women Survey." The Daily, November 18.

_____. 2000. "Family Violence." The Daily, July 25.

_____. 2005. "General Social Survey: Victimization." The Daily, July 7.

_____. 2010. "General Social Survey: Self-Reported Victimization, by Type of Offence and Province, 2009." Web.

_____. 2011a. "Cases in Adult Criminal Court, by Province and Territory, 2009/2010." Web.

_____. 2011b. "Police-Reported Crime for Selected Offences, 2009 and 2010." Web.

Steffensmeier, Darrell, and John H. Kramer. 1982. "Sex-Based Differences in the Sentencing of Adult Criminal Defendants." Sociology and Social Research 663: 289–304.

Steinmetz, Suzanne. 1981. "A Cross-cultural Comparison of Marital

Abuse." Journal of Sociology and Social Welfare 8: 404–14.

Straus, Murray A. 1979. "Measuring Intrafamily Conflict and Violence: The Conflict Tactics (CT) Scales." Journal of Marriage and the Family 41, no.1.

Straus, Murray, and Richard Gelles. 1986. "Societal Changes and Change in Family Violence from 1975 to 1985 as Revealed by Two National Surveys." Journal of Marriage and the Family 48: 465–80.

Straus, Murray, Richard Gelles, and Suzanne Steinmetz. 1980. Behind Closed Doors: Violence in the American Family. New York: Doubleday.

Taylor, Ian, Paul Walton, and Jock Young. 1973. The New Criminology. London: Routledge and Kegan Paul.

The War Against Women. 1991 (June). Report of the Standing Committee on Health and Welfare, Social Affairs, Seniors and the Status of Women. Barbara Greene, Chair. Ottawa: House of Commons.

Thomas, William I. 1967. The Unadjusted Girl. New York: Harper and Row.

Ursel, Jane. 1994. "The Winnipeg Family Violence Court." Juristat 14, no. 12.

———. 1998. "Eliminating Violence Against Women: Reform or Co-Optation in State Institutions." In Power and Resistance: Critical Thinking About Canadian Social Issues, 2nd ed., ed. L. Samuelson and W. Antony. Halifax: Fernwood.

Walker, Lenore. 1979. The Battered Woman. New York: Harper and Row.

———. 1987. Terrifying Love: Why Battered Women Kill and How Society Responds. New York: HarperCollins.

Wallace, Marnie. 2004. "Crime Statistics in Canada, 2003." Juristat 24, no. 6.

West, Candace, and Don Zimmerman. 1987. "Doing Gender." Gender & Society 1, no. 2: 125–51.

Zingraff, Matthew, and Randall Thomson. 1984. "Differential Sentencing of Women and Men in the USA." International Journal of the Sociology of Law 12: 401–13.

CHAPTER 7

Allen, Mary. 2014. "Victim Services in Canada, 2011/2012." Juristat. Statistics Canada, Cat. no. 85-002X.

Amernic, Jerry. 1984. Victims: Orphans of Justice. Toronto: McClelland and Stewart.

Besserer, Sandra, and Catherine Trainor. 2000. "Criminal Victimization in Canada, 1999." Juristat 20, no. 10.

Black, M.C., K.C. Basile, M.J. Breiding, S.G. Smith, M.L. Walters, M.T. Merrick, J. Chen, and M.R. Stevens. The National Intimate Partner and Sexual Violence Survey (NISVS): 2010 Summary Report. Atlanta: National Center for Injury Prevention and Control, Centers for Disease Control and Prevention, 2011.

Campbell, Rebecca. 2006. "Rape Survivors' Experiences with the Legal and Medical Systems: Do Rape Victim Advocates Make a Difference?" Violence Against Women 12, no. 1: 30–35.

Canada, Department of Justice. 2004. "Canadian Statement of Basic Principles of Justice for Victims of Crime, 2003." Ottawa: Department of Justice Canada. Web.

Canada, Canadian Federal–Provincial Task Force on Justice for Victims of Crime. 1983. Final Report. Ottawa.

Canada, Standing Committee on Justice and Human Rights. 2000. Victims' Rights—A Voice Not a Veto. Ottawa: Parliament of Canada.

Clarke, Lorenne, and Debra Lewis. 1977. Rape: The Price of Coercive Sexuality. Toronto: Women's Press.

Crooks, Claire, D., Wolfe, R. Hughes, P. Jaffe, and D. Chiodo. 2008. Development, Evaluation, and National Implementation of a School-Based Program to Reduce Violence and Related Risk Behaviours: Lessons from the 4th R. Ottawa: Institute for the Prevention of Crime.

European Council. 2001. Framework Decision of 15 March 2001 on the Standing of Victims in Criminal Proceedings (2001/220/JHA). Brussels: Commission of the European Communities.

European Union. 2012. Council Directive 2012/29/EU of the European Parliament and of the Council of 25 October 2012 Establishing Minimum Standards on the Rights, Support, and Protection of Victims of Crime, and Replacing Council Framework Decision 2001/220/JHA.

Fisher, Bonnie, and John J. Sloan. 2007. Campus Crime: Legal, Social, and Policy Perspectives. Springfield: Charles C. Thomas.

Gannon, Maire, and Karen Mihorean. 2005. "Criminal Victimization in Canada, 2004." Juristat 25, no. 7.

Gaudreault, Arlène, and Irvin Waller. 2001. "Xe Symposium international de victimologie: Textes choisies du Symposium." Paper presented at the Association québécoise Plaidoyer-Victimes, Montreal, August.

Groenhuijsen, Marc, and Rianne Letschert, eds.. 2009. Compilation of International Victims' Rights Instruments. Nijmegen: Wolf Legal Publishers.

Institute for the Prevention of Crime. 2009 (March). Making Cities Safer: Action Briefs for Municipal Stakeholders, Number 3. Ottawa: University of Ottawa.

International Association of Chiefs of Police. 2008. Enhancing Law Enforcement Response to Victims: A 21st Century Strategy. Alexandria: International Association of Chiefs of Police.

International Victimology Institute Tilburg. 2006. "Towards Implementation of the UN Declaration on Basic Principles of Justice for Victims of Crime and Abuse of Power—Preparing a Draft Convention on the Rights of Victims of Crime, Abuse of Power and Terrorism." Report on Expert Group Meeting. University of Tilburg.

Kilpatrick, Dean, Heidi Resnick, Kenneth J. Ruggiero, Lauren Conoscenti, and Jenna McCauley. 2007. Drug-Facilitated, Incapacitated, and Forcible Rape: A National Study. Washington: US Department of Justice, National Institute of Justice.

MADD (Mothers Against Drunk Driving Canada). 2010. "The Magnitude of the Alcohol/Drug-Related Crash Problem in Canada." Web.

Mazowita, Benjamin, and Marta Burczycka. 2014. "Shelters for Abused Women in Canada, 2012." Web.

McMurtry, Roy. 2008. "Report on Financial Assistance for Victims of Crime in Ontario." Toronto: Ontario Ministry of the Attorney General. Web.

Miller, Ted, Mark Cohen, and Brian Wiersema. 1996. Victim Costs and Consequences: A New Look. Washington: National Institute of Justice.

National Crime Victim Bar Association. 2007. Civil Justice for Victims of Crime. Washington: National Center for Victims of Crime.

National Sheriffs' Association. 2008. First Response to Victims of Crime: A Guide Book for Law Enforcement Officers. Washington: US Department of Justice.

Newmark, Lisa. 2006. Crime Victims' Needs and VOCA-Funded Services: Findings and Recommendations from Two National Studies. Washington: National Institute of Justice.

Newmark, Lisa, Judy Bonderman, Barbara Smith, and E. Blaine Liner. 2006. The National Evaluation of State Victims of Crime Act Assistance and Compensation Programs: Trends and Strategies for the Future. Washington: National Institute of Justice.

Nina's Place. 2011. http://www.jbmh.com. Web.

Ombudsman of Ontario. 2007. Adding Insult to Injury: Investigation into the Treatment of Victims by the Criminal Injuries Compensation Board. Toronto: Ombudsman of Ontario.

Ontario, Criminal Injuries Compensation Board. 2010. 35th Annual Report—2009/2010. Web.

Ontario. 1984. Government Consultation on Victims of Violent Crime. Toronto: Secretary for Justice.

Parliamentary Budget Officer. 2013. Expenditure Analysis of Criminal Justice in Canada. Ottawa: Office of the Parliamentary Budget Officer.

Perreault, Samuel, and Shannon Brennan. 2010. "Criminal Victimization in Canada, 2009." Juristat 30, no. 2.

Safe Horizons. 2011. Web.

Saskatchewan. 2011. Restitution Civil Enforcement Program. Regina: Justice and Attorney General. Web.

Schweinhart, Lawrence. 2003. "Benefits, Costs, and Explanation of the High/Scope Perry Preschool Program." Presented at the Meeting of the Society for Research in Child Development, Tampa, April 26.

Seymour, Anne, and Steve Derene. 2003. "An Oral History of the Crime Victim Assistance Field." University of Akron. Web.

Skogan, W., and K. Frydl. 2004. Fairness and Effectiveness in Policing: The Evidence. Washington: National Academies Press.

Statistics Canada. 2009. Police Personnel and Expenditures. Ottawa: Canadian Centre for Justice Statistics. Web.

Sauvé, Julie. "Victim Services in Canada: Results from the Victim Services Survey 2007/2008." Justice Canada, Victims of Crime Research Digest. Web.

_____. 2005. "Crime Statistics in Canada, 2004." Juristat 25, no. 5.

Strang, Heather, and Lawrence W. Sherman. 2007. Restorative Justice: The Evidence. London: Smith Institute.

Thomas, Mikhail. 2004. "Adult Criminal Court Statistics, 2003/2004." Juristat 24, no. 12.

UN, General Assembly. 1985. Declaration of Basic Principles of Justice for Victims of Crime and Abuse of Power (GA/res/40/34). New York. Web.

UN, Office for Drugs and Crime. 1999. Guide for Policy Makers on the Implementation of the Declaration of Basic Principles of Justice for Victims of Crime and Abuse of Power. New York.

_____. 1999. Handbook on Justice for Victims on the Use and Application of the Declaration of Basic Principles of Justice for Victims of Crime and Abuse of Power. New York.

_____. 2005. Guidelines on Justice for Child Victims and Witnesses. New York.

US Department of Justice. Bureau of Justice Statistics. 2010. "Criminal Victimization in the United States, 2007 Statistical Tables." Web.

_____. Bureau of Justice Statistics. 2009. Criminal Victimization, 2008. Washington: Office of Justice Programs.

_____. Office for Victims of Crime. 1999. International Crime Victim Compensation Directory. Washington.

_____. 2002. Restitution: Making It Work. Washington.

_____. 2009. "Nation-Wide Analysis—Performance Reports." Web.

_____. Office on Violence Against Women. (2007). 2006 Biennial Report to Congress on the Effectiveness of Grant Programs Under the Violence Against Women Act. Washington.

_____. 2006. S.T.O.P. Program Services, Training, Officers, Prosecutors, Annual Report 2006. Washington.

US Government Accountability Office. 2009. Crime Victim Rights Act: Increasing Victim Awareness and Clarifying Applicability to the District of Columbia Will Improve Implementation of the Act. Washington.

United States. 1982. President's Task Force on Victims of Crime Final Report. Washington.

van Dijk, Jan, Robert Manchin, John van Kesteren, and Gergely Hideg. 2007. The Burden of Crime in the EU: A Comparative Analysis of the European Survey of Crime and Safety. Brussels: Gallup Europe.

Victim Support Europe. 2010. Victims in Europe: Implementation of the EU Framework Decision on the Standing of Victims in the Criminal Proceedings in the Member States of the European Union. Lisbon: Associação Portuguesa de Apoio à Vítima.

Victims of Violence Canadian Centre for Missing Children. 2014. An Exploration of the Victims' Movement in Canada, Ottawa.

Waller, Irvin. 2014. Smarter Crime Control: A Guide to a Safer Future for Citizens, Communities, and Politicians. New York: Rowman and Littlefield.

_____. 2010. Rights for Victims of Crime: Rebalancing Justice. New York: Rowman and Littlefield.

_____. 2008. Less Law, More Order: The Truth About Reducing Crime. Westport: Praeger.

_____. 2004. "Harnessing Criminology and Victimology Internationally." In Lessons from International/Comparative Criminology/Criminal Justice, ed. John Winterdyk and Liqun Cao. 233–48. Toronto: De Sitter.

Waller, Irvin, and Norm Okihiro. 1978. Burglary, the Victim, and the Public. Toronto: University of Toronto Press.

Wang, Ching-Tung, and John Holton. 2007. "Total Estimated Cost of Child Abuse and Neglect in the United States." Prevent Child Abuse America. Web.

Wemmers, Jo-Anne. 2003. Introduction a la victimologie. Montreal: Les Presses de l'Université de Montreal.

Wing-Cheong Chan, ed. 2008. Support for Victims of Crime in Asia. London: Routledge.

World Health Organization. 2002. World Report on Violence and Health. Geneva.

_____. 2004. Economic Dimensions of Interpersonal Violence. Geneva.

_____. 2009. Violence Prevention: The Evidence. Geneva.

_____. 2010. Preventing Intimate Partner and Sexual Violence Against Women: Taking Action and Generating Evidence. Geneva.

Zhang, Ting. 2011. Costs of Crime in Canada, 2008. Ottawa: Department of Justice Canada. Web.

CHAPTER 8

Angell, Robert. 1965. Free Society and Moral Crisis. Ann Arbor: University of Michigan Press.

Archer, Dane, Rosemary Gartner, and Marc Beittel. 1983. "Homicide and the Death Penalty: A Cross-National Test of a Deterrence Hypothesis." Journal of Criminal Law and Criminology 74: 991–1014.

Beccaria, Cesare. 1963. On Crimes and Punishments. Translated by H. Paolucci. Indianapolis: Bobbs-Merrill. (First published as Dei Delitti E Delle Pene in 1764.)

Beirne, Piers. 1993. Inventing Criminology. Albany: SUNY Press.

Best, Michael. 1998. "What Did Elizabethans Consider a Crime?" Internet Shakespeare Editions 2001. http://web.uvic.ca/shakespeare/Library/SLTnoframes/history/crime.html. Accessed July 14, 2003.

Driver, Edwin D. 1972. "Charles Buckman Goring." In Pioneers in Criminology, ed. Hermann Mannheim. 429–42. Montclair: Patterson Smith.

Empey, LaMar T. 1982. American Delinquency: Its Meaning and Construction. Homewood,: Dorsey.

Gibbs, Jack R. 1975. Crime, Punishment, and Deterrence. New York: Elsevier.

Goddard, H.H. 1912. The Kallikak Family: A Study in the Heredity of Feeble-Mindedness. New York: Macmillan.

_____. 1914. Feeble-Mindedness: Its Causes and Consequences. New York: Macmillan.

Goring, Charles. 1913. The English Convict. London: HMSO.

_____. 1972. The English Convict. Montclair: Patterson Smith.

Gould, Stephen Jay. 1996. The Mismeasure of Man: Revised and Expanded. New York: W.W. Norton.

Harris, Marvin. 1974. Cows, Pigs, Wars, and Witches. New York: Vintage.

Hobbes, Thomas. 1958. Leviathan, Parts I and II. Indianapolis: Bobbs-Merrill. (First published in 1651.)

Hogan, Margaret Monahan. n.d. "Medical Ethics: The New Eugenics: Therapy—Enhancement—Screening—Testing." International Catholic University. Web.

Hooker, Richard. n.d.. "The European Enlightenment." World Civilizations. Washington State University. Web.

Hooton, Ernest Albert. 1939. The American Criminal: An Anthropological Study. Cambridge, MA: Harvard University Press.

Hostettler, John. 2011. Cesare Beccaria: The Genius of "On Crimes and Punishment." Sherfield on Loddon: Waterside.

Langbein, John H. 1976. Torture and the Law of Proof. Chicago: University of Chicago Press.

Lilly, J. Robert, Frances T. Cullen, and Richard A. Ball. 2007. Criminological Theory: Context and Consequences, 4th ed. Thousand Oaks: Sage.

Lombroso, Cesare. 1912. Crime: Its Causes and Remedies. Boston: Little, Brown.

_____. 1972. "Criminal Man." In The Heritage of Modern Criminology, ed. S.F. Sylvester. 67–78. Cambridge: Schenkman.

Lombroso-Ferrero, Gina. 1972. Criminal Man According to the Classification of Cesare Lombroso. Montclair: Patterson Smith.

Monachesi, Elio. 1972. "Cesare Beccaria." In Pioneers in Criminology, ed. Hermann Mannheim. Montclair: Patterson Smith.

Newman, Graeme. 1978. The Punishment Response. New York: J.B. Lippincott.

Newman, Graeme, and Pietro Marongiu. 1990. "Penological Reform and the Myth of Beccaria." Criminology (May): 325–46.

Parmelee, Maurice. 1912. "Introduction to the English Version." In Cesare Lombroso, Crime: Its Causes and Remedies. xi–xxxii. Boston: Little, Brown.

Pfohl, Stephen J. 1985. Images of Deviance and Social Control. New York: McGraw-Hill.

Radzinowicz, Sir Leon. 1966. Ideology and Crime. London: Heinemann.

Radzinowicz, Sir Leon, and Joan King. 1977. The Growth of Crime. London: Pelican.

Rafter, Nicole Hahn. 1997. Creating Born Criminals. Urbana: University of Illinois Press.

Rosenhaft, Eve. "The Nazi Persecution of Deaf People." Panel presentation, US Holocaust Memorial Museum, August 14, 2001. Web.

Roshier, Bob. 1989. Controlling Crime: The Classical Perspective in Criminology. Philadelphia: Open University Press.

Sylvester, F. Sawyer, Jr. 1972. The Heritage of Modern Criminology. Cambridge: Schenkman.

Taylor, Ian, Paul Walton, and Jock Young. 1973. The New Criminology: For a Social Theory of Deviance. London: Routledge and Kegan Paul.

Thomas, Charles W., and John R. Hepburn. 1983. Crime, Criminal Law, and Criminology. Dubuque: Wm. C. Brown.

Wetzell, Richard. 2000. Inventing the Criminal: A History of German Criminology, 1880–1945. Chapel Hill: University of North Carolina Press.

Wolf, Leonard. 1981. In Stephen Jay Gould, The Mismeasure of Man. New York: W.W. Norton.

Wolfgang, Marvin E. 1972. "Cesare Lombroso." In Pioneers in Criminology, ed. Hermann Mannheim. 232–91. Montclair: Patterson Smith.

Zilborg, Gregory. 1969. The Medical Man and the Witch During the Renaissance. New York: Cooper Square.

CHAPTER 9

Abrahamsen, D. 1944. Crime and the Human Mind. New York: Columbia University Press.

Abram, K.M., and L.A. Teplin. 1991. "Co-Occurring Disorders Among Mentally Ill Jail Detainees: Implications for Public Policy." American Psychologist 46: 1036–45.

Abram, K.M., L.A. Teplin, and G.M. McClelland. 2003. "Comorbidity of Severe Psychiatric Disorders and Substance Use Disorders Among Women in Jail." American Journal of Psychiatry 160: 1007–10.

Akers, R. 1990. "Rational Choice, Deterrence, and Social Learning Theories in Criminology: The Path Not Taken." Journal of Criminal Law and Criminology 81: 653–76.

Akers, R.L., and G.F. Jensen. 2006. "Empirical Status of Social Learning Theory of Crime and Deviance: The Past, Present, and Future." In Taking Stock: The Status of Criminological Theory, ed. K. Blevins, F. Cullen, and J. Wright. 37–76. Beverly Hills: Sage.

Alexander, F., and M. Healey. 1935. Roots of Crime. New York: Alfred A. Knopf.

Allodi, F., H. Kedward, and M. Robertson. 1977. "Insane But Guilty: Psychiatric Patients in Jail." Canada's Mental Health 25: 3–7.

Anderson, C.A., A. Shibuya, N. Ihori, E.L. Swing, B.J. Bushman, A. Sakamoto, H.R. Rothstein, and M. Saleem. 2010. "Violent Video Game Effects on Aggression, Empathy, and Prosocial Behavior in Eastern and Western Countries." Psychological Bulletin 136: 151–73.

APA (American Psychiatric Association). 2000. Psychiatric Services in Jails and Prisons, 2nd ed. Washington.

Arboleda-Florez, J., A. Crisanti, and H. Holley. 1995. "The Effects of Changes in the Law Concerning Mentally Disordered Offenders: The Alberta Experience with Bill C-30." Canadian Journal of Psychiatry 40: 225–33.

———. 2013. Diagnostic and Statistical Manual of Mental Disorders, 5th ed. Washington.

Babiak, Paul, and Robert Hare. 2006. Snakes in Suits: When Psychopaths Go to Work. New York: HarperBusiness.

Bandura, A. 1986. Social Foundations of Thought and Action: A Social Cognitive Theory. Englewood Cliffs: Prentice Hall.

———. 2000. "Social-Cognitive Theory." In Encyclopedia of Psychology, Vol. VII, ed. A.E. Kazdin. 329–32. Washington: America Psychological Association.

Bartol, C.R. 1980. Criminal Behavior: A Psychosocial Approach. Englewood Cliffs: Prentice Hall.

Birmingham, L., J. Gray, D. Mason, and D. Grubin. 2000. "Mental Illness at Reception into Prison." Criminal Behaviour and Mental Health 10: 77–87.

Blair, R.J.R. 2006. "Subcortical Brain Systems in Psychopathy." In Handbook of Psychopathy, ed. C.J. Patrick. 296–312. New York: Guilford.

Blasi, A. 1980. "Bridging Moral Cognition and Moral Action: A Critical Review of the Literature." Psychological Bulletin 88: 1–45.

Bonta, J., M. Law, and K. Hanson. 1998. "The Prediction of Criminal and Violent Recidivism Among Mentally Disordered Offenders: A Meta-Analysis." Psychological Bulletin 123: 123–42.

Borum, R. 1996. "Improving the Clinical Practice of Violence Risk Assessment: Technology Guidelines and Training." American Psychologist 51: 945–46.

Borzecki, M., and J.S. Wormith. 1985. "The Criminalization of Psychiatrically Ill People: A Review with a Canadian Perspective." Psychiatric Journal of the University of Ottawa 10: 241–47.

Bowlby, J. 1953. Child Care and the Growth of Love. New York: Penguin.

Braukman, C.J., K.A. Kirigin, and M.M. Wolf. 1980. "Group Homes Treatment Research: Social Learning and Social Control Perspectives." In Understanding Crime: Current Theory and Research, ed. T. Hirschi and M. Gottfredson. Beverly Hills: Sage.

Braukman, C.J., and M.M. Wolf. 1987. "Behaviorally Based Group Homes for Juvenile Offenders." In Behavioral Approaches to Crime and Delinquency, ed. Braukman and Wolf. New York: Plenum.

Braukman, C.J., K.A. Kirigin, and M.M. Wolf. 1980. "Group Home Treatment Research: Social Learning and Social Control Perspectives." In Understanding Crime, ed. Travis Hirschi and Michael Gottfredson, Beverly Hills: Sage.

Braukman, C.J., M.M. Wolf, and K.K. Ramp. 1985. "Follow-Up of

Group Home Youths into Young Adulthood." Progress Report, Grant MA 20030. Achievement Place Research Project, University of Kansas, Lawrence.

Brodsky, S.L. 1977. "Crime and Dangerous Behavior." In Abnormal Psychology, ed. D.C. Rimm and J.W. Somervill. New York: Academic Press.

Burgess, R.L., and R.L. Akers. 1966. "A Differential Association Reinforcement Theory of Criminal Behavior." Social Problems 14: 128–47.

Buttell, F.P. 2002. "Exploring Levels of Moral Development Among Sex Offenders Participating in Community-Based Treatment." Journal of Offender Rehabilitation 34: 85–95.

Chaiklin, H. 2001. "Current and Prior Mental Health Treatment of Jail Inmates: The Use of the Jail as an Alternative Shelter". Journal of Social Distress and the Homeless 10: 255–68.

Clastner, D.S. 1967. "Comparison of Risk Perception Between Delinquents and Nondelinquents." Journal of Criminal Law, Criminology, and Police Science 58: 80–86.

Cleckley, H. 1976. The Mask of Sanity. St. Louis: Mosby.

Cohen, A.K. 1966. Deviance and Control. Englewood Cliffs: Prentice Hall.

Conger, R.D. 1976. "Social Control and Social Learning Models of Delinquent Behavior: A Synthesis." Criminology 14: 17–40.

Cook, T.D., D.A. Kendzierski, and S.V. Thomas. 1983. "The Implicit Assumptions of Television Research: An Analysis of the 1982 NIMH Report on Television and Behavior." Public Opinion Quarterly 47: 161–201.

Corrado, R.R., I. Cohen, S.D. Hart, and R. Roesch. 2000. "Comparative Examination of the Prevalence of Mental Disorders Among Jailed Inmates in Canada and the United States." International Journal of Law and Psychiatry 23: 633–47.

Cotton, D., and T.G. Coleman. 2010. "Canadian Police Agencies and Their Interactions with Persons with a Mental Illness: A Systems Approach." Police Practice and Research: An International Journal 11: 301–14.

Craddick, R. 1962. "Selection of Psychopathic from Non-Psychopathic Prisoners within a Canadian Prison." Psychological Reports 10: 495–99.

DeMatteo, D., and J. Edens. 2006. "The Role and Relevance of the Psychopathy Checklist-Revised in Court: A Case Law Survey of U.S. Courts". Psychology, Public Policy, and Law 24: 133–46.

Diamond, P.M., W.W. Eugene, C.E. Holzer, C. Thomas, and D.A. Cruser. 2001. "The Prevalence of Mental Illness in Prison." Administration and Policy in Mental Health 29: 21–40.

Drewett, A. and Shepperdson, B. 1995. A Literature Review of Services for Mentally Disordered Offenders. Leicester: Nuffield Community Care Studies Unit, University of Leicester.

Einstadter, W., and S. Henry. 1995. Criminological Theory: An Analysis of Its Underlying Assumptions. Fort Worth: Harcourt Brace.

Ewen, R.B. 1988. An Introduction to Theories of Personality. Hillside: Lawrence Erlbaum.

Eysenck, H.J. 1977. Crime and Personality. London: Routledge and Kegan Paul.

———. 1990. "Crime and Personality." In Clinical Criminology: Theory Research and Practice, ed. N.Z. Hilton, M.A. Jackson, and C.D. Webster. 85–99. Toronto: Canadian Scholars' Press.

Eysenck, H.J., and S.B. Eysenck. 1976. Psychoticism as a Dimension of Personality. London: Hodder and Stoughton.

Eysenck, H.J., and G.H. Gudjonsson. 1989. The Causes and Cures of Criminality. New York and London: Plenum.

Falissard, B., J. Loze, Y. Gasquet, I. Duburc, A. de Beaurepaire, C. Fagnani, and F. Rouillon. 2006. "Prevalence of Mental Disorders in French Prisons for Men." BMC Psychiatry 6: 33–38.

Farrington, D.P. 1978. "The Family Background of Aggressive Youths." In Aggression and Antisocial Behavior in Childhood and Adolescence, ed. L.A. Hersov, M. Berger, and D. Shaffer. Oxford: Pergamon.

———. 1979. "Environmental Stress, Delinquent Behavior, and Conviction." In Stress and Anxiety, Vol. 6, ed. I.G. Sarason and C.D. Spielberger. Washington: Hemisphere.

———. 2002. "Multiple Risk Factors for Multiple Problem Violent Boys." In Multi-Problem Violent Youth: A Foundation for Comparative Research on Needs, Interventions and Outcomes, ed. R.R. Corrado, R. Roesch, S.D. Hart, and J.K. Gierowski. 23–34. Amsterdam: IOS.

Farrington, D.P., L. Biron, and M. LeBlanc. 1982. "Personality and Delinquency in London and Montreal." In Abnormal Offenders, Delinquency, and the Criminal Justice System, ed. J. Gunn and D.P. Farrington. Chichester: Wiley.

Fazel, Seena, and John Danesh. 2002. "Serious Mental Disorder in 23,000 Prisoners: A Systematic Review of 62 Surveys." The Lancet 359: 545–50.

Friedlander, K. 1947. The Psychoanalytic Approach to Juvenile Delinquency. New York: International Universities Press.

Geen, R.G. 1983. "Aggression and Television Violence." In Aggression: Theoretical and Empirical Reviews, ed. R.G. Geen and E.I. Donnerstein. New York: Academic Press.

Gilligan, C. 1982. In a Different Voice: Psychological Theory and Women's Development. Cambridge, MA: Harvard University Press.

Gunn, J. 1977. "Criminal Behaviour and Mental Disorder." British Journal of Psychiatry 130: 317–29.

Gunn, J., A Maden, and M. Swinton. 1991. "Treatment Needs of Prisoners with Psychiatric Disorders." BMJ 303: 338–41.

Hails, J., and R. Borum. 2006. "Police Training and Specialized Approaches to Respond to People With Mental Illnesses." Crime and Delinquency 49: 52–61.

Hakeem, M. 1958. "A Critique of the Psychiatric Approach to Crime and Correction." Law and Contemporary Problems 23: 650–82.

Haney, C. 2002. "Making Law Modern: Toward a Contextual Model of Justice." Psychology, Public Policy, and Law 7: 3–63.

Hare, R.D. 1970. Psychopathy: Theory and Research. New York: Wiley.

———. 1982. "Psychopathy and the Personality Dimensions of Psychoticism, Extraversion, and Neuroticism." Personality and Individual Differences 3: 35–42.

———. 1983. "Diagnosis of Antisocial Personality Disorder in Two Prison Populations." American Journal of Psychiatry 140: 887–90.

———. 1991. The Hare Psychopathy Checklist—Revised. Toronto: Multi-Health Systems.

———. 1998a. Without Conscience: The Disturbing World of the Psychopaths Among Us. New York: Guilford.

———. 1998b. "Psychopathy, Affect and Behavior." In Psychopathy: Theory, Research and Implications for Society, ed. D.J. Cooke, A.E. Forth, and R. Hare. 105–37. Dordrecht: Kluwer.

———. 1998c. "The Hare PCL-R: Some Issues Concerning Its Use and Misuse." Legal and Criminological Psychology 3: 101–19.

Hare, R.D., and D.N. Cox. 1978. "Clinical and Empirical Conceptions of Psychopathy, and the Selection of Subjects for Research." In Psychopathic Behavior: Approaches to Research, ed. R.D. Hare and D. Schalling. Chichester: Wiley.

Harris, G. and M. Rice. 1997. "Risk Appraisal and Management of Violent Behavior. Psychiatric Services 48: 1168–76.

Hart, S.D., D.N. Cox, and R.D. Hare. 1995. The Hare Psychopathy Checklist: Screening Version. Toronto: Multi-Health Systems.

Hodgins, S. 1995. "Assessing Mental Disorder in the Criminal Justice System: Feasibility versus Clinical Accuracy."

International Journal of Law and Psychiatry 18: 15–28.

Heilbrun, A.B., Jr. 1979. "Psychopathy and Violent Crime." Journal of Consulting and Clinical Psychology 47: 509–16.

Hodgins, S., and G. Côté. 1990. "Prevalence of Mental Disorders among Penitentiary Inmates in Quebec." Canada's Mental Health (March): 1–4.

Hoge, Robert, Nancy Guerra, and Paul Boxer. 2008. Treating the Juvenile Offender. New York: Guilford Press.

Human Rights Watch. 2003. Ill-Equipped: US Prisons and Offenders with Mental Illness. New York.

Jacobsen, D., W. Craven, and S. Kushner. 1973. "A Study of Police Referral of Allegedly Mentally Ill Persons to a Psychiatric Unit." In The Urban Policeman in Transition: A Psychological and Sociological Review, ed. J.R. Snibbe and H.M. Snibbe. Springfield: C.C. Thomas.

James, D.J., and L.E. Glaze. 2006. "Mental Health Problems in Prison and Jail Inmates." Bureau of Justice Statistics Bulletin, NCJ 213600. Web.

Jeffery, C.R. 1965. "Criminal Behavior and Learning Theory." Journal of Criminal Law and Criminology 56: 294–300.

Jennings, W.S., R. Kilkenny, and L. Kohlberg. 1983. "Moral-Development Theory and Practice for Youthful and Adult Offenders." In Personality Theory, Moral Development, and Criminal Behavior, ed. W.S. Laufer and S.M. Day. 281–94. Lexington: Lexington.

Kiriakidis, S. 2008. "Moral Disengagement: Relation to Delinquency and Independence from Indices of Social Dysfunction." International Journal of Offender Therapy and Comparative Criminology 52: 571–83.

Kohlberg, L., and R. Kramer. 1969. "Continuities and Discontinuities in Child and Adult Moral Development." Human Development 12: 93–120.

Kropp, P.R., D.N. Cox, R. Roesch, and D. Eaves. 1989. "The Perceptions of

Correctional Officers Towards Mentally Disordered Offenders." International Journal of Law and Psychiatry 12: 181–88.

Lamb, H.R., R. Shaner, D.M. Elliott, W.J. DeCuir, and J.T. Foltz. 1995. "Outcome for Psychiatric Emergency Patients Seen by an Outreach Police—Mental Health Team." Psychiatric Services 46: 1267–71.

Lamb, H.R., and L.E. Weinberger. 1998. "Persons with Severe Mental Illness in Jails and Prisons: A Review." Psychiatric Services 49: 483–92.

Lev, J. 1998. "Jail as a Psychiatric Emergency Room." American Jails 12: 72–74.

Loeber, R., and D.P. Farrington. 2012. "Advancing Knowledge about Direct Protective Factors That May Reduce Youth Violence." American Journal of Preventive Medicine 43: S24–S27.

Loeber, R., D.P. Farrington, and M. Stouthamer-Loeber. 2001a. "Male Mental Health Problems, Psychopathy, and Personality Traits: Key Findings from the First 14 years of the Pittsburgh Youth Study." Clinical Child and Family Psychology Review 4: 273–97.

———. 2001b. "The Development of Male Offending: Key Findings from the First Decade of the Pittsburgh Youth Study." In Children and the Law: The Essential Readings, ed. R. Bull. 336–78. Malden: Blackwell.

Losel, F. 1998. "Treatment and Management of Psychopaths." In Psychopathy: Theory, Research and Implications for Society, ed. D.J. Cooke, A.E. Forth, and R. Hare. 303–54. Dordrecht: Kluwer.

Malamuth, N.M., and J.V.P. Check. 1981. "The Effects of Mass Media Exposure on Acceptance of Violence Against Women: A Field Experiment." Journal of Research in Personality 15: 436–46.

Markowitz, F.E. 2011. "Mental Illness, Crime, and Violence: Risk, Context, and Social Control." Aggression and Violent Behavior 16: 36–44.

Martin, S.E., L.E. Sechrest, and R. Redner, eds. 1981. New Directions in the Rehabilitation of Criminal Offenders. Washington: National Press Academy.

McIntyre, Mike. 2009. "Only One Verdict Possible: Judge, Killer Ruled Not Responsible for Grisly Deed." Winnipeg Free Press, March 6.

Monahan, J., and S. Splane. 1980. "Psychological Approaches to Criminal Behavior." In Criminology Review Yearbook, ed. E. Bittner and S. Messinger. Beverly Hills: Sage.

Monahan, J., and H.J. Steadman. 1983. "Crime and Mental Disorder: An Epidemiological Approach." In Crime and Justice: An Annual Review of Research, ed. M. Tonry and N. Morris. Chicago: University of Chicago Press.

Morash, M. 1983. "An Explanation of Juvenile Delinquency: The Integration of Moral Reasoning, Theory, and Social Knowledge." In Personality Theory, Moral Development, and Criminal Behavior, ed. W.S. Laufer and J.M. Day. 385–409. Lexington: Lexington.

Moretti, Marlene, Margaret Jackson, and Ingrid Obsuth. 2010. "Translating Research into Intervention: Lessons Learned and New Directions". Court Review 46: 58–63.

Nathan, P.E., and S.L. Harris. 1975. Psychopathology and Society. New York: McGraw-Hill.

National Commission on Correctional Health Care 2003. Standards for Health Services in Jails. Chicago.

Newman, J.P. 1998. "Psychopathic Behavior: An Information Processing Perspective." In Psychopathy: Theory, Research and Implications for Society, ed. D.J. Cooke, A.E. Forth, and R. Hare. 81–104. Dordrecht: Kluwer.

Nicholls, T.L., R. Roesch, M.C. Olley, J.R.P. Ogloff, and J.F. Hemphill. 2005. Jail Screening Assessment Tool (JSAT): Guidelines for Mental Health Screening in Jails. Burnaby: Mental Health, Law, and Policy Institute, Simon Fraser University.

Nietzel, M.T. 1979. Crime and Its Modification: A Social Learning Perspective. New York: Pergamon.

Ogloff, J.R.P. 1996. The Surrey Pretrial Mental Health Program: Community Component Evaluation. Surrey: BC Forensic Psychiatric Services Commission.

Ogloff, J.R.P. 2002. Identifying and Accommodating the Needs of Mentally Ill People in Gaols and Prisons. Psychiatry, Psychology, and Law 9: 1–33.

Ogloff, J.R.P., S. Wong, and A. Greenwood. 1990. "Treating Criminal Psychopaths in a Therapeutic Community Program." Behavioral Sciences and the Law 8: 181–90.

Osher, F., H.J. Steadman, and H. Barr. 2003. "A Best Practice Approach to Community Re-entry from Jails for Inmates with Co-occurring Disorders: The APIC Model." Crime and Delinquency 49: 79–96.

Piaget, J. 1932. The Moral Judgment of the Child. New York: Free Press.

Polansky, N., R. Lippitt, and F. Redl. 1950. "An Investigation of Behavioral Contagion in Groups." Human Relations 3: 319–48.

Power, C. 2010. "The Moral Education Miracle at the Franklin County Community-Based Corrections Facility: The Influence of Moral Culture." Journal of Research in Character Education 8: xiii–xxii.

Pritchard, Dean. 2009. "Beheading Verdict No Surprise: Family." Winnipeg Sun, March 5.

Province of Manitoba Review Board. 2009. "A Disposition Hearing Held in Winnipeg, Manitoba on Monday, June 1, 2009." Winnipeg: Manitoba Review Board.

———. 2010. "A Disposition Review Hearing Held in Winnipeg, Manitoba on Monday, May 31, 2010." Winnipeg: Manitoba Review Board.

Queen's Bench, Winnipeg Centre. n.d.. Between Her Majesty the Queen and Vince Weiguang Li—Agreed Statement of Facts. n.d. Winnipeg: Queen's Bench.

Raine, A., and Y. Yang. 2006. "The Neuroanatomical Basis of Psychopathy." In Handbook of Psychopathy, ed. C.J. Patrick. 278–95. New York: Guilford.

Rappaport, J. 1977. Community Psychology: Values, Research, and Action. New York: Holt, Rinehart and Winston.

Reid, C.L. 2003. "Do Minority and Female Offenders Have Distinct 'Criminal Personalities'?: A Critique of Yochelson-Samenow's Theory of Criminality." Criminal Justice Studies 16: 233–44.

Redl, F., ed. 1966. When We Deal with Children: Selected Writings. New York: Free Press.

Reppucci, N.D., and W.G. Clingempeel. 1978. "Methodological Issues in Research with Correctional Populations." Journal of Consulting and Clinical Psychology 46: 727–46.

Roesch, R. 1988. "Community Psychology and the Law." American Journal of Community Psychology 16: 451–63.

———. 1995. "Mental Health Interventions in Pretrial Jails." In Psychology and Law: Advances in Research, ed. G.M. Davies, S. Lloyd-Bostock, M. McMurran, and C. Wilson. 520–31. Berlin: De Greuter.

Roesch, R., and S.L. Golding. 1985. "The Impact of Deinstitutionalization." In Aggression and Dangerousness, ed. D.P. Farrington and J. Gunn. New York: Wiley.

Salekin, R.T., C. Worley, and R.D. Grimes. 2010. "Treatment of Psychopathy: A Review and Brief Introduction to the Mental Model Approach for Psychopathy." Behavioral Sciences and the Law 28: 235–66.

Schoenfeld, C.G. 1971. "A Psychoanalytic Theory of Juvenile Delinquency." Crime and Delinquency 19: 469–80.

Scott, C., and B. McDermott. "International Perspectives (I): An Overview of US Correctional Mental Health." In Psychiatry in Prisons: A Comprehensive Handbook, ed. S. Wilson & I. Cumming. 239–45. London: Jessica Kingsley.

Seidman, E., and B. Rabkin. 1983. "Economics and Psychosocial Dysfunction: Toward a Conceptual Framework and Prevention Strategies." In Preventive Psychology, ed. R.D. Felner et al. 175–98. Elmsford: Pergamon.

Shenson, D., N. Dubler, and D. Michaels. 1990. "Jails and Prisons: The New Asylums?" American Journal of Public Health 80: 655–56.

Skeem, J., and D. Cooke. 2010. "Is Criminal Behavior a Central Component of Psychopathy? Conceptual Directions for Resolving the Debate." Psychological Assessment 22: 433–45.

Skilling, T.A., G.T. Harris, M.E. Rice, and V.L. Quinsey. 2002. "Identifying Persistently Antisocial Offenders Using the Hare Psychopathy Checklist and DSM Antisocial Personality Disorder Criteria." Psychological Assessment 14: 27–38.

Skoler, G.D., A. Bandura, and D. Ross. 1994. "Aggression." In Readings in Social Psychology: General, Classic, and Contemporary Selections, 2nd ed., ed. W.A. Lesko. 296–326. Boston: Allyn & Bacon.

Slinger, E., and R. Roesch. 2010. "Problem-Solving Courts in Canada: A Review and a Call for Empirically-Based Evaluation Methods." International Journal of Law and Psychiatry 33: 258–64.

Smith, S.L., and A.R. Boyson. 2002. "Violence in Music Videos: Examining the Prevalence and Context of Physical Aggression." Journal of Communication 52: 61–83.

Somers, J.M., Cartar, L. and Russo, J. 2008. Corrections, Health and Human Services: Evidence-Based Planning and evaluation. Center for Applied Research in Mental Health and Addiction, Simon Fraser University.

Steadman, H.J., D.W. McCarty, and J.P. Morrissey. 1988. The Mentally Ill in Jail: Planning for Essential Services. New York: Guilford.

Steadman, H.J., J.E. Scott, F. Osher, T.K. Agnese, and P.C. Robbins. 2005. "Validation of the Brief Jail Mental Health Screen." Psychiatric Services 56: 816–22.

Suedfeld, P., and P.B. Landon. 1978. "Approaches to Treatment." In Psychopathic Behaviour: Approaches

to Research, ed. R.D. Hare and D. Schalling. 347–76. Chichester: Wiley.

Teevan, J.J., and T.F. Hartnagel. 1976. "The Effects of Television Violence on the Perceptions of Crime by Adolescents." Sociology and Social Research 60: 337–48.

Teplin, Linda. 1984. "Criminalizing Mental Disorder: The Comparative Arrest Rate of the Mentally Ill." American Psychologist 7: 794–803.

———. 1991. "The Criminalization Hypothesis: Myth, Misnomer, or Management Strategy." In Law and Mental Health: Major Developments and Research Needs, ed. S.A. Shah and B.D. Sales. 149–83. Rockville: US Department of Health and Human Services.

Thomas, M.H., R.W. Horton, E.C. Lippincott, and R.S. Drabman. 1979. "Desensitization to Portrayals of Real-Life Aggression as a Function of Exposure to Television Violence." Journal of Personality and Social Psychology 35: 450–58.

Thompson, S. 2010. Policing Vancouver's Mentally Ill: The Disturbing Truth. Vancouver: Vancouver Police Department.

Thornberry, T.P., and M.D. Krohn. 2000. "The Self-Report Method for Measuring Delinquency and Crime." Criminal Justice 4: 33–83.

Torrey, E. Fuller. 1995. "Jails and Prisons: America's New Mental Hospitals." American Journal of Public Health 85: 1611–13.

Walter, G.D. 2004. "The Trouble with Psychopathy as a General Theory of Crime." International Journal of Offender Therapy and Comparative Criminology 48: 133–48.

Warren, M.Q., and M.J. Hindelang. 1979. "Current Explanations of Offender Behavior." In Psychology of Crime and Criminal Justice, ed. H. Toch. 166–82. New York: Holt, Rinehart and Winston.

Webster, C.D., T.L. Nicholls, M.L. Martin, S.L. Desmarais, and J. Brink. 2006. "Short-Term Assessment of Risk and Treatability (START): The Case for a New Structured Profes-

sional Judgment Scheme." Behavioral Sciences and the Law 24: 747–66.

Widom, C. 1977. "A Methodology for Studying Non-Institutionalized Psychopaths." Clinical Psychology 45: 674–83.

Widom, C., and J.P. Newman. 1985. "Characteristics of Non-Institutionalized Psychopaths." In Aggression and Dangerousness, ed. D.P. Farrington and J. Gunn. 57–80. New York: Wiley.

Wilson, M. 2004. "The Community and Family Context in Understanding Juvenile Crime." In Applying Psychology to Forensic Practice, ed. A. Needs & G. Towl. 18–33. Glasgow: Malden Blackwell.

Wilson-Bates, F. 2008. Lost in Transition: How a Lack of Capacity in the Mental Health System Is Failing Vancouver's Mentally Ill and Draining Police Resources. Vancouver: Vancouver Police Board.

CHAPTER 10

Agnew, Robert. 2001. "Building on the Foundation of General Strain Theory: Specifying the Types of Strain Most Likely to Lead to Crime and Delinquency." Journal of Research in Crime and Delinquency 38: 319–61.

Agnew, Robert. 2002. "Experienced, Vicarious, and Anticipated Strain." Justice Quarterly. 19: 603–32.

Agnew, Robert. 2006. Pressured into Crime: An Overview of General Strain Theory. New York: Oxford University Press.

Agnew, Robert. 2009. Juvenile Delinquency: Causes and Control. New York: Oxford University Press.

———. 2010. "Controlling Crime: Recommendations from General Strain Theory." In Criminology and Public Policy: Putting Theory to Work, ed. Hugh Barlow and Scott Decker. Philadelphia: Temple University Press.

Anderson, Elijah. 1999. Code of the Street: Decency, Violence, and the Moral Life of the Inner City. New York: W.W. Norton.

Andrews, Donald A., and James Bonta. 1998. The Psychology of Criminal

Conduct, 2nd ed. Cincinnati: Anderson.

Babiak, Paul, Craig Neuman, and Robert Hare. 2010. "Corporate Psychopathy: Talking the Walk." Behavioral Sciences and the Law 28, no. 2:174–93.

Bernard, Thomas. 1987. "Testing Structural Strain Theories." Journal of Research in Crime and Delinquency 24: 262–80.

Blau, Judith, and Peter Blau. 1982. "The Cost of Inequality: Metropolitan Structure and Violent Crime." American Sociological Review 47: 114–29.

Braithwaite, John. 1979. Inequality, Crime and Public Policy. London: Routledge and Kegan Paul.

Braithwaite, John. 1989. Crime, Shame, and Reintegration. Cambridge: Cambridge University Press.

Cao, Liqun. 2004. "Is American Society More Anomic? A Test of Merton's Theory with Cross-National Data." International Journal of Comparative and Applied Criminal Justice 28, no. 1: 15–32.

Cloward, Richard, and Lloyd Ohlin. 1960. Delinquency and Opportunity. Glencoe: Free Press.

Comack, Elizabeth. 2009. "Women and Crime." In Criminology: A Canadian Perspective, 6th ed. Rick Linden. Toronto: Harcourt Brace.

Crutchfield, Robert D. 1995. "Ethnicity, Labor Markets and Crime." In Ethnicity, Race, and Crime: Perspectives Across Time and Place, ed. Darnell F. Hawkins. Albany: SUNY Press.

Cullen, Francis. 1984. Rethinking Crime and Deviance Theory: The Emergence of a Structuring Tradition. Totowa: Rowman and Allanheld.

———. 1988. "Were Cloward and Ohlin Strain Theorists? Delinquency and Opportunity Revisited." Journal of Research in Crime and Delinquency 25: 214–41.

Desroches, Fred. 1995. "Tearoom Trade: A Law Enforcement Problem." Canadian Journal of Criminology 33, no. 1: 1–21.

Durkheim, Émile. 1893/1933. The Division of Labor in Society. New York: Free Press.

———. 1897/1951. Suicide. New York: Free Press.

El Akkad, Omar. 2014. "When Speed Is Greed." Globe and Mail, April 12, F4.

Farnworth, Margaret, and Michael Leiber. 1989. "Strain Theory Revisited." American Sociological Review 54: 263–74.

Galloway, Gloria. 2010. "Tory-Appointed Watchdogs Reluctant to Probe Wrongdoing, Critics Charge." Globe and Mail, January 28, A4.

Gooch, Charmian. 2014. "No Anonymity, No Exploitation." Globe and Mail, March 20, A15.

Grabosky, Peter, and Neal Shover. 2010. "Forestalling the Next Epidemic of White Collar Crime: Linking Policy to Theory." Criminology and Public Policy 9: 641–54.

Hackler, James C. 1966. "Boys, Blisters, and Behavior." Journal of Research in Crime and Delinquency 3 (July): 155–64.

———. 2006. Canadian Criminology: Strategies and Perspectives, 4th ed.. Toronto: Prentice Hall Canada.

Hackler, James C., and Eric Linden. 1970. "The Response of Adults to Delinquency Prevention Programs: The Race Factor." Journal of Research in Crime and Delinquency 7 (January): 31–45.

Hackler, Jim. 2011. "Reducing Crime the Intelligent Way: Building Parenting Not Prisons." Justice Report 26, no. 3: 3–6.

Hagan, John. 2010. Who Are the Criminals? Princeton: Princeton University Press.

Hagan, John, and Bill McCarthy. 1997. Mean Streets: Youth Homelessness and Crime. New York: Cambridge University Press.

Heinze, P., R. Allen, C. Magai, and B. Ritzler. 2010. "Let's Get Down to Business: A Validation Study of the Psychopathic Personality Inventory Among a Sample of MBA students." Journal of Personality Disorders 24, no. 4: 487–98.

Hellenbach, Michael. 2006. Arbeitsmotivation in Ost- und West Deutsch-
land: Grundlagen und Vergleiche. Saarbruecken: VDM.

Hongming Cheng. 2011. "Academic Fraud in China: Assessing the Applicability of Merton's Strain Theory." Western Society of Criminology Conference, Vancouver, February 3–5.

Konty, Mark. 2005. "Microanomie: The Cognitive Foundations of the Relationship Between Anomie and Deviance." Criminology 43 (February): 107–31.

Leblanc, Daniel. 2011. "Bloc Takes Tories to Task on Fraudster's Release." Globe and Mail, January 31.

McFarland, Janet. 2010. "Drabinsky, Gottlieb Argue Appeals Judge Erred." Globe and Mail, November 27.

———. 2014. OSC Seeks Wiretap Rule Changes: Globe and Mail, March 28, B4.

McGrath, John Michael. 2011. "The Son Also Stumbles: Edgar Bronfman Jr. Not Going to Jail After All." Toronto Life, January 24.

Merton, Robert K. 1938. "Social Structure and Anomie." American Sociological Review 3 (October): 672–82.

Messner, Steven F., and Richard Rosenfeld. 2007. Crime and the American Dream, 4th ed. Belmont: Thomson Wadsworth.

Morris, Alison. 1987. Women, Crime, and Criminal Justice. Oxford: Basil Blackwell.

Naffine, Ngaire. 1987. Female Crime: The Construction of Women in Criminology. Sydney: Allen and Unwin.

Pinker, Stephen. 2011. The Better Angels of Our Nature. New York: Viking.

Quinney, Richard. 1963. "Occupational Structure and Criminal Behavior: Prescription Violation by Retail Pharmacists." Social Problems 11 (Fall): 179–95.

Schwartz, Robert G., and Marsha Levick. 2010. "When a 'Right' Is Not Enough: Implementation of the Right to Counsel in an Age of Ambivalence." Criminology and Public Policy 9, no. 20: 365–73.

Schweinhart, L.L., H.V. Barnes, and D.P. Weikart. 1993. Significant Benefits: The High/Scope Perry Preschool Study Through Age 27. Ypsilanti: High/Scope.

Slater, Joanna. 2011. "After the Financial Crisis: A Dearth of Prosecutions." Globe and Mail, April 19, B11.

Snider, Laureen. 2003. "Resisting Neo-Liberalism: The Poisoned Water Disaster in Walkerton, Ontario." Social and Legal Studies 5, no. 2: 27–47.

Sutherland, Edwin. 1949. White Collar Crime. New York: Dryden.

Thornberry, Terence P. 1987. "Toward an Interactional Theory of Delinquency." Criminology 25: 863–91.

Tremblay, Richard E., and Wendy M. Craig. 1995. "Developmental Crime Prevention." In Building a Safer Society: Strategic Approaches to Crime Prevention, Vol. 19, ed. M. Tonry and D.P. Farrington. Chicago: University of Chicago Press.

Wilkinson, Richard, and Kate Picket. 2009. The Spirit Level: Why More Equal Societies Almost Always Do Better. London: Allen Lane.

Zhao, Ruohui, and Liquin Cao. 2010. "Social Change and Anomie: A Cross Nation Study." Social Forces 89, no. 3: 1209–29.

CHAPTER 11

Althusser, L. 1969. For Marx. New York: Vintage.

Bartholomew, Amy, and Susan Boyd. 1989. "Towards a Political Economy of Law." In The New Canadian Political Economy, ed. Wallace Clement and Glen Williams. 212–39. Montreal and Kingston: McGill–Queen's University Press.

Bill C-13: Protecting Canadians from Online Crime Act. 2013. 1st Reading. November 20, 2013, 41st Parliament, 2nd Session. http://www.parl.gc.ca/HousePublications/Publication.aspx?Language=E&Mode=1&DocId=6311444.

Bohm, Robert M. 1982. "Radical Criminology: An Explication." Criminology 19, no. 4: 565–89.

Brickey, Stephen, and Elizabeth Comack. 1989. "The Role of Law in Social Transformation: Is a Jurisprudence of Insurgency Possible?" In Law and Society: A Critical Perspective, ed. Tullio Caputo, Mark Kennedy, Charles E. Reasons, and Augustine Brannigan. 316–30. Toronto: Harcourt Brace Jovanovich.

Cain, Maureen, and Alan Hunt. 1979. Marx and Engels on Law. London: Academic Press.

Canadian Press. (2013. "Canada to Get New Cyberbullying Legislation in the Fall." September 26.

CCMW (Canadian Council of Muslim Women). 2012. "CCMW Position on Femicide (not honour killing)." Web.

Chambliss, William, and Robert Siedman. 1982. Law, Order, and Power. Reading: Addison-Wesley.

Chu, Jim. 2014. "Police Chiefs Support Cyberbullying Bill." Vancouver Sun, January 23.

Cohen, Tobi. 2013. "Cyberbullying Bill Introduces Sweeping Changes to Bring Criminal Code into Modern Era." Canada.com. November 20.

Comack, Elizabeth, and Stephen Brickey, eds. 1991. The Social Basis of Law: Critical Readings in the Sociology of Law. Halifax: Garamond.

Cook, Ramsey, and Wendy Mitchinson, eds. 1976. "Sweet Girl Graduates." In The Proper Sphere: Women's Place in Canadian Society. Toronto: Oxford University Press.

———. 1991. "Realist Criminology, Women, and Social Transformation in Canada." In New Directions in Critical Criminology, ed. Brian D. MacLean and Dragan Milovanovic. 9–14. Vancouver: Collective Press.

Currie, Dawn, Walter S. DeKeseredy, and Brian D. MacLean. 1990. "Reconstructing Social Order and Social Control: Police Accountability in Canada." Journal of Human Justice 2, no. 1: 29–53.

DeKeseredy, Walter S. 1991. "Confronting Woman Abuse: A Brief Overview of the Left Realist Approach." In New Directions in Critical Criminology, ed. Brian D.

MacLean and Dragan Milovanovic. 27–30. Vancouver: Collective Press.

Domhoff, G. William. 1970. The Higher Circles: The Governing Class in America. New York: Random House.

Einstadter, Werner, and Stuart Henry. 2006. Criminological Theory: An Analysis of Its Underlying Assumptions. Lanham: Rowman and Littlefield.

Fine, Sean. 2013. "Conservatives Reviving Old Controversy with Proposal of Cyberbullying Law, Critics Say." Globe and Mail, November 21.

Fisk, Robert. 2010. "The Crimewave That Shames the World." The Independent, September 7.

France, Anatole. 1897. The Red Lily. London: John Lane.

Friscolanti, Michael. 2012. "Transcripts: The Crown's Case." The Shafia Honour Killing Trial. Macleans e-book. 86–104.

Geist, Michael. 2013. "The Privacy Threats in Bill C-13, Part One: Immunity for Personal Info Disclosures Without a Warrant." Law Blog. November 25. Web.

Glasbeek, Harry. 1989. "Why Corporate Deviance Is Not Treated as a Crime: The Need to Make Profits a Dirty Word." In Law and Society: A Critical Perspective, ed. Tullio Caputo, Mark Kennedy, Charles E. Reasons, and Augustine Brannigan. 126–45. Toronto: Harcourt Brace Jovanovich.

Goff, Colin, and Charles Reasons. 1978. Corporate Crime in Canada: A Critical Analysis of Anti-Combines Legislation. Toronto: Prentice Hall Canada.

Gold, David, Clarence Y.H. Lo, and Erik O. Wright. 1975. "Recent Developments in Marxist Theories of the Capitalist State." Monthly Review 27 (October–November): 29–43.

Gordon, Robert, and Ian Coneybeer. 1999. "Corporate Crime." In Law in Society: Canadian Readings, ed. N. Larsen and B. Burtch. 101–27. Toronto: Nelson Thomson Learning.

Gossner, Céline, Jorgen Schlundt, Peter Embarek, Susan Hird, Danilo Wong,

Jose Beltran, Keng Ngee Teoh, and Angelika Tritscher. 2009. "The Melamine Incident: Implications for International Food and Feed Safety." Environmental Health Perspectives 117, no. 12: 1803–08.

Greenberg, David F. 1993. Crime and Capitalism: Readings in Marxist Criminology, 2nd ed. Philadelphia: Temple University Press.

Henry, Frank. 1986. "Crime—A Profitable Approach." In The Political Economy of Crime, ed. Brian D. Maclean. 182–203. Toronto: Prentice Hall.

Hunt, Alan. 1993. Explorations in Law and Society: Towards a Constitutive Theory of Law. New York: Routledge.

Ingelfinger, Julie. 2008. "Melamine and the Global Implications of Food Contamination." New England Journal of Medicine 359: 2745–48.

Jiwani, Yasmin, and Homa Hoodfar. 2012. "Should We Call It 'Honour Killing'? No!" The Gazette Montreal), January 30.

Jones, Trevor, Brian D. MacLean, and Jock Young. 1986. The Islington Crime Survey: Crime, Victimization and Policing in Inner-City London. Aldershot: Gower.

Korteweg, Anna. 2012. "Understanding Honour Killing and Honour-Related Violence in the Immigration Context: Implications for the Legal Profession and Beyond." Canadian Criminal Law Review 16, no. 2: 135–60.

Kuehn, Bridget. 2009. "Melamine Scandals Highlight Hazards of Increasingly Globalized Food Chain." JAMA 301, no. 5: 473–75.

Lea, John, and Jock Young. 1984. What Is to Be Done About Law and Order? Harmondsworth: Penguin.

Lea, John, and Jock Young. 1986. "A Realistic Approach to Law and Order." In The Political Economy of Crime: Readings for a Critical Criminology, ed. Brian D. MacLean. Toronto: Prentice Hall Canada.

Lowman, John, and Brian D. MacLean. 1992. "Introduction: Left Realism, Crime Control, and Policing in the 1990s." In Realist Criminology:

Crime Control and Policing in the 1990s, ed. John Lowman and Brian D. MacLean. 3–29. Toronto: University of Toronto Press.

Mackay, Peter. 2013, "Protecting Canadians from Online Crime." Canada. Parliament. House of Commons. Edited Hansard 147 025, 41st Parliament, 2nd session. November 27. http://www.parl.gc.ca/HousePublications/Publication.aspx?Language=E &Mode=1&Parl=41&Ses=2&DocId=6339212.

MacLean, Brian D. 1991. "The Origins of Left Realism." In New Directions in Critical Criminology, ed. Brian D. MacLean and Dragan Milovanovic. 9–14. Vancouver: Collective Press.

Mandel, Michael. 1987. "'Relative Autonomy' and the Criminal Justice Apparatus." In State Control: Criminal Justice Politics in Canada, ed. R.S. Ratner and John McMullan. 149–64. Vancouver: UBC Press.

Marx, Karl, and Friedrich Engels. 1992/1848. The Communist Manifesto. Oxford: Oxford University Press.

Matthews, Roger, and Jock Young. 1992. "Reflections on Realism." In Rethinking Criminology: The Realist Debate, ed. Jock Young and Roger Matthews. 1–23. London: Sage.

McLeod, Paul. 2013. "Impact of Cyberbullying Worries Experts." Halifax Chronicle Herald, November 21.

McMullan, John. 1992. Beyond the Limits of the Law: Corporate Crime and Law and Order. Halifax: Fernwood.

Macphail, Andrew. 1976. "On Certain Aspects of Feminism." In The Proper Sphere: Women's Place in Canadian Society, ed. R. Cook and W. Mitchinson. 301–4. Toronto: Oxford University Press.

Meyer, Andrew. 2013. "Cyberbullying Bill Won't Stop Online Taunts, Critics Say." CBC News: Technology and Science, November 27.

Michalowski, Raymond. 1985. Order, Law, and Crime: An Introduction to Criminology. New York: Random House.

Miliband, Ralph. 1969. The State in Capitalist Society. London: Weidenfeld and Nicolson.

Mojab, Shahrzad. 2012. "The Politics of Culture, Racism, and Nationalism in Honour Killing." Canadian Criminal Law Review 16, no. 2: 115–34.

Mundell, E.J., and Steven Reinberg. 2007. "FDA: Millions of Chickens Fed Contaminated Pet Food." Washington Post, May 2.

Mugford, Stephen, and Pat O'Malley. 1991. "Heroin Policy and Deficit Models." Crime, Law, and Social Change 15, no. 1: 19–36.

Nestle, Marion. 2008. Pet Food Politics: The Chihuahua in the Coal Mine. Berkeley: University of California Press.

O'Reilly-Fleming, Thomas. 1996. "Left-Realism as Theoretical Retreatism or Paradigm Shift: Toward Post-Critical Criminology." In Post-Critical Criminology, ed. Thomas O'Reilly-Fleming. 1–25. Scarborough: Prentice-Hall.

Papp, Aruna. 2010. "Culturally Driven Violence Against Women: A Growing Problem in Canada's Immigrant Communities." Frontier Centre for Public Policy. FCPP Policy Series no. 92: 1–20.

Pearce, Frank. 1976. Crimes of the Powerful. London: Pluto.

Poulantzas, N. 1975. Classes in Contemporary Capitalism. London: New Left.

Prentice, Alison, Paula Bourne, Gail Cuthbert Brandt, Beth Light, Wendy Mitchinson, and Naomi Black. 1996. Canadian Women: A History, 2nd ed.. Toronto: Harcourt Brace.

Puschner, Birgit, and Renate Reimschuessel. 2011. "Toxicosis Caused by Melamine and Cyanuric Acid in Dogs and Cats: Uncovering the Mystery and Subsequent Global Implications." Clinics in Laboratory Medicine. In Press.

Quinney, Richard. 1970. The Social Reality of Crime. Boston: Little, Brown.

———. 1974. Critique of the Legal Order. Boston: Little, Brown.

Roth, Aleda, Andy Tsay, Madeline Pullman, and John Grey. 2008. "Unravelling the Food Supply Chain: Strategic Insights from China and the 2007 Recalls." Journal of Supply Chain Management 44, no. 1: 22–39.

Sargent, Neil. 1991. "Law, Ideology, and Social Change: An Analysis of the Role of Law in the Construction of Corporate Crime." In The Social Basis of Law: Critical Readings in the Sociology of Law, ed. Elizabeth Comack and Stephen Brickey. 289–309. Halifax: Garamond.

Schmit, Julie. 2007. "Pet Food Probe: Who Was Watching Suppliers?" USA Today, July 5.

Schmitz, Cristin. 2013. "Privacy and Press Freedom Cites as Concerns with Cyberbully Bill." Lawyers Weekly, December 13.

Sellin, Thorsten. 1938. Culture Conflict and Crime. New York: Social Science Research Council.

Sharma, Kirti, and Manish Paradkar. 2010. "The Melamine Adulteration Scandal." Food Security 2: 97–107.

Smandych, Russell. 1985. "Marxism and the Creation of Law: Re-examining the Origins of Canadian Anti-Combines Legislation, 1890–1910." In The New Criminology in Canada: State, Crime and Control, ed. Thomas Fleming. 87–99. Toronto: Oxford University Press.

Snider, Laureen. 1979. "Revising the Combines Investigation Act: A Study in Corporate Power." In Structure, Law, and Power: Essays in the Sociology of Law, ed. Paul Brantingham and Jack Kress. 105–19. Beverly Hills: Sage.

_____. 1989. "Ideology and Relative Autonomy in Anglo-Canadian Criminology." Journal of Human Justice 1, no. 1: 27–42.

_____. 1993. Bad Business: Corporate Crime in Canada. Toronto: Nelson.

Spitzer, Steven. 1975. "Towards a Marxian Theory of Analysis." Social Problems 22, no. 5: 638–51.

Spratt, Michael. 2013a. "Bill C-13: Cyberbullying—a Wolf in Sheep's Clothing." Law Blog. November 26.

_____. 2013b. "Bill C-13: Voluntary Disclosure." Law Blog. November 28.

"Sweet Girl Graduates." 1976. In The Proper Sphere: Women's Place in Canadian Society, ed. Ramsey Cook and Wendy Mitchinson. 123. Toronto: Oxford University Press.

Terman, Rochelle L. 2010. "To Specify or Single Out: Should We Use the Term 'Honor Killing?'" Muslim World Journal of Human Rights 7, no. 1: 1–39.

Tierney, John. 1996. Criminology: Theory and Context. London: Prentice-Hall.

Todd, Carol. 2013. "Could the Cyberbullying Bill Have Saved Amanda? Yes." Huffington Post Canada, November 25.

UN Population Fund. 2000. "Ending Violence Against Women and Girls." The State of World Population 2000. http://www.unfpa.org/swp/2000/english/ch03.html.

Vold, George. 1958. Theoretical Criminology. New York: Oxford University Press.

Warrick, Catherine. 2005. "The Vanishing Victim: Criminal Law and Gender in Jordan." Law and Society Review 39, no. 2: 315–48.

Weiss, Rick. 2007. "Farm Raised Fish Given Tainted Food." Washington Post, May 9.

West, W. Gordon, and Laureen Snider. 1985. "A Critical Perspective on Law and the Canadian State: Delinquency and Corporate Crime." In The New Criminology in Canada: State, Crime and Control, ed. Thomas Fleming. 138–70. Toronto: Oxford University Press.

Young, Jock. 1979. "Left Idealism, Reformism, and Beyond." In Capitalism and the Rule of Law, ed. Bob Fine, Richard Kinsey, John Lea, Sol Picciotto, and Jock Young. 11–28. London: Hutchinson.

_____. 1992. "Ten Points of Realism." In Rethinking Criminology: The Realist Debate, ed. Roger Matthews and Jock Young. 24–68. London: Sage.

Young, Jock, and Roger Matthews. 1992. "Questioning Left Realism." In Issues in Realist Criminology, ed. Roger Matthews and Jock Young. 1–18. London: Sage.

CHAPTER 12

Ackerman, Spencer, and Dan Roberts. 2014. "US Government Privacy Board Says NSA Bulk Collection of Phone Data is Illegal." The Guardian, January 23.

Andrews, D.A., and J. Bonta. 1998. The Psychology of Criminal Conduct, 2nd ed. Cincinnati: Anderson.

Balke, Friedrich. 2005. "Derrida and Foucault on Sovereignty." German Law Journal 6, no. 1: 71–85.

Bauman, Zymunt. 2000. Liquid Modernity. Cambridge: Cambridge University Press.

Beck, Ulrich. 1992. "From Industrial to Risk Society: Questions of Survival, Social Structure, and Ecological Enlightenment." Theory, Culture, and Society 9: 97–123.

Bosworth, Mary. 2004. "Gender, Risk, and Recidivism." Criminology and Public Policy 3, no. 2: 181–84.

Bourdieu, Pierre. 1984. Distinction: A Social Critique of the Judgement of Taste. Cambridge, MA: Harvard University Press.

_____. 1986. "The Forms of Capital." In Handbook of Theory and Research for the Sociology of Education, ed. John Richardson. 241–58. New York: Greenwood.

_____. 1990a. The Logic of Practice. Cambridge: Polity.

_____. 1990b. In Other Words: Essays Toward a Reflexive Sociology. Stanford: Stanford University Press.

_____. 1991. Language and Symbolic Power. Cambridge: Harvard University Press.

_____. 1992. An Invitation to Reflexive Sociology. Chicago: University of Chicago Press.

Brubaker, Rogers. 1985. "Rethinking Classical Theory: The Sociological Vision of Pierre Bourdieu." Theory and Society 14: 745–75.

Caputo, John. 1997. Deconstruction in a Nutshell: A Conversation with Jacques Derrida. New York: Fordham.

Chambliss, William. 1969. "The Law of Vagrancy." In Crime and the Legal Process, ed. William Chambliss. 51–63. New York: McGraw-Hill.

Dean, Mitchell. 1999. Governmentality: Power and Rule in Modern Society. London: Sage.

Dekeseredy, Walter, and Brian D. MacLean. 1993. "Critical Criminological Pedagogy in Canada: Strengths, Limitations, and Recommendations for Improvements." Journal of Criminal Justice Education 4: 361–76.

Derrida, Jacques. 1976. Of Grammatology. Translated by Gayatri Chakravorty Spivak. Baltimore: Johns Hopkins University Press.

———. 1981. Positions. Chicago: University of Chicago Press.

———. 1987. "Some Questions and Responses." In The Linguistics of Writing: Arguments between Language and Literature, ed. N. Fabb. Manchester: Manchester University Press.

———. 1994. Specters of Marx: The State of the Debt, the Work of Mourning, and the New International. London: Routledge.

———. 2005. Rogues: Two Essays on Reason. Stanford: Stanford University Press.

DiMaggio, Paul. 1979. "Review Essay: On Pierre Bourdieu." American Journal of Sociology 84: 1460–74.

Ek, Richard. 2006. "Giorgio Agamben and the Spatialities of the Camp." Geografiska Annaler: Series B, Human Geography 88, no. 4: 363–86.

Ericson, Richard, and Kevin Haggerty. 1997. Policing the Risk Society. Toronto: University of Toronto Press.

Ewald, Francois. 1991. "Insurance and Risk." In The Foucault Effect: Studies in Governmentality, ed. Graham Burchell, Colin Gordon, and Peter Miller. Chicago: University of Chicago Press.

Feeley, Malcolm, and Jonathan Simon. 1994. "Actuarial Justice: The Emerging Criminal Law." In The Futures of Criminology, ed. David Nelken. New York: Sage.

Ferrell, Jeff. 1998. "Criminological Verstehen." In Ethnography at the Edge, ed. Jeff Ferrell and Mark Hamm. Boston: Northeastern University Press.

———. 2004. "Boredom, Crime and Criminology." Theoretical Criminology 8, no. 3: 287–302.

Foucault, Michel. 1979. The History of Sexuality, Vol. 1. New York: Vintage.

———. 1980. Power/Knowledge: Selected Interviews and Other Writings. New York: Pantheon.

———. 1982. "The Subject and Power." In Michel Foucault: Beyond Structuralism and Hermeneutics, ed. Hubert Dreyfus and Paul Rabinow. Chicago: University of Chicago Press.

———. 1991. "Governmentality." In The Foucault Effect: Studies in Governmentality, ed. Graham Burchell, Colin Gordon, and Peter Miller. Chicago: University of Chicago Press.

———. 1997. The Essential Works, 1954–1985, Vol. 1: Ethics, Subjectivity, and Truth. New York: New Press.

Garland, David. 1997. "Governmentality and the Problem of Crime: Foucault, Criminology, Sociology." Theoretical Criminology 1, no. 2: 173–214.

Hannah-Moffat, Kelly, and Paula Maurutto. 2003. Youth Risk/Need Assessment: An Overview of Issues and Practices. Ottawa: Department of Justice.

Hannah-Moffat, Kelly, and Margaret Shaw. 2001. Taking Risks: Incorporating Gender and Culture into the Classification and Assessment of Federally Sentenced Women in Canada. Ottawa: Status of Women.

Hayward, Keith J., and Jock Young. 2004. "Cultural Criminology: Some Notes on the Script." Theoretical Criminology 8, no. 3: 259–73.

Hogeveen, Bryan. 2006. "Memoir of a/ the Blind." Punishment and Society 8, no. 4: 469–76.

Hogeveen, Bryan, and Andrew Woolford. 2006. "Critical Criminology and Possibility in the Neoliberal Ethos." Canadian Journal of Criminology and Criminal Justice 48, no. 5: 681–702.

Katz, Jack. 1988. Seductions of Crime: Moral and Sensual Attractions in Doing Crime. New York: Basic.

Lippert, Randy, and James Williams. 2006. "Governing on the Margins: Exploring the Contributions of Governmentality Studies to Critical Criminology in Canada." Canadian Journal of Criminology and Criminal Justice 48, no. 5: 703–19.

Minaker, Joanne, and Bryan Hogeveen. 2009. Youth, Crime, and Society: Critical Reflections. Toronto: Pearson.

Minca, Claudio. 2006. "Giorgio Agamben and the New Biopolitical Nomos." Geografiska Annaler: Series B, Human Geography 88, no. 4: 387–403.

Morrison, Wayne. 2007. Criminology and the New World Order. London: Glasshouse.

O'Connor, D. 2006. Report of the Events Relating to Maher Arar: Analysis and Recommendations of the Commission of Inquiry in the Actions of Canadian Officials in Relation to Maher Arar. Ottawa: Queen's Printer.

Office of the Privacy Commissioner of Canada. 2014. "Interim Privacy Commissioner Provides Recommendations to Parliament for the Protection of Privacy Rights in National Security Efforts." News Release, 28 January.

O'Malley Pat. 1992. "Risk, Power and Crime Prevention." Economy and Society 21: 252–75

———. 1996. "Risk and Responsibility." In Foucault and Political Reason: Liberalism, Neoliberalism, and Rationalities of Government, ed. Andrew Barry, Thomas Osbourne, and Nikoas Rose. Chicago: University of Chicago Press.

O'Neill, Maggie. 2004. "Crime, Culture, and Visual Methodologies: Ethno-Mimesis as Performative Praxis." In Cultural Criminology Unleashed, ed. Jeff Ferrell, Keith Hayward,

Wayne Morrison, and Mike Presdee. London: Glasshouse.

O'Reilly-Fleming, Thomas, ed. 1985. The New Criminologies in Canada: State, Crime, and Control. Toronto: Oxford University Press.

Pavlich, George. 1999. "Criticism and Criminology: In Search of Legitimacy." Theoretical Criminology 3, no. 1: 29–51.

———. 2000. Critique and Radical Discourses on Crime. Aldershot: Ashgate.

———. 2005. Governing Paradoxes of Restorative Justice. London: Glasshouse.

———. 2007. "Deconstruction." Blackwell Encyclopedia of Sociology. London: Blackwell.

Raban, Jonathan. 1974. The Soft City. London: Hamilton.

Ratner, R.S. 1971. "Criminology in Canada: Conflicting Objectives." Unpublished manuscript.

———. 1984. "Inside the Liberal Boot: The Criminological Enterprise in Canada." Studies in Political Economy 13: 145–64.

———. 1989. "Critical Criminology— A Splendid Oxymoron." Journal of Human Justice 1: 3–8.

Schmitt, Carl. 1985. Political Theology: Four Chapters on the Concept of Sovereignty. Chicago: University of Chicago Press.

Simon, Jonathan. 1988. "The Ideological Effects of Actuarial Practices." Law and Society Review 22, no. 4: 772–800.

Taylor, Ian, Paul Walton, and Jock Young. 1973. The New Criminology: For a Social Theory of Deviance. London: Routledge and Kegan Paul.

van Swaaningen, Rene. 1997. Critical Criminology: Visions from Europe. London: Sage.

Wacquant, Loïc. 2001. "Deadly Symbiosis: When Ghetto and Prison Meet and Mesh." Punishment and Society 3, no. 1: 95–134.

———. 2009. Punishing the Poor: The Neoliberal Government of Social Insecurity. Durham: Duke University Press.

———. 2010. "Crafting the Neoliberal State: Workfare, Prisonfare, and Social Insecurity." Sociological Forum 25, no. 2: 197–220.

Young, Jock. 1979. "Left Idealism, Reformism, and Beyond: From New Criminology to Marxism." In Capitalism and the Rule of Law, ed. B. Fine, R. Kinsey, J. Lea, S. Picciotto, and J. Young. 11–28. London: Hutchinson.

———. 1998. "From Inclusive to Exclusive Society: Nightmares in the European Dream." In The New European Criminology: Crime and Social Order in Europe, ed. Vincent Riggiero, N. South, and Ian Taylor. London: Routledge.

CHAPTER 13

Becker, Howard S. 1963. Outsiders: Studies in the Sociology of Deviance. New York: Free Press.

Birkbeck, Christopher, and Gary LaFree. 1993. "The Situational Analysis of Crime and Deviance." In Annual Review of Sociology 19, ed. Judith Blake and John Hagan. Palo Alto: Annual Reviews.

Blumer, Herbert. 1986. Symbolic Interactionism. Berkeley: University of California Press.

CBC News Toronto. 2007. "Toronto Police Corruption Probe Laid a Fraction of Charges: Report." Web.

Cohen, Albert K. 1965. "The Sociology of the Deviant Act." American Sociological Review 30: 5–14.

CTV News. 2013. "Toronto Police to Review Violent Arrest Captured on Video." September 25. Web.

Davis, Nanette J. 1980. Sociological Constructions of Deviance, 2nd ed.. Dubuque: Wm. C. Brown.

Empey, Lamar T., Mark C. Stafford, and Carter H. Hay. 1999. American Delinquency: Its Meaning and Construction, 4th ed.. Belmont: Wadsworth.

Glassner, Barry. 1982. "Labelling Theory." In The Sociology of Deviance, ed. M. Michael Rosenberg, Robert A. Stebbins, and Allan Turowetz. New York: St. Martin's.

Goffman, Erving. 1986. Stigma: Notes on the Management of Spoiled Identity. Oneonta: Touchstone.

Griffiths, Curt T., and Simon N. Verdun-Jones. 1994. Canadian Criminal Justice, 2nd ed.. Toronto: Harcourt Brace Canada.

Hewitt, John P., and Peter M. Hall. 1973. "Social Problems, Problematic Situations, and Quasi-Theories." American Sociological Review 38: 367–74.

Hirschi, Travis. 2001. Causes of Delinquency. New Brunswick: Transaction.

Inciardi, James A. 1974. "Vocational Crime." In Handbook of Criminology, ed. Daniel Glaser. Chicago: Rand McNally.

Jankowski, Martin S. 1991. Islands in the Street: Gangs and American Urban Society. Berkeley: University of California Press.

Katz, Jack. 1990. Seductions of Crime: Moral and Sensual Attractions in Doing Evil. New York: Basic.

Keel, Robert O. 2001. "Ethnomethodological Perspective (on Crime and Deviance)." In Encyclopedia of Criminology and Deviance, ed. Clifton Bryant. New York: Taylor & Francis.

Lemert, Edwin. 1951. Social Pathology. New York: McGraw-Hill.

———. 1972. Human Deviance, Social Problems, and Social Control, 2nd ed. Englewood Cliffs: Prentice Hall.

Letkemann, Peter. 1973. Crime as Work. Englewood Cliffs: Prentice Hall.

Liberman, Akiva M., David S. Kirk, and Kim Kideuk. 2014. "Labeling Effects of First Juvenile Arrests: Secondary Deviance and Secondary Sanctioning." Criminology 52: 345–70.

Linden, Rick, and Cathy Fillmore. 1981. "A Comparative Study of Delinquency Involvement." Canadian Review of Sociology and Anthropology 18: 343–61.

Link, Bruce G., and Jo C. Phelan. 2001. "Conceptualizing Stigma." In Annual Review of Sociology 27, ed. Karen S. Cook and John Hagan. Palo Alto: Annual Reviews.

Matsueda, Ross L. 2001. "Differential Association Theory." In Encyclopedia of Criminology and Deviant Behavior, Vol. 1, ed. Patricia A. Adler, Peter Adler, and Jay Corzine. Philadelphia: Brunner-Routledge.

Matza, David. 1990. Delinquency and Drift. New Brunswick: Transaction.

———. 2010. Becoming Deviant, rev. ed. New Brunswick: Transaction.

Moharib, Nadia. 2012. "Wheel and Weed Don't Mix, Says Study." Calgary Sun. May 17.

Prus, Robert C., and C.R.D. Sharper. 1991. Road Hustler: Grifting, Magic, and the Thief Subculture, expanded ed. New York: Kaufman and Greenberg.

Schwendinger, Herman, and Julia S. Schwendinger. 1985. Adolescent Subcultures and Delinquency. New York: Praeger.

Shannon, Lyle W. 1988. Criminal Career Continuity. New York: Human Sciences Press.

Short, James F. 1990. Delinquency and Society. Englewood Cliffs: Prentice Hall.

Shover, Neal. 1983. "The Later Stages of Ordinary Property Offender Careers." Social Problems 31: 208–18.

Small, Peter. "Toronto Police Corruption Trial: Guilty Verdicts on Obstructing Justice Charges." Web.

Sommers, Ira B. 2001. "Criminal Careers." In Encyclopedia of Criminology and Deviant Behavior, Vol. 2, ed. David Luckenbill and Dennis Peck. Philadelphia: Brunner-Routledge.

Spector, Malcom, and John I. Kitsuse. 2000. Constructing Social Problems. New Brunswick: Transaction.

Stebbins, Robert A. 1970. "On Misunderstanding the Concept of Commitment: A Theoretical Clarification." Social Forces 48: 526–29.

———. 1976. Commitment to Deviance: The Nonprofessional Criminal in the Community. Westport: Greenwood.

———. 1997. "Lifestyle as a Generic Concept in Ethnographic Research." Quality and Quantity 31: 347–60.

———. 2007. Serious Leisure: A Perspective for Our Time. New Brunswick: Transaction.

Sutherland, Edwin H., and David R. Cressey. 1978. Principles of Criminology, 10th ed. Philadelphia: Lippincott.

Ulmer, Jeffery T. 1994. "Revisiting Stebbins: Labeling and Commitment to Deviance." Sociological Quarterly 35: 135–57.

Watson, J. Mark. 1984. "Outlaw Motorcyclists: An Outgrowth of Lower Class Cultural Concerns." In Deviant Behavior, 2nd ed., ed. Delos H. Kelly. New York: St. Martin's.

West, W. Gordon. 1980. "The Short Term Careers of Serious Thieves." In Crime in Canadian Society, 2nd ed., ed. Robert A. Silverman and James J. Teevan, Jr. Toronto: Butterworths.

Wolf, Daniel R. 1991. The Rebels: A Brotherhood of Outlaw Bikers. Toronto: University of Toronto Press.

Wolfgang, Marvin E., Terence P. Thornberry, and Robert M. Figlio. 1987. From Boy to Man, from Delinquency to Crime. Chicago: University of Chicago Press.

CHAPTER 14

Anderson, Elijah. 1994. "The Code of the Streets." The Atlantic Monthly (May), 81–94.

Aronson, Elliot. 1984. The Social Animal. New York: W.H. Freeman.

Arum, Richard, and Irenee R. Beattie. 1999. "High School Experience and the Risk of Adult Incarceration." Criminology 37, no. 3: 515–36.

Baier, Colin, and Bradley Wright. 2000. "'If You Love Me, Keep my Commandments': A Meta-Analysis of the Effect of Religion on Crime." Journal of Research on Crime and Delinquency 38: 1–21.

Biron, Louise, and Marc LeBlanc. n.d. "Family and Delinquency." Unpublished paper, Université de Montréal.

Bohm, Robert. 1987. "Comment on 'Traditional Contributions to Radical Criminology' by Groves and Sampson." Journal of Research in Crime and Delinquency 24 (November): 324–31.

Box, Steven. 1971. Deviance, Reality and Society. London: Holt, Rinehart and Winston.

Brody, Hugh. 1975. The People's Land. Markham: Penguin.

Burns, Ausra. 2006. "Moving and Moving Forward: Mushuau Innu Relocation from Davis Inlet to Natuashish." Acadiensis 2 (Spring): 64–84.

Caplan, Aaron. 1977. "Attachment to Parents and Delinquency." Paper presented at the annual meeting of the Canadian Sociology and Anthropology Association, Fredericton.

Caplan, Aaron, and Marc LeBlanc. 1985. "A Cross-Cultural Verification of a Social Control Theory." International Journal of Comparative and Applied Criminal Justice 9, no. 2: 123–38.

CBC News. 2013. "More Children Sniffing Gas, Natuashish Official Says." Web.

Chambliss, William. 1973. "The Saints and the Roughnecks." Society 11: 24–31.

Denov, Myriam, and Kathryn Campbell. 2002. "Casualties of Aboriginal Displacement in Canada: Children at Risk Among the Innu of Labrador." Refuge 20, no. 2: 21–33.

Durkheim, Émile. 1951. Suicide. Translated by John A. Spaulding and George Simpson. New York: Free Press.

Elifson, Kirk W., David M. Petersen, and C. Kirk Hadaway. 1983. "Religiosity and Delinquency: A Contextual Analysis." Criminology 21: 505–27.

Engstad, Peter A. 1975. "Environmental Opportunities and the Ecology of Crime." In Crime in Canadian Society, ed. Robert A. Silverman and James J. Teevan. 193–211. Toronto: Butterworths.

Fischer, Donald G. 1980. Family Relationship Variables and Programs Influencing Juvenile Delinquency. Ottawa: Solicitor General.

Fitzgerald, Robin, and Peter Carrington. 2008. "The Neighbourhood Context of Urban Aboriginal Crime." Canadian Journal of Criminology and Criminal Justice 50: 523–57.

Fréchette, M., and Marc LeBlanc. 1985. Des délinquantes: émergence et développement. Chicoutimi: Gaëtan Morin.

Glueck, Sheldon, and Eleanor Glueck. 1950. Unraveling Juvenile Delinquency. Cambridge, MA: Harvard University Press.

Gomme, Ian. 1985. "Predictors of Status and Criminal Offences Among Male and Female Delinquency in an Ontario Community." Canadian Journal of Criminology 26: 313–23.

Gottfredson, Michael R., and Travis Hirschi. 1990. A General Theory of Crime. Stanford: Stanford University Press.

Hagan, John. 1985. Modern Criminology: Crime, Criminal Behavior and Its Control. New York: McGraw-Hill.

Hagan, John, and Bill McCarthy. 1997. Mean Streets: Youth Crime and Homelessness. Cambridge: Cambridge University Press.

Hamilton, A.C., and C.M. Sinclair. 1991. Report of the Aboriginal Justice Inquiry of Manitoba, Vol. 1. Winnipeg: Queen's Printer.

Hardwick, Kelly. 2002. "Unravelling 'Crime in the Making': Re-examining the Role of Informal Social Control in the Genesis and Stability of Delinquency and Crime." Ph.D. diss., University of Calgary.

Hargreaves, David H. 1967. Social Relations in a Secondary School. London: Routledge and Kegan Paul.

Hargreaves, David H., Stephen K. Hester, and Frank J. Mellor. 1975. Deviance in Classrooms. London: Routledge and Kegan Paul.

Hirschi, Travis. 1969. Causes of Delinquency. Berkeley: University of California Press.

———. 1983. "Crime and the Family." In Crime and Public Policy, ed. James Q. Wilson. 53–68. San Francisco: ICS.

Hirschi, Travis, and Rodney Stark. 1969. "Hellfire and Delinquency." Social Problems 17: 202–13.

Ho, Caroline, Deborah Bluestein, and Jennifer Jenkins. 2008. "Cultural Differences in the Relationship Between Parenting and Children's Behavior." Developmental Psychology 44: 507–22.

Hutchings, Judy, Pam Martin-Forbes, David Daley, and Margiad Williams.

2013. "A Randomized Controlled Trial of the Impact of a Teacher Management Program on the Classroom Behavior of Children with Behavior Problems." 51: 571–85.

Johnson, Byron, Spencer De Li, David Larson, and Michael McCullough. 2000. "A Systematic Review of the Religiosity and Delinquency Literature: A Research Note." Journal of Contemporary Criminal Justice 16: 32–51.

Keane, Carl, Paul S. Maxim, and James J. Teevan. 1993. "Drinking and Driving, Self-Control, and Gender: Testing a General Theory of Crime." Journal of Research in Crime and Delinquency 30: 30–46.

Kornhauser, Ruth Rosner. 1978. Social Sources of Delinquency. Chicago: University of Chicago Press.

Kupfer, George. 1966. "Middle Class Delinquency in a Canadian City." Ph.D. diss., Department of Sociology, University of Washington.

LaGrange, Theresa, and Robert Silverman. 1999. "Low Self-Control and Opportunity: Testing the General Theory of Crime as an Explanation for Gender Differences in Delinquency." Criminology 37, no. 1: 41–72.

Laub, John, and Robert Sampson. 2003. Shared Beginnings, Divergent Lives. Cambridge. MA: Harvard University Press.

LeBlanc, Marc. 1983. "Delinquency as an Epiphenomenon of Adolescence." In Current Issues in Juvenile Justice, ed. Raymond R. Corrado, Marc LeBlanc, and Jean Trepanier. 31–48. Toronto: Butterworths.

———. 1997. "A Generic Control Theory of the Criminal Phenomenon." In Developmental Theories of Crime and Delinquency, ed. Terence P. Thornberry. 215–85. New Brunswick: Transaction.

LeBlanc, Marc, Marc Ouimet, and Richard Tremblay. 1988. "An Integrative Control Theory of Delinquent Behavior: A Validation 1976–1985." Psychiatry 51: 164–76.

Lehrer, Jonah. 2009. "Don't: The Secret of Self-Control." The New Yorker, May 18, 26–32.

Linden, Eric. 1974. "Interpersonal Ties and Delinquent Behavior." Unpublished Ph.D. diss., University of Washington.

Linden, Rick, and Raymond Currie. 1977. "Religiosity and Drug Use: A Test of Social Control Theory." Canadian Journal of Criminology and Corrections 19: 346–55.

Linden, Rick, and Cathy Fillmore. 1981. "A Comparative Study of Delinquency Involvement." Canadian Review of Sociology and Anthropology 18: 343–61.

Linden, Rick, and James C. Hackler. 1973. "Affective Ties and Delinquency." Pacific Sociological Review 16: 27–46.

Lynch, Michael, and W. Byron Groves. 1989. A Primer in Radical Criminology, 2nd ed. Albany: Harrow and Heston.

Matza, David. 1964. Delinquency and Drift. New York: Wiley.

Maume, Michael, Graham Ousey, and Kevin Beaver. 2005. "Cutting the Grass: A Re-examination of the Link Between Marital Attachment, Delinquent Peers and Desistance from Marijuana Use." Journal of Quantitative Criminology 21 (March): 27–53.

Miller, James. 1996. Shingwauk's Vision: A History of Native Residential Schools. Toronto: University of Toronto Press.

Mischel, Walter, Ozlem Ayduk, Marc Berman, B.J. Casey, Ian Gotlib, John Jonides, Ethan Kross, Theresa Teslovich, Nicole Wilson, Vivian Zayas, and Yuichi Shoda. 2011. "'Willpower' Over the Life Span: Decomposing Self-Regulation." Social Cognitive and Affective Neuroscience 6: 252–56.

Moore, D.R., B.P. Chamberlain, and L. Mukai. 1979. "Children at Risk for Delinquency: A Follow-up Comparison of Aggressive Children and Children Who Steal." Journal of Abnormal Child Psychology 7: 345–55.

Nixon, Reginald, Lynne Sweeney, Deborah Erickson, and Stephen Touyz. 2003. "Parent–Child Interaction Therapy: A Comparison of Standard and Abbreviated Treatments for

Oppositional Defiant Preschoolers." Journal of Consulting and Clinical Psychology 71: 251–60.

Nye, F. Ivan. 1958. Family Relationships and Delinquent Behavior. New York: Wiley.

Olds, D., C.R. Henderson, R. Cole, J. Eckenrode, J. Kitzman, D. Luckey. 1998. "The Long-Term Effects of Nurse Home Visitation and Children's Criminal and Antisocial Behavior: 15-Year Follow-Up of a Randomized Controlled Trial." Journal of the American Medical Association, 280: 1238–44.

Patterson, G.R. 1980. "Children Who Steal." In Understanding Crime: Current Theory and Research, ed. Travis Hirschi and Michael Gottfredson. Beverly Hills: Sage.

Pearson, Ashley. 2012. An Evaluation of Winnipeg's Electronic Monitoring Program for Youth Auto Theft Offenders. Unpublished M.A. Thesis. Winnipeg: University of Manitoba.

Polk, Kenneth, and F. Lynn Richmond. 1972. "Those Who Fail." In Schools and Delinquency, ed. Kenneth Polk and Walter E. Schafer, 55–69. Englewood Cliffs: Prentice Hall.

Polk, Kenneth, and Walter E. Schafer. 1972. Schools and Delinquency. Englewood Cliffs: Prentice Hall.

Reiss, Albert J., Jr. 1951. "Delinquency as the Failure of Personal and Social Controls." American Sociological Review 16: 196–207.

Rothman, David J. 1971. The Discovery of the Asylum. Boston: Little, Brown.

Rutter, Michael, and Henri Giller. 1984. Juvenile Delinquency: Trends and Perspectives. New York: Guilford.

Salas-Wright, Christopher, Michael Vaughn, and Brandy Maynard. 2014. "Buffering Effects of Religiosity on Crime: Testing the Invariance Hypothesis Across Gender and Developmental Period." Criminal Justice and Behavior 41: 673–91.

Sampson, Robert J., and John H. Laub. 1993. Crime in the Making: Pathways and Turning Points Through Life. Cambridge, MA: Harvard University Press.

Samson, Colin. 2003. A Way of Life That Does Not Exist: Canada and the Extinguishment of the Innu. London: Verso.

Samson, Colin, James Wilson, and Jonathan Mazower. 1999. Canada's Tibet: The Killing of the Innu. London: Survival.

Savoie, Josee. 2008. "Neighbourhood Characteristics and the Distribution of Crime." Ottawa: Statistics Canada. Web.

Schafer, Walter E., and Kenneth Polk. 1967. "Delinquency and the Schools." In The President's Commission on Law Enforcement and Administration of Justice, Task Force Report: Juvenile Delinquency and Crime. 222–77. Washington: US GPO.

Shaw, Clifford, and Henry McKay. 1942. Juvenile Delinquency in Urban Areas. Chicago: University of Chicago Press.

Shoda, Yuichi, Walter Mischel, and Philip Peake. 1990. "Predicting Adolescent Cognitive and Self-Regulatory Competencies from Preschool Delay of Gratification Identifying Diagnostic Conditions." Developmental Psychology 26, no. 6: 978–86.

Simons, Ronald, L.Chyi-In Wu, Kuei-Hsui Lin, Leslie Gordon, and Rand D. Conger. 2000. "A Cross-Cultural Examination of the Link Between Corporal Punishment and Adolescent Antisocial Behavior." Criminology 38: 47–80.

Shkilnyk, Anastasia M. 1985. A Poison Stronger Than Love: The Destruction of an Ojibwa Community. New Haven: Yale University Press.

Short, James, Jr., and Fred Strodtbeck. 1965. Group Process and Gang Delinquency. Chicago: University of Chicago Press.

Sorenson, Ann Marie, and David Brownfield. 1995. "Adolescent Drug Use and a General Theory of Crime: An Analysis of a Theoretical Integration." Canadian Journal of Criminology 37: 19–37.

Sprott, Jane. 2004. "The Development of Early Delinquency: Can Classroom and School Climates Make a Difference?" Canadian Journal of Criminology and Criminal Justice 46: 553–72.

Sprott, Jane, and Anthony Doob. 2000. "Bad, Sad, and Rejected: The Lives of Aggressive Children." Canadian Journal of Criminology 42: 123–33.

Stark, Rodney, Daniel P. Doyle, and Lori Kent. 1980. "Rediscovering Moral Communities: Church Membership and Crime." In Understanding Crime: Current Theory and Research, ed. Travis Hirschi and Michael Gottfredson. 43–52. Beverly Hills: Sage.

———. 1982. "Religion and Delinquency: The Ecology of a 'Lost' Relationship." Journal of Research in Crime and Delinquency 19: 4–24.

Statistics Canada. 1998. "National Longitudinal Study of Children and Youth." The Daily, October 28.

Steinmetz, Suzanne K., and Murray A. Straus. 1980. "The Family as a Cradle of Violence." In Criminal Behavio, ed. Delos H. Kelly. 130–42. New York: St. Martin's.

Thornberry, Terence P., Marvin D. Krohn, Alan J. Lizotte, and Deborah Chard-Wierschem. 1993. "The Role of Juvenile Gangs in Facilitating Delinquent Behavior." Journal of Research in Crime and Delinquency 30: 55–87.

Thrasher, Frederic M. 1963. The Gang. Chicago: University of Chicago Press.

Topalli, Volkan, Timothy Brezina, and Mindy Bernhardt. 2012. "With God on My Side: The Paradoxical Relationship Between Religious Belief and Criminality Among Hardcore Street Offenders." Theoretical Criminology 17: 49–69.

Tremblay, Richard E., Joan McCord, Helene Boileau, Pierre Charlebois, Claude Gagnon, Marc LeBlanc, and Serge Larivee. 1991. "Can Disruptive Boys Be Helped to Become Competent?" Psychiatry 54: 148–61.

Velarde, Albert J. 1978. "Do Delinquents Really Drift?" British Journal of Criminology 18, no. 1: 23–39.

West, D.J. 1982. Delinquency: Its Roots, Careers, and Prospects. London: Heinemann.

West, D.J., and D.P. Farrington. 1973. Who Becomes Delinquent? London: Heinemann.

———. 1977. The Delinquent Way of Life. London: Heinemann.

West, W. Gordon. 1984. Young Offenders and the State: A Canadian Perspective on Delinquency. Toronto: Butterworths.

Wilson, Harriet. 1980. "Parental Supervision: A Neglected Aspect of Delinquency." British Journal of Criminology 20: 30–39.

Wilson, James Q. 1983. "Raising Kids." The Atlantic Monthly, (October), 45–56.

CHAPTER 15

Anderson, Jeff, and Rick Linden. 2014. "Why Steal Cars: A Study of Young Offenders Involved in Auto Theft." Canadian Journal of Criminology and Criminal Justice 56: 241–59.

Archer, D., R. Gartner, and M. Beitel. 1983. "Homicide and the Death Penalty: A Cross-National Test of a Deterrence Hypothesis." Journal of Criminal Law and Criminology 74: 991–1013.

Bennett, Trevor, and Richard Wright. 1984a. Burglars on Burglary. Brookfield: Gower.

———. 1984b. "Constraints to Burglary: The Offender's Perspective." In Coping with Burglary, ed. Ronald Clarke and Tim Hope. 181–200. Boston: Kluwer-Nijhoff.

Beavon, Daniel, Patricia Brantingham, and Paul Brantingham. 1994. "The Influence of Street Networks on the Patterning of Property Offenses." In Crime Prevention Studies, ed. Ronald V. Clarke. Monsey: Criminal Justice Press.

Blatchford, Christie. 2002. "Doesn't Take a Lot to Get You Killed." National Post, November 27. Web.

Braga, Anthony. 2008. "Police Enforcement Strategies to Prevent Crime in Hot Spot Areas." Crime Prevention Research Review no. 2. Washington: Office of Community Oriented Policing, US Department of Justice.

Braga, Anthony, David Hureau, Andrew Papachristo. 2011. "The Relevance of Micro Places to Citywide Robbery Trends: A Longitudinal Analysis of Robbery Incidents at Street Corners and Block Faces in Boston." Journal of Research in Crime and Delinquency 48, no. 1: 7–32.

Brantingham, Patricia, and Paul Brantingham. 1995. "Criminality of Place: Crime Generators and Crime Attractors. European Journal of Criminal Policy and Research 3: 5–26.

Bureau of Justice Statistics. 2009. Sourcebook of Criminal Justice Statistics. http://www.albany.edu/sourcebook/tost_6.html#6_a.

California State Auditor. 2010. "California Department of Corrections and Rehabilitation: Inmates Sentenced Under the Three Strikes Law and a Small Number of Inmates Receiving Specialty Health Care Represent Significant Costs." Report 2009-107.2, May 2010. Web.

Chen, Elsa. 2008. "Impacts of 'Three Strikes and You're Out' on Crime Trends in California and Throughout the United States." Journal of Contemporary Criminal Justice 24: 345–70.

Clarke, Ronald. 1995. "Situational Crime Prevention." In Building a Safer Society: Strategic Approaches to Crime Prevention, ed. Michael Tonry and David Farrington. 91–150. Chicago: University of Chicago Press.

Clarke, Ronald. 2005. "Seven Misconceptions of Situational Crime Prevention." In Handbook of Crime Prevention and Public Safety, ed. Nick Tilley. 39–70. Portland: Willan.

Clarke, Ronald V., and John Eck. 2003. Becoming a Problem-Solving Crime Analyst. London: Jill Dando Institute of Crime Science.

CNN. 2010. "Mexican Drug War Deaths Surpass 30,100." December 17. Web.

Cohen, Lawrence E., and Marcus Felson. 1979. "Social Change and Crime Rate Trends." American Sociological Review 44: 588–607.

Cornish, Derek, and Ronald Clarke. 1986. The Reasoning Criminal: Rational Choice Perspectives on Offending. New York: Springer.

Dauvergne, Mia. 2010. "Police-Reported Robbery in Canada, 2008." Juristat 30, no. 1. Web.

Desroches, Frederic J. 1995. Force and Fear: Robbery in Canada. Toronto: Nelson.

Durlauf, Steven, and Daniel Nagin 2011a. "The Deterrent Effect of Imprisonment." Web.

———. 2011b. "Imprisonment and Crime: Can Both Be Reduced?" Criminology and Public Policy 10, no. 1: 13–54.

Engstad, Peter. 1975. "Environmental Opportunities and the Ecology of Crime." In Crime in Canadian Society, ed. Robert Silverman and James Teevan. 193–211. Toronto: Nelson.

Federal Communications Commission. 2014. Announcement of New Initiatives to Combat Smartphone and Data Theft. Web.

Feeney, Floyd. 1986. "Robbers and Decision-Makers." In The Reasoning Criminal: Rational Choice Perspectives on Offending, ed. Derek Cornish and Ronald Clarke. 53–71. New York: Springer.

Felson, Marcus. 1986. "Linking Criminal Choices, Routine Activities, Informal Control, and Criminal Outcomes." In The Reasoning Criminal: Rational Choice Approaches on Offending, ed. D.B. Cornish and R.V. Clarke. New York: Springer.

Felson, Marcus, and Ronald Clarke. 1998. Opportunity Makes the Thief: Practical Theory for Crime Prevention. Police Research Series Paper 98. London: Home Office.

Gabor, Thomas, Micheline Baril, Maurice Cusson, Daniel Elie, Marc LeBlanc, and Andre Normandeau. 1987. Armed Robbery: Cops, Robbers, and Victims. Springfield: Charles C. Thomas.

Gannon, Maire, and Karen Mihorean. 2005. "Criminal Victimization in Canada, 2004." Juristat 25, no. 7. Web.

Ha, Tu Thanh. 2002. "The Demise of the Bank Heist." Globe and Mail, November 11, A1, A7.

Hawken, Angela, and Mark Kleiman. 2009. Managing Drug-Involved Probationers with Swift and Certain Sanctions: Evaluating Hawaii's HOPE. Washington: US Department of Justice.

Hayward, Keith. 2007. "Situational Crime Prevention and Its Discontents: Rational Choice Theory Versus the 'Culture of Now.'" Social Policy and Administration 41, no. 3: 232–50.

Hindelang, Michael J., Michael R. Gottfredson, and James Garofalo. 1978. Victims of Personal Crime: An Empirical Foundation for a Theory of Personal Victimization. Cambridge, MA: Ballinger.

Kennedy, David. 2009. Deterrence and Crime Prevention: Reconsidering the Prospect of Sanction. London: Routledge.

Kennedy, David, Anthony Braga, Anne Piehl, and Elin Waring. 2001. Reducing Gun Violence: The Boston Gun Project's Operation Ceasefire. Washington: National Institute of Justice.

Koenig, Daniel J. 1977. "Correlates of Self-Reported Victimization and Perceptions of Neighbourhood Safety." In Selected Papers from the Social Indicators Conference, 1975, ed. Lynn Hewitt and David Brusegard. 77–90. Edmonton: Alberta Bureau of Statistics.

Kovandzic, Tomislav, John Sloan, and Lynne Vieraitis. 2004. "Striking Out as Crime Reduction Policy: The Impact of 'Three Strikes' on Crime Rates in U.S. Cities (1980–1999)." Justice Quarterly 21, no. 2: 399–424.

Legislative Analyst's Office, California Legislature. 2005. A Primer: Three Strikes: The Impact After More Than a Decade. Sacramento.

Luckenbill, David. 1977. "Criminal Homicide as a Situated Transaction." Social Problems 25, no. 2: 176–86.

Marvell, Thomas, and Calisle Moody. 2001. "The Lethal Effects of Three Strikes Laws." Journal of Legal Studies 30, no. 1: 89–106.

McLean, Gene. 2000. "The New Age of Bank Security." Canadian Banker 107, no. 4.

Perreault, Samuel. 2013. "Police-Reported Crime Statistics in Canada, 2012." Juristat, July 25. Web.

Perreault, Samuel, and Shannon Brennan. 2010. "Criminal Victimization in Canada, 2009." Juristat 30, no. 2. Web.

Pollack, Stanley. 2006. "Bringing Peace to Boston's Streets." Boston Globe, July 18.

Public Safety Canada. 2013. Corrections and Conditional Release Statistical Overview—2013. Ottawa: Public Safety Canada.

Roberts, Julian. 2005. Mandatory Sentences of Imprisonment in Common Law Jurisdictions: Some Representative Models. Ottawa: Minister of Justice.

Roehl, Jan, Dennis Rosenbaum, Sandra Costello, James Coldren, Amie Schuck, Laura Kunard, and David Forde. 2006. Strategic Approaches to Community Safety Initiative (SACSI) in 10 U.S. Cities: The Building Blocks for Project Safe Neighborhoods. Washington: US Department of Justice.

Sacco, Vincent F., and Holly Johnson. 1990. Patterns of Criminal Victimization in Canada. Ottawa: Statistics Canada.

Schneider, Stephen. 2007. Refocusing Crime Prevention: Collective Action and the Quest for Community. Toronto: University of Toronto Press.

Schweinhart, L.J., J. Montie, Z. Xiang, W.S. Barnett, C.R. Belfield, and M. Nores. 2005. Lifetime Effects: The High/Scope Perry Preschool Study Through Age 40. Ypsilanti: High/Scope.

Shaw, Hollie. 2014. "Target Data Breach Could Have Been Avoided with Chip Technology Widespread in Canada." National Post, January 21.

Sherman, Lawrence, Patrick Gartin, and Michael Buerger. 1989. "Hot Spots of Predatory Crime: Routine Activities and the Criminology of Place." Criminology 27: 27–55.

Sparks, Richard F. 1981. "Multiple Victimization: Evidence, Theory and Future Research." In Victims of Crime: A Review of Research Issues and Methods. Washington: US Department of Justice.

Tonry, Michael. 2009. "The Mostly Unintended Effects of Mandatory Minimum Penalties: Two Centuries of Consistent Findings." In Crime and Justice: A Review of Research, Vol. 38, ed. Michael Tonry. 65–114. Chicago: University of Chicago Press.

US Department of Justice. 1974a. Crime in Eight American Cities. Advance Report. Washington: US Department of Justice.

———. 1974b. Crimes and Victims: A Report on the Dayton–San Jose Pilot Study of Victimization. Washington: US Department of Justice.

Wasserman, Gail, Kate Keenan, Richard Tremblay, John Coie, Todd Herrenkohl, Rolf Loeber, and David Petechuk. 2003. Risk and Protective Factors of Child Delinquency. Washington: Office of Juvenile Justice and Delinquency Prevention.

Werb, Dan, Thomas Kerr, Bohdan Nosyk, Steffanie Strathdee, and Julio Montaner. 2013. "The Temporal Relationship Between Drug Supply Indicators: An Audit of International Government Surveillance Systems." BMJ Open. Web.

Wright, Richard T., and Scott H. Decker. 1992. Burglars on the Job: Streetlife and Residential Break-Ins. Evanston: Northeastern University Press.

Young, Jock. 1997. "The Left and Crime Control." http://www.malcolmread.co.uk/JockYoung.

CHAPTER 16

Abadinsky, Howard. 2000. Organized Crime. New York: Wadsworth.

———. 2012. Organized Crime, 10th ed.. Belmont: Thomson Wadsworth.

Albini, Joseph L. 1971. American Mafia: Genesis of a Legend. New York: Appleton- Century-Crofts.

Anderson, Annelise G. 1979. The Business of Organized Crime: A Cosa

Nostra Family. Stanford: Hoover Institution Press.

Arlacchi, Pino. 1979. "The Mafioso: From Man of Honour to Entrepreneur [Social Basis of Mafioso Traditions]." New Left Review, November–December, 53–72.

Bandidos MC Randers. Web.

Beare, Margaret, and Stephen Schneider. 1990. Tracing of Illicit Funds: Money Laundering in Canada. Ottawa: Solicitor General.

Bell, Daniel. 1953. "Crime as an American Way of Life." Antioch Review 13 (June): 131–54.

Brown, Bob. 2007. "Cybercrime Update: Is Organized Crime Moving into Cybersphere?" NetworkWorld.com, May 9.

Canadian Association of Chiefs of Police. 1994. Organized Crime Committee Report, 1994: Smuggling Activities in Canada. Ottawa.

Canadian Press. 2002. "Montreal Trial Told Hells Angels Videotaped Funeral of Cotroni Family Member." July 9.

_____. 2010. "Border Agents Intercept 10 million Counterfeit Cigarettes in B.C." November 30.

_____. 2012. "Mafia 'Tax' on Construction Projects Hit 30% at Height of Rizzutos' Power, Quebec Inquiry hears." September 26.

_____. 2013. "Quebec Union Had Big Ties to Organized Crime, Inquiry Hears." October 2.

Canadian Tobacco Manufacturers Council. n.d. Cigarette Export Statistics. Ottawa.

Carrigan, D. Owen. 1991. Crime and Punishment in Canada: A History. Toronto: McClelland and Stewart.

Caulkins, J., and P. Reuter. 1998. "What Price Data Tell Us About Drug Markets." Journal of Drug Issues 28, no. 3: 593–612.

CCSA (Canadian Convenience Store Association). 2009. Contraband Tobacco in Canada: Time for Action: 2009 Status Report.

CFSEU (Combined Forces Special Enforcement Unit British Columbia).

2013. B.C.'s Anti-Gang Police. Vancouver.

Charbonneau, Jean-Pierre. 1975. The Canadian Connection. Trans. James Stewart. Ottawa: Optimum Publishing, 1975.

CISC (Criminal Intelligence Service Canada). 2002. Annual Report on Organized Crime in Canada, 2002. Ottawa.

_____. 2004. Annual Report on Organized Crime in Canada, 2004. Ottawa.

_____. 2006. Criminal Intelligence Service Canada Annual Report, 2006. Ottawa.

_____. 2007. Criminal Intelligence Service Canada Annual Report, 2007. Ottawa.

_____. 2009. Annual Report on Organized Crime in Canada, 2009. Ottawa.

_____. 2010. Annual Report on Organized Crime in Canada, 2009. Ottawa.

Clarke, Ronald, and Derek Cornish. 1985. "Modeling Offender's Decisions: A Framework for Policy and Research." In Crime and Justice: An Annual Review of Research, Vol. 6, ed. M. Tonry and N. Morris. 147–85. Chicago: University of Chicago Press.

Commission of the European Communities and EUROPOL. 2001. Towards a European Strategy to Prevent Organised Crime. March. Brussels.

Constantine, Thomas. 1994. "Statement Before the U.S. Senate Drug Caucus." February 24. Washington: US Drug Enforcement Administration.

Cressey, Donald. 1969. Theft of a Nation: The Structure and Operations of Organized Crime in America. New York: Harper and Row.

Dickie, Phil, and Paul Wilson. 1993. "Defining Organized Crime: An Operational Perspective." Current Issues in Criminology 4 (March): 215–24.

Dubro, James. 1986. Mob Rule: Inside the Canadian Mafia. Toronto: Totem.

_____. 1992. Dragons of Crime: Inside the Asian Underworld. Toronto: McClelland and Stewart.

Edwards, Peter. 1990. Blood Brothers: How Canada's Most Powerful Mafia

Family Runs Its Business. Toronto: McClelland.

Edwards, Peter, and Antonio Nicaso. 1993. Deadly Silence: Canadian Mafia Murders. Toronto: Macmillan Canada.

FBI (Federal Bureau of Investigation). 1995. "Eurasian Criminal Enterprises." In Overview of International Organized Crime. 13–37. Washington: Federal Bureau of Investigation.

Ferracuti, Franco, and Marvin E. Wolfgang. 1967. Subcultures of Violence: Towards an Integrated Theory in Criminology. Tavistock.

Finckenauer, James. 2004. "The Russian 'Mafia.'" Society 41, no. 5: 61–64.

_____. 2005. "Problems of Definition: What Is Organized Crime." Trends in Organized Crime 8, no. 3: 63–83.

Freedman, David. 2006. "The New Law of Criminal Organizations in Canada." Canadian Bar Review 85, no. 2: 172–219.

Gambetta, Diego. 1993. The Sicilian Mafia: The Business of Private Protection. Cambridge, MA: Harvard University Press.

Globe and Mail. 1972. "Metro Police Raid Turned Up Copy of Mafia Linked Society's Secret Rituals, Court Is Told." Globe and Mail, June 2.

_____. 1998. "Canada Braces for Eastern European Mafia Flood." November 30.

_____. 2010a. "B.C. RCMP Seize 60,000 Poppy Plants in Record Haul." August 26.

_____. 2010b. "Delta Police Seize Opium Poppy Pods Worth $760,000." September 15.

_____. 2012. "More Arrests Made in Massive Human-Trafficking Ring." July 13.

Haller, Mark. 1990. "Illegal Enterprise: A Theoretical and Historical Interpretation." Criminology 28, no. 2: 207–234.

Hess, Henner. 1973. Mafia and Mafiosi: The Structure of Power. Lexington: Heath Lexington.

Ianni, Francis. 1974. Black Mafia: Ethnic Succession in Organized Crime. New York: Simon and Schuster.

Ianni, Francis, and Elizabeth Reuss-Ianni. 1972. A Family Business: Kinship and Social Control in Organized Crime. New York: Russell Sage Foundation.

Ianni, Francis, and Elizabeth Reuss-Ianni. 1983. "Organized Crime." In Encyclopedia of Crime and Social Justice, ed. Sanford Kadish. 1094–106. New York: Free Press.

International Labour Organization. 2012. ILO Global Estimate of Forced Labour. Results and Methodology. Geneva.

Kaihla, Paul. 2002. "The Technology Secrets of Cocaine Inc." Web.

Kelly, Robert. 1987. "The Nature of Organized Crime." In Major Issues in Organized Crime Control, ed. Herbert Edelhertz. 5–43. Washington: National Institute of Justice.

Krukowska, Ewa, and Mathew Carr. 2011. "Organized Crime Blamed for Roiling $110 Billion Carbon Market." Bloomberg.com, January 31. Web.

Lamothe, Lee, and Adrian Humphreys. 2006. The Sixth Family: The Collapse of the New York Mafia and the Rise of Vito Rizzuto. Toronto: Wiley.

Lamothe, Lee, and Antonio Nicaso. 1994. Global Mafia. Toronto: MacMillan Canada.

Lavigne, Yves. 1996. Hells Angels: Into the Abyss. New York: HarperCollins.

Lupsha, Peter. 1981. "Individual Choice, Material Culture and Organized Crime." Criminology: An Interdisciplanary Journal 19, no. 3: 3–24.

Martens, Frederick, and Colleen Miller-Longfellow. 1982. "Shadows of Substance: Organized Crime Reconsidered." Federal Probation 46 (December): 3–9.

Montreal Gazette. 1996. "Smuggling Illegal Immigrants Increasing, U.S. Cop Says." October 5.

_____. 2011. "Cops Comb Woods Behind Rizzuto Home." January 10.

_____. 2012. "Charbonneau Commission: Detective lists Construction Firms Linked to Mafia." September 27.

Morselli, Carlo. 2005. Contacts, Opportunities, and Criminal Enterprise. Toronto: University of Toronto Press.

_____. 2009. Inside Criminal Networks. New York: Springer.

Morselli, Carlo, and Julie Roy. 2008. "Brokerage Qualifications in Ringing Operations." Criminology 46, no. 1: 71–98.

National Post. 2003. "Tobacco Company Accused of Smuggling," February 28.

_____. 2010a. "'There's Nothing We've Done That's Illegal': Mohawk Leaders Deny That Organized Crime Is Involved in the Industry." September 21.

_____. 2010b. "A New Mafia: Crime Families Ruling Toronto, Italy Alleges." September 24.

_____. 2010c. "Mafia 'Ndrangheta in Canada." September 25.

Naylor, Tom. 2002. Wages of Crime: Black Markets, Illegal Finance, and the Underworld Economy. Ithaca: Cornell University Press.

New York Times. 2012. "Smugglers Go Under the Sea to Move Drugs." September 10.

Nicaso, Antonio. 2001. "Angels with Dirty Faces: Part 15—How the World's Richest and Most Ferocious Motorcycle Gang Is Expanding Its Wings in Canada." Tandem News, June 24.

Office of National Drug Control Policy. 2004. Technical Report for the Price and Purity of Illicit Drugs: 1981 Through the Second Quarter of 2003. Washington: Executive Office of the President (Publication no. NCJ 207769).

Ottawa Sun. 2012. "Police Are Warning Ottawans to Be on the Alert for a Gang of Thieves That Distract." September 29.

Perreault, S. 2012. Homicide in Canada, 2011. Ottawa: Statistics Canada.

Pileggi, Nicholas. 1985. Wise Guy: Life in a Mafia Family. New York, NY: Pocket Books.

Potter, Gary. 1994. Criminal Organizations: Vice, Racketeering, and Politics in an American City. Prospect Heights: Waveland Press.

President's Commission on Law Enforcement and Administration of Justice. 1967. Task Force Report: Organized Crime. Washington, DC: United States Government Printing Office.

President's Commission on Organized Crime. 1984. Organized Crime and Cocaine Trafficking. Record of Hearing IV, November 27–29, 1984. Washington: U.S. Government Printing Office.

_____. 1986. America's Habit. Drug Abuse, Drug Trafficking, & Organized Crime. Washington, DC: United States Government Printing Office.

Quebec Police Commission. 1977. The Fight Against Organized Crime in Quebec: Report of the Commission on Organized Crime and Recommendations. Québec: Editeur officiel du Québec.

Rawlinson, Patricia. 1997. "Russian Organized Crime: A Brief History." In Phil Williams (ed.) Russian Organized Crime: The New Threat? 28–52. London: Frank Cass.

Roach, Wilfrid. 1962. Report of The Honourable Mr. Justice Wilfrid D. Roach as a Commissioner Appointed Under the Public Inquiries Act by Letters Patent Dated December 11, 1961. Toronto: Commission of Inquiry.

Reppetto, T. 2007. Bring Down the Mob : The War Against the American Mafia. New York: Holt Paperbacks.

RCMP (Royal Canadian Mounted Police). 1945. Report of the Royal Canadian Mounted Police for the Year Ended March 31, 1945. Ottawa, ON: F.A. Acland.

_____. 1987. "Outlaw Motorcycle Gangs: Modern profiles." RCMP Gazette. 49, no. 5: 9–10.

_____. 2007. Drug Situation Report, 2007. Ottawa: RCMP, Criminal Intelligence Directorate.

_____. 2008. 2008 Contraband Tobacco Enforcement Strategy. Web.

Salerno, Ralph. 1967. "Syndicate Personnel Structure." Canadian Police Chief 55, no. 3.

Schneider, S. 2003. Money Laundering in Canada: An Analysis of RCMP Cases. Toronto: Nathanson Centre for the Study of Organized Crime and Corruption, York University.

_____. 2009. Iced: The Story of Organized Crime in Canada. Toronto: John Wiley & Sons.

Sher, Julian, and William Marsden. 2004. The Road to Hell: How the Biker Gangs Conquered Canada. Toronto: Knopf Canada.

Smith, Dwight. 1975. The Mafia Mystique. New York: Basic Books.

Toronto Star. 1895. "Smuggle the Vile Cigarette." August 2.

_____. 1948. "Windsor Grills Detroit's Chief on Race Data." February 27.

_____. 1996. "Russian Crime Hits Metro Area." June 1.

_____. 2005. "Being Hells Angel Is Now a Crime: Court Case a Test of Anti-gang Law." July 1.

Toronto Telegram. 1961. "RCMP, FBI Suspect Mafia of Ruling Metro Gangland." April 14.

Tyler, Gus. 1962. Organized Crime in America. Ann Arbor: University of Michigan Press.

UN. 2012. Global Report on Trafficking in Persons, 2012. Vienna: UN Office on Drugs and Crime.

_____. 2013. World Drug Report, 2013. Vienna: UN Office on Drugs and Crime.

UN News Centre. 2012. "New UN Campaign Highlights Financial and Social Costs of Transnational Organized Crime" July 16. Web.

US Congress. Senate. 1951. Special Committee to Investigate Organized Crime in Interstate Commerce. Final Report of the Special Committee to Investigate Organized Crime in Interstate Commerce. Pursuant to S. Res. 202 (81st Cong.) As amended by S. Res. 60 and S. Res. 129 (82d Cong.. Washington, DC: U.S. Government Printing Office.

US Congress. United States House of Representatives, Committee on the Judiciary, Subcommittee on Immigration and Claims. 2000.

Law Enforcement Problems at the Border Between the United States and Canada: Drug Smuggling, Illegal Immigration and Terrorism. One Hundred Sixth Congress, First Session, April 14, 1999. -Washington, DC: U.S. Government Printing Office, p. 158.

US Senate Committee on Governmental Affairs. Permanent subcommittee on Investigations. 1989. Structure of International Drug Trafficking Organizations Hearings. Washington, DC: United States Printing Office.

US Comptroller General. 1989. Non-traditional Organized Crime: Law Enforcement Officials Perspectives on Five Criminal Groups. Washington: US GPO.

US Department of State. 2002. International Narcotics Control Strategy Report, 2002. Washington. Web.

US Drug Enforcement Administration. n.d.. Major Traffickers and Their Organizations. Washington, DC: U.S. Drug Enforcement Administration.

_____. 2001. Drug Trafficking in the United States. September. Washington.

Vancouver Sun. 2005. "Ruling Hobbles Organized Crime Battle, Police Say." December 13.

_____. 2010. "Police Fear More Drugs and Violence Are Coming as Mexican Cartels Begin Operating in B.C." October 18.

Verizon Business Risk Team. 2009. 2009 Data Breach Investigation Report, New York: Verizon Business. Web.

Victoria Times-Colonist. 2005. "Police Net Can Be Cast Too Wide." December 14.

Windsor Star. 2012. "Windsor Police Foil Plans for Human Smuggling, Fraud, Escape to Mexico." August 9.

Wolf, Daniel. 1991. The Rebels: A Brotherhood of Outlaw Bikers. Toronto: University of Toronto Press.

Young, J. 2001. "Identity, Community and Social Exclusion." In Crime, Disorder, and Community Safety: A New Agenda?, ed. M. Roger and J. Pitts. 26–53. London: Routledge.

CHAPTER 17

Akers, Ronald. 1973. Deviant Behavior: A Social Learning Approach. Belmont: Wadsworth.

Auditor General of Canada. 1999. "The Underground Economy Initiative." Report of the Auditor General of Canada. Ottawa.

Baumhart, Raymond. 1961. "How Ethical Are Businessmen?" Harvard Business Review 39: 5–176.

Benson, M.L. 1989. "The Influence of Class Position on the Formal and Informal Sanctioning of White-Collar Offenders." Sociological Quarterly 30: 465–79.

Benson, M.L., W.J. Maakestad, F.T. Cullen, and G. Geis. 1988. "District Attorneys and Corporate Crime: Surveying the Prosecutorial Gatekeepers." Criminology 26: 505–18.

Bittle, Steven, and Laureen Snider. 2014. "The Breakdown of Canada's Corporate Crime Laws." In Locating Law, ed. Elizabeth Comack. 178–97. Halifax: Fernwood.

Butler, Steve. 2002. "Colossal Enron Collapse a Good Thing for the Rest of Us." Winnipeg Free Press, February 22, A15.

Canadian Bankers Association. 2013. Credit Card Fraud and Interac Debit Card Statistics—Canadian Issued Cards. Web.

Canadian Press. 2000. "CEO Jailed for Insider Trading." Winnipeg Free Press, September 19, B8.

Casey, John. 1985. "Corporate Crime and the State: Canada in the 1980s." In The New Criminologies in Canada, ed. Thomas Fleming. 100–1. Toronto: Oxford University Press.

CBC. 2001. "Study Shows Employee Fraud Prevalent in Workplace." Web.

_____. 2004. "Auditor-General's Report 2004." Web.

Clinard, Marshall. 1952. The Black Market: A Study of White Collar Crime. New York: Holt, Rinehart and Winston.

Clinard, Marshall, and Peter Yeager. 1980. Corporate Crime. New York: Free Press.

CMPA (Canadian Medical Protective Association). 2013. 2010 Annual Report. Ottawa.

Coleman, James. 1974. Power and the Structure of Society. New York: W.W. Norton.

———. 1985. The Criminal Elite. New York: St. Martin's.

College of Physicians and Surgeons of Ontario. 2011. Yazdanfar, Behnaz CPSO #: 67947. http://www.cpso.on.ca/docsearch/details.aspx?view=4&id=%2067947.

Corrado, Raymond. 1996. "Political Crime in Canada." In Criminology: A Canadian Perspective, 3rd ed., ed. Rick Linden. 459–93. Toronto: Harcourt Brace.

Corkery, Michael. 2014. "Citi Settles Mortgage Securities Inquiry for $7 Billion." International New York Times. July 14.

CRA (Canada Revenue Agency). 2008. "Businesses Warned Against Using Tax Cheating Software." Tax Alert. Ottawa.

Cullen, Francis, Bruce Link, and Craig Polanzi. 1982. "The Seriousness of Crime Revisited: Have Attitudes Toward White Collar Crime Changed?" Criminology 20: 83–102.

Daly, Kathleen. 1989. "Gender and Varieties of White-Collar Crime." Criminology 27: 769–93.

DeCloet, Derek. 2002. "Deceit Began This Scandalous Rot." National Post, July 11.

Donovan, Kevin. 2007. "$1.4B Tax Scams Nail Donors." TheStar.com, September 29.

Drohan, Madelaine. 1995. "Barings Was Warned of Risk." Globe and Mail, March 6, A1.

Duffy, Andrew. 2014. "B.C. Securities Commission Rules Victoria Man Committed $65 Million Fraud." Victoria Times Colonist. August 13.

Ermann, M. David, and Richard Lundman. 1982. Corporate Deviance. New York: Holt, Rinehart and Winston.

Evola, K., and N. O'Grady. 2009. "As Fraud Schemes Proliferate—Are You the Next Investor to Crash and Burn?" Journal of Investment Compliance 10: 14–17.

Farberman, Harvey. 1975. "A Criminogenic Market Structure: The Automobile Industry." Sociological Quarterly 16: 438–57.

Fitzgerald, Rory. 2011. "Enda Kenny's Attack on the Vatican Reflects Ferocious Public Anger." Catholic Herald, July 21. Web.

Freeze, Colin, and Alexandra Posadzki. 2014. "Canadian Resident Charged in U.S. for Directing Chinese Spy Ring." Globe and Mail. July 22.

Gabor, Thomas. 1994. Everybody Does It. Toronto: University of Toronto Press.

Geis, Gilbert. 1962. "Toward a Delineation of White-Collar Offenses." Sociological Inquiry 32: 160–71.

———. 1984. "White Collar Crime and Corporate Crime." In Major Forms of Crime, ed. Robert F. Meier. Beverly Hills: Sage.

Giesbrecht, Matthew. 2012. Canadian Corporate Criminal Liability in Workplace Fatalities Evaluating Bill C-45. MA thesis, University of Manitoba.

Glasbeek, Harry, and Eric Tucker. 1994. "Corporate Crime and the Westray Tragedy." Canadian Dimension, January–February, 11–14.

Gomery, Mr. Justice John. 2005. Who Is Responsible? Fact Finding Report. Montreal: Commission of Inquiry into the Sponsorship Program and Advertising Activities.

Goudge, Mr. Justice Stephen. 2008. Inquiry in Pediatric Forensic Pathology in Ontario. Vol. 1: Executive Summary. Web.

Hagan, John. 1982. "The Corporate Advantage: The Involvement of Individual and Organizational Victims in the Criminal Justice Process." Social Forces 60, no. 4: 993–1022.

Hagan, John, and Celesta Albonetti. 1982. "Race, Class, and the Perception of Criminal Injustice in America." American Journal of Sociology 88: 329–55.

Hagan, John, and Fiona Kay. 1990. "Gender and Delinquency in White-Collar Families: A Power–Control Perspective." Crime and Delinquency 36, no. 3: 391–407.

Hagan, John, and Ilene Nagel. 1982. "White Collar Crime, White Collar Time: The Sentencing of White Collar Criminals in the Southern District of New York." American Criminal Law Review 20, no. 2: 259–301.

Hagan, John, and Alberto Palloni. 1983. "The Sentencing of White Collar Offenders Before and After Watergate." Paper presented at the American Sociological Association Meetings, Detroit.

Hagan, John, and Patricia Parker. 1985. "White Collar Crime and Punishment: The Class Structure and Legal Sanctioning of Securities Violations." American Sociological Review 50, no. 3: 302–16.

Hartung, Frank E. 1950. "White Collar Offenses in the Wholesale Meat Industry in Detroit." American Journal of Sociology 56: 25–34.

Henderson, Tanya. 2000. "Delivered and Signed." http://abcnews.go.com/onair/2020/2020_000428_zorro_feature.html.

Howlett, Karen. 2002. "The Two Faces of YBM Magnex." Globe and Mail, December 29, B13.

Hu, Jane. 2014. "Why Do Scientists Commit Fraud?" Slate. August 6.

Kadlec, Daniel. 2002. "WorldCon." Time, July 8, 15–20.

Katz, Jack. 1980. "The Movement Against White-Collar Crime." In Criminology Review Yearbook, Vol. 2., ed. Egon Bittner and Sheldon Messinger. Beverly Hills: Sage.

Kranhold, Kathryn, and Mitchell Pacelle. 2002. "Enron Paid Top Managers $681 Million, Even as Stock Slid." Wall Street Journal, June 17, B1, B4.

Lagarde, Christine. 2014. "Economic Inclusion and Financial Integrity." An Address to the Conference on Inclusive Capitalism. London, May 27.

Law Commission of Canada. 2000. Restoring Dignity: Responding to

Child Abuse in Canadian Institutions. Ottawa.

Le Pan, Nick. 2007. Enhancing Integrated Market Enforcement Teams, Achieving Results in Fighting Capital Markets Crime. Report submitted to the Commissioner of the RCMP.

Leslie, Gabriel. 2014. "The True Cost of Hidden Money." New York Times. June 15.

Mann, Kenneth, Stanton Wheeler, and Austin Sarat. 1980. "Sentencing the White Collar Offender." American Criminal Law Review 17, no. 4: 479.

McIntyre, Mike. 2001. "Deaths Cost Firms Dearly." Winnipeg Free Press, March 3, A1, A4.

Menzies, David. 2000. "Looking for Mr. Goodwrench." National Post, September 23.

Morgenson, Gretchen, and Louise Story. 2011. "In Financial Crisis, No Prosecutions of Top Figures." New York Times, April 14.

Morton, Brian. 2014. "Sawmill Owner to Appeal Record $1.01 Million Fine for Fatal Explosion." Vancouver Sun. April 3.

Oliphant, Jeffrey. 2010. Commission of Inquiry into Certain Allegations Respecting Business and Financial Dealings between Karlheinz Schreiber and the Right Honourable Brian Mulroney. Ottawa: Minister of Public Works and Government Services.

Olive, David. 2007. "The World According to Conrad Black." Toronto Star, March 11. http://www.thestar.com/News/article/190677.

Pontell, Henry, and Gilbert Geis. 2013. "The Trajectory of White-Collar Crime Following the Great Economic Meltdown." Journal of Contemporary Criminal Justice 30: 70–82.

Posner, Richard A. 1980. "Optimal Sentences for White Collar Criminals." American Criminal Law Review 17, no. 4: 409–18.

PWC. 2012. Canadian Retail Security Survey, 2012. Web.

Reasons, C., L. Ross, and C. Paterson. 1981. Assault on the Worker:

Occupational Health and Safety in Canada. Toronto: Butterworths.

Reiss, Albert. 1980. Data Sources on White Collar Law Breaking. Washington: National Institute of Justice.

Retail Council of Canada. 2002. 2001 Canadian Retail Security Report. Toronto.

Richard, Justice K. Peter. 1997. The Westray Story: A Predictable Path to Disaster, Executive Summary. Halifax: Government of Nova Scotia.

Ross, E.A. 1907. Sin and Society. Boston: Houghton Mifflin.

Rubin, Sandra. 1999. "RCMP Investigated YBM in Early 1995." Financial Post, January 9.

Rugaber, Christopher, and Derek Kravitz. 2011. "Wells Fargo Fined in Mortgage Case." Globe and Mail, July 21, B7.

Sargeant, Malcolm, and Eric Tucker. 2010. "Layers of Vulnerability in Occupational Health and Safety for Migrant Workers." Policy and Practice in Occupational Health and Safety 7: 51–73.

Sandborn, Tom. 2010. "Hard Thanksgiving for Injured Farm Workers." The Tyee, October 11. Web.

Shapiro, Susan P. 1990. "Collaring the Crime, Not the Criminal: Reconsidering the Concept of White-Collar Crime." American Sociological Review 55: 346–65.

Sharpe, Andrew, and Jill Hardt. 2006. "Five Deaths a Day: Workplace Fatalities in Canada, 1993–2005." CSLS Research Paper 2006–04. Ottawa: Centre for the Study of Living Standards.

Shover, Neal, and Andy Hochstetler. 2006. Choosing White-Collar Crime. New York: Cambridge University Press.

Sikorsky, Robert. 1990. "Highway Robbery: Canada's Auto Repair Scandal." Reader's Digest (February): 55–63.

Sinclair, Judge Murray. 2000. The Report of the Manitoba Pediatric Surgery Inquest. Winnipeg: Provincial Court of Manitoba. Web.

Snider, Laureen. 1979. "Revising the Combines Investigation Act: A Study

in Corporate Power." In Structure, Law, and Power: Essays in the Sociology of Law, ed. Paul J. Brantingham and Jack M. Kress. 105–19. Beverly Hills: Sage.

———. 1988. "Commercial Crime." In Conformity and Control in Canadian Society, ed. Vincent F. Sacco. 231–83. Scarborough: Prentice Hall.

Statistics Canada. 2011. "Study: The Underground Economy in Canada." The Daily, June 27. Ottawa.

Stone, Christopher. 1975. Where the Law Ends: The Social Control of Corporate Behavior. New York: Harper and Row.

Sutherland, Anne. 2009. "Montreal Man's $50M Disappearance 'Shatters' Friends. Gazette (Montreal), July 13.

Sutherland, Edwin. 1940. "White Collar Criminality." American Sociological Review 5: 1–12.

———. 1945. "Is 'White Collar Crime' Crime?" American Sociological Review 10: 132–39.

Swartz, Joel. 1978. "Silent Killers at Work." In Corporate and Governmental Deviance, ed. M. David Ermann and Richard Lundman. 114–28. New York: Oxford University Press.

Taibbi, Matt. 2009. "The Great American Bubble Machine." Rolling Stone, July 9–23. Web.

Vancouver Sun. 2014. "Calgary Law Firm Under Investigation Stands to Earn $16.6 million." June 14.

Weisburd, David, Elin Waring, and Stanton Wheeler. 1990. "Class, Status and the Punishment of White-Collar Criminals." Law and Social Inquiry 15, no. 2: 223–46.

Wells, Jennifer. 1998. Fever: The Dark Mystery of the Bre-X Gold Rush. Toronto: Viking.

Wente, Margaret. 2000. "Dr. Bloody and Mr. Whizzo." Globe and Mail, July 25, A17.

Wheeler, Stanton, and Mitchell Rothman. 1982. "The Organization as Weapon in White-Collar Crime." Michigan Law Review 80: 1403–26.

Wheeler, Stanton, David Weisburd, and Nancy Bode. 1982. "Sentencing the

White Collar Offender: Rhetoric and Reality." American Sociological Review 47: 641–59.

CHAPTER 18

Arntfield, Michael. 2014. "Towards a Cybervictimology: Cyberbullying, Routine Activities Theory, and the Anti-Sociality of Social Media." Canadian Journal of Communication (in press).

———. 2013. "1921–1940" In The Social History of Crime and Punishment in America, ed. Wilbur R. Miller. 2201–19). Thousand Oaks: Sage.

Aggrawal, Anil. 2008. Forensic and Medico-Legal Aspects of Sexual Crimes and Unusual Sexual Practices. Boca Raton: CRC.

Baranetsky, Victoria. 2009. "What Is Cyberterrorism? Even Experts Can't Agree." Harvard Law Review. Web.

Bogart, Nicole. 2014. "Hacker Charged in CRA Heartbleed Breach 'Straight-A' Engineering Student." Global News. Web.

Cohen, Lawrence E., and Marcus Felson. 1979. "Social Change and Crime Rate Trends: A Routine Activity Approach." American Sociological Review 44: 588–608.

CyberSCAN. 2014. Nova Scotia Cyber Safety. http://cyberscan.novascotia.ca. Accessed July 23, 2014.

Dalby, J. Thomas. 1988. "Is Telephone Scatologia a Variant of Exhibitionism?" International Journal of Offender Therapy and Comparative Criminology 32: 45–48.

Department of Justice. 2014a. "Backgrounder: Cyberbullying and the Non-Consensual Distribution of Intimate Images." Government of Canada. http://www.justice.gc.ca/engl. /news-nouv/nr-cp/2013/doc_32995.html. Accessed July 23, 2014.

———. 2014b. "Voyeurism as a Criminal Offence: A Consultation Paper." Government of Canada. http://www.justice.gc.ca/eng/cons/voy/part1_context.html. Accessed July 23, 2014.

Durkin, Keith F. 2007. "Show Me the Money: Cybershrews and On-Line Money Masochists." Deviant Behavior 2: 355–78.

———. 2009. "There Must Be Some Type of Misunderstanding, There Must be Some Kind of Mistake: The Deviance Disavowal Strategies of Men Arrested in Internet Sex Stings." Sociological Spectrum 29: 661–76.

Ellul, Jacques. 1964. The Technological Society. New York: Alfred A. Knopf.

Freiberger, Kimberley L. 2008. "Examining Incidents of Cyberstalking: An Exploration of an Emerging Crime." Ph.D. diss., Virginia Commonwealth University. Richmond.

Freund, Kurt, and Robin Watson. 1990. "Mapping the Boundaries of Courtship Disorder." Journal of Sex Research 27, no. 4: 589–606.

Harris, Elizabeth A., and Nicole Perlroth. 2014. "Target Missed Signs of a Data Breach." New York Times. Web.

Hayward, K. 2012. "Pantomime Justice: A Cultural Criminological Analysis of 'Life Stage Devolution.'" Crime, Media, Culture 8, no.. 2: 213–29.

Hazelwood, Robert R., and Janet I. Warren. 2004. "Linkage Analysis: Modus Operandi, Ritual, and Signature in Serial Sexual Crime." Aggression and Violent Behavior 9: 307–18.

Hickey, E.W. 2010. Serial Murderers and Their Victims, 6th ed. Belmont: Wadsworth.

Hinduja, Sarneer, and Justin W. Patchin. 2009. Bullying Beyond the Schoolyard: Preventing and Responding to Cyberbullying. Thousand Oaks: Sage.

———. 2008. "Cyberbullying: An Exploratory Analysis of Factors Related to Offending and Victimization." Deviant Behavior 29: 129–56.

Holt, Thomas J., and Adam M. Bossler. 2009. "Exploring the Applicability of Lifestyle-Routine Activities Theory for Cybercrime Victimization." Deviant Behavior 30: 1–25.

Hootsen, Jan-Albert, and Roeland Roovers. 2014. "Man Accused in Amanda Todd Case Vows to Fight Extradition to Canada." Globe and Mail. Web.

Kaplan, Meg S., and Richard B. Krueger. 1997. "Voyeurism: Psychopathology and Theory." In Sexual Deviance: Theory, Assessment, and Treatment, ed. D. Richard Laws and William T. O'Donohue. 297–310. New York: Guilford.

Kirchen, Rich. 2008. "Mayfair Mall's Teen Chaperone Policy Paying Off." Business Journal of Milwaukee. Web.

Kucera, H. 1967. Computational Analysis of Present-Day American English. Providence: Brown University Press.

Manovich, L. 2001. The Language of New Media. Cambridge: MIT Press.

Mautner, Gerlinde. 2009. "Corpora and Critical Discourse Analysis." In Contemporary Corpus Linguistics, ed. Paul Baker. 32–46. London: Continuum.

Miller, Brooke N., and Robert G. Morris. 2012. "Cyber-Related Violence." In Violent Offenders: Theories, Research, Police, and Practice, 2nd ed., ed. Matt DeLisi and Peter J. Conis. 75–94. Burlington: Jones and Bartlett.

Moore, Robert. 2005. Cybercrime: Investigating High-Technology Computer Crime. Burlington: Anderson.

Olweus, Dan. 1993. Bullying at School: What We Know and What We Can Do. Cambridge: Blackwell.

———. 2012. "Cyberbullying: An Overrated Phenomenon?" European Journal of Developmental Psychology 9, no. 5: 520–38.

Pelfrey, William V., Jr., & Nicole L. Weber. 2013. "Keyboard Gangsters: Analysis of Incidence and Correlates of Cyberbullying in a Large Urban Student Population." Deviant Behavior 34: 68–84.

Press, Jordan. 2012. "Canadian Government Under International Pressure to Pass Controversial Internet Surveillance Bill." National Post. Web.

Quayle, Ethel, and Max Taylor. 2002. "Child Pornography and the Internet: Perpetuating a Cycle of Abuse." Deviant Behavior 8: 47–63.

Quinn, James F., and Craig J. Forsyth. 200. "Describing Sexual Behavior in the Era of the Internet: A Typology for Empirical Research." Deviant Behavior 26: 191–207.

Raskauskas, Juliana, and Ann D. Stoltz. 2007. "Involvement in Electronic and Traditional Bullying Among Adolescents." Developmental Psychology 7: 22–43.

Reyns, Bradford W., Billy Henson, and Bonnie S. Fisher. 2011. "Being Pursued Online: Applying Cyber-lifestyle-Routine Activities Theory to Cyberstalking Victimization."

Criminal Justice and Behavior 38, no. 11: 1149–69.

Roberts, Joshua W., and Scott A. Hunt. 2012. "Social Control in a Sexually Deviant Cybercommunity: A Cappers' Code of Conduct." Deviant Behavior 33, no. 10: 757–73.

Rufo, Ronald A. 2012. Sexual Predators Amongst Us. Boca Raton: CRC.

Sankin, Aaron. 2014. "Lonely People Share More on Facebook." Salon.com. Web.

Saunders, Elisabeth B., and George A. Awad. 1991. "Male Adolescent Sexual Offenders: Exhibitionism and Obscene Phone Calls." Child Psychiatry and Human Development 21: 169–78.

Schmidt, Michael, and David E. Sanger. 2014. "8 in China Army Face U.S. Charges of Cyberattacks." New York Times. Web.

Zetter, Kim. 2009. "Prosecutors Drop Plan to Appeal Lori Drew Case." Wired. Web.

Index

Page numbers in italics refer to figures and tables.

S